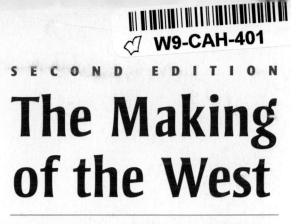

SECOND EDITION

The Making of the West

PEOPLES AND CULTURES

SECOND EDITION

The Making of the West

PEOPLES AND CULTURES

Volume C: Since 1740

Lynn Hunt
University of California,
Los Angeles

Thomas R. Martin
College of the Holy Cross

Barbara H. Rosenwein
Loyola University Chicago

R. Po-chia Hsia
Pennsylvania State University

Bonnle G. Smith
Rutgers University

BEDFORD/ST. MARTIN'S
Boston ◆ New York

FOR BEDFORD/ST. MARTIN'S

Executive Editor for History: Mary Dougherty
Director of Development for History: Jane Knetzger
Developmental Editor: Sara Wise
Senior Production Editor: Anne Noonan
Senior Production Supervisor: Dennis Conroy
Senior Marketing Manager: Jenna Bookin Barry
Editorial Assistant: Rachel L. Safer
Production Assistant: Kristen Merrill
Copyeditor: Janet Renard
Text Design: Wanda Kossak
Page Layout: DeNee Reiton Skipper
Photo Researchers: Elsa Peterson and Judy Brody
Cover Design: Billy Boardman
Cartography: Mapping Specialists Limited
Composition: TechBooks
Printing and Binding: R.R. Donnelley & Sons Company

President: Joan E. Feinberg
Editorial Director: Denise B. Wydra
Director of Marketing: Karen Melton Soeltz
Director of Editing, Design, and Production: Marcia Cohen
Managing Editor: Elizabeth M. Schaaf

Library of Congress Control Number: 2004102164

Manufactured in the United States of America.

9 8 7 6 5
f   e   d   c   b

For information, write: Bedford/St. Martin's, 75 Arlington Street, Boston, MA 02116
(617-399-4000)

ISBN: 0-312-40959-1 (hardcover edition)   EAN: 978-0-312-40959-3
ISBN: 0-312-41740-3 (paperback Vol. I)   EAN: 978-0-312-41740-6
ISBN: 0-312-41761-6 (paperback Vol. II)   EAN: 978-0-312-41761-1
ISBN: 0-312-41767-5 (paperback Vol. A)   EAN: 978-0-312-41767-3
ISBN: 0-312-41768-3 (paperback Vol. B)   EAN: 978-0-312-41768-0
ISBN: 0-312-41769-1 (paperback Vol. C)   EAN: 978-0-312-41769-7

Cover Art: *July 14 in Avignon,* 1930 by André Lhote (1885–1962). Musée National d'Art Modern, Center Georges Pompidou, Paris. © 2004 Artist Rights Society (ARS), New York/ADAGP, Paris and Réunion des Musées Nationaux/Art Resource, New York.

Preface

THE IDEA OF "THE WEST" is now urgently under discussion. The end of the cold war after 1989 presented new challenges for historical interpretation, but these had hardly been digested when the shock of September 11, 2001, reverberated throughout the world. These momentous events present extraordinary challenges for authors of Western civilization textbooks. We welcome the challenges, for they have deepened our commitment to our project's basic goal and approach. From the very beginning, we have insisted on an expanded vision of the West that includes the United States, fully incorporates eastern Europe, and emphasizes Europe's relationship with the rest of the world, whether through trade, colonization, migration, cultural exchange, or religious and ethnic conflict.

Every generation of students needs new textbooks that synthesize recent findings. Textbooks conceived during the era of the cold war are, of course, oriented toward explaining the clash between a West unquestionably identified as western Europe and the United States and its eastern-bloc opponents, eastern Europe and the Soviet Union. Since much of eastern Europe has now joined the European Union, the notion of Europe—and the West—has to change. Conflict now takes place on a global stage, and globalization of the economy and culture has become a subject of passionate debate. Nowhere is that debate more crucial than over relations between the West and Islam precipitated by the September 11, 2001, attacks by Islamic radicals. How to respond to such global threats sharply divides the West. The United States and Great Britain's decision to invade Iraq despite strong opposition from allies in western Europe tests long-standing alliances and suggests significant international realignments. New histories must reflect these dramatic changes, and we feel confident that ours meets the challenge. In every chapter, we develop these new perspectives and show how they offer a more coherent and convincing view of the important issues in the making of the West.

Central Themes and Approach

Our title, *The Making of the West: Peoples and Cultures*, makes two enduring points about our themes and approach: (1) that the history of the West is the story of a process that is still ongoing, not a finished result with only one fixed meaning; and (2) that "the West" includes many different peoples and cultures, that is, that there is no one Western people or culture that has existed from the beginning until now. To understand the historical development of the West and its position in the world today, it is essential to place the West's emergence in a larger, global context that reveals the cross-cultural interactions fundamental to the shaping of the Western identity. Our task as authors, moreover, is to integrate the best of social and cultural history with the enduring developments of political, military, and diplomatic history, offering a clear, compelling narrative that sets all the key events and stages of the West's evolution in a broad, meaningful context.

We know from our own teaching that introductory students need a solid chronological framework, one with enough familiar benchmarks to make the material readily assimilable, but also one with enough flexibility to incorporate the new varieties of historical research. That is one reason why we present our account in a straightforward, chronological manner. Each chapter treats all the main events, people, and themes of a period in which the West significantly changed; thus students are not required to learn about political events in one chapter, then backtrack to concurrent social and cultural developments in the next. The chronological organization also accords with our belief that it is important, above all else, for students to see the interconnections among varieties of historical experience—between politics and cultures, between public events and private experiences, between wars and diplomacy and everyday life. Our chronological synthesis allows students to appreciate these relationships while it, we hope, captures the spirit of each age and sparks students' historical imaginations. For teachers, our chronological approach ensures a balanced account, allows the flexibility to stress themes of one's own choosing, and perhaps best of all, provides a text that reveals history not as a settled matter but as a process that is constantly alive, subject to pressures, and able to surprise us. In writing *The Making of the West: Peoples and Cultures*, it has been our aim to communicate the vitality and excitement as well as the fundamental importance of history. If we have succeeded in conveying some of the vibrancy of the past and the thrill of historical investigation, we will be encouraged to start rethinking and revising—as historians always must—once again.

Pedagogy and Features

More and more is required of students these days, and not just in Western civilization courses. We know from our own teaching that students need all the help they can get in assimilating information, acquiring skills, learning about historical debate, and sampling the newest approaches to historical thinking. With these goals in mind, we retained the class-tested learning and teaching aids that contributed to the first edition, but we have also added more such features.

Each chapter begins with a **vivid anecdote** that draws readers into the atmosphere and issues of the period and raises the chapter's main themes, supplemented by a full-page illustration that echoes the anecdote and similarly reveals the temper of the times. We have added **new chapter outlines** and **timelines** to introduce students to each chapter. As they read, students now encounter **review questions** strategically placed at the end of each major section to check their comprehension of main ideas, plus bolded **key terms** in the text with corresponding **glossary** definitions at the end of the book and a running **pronunciation guide**. Each chapter closes with a strong **chapter conclusion** that reviews main topics and ties together the chapter's thematic strands. An all-new **chapter review** section provides a clear study plan with a table of important events, list of key terms, review questions, and "Making Connections" questions, which encourage students to analyze chapter material or make comparisons within or beyond the chapter.

But like a clear narrative synthesis, strong pedagogical support is not enough on its own to encourage active learning. To reflect the richness of the themes in the text and to enliven the past with many more original sources, in the second edition we have added **sixty new single-source documents** (two per chapter). Nothing can give a more direct experience of the past than original voices, and we have each endeavored, sometimes through our own retranslation, to let those voices speak, whether it is Seneca describing everyday life in the Roman Empire, Frederick Barbarossa replying to the Romans when they offer him the emperor's crown, or an ordinary person's account of one of Stalin's pogroms. At the same time, we have retained our unique, proven features that extend the narrative by revealing the process of interpretation, providing a solid introduction to the principles of historical argument, and capturing the excitement of historical investigation:

- **Contrasting Views** provide three or four often conflicting eyewitness accounts of a central event, person, or development, such as Martin Luther, the English Civil War, and late-nineteenth-century migration.
- **New Sources, New Perspectives** show students how historians continue to develop

new kinds of evidence about the past, from tree rings to Holocaust museums.

- **Terms of History** explain the meanings of some of the most important and contested terms in the history of the West and show how those meanings have developed—and changed—over time. For example, the discussion of *progress* shows how the term took root in the eighteenth century and has been contested in the twentieth.

- **Did You Know?** is a short, illustrated feature that emphasizes the interactions between the West and the broader world, offering unexpected and sometimes startling examples of cultural interchange, from the invention of "smoking" (derived from the New World) to the creation of polo (adapted from South Asia).

- **Taking Measure** highlights a chart, table, graph, or map of historical statistics that illuminates an important political, social, or cultural development.

The map program of the first edition was widely praised as the most comprehensive in any survey text. In each chapter we offer a set of three types of maps, each with a distinct role in conveying information to students. Four to five **full-size maps** show major developments, two to four **"spot" maps**—small maps that emphasize a detailed area from the discussion—aid students' understanding of specific but crucial issues, and **"Mapping the West"** summary maps at the end of each chapter provide a snapshot of the West at the close of a transformative period and help students visualize the West's changing contours over time. For this edition, we have carefully considered each map, improved the colors for better contrast, and clarified and updated borders and labels where needed.

It has been our intention to integrate art as fully as possible into the narrative and to show its value for teaching and learning. **Over 400 illustrations**, carefully chosen to reflect this edition's broad topical coverage and geographic inclusion, reinforce the text and show the varieties of visual sources from which historians build their narratives and interpretations. All artifacts, illustrations, paintings, and photographs are contemporaneous with the chapter; there are no anachronistic illustrations—no fifteenth-century peasants

tilling fields in a chapter on the tenth century! We know that today's students are very attuned to visual sources of information, yet they do not always receive systematic instruction in how to "read" or think critically about such visual sources. Our substantive captions for the maps and art help them learn how to make the most of these informative materials, and now in the second edition, we have frequently included specific questions or suggestions for comparisons that might be developed. Specially designed visual exercises in the *Online Study Guide* supplement this approach in an especially thought-provoking fashion. A new page design for the second edition supports our goal of intertwining the art and the narrative and lends more interest and dynamism to the page.

Textual Changes

A textbook, unlike most scholarly books, offers historians the rare chance to revise the original work, to keep it fresh, and to make it better. It has been a privilege to bring our own scholarship and teaching to bear on this rewriting. In this second edition, we have kept our emphasis on a strong central story line that incorporates the best of new research, but we have worked to make the narrative even more focused and accessible by reviewing every line of text and recrafting the headings to provide better signposts for readers.

Our book now begins with a new prologue that examines the lives of early human beings in the Paleolithic and Neolithic eras. Here we discuss the archeological evidence that points to the technology, trade, religious practices, and social traditions of people who left no written history. The prologue is designed for maximum flexibility. It contains full chapter pedagogy to support instructors who choose to assign this period. Alternatively, it can be used as introductory or extra reading for those instructors who begin their courses with Mesopotamia.

To illustrate our conception of the history of the West as an ongoing process, the first chapter opens with a new section on the origins and contested meaning of *Western civilization*. In this conversation, we emphasize our theme of cultural borrowing between the peoples of Europe and their neighbors that has characterized Western civilization from the beginning. We continue to incorporate the experiences of borderland regions and the importance of global interactions into the historical narrative and in many of our new art selections.

Of course, the recent past is the most pressing arena in which to examine the West as an evolving construct. The impact of recent events is reflected most dramatically in the last two chapters, which have been completely rewritten and now divide at 1989, the year that marks the beginning of a new era after the cold war.

Throughout each chapter, we've added new material and drawn on new scholarship on topics such as the demise of the Akkadian Empire and the succeeding Ur III dynasty (Chapter 1); Zoroastrianism and the influence of Persian religion on later faiths (Chapter 2); criticisms of radical democracy (Chapter 3); diversity among the non-Roman peoples who flooded into the Roman Empire (Chapter 7); the origins of Islam (Chapter 8); Byzantine court culture and the *dynatoi* (Chapter 9); the prominence of the flagellant movement (Chapter 13); Spanish exploration of the Pacific Coast of North America (Chapter 16); the promotion of women's emigration to the new colonies (Chapter 17); sugar grinding in the colonies (Chapter 18); the role of peasants in the French Revolution (Chapter 20); nineteenth-century French efforts to transform Saigon (Chapter 23); Japan's imperialist activity in the 1920s (Chapter 26); discontent in the colonies during the depression (Chapter 27); postwar recovery in Scandinavia and the contributions of immigrants to postwar European economies (Chapter 28); the rise in the study of social sciences (Chapter 29); and the impact of global outsourcing (Chapter 30).

Supplements

As with the first edition, a well-integrated ancillary program supports *The Making of the West: Peoples and Cultures.* Each print and electronic resource has been carefully revised to provide a host of practical teaching and learning aids.

For Students

***Sources of* The Making of the West, Second Edition**—Volumes I (to 1740) and II (since 1500)—by Katharine J. Lualdi, University of Southern Maine. For each chapter in *The Making of the West*, this companion sourcebook features four or five important political, social, and cultural documents that reinforce or extend discussions in the textbook, encouraging students to make connections between narrative history and primary sources. Short chapter summaries and document headnotes contextualize the wide array of sources and perspectives represented, while discussion and comparative questions guide students' reading and promote historical thinking skills. The second edition provides instructors with even more flexibility, as the nearly one-third new selections feature visual sources for the first time. This edition also features more attention to geographic areas beyond Europe and includes an improved balance between traditional documents and selections that provide a fresh perspective.

***Study Guide to Accompany* The Making of the West, Second Edition**—Volumes I (to 1740) and II (since 1500)—by Victoria Thompson, Arizona State University, and Eric Johnson, University of California, Los Angeles. For each chapter in the textbook, the *Study Guide* offers overview questions; a chapter summary; an expanded timeline with questions; a glossary of key terms with a related exercise; multiple-choice and short-answer questions; plus map, illustration, and source exercises that help students synthesize information and practice analytical skills. Answers for all exercises are provided.

***Online Study Guide* at bedfordstmartins .com/hunt** The popular *Online Study Guide* for *The Making of the West* is a free and uniquely personalized learning tool to help students master themes and information in the textbook and improve their historical skills. Instructors can monitor student progress through the online *Quiz Gradebook* or receive e-mail updates.

The Bedford Series in History and Culture—Advisory Editors Natalie Zemon Davis, Princeton University; Ernest R. May, Harvard University; David W. Blight, Yale University; and Lynn Hunt, University of California, Los Angeles. European titles in this highly praised series combine first-rate scholarship, historical narrative, and important primary documents for undergraduate courses. Each book is brief, inexpensive, and focused on a specific topic or period. Packaged discounts are available. European titles include *Spartacus and the Slave Wars*, *Utopia*, *Candide*, *The French Revolution and Human Rights*, *The Enlightenment*, and *The Communist Manifesto*.

DocLinks at bedfordstmartins.com/doclinks This Web site provides over 400 annotated Web links with single-click access to primary documents online, including speeches, legislation, treaties, social commentary, essays, travelers' accounts, personal narratives and testimony, newspaper articles, visual artifacts, songs, and poems. Searchable by topic, date, or specific chapter of *The Making of the West*.

HistoryLinks at bedfordstmartins.com/historylinks HistoryLinks directs instructors and students to over 500 carefully selected and annotated history-related Web sites, including those containing image galleries, maps, and audio and video clips for supplementing lectures or making assignments. Searchable by date, subject, medium, keyword, or specific chapter in *The Making of the West*.

A Student's Online Guide to History Reference Sources at bedfordstmartins.com/benjamin This collection of links provides access to history-related electronic reference sources such as databases, indexes, and journals, plus contact information for state, provincial, local, and professional history organizations. Based on the appendix to Jules Benjamin's *A Student's Guide to History*, Ninth Edition.

For Instructors

***Instructor's Resource Manual to Accompany* The Making of the West, Second Edition**—Volumes I (to 1740) and II (since 1500)—by Dakota Hamilton, Humboldt State University. This helpful manual offers both first-time and experienced teachers a wealth of tools for structuring and customizing Western civilization history courses of different sizes. For each chapter in the textbook, the *Instructor's Resource Manual* includes an outline of chapter themes; a chapter summary; lecture and discussion topics; film and literature suggestions; writing and class-presentation assignments; research topic suggestions; and in-class exercises for working with maps, illustrations, and sources.

Transparencies A set of over 200 full-color acetate transparencies for *The Making of the West* includes all full-sized maps and many images from the text.

Computerized Test Bank—by Joseph Coohill, Pennsylvania State University at New Kensington, and Frances Mitilineos, Loyola University Chicago; available on CD-ROM. This fully updated test bank offers over 80 exercises per chapter, including multiple-choice, identification, timelines, map labeling and analysis, source analysis, and full-length essay questions. Instructors can customize quizzes, edit both questions and answers, as well as export them to a variety of formats, including WebCT and Blackboard. The disc includes answer keys and essay outlines.

Instructor's Resource CD-ROM This disc provides instructors with ready-made and easily customized PowerPoint multimedia presentations built around chapter outlines, maps, figures, and selected images from the textbook. The disc also contains images in JPEG format, an electronic version of the *Instructor's Resource Manual*, outline maps in PDF format for quizzing or handouts, and quick-start guides to the *Online Study Guide*.

Book Companion Site at bedfordstmartins.com/hunt The companion Web site for

The Making of the West gathers all the electronic resources for the text, including the *Online Study Guide* and related *Quiz Gradebook*, at a single Web address. It provides convenient links to such helpful lecture and research materials as PowerPoint chapter outlines from the textbook, DocLinks, HistoryLinks, and Map Central.

Map Central at bedfordstmartins.com/mapcentral Map Central is a searchable database of more than 750 maps from Bedford/St. Martin's history texts for classroom presentations and more than 50 basic political and physical outline maps for quizzes or handouts.

***Using the Bedford Series in History and Culture with* The Making of the West, Second Edition** This short guide gives practical suggestions for using the volumes in The Bedford Series in History and Culture in conjunction with *The Making of the West*. This reference supplies connections between the text and the supplements and ideas for starting discussions focused on a single primary-source volume. Available in print as well as online at bedfordstmartins.com/usingseries.

Blackboard and WebCT content is available for *The Making of the West*.

Videos and Multimedia A wide assortment of videos and multimedia CD-ROMs on various topics in European history is available to qualified adopters.

Acknowledgments

In the vital process of revision, the authors have benefited from repeated critical readings by many talented scholars and teachers. Our sincere thanks go to the following instructors, whose comments often challenged us to rethink or justify our interpretations and who always provided a check on accuracy down to the smallest detail.

Stephen J. Andrews, *Albuquerque Technical Vocational Institute*

Laetitia Argenteri, *San Diego Mesa College*

Sharon Arnoult, *Midwestern State University*

Wayne C. Bartee, *Southwest Missouri State University*

S. Jonathan Bass, *Samford University*

Joel D. Benson, *Northwest Missouri State University*

Marjorie Berman, *Red Rocks Community College*

Lyn A. Blanchfield, *Le Moyne College*

Stephen Blumm, *Montgomery County Community College*

Ronald G. Brown, *College of Southern Maryland*

J. Laurel Carrington, *St. Olaf College*

Joseph Coohill, *Pennsylvania State University, New Kensington*

Cassandra B. Cookson, *Brazosport College*

Paul Cullity, *Keene State College*

Marianne Eve Fisher, *South Dakota State University*

Malia Formes, *Western Kentucky University*

James Genova, *Indiana State University*

Karen Graubert, *Cornell University*

William G. Gray, *Texas Tech University*

Ginger Guardiola, *Colorado State University*

David Halahmy, *Cypress College*

Paul Halsall, *University of North Florida*

Dakota Hamilton, *Humboldt State University*

Carmen Harris, *University of South Carolina, Spartanburg*

L. Edward Hicks, *Faulkner University*

Christine Holden, *University of Southern Maine*

David Hood, *California State University, Long Beach*

Chris Howell, *Red Rocks Community College*

David Hudson, *California State University, Fresno*

Paul J. Hughes, *Sussex County Community College*

Marsh W. Jones, *Parkland College*

Erin Jordan, *University of Northern Colorado*

Gerald Kadish, *State University of New York, Binghamton*

Ruth Mazo Karras, *University of Minnesota*

Frances A. Kelleher, *Grand Valley State University*

Jason Knirck, *Humboldt State University*

Anne Kelly Knowles, *Middlebury College*

John Krapp, *Hofstra University*

David Kutcha, *University of New England*

Ann Kuzdale, *Chicago State University*

Michelle Laughran, *Saint Joseph's College of Maine*

Alison Williams Lewin, *St. Joseph's University*

Janice Liedl, *Laurentian University*

Paul Douglas Lockhart, *Wright State University*

David W. Madsen, *Seattle University*

Steven G. Marks, *Clemson University*

Andrew McMichael, *Western Kentucky University*

Gary M. Miller, *Southern Oregon University*

Eva Mo, *Modesto Junior College*

David B. Mock, *Tallahassee Community College*

Scott Morschauser, *Rowan University*

Johanna Moyer, *State University of New York, Oswego*

Peter Parides, *New York City College of Technology*

Paulette L. Pepin, *University of New Haven*

Norman Raiford, *Greenville Technical College*

Salvador Rivera, *State University of New York, Cobleskill*

Kenneth W. Rock, *Colorado State University*

Anna Marie Roos, *University of Minnesota, Duluth*

Patricia C. Ross, *Columbus State Community College*

Jon Rudd, *Prince George's Community College*

Brian Rutishauser, *Fresno City College*

Daniella Sarnoff, *Xavier University*

Lynn Schibeci, *University of New Mexico*

Kim Schutte, *Missouri Western State College*

David Shafer, *California State University, Long Beach*

Jessica A. Sheetz-Nguyen, *Oklahoma City Community College*

William A. Sherrard, *Creighton University*

Charlie R. Steen, *University of New Mexico*

Nicholas Steneck, *Ohio State University*

Robert E. Stiefel, *University of New Hampshire*

Ann Sullivan, *Tompkins Cortland Community College*

Paul Teverow, *Missouri Southern State College*

Michael E. Thede, *Florida Gulf Coast University*

Frances Titchener, *Utah State University*

Tracey Trenam, *Aims Community College*

David G. Troyansky, *Texas Tech University*

Timothy Vogt, *University of San Francisco*

James J. Ward, *Cedar Crest College*

Theodore Weeks, *Southern Illinois University*

Michael Weiss, *Linn-Benton Community College*

Stephen J. White Sr., *College of Charleston*

Anne Will, *Skagit Valley College*

Andrea Winkler, *Whitman College*

Robinson Yost, *Kirkwood Community College*

Each of us has also benefited from the close readings and valuable criticisms of our coauthors, though we all assume responsibility for our own chapters. Thomas Martin has written Chapters 1–7; Barbara Rosenwein, Chapters 8–12; Ronnie Hsia, Chapters 13–15; Lynn Hunt, Chapters 16–22; and Bonnie Smith, Chapters 23–30.

Many colleagues, friends, and family members have helped us develop this work as well. They know how grateful we are. We also wish to acknowledge and thank the publishing team at Bedford/St. Martin's who did so much to bring this revised edition to completion: Joan Feinberg, Denise Wydra, Elizabeth Welch, Mary Dougherty, Jane Knetzger, Sara Wise, Anne Noonan, Kristen Merrill, Jenna Bookin Barry, Rachel Safer, Bryce Sady, Jan Fitter, Dale Anderson, Gretchen Boger, Elsa Peterson, and Judy Brody.

Our students' questions and concerns have shaped much of this work, and we welcome all our readers' suggestions, queries, and criticisms. Please contact us at our respective institutions or via history@bedfordstmartins.com.

L.H.   T.R.M.   B.H.R.   R.P.H.   B.G.S.

Contents

The New Globalism: Opportunities and Dilemmas, 1989 to the Present   1185

Maps and Figures

Maps

Special Features

Individual Documents

Contrasting Views

New Sources, New Perspectives

Terms of History

Did You Know?

Taking Measure

To the Student

This guide to your textbook introduces the unique features that will help you understand the fascinating story of Western civilization.

Renaissance Europe, 1400–1500

CHAPTER 14

Widening Intellectual Horizons
• The Humanist Renewal
• The Advent of Printing

Revolution in the Arts
• From Artisan to Artist
• The Human Figure

Read the **chapter outlines** to preview topics and themes to come.

IN 1461, THE OTTOMAN RULER MEHMED II sent a letter to Sigismondo Malatesta, the lord of the Italian city-state of Rimini, asking the Italian prince to lend him court painter and architect Matteo de Pasti. The Ottoman sultan was planning to but recently conquered capital, Constantinople (a fitting symbol of his imperial dominion, and Pasti's reputation. The Rimini painter had no minated manuscripts and portrait medals of tress but also designed a monument to the p which was modeled after the principles descrit tise *On Architecture* (first century B.C.E.). This w in Italy in 1414.

Armed with a letter from Sigismondo, ma set out for Constantinople, ready to court favo was eager to form an alliance with the Turkis thorities, however, intercepted the artist in Cre a political connection between another Italian the Venetians confiscated the gifts and sent de Thus, Mehmed's new palace was constructe help—but with the aid of several Venetian p palace came to be called the Topkapi Saray a looking across the Bosporus, the strait that c Asian Turkey.

The story of Matteo de Pasti's failed missi tral theme of the Renaissance: the connection fame in an age that was discovering

Keep track of the dates and topics with **two-tiered running heads** that link subject matter to the time frame.

TRADITION AND INNOVATION IN ATHENS'S GOLDEN AGE 111

c. 500–c. 400 B.C.E.

Vase Painting of a Doctor at Work
This piece of pottery, apparently used to hold perfume or ointment, is decorated with a picture of a physician treating a patient's arm. The prevalence of war gave Greek doctors much experience with wounds and trauma, and they could stop bleeding, set bones, perform minor surgery, and offer some pain relief with drugs derived from plants. Still, the effectiveness of their treatment was limited because they had no cure for infections. *Photo Réunion des Musées Nationaux—Herve Lewandowski.*

medicine, that four humors (fluids) made up the human body: blood, phlegm, black bile, and yellow bile. Health therefore depended on keeping the proper balance among them; being healthy was to be in "good humor." This system for understanding the body corresponded to the division of the inanimate world into four parts: the elements earth, air, fire, and water.

Hippocrates taught that the physician's most important duty was to base his knowledge on careful observation of patients and their response to different treatments. He insisted that clinical experience, not abstract theory or religious belief, was the proper principle for establishing effective cures. By putting his innovative ideas and practices to the test in competition with those of traditional medicine, Hippocrates established the truth of his principle, which later became a cornerstone of scientific medicine.

Review: How did new ways of thinking in the Golden Age threaten cherished traditions?

Use the **review questions** at the end of each major section to check your understanding of key concepts.

Use **boldface key terms** to identify important ideas.

shameful actions (such as the Athenian punishment of Melos in the Peloponnesian War—see page 117) as of glorious achievements.

Hippocrates and the Birth of Scientific Medicine. Hippocrates* of Cos, a fifth-century contemporary of Thucydides, challenged tradition by grounding medical diagnosis and treatment in clinical observation; his fame continues today in the oath bearing his name that doctors swear at the beginning of their professional careers. Previously, medicine had depended on magic and ritual; illness was believed to be caused by evil spirits, and various cults in Greek religion offered healing to patients through divine intervention. Competing to refute these earlier doctors' theories, Hippocrates insisted that only physical factors caused disease. He may have been the author of the view, dominant in later

The Development of Greek Tragedy
The problematic relationship between gods and humans inspired Golden Age Athens's most prominent cultural innovation: tragic drama. Plays called tragedies were presented over three days at the major annual festival of the god Dionysus in a contest for playwrights, in keeping with the competitive spirit characteristic of Greek cultural life. The word *tragedy*—derived, for unknown reasons, from the Greek words for "goat" and "song"—referred to a play involving fierce conflict and characters representing powerful forces. Tragedies presented shocking stories, usually from myth but occasionally from history, that could be related to controversial issues in contemporary Athens. Therefore, these plays stimulated their large audiences to ponder the danger that ignorance, arrogance, and violence presented to the city-state's democratic society. Following the tradition of Homer and Hesiod, Golden Age playwrights explored topics ranging from the roots of good and evil to the nature of individual freedom and responsibility in the family and the political community. As with other ancient

Consult the **pronunciation guide** for hard-to-pronounce words.

*Hippocrates: hih PAH kruh teez

THE GREEK DARK AGE, c. 1000–750 B.C.E.

c. 1000 B.C.E.	Almost all important Mycenaean sites except Athens destroyed by now
c. 1000–900 B.C.E.	Greatest depopulation and economic loss
900–800 B.C.E.	Early revival of population and agriculture; iron now beginning to be used for tools and weapons
c. 800 B.C.E.	Greek trading contacts initiated with Al Mina in Syria
776 B.C.E.	First Olympic Games held
c. 775 B.C.E.	Euboeans found trading post on Ischia in the Bay of Naples
c. 750 B.C.E.	Homeric poetry recorded in writing after Greeks learn to write again; Hesiod composes his poetry; Oracle of Apollo at Delphi already famous

Keep track of time with **chapter timelines** and **topical chronologies**.

486   751 Merovingian dynasty

◆ c. 570–632 Life of Muhammad, prophet of Islam   ◆ c. 590 Arrival of Irish monk Columbanus in Gaul   ◆ 661–750 Umayyad caliphate

◆ 572 Lombards conquer northern Italy   ◆ 624 Battle of Badr   ◆ 664 Synod of Whitby; English king adopts Roman Christianity

575   600   625   650   675   700   725   750

◆ r. 573–c. 594 Bishop Gregory of Tours   ◆ 622 Hijra to Medina; start of the Islamic calendar   ◆ 726–787 Period of iconoclasm at Byzantium

◆ 587 Conversion of Visigothic king Reccared

◆ r. 590–604 Pope Gregory the Great

◆ 603–623 Byzantium/Persia War

Special features show you how historians think and work.

The document program reveals the range of sources that historians use to learn about the past and to draw conclusions.

Numerous **individual documents** offer direct experiences of the past including personal letters, poems, songs, political statements, and speeches.

Contrasting Views provide three or four often-conflicting eyewitness accounts of a central event, person, or development.

New Sources, New Perspectives show how new evidence leads historians to fresh insights—and sometimes new interpretations.

A Merchant's Advice to His Sons

Giovanni Rucellai, one of the most successful merchants of fifteenth-century Florence, kept an extensive diary that reveals life among the city's urban elite. In this selection, Rucellai warns his sons against pursuing political power for self-serving reasons. Rucellai's comments on political of- in order to convert the treasure of the state into your own, for such an action is not good and I shall not approve it. He who aspires to a political position with this goal in mind has always been destroyed by the state itself regardless of the power of ingenuity which he might command. Everyone who

CONTRASTING VIEWS

Christians in the Empire: Conspirators or Faithful Subjects?

Ancient Romans worried that new religions might disrupt the long-standing "peace with the gods" that guaranteed their national safety and prosperity. Groups whose religious creed seemed likely to offend the traditional deities could therefore be accused of treason, but Christians insisted that they were loyal subjects who prayed for the safety of the em... Looking up to heaven, the Christians—with hands outspread, because innocent, with head bare because we do not blush, yes! and without a prompter because we pray from the heart—are ever praying for all the emperors. We pray for a fortunate life for them, a secure rule, a safe house, brave armies, a faithful senate, a virtuous people.

NEW SOURCES, NEW PERSPECTIVES

The Cairo Geniza

What do historians know about the daily life of ordinary people in the Middle Ages? Generally speaking, very little. We have writings from the intellectual elite and administrative documents from monasteries, churches, and courts. But these rarely mention ordinary folk, and if they do, it is always from the standpoint of those who are not ordinary themselves. Glimpsing the concerns, occupations, and family relations of medieval people as they went about their daily lives is very difficult—except at old Cairo (now called Fustat), in Egypt.

Cairo is exceptional because of a cache of un...

Many of these documents were purchased by American and English collectors and ended up in libraries in New York, Philadelphia, and Cambridge, England, where they remain. As is often the case in historical research, the questions that scholars ask are just as important as the sources themselves. At first, historians did not ask what the documents could tell them about everyday life. They wanted to know how to transcribe and read them; they wanted to study the evolution of their writing style (a discipline called paleography). They also needed to organize the material. Dispersed among various libraries, the documents were a...

Other engaging features investigate historical terms, evidence of cultural exchange, and qualitative data.

Terms of History identify a term central to history writing yet hotly debated.

Did You Know? features offer unexpected examples of cultural interchange between the West and the wider world.

Taking Measure data reveal how individual facts add up to broad trends and introduce important quantitative analysis skills.

TERMS OF HISTORY

Progress

Believing as they did in the possibilities of improvement, many Enlightenment writers preached a new doctrine about the meaning of human history. They challenged the traditional Christian belief that the original sin of Adam and Eve condemned human beings to un- you was a bottomless pit." In the movement toward postmodernism, which began in the 1970s, critics argued that we should no longer be satisfied with the modern; the modern brought us calamity and disaster, not reason and freedom. They wanted to go beyond the modern, hence ... The most influential ... Frenchman Michel ... 970s and 1980s that

DID YOU KNOW?

Tobacco and the Invention of "Smoking"

In the early seventeenth century, a "new astonishing fashion," wrote a German ambassador, came to the Dutch Republic from the New World. The term *smoking* gradually evolved in the seventeenth century out of "a fog-drinking bout," "drinking smoke," or "drinking tobacco." One Jesuit preacher called it "dry drunkenness." The analogy to inebriation is not entirely far-fetched, for nicotine (named after the French ambassador to Portugal, panded their exports of tobacco sixfold between 1663 and 1699. Until 1700, Amsterdam dominated the curing process; half the tobacco factories in Amsterdam were owned by Jewish merchants of Spanish or Portuguese descent.

Smoking spread geographically from western to eastern Europe, socially from the upper classes downward, and from men to women. At first the Spanish preferred cigars, the British pipes, and

TAKING MEASURE

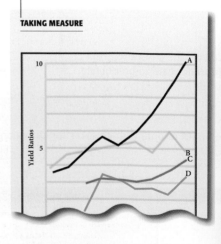

Read the **art and map captions** to help you analyze images and place events.

The Exotic as Consumer Item
This painting by the Venetian artist Rosalba Carriera (1675–1757) is titled *Africa*. The young black girl wearing a turban represents the African continent. Carriera was known for her use of pastels. In 1720, she journeyed to Paris where she became an associate of Antoine Watteau and helped inaugurate the rococo style in painting. Why did the artist choose to paint an African girl for this picture? **For more help analyzing this image,** see the visual activity for this chapter in the Online Study Guide at **bedfordstmartins.com/hunt.** *Staatliche Kunstsammlungen Dresden, Gemaldegalerie Alte Meister.*

Web references direct you to visual activities at the Online Study Guide.

MAP 17.2 State Building in Central and Eastern Europe, 1648–1699
The Austrian Habsburgs had long contested the Ottoman Turks for dominance of eastern Europe, and by 1699 they had pushed the Turks out of Hungary. In central Europe, the Austrian Habsburgs confronted the growing power of Brandenburg-Prussia, which had emerged from relative obscurity after the Thirty Years' War to begin an aggressive program of expanding its military and its territorial base. As emperor of the Holy Roman Empire, the Austrian Habsburg ruler governed a huge expanse of territory, but the emperor's control was in fact only partial because of guarantees of local autonomy.

Full-size maps show major historical developments and carry informative captions.

Mapping the West summary maps provide a snapshot of the West at the close of each chapter.

"Spot" maps offer geographic details right where you need them.

officers, in fact the dukes of Benevento and Spoleto ruled on their own behalf. Although many Lombards were Catholics, others, including important kings and dukes, were Arian. The "official" religion of **Lombard Italy** varied with the ruler in power. Rather than signal a major political event, the conversion of the Lombards to Catholic Christianity occurred gradually, ending only around the mid-seventh century. Partly as a result of this slow development, the Lombard kings, unlike the Visigoths, Franks, or even the

Lombard Italy, Early Eighth Century

MAPPING THE WEST Europe and Byzantium, C. 1215
The major transformation in the map of the West between 1150 and 1215 was the conquest of Constantinople and the setting up of European rule there until 1261. The Byzantine Empire was now a mere shell. A new state, Epirus, emerged in the power vacuum to dominate Thrace. Bulgaria once again gained its independence. If Venice had hoped to control the Adriatic by conquering Constantinople, it must have been disappointed, for Hungary became its rival over the ports of the Dalmatian coast.

Organize your study plans with review sections at the end of each chapter.

Chapter conclusions tie together the chapter's thematic strands, review main topics, and point you onward.

Annotated lists of suggested references provide print and web resources for papers, research projects, or further study.

Important Events lists help you review key happenings at a glance.

Key terms highlight important concepts with page references that point to the text discussion. Each term is defined in the **glossary** at the end of the book.

Review Questions offer section-by-section comprehension prompts.

Making Connections analytical questions help you link ideas within or across chapters.

For Further Exploration points you to free online activities that help you master the chapter material and to additional chapter-related primary sources.

(Sample textbook page 39, Chapter 1 • Foundations of Western Civilization, c. 4000–c. 1000 B.C.E.)

forced them to wander abroad in search of new places to settle. Like people from the earliest times, these devastated ancestors of Western civilization had to move to build a better life.

Review: How did war determine the fates of the early civilizations of Crete, Anatolia, and Greece?

Conclusion

Western civilization emerged in Mesopotamia and Egypt; these cultures in turn influenced the later civilization of Greece. Cities first arose in Mesopotamia by around 3000 B.C.E. Hierarchy characterized society to some degree from the very beginning, but it grew more pronounced once civilization emerged. Trade and war were constants, both aiming in different ways at profit and glory. Indirectly, they often generated energetic cultural interaction by putting civilizations into close contact to learn from one another. Technological innovation was also a prominent characteristic of this long period. The invention of metallurgy, monumental architecture, mathematics, and alphabetic writing greatly affected the future. Religion was at the center of people's lives, with the gods seen as demanding just and righteous conduct from everyone. The emergence of monotheism set the stage for the leading faiths of later Western history.

have seemed destined for irreversible economic and social decline, even oblivion. Chapter 2 shows how wrong this prediction would have been. After a dark period of economic and population decline called the Dark Age, Greeks invented a new form of social and political organization and breathed renewed life into their culture, inspired by their neighbors in the Near East and Egypt.

Suggested References

Mesopotamia, Home of the First Civilization, c. 4000–c. 1000 B.C.E.

Archaeological exploration in Mesopotamia (present-day Iraq) has been almost completely halted for more than a decade. Scholars have therefore been limited to studying already excavated material and texts. Modern translations have made Mesopotamian myths more accessible to today's readers.

Alcock, Susan, et al., eds. *Empires.* 2001.
Ancient Near East: http://www.etana.org/abzu.
Aruz, Joan. ed. *Art of the First Cities: The Third Millennium B.C. from the Mediterranean to the Indus.* 2003.
Bertman, Stephen. *Handbook to Life in Ancient Mesopotamia.* 2003.
Bienkowski, Piotr, and Alan Millard, eds. *Dictionary of the Ancient Near East.* 2000.
Bottéro, Jean. *Everyday Life in Mesopotamia.* Trans. Antonia Nevill. 2001.
Collins, Billie Jean. *A History of the Animal [Wo]rld in the Ancient Near East.* 2002.
[...]ord, Harriet. *Sumer and the Sumerians.*
[...]y, Stephanie, trans. *Myths from Mesopotamia: Creation, The Flood, Gilgamesh, and [oth]ers.* 1991.
[...]ews, Roger. *Archaeology of Mesopotamia: [The]ories and Approaches.* 2003.
[...]rdson, M. E. J. *Hammurabi's Laws: Text, [Tra]nslation and Glossary.* 2000.
[...]ng, William H., Jr. *Ancient Near Eastern [His]tory and Culture.* 2003.
[...]rian literature. http://www-etcsl.orient [...].ac.uk.

(Sample textbook page 121, Chapter Review, c. 500–c. 400 B.C.E.)

CHAPTER REVIEW

IMPORTANT EVENTS

c. 500–323 B.C.E.	Classical Age of Greek History
499–479 B.C.E.	Wars between Persia and Greece
490 B.C.E.	Battle of Marathon
480–479 B.C.E.	Xerxes' invasion of Greece
480 B.C.E.	Battle of Salamis
479 B.C.E.	Battles of Plataea and Mycale
461 B.C.E.	Ephialtes reforms the Athenian court system
Early 450s B.C.E.	Pericles introduces pay for office holders in Athenian democracy
454 B.C.E.	Catastrophic defeat of Athenian fleet by Persians in Egypt kills tens of thousands of oarsmen
451 B.C.E.	Pericles sponsors law to restrict Athenian citizenship to children whose parents are both citizens
c. 450 B.C.E.	Protagoras and other Sophists begin to move to Athens to teach
446–445 B.C.E. (winter)	Peace treaty between Athens and Sparta; intended to last thirty years
431 B.C.E.	Euripides presents the tragedy *Medea*
431–404 B.C.E.	Peloponnesian War
420s B.C.E.	Herodotus finishes *Histories,* the first great Greek work of history writing
415–413 B.C.E.	Enormous Athenian military expedition against Sicily
411 B.C.E.	Aristophanes presents the comedy *Lysistrata*
404–403 B.C.E.	Rule of the Thirty Tyrants at Athens
403 B.C.E.	Restoration of democracy

KEY TERMS

agora (93)
Delian League (88)
frieze (95)
hetaira (99)
hubris (114)
metic (97)
mystery cult (97)
ostracism (91)
radical democracy (90)
Socratic method (109)
Sophists (106)
subjectivism (106)
symposium (plural "symposia") (99)
trireme (89)

REVIEW QUESTIONS

1. What differences in Greek and Persian political and military organization determined the course of the Persian Wars?

2. What factors prompted political change in fifth-century B.C.E. Athens?
3. How did new ways of thinking in the Golden Age threaten cherished traditions?
4. How did unexpected events contribute to the outcome of the Peloponnesian War?

MAKING CONNECTIONS

1. What were the most significant differences between Greece in the Archaic Age and in the Golden Age?
2. What did Greeks of the Golden Age believe it was worth spending public funds to pay for and why?

FOR FURTHER EXPLORATION

To assess your mastery of the material in this chapter, see the Online Study Guide at bedfordstmartins.com/hunt.

To read additional primary-source material from this period, see Chapter 3 in *Sources of The Making of the West,* Second Edition.

See the preface for a full list of student resources, including the Online Study Guide, that accompany *The Making of the West: Peoples and Cultures,* Second Edition.

How to Read Primary Sources

In each chapter of this textbook you will find many primary sources to broaden your understanding of the development of the West. Primary sources refer to firsthand, contemporary accounts or direct evidence about a particular topic. For example, speeches, letters, diaries, song lyrics, and newspaper articles are all primary sources that historians use to construct accounts of the past. Nonwritten materials such as maps, paintings, artifacts, and even architecture and music can also be primary sources. Both types of historical documents in this textbook—written and visual—provide a glimpse into the lives of the men and women who influenced or were influenced by the course of Western history.

To guide your interpretation of any source, you should begin by asking several basic questions, listed below, as starting points for observing, analyzing, and interpreting the past. Your answers should prompt further questions of your own.

1. **Who is the author?** Who wrote or created the material? What was his or her authority? (Personal? institutional?) Did the author have specialized knowledge or experience? If you are reading a written document, how would you describe the author's tone of voice? (Formal, personal, angry?)

2. **Who is the audience?** Who were the intended readers, listeners, or viewers? How does the intended audience affect the ways that the author presents ideas?

3. **What are the main ideas?** What are the main points that the author is trying to convey? Can you detect any underlying assumptions of values or attitudes? How does the form or medium affect the meaning of this document?

4. **In what context was the document created?** From when and where does the document originate? What was the interval between the initial problem or event and this document, which responded to it? Through what form or medium was the document communicated? (For example, a newspaper, a government record, an illustration.) What contemporary events or conditions might have affected the creation of the document?

5. **What's missing?** What's missing or cannot be learned from this source, and what might this omission reveal? Are there other sources that might fill in the gaps?

Now consider these questions as you read the following document, "Columbus Describes His First Voyage, 1493." Compare your answers to the sample observations provided.

Columbus Describes His First Voyage, 1493

In this famous letter to Raphael Sanchez, treasurer to his patrons, Ferdinand and Isabella, Columbus recounts his initial journey to the Bahamas, Cuba, and Hispaniola (today Haiti and the Dominican Republic), and tells of his achievements. This passage reflects the first contact between Native Americans and Europeans; already the themes of trade, subjugation, gold, and conversion all emerge in Columbus's own words.

Indians would give whatever the seller required; . . . Thus they bartered, like idiots, cotton and gold for fragments of bows, glasses, bottles, and jars; which I forbad as being unjust, and myself gave them many beautiful and acceptable articles which I had brought with me, taking nothing from them in return; I did this in order that I might the more easily conciliate them, that they might be led to become Christians, and be inclined to entertain a regard for the King and Queen, our Princes and all Spaniards, and that I might induce them to take an interest in seeking out, and collecting, and delivering to us such things as they possessed in abundance, but which we greatly needed. They practise no kind of idolatry, but have a firm belief that all strength and power, and indeed all good things, are in heaven, and that I had descended from thence with these ships and sailors, and under this impression was I received after they had thrown aside their fears. Nor are they slow or stupid, but of very clear understanding; and those men who have crossed to the neighbouring islands give an admirable description of everything they observed; but they never saw any people clothed, nor any ships like ours. On my arrival at that sea, I had taken some Indians by force from the first island that I came to, in order that they might learn our language, and communicate to us what they know respecting the country; which plan succeeded excellently, and was a great advantage to us, for in a short time, either by gestures and signs, or by words, we were enabled to understand each other. These men are still travelling with me, and although they have been with us now a long time, they continue to entertain the idea that I have descended from heaven.

Source: Christopher Columbus, *Four Voyages to the New World.* Translated by R. H. Major (New York: Corinth Books, 1961), 8–9.

1. **Who is the author?** The title and headnote that precede each document contain information about the authorship and date of its creation. In this case, the Italian explorer Christopher Columbus is the author. His letter describes events in which he was both an eyewitness and a participant.

2. **Who is the audience?** Columbus sent the letter to Raphael Sanchez, treasurer to Ferdinand and Isabella—someone who Columbus knew would be keenly interested in the fate of his patrons' investment. Because the letter was also a public document written to a crown official, Columbus would have expected a wider audience beyond Sanchez. How might his letter have differed had it been written to a friend?

3. **What are the main ideas?** In this segment, Columbus describes his encounter with the native people. He speaks of his desire to establish good relations by treating them fairly, and he offers his impressions of their intelligence and naiveté—characteristics he implies will prove useful to Europeans. He also expresses an interest in converting them to Christianity and making them loyal subjects of the crown.

4. **In what context was the document was created?** Columbus wrote the letter in 1493, within six months of his first voyage. He would have been eager to announce the success of his endeavor.

5. **What's missing?** Columbus's letter provides just one view of the encounter. We do not have a corresponding account from the Native Americans' perspective nor from anyone else travelling with Columbus. With no corroboration evidence, how reliable is this description?

Note: You can use these same questions to analyze visual images. Start by determining who created the image—whether it's a painting, photograph, sculpture, map, or artifact—and when it was made. Then consider the audience for whom the artist might have intended the work and how viewers might have reacted. Consult the text for information about the time period, and look for visual cues such as color, artistic style, and use of space to determine the central idea of the work. As you read, consult the captions in this book to help you evaluate the images and to ask more questions of your own.

About the Authors

LYNN HUNT, Eugen Weber Professor of Modern European History at the University of California, Los Angeles, received her B.A. from Carleton College and her M.A. and Ph.D. from Stanford University. She is the author of *Revolution and Urban Politics in Provincial France* (1978); *Politics, Culture, and Class in the French Revolution* (1984); and *The Family Romance of the French Revolution* (1992). She is also the coauthor of *Telling the Truth about History* (1994); coauthor of *Liberty, Equality, Fraternity: Exploring the French Revolution* (2001, with CD-ROM); editor of *The New Cultural History* (1989); editor and translator of *The French Revolution and Human Rights* (1996); and coeditor of *Histories: French Constructions of the Past* (1995), *Beyond the Cultural Turn* (1999), and *Human Rights and Revolutions* (2000). She has been awarded fellowships by the Guggenheim Foundation and the National Endowment for the Humanities and is a fellow of the American Academy of Arts and Sciences. She served as president of the American Historical Association in 2002.

THOMAS R. MARTIN, Jeremiah O'Connor Professor in Classics at the College of the Holy Cross, earned his B.A. at Princeton University and his M.A. and Ph.D. at Harvard University. He is the author of *Sovereignty and Coinage in Classical Greece* (1985) and *Ancient Greece* (1996, 2000) and one of the originators of *Perseus 1.0: Interactive Sources and Studies on Ancient Greece* (1992, 1996, and www.perseus.tufts.edu), which, among other awards, was named the EDUCOM Best Software in Social Sciences (History) in 1992. He also wrote the lead article on ancient Greece for the revised edition of the *Encarta* electronic encyclopedia. He serves on the editorial board of STOA (www.stoa.org) and as codirector of its DEMOS project (online resources on ancient Athenian democracy). A recipient of fellowships from the National Endowment for the Humanities and the American Council of Learned Societies, he is currently conducting research on the comparative historiography of ancient Greece and ancient China.

BARBARA H. ROSENWEIN, professor of history at Loyola University Chicago, earned her B.A., M.A., and Ph.D. at the University of Chicago. She is the author of *Rhinoceros Bound: Cluny in the Tenth Century* (1982); *To Be the Neighbor of Saint Peter: The Social Meaning of Cluny's Property, 909–1049* (1989); *Negotiating Space: Power, Restraint, and Privileges of Immunity in Early Medieval Europe* (1999); and *A Short History of the Middle Ages* (2001). She is the editor of *Anger's Past: The Social Uses of an Emotion in the Middle Ages* (1998) and coeditor of *Debating the Middle Ages: Issues and Readings* (1998) and *Monks and Nuns, Saints and Outcasts: Religion in Medieval Society* (2000). A recipient of Guggenheim and National Endowment for the Humanities fellowships, she is currently working on a history of emotions in the early Middle Ages.

R. PO-CHIA HSIA, Edwin Erle Sparks Professor of History at Pennsylvania State University, received his B.A. from Swarthmore College and his M.A. and Ph.D. from Yale University. He is the author of *Society and Religion in Münster, 1535–1618* (1984); *The Myth of Ritual Murder: Jews and Magic in Reformation Germany* (1988); *Social Discipline in the Reformation: Central Europe 1550–1750* (1989); *Trent 1475: Stories of a Ritual Murder Trial* (1992); and *The World of the Catholic Renewal* (1997). He has edited *The German People and the Reformation* (1998); *In and Out of the Ghetto: Jewish-Gentile Relations in Late Medieval and Early Modern Germany* (1995); *Calvinism and Religious Toleration in the Dutch Golden Age* (2002); and *A Blackwell Companion to the Reformation World* (Blackwell Companion Series, 2004). An academician at the Academia Sinica, Taiwan, he has also been awarded fellowships by the Woodrow Wilson

International Society of Scholars, the National Endowment for the Humanities, the Guggenheim Foundation, the Davis Center of Princeton University, the Mellon Foundation, the American Council of Learned Societies, and the American Academy in Berlin. Currently he is working on the cultural contacts between Europe and Asia between the sixteenth and eighteenth centuries.

BONNIE G. SMITH, Board of Governors Professor of History at Rutgers University, earned her B.A. at Smith College and her Ph.D. at the University of Rochester. She is the author of *Ladies of the Leisure Class* (1981); *Confessions of a Concierge: Madame Lucie's History of Twentieth-Century France* (1985); *Changing Lives: Women in European History Since 1700* (1989); *The Gender of History: Men, Women, and Historical Practice* (1998); and *Imperialism* (2000). She is also the coauthor and translator of *What Is Property?* (1994); editor of *Global Feminisms since 1945* (2000); and coeditor of *Objects of Modernity: Selected Writings of Lucy Maynard Salmon, Gendering Disability* (2004) and the forthcoming *Oxford Encyclopedia of Women in World History.* She has received fellowships from the Guggenheim Foundation, the National Endowment for the Humanities, the National Humanities Center, the Davis Center of Princeton University, and the American Council of Learned Societies. Currently she is studying the globalization of European culture since the seventeenth century.

The Promise of Enlightenment,
1740–1789

The Enlightenment at Its Height
- Men and Women of the Republic of Letters
- Conflicts with Church and State
- The Individual and Society
- Spreading the Enlightenment
- The Limits of Reason: Roots of Romanticism and Religious Revival

Society and Culture in an Age of Enlightenment
- The Nobility's Reassertion of Privilege
- The Middle Class and the Making of a New Elite
- Life on the Margins
- The Roots of Industrialization

State Power in an Era of Reform
- War and Diplomacy
- State-Sponsored Reform
- Limits of Reform

Rebellions against State Power
- Food Riots and Peasant Uprisings
- Public Opinion and Political Opposition
- Revolution in North America

IN THE SUMMER OF 1766, Empress Catherine II ("the Great") of Russia wrote to Voltaire, one of the leaders of the Enlightenment:

> It is a way of immortalizing oneself to be the advocate of humanity, the defender of oppressed innocence. . . . You have entered into combat against the enemies of mankind: superstition, fanaticism, ignorance, quibbling, evil judges, and the powers that rest in their hands. Great virtues and qualities are needed to surmount these obstacles. You have shown that you have them: you have triumphed.

Over a fifteen-year period Catherine corresponded regularly with Voltaire, a writer who, at home in France, found himself in constant conflict with authorities of church and state. Her admiring letter shows how influential Enlightenment ideals had become by the middle of the eighteenth century. Even an absolutist ruler such as Catherine endorsed many aspects of the Enlightenment call for reform; she too wanted to be an "advocate of humanity."

Catherine's letter aptly summed up Enlightenment ideals: progress for humanity could be achieved only by rooting out the wrongs left by superstition, religious fanaticism, ignorance, and outmoded forms of justice. Enlightenment writers used every means at their disposal—from encyclopedias to novels to personal interaction with rulers—to argue for reform. Everything had to be examined in the cold light of reason, and anything that did not promote the improvement of humanity was to be jettisoned. As a result, Enlightenment writers attacked the legal use of torture to extract confessions, supported religious toleration, favored the spread of education to eliminate ignorance, and criticized censorship by state or church. The book trade and new places for urban socializing, such as coffeehouses and learned societies, spread these ideas within a new elite of middle- and upper-class men and women.

Catherine the Great
In this portrait by the Danish painter Vigilius Eriksen, the Russian empress Catherine the Great is shown on horseback (c.1752), much like any male ruler of the time. Born Sophia Augusta Frederika of Anhalt-Zerbst in 1729, Catherine was the daughter of a minor German prince. When she married the future tsar Peter III in 1745, she promptly learned Russian and adopted Russian Orthodoxy. Peter, physically and mentally frail, proved no match for her; in 1762 she staged a coup against him and took his place when he was killed. *Bridgeman–Giraudon/Art Resource, NY.*

The lower classes had little contact with Enlightenment ideas. Their lives were shaped more profoundly by the continuing rise in population, the development of factories to produce cotton cloth, and wars among the great powers. States had to balance conflicting social pressures: rulers pursued Enlightenment reforms that they believed might enhance state power, but they feared changes that might unleash popular discontent. For example, Catherine aimed to bring Western ideas, culture, and reforms to Russia, but when faced with a massive uprising of the serfs, she not only suppressed the revolt but also increased the powers of the nobles over their serfs. All reform-minded rulers faced similar potential challenges to their authority.

Even if the movement for reform had its limits, governments now needed to respond to a new force: "public opinion." Rulers wanted to portray themselves as modern, open to change, and responsive to the segment of the public that was reading newspapers and closely following political developments. Enlightenment writers appealed to public opinion, but they still looked to rulers to effect reform. Writers such as Voltaire expressed little interest in the future of peasants or lower classes; they favored neither revolution nor political upheaval. Yet their ideas paved the way for something much more radical and unexpected. The American Declaration of Independence in 1776 showed how Enlightenment ideals could be translated into democratic political practice. After 1789, democracy would come to Europe as well.

❖ The Enlightenment at Its Height

The Enlightenment emerged as an intellectual movement before 1740 but reached its peak only in the second half of the eighteenth century. The writers of the Enlightenment called themselves **philosophes**◆ (French for "philosophers"), but that term is somewhat misleading. Whereas philosophers concern themselves with abstract theories, the philosophes were public intellectuals dedicated to solving the real problems of the world. They wrote on subjects ranging from current affairs to art criticism, and they wrote in every conceivable format. The Swiss philosophe Jean-Jacques Rousseau,◆ for example, wrote a political tract, a treatise on education, a constitution for Poland, an analysis of the effects of the theater on public morals, a best-selling novel, an opera, and a notorious autobiography. The philosophes wrote for a broad educated public of readers who snatched up every Enlightenment book they could find at their local book sellers, even when rulers or churches tried to forbid such books. Between 1740 and 1789, the Enlightenment acquired its name and, despite heated conflicts between the philosophes and state and religious authorities, gained support in the highest reaches of government. (See "Terms of History," page 710.)

◆**philosophes:** fee luh ZAWFS
◆**Jean-Jacques Rousseau:** zhahn zhawk roo SOH

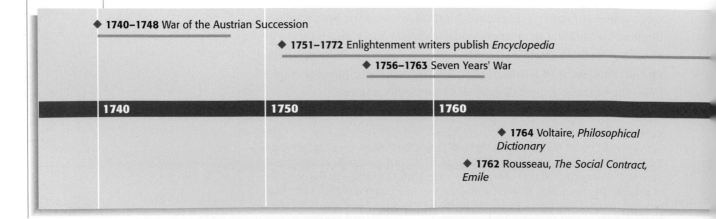

◆ **1740–1748** War of the Austrian Succession

◆ **1751–1772** Enlightenment writers publish *Encyclopedia*

◆ **1756–1763** Seven Years' War

1740	1750	1760

◆ **1764** Voltaire, *Philosophical Dictionary*

◆ **1762** Rousseau, *The Social Contract, Emile*

Men and Women of the Republic of Letters

Although *philosophe* is a French word, the Enlightenment was distinctly cosmopolitan; philosophes could be found from Philadelphia to Moscow. The philosophes considered themselves part of a grand "republic of letters" that transcended national political boundaries. They were not republicans in the usual sense, that is, people who supported representative government and opposed monarchy. What united them were the ideals of reason, reform, and freedom. In 1784, the German philosopher Immanuel Kant summed up the program of the Enlightenment in two Latin words: *sapere aude*, "dare to know"—have the courage to think for yourself.

The philosophes used reason to attack superstition, bigotry, and religious fanaticism, which they considered the chief obstacles to free thought and social reform. Voltaire took religious fanaticism as his chief target: "Once fanaticism has corrupted a mind, the malady is almost incurable. . . . The only remedy for this epidemic malady is the philosophical spirit." Enlightenment writers did not necessarily oppose organized religion, but they strenuously objected to religious intolerance. They believed that the systematic application of reason could do what religious belief could not: improve the human condition by pointing to needed reforms. Reason meant critical, informed, scientific thinking about social issues and problems. Many Enlightenment writers collaborated on a new multivolume *Encyclopedia* (published 1751–1772) that aimed to gather together knowledge about science, religion, industry, and society (see the illustration on this page). The chief editor of the

Bookbinding

In this plate from the *Encyclopedia*, the various stages in bookbinding are laid out from left to right. Binding was not included in the sale of books; owners had to order leather bindings from a special shop. The man at (a) is pounding the pages to be bound on a marble block. The woman at (b) is stitching the pages with a special frame. The worker at (c) cuts the pages, and at (d) the volumes are pressed to prevent warping. In what ways is this illustration representative of the aims of the *Encyclopedia*?

◆ **1770** Louis XV's legal reform fails

◆ **1772** First partition of Poland

◆ **1773** Pugachev rebellion

◆ **1776** American Declaration of Independence; Watt's steam engine; Smith, *Wealth of Nations*

1770	1780	1790	1800

◆ **1780** Joseph II's reforms

◆ **1781** Kant, *The Critique of Pure Reason*

◆ **1785** Charter of the Nobility

◆ **1707** U.S. Constitution

TERMS OF HISTORY

Enlightenment

In 1784, in an essay titled "What Is Enlightenment?" the German philosopher Immanuel Kant gave widespread currency to a term that had been in the making for several decades. The term *enlightened century* had become common in the 1760s. Closely related to Enlightenment was the French term *philosophe*, which was first used to mean "proponent of Enlightenment" in the 1740s. A clandestine tract of 1743 titled *Le Philosophe* explained that the philosophe was the man who saw through popular errors.

The Enlightenment gave itself its own name, and the name clearly had propaganda value. The philosophes associated Enlightenment with philosophy, reason, and humanity; religious tolerance; natural rights; and criticism of outmoded customs and prejudices. They tied Enlightenment to "progress" and to the "modern," and it came into question, just as these other terms did, when events cast doubt on the benefits of progress and the virtues of modernity. Although some opposed the Enlightenment from the very beginning as antireligious, undermining of authority, and even atheistic and immoral, the French Revolution of 1789 galvanized the critics of Enlightenment who blamed every excess of revolution on Enlightenment principles.

For most of the nineteenth century, condemnation of the Enlightenment came from right-wing sources. Some of the more extreme of these critics denounced a supposed "Jewish-Masonic conspiracy," believing that Jews and Freemasons benefited most from the spread of Enlightenment principles and worked secretly to jointly undermine Christianity and established monarchical authorities. Adolf Hitler and his followers shared these suspicions, and during World War II the Germans confiscated the records of Masonic lodges in every country they occupied. They sent the documents back to Berlin so that a special office could trace the links of this supposed conspiracy. They found nothing.

After the catastrophes of World War II, the Enlightenment came under attack for the first time from left-wing critics. In a book published right after World War II, *Dialectic of Enlightenment*, Max Horkheimer and Theodor W. Adorno, two German Jewish refugees from Hitler's regime who had fled to the United States, denounced the Enlightenment as "self-destructive" and even "totalitarian" because its belief in reason led not to freedom but to greater bureaucratic control. They asked "why mankind, instead of entering into a truly human condition, is sinking into a new kind of barbarism," and they answered, because we have trusted too much in the Enlightenment and its belief in reason and science. Reason provided the technology to transport millions of Jews to their deaths in scientifically sound gas chambers. Reason invented the atomic bomb and gave us the factories that pollute the atmosphere. The masses did not rise up against these uses of reason because they were distracted by a mass culture that emphasized entertainment rather than reflection. These criticisms of the Enlightenment, however extreme and sometimes outlandish, show how central the Enlightenment remains to the very definition of modern history.

Sources: Max Horkheimer and Theodor W. Adorno, *Dialectic of Enlightenment*, trans. John Cumming (New York: Continuum, 1993; first published 1947), xi, 6.

Encyclopedia, Denis Diderot♦ (1713–1784), explained the goal: "All things must be examined, debated, investigated without exception and without regard for anyone's feelings."

♦**Diderot:** deed ROH

The philosophes believed that the spread of knowledge would encourage reform in every aspect of life, from the grain trade to the penal system. Chief among their desired reforms was intellectual freedom, the freedom to use one's own reason and to publish the results. The philosophes wanted freedom of

Madame Geoffrin's Salon in 1755
This 1812 painting by Anicet Charles Lemonnier claims to depict the best-known Parisian salon of the 1750s. Lemonnier was only twelve years old in 1755 and so could not have based his rendition on firsthand knowledge. Madame Geoffrin is the figure in blue on the right facing the viewer. The bust is of Voltaire. Rousseau is the fifth person to the left of the bust (facing right) and behind him (facing left) is Raynal. *Bridgeman–Giraudon/Art Resource, NY.*

the press and freedom of religion, which they considered "natural rights" guaranteed by "natural law." In their view, progress depended on these freedoms. As Voltaire asserted, "I quite understand that the fanatics of one sect slaughter the enthusiasts of another sect . . . [but] that Descartes should have been forced to flee to Holland to escape the fury of the ignorant . . . these things are a nation's eternal shame."

Most philosophes, like Voltaire, came from the upper classes, yet Rousseau's father was a modest watchmaker in Geneva, and Diderot was the son of a cutlery maker. Although it was a rare phenomenon, some women were philosophes, such as the French noblewoman Émilie du Châtelet♦ (1706–1749), who wrote extensively about the mathematics and physics of Gottfried Wilhelm Leibniz♦ and Isaac Newton. (Her lover Voltaire learned much of his science from her.) Few of the leading writers held university positions, except those who were German or Scottish. Universities in France were dominated by the Catholic clergy and unreceptive to Enlightenment ideals.

Enlightenment ideas developed instead through personal contacts; through letters that were hand-copied, circulated, and sometimes published; through informal readings of manuscripts; and through letters to the editor and book reviews in periodicals. **Salons**♦—informal gatherings, usually sponsored by middle-class or aristocratic women, that provided a forum for new ideas—gave intellectual life an anchor outside the royal court and the church-controlled universities. (*Salon* is French for "living room.") Best known was the Parisian salon of Madame Marie Thérèse Geoffrin♦ (1699–1777), a wealthy middle-class widow who had been raised by her grandmother and married off at fourteen to a much older man (see Madame Geoffrin's Salon on this page). Creating a salon was her way of educating herself and participating directly in the movement for reform. She brought together the most exciting thinkers and artists of the time; her social gatherings provided a forum for new ideas and an opportunity to establish new intellectual contacts. In the salon the philosophes could discuss ideas they might hesitate to put into print, testing public opinion and even pushing it in new directions. Madame Geoffrin corresponded extensively with influential people across Europe, including

♦**Émilie du Châtelet:** AY mee lee du SHAHT leh
♦**Leibniz:** LYB nuhts

♦**Salons:** suh LAHNS
♦**Marie-Thérèse Geoffrin:** ma ree tay rehz zhaw FRAN

Catherine the Great. One Italian visitor commented, "There is no way to make Naples resemble Paris unless we find a woman to guide us, organize us, *Geoffrinize* us."

Women's salons provoked criticism from men who resented their power. (See "Contrasting Views," page 714.) Nevertheless, the gatherings helped galvanize intellectual life and reform movements all over Europe. Wealthy Jewish women created nine of the fourteen salons in Berlin at the end of the eighteenth century, and in Warsaw, Princess Zofia Czartoryska♦ gathered around her the reform leaders of Poland-Lithuania. Some of the aristocratic women in Madrid who held salons had lived in France, and they combined an interest in French culture and ideas with their efforts to promote the new ideas in Spain. Middle-class women in London used their salons to raise money to publish women's writings. Salons could be tied closely to the circles of power: in France, for example, Louis XV's mistress, Jeanne-Antoinette Poisson, first made her reputation as hostess of a salon frequented by Voltaire and Montesquieu. When she became Louis XV's mistress in 1745, she gained the title Marquise de Pompadour and turned her attention to influencing artistic styles by patronizing architects and painters.

Conflicts with Church and State

Madame Geoffrin did not approve of discussions that attacked the Catholic church, but elsewhere voices against organized religion could be heard. Criticisms of religion required daring because the church, whatever its denomination, wielded enormous power in society, and most influential people considered religion an essential foundation of good society and government. Defying such opinion, the Scottish philosopher David Hume (1711–1776) boldly argued in *The Natural History of Religion* (1755) that belief in God rested on superstition and fear rather than on reason. Hume soon met kindred spirits while visiting Paris; he attended a dinner party consisting of "fifteen atheists, and three who had not quite made up their minds."

Before the scientific revolution, virtually every European believed in God. After

♦**Zofia Czartoryska:** ZAW fya char taw RIHS kee

Newton, however, and despite Newton's own deep religiosity, people could conceive of the universe as an eternally existing, self-perpetuating machine, in which God's intervention was unnecessary. In short, such people could become either **atheists**, people who do not believe in any kind of God, or **deists**, people who believe in God but give him no active role in earthly affairs. For the first time, writers claimed the label *atheist* and disputed the common view that atheism led inevitably to immorality.

Deists continued to believe in a benevolent, all-knowing God who had designed the universe and set it in motion. But they usually rejected the idea that God directly intercedes in the functioning of the universe, and they often criticized the churches for their dogmatic intolerance of dissenters. Voltaire was a deist, and in his popular *Philosophical Dictionary* (1764) he attacked most of the claims of organized Christianity, both Catholic and Protestant. Christianity, he argued, had been the prime source of fanaticism and brutality among humans. Throughout his life, Voltaire's motto was *Ecrasez l'infâme*—"Crush the infamous thing" (the "thing" being bigotry and intolerance). French authorities publicly burned his *Philosophical Dictionary.*

Criticism of religious intolerance involved more than simply attacking the churches. Critics also had to confront the states to which churches were closely tied. In 1761, a judicial case in Toulouse provoked an outcry throughout France that Voltaire soon joined. When the son of a local Calvinist was found hanged (he had probably committed suicide), magistrates accused the father, Jean Calas, of murdering him to prevent his conversion to Catholicism. (Since Louis XIV's revocation of the Edict of Nantes in 1685, it had been illegal to practice Calvinism publicly in France.) The all-Catholic parlement of Toulouse tried to extract a confession using torture—breaking all Calas's bones—and then executed him even though he refused to confess. Voltaire launched a successful crusade to rehabilitate Jean Calas's good name and to restore the family's properties, which had been confiscated after his death. Voltaire's efforts eventually helped bring about the extension of civil rights to French

Protestants and encouraged campaigns to abolish the legal use of torture.

Critics also assailed state and church support for European colonization and slavery. One of the most popular books of the time was the *Philosophical and Political History of European Colonies and Commerce in the Two Indies*, published in 1770 by Abbé Guillaume Raynal (1713–1796), a French Catholic clergyman. Raynal and his collaborators described in excruciating detail the destruction of native populations by Europeans and denounced the slave trade. Raynal's criticism did not stop European exploration and colonization. British explorer James Cook (1728–1779) charted the coasts of New Zealand and Australia, discovered New Caledonia, and visited the ice fields of Antarctica. In 1787 part of Australia was designated a convict colony for the transportation of British offenders.

Some Enlightenment thinkers took a negative view of Africans. Hume judged blacks to be "naturally inferior to the whites," concluding, "There never was a civilized nation of any other complexion than white." Nevertheless, the Enlightenment belief in natural rights helped fuel the antislavery movement, which began to organize political campaigns against slavery in Britain, France, and the new United States in the 1780s. Advocates of the abolition of slavery encouraged freed slaves to write the story of their enslavement. One such freed slave, Olaudah Equiano, wrote of his kidnapping and enslavement in Africa and his long effort to free himself. *The Interesting Narrative of the Life of Olaudah Equiano*, published in 1788, became an international best seller; it had appeared in English, Dutch, Russian, and French by the time Equiano died in 1797. Armed with such firsthand accounts of slavery, **abolitionists** began to petition their governments for the abolition of the slave trade and then of slavery itself.

Enlightenment critics of church and state usually advocated reform, not revolution. For example, though he lived near the French-Swiss border in case he had to flee, Voltaire made a fortune in financial speculations, wrote a glowing history called *The Age of Louis XIV* (1751), and lived to be celebrated in his last years as a national hero even by many former foes. Other philosophes also lived respectably,

believing that published criticism, rather than violent action, would bring about necessary reforms. As Diderot said, "We will speak against senseless laws until they are reformed; and, while we wait, we will abide by them." Those few who lived long enough to see the French Revolution in 1789 resisted its radical turn, for the philosophes generally regarded the lower classes—"the people"—as ignorant, violent, and prone to superstition, hence in need of leadership from above. They pinned their hopes on educated elites and enlightened rulers.

Despite the philosophes' preference for reform, in the long run their books often had a revolutionary impact. For example, Montesquieu's widely reprinted *Spirit of the Laws* (1748) warned against the dangers of despotism, opposed the divine right of kings, and favored constitutional government. In his somewhat rosy view, Great Britain was "the one nation in the world which has political liberty as the direct object of its constitution." His analysis of British constitutionalism inspired French critics of absolutism and would greatly influence the American revolutionaries.

The Individual and Society

The controversy created by the most notorious conflicts between the philosophes and the various churches and states of Europe drew attention away from a subtle but profound transformation in worldviews. In previous centuries, questions of theological doctrine and church organization had been the main focus of intellectual and even political interest. The Enlightenment writers shifted attention away from religious questions and toward the secular study of society and the individual's role in it. Religion did not drop out of sight, but the philosophes tended to make religion a private affair of individual conscience, even while rulers and churches still considered religion very much a public concern.

The Enlightenment interest in secular society produced two major results: it advanced the secularization of European political life that had begun after the Wars of Religion of the sixteenth and seventeenth centuries, and it laid the foundations for the social sciences of the modern era. Not surprisingly, then, many historians and philosophers consider the Enlightenment to be the

CONTRASTING VIEWS

Women and the Enlightenment

During the Enlightenment, women's roles in society became the subject of heated debates. Some men resented what they saw as the growing power of women, especially in the salons. Rousseau railed against their corrupting influence: "Every woman at Paris gathers in her apartment a harem of men more womanish than she." Rousseau's Emile *(Document 1) offered his own influential answer to the question of how women should be educated. The* Encyclopedia *ignored the contributions of salon women and praised women who stayed at home; in the words of one typical contributor, women "constitute the principal ornament of the world. . . . May they, through submissive discretion and through simple, adroit, artless cleverness, spur us [men] on to virtue." Many women objected to these characterizations. The editor of a prominent newspaper for women, Madame de Beaumer, wrote editorials blasting the masculine sense of superiority (Document 2). Many prominent women writers specifically targeted Rousseau's book because it proved to be the most influential educational treatise of the time (Document 3). Their ideas formed the core of nineteenth-century feminism.*

1. JEAN-JACQUES ROUSSEAU, *EMILE* (1762)

Rousseau used the character of Emile's wife-to-be, Sophie, to discuss his ideas about women's education. Sophie is educated for a domestic role as wife and mother, and she is taught to be obedient, always helpful to her husband and family, and removed from any participation in the public world. Despite his insistence on the differences between men's and women's roles, many women enthusiastically embraced Rousseau's ideas, for he placed great emphasis on maternalism, breast-feeding, and child rearing. Rousseau's own children, however, suffered the contradictions that characterized his life. By his own admission, he abandoned to a foundling hospital all the children he had by his lower-class common-law wife because he did not think he could support them properly; if their fate was like that of most abandoned children of the day, they met an early death.

There is no parity between man and woman as to the importance of sex. The male is only a male at certain moments; the female all her life, or at least throughout her youth, is incessantly reminded of her sex and in order to carry out its functions she needs a corresponding constitution. She needs to be careful during pregnancy; she needs rest after childbirth; she needs a quiet and sedentary life while she nurses her children; she needs patience and gentleness in order to raise them; a zeal and affection that nothing can discourage. . . .

On the good constitution of mothers depends primarily that of the children; on the care of women depends the early education of men; and on women, again, depend their morals, their passions, their tastes, their pleasures, and even their happiness. Thus the whole education of women ought to be relative to men. To please them, to be useful to them, to make themselves loved and honored by them, to educate them when young, to care for them when grown, to counsel them, to console them, and to make life agreeable and sweet to them—these are the duties of women at all times, and should be taught them from their infancy.

Source: Susan Groag Bell and Karen M. Offen, *Women, the Family, and Freedom: The Debate in Documents,* vol. 1, *1750–1880* (Stanford: Stanford University Press, 1983), 46–49.

2. MADAME DE BEAUMER, EDITORIAL IN *LE JOURNAL DES DAMES* (1762)

Madame de Beaumer (d. 1766) was the first of three women editors of Le Journal des Dames *(The Ladies' Journal). She ran it for two years and published many editorials defending women against their male critics.*

The success of the *Journal des Dames* allows us to triumph over those frivolous persons who have regarded this periodical as a petty work containing only a few bagatelles suited to help them kill time. In truth, Gentlemen, you do us much honor to think that we could not provide things that unite the useful to the agreeable. To rid you of your error, we have made our Journal historical, with a view to putting before the eyes of youth striking images that will guide them toward virtue. . . . An historical *Journal des Dames*! these Gentlemen reasoners reply. How ridiculous! How out of character with the nature of this work, which calls only for little pieces to amuse [ladies] during their toilette. . . . Please, Gentlemen *beaux esprits* [wits], mind your own business and let us write in a manner worthy of our sex; I love this sex, I am jealous to uphold its honor and its rights. If we have not been raised up in the sciences as you have, it is you who are the guilty ones.

Source: Bell and Offen, 27–28.

3. CATHARINE MACAULAY, *LETTERS ON EDUCATION* (1787)

Catharine Sawbridge Macaulay-Graham (1731–1791) was one of the best-known English writers of the 1700s. She wrote immensely popular histories of England and also joined in the debate provoked by Rousseau's Emile.

There is another prejudice . . . which affects yet more deeply female happiness, and female importance; a prejudice, which ought ever to have been confined to the regions of the east, because [of the] state of slavery to which female nature in that part of the world has been ever subjected, and can only suit with the notion of a positive inferiority in the intellectual powers of the female mind. You will soon perceive, that the prejudice which I mean, is that degrading difference in the culture of the understanding, which has prevailed for several centuries in all European societies. . . .

Among the most strenuous asserters of a sexual difference in character, Rousseau is the most conspicuous, both on account of that warmth of sentiment which distinguishes all his writing, and the eloquence of his compositions: but never did enthusiasm and the love of paradox, those enemies of philosophical disquisition, appear in more strong opposition to plain sense than in Rousseau's definition of this difference. He sets out with a supposition, that Nature intended the subjection of the one sex to the other; that consequently there must be an inferiority of intellect in the subjected party; but as man is a very imperfect being, and apt to play the capricious tyrant, Nature, to bring things nearer to an equality, bestowed on the woman such attractive graces, and such an insinuating address, as to turn the balance on the other scale. . . .

The situation and education of women . . . is precisely that which must necessarily tend to corrupt and debilitate both the powers of mind and body. From a false notion of beauty and delicacy, their system of nerves is depraved before they come out of the nursery; and this kind of depravity has more influence over the mind, and consequently over morals, than is commonly apprehended.

Source: Bell and Offen, 54–55.

QUESTIONS TO CONSIDER

1. Why would women in the eighteenth century read Rousseau with such interest and even enthusiasm?

2. Why does Madame de Beaumer address herself to male readers if the *Journal des Dames* is intended for women?

3. Why would Macaulay focus so much of her analysis on Rousseau? Why does she not just ignore him?

4. Was the Enlightenment intended only for men?

MAJOR WORKS OF THE ENLIGHTENMENT

1748   Charles-Louis de Secondat, baron of Montesquieu, *Spirit of Laws*

1751   Beginning of publication of the French *Encyclopedia*

1755   David Hume, *The Natural History of Religion*

1762   Jean-Jacques Rousseau, *The Social Contract* and *Emile*

1764   Voltaire, *Philosophical Dictionary*

1770   Abbé Guillaume Raynal, *Philosophical and Political History of European Colonies and Commerce in the Two Indies*

1776   Adam Smith, *An Inquiry into the Nature and Causes of the Wealth of Nations*

1781   Immanuel Kant, *The Critique of Pure Reason*

origin of modernity, which they define as the belief that human reason, rather than theological doctrine, should set the patterns of social and political life. This belief in reason as the sole foundation for secular authority has often been contested, but it has also proved to be a powerful force for change.

Although most of the philosophes believed that human reason could understand and even remake society and politics, they disagreed about what that reason revealed. Among the many different approaches were two that proved enduringly influential, those of the Scottish philosopher Adam Smith and the Swiss writer Jean-Jacques Rousseau. Smith provided a theory of modern capitalist society and devoted much of his energy to defending free markets as the best way to make the most of individual efforts. The modern discipline of economics took shape around the questions raised by Smith. Rousseau set out the principles of a more communitarian philosophy, one that emphasized the needs of the community over those of the individual. His work, which led both toward democracy and toward communism, continues to inspire heated debate in political science and sociology.

Adam Smith. Adam Smith (1723–1790) optimistically believed that individual interests naturally harmonized with those of the whole society. He claimed, "The study of his [the individual's] own advantage necessarily leads him to prefer what is most advantageous to the society." To explain how this natural harmonization worked, he published *An Inquiry into the Nature and Causes of the Wealth of Nations* in 1776. Smith insisted that individual self-interest, even greed, was quite compatible with society's best interest: the laws of supply and demand served as an "invisible hand" ensuring that individual interests would be synchronized with those of the whole society. Market forces—"the propensity to truck, barter, and exchange one thing for another"—naturally brought individual and social interests in line.

Smith rejected the prevailing mercantilist views that the general welfare would be served by accumulating national wealth through agriculture or the hoarding of gold and silver. Instead, he argued that the division of labor in manufacturing increased productivity and generated more wealth for society and well-being for the individual. In his much-cited example of the manufacture of pins, Smith showed that when the manufacturing process was broken down into separate operations—one man to draw out the wire, another to straighten it, a third to cut it, a fourth to point it, and so on—workers who could make only one pin a day on their own could make thousands by pooling their labor.

To maximize the effects of market forces and the division of labor, Smith endorsed a concept called **laissez-faire◆** (that is, "to leave alone") to free the economy from government intervention and control. He insisted that governments eliminate all restrictions on the sale of land, remove restraints on the grain trade, and abandon duties on imports. Free international trade, he argued, would stimulate production everywhere and thus ensure the growth of national wealth: "The natural effort of every individual to better his own condition, when suffered to exert itself with freedom and security, is so powerful a principle that it is alone, and without any assistance, not only capable of carrying the society to wealth and prosperity, but of surmounting a hundred impertinent obstruc-

---

◆**laissez-faire:** leh say FEHR

tions with which the folly of human laws too often encumbers its operations." Governments should restrict themselves to providing "security," that is, national defense, internal order, and public works. Smith recognized that government had an important role in providing a secure framework for market activity, but he placed most emphasis on freeing individual endeavor from what he saw as excessive government interference.

Jean-Jacques Rousseau.   Much more pessimistic about the relation between individual self-interest and the good of society was Jean-Jacques Rousseau (1712–1778). In Rousseau's view, society itself threatened natural rights or freedoms: "Man is born free, and everywhere he is in chains." Rousseau first gained fame by writing a prize-winning essay in 1749 in which he argued that the revival of science and the arts had corrupted social morals, not improved them. This startling conclusion seemed to oppose some of the Enlightenment's most cherished beliefs. Rather than improving society, he claimed, science and art raised artificial barriers between people and their natural state. Rousseau's works extolled the simplicity of rural life over urban society. Although he participated in the salons, Rousseau always felt ill at ease in high society, and he periodically withdrew to live in solitude far from Paris. Paradoxically, his solitude was often paid for by wealthy upper-class patrons who lodged him on their estates, even as his writings decried the upper-class privilege that made his efforts possible.

Rousseau explored the tension between the individual and society in a best-selling novel (*The New Heloise*, 1761), in an influential work on education (*Emile*, 1762), and in a treatise on political theory (*The Social Contract*, 1762). He wrote *Emile* in the form of a novel in order to make his educational theories easily comprehensible. Free from the supervision of the clergy, who controlled most schools, the boy Emile works alone with his tutor to develop practical skills and independent ways of thinking. After developing his individuality, Emile joins society through marriage to Sophie, who received the education Rousseau thought appropriate for women. (See "Contrasting Views," page 714.)

Whereas earlier Rousseau had argued that society corrupted the individual by taking him out of nature, in *The Social Contract* he aimed to show that the right kind of political order could make people truly moral and free. (See *The Social Contract*, page 718.) Individual moral freedom could be achieved only by learning to subject one's individual interests to "the general will," that is, the good of the community. Individuals did this by entering into a social contract not with their rulers, but with one another. If everyone followed the general will, then all would be equally free and equally moral because they lived under a law to which they had all consented.

These arguments threatened the legitimacy of eighteenth-century governments. Rousseau derived his social contract from human nature, not from history, tradition, or the Bible. He implied that people would be most free and moral under a republican form of government with direct democracy, and his abstract model included no reference to differences in social status. He roundly condemned slavery: "To decide that the son of a slave is born a slave is to decide that he is not born a man." Not surprisingly, authorities in both Geneva and Paris banned *The Social Contract* for undermining political authority. Rousseau's works would become a kind of political bible for the French revolutionaries of 1789, and his attacks on private property inspired the communists of the nineteenth century such as Karl Marx. Rousseau's rather mystical concept of the general will remains controversial. The "greatest good of all," according to Rousseau, was liberty combined with equality, but he also insisted that the individual could be "forced to be free" by the terms of the social contract. He provided no legal protections for individual rights. In other words, Rousseau's version of democracy did not preserve the individual freedoms so important to Adam Smith.

Spreading the Enlightenment

The Enlightenment flourished in places where an educated middle class provided an eager audience for ideas of constitutionalism and reform. It therefore found its epicenter in the triangle formed by London, Amsterdam, and Paris and diffused outward to eastern and southern Europe and North America

Jean-Jacques Rousseau, *The Social Contract* (1762)

In this work, Rousseau took the notion of a social contract first developed by Thomas Hobbes and John Locke in the seventeenth century and made it the foundation for a theory of democratic politics. All "men" (which in French can mean either humans or males) participate in the social contract or social compact; they are therefore equal in civil society. Although Rousseau argued that monarchy could be a suitable form of government in rich nations, he hardly ever refers to kings or nobles in this work and speaks almost always of all men. In this section, he makes clear that the social contract unites equal citizens, not the ruler and his subjects. He also dismisses slavery as incompatible with the natural liberty of mankind.

There is but one law which, from its nature, needs unanimous consent. This is the social compact; for civil association is the most voluntary of all acts. Every man being born free and his own master, no one, under any pretext whatsoever, can make any man subject without his consent. To decide that the son of a slave is born a slave is to decide that he is not born a man.

If then there are opponents when the social compact is made, their opposition does not invalidate the contract, but merely prevents them from being included in it. They are foreigners among citizens. When the State is instituted, residence constitutes consent; to dwell within its territory is to submit to the Sovereign.

Apart from this primitive contract, the vote of the majority always binds all the rest. This follows from the contract itself. But it is asked how a man can be both free and forced to conform to wills that are not his own. How are the opponents at once free and subject to laws they have not agreed to?

I retort that the question is wrongly put. The citizen gives his consent to all the laws, including those which are passed in spite of his opposition, and even those which punish him when he dares to break any of them. The constant will of all the members of the State is the general will; by virtue of it they are citizens and free. When in the popular assembly a law is proposed, what the people is asked is not exactly whether it approves or rejects the proposal, but whether it is in conformity with the general will, which is their will. Each man, in giving his vote, states his opinion on that point; and the general will is found by counting votes. When therefore the opinion that is contrary to my own prevails, this proves neither more nor less than that I was mistaken, and that what I thought to be the general will was not so. If my particular opinion had carried the day I should have achieved the opposite of what was my will; and it is in that case that I should not have been free.

Source: Jean-Jacques Rousseau, *The Social Contract and Discourses*, trans. G. D. H. Cole (New York: E. P. Dutton, 1947), 87–88.

(Map 19.1). Where constitutionalism and the guarantee of individual freedoms were most advanced, as in Great Britain and the Dutch Republic, the movement had less of an edge because there was, in a sense, less need for it. Scottish and English writers concentrated on economics, philosophy, and history rather than on politics or social relations. Dutch printers made money publishing the books that were forbidden in France. In British North America, Enlightenment ideas helped stiffen growing colonial resistance to British rule after 1763. In places with small middle classes, such as Spain, the Italian states, and Russia, governments successfully suppressed writings they did not like. Italian philosophes, such as the Milanese penal reformer Cesare Beccaria◆ (1738–1794), got moral support from their French counterparts in the face of stern censorship at home.

The French Enlightenment. The hot spot of the Enlightenment was France. French writers published the most daring critiques

◆**Cesare Beccaria:** CHAY zahr ay bayk kah REE uh

of church and state and often suffered harassment and persecution. Voltaire, Diderot, and Rousseau all faced arrest, exile, or even imprisonment. The Catholic church and royal authorities routinely forbade the publication of their books, and the police arrested publishers who ignored the warnings. Yet the French monarchy was far from the most autocratic in Europe, and Voltaire, Diderot, and Rousseau all ended their lives as cultural heroes. France seems to have been curiously caught in the middle during the Enlightenment: with fewer constitutional guarantees of individual freedom than Great Britain, it still enjoyed much higher levels of prosperity and cultural development than most other European countries. In short, French elites had reason to complain, the means to make their complaints known, and a government torn

between the desires to censor dissident ideas and to appear open to modernity and progress. The French government controlled publishing—all books had to get official permissions—but not as tightly as in Spain, where the Catholic Inquisition made up its own list of banned books, or in Russia, where Catherine the Great allowed no opposition.

By the 1760s, the French government regularly ignored the publication of many works once thought offensive or subversive. In addition, a growing flood of works printed abroad poured into France and circulated underground. In the Dutch Republic and Swiss cities, private companies made fortunes smuggling illegal books into France over mountain passes and back roads. Foreign printers provided secret catalogs of their offerings and sold their products through booksellers who

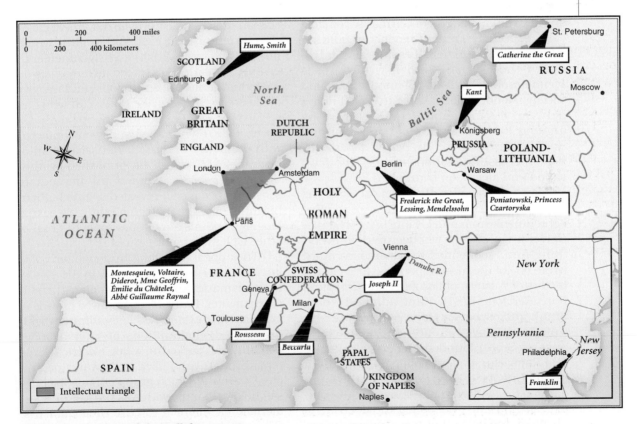

MAP 19.1 Centers of the Enlightenment
Paris was the heart of the Enlightenment because most philosophes, whatever their nationality, spoke and wrote French. Both Catherine the Great and Frederick the Great corresponded in French with their favorite French philosophes. Many French philosophes traveled to London, where they met with their English and Scottish counterparts. Montesquieu and Voltaire wrote extensively about English customs. Dutch printers published books censored in France and made them available throughout Europe and the American colonies.

were willing to market forbidden books for a high price—among them, not only philosophical treatises of the Enlightenment but also pornographic books and pamphlets (some by Diderot) lampooning the Catholic clergy and leading members of the royal court. In the 1770s and 1780s, lurid descriptions of sexual promiscuity at the French court helped undermine the popularity of the throne.

The German Enlightenment. Whereas the French philosophes often took a violently anticlerical and combative tone, their German counterparts avoided direct political confrontations with authorities. Gotthold Lessing (1729–1781) complained in 1769 that Prussia was still "the most slavish society in Europe" in its lack of freedom to criticize government policies. As a playwright, literary critic, and philosopher, Lessing promoted religious toleration for the Jews and spiritual emancipation of Germans from foreign, especially French, models of culture, which still dominated. Lessing also introduced the German Jewish writer Moses Mendelssohn (1729–1786) into Berlin salon society. Mendelssohn labored to build bridges between German and Jewish culture by arguing that Judaism was a rational and undogmatic religion. He believed persecution and discrimination against the Jews would end as reason triumphed.

Reason was also the chief focus of the most influential German thinker of the Enlightenment, Immanuel Kant (1724–1804). A university professor who lectured on everything from economics to astronomy, Kant wrote one of the most important works in the history of Western philosophy, *The Critique of Pure Reason* (1781). Kant admired Adam Smith and especially Rousseau, whose portrait he displayed proudly in his lodgings. Just as Smith founded modern economics and Rousseau modern political theory, Kant in *The Critique of Pure Reason* set the foundations for modern philosophy. In this complex book, Kant established the doctrine of idealism, the belief that true understanding can come only from examining the ways in which ideas are formed in the mind. Ideas are shaped, Kant argued, not just by sensory information (a position central to empiricism, a philosophy based on John Locke's

writings) but also by the operation on that information of mental categories such as space and time. In Kant's philosophy these "categories of understanding" were neither sensory nor supernatural; they were entirely ideal and abstract and located in the human mind. For Kant the supreme philosophical questions—Does God exist? Is personal immortality possible? Do humans have free will?—were unanswerable by reason alone. But like Rousseau, Kant insisted that true moral freedom could be achieved only by living in society and obeying its laws.

The Limits of Reason: Roots of Romanticism and Religious Revival

As Kant showed, reason had its limits: it could not answer all of life's pressing questions. In reaction to what some saw as the Enlightenment's excessive reliance on the authority of human reason, a new artistic movement called **romanticism** took root. Although it would not fully flower until the early nineteenth century, romanticism traced its emphasis on individual genius, deep emotion, and the joys of nature to thinkers like Rousseau who had scolded the philosophes for ignoring those aspects of life that escaped and even conflicted with the power of reason. Rousseau's autobiographical *Confessions*, published posthumously in 1782, caused an immediate sensation because it revealed so much about his inner emotional life, including his sexual longings and his almost paranoid distrust of other Enlightenment figures.

The appeal to feelings and emotions also increased interest in the occult. In the 1780s, a charismatic Austrian physician-turned-experimenter, Franz Mesmer, awed crowds of aristocrats and middle-class admirers with his Paris demonstrations of "animal magnetism." He passed a weak electrical current through tubs filled with water or iron filings, around which groups of his disciples sat, holding hands; with this process of "mesmerism" he claimed to cure their ailments. (The word *mesmerize* has come to mean "hypnotize" or "hold spellbound.")

A novel by the young German writer Johann Wolfgang von Goethe♦ (1749–1832)

♦**Goethe:** GUR tuh

captured the early romantic spirit with its glorification of emotion. *The Sorrows of Young Werther* (1774) told of a young man who loves nature and rural life and is unhappy in love. When the woman he loves marries someone else, he falls into deep melancholy and eventually kills himself. Reason cannot save him. The book spurred a veritable Werther craze: in addition to Werther costumes, engravings, embroidery, and medallions, there was even a perfume called Eau de Werther. Tragically, a few people imitated Werther's suicide. The young Napoleon Bonaparte, who was to build an empire for France, claimed to have read Goethe's novel seven times.

Religious revivals underlined the limits of reason in a different way. Much of the Protestant world experienced an "awakening" in the 1740s. In the German states, Pietist groups founded new communities; and in the British North American colonies, revivalist Protestant preachers drew thousands of fervent believers in a movement called the Great Awakening. In North America bitter conflicts between revivalists and their opponents in the established churches prompted the leaders on both sides to set up new colleges to support their beliefs. These included Princeton, Columbia, Brown, and Dartmouth, all founded between 1746 and 1769.

Revivalism also stirred eastern European Jews at about the same time. Israel ben Eliezer (c. 1700–1760), later known as Ba'al Shem Tov (or the Besht, from the initials), laid the foundation for a new sect in the 1740s and 1750s. Teaching outside the synagogue system, Ba'al Shem Tov traveled the Polish countryside offering to cure men of their evil spirits. He invented a new form of popular prayer, in which the believer aimed to annihilate his own personality in order to let the supernatural speak through him. His followers, the **Hasidim** (Hebrew for "most pious"), often prayed at the top of their lungs, joyfully swaying and clapping their hands. They scorned the formality of the regular synagogues in favor of their own prayer houses, where they gathered in rustic clothing and broad fur hats to emphasize their piety and simplicity. Their practices soon spread all over Poland-Lithuania.

Most of the waves of Protestant revivalism ebbed after the 1750s, but in Great

A Hasid and His Wife
The followers of Ba'al Shem Tov were known as Hasidim ("most pious Jews"). They insisted on wearing Polish peasant-style clothing even if they themselves were not peasants. The Hasidim stressed devotion to the rebbe ("teacher and spiritual guide"). *Encyclopedia of Jewish History.*

Britain one movement continued to grow through the end of the century. John Wesley (1703–1791), the Oxford-educated son of an Anglican cleric, founded **Methodism**, a term evoked by Wesley's insistence on strict self-discipline and a methodical approach to religious study and observance. In 1738, Wesley began preaching a new brand of Protestantism that emphasized an intense personal experience of salvation and a life of thrift, abstinence, and hard work. Traveling all over the British Isles, Wesley would mount a table or a box to speak to the ordinary people of the village or town. He slept in his followers' homes, ate their food, and treated their illnesses with various remedies, including small electric shocks for nervous diseases (Wesley eagerly followed Benjamin Franklin's experiments with electricity). In fifty years, Wesley preached forty thousand sermons, an average of fifteen a week. Not surprisingly, his preaching disturbed the Anglican authorities, who refused to let him preach in the churches. In response, Wesley began to ordain his own clergy. Nevertheless, during Wesley's lifetime the Methodist leadership remained politically conservative; Wesley himself wrote many pamphlets urging order, loyalty, and submission to higher authorities.

Review: Why was France the center of the Enlightenment?

❖ Society and Culture in an Age of Enlightenment

Religious revivals and the first stirrings of romanticism show that not all intellectual currents of the eighteenth century were flowing in the same channel. Some social and cultural developments, too, manifested the influence of Enlightenment ideas, but others did not. The traditional leaders of European societies—the nobles—responded to Enlightenment ideals in contradictory fashion: many simply reasserted their privileges and resisted the influence of the Enlightenment, but an important minority embraced change and actively participated in reform efforts. The expanding middle classes saw in the Enlightenment a chance to make their claim for joining society's governing elite. They bought Enlightenment books, joined Masonic lodges, and patronized new styles in art, music, and literature. The lower classes were more affected by economic growth than by ideas. Population increases contributed to a rise in prices for basic goods, but the mechanization of textile manufacturing, which began in this period, made cotton clothing more accessible to those at the bottom of the social scale.

The Nobility's Reassertion of Privilege

Nobles made up about 3 percent of the European population, but their numbers and ways of life varied greatly from country to country. At least 10 percent of the population in Poland and 7 to 8 percent in Spain was noble, in contrast to only 2 percent in Russia and between 1 and 2 percent in the rest of western Europe. Many Polish and Spanish nobles lived in poverty; titles did not guarantee wealth. Still, the wealthiest European nobles luxuriated in almost unimaginable opulence. Many of the English peers, for example, owned more than ten thousand acres of land; invested widely in government bonds and trading companies; kept several country residences with scores of servants, as well as houses in London; and occasionally even had their own private orchestras to complement libraries of expensive books, greenhouses for exotic plants, kennels of pedigreed dogs, and collections of antiques, firearms, and scientific instruments.

To support an increasingly expensive lifestyle in a period of inflation, European aristocrats sought to cash in on their remaining legal rights (called seigneurial dues, from the French *seigneur*, for "lord"). Peasants felt the squeeze as a result. French landlords required their peasants to pay dues to grind grain at the lord's mill, bake bread in his oven, press grapes at his winepress, or even pass on their own land as inheritance. In addition, peasants had to work without compensation for a specified number of days every year on the public roads. They also paid taxes to the government on salt, an essential preservative, and on the value of their land; customs duties if they sold produce or wine in town; and the tithe on their grain (one-tenth of the crop) to the church.

In Britain, the landed gentry could not claim these same onerous dues from their tenants, but they tenaciously defended their exclusive right to hunt game. The game laws kept the poor from eating meat and helped protect the social status of the rich. The gentry enforced the game laws themselves by hiring gamekeepers who hunted down poachers and even set traps for them in the forests. According to the law, anyone who poached deer or rabbits while armed or disguised could be sentenced to death. After 1760, the number of arrests for breaking the game laws increased dramatically. In most other countries, too, hunting was the special right of the nobility, a cause of deep popular resentment.

Even though Enlightenment writers sharply criticized nobles' insistence on special privileges, most aristocrats maintained their marks of distinction. The male court nobility continued to sport swords, plumed hats, makeup, and powdered hair, while middle-class men wore simpler and more somber clothing. Aristocrats had their own seats in church and their own quarters in the universities. Frederick II ("the Great") of Prussia (r. 1740–1786) made sure that nobles dominated both the army officer corps and the civil bureaucracy. Catherine II of Russia (r. 1762–1796) granted the nobility vast tracts of land, the exclusive right to own serfs, and exemption from personal taxes and corporal punishment. Her Charter of the Nobility of 1785 codified these privileges in exchange for the nobles' political subservience to the state. In Austria, Spain, the Italian states, Poland-Lithuania, and Russia, most nobles consequently cared little about Enlightenment ideas; they did not read the books of the philosophes and feared reforms that might challenge their dominance of rural society.

In France, Britain, and the western German states, however, the nobility proved more open to the new ideas. Among those who personally corresponded with Rousseau, for example, half were nobles, as were 20 percent of the 160 contributors to the *Encyclopedia*. It had not escaped their notice that Rousseau had denounced inequality. In his view, it was "manifestly contrary to the law of nature . . . that a handful of people should gorge themselves with superfluities while the hungry multitude goes in want of necessities." The nobles of western Europe sometimes married into middle-class families and formed with them a new mixed elite, united by common interests in reform and new cultural tastes.

The Middle Class and the Making of a New Elite

The Enlightenment offered middle-class people an intellectual and cultural route to social improvement. The term *middle class* referred to the middle position on the social ladder; middle-class families did not have legal titles like the nobility above them, but neither did they work with their hands like the peasants, artisans, or workers below them. Most middle-class people lived in towns or cities and earned their living in the professions—as doctors, lawyers, or lower-level officials—or through investment in land, trade, or manufacturing. In the eighteenth century, the ranks of the middle class—also known as the bourgeoisie◆ after *bourgeois*, the French word for "city dweller"—grew steadily in western Europe as a result of economic expansion. In France, for example, the overall population grew by about one-third in the 1700s, but the bourgeoisie nearly tripled in size. Although middle-class people had many reasons to resent the nobles, they also aspired to be like them.

◆**bourgeoisie:** bawrzh wah ZEE

Lodges and Learned Societies. Nobles and middle-class professionals mingled in Enlightenment salons and joined the new Masonic lodges and local learned societies. The Masonic lodges began as social clubs organized around elaborate secret rituals of stonemasons' guilds. They called their members **Freemasons** because that was the term given to apprentice masons when they were deemed "free" to practice as masters of their guild. Although not explicitly political in aim, the lodges encouraged equality among members, and both aristocrats and middle-class men could join. Members wrote constitutions for their lodges and elected their own officers, thus promoting a direct experience of constitutional government.

Freemasonry arose in Great Britain and spread eastward: the first French and Italian lodges opened in 1726; Frederick II of Prussia founded a lodge in 1740; and after 1750, Freemasonry spread in Poland, Russia, and British North America. In France, women set up their own Masonic lodges. Despite the papacy's condemnation of Freemasonry in 1738 as subversive of religious and civil authority, lodges continued to multiply throughout the eighteenth century because they offered a place for socializing outside of the traditional channels and a way of declaring one's interest in the Enlightenment and reform. In short, Freemasonry offered a kind of secular religion. After 1789 and the outbreak of the French Revolution, conservatives would blame the lodges for every kind of political upheaval, but in the 1700s many high-ranking nobles became active members and saw no conflict with their privileged status.

Nobles and middle-class professionals also met in local learned societies, which greatly increased in number in this period. They gathered to discuss such practical issues as new scientific innovations or methods to eliminate poverty. The societies, sometimes called academies, brought the Enlightenment down from the realm of books and ideas to the level of concrete reforms. They sponsored essay contests, such as the one won by Rousseau in 1749, or the one set by the society in Metz in 1785 on the question "Are there means for making the Jews happier and more useful in France?" The Metz society approved essays that argued for granting civil rights to Jews.

New Cultural Styles.   Shared tastes in travel, architecture, the arts, and even reading helped strengthen the links between nobles and members of the middle class. "Grand tours" of Europe often led upper-class youths to recently discovered Greek and Roman ruins at Pompeii, Herculaneum, and Paestum in Italy. These excavations aroused enthusiasm for the neoclassical style in architecture and painting, which began pushing aside the rococo and the long dominant baroque. Urban residences, government buildings, furniture, fabrics, wallpaper, and even pottery soon reflected the neoclassical emphasis on purity and clarity of forms. As one German writer noted, with considerable exaggeration, "Everything in Paris is in the Greek style." Employing neoclassical motifs, the English potter Josiah Wedgwood (1730–1795) almost single-handedly created a mass market for domestic crockery and

appealed to middle-class desires to emulate the rich and royal. His designs of special tea sets for the British queen, for Catherine the Great of Russia, and for leading aristocrats allowed him to advertise his wares as fashionable. By 1767, he claimed that his Queensware pottery had "spread over the whole Globe," and indeed by then his pottery was being marketed in France, Russia, Venice, the Ottoman Empire, and British North America.

This period also supported artistic styles other than neoclassicism. Frederick II of Prussia built himself a palace in the earlier rococo style, gave it a French name, Sanssouci◆ ("worry-free"), and filled it with the works of French masters of the rococo. A growing taste for moralistic family scenes in painting reflected the same middle-class preoccupation with the emotions of ordinary private life that could be seen in novels. The middle-class public now attended the official painting exhibitions in France that were held regularly every other year after 1737. Court painting nonetheless remained much in demand. Marie-Louise-Elizabeth Vigée-Lebrun◆ (1755–1842), who painted portraits at the French court, reported that in the 1780s "it was difficult to get a place on my waiting list. . . . I was the fashion."

Although wealthy nobles still patronized Europe's leading musicians, music too began to reflect the broadening of the elite and the spread of Enlightenment ideals as classical forms replaced the baroque style. Complex polyphony gave way to melody, which made the music more accessible to ordinary listeners. Large sections of string instruments became the backbone of professional orchestras, which now played to large audiences of well-to-do listeners in sizable concert halls. The public concert gradually displaced the private recital, and a new attitude toward "the classics" developed: for the first time in the 1770s and 1780s, concert groups began to play older music rather than simply playing the latest commissioned works.

This laid the foundation for what we still call classical music today, that is, a repertory of the greatest music of the eighteenth and early nineteenth centuries. Because composers

Neoclassical Style

In this Georgian interior of Syon House on the outskirts of London, various neoclassical motifs are readily apparent: Greek columns, Greek-style statuary on top of the columns, and Roman-style mosaics in the floor. The Scottish architect Robert Adam created this room for the duke of Northumberland in the 1760s. Adam had spent four years in Italy and returned in 1758 to London to decorate homes in the "Adam style," meaning the neoclassical manner. *Fotomas Index, UK.*

◆**Sans-souci:** SAHN soo SEE
◆**Vigée-Lebrun:** vee ZHAY luh BRUHN

now created works that would be performed over and over again as part of a classical repertory, rather than occasional pieces for the court or noble patrons, they deliberately attempted to write lasting works. As a result, the major composers began to produce fewer symphonies: the Austrian composer Franz Joseph Haydn (1732–1809) wrote more than one hundred symphonies, but his successor Ludwig van Beethoven (1770–1827) would create only nine.

The two supreme masters of the new musical style of the eighteenth century show that the transition from noble patronage to classical concerts was far from complete. Haydn and his fellow Austrian Wolfgang Amadeus Mozart (1756–1791) both wrote for noble patrons, but by the early 1800s their compositions had been incorporated into the canon of concert classics all over Europe. Incredibly prolific, both excelled in combining lightness, clarity, and profound emotion. Both also wrote numerous Italian operas, a genre whose popularity continued to grow: in the 1780s, the Papal States alone boasted forty opera houses. Haydn spent most of his career working for a Hungarian noble family, the Eszterházys.♦ Asked why he had written no string quintets (at which Mozart excelled), he responded simply: "No one has ordered any."

Interest in reading, like attending public concerts, took hold of the middle classes and fed a frenzied increase in publication. By the end of the eighteenth century, six times as many books were being published in the German states, for instance, as at the beginning. One Parisian author commented that "people are certainly reading ten times

Jean-Baptiste Greuze, *Broken Eggs* (1756)
Greuze made his reputation as a painter of moralistic family scenes. In this one, an old woman (perhaps the mother) confronts the lover of a young girl and points to the eggs that have fallen out of a basket. The broken eggs are a symbol of lost virginity. Diderot praised Greuze's work as "morality in paint," but the paintings often had an erotic subtext. **For more help analyzing this image,** see the visual activity for this chapter in the Online Study Guide at **bedfordstmartins.com/hunt**. *© Francis G. Mayer/CORBIS.*

as much in Paris as they did a hundred years ago." Provincial towns in western Europe published their own newspapers; by 1780, thirty-seven English towns had local newspapers. Lending libraries and book clubs multiplied. Despite the limitations of women's education, which emphasized domestic skills, women benefited as much as men from the spread of print. As one Englishman observed, "By far the greatest part of ladies now have a taste for books." Women also wrote them. Catherine Macaulay (1731–1791) published best-selling histories of Britain, and in France Stéphanie de Genlis (1746–1830) wrote children's books—a genre that was growing in importance as middle-class parents became more interested in education. The universities had little impact on these new tastes. An Austrian reformer complained about the universities in his country: "Critical history, natural sciences—which

♦**Eszterházys:** EHS tur hah zees

TAKING MEASURE

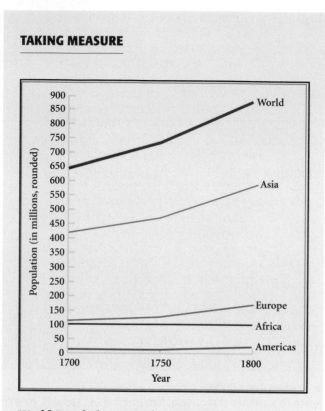

World Population Growth, 1700–1800
This graph gives a very crude comparison of regional population growth in the 1700s. Precise statistical data are impossible to develop for this period on a worldwide scale. Asia had many more people than Europe, and both Asia and Europe were growing much more rapidly in the 1700s than Africa or the Americas. The population stagnation in Africa has been the subject of much scholarly controversy; it seems likely that it was the result of the slave trade, which transported millions across the ocean to the Americas. The native population in the Americas died because of disease and was only partially replaced by the import of African slaves. What are the advantages of a growing population? What are the disadvantages? *Adapted from Andre Gundar Frank,* Reorient: Global Economy in the Asian Age *(Berkeley: University of California Press), 1998.*

are supposed to make enlightenment general and combat prejudice—were neglected or wholly unknown."

Life on the Margins

Booming foreign trade fueled a dramatic economic expansion—French colonial trade increased tenfold in the 1700s—but the results did not necessarily trickle all the way down the social scale. The population of Europe grew by nearly 30 percent, with especially striking gains in England, Ireland, Prussia, and Hungary. (See "Taking Measure," on this page.) Even though food production increased, shortages and crises still occurred periodically. Prices went up in many countries after the 1730s and continued to rise gradually until the early nineteenth century; wages in many trades rose as well, but less quickly than prices. Some people prospered—for example, peasants who produced surpluses to sell in local markets and shopkeepers and artisans who could increase their sales to meet growing demand. But those at the bottom of the social ladder—day laborers in the cities and peasants with small holdings—lived on the edge of dire poverty, and when they lost their land or work, they either migrated to the cities or wandered the roads in search of food and work. In France alone, 200,000 workers left their homes every year in search of seasonal employment elsewhere. At least 10 percent of Europe's urban population depended on some form of charity.

The growing numbers of poor overwhelmed local governments. In some countries, beggars and vagabonds had been locked up in workhouses since the mid-1600s. The expenses for running these overcrowded institutions increased by 60 percent in England between 1760 and 1785. After 1740, most German towns created workhouses that were part workshop, part hospital, and part prison. Such institutions also appeared for the first time in Boston, New York, and Philadelphia. To supplement the inadequate system of religious charity, offices for the poor, public workshops, and workhouse-hospitals, the French government created *dépôts de mendicité,*♦ or beggar houses, in 1767. The government sent people to these new workhouses to labor in manufacturing, but most were too weak or sick to work, and 20 percent of them died within a few months of incarceration. The ballooning number of poor people created fears about rising crime. To officials, beggars seemed more aggressive than ever. The handful of police assigned to keep

♦*dépôts de mendicité:* day POH duh mehn dee see TAY

order in each town or district found themselves confronted with increasing incidents of rural banditry and crimes against property.

The Persistence of Popular Culture. Those who were able to work or keep their land fared better: an increase in literacy, especially in the cities, allowed some lower-class people to participate in new tastes and ideas. One French observer insisted, "These days, you see a waiting-maid in her backroom, a lackey in an ante room reading pamphlets. People can read in almost all classes of society." In France, however, only 50 percent of men and 27 percent of women could read and write in the 1780s (although that was twice the rate of a century earlier). Literacy rates were higher in England and the Dutch Republic, much lower in eastern Europe. About one in four Parisians owned books, but the lower classes overwhelmingly read religious books, as they had in the past.

Whereas the new elite might attend salons, concerts, or art exhibitions, peasants enjoyed their traditional forms of popular entertainment, such as fairs and festivals, and the urban lower classes relaxed in cabarets and taverns. Sometimes pleasures were cruel. In Britain, bullbaiting, bearbaiting, dogfighting, and cockfighting were all common forms of entertainment that provided opportunities for organized gambling. Even "gentle" sports frequented by the upper classes had their violent side, showing that the upper classes had not become so different as they sometimes thought. Cricket matches, whose rules were first laid down in 1744, were often accompanied by brawls among fans (not unlike soccer matches today, though on a much smaller scale). Many Englishmen enjoyed what one observer called a "battle royal with sticks, pebbles and hog's dung."

Changes in Sexual Behavior. As population increased and villagers began to move to cities to better their prospects, sexual behavior changed too. The rates of births out of wedlock soared, from less than 5 percent of all births in the seventeenth century to nearly 20 percent at the end of the eighteenth. Historians have disagreed about the causes and meaning of this change. Some detect in this pattern a sign of sexual liberation and the beginnings of a modern sexual revolution: as women moved out of the control of their families, they began to seek their own sexual fulfillment. Others view this change more bleakly, as a story of seduction and betrayal: family and community pressure had once forced a man to marry a woman pregnant with his child, but now a man could abandon a pregnant lover by simply moving away.

Increased mobility brought freedom for some women, but it also aggravated the vulnerability of those newly arrived in cities from the countryside. Desperation, not reason, often ruled their choices. Women who came to the city as domestic servants had little recourse against masters or fellow servants who seduced or raped them. The result was a startling rise in abandoned babies. Most European cities established foundling hospitals in the 1700s, but infant and child mortality was 50 percent higher in such institutions than for children brought up at home. Some women tried herbs, laxatives, or crude surgical means of abortion; a few, usually servants who would lose their jobs if their employers discovered they had borne a child, resorted to infanticide.

European states had long tried to regulate sexual behavior; every country had laws against prostitution, adultery, fornication, sodomy, and infanticide. Reformers criticized the harshness of laws against infanticide, but they showed no mercy for "sodomites" (as male homosexuals were called), who in some places, in particular the Dutch Republic, were systematically persecuted and imprisoned or even executed. Male homosexuals attracted the attention of authorities because they had begun to develop networks and special meeting places. The stereotype of the effeminate, exclusively homosexual male seems to have appeared for the first time in the eighteenth century, perhaps as part of a growing emphasis on separate roles for men and women.

The Enlightenment's emphasis on reason, self-control, and childhood innocence made parents increasingly anxious about their children's sexuality. Moralists and physicians wrote books about the evils of masturbation, "proving" that it led to physical and mental degeneration and even madness. One English writer linked masturbation to debility of body and of mind; infertility;

epilepsy; loss of memory, sight, and hearing; distortions of the eyes, mouth, and face; a pale, sallow, and bluish complexion; wasting of the limbs; idiotism; and death itself.

While the Enlightenment thus encouraged excessive concern about children being left to their own devices, it nevertheless taught the middle and upper classes to value their children and to expect their improvement through education. Writers such as de Genlis and Rousseau drew attention to children, who were no longer viewed only as little sinners in need of harsh discipline. Paintings now showed individual children playing at their favorite activities rather than formally posed with their families. Books about and for children became popular. *The Newtonian System of the Universe Digested for Young Minds*, by "Tom Telescope," was published in Britain in 1761 and reprinted many times. Children's toys, jigsaw puzzles, and clothing designed for children all appeared for the first time in the 1700s. Children were no longer considered miniature adults.

The Roots of Industrialization

Although it was only starting to take hold, **industrialization** would eventually transform European society. The process began in

England in the 1770s and 1780s and included four interlocking trends: (1) population increased dramatically, by more than 50 percent in England in the second half of the eighteenth century; (2) manufacturers introduced steam-driven machinery to increase output; (3) manufacturers also established factories to concentrate the labor of their workers; and (4) the production of cotton goods, which were lighter and more versatile than woolens, increased tenfold. Together these factors sparked the Industrial Revolution, which would change the face of Europe—indeed, of the entire world—in the nineteenth century.

Innovations in the technology of cotton production permitted manufacturers to make use of the growing supply of raw cotton shipped from the plantations of North America and the Caribbean. In 1733, the Englishman John Kay patented the flying shuttle, which weavers operated by pulling a cord that drove the shuttle to either side, enabling them to "throw" yarn across the loom rather than draw it back and forth by hand. When the flying shuttle came into widespread use in the 1760s, weavers began producing cloth more quickly than spinners could produce the thread. The shortage of spun thread propelled the invention of machines to speed the process of spinning: the spinning jenny and the water frame, a power-driven spinning machine, were introduced in the 1760s. In the following decades, water frames replaced thousands of women spinners working at home by hand. In 1776, the Scottish engineer James Watt developed an improved steam engine, and, in the 1780s, Edmund Cartwright, an English clergyman and inventor, designed a mechanized loom, which when perfected could be run by a small boy and yet yield fifteen times the output of a skilled adult weaver working a handloom. By the end of the century, all the new power machinery was assembled in large factories that hired semiskilled men, women, and children to replace skilled weavers.

Historians have no single explanation for why England led the

Spinning Jenny
James Hargreaves invented the spinning jenny in the mid-1760s. It was capable of spinning 8 threads from the motion of one wheel, thus increasing the output of a spinner who previously spun one thread at a time. © *Bettmann/CORBIS.*

Industrial Revolution. Some have emphasized England's large internal market, increasing population, supply of private investment capital from overseas trade and commercial profits, or natural resources such as coal and iron. Others have cited England's greater opportunities for social mobility, its relative political stability in the eighteenth century, or the pragmatism of the English and Scottish inventors who designed the necessary machinery. These early industrialists hardly had a monopoly on ingenuity, but they did come out of a tradition of independent capitalist enterprise. They also shared a culture of informal scientific education through learned societies and popular lectures (one of the prominent forms of the Enlightenment in Britain). For whatever reasons, the combination of improvements in agricultural production, growth in population and foreign trade, and willingness to invest in new machines and factories appeared first in this relatively small island.

Although the rest of Europe did not industrialize until the nineteenth century, textile manufacturing—long a linchpin in the European economy—expanded dramatically in the eighteenth century even without the introduction of new machines and factories. Textile production increased because of the spread of the "putting-out" or "domestic" system. Hundreds of thousands of families manufactured cloth in every country from Britain to Russia. Under the putting-out system, manufacturers supplied the families with raw materials, such as woolen or cotton fibers. Working at home in a dimly lit room, a whole family labored together. The mother and her children washed the fibers and carded and combed them. Then the mother and oldest daughters spun them into thread. The father, assisted by the children, wove the cloth. The cloth was then finished (bleached, dyed, smoothed, and so on) under the supervision of the manufacturer in a large workshop, located either in town or in the countryside. This system had existed in the textile industry for hundreds of years, but in the eighteenth century it expanded immensely, and it included not only textiles but also the manufacture of such products as glassware, baskets, nails, and guns.

The spread of the domestic system of manufacturing is sometimes called proto-industrialization to signify that the process helped pave the way for the full-scale Industrial Revolution.

All across Europe, thousands of people who worked in agriculture became part-time or full-time textile workers. Peasants turned to putting-out work because they did not have enough land to support their families. Men labored off-season and women often worked year-round to augment their meager incomes. At the same time, population growth and general economic improvement meant that demand for cloth increased because more people could afford it. Studies of wills left by working-class men and women in Paris at the end of the eighteenth century show that people owned more clothes of greater variety than previously. Working-class men in Paris began to wear underclothes, something rare at the beginning of the century. Men and women now bought nightclothes; before, Europeans had slept naked except in cold weather. And white, red, blue, yellow, green, and even pastel shades of cotton now replaced the black, gray, or brown of traditional woolen dress.

Review: What were the major differences in the impact of the Enlightenment on nobles, middle classes, and lower classes?

❖ State Power in an Era of Reform

All rulers recognized that manufacturing created new sources of wealth, but the start of industrialization had not yet altered the standard forms of competition between states: commerce and war. The diffusion of Enlightenment ideas of reform had a more immediate impact on the ways European monarchs exercised power than did industrialization. Historians label many of the sovereigns of this time **enlightened despots** or enlightened absolutists, for they aimed to promote Enlightenment reforms without giving up their absolutist powers. Catherine the Great's admiring relationship with Voltaire showed how even the most absolutist rulers championed reform when it suited their own goals. Implementation of reforms was directly affected by success or failure in the competition for trade and territory. French losses in the Seven Years' War, for example, prompted the French crown to introduce far-reaching reforms that provoked violent resistance and helped pave the way for the French Revolution of 1789. Reform proved to be a two-edged sword.

War and Diplomacy

Europeans no longer fought devastating wars over religion that killed hundreds of thousands of civilians; instead, professional armies and navies battled for control of overseas empires and for dominance on the European continent. Rulers continued to expand their armies: the Prussian army, for example, nearly tripled in size between 1740 and 1789. Widespread use of flintlock muskets required deployment in long lines, usually three men deep, with each line in turn loading and firing on command. Military strategy became cautious and calculating, but this did not prevent the outbreak of hostilities. The instability of the European balance of power resulted in two major wars, a diplomatic reversal of alliances, and the partition of Poland-Lithuania among Russia, Austria, and Prussia.

War of the Austrian Succession, 1740–1748. The difficulties over the succession to the Austrian throne typified the dynastic complications that repeatedly threatened the European balance of power. In 1740, Holy Roman Emperor Charles VI died without a male heir. Most European rulers recognized the emperor's chosen heiress, his daughter Maria Theresa, because Charles's Pragmatic Sanction of 1713 had given a woman the right to inherit the Habsburg crown lands. The new king of Prussia, Frederick II, who had just succeeded his father a few months

Maria Theresa and Her Family
In this portrait by Martin van Meytens (1695–1770), Austrian empress Maria Theresa is shown with her husband, Francis I, and twelve of their sixteen children. Their eldest son eventually succeeded to the Austrian throne as Joseph II, and their youngest daughter, Maria Antonia, or Marie-Antoinette, became the queen of France. *Bridgeman–Giraudon/Art Resource, NY.*

earlier in 1740, saw his chance to grab territory and immediately invaded the rich Austrian province of Silesia. France joined Prussia in an attempt to further humiliate its traditional enemy Austria, and Great Britain allied with Austria to prevent the French from taking the Austrian Netherlands (Map 19.2). The War of the Austrian Succession (1740–1748) soon expanded to the overseas colonies of Great Britain and France as well. French and British colonials in North America fought each other all along their boundaries, enlisting native American auxiliaries. Britain tried but failed to isolate the French Caribbean colonies during the war, and hostilities broke out in India too.

Maria Theresa (r. 1740–1780) survived only by conceding Silesia to Prussia in order to split the Prussians off from France. The Peace of Aix-la-Chapelle of 1748 recognized Maria Theresa as the heiress to the Austrian lands, and her husband, Francis I, became Holy Roman Emperor, thus reasserting the integrity of the Austrian Empire. The peace of 1748 failed to resolve the colonial conflicts between Britain and France, and fighting for domination continued unofficially.

MAP 19.2 War of the Austrian Succession, 1740–1748
The accession of a twenty-three-year-old woman, Maria Theresa, to the Austrian throne gave the new king of Prussia, Frederick II, an opportunity to invade the province of Silesia. France joined on Prussia's side, Great Britain on Austria's. In 1745, the French defeated the British in the Austrian Netherlands and helped instigate a Jacobite uprising in Scotland. The rebellion failed and British attacks on French overseas shipping forced the French to negotiate. The peace treaties guaranteed Frederick's conquest of Silesia, which soon became the wealthiest province of Prussia. France came to terms with Great Britain to protect its overseas possessions; Austria had to accept the peace settlement after a formal public protest.

Seven Years' War, 1756–1763. In 1756, a major reversal of alliances—what historians call the Diplomatic Revolution—reshaped relations among the great powers. Prussia and Great Britain signed a defensive alliance, prompting Austria to overlook two centuries of hostility and ally with France. Russia and Sweden soon joined the Franco-Austrian alliance. When Frederick II invaded Saxony, an ally of Austria, with his bigger and better-disciplined army, the long-simmering hostilities between Great Britain and France over colonial boundaries flared into a general war that became known as the Seven Years' War (1756–1763).

Fighting soon raged around the world (Map 19.3 on the next page). The French and British battled on land and sea in North America (where the conflict was called the French and Indian War), the West Indies, and India. The two coalitions also fought each other in central Europe. At first, in 1757, Frederick the Great surprised Europe with a spectacular victory at Rossbach in Saxony over a much larger Franco-Austrian

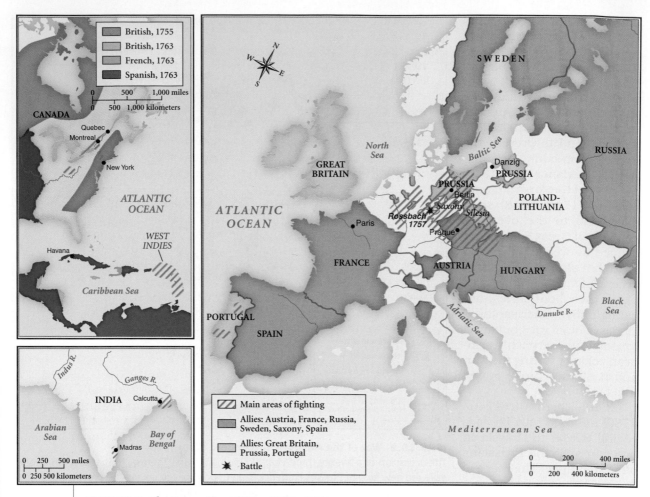

MAP 19.3 The Seven Years' War, 1756–1763

In what might justly be called the first worldwide war, the French and British fought each other on the European continent, in the West Indies, in North America, and in India. Skirmishing in North America helped precipitate the war, which became more general when Austria, France, and Russia allied to check Prussian influence in central Europe. Fearing, with reason, a joint Austrian-Russian attack, Frederick II of Prussia invaded Saxony in August 1756. Despite overwhelming odds, Frederick managed time and again to emerge victorious, until the Russians withdrew and the coalition against Prussia fell apart. The treaty between Austria and Prussia simply restored the status quo. The changes overseas were much more dramatic. Britain gained control over Canada and India but gave back to France the West Indian islands of Guadeloupe and Martinique. Britain was now the dominant power of the seas.

army. But in time, Russian and Austrian armies encircled his troops. Frederick despaired: "I believe all is lost. I will not survive the ruin of my country." A fluke of history saved him. Empress Elizabeth of Russia (r. 1741–1762) died and was succeeded by the mentally unstable Peter III, a fanatical admirer of Frederick and things Prussian. Peter withdrew Russia from the war. (This was practically his only accomplishment as tsar. He was soon mysteriously murdered, probably at the instigation of his wife, Catherine the Great.) In a separate peace treaty Frederick kept all his territory, including Silesia.

The Anglo-French overseas conflicts ended more decisively than the continental land wars. British naval superiority, fully achieved only in the 1750s, enabled Great

Britain to rout the French in North America, India, and the West Indies. In the Treaty of Paris of 1763, France ceded Canada to Great Britain and agreed to remove its armies from India, in exchange for keeping its rich West Indian islands. Eagerness to avenge this defeat would motivate France to support the British North American colonists in their War of Independence just fifteen years later.

Prussia's Revival and the First Partition of Poland.

Although Prussia suffered great losses in the Seven Years' War—some 160,000 Prussian soldiers died either in action or of disease—the army helped vault Prussia to the rank of leading powers. In 1733, Frederick II's father, Frederick William I, had instituted the "canton system," which enrolled peasant youths in each canton (or district) in the army, gave them two or three months of training annually, and allowed them to return to their family farms the rest of the year. They remained "cantonists" (reservists) as long as they were able-bodied. In this

The First Partition of Poland, 1772

fashion, the Prussian military steadily grew in size; by 1740, Prussia had the third or fourth largest army in Europe even though it was tenth in population and thirteenth in land area. Under Frederick II, Prussia's military expenditures rose to two-thirds of the state's revenue. Virtually every nobleman served in the army, paying for his own support as officer and buying a position as company commander. Once retired, the officers returned to their estates, coordinated the canton system, and served as local officials. In this way, the military permeated every aspect of rural society, fusing army and agrarian organization. The army gave the state great power, but the militarization of Prussian society also had a profoundly conservative effect: it kept the peasants enserfed to their lords and blocked the middle classes

from access to estates or high government positions.

Prussia's power grew so dramatically that in 1772 Frederick the Great proposed that large chunks of Polish-Lithuanian territory be divided among Austria, Prussia, and Russia. Despite the protests of the Austrian empress Maria Theresa that the partition would spread "a stain over my whole reign," she agreed to split one-third of Poland-Lithuania's territory and half of its people among the three powers. Austria feared growing Russian influence in Poland and in the Balkans, where Russia had been successfully battling the Ottoman Empire. Conflicts between Catholics, Protestants, and Orthodox Christians in Poland were used to justify this cynical move. Russia took over most of Lithuania, effectively ending the large but weak Polish-Lithuanian commonwealth.

State-Sponsored Reform

In the aftermath of the Seven Years' War, all the belligerents faced pressing needs for more money to fund their growing armies, to organize navies to wage overseas conflicts, and to counter the impact of inflation. To make tax increases more palatable to public opinion, rulers appointed reform-minded ministers and gave them a mandate to modernize government. As one adviser to the Austrian ruler Joseph II put it, "A properly constituted state must be exactly analogous to a machine . . . and the ruler must be the foreman, the mainspring . . . which sets everything else in motion." Such reforms always threatened the interests of traditional groups, however, and the spread of Enlightenment ideas aroused sometimes unpredictable desires for more change.

Administrative and Legal Reforms.

Reforming monarchs did not invent government bureaucracy, but they did insist on greater attention to merit, hard work, and professionalism, which made bureaucrats more like modern civil servants. In this view, the ruler should be a benevolent, enlightened administrator who worked for the general well-being of his or her people. Frederick II of Prussia, who drove himself as hard as he drove his officials, boasted, "I am the first servant of the state."

Legal reform, both of the judicial system and of the often disorganized and irregular law codes, was central to the work of many reform-minded monarchs. Although Frederick II favored all things French in culture—he insisted on speaking French in his court and prided himself on his personal friendship with Voltaire—he made Prussian justice the envy of Europe. His institution of a uniform civil justice system created the most consistently administered laws and efficient judiciary of the time. Joseph II of Austria (r. 1780–1790) also ordered the compilation of a unified law code, a project that required many years for completion. Catherine II of Russia began such an undertaking even more ambitiously. In 1767, she called together a legislative commission of 564 deputies and asked them to consider a long document called the *Instruction*, which represented her hopes for legal reform based on the ideas of Montesquieu and the Italian writer Cesare Beccaria. Montesquieu had insisted that punishment should fit the crime; he criticized the use of torture and brutal corporal punishment. In his influential book *On Crimes and Punishments* (1764), Beccaria argued that laws should be printed for everyone to read and administered in rational procedures, that torture should be abolished as inhumane, and that the accused should be presumed innocent until proven guilty. Despite much discussion and hundreds of petitions and documents about local problems, little came of Catherine's commission because the monarch herself—despite her regard for Voltaire and his fellow philosophes—proved ultimately unwilling to see through far-reaching legal reform.

The Church, Education, and Religious Toleration. Rulers everywhere wanted more control over church affairs, and they used Enlightenment criticisms of the organized churches to get their way. In Catholic countries, many government officials resented the influence of the Jesuits, the major Catholic teaching order. The Jesuits trained the Catholic intellectual elite, ran a worldwide missionary network, enjoyed close ties to the papacy, and amassed great wealth.

Critics mounted campaigns against the Jesuits in many countries, and by the early 1770s the Society of Jesus had been dissolved in Portugal, France, and Spain. In 1773, Pope Clement XIV (r. 1769–1774) agreed under pressure to disband the order, an edict that held until a reinvigorated papacy restored the society in 1814. Joseph II of Austria not only applauded the suppression of the Jesuits but also required Austrian bishops to swear fidelity and submission to him. Joseph had become Holy Roman Emperor and co-regent with his mother, Maria Theresa, in 1765. After her death in 1780 he initiated a wide-ranging program of reform. Under him, the Austrian state supervised Catholic seminaries, abolished comtemplative monastic orders, and confiscated monastic property to pay for education and poor relief.

Joseph II launched the most ambitious educational reforms of the period. In 1774, once the Jesuits had been disbanded, a General School Ordinance in Austria ordered state subsidies for local schools, which the state would regulate. By 1789, one-quarter of the school-age children attended school. In Prussia the school code of 1763 required all children between the ages of five and thirteen to attend school. Although not enforced uniformly, the Prussian law demonstrated Frederick II's belief that modernization depended on education. Catherine II of Russia also tried to expand elementary education—and the education of women in particular—and founded engineering schools.

No ruler pushed the principle of religious toleration as far as Joseph II of Austria, who in 1781 granted freedom of religious worship to Protestants, Orthodox Christians, and Jews. For the first time these groups were allowed to own property, build schools, enter the professions, and hold political and military offices. The efforts of other rulers to extend religious toleration proved more limited. Louis XVI signed an edict in 1787 restoring French Protestants' civil rights—but still they could not hold political office. Great Britain continued to deny Catholics freedom of open worship and the right to sit in Parliament. Most European states limited the rights and opportunities available to Jews. In Russia, only wealthy Jews could hold municipal office, and in the Papal

States, the pope encouraged forced baptism. Even in Austria, where Joseph encouraged toleration, the laws forced Jews to take German-sounding names. The leading philosophes opposed persecution of the Jews in theory but often treated them with undisguised contempt. Diderot's comment was all too typical: the Jews, he said, bore "all the defects peculiar to an ignorant and superstitious nation."

Limits of Reform

When enlightened absolutist leaders introduced reforms, they often ran into resistance from groups threatened by the proposed changes. The most contentious area of reform was agricultural policy. Whereas Frederick II and Catherine II reinforced the authority of nobles over their serfs, Joseph II tried to remove the burdens of serfdom in the Habsburg lands. In 1781, he abolished the personal aspects of serfdom: serfs could now move freely, enter trades, or marry without their lords' permission. Joseph abolished the tithe to the church, shifted more of the tax burden to the nobility, and converted peasants' labor services into cash payments.

The Austrian nobility furiously resisted these far-reaching reforms. When Joseph died in 1790, his brother Leopold II had to revoke most reforms to appease the nobles. On his deathbed, Joseph recognized the futility of many of his efforts; as his epitaph he suggested, "Here lies Joseph II, who was unfortunate in all his enterprises." Prussia's Frederick II, like Joseph, encouraged such agricultural innovations as planting potatoes and turnips (new crops that could help feed a growing population), experimenting with cattle breeding, draining swamplands, and clearing forests. But Prussia's noble landlords, the Junkers, continued to expand their estates at the expense of poorer peasants, and Frederick did nothing to ameliorate serfdom except on his own domains.

Reforming ministers also tried to stimulate agricultural improvement in France. Unlike most other western European countries, France still had about a hundred thousand serfs; though their burdens weighed less heavily than those in eastern Europe, serf-

Dividing Poland, 1772
In this contemporary depiction, Catherine the Great, Joseph II, and Frederick II point on the map to the portion of Poland-Lithuania each plans to take. The artist makes it clear that Poland's fate rested in the hands of neighboring rulers, not its own people. Can you infer the sentiments of the artist from the content of this engraving? *Mansell/Time Life Pictures/Getty Images.*

dom did not entirely disappear until 1789. A group of economists called the physiocrats urged the French government to deregulate the grain trade and make the tax system more equitable to encourage agricultural productivity. In the interest of establishing a free market, they also insisted that urban guilds be abolished because the guilds prevented free entry into the trades. Their proposed reforms applied the Enlightenment emphasis on individual liberties to the economy; Adam Smith took up many of the physiocrats' ideas in his writing in favor of free markets. The French government heeded some of this advice and gave up its system of price controls on grain in 1763, but it had to reverse the decision in 1770 when grain shortages caused a famine.

French reform efforts did not end there. In 1770 Louis XV tried to replace the parlements, the thirteen high courts of law, with courts in which the judges no longer owned their offices and thus could not sell them or pass them on as an inheritance. Justice would then be more impartial. Nevertheless, the judges of the displaced parlements aroused widespread opposition to what they portrayed as tyrannical royal policy. The furor calmed down only when Louis XV died in 1774 and his successor, Louis XVI (r. 1774–1792), yielded to aristocratic demands and restored the old parlements. Louis XV died one of the most despised kings in French history, resented both for his high-handed reforms and his private vices. Underground pamphlets lampooned him, describing his final mistress, Madame Du Barry, as a prostitute who pandered to the elderly king's well-known taste for young girls. This often pornographic literature linked despotism to the supposedly excessive influence of women at court.

Louis XVI tried to carry out part of the program suggested by the physiocrats, and he chose one of their disciples, Jacques Turgot (1727–1781), as his chief minister. A contributor to the *Encyclopedia*, Turgot pushed through several edicts that again freed the grain trade, suppressed guilds, converted the peasants' forced labor on roads into a money tax payable by all landowners, and reduced court expenses. He also began making plans to introduce a system of elected local assemblies, which would have made government much more representative. Faced with broad-based resistance led by the parlements and his own courtiers, as well as with riots against rising grain prices, Louis XVI dismissed Turgot, and one of the last possibilities to overhaul France's government collapsed.

The failure of reform in France paradoxically reflected the power of Enlightenment thinkers; everyone now endorsed Enlightenment ideas but used them for different ends. The nobles in the parlements blocked the French monarchy's reform efforts using the very same Enlightenment language spoken by the crown's ministers. But unlike Austria, the other great power that faced persistent aristocratic resistance to reform, France had a large middle-class public that was increasingly frustrated by the failure to institute social change, a failure that ultimately helped undermine the monarchy itself. Where Frederick II, Catherine II, and even Joseph II used reform to bolster the efficiency of absolutist government, attempts at change in France backfired. French kings found that their ambitious programs for reform succeeded only in arousing unrealistic hopes.

Review: What prompted enlightened absolutists to undertake reforms in the second half of the eighteenth century?

❖ Rebellions against State Power

Although traditional forms of popular discontent had not disappeared, Enlightenment ideals and reforms changed the rules of the game in politics. Governments had become accountable for their actions to a much wider range of people than ever before. In Britain and France, ordinary people rioted when they perceived government as failing to protect them against food shortages. The growth of informed public opinion had its most dramatic consequences in the North American colonies, where a struggle over the British Parliament's right to tax turned into a full-scale war for independence. The American War of Independence showed that once put into practice, Enlightenment ideals could have revolutionary implications.

Food Riots and Peasant Uprisings

Population growth, inflation, and the extension of the market system put added pressure on the already beleaguered poorest classes of people. Seventeenth-century peasants and townspeople had rioted to protest new taxes. In the last half of the eighteenth century, the food supply became the focus of political and social conflict. Poor people in the villages and the towns believed that it was the government's responsibility to ensure they had enough food, and many governments did stockpile grain to make up for the occa-

A Cossack

Pugachev and many of his followers were Cossacks, Ukrainians who set up nomadic communities of horsemen to resist outside control, whether from Turks, Poles, or Russians. This eighteenth-century engraving captures the common view of Cossacks as horsemen always ready for battle but with a fondness for music too. *Bridgeman Art Library.*

sional bad harvest. At the same time, in keeping with Adam Smith's and the French physiocrats' free-market proposals, governments wanted to allow grain prices to rise with market demand, because higher profits would motivate producers to increase the overall supply of food.

Free trade in grain meant selling to the highest bidder even if that bidder was a foreign merchant. In the short run, in times of scarcity, big landowners and farmers could make huge profits by selling grain outside their hometowns or villages. This practice enraged poor farmers, agricultural workers, and city wage workers, who could not afford the higher prices. Lacking the political means to affect policy, they could enforce

their desire for old-fashioned price regulation only by rioting. Most did not pillage or steal grain but rather forced the sale of grain or flour at a "just" price and blocked the shipment of grain out of their villages to other markets. Women often led these "popular price fixings," as they were called in France, in desperate attempts to protect the food supply for their children.

Such food riots occurred regularly in Britain and France in the last half of the eighteenth century. One of the most turbulent was the so-called Flour War in France in 1775. Turgot's deregulation of the grain trade in 1774 caused prices to rise in several provincial cities. Rioting spread from there to the Paris region, where villagers attacked grain convoys heading to the capital city. Local officials often ordered merchants and bakers to sell at the price the rioters demanded, only to find themselves arrested by the central government for overriding free trade. The government brought in troops to restore order and introduced the death penalty for rioting.

Frustrations with serfdom and hopes for a miraculous transformation provoked the Pugachev rebellion in Russia beginning in 1773. An army deserter from the southeast frontier region, Emelian Pugachev◆ (1742–1775) claimed to be Tsar Peter III, the dead husband of Catherine II. Pugachev's appearance seemed to confirm peasant hopes for a "redeemer tsar" who would save the people from oppression. He rallied around him Cossacks like himself who resented the loss of their old tribal independence. Now increasingly enserfed or forced to pay taxes and endure army service, these nomadic bands joined with other serfs, rebellious mineworkers, and Muslim minorities. Catherine dispatched a large army to squelch

◻ Area of rebellion
← Pugachev's route

0   150   300 miles
0 150 300 kilometers

Moscow

Don R.

Volga R.

RUSSIA

Black Sea

Caspian Sea

Aral Sea

The Pugachev Rebellion, 1773

◆**Emelian Pugachev:** yihm yihl YAN poo guh CHAWF

the uprising, but Pugachev eluded them and the fighting spread. Nearly three million people eventually participated, making this the largest single rebellion in the history of tsarist Russia. When Pugachev urged the peasants to attack the nobility and seize their estates, hundreds of noble families perished. Foreign newspapers called it "the revolution in southern Russia" and offered fantastic stories about Pugachev's life history. Finally, the army captured the rebel leader and brought him in an iron cage to Moscow, where he was tortured and executed. In the aftermath, Catherine tightened the nobles' control over their serfs and harshly punished those who dared to criticize serfdom.

Public Opinion and Political Opposition

Peasant uprisings might briefly shake even a powerful monarchy, but the rise of public opinion as a force independent of court society caused more enduring changes in European politics. Across much of Europe and in the North American colonies, demands for broader political participation reflected Enlightenment notions about individual rights. Aristocratic bodies such as the French parlements, which had no legislative role like that of the British Parliament, insisted that the monarch consult them on the nation's affairs, and the new educated elite wanted more influence too. Newspapers began to cover daily political affairs, and the public learned the basics of political life, despite the strict limits on political participation in most countries. Monarchs turned to public opinion to seek support against aristocratic groups that opposed reform. Gustavus III of Sweden (r. 1771–1792) called himself "the first citizen of a free people" and promised to deliver the country from "insufferable aristocratic despotism." Shortly after coming to the throne, Gustavus proclaimed a new constitution that divided power between the king and the legislature, abolished the use of torture in the judicial process, and assured some freedom of the press.

In France both the parlements and the monarch appealed to the public through the printed word. The crown hired writers to make its case; the magistrates of the parle-

ments wrote their own rejoinders. French-language newspapers published in the Dutch Republic provided many people in France with detailed accounts of political news and also gave voice to pro-parlement positions. One of the new French-language newspapers printed inside France, *Le Journal des Dames* (The Ladies' Journal), was published by women and mixed short stories and reviews of books and plays with demands for more women's rights.

The Wilkes affair in Great Britain showed that public opinion could be mobilized to challenge a government. In 1763, during the reign of George III (r. 1760–1820), John Wilkes, a member of Parliament, attacked the government in his newspaper, *North Briton*, and sued the crown when he was arrested. He won his release as well as damages. When he was reelected, Parliament denied him his seat, not once but three times.

The Wilkes episode soon escalated into a major campaign against the corruption and social exclusiveness of Parliament, complaints the Levellers had first raised during the English Revolution of the late 1640s. Newspapers, magazines, pamphlets, handbills, and cheap editions of Wilkes's collected works all helped promote his cause. Those who could not vote demonstrated for Wilkes. In one incident eleven people died when soldiers broke up a huge gathering of his supporters. The slogan "Wilkes and Liberty" appeared on walls all over London. Middle-class voters formed a Society of Supporters of the Bill of Rights, which circulated petitions for Wilkes; they gained the support of about one-fourth of all the voters. The more determined Wilkesites proposed sweeping reforms of Parliament, including more frequent elections, more representation for the counties, elimination of "rotten boroughs" (election districts so small that they could be controlled by one big patron), and restrictions of pensions used by the crown to gain support. These demands would be at the heart of agitation for parliamentary reform in Britain for decades to come.

Popular demonstrations did not always support reforms. In 1780, the Gordon riots devastated London. They were named after the fanatical anti-Catholic crusader Lord George Gordon, who helped organize huge marches and petition campaigns against a bill the House of Commons passed to grant limited toleration to Catholics. The demonstrations culminated in a seven-day riot that left fifty buildings destroyed and three hundred people dead. Despite the continuing limitation on voting rights in Great Britain, British politicians were learning that they could ignore public opinion only at their peril.

Political opposition also took artistic forms, particularly in countries where governments restricted organized political activity. A striking example of a play with a political message was *The Marriage of Figaro* (1784) by Pierre-Augustin Caron de Beaumarchais♦ (1732–1799), a watchmaker, a judge, a gunrunner in the American War of Independence, and a French spy in Britain. *The Marriage of Figaro* was first a hit at court, when Queen Marie-Antoinette had it read for her friends. But when her husband, Louis XVI, read it, he forbade its production on the grounds that "this man mocks at everything that should be respected in government." When finally performed publicly, the play caused a sensation. The chief character, Figaro, is a clever servant who gets the better of his noble employer. When speaking of the count, he cries, "What have you done to deserve so many rewards? You went to the trouble of being born, and nothing more." Two years later, Mozart based an equally famous but somewhat tamer opera on Beaumarchais's story.

Revolution in North America

Oppositional forms of public opinion came to a head in Great Britain's North American colonies, where the result was American independence and the establishment of a republican constitution that stood in stark contrast to most European regimes. The successful revolution was the only blow to Britain's increasing dominance in world affairs in the eighteenth century, and as such it was another aspect of the power rivalries existing at that time. Yet many Europeans saw the American War of Independence, or the American Revolution, as a triumph for Enlightenment ideas. As one

♦**Beaumarchais:** boh mahr SHAY

German writer exclaimed in 1777, American victory would give "greater scope to the Enlightenment, new keenness to the thinking of peoples and new life to the spirit of liberty."

The American revolutionary leaders had been influenced by a common Atlantic civilization; they participated in the Enlightenment and shared political ideas with the opposition Whigs in Britain. Supporters demonstrated for Wilkes in South Carolina and Boston, and the South Carolina legislature donated a substantial sum to the Society of Supporters of the Bill of Rights. In the 1760s and 1770s, both British and American opposition leaders became convinced that the British government was growing increasingly corrupt and despotic. British radicals wanted to reform Parliament so that the voices of a broader, more representative segment of the population would be heard. The colonies had no representatives in Parliament, and colonists claimed that "no taxation without representation" should be allowed. Indeed, they denied that Parliament had any jurisdiction over the colonies, insisting that the king govern them through colonial legislatures and recognize their traditional British liberties. The failure of the "Wilkes and Liberty" campaign to produce concrete results convinced many Americans that Parliament was hopelessly tainted and that they would have to stand up for their rights as British subjects.

The British colonies remained loyal to the crown until Parliament's encroachment on their autonomy and the elimination of the French threat at the end of the Seven Years' War transformed colonial attitudes. Unconsciously, perhaps, the colonies had begun to form a separate nation; their economies generally flourished in the eighteenth century, and between 1750 and 1776 their population almost doubled. With the British clamoring for lower taxes and the colonists paying only a fraction of the tax rate paid by the Britons at home, Parliament passed new taxes, including the Stamp Act in 1765, which required a special tax stamp on all legal documents and publications. After violent rioting in the colonies, the tax was repealed, but in 1773 a new Tea Act revived colonial resistance, which culminated in the so-called Boston Tea Party of 1773. Colonists dressed

Thomas Jefferson, Declaration of Independence (July 4, 1776)

Although others helped revise the Declaration of Independence of the thirteen North American colonies from Great Britain, Jefferson wrote the original draft himself. A Virginia planter and lawyer, Jefferson went on to become governor of Virginia, minister to France, Secretary of State, vice president and president of the United States (1801–1809). The Declaration begins with a stirring expression of the belief in natural or human rights.

When in the Course of human events, it becomes necessary for one people to dissolve the political bands which have connected them with another, and to assume among the powers of the earth, the separate and equal station to which the Laws of Nature and of Nature's God entitle them, a decent respect to the opinions of mankind requires that they should declare the causes which impel them to the separation.

We hold these truths to be self-evident, that all men are created equal, that they are endowed by their Creator with certain unalienable Rights, that among these are Life, Liberty and the pursuit of Happiness.—That to secure these rights, Governments are instituted among Men, deriving their just powers from the consent of the governed,—That whenever any Form of Government becomes destructive of these ends, it is the Right of the People to alter or to abolish it, and to institute new Government, laying its foundation on such principles and organizing its powers in such form, as to them shall seem most likely to effect their Safety and Happiness. Prudence, indeed, will dictate that Governments long established should not be changed for light and transient causes; and accordingly all experience hath shewn, that mankind are more disposed to suffer, while evils are sufferable, than to right themselves by abolishing the forms to which they are accustomed. But when a long train of abuses and usurpations, pursuing invariably the same Object evinces a design to reduce them under absolute Despotism, it is their right, it is their duty, to throw off such Government, and to provide new Guards for their future security.—Such has been the patient sufferance of these Colonies; and such is now the necessity which constrains them to alter their former Systems of Government. The history of the present King of Great Britain is a history of repeated injuries and usurpations, all having in direct object the establishment of an absolute Tyranny over these States. . . .

Source: U.S. National Archives and Records Administration, Washington, D.C.

---

as Indians boarded British ships and dumped the imported tea (by this time an enormously popular beverage) into Boston's harbor. The British government tried to clamp down on the unrest, but British troops in the colonies soon found themselves fighting locally organized militias.

Political opposition in the American colonies turned belligerent when Britain threatened to use force to maintain control. In 1774, the First Continental Congress convened, composed of delegates from all the colonies, and unsuccessfully petitioned the crown for redress. The next year the Second Continental Congress organized an army with George Washington in command. After actual fighting had begun, in 1776, the congress proclaimed the Declaration of Independence. An eloquent statement of the American cause written by Thomas Jefferson, the Declaration of Independence was couched in the language of universal human rights, which enlightened Europeans could be expected to understand. (See

"Declaration of Independence," opposite.) George III denounced the American "traitors and rebels." But European newspapers enthusiastically reported on every American response to "the cruel acts of oppression they have been made to suffer." In 1778 France boosted the American cause by entering on the colonists' side. Spain, too, saw an opportunity to check the growing power of Britain, though without actually endorsing American independence out of fear of the response of its Latin American colonies. Spain declared war on Britain in 1779; in 1780, Great Britain declared war on the Dutch Republic in retaliation for Dutch support of the rebels. The worldwide conflict that resulted was more than Britain could handle. The American colonies achieved their independence in the peace treaty of 1783.

The newly independent states still faced the challenge of republican self-government.

The Articles of Confederation, drawn up in 1777 as a provisional constitution, proved weak because they gave the central government few powers. In 1787, a constitutional convention met in Philadelphia to draft a new constitution. It established a two-house legislature, an indirectly elected president, and an independent judiciary. The U.S. Constitution's preamble insisted explicitly, for the first time in history, that government derived its power solely from the people and did not depend on divine right or on the tradition of royalty or aristocracy. The new educated elite of the eighteenth century had now created government based on a "social contract" among male, property-owning, white citizens. It was by no means a complete democracy (women and slaves were excluded from political participation), but the new government represented a radical departure from European models. In 1791, the Bill of

Overthrowing British Authority
The uncompromising attitude of the British government went a long way toward dissolving long-standing loyalties to the home country. During the American War of Independence, residents of New York City pulled down the statue of the hated George III. *Lafayette College Art Collection, Easton, Pennsylvania.*

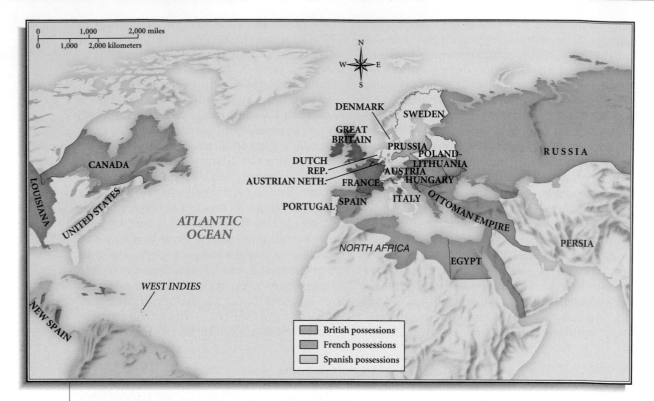

MAPPING THE WEST Europe and the World, c. 1780
Although Great Britain lost control over the British North American colonies, which became the new United States, European influence on the rest of the world grew dramatically in the eighteenth century. The slave trade linked European ports to African slave-trading outposts and to plantations in the Caribbean, South America, and North America. The European countries on the Atlantic Ocean benefited most from this trade. Yet almost all of Africa, China, Japan, and large parts of India still resisted European incursion, and the Ottoman Empire, with its massive territories, still presented Europe with a formidable military challenge.

Rights was appended to the Constitution outlining the essential rights (such as freedom of speech) that the government could never overturn. Although slavery continued in the American republic, the new emphasis on rights helped fuel the movement for its abolition in both Britain and the United States.

Interest in the new republic was greatest in France. The U.S. Constitution and various state constitutions were published in French with commentary by leading thinkers. Even more important in the long run were the effects of the American war. Dutch losses to Great Britain aroused a widespread movement for political reform in the Dutch Republic, and debts incurred by France in supporting the American colonies would soon

force the French monarchy to the edge of bankruptcy and then to revolution. Ultimately, the entire European system of royal rule would be challenged.

Review: Why did public opinion become a new factor in politics in the second half of the eighteenth century?

Conclusion

When Thomas Jefferson looked back many years later on the Declaration of Independence, he said he hoped it would be "the signal of arousing men to burst the chains under which monkish ignorance and superstition had persuaded them to bind themselves." What began as a cosmopolitan movement of a few intellectuals in the first half of the eighteenth century had reached a relatively wide audience among the educated elite of men and women by the 1770s and 1780s. The spirit of Enlightenment swept from the coffeehouses and Masonic lodges into the halls of government from Philadelphia to Vienna. Reasoned, scientific inquiry into the causes of social misery and laws defending individual rights and freedoms gained adherents even among the rulers and ministers responsible for censoring Enlightenment works.

For most Europeans, however, the promise of the Enlightenment did not become a reality. Rulers such as Catherine the Great had every intention of retaining their full, often unchecked, powers, even as they corresponded with leading philosophes and entertained them at their courts. Moreover, would-be reformers often found themselves thwarted by the resistance of nobles, by the priorities rulers gave to waging wars, or by popular resistance to deregulation of trade that increased the uncertainties of the market. Yet even the failure of reform contributed to the ferment in Europe after 1770. Peasant rebellions in eastern Europe, the "Wilkes and Liberty" campaign in Great Britain, the struggle over reform in France, and the revolution in America all occurred around the same time, and their conjunction convinced many Europeans that change was brewing. Just how much could change, and whether change made life better or worse, would come into question in the next ten years.

Suggested References

The Enlightenment at Its Height

The interpretive study by Gay remains useful even though it is over thirty years old, but the Kors volumes give the most up-to-date views. Equiano, a freed slave, offers one of the earliest firsthand views of the experience of slavery, but some scholars now question whether he was born in Africa (and not the New World).

*Equiano, Olaudah. *The Interesting Narrative and Other Writings.* Ed. Vincent Carretta. 1995.

Gay, Peter. *The Enlightenment: An Interpretation.* 2 vols. 1966, 1969.

Goodman, Dena. *The Republic of Letters: A Cultural History of the French Enlightenment.* 1994.

Jacob, Margaret C. *Living the Enlightenment: Freemasonry and Politics in Eighteenth-Century Europe.* 1991.

Kors, Alan Charles, ed. *Encyclopedia of the Enlightenment.* 4 vols. 2003.

Porter, Roy. *The Creation of the Modern World: The Untold Story of the British Enlightenment.* 2000.

*Voltaire. *Candide.* Ed. and trans. Daniel Gordon. 1999.

Voltaire Foundation: http://www.voltaire.ox.ac.uk.

Society and Culture in an Age of Enlightenment

Recent work has drawn attention to the lives of ordinary people. The personal journal of the French glassworker Ménétra is a rarity: it offers extensive documentation of the inner life of an ordinary person during the Enlightenment. Ménétra claimed to have met Rousseau. Even if not true, the claim shows that Rousseau's fame was not limited to the upper classes.

Adams, Christine. *A Taste for Comfort and Status: A Bourgeois Family in Eighteenth-Century France.* 2000.

Darnton, Robert. *The Great Cat Massacre and Other Episodes in French Cultural History.* 1984.

Hull, Isabel V. *Sexuality, State, and Civil Society in Germany, 1700–1815.* 1996.

*Ménétra, Jacques Louis. *Journal of My Life.* Trans. Arthur Goldhammer. Intro. Daniel Roche. 1986.

Mozart Project: http://www.mozartproject.org.

Smith, Douglas. *Working the Rough Stone: Freemasonry and Society in Eighteenth-Century Russia.* 1999.

Stone, Lawrence. *The Family, Sex, and Marriage in England, 1500–1800.* Abridged ed. 1979.

State Power in an Era of Reform

Biographies and general histories of this period tend to overemphasize the individual decisions of rulers. Although these decisions are incontestably important, side-by-side reading of Büsch,

*Primary source.

Frederick II's writings on war, and Showalter's book on the wars themselves offers a broader view that puts Frederick II's policies into the context of military growth and its impact on society.

Blanning, T. C. W. *Joseph II and Enlightened Despotism.* 1994.

Büsch, Otto. *Military System and Social Life in Old Regime Prussia, 1713–1807: The Beginnings of the Social Militarization of Prusso-German Society.* Trans. John G. Gagliardo. 1997.

Crankshaw, Edward. *Maria Theresa.* 1996.

Dixon, Simon. *Catherine the Great.* 2001.

*Frederick II, King of Prussia. *Frederick the Great on the Art of War.* Ed. and trans. Jay Luvaas. 1999.

Showalter, Dennis E. *The Wars of Frederick the Great.* 1996.

Venturi, Franco. *The End of the Old Regime in Europe, 1768–1776: The First Crisis.* Trans. R. Burr Litchfield. 1989.

Rebellions against State Power

Historians have recently shown great interest in the riots and rebellions of this era, but most have focused on one national case. Palmer's overview of political movements therefore remains valuable for its comparative aspects.

Alexander, John T. *Autocratic Politics in a National Crisis: The Imperial Russian Government and Pugachev's Revolt, 1773–1775.* 1969.

Palmer, R. R. *The Age of Democratic Revolution: A Political History of Europe and America, 1760–1800.* Vol. 1, *The Challenge.* 1959.

*Rakove, Jack N. *Declaring Rights: A Brief History with Documents.* 1998.

Thomas, P. D. G. *John Wilkes: A Friend to Liberty.* 1996.

Thompson, E. P. *Whigs and Hunters: The Origin of the Black Act.* 1975.

Wood, Gordon S. *The Radicalism of the American Revolution.* 1992.

CHAPTER REVIEW

IMPORTANT EVENTS

1740–1748 War of the Austrian Succession: France, Spain, and Prussia versus Austria and Great Britain

1751–1772 *Encyclopedia* published in France

1756–1763 Seven Years' War fought in Europe, India, and the American colonies

1762 Jean-Jacques Rousseau, *The Social Contract* and *Emile*

1764 Voltaire, *Philosophical Dictionary*

1770 Louis XV of France fails to break the power of the French law courts

1772 First partition of Poland

1773 Pugachev rebellion of Russian peasants

1776 American Declaration of Independence from Great Britain; James Watt improves the steam engine, making it suitable for new industrial projects; Adam Smith, *The Wealth of Nations*

1780 Joseph II of Austria undertakes a wide-reaching reform program

1781 Immanuel Kant, *The Critique of Pure Reason*

1785 Catherine the Great's Charter of the Nobility grants nobles exclusive control over their serfs in exchange for subservience to the state

1787 Delegates from the states draft the U.S. Constitution

KEY TERMS

abolitionists (713)

atheist (712)

deist (712)

enlightened despots (or enlightened absolutists) (729)

Freemasons (723)

Hasidim (721)

industrialization (728)

laissez-faire (716)

Methodism (721)

philosophes (708)

romanticism (720)

salons (711)

REVIEW QUESTIONS

1. Why was France the center of the Enlightenment?
2. What were the major differences in the impact of the Enlightenment on nobles, middle classes, and lower classes?
3. What prompted enlightened absolutists to undertake reforms in the second half of the eighteenth century?

4. Why did public opinion become a new factor in politics in the second half of the eighteenth century?

MAKING CONNECTIONS

1. Why would rulers feel ambivalent about the Enlightenment, supporting reform on the one hand, while clamping down on political dissidents on the other hand?
2. Which major developments in this period ran counter to the influence of the Enlightenment?
3. In what ways had politics changed, and in what ways did they remain the same during the Enlightenment?

FOR FURTHER EXPLORATION

To assess your mastery of the material in this chapter, see the Online Study Guide at **bedfordstmartins.com/hunt**.

To read additional primary-source material from this period, see Chapter 19 in *Sources of The Making of the West*, Second Edition.

The Cataclysm of Revolution, 1789–1800

ON OCTOBER 5, 1789, a crowd of several thousand women marched in a drenching rain twelve miles from the center of Paris to Versailles. They demanded the king's help in securing more grain for the hungry and his reassurance that he did not intend to resist the emerging revolutionary movement. Joined by thousands of men who came from Paris to reinforce them, the next morning they broke into the royal family's private apartments. To prevent further bloodshed—two of the royal bodyguards had already been killed and their heads paraded on pikes—the king agreed to move his family and his government to Paris. A dramatic procession guarded by thousands of ordinary men and women made its slow way back to the capital. The people's proud display of cannons and pikes underlined the fundamental transformation that was occurring. Ordinary people had forced the king of France to respond to their grievances. The French monarchy was in danger, and if such a powerful and long-lasting institution could come under fire, then could any monarch of Europe rest easy?

Although even the keenest political observer did not predict its eruption in 1789, the French Revolution had its immediate origins in a constitutional crisis provoked by a growing government deficit, traceable to French involvement in the American War of Independence. The constitutional crisis came to a head on July 14, 1789, when armed Parisians captured the Bastille,◆ a royal fortress and symbol of monarchical authority in the center of the capital. The fall of the Bastille, like the women's march to Versailles three months later, showed the determination of the common people to put their mark on events.

The French Revolution first grabbed the attention of the entire world because it seemed to promise universal human rights, constitutional

---

◆**Bastille:** ba STEEL

Women's March to Versailles
Thousands of prints broadcast the events of the French Revolution to the public in France and elsewhere. They varied from fine art engravings signed by the artist to anonymous simple woodblock prints. This colored etching shows a crowd of armed women marching to Versailles on October 5, 1789, to confront the king. The sight of armed women frightened many observers and demonstrated that the Revolution was not only a men's affair. *AKG-Images.*

government, and broad-based political participation. Its most famous slogan pledged "Liberty, Equality, and Fraternity" for all. An enthusiastic German wrote, "One of the greatest nations in the world, the greatest in general culture, has at last thrown off the yoke of tyranny." The revolutionaries used a blueprint based on the Enlightenment idea of reason to remake all of society and politics: they executed the king and queen, established a republic for the first time in French history, abolished nobility, and gave the vote to all adult men. Even as the Revolution promised democracy, however, it also inaugurated a cycle of violence and intimidation. When the revolutionaries encountered resistance to their programs, they set up a government of terror to compel obedience. Some historians therefore see in the French Revolution the origins of modern totalitarianism—that is, governments that try to control every aspect of life, including daily activities, while limiting all forms of political dissent. As events unfolded after 1789, the French Revolution became the model of modern revolution; republicanism, democracy, terrorism, nationalism, and military dictatorship all took their modern forms during the French Revolution.

The Revolution might have remained a strictly French affair if war had not involved the rest of Europe. After 1792, huge French republican armies, fueled by patriotic nationalism, marched across Europe, promising liberation from traditional monarchies but often delivering old-fashioned conquest and annexation. French victories spread revolutionary ideas far and wide, from the colonies in the Caribbean, where the first successful slave revolt established the republic of Haiti, to Poland and Egypt. The army's success ultimately undermined the republic and made possible the rise of Napoleon Bonaparte, a remarkable young general from Corsica, an island off Italy, who brought France more wars, more conquests, and a form of military dictatorship.

The breathtaking succession of regimes in France between 1789 and 1799 and the failure of the republican experiment after ten years of upheaval raised disturbing questions about the relationship between rapid political change and violence. Do all revolutions inevitably degenerate into terror or wars of conquest? Is a regime democratic if it does not allow poor men, women, or blacks to vote? The French Revolution raised these questions and many more. The questions resonated in many countries because the French Revolution seemed to be only the most extreme example of a much broader political and social movement at the end of the eighteenth century.

❖ The Revolutionary Wave, 1787–1789

Between 1787 and 1789, revolts in the name of liberty broke out in the Dutch Republic, the Austrian Netherlands (present-day Belgium and Luxembourg), and Poland, as well as in France. At the same time, the

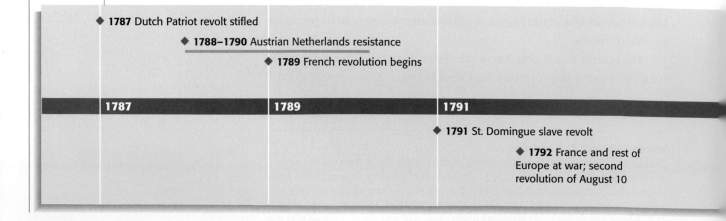

◆ **1787** Dutch Patriot revolt stifled

◆ **1788–1790** Austrian Netherlands resistance

◆ **1789** French revolution begins

| 1787 | 1789 | 1791 |

◆ **1791** St. Domingue slave revolt

◆ **1792** France and rest of Europe at war; second revolution of August 10 newly independent United States of America prepared a new federal constitution. Historians have sometimes referred to these revolts as the **Atlantic revolutions** because so many protest movements arose in countries on both shores of the North Atlantic in the late 1700s. These revolutions were the product of long-term prosperity and high expectations: Europeans in general were wealthier, healthier, more numerous, and better educated than they had ever been before; and the Dutch, Belgian, and French societies were among the wealthiest and best educated within Europe. Most scholars agree, however, that the French Revolution differed greatly from the others. Not only was France the richest, most powerful, and most populous state in western Europe, but its revolution was also more violent, more long-lasting, and ultimately more influential. (See "Terms of History," page 750.)

Protesters in the Low Countries and Poland

Political protests in the Dutch Republic attracted European attention because Dutch banks still controlled a hefty portion of the world's capital at the end of the eighteenth century, even though the Dutch Republic's role in international politics had diminished. Revolts also broke out in the neighboring Austrian Netherlands and Poland. Although none of these movements ultimately succeeded, they showed how quickly political discontent could boil over in this era of rising economic and political expectations.

The Dutch Patriot Revolt, 1787. The Dutch Patriots, as they chose to call themselves, wanted to reduce the powers of the prince of Orange, the kinglike stadholder who favored close ties with Great Britain. Government-sponsored Dutch banks owned 40 percent of the British national debt, and by 1796 they held the entire foreign debt of the United States. Relations with the British deteriorated during the American War of Independence, however, and by the middle of the 1780s, agitation in favor of the Americans had boiled over into an attack on the stadholder.

Building on support among middle-class bankers, merchants, and writers who sympathized with the American cause, the Patriots soon gained a more popular audience by demanding political reforms and organizing armed citizen militias of men, called Free Corps. Parading under banners that read "Liberty or Death," the Free Corps forced local officials to set up new elections to replace councils that had been packed with Orangist supporters through patronage or family connections. The future American president John Adams happened to be visiting Utrecht when such a revolt occurred. He wrote admiringly to Thomas Jefferson that "in no instance of ancient or modern History, have the People ever asserted more unequivocally their own inherent and unalienable Sovereignty."

The Low Countries in 1787

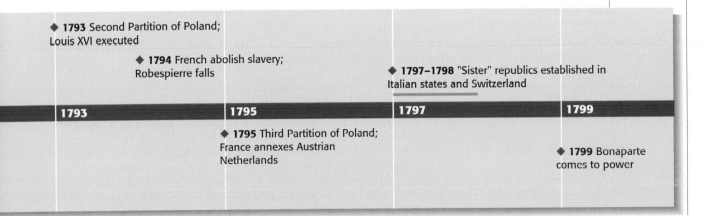

♦ **1793** Second Partition of Poland; Louis XVI executed

♦ **1794** French abolish slavery; Robespierre falls

♦ **1797–1798** "Sister" republics established in Italian states and Switzerland

| 1793 | 1795 | 1797 | 1799 |

♦ **1795** Third Partition of Poland; France annexes Austrian Netherlands

♦ **1799** Bonaparte comes to power

TERMS OF HISTORY

Revolution

Revolution had previously meant cyclical change that brought life back to a starting point, as a planet makes a revolution around the sun. Revolutions could come and go, by this definition, and change nothing fundamental in the structure of society. After 1789, *revolution* came to mean a self-conscious attempt to leap into the future by reshaping society and politics and even the human personality. A revolutionary official analyzed the meaning of the word in 1793: "A revolution is never made by halves; it must either be total or it will abort. . . . *Revolutionary* means outside of all forms and all rules; *revolutionary* means that which affirms, consolidates the revolution, that which removes all the obstacles which impede its progress." In short, *revolution* soon had an all-or-nothing meaning; you were either for the revolution or against it. There could be no in between.

Revolution still has the same meaning given it by the French revolutionaries, but it is now an even more contested term because of its association with communist theory. In the nineteenth century, Karl Marx incorporated the French Revolution into his new doctrine of communism. In his view, the middle-class French revolutionaries had overthrown the monarchy and the "feudal" aristocracy to pave the way for capitalist development. In the future, the proletariat (industrial workers) would overthrow the capitalist middle class to install a communist government that would abolish private property. Since Marxists claimed the French Revolution as the forerunner of the communist revolution in the nineteenth and twentieth centuries, it was perhaps inevitable that those who

opposed communism would also criticize the French Revolution.

The most influential example of this view is that of the French scholar François Furet. An ex-communist, Furet argued that the French Revolution can be seen as the origin of totalitarianism: "Today the Gulag [the Soviet system of prison camps for dissidents] is leading to a rethinking of the Terror precisely because the two undertakings are seen as identical." The Soviet Gulag and the Terror were identical systems for repressing all avenues of dissent. The French Revolution ended up in totalitarianism during the Terror because it incarnated what Furet calls "the illusion of politics," that is, the belief that people can transform social and economic relationships through political revolution. However, the French revolutionaries became totalitarian, in Furet's view, because they wanted to establish a kind of political and social utopia (a perfect society), in which reason alone determined the shape of political and social life. Because this dream was impossible given human resistance to rapid change, the revolutionaries had to use force to achieve their goals. In other words, revolution itself was a problematic idea, according to Furet.

Controversy about the relationship between the French Revolution and totalitarianism continues. *Revolution* as a term remains as contested as the events that gave rise to it.

FURTHER READING

Furet, François. *Interpreting the French Revolution.* Trans. Elborg Forster. 1981.

Hunt, Lynn. *Politics, Culture, and Class in the French Revolution.* 1984.

In 1787, the protesters demanded "the true republican form of government in our commonwealth," that is, the reduction of stadholder powers. The Free Corps took on the troops of the prince of Orange and got the upper hand. In response, Frederick William II of Prussia, whose sister had married the stad-

holder, intervened with tacit British support. Thousands of Prussian troops soon occupied Utrecht and Amsterdam, and the House of Orange regained its former position.

Internal social divisions paved the way for successful outside intervention. Many of the Patriots from the richest merchant families feared the growing power of the Free Corps. The Free Corps wanted a more democratic form of government, and to get it they encouraged the publication of pamphlets and cartoons attacking the prince and his wife, promoted the rapid spread of clubs and societies made up of common people, and organized crowd-pleasing public ceremonies, such as parades and bonfires, that sometimes turned into riots. In the aftermath of the Prussian invasion in September 1787, the Orangists got their revenge: lower-class mobs pillaged the houses of prosperous Patriot leaders, forcing many to flee to the United States, France, or the Austrian Netherlands. Those Patriots who remained nursed their grievances until the French republican armies invaded in 1795.

The Belgian Independence Movement.

If Austrian emperor Joseph II had not tried to introduce Enlightenment-inspired reforms, the Belgians of the ten provinces of the Austrian Netherlands might have remained tranquil. Joseph abolished torture, decreed toleration for Jews and Protestants (in this resolutely Catholic area), and suppressed monasteries. His reorganization of the administrative and judicial systems eliminated many offices that belonged to nobles and lawyers, sparking resistance among the upper classes in 1788. The countess of Yves,♦ for example, wrote pamphlets against Joseph's reforms and provided meeting places for the rebels.

Upper-class protesters intended only to defend historic local liberties against an overbearing government. Nonetheless, their resistance galvanized democrats, who wanted a more representative government and organized clubs to give voice to their demands. At the end of 1788, a secret society formed armed companies to prepare an uprising. By late 1789, each province had separately declared its independence, and the Austrian administration had collapsed. Delegates from the various provinces declared themselves the United States of Belgium, a clear reference to the American precedent.

Once again, however, social divisions doomed the rebels. Emboldened by the revolt's success, the democrats began to challenge

aristocratic authority. "The nobles have no acquired right over the people," one writer proclaimed. In the face of increasing democratic ferment, aristocratic leaders drew to their side the Catholic clergy and peasants, who had little sympathy for the democrats of the cities. Every Sunday in May and June 1790, thousands of peasant men and women, led by their priests, streamed into Brussels carrying crucifixes, nooses, and pitchforks to intimidate the democrats and defend the church. Faced with the choice between the Austrian emperor and "our current tyrants," the democrats chose to support the return of the Austrians under Emperor Leopold II (r. 1790–1792), who had succeeded his brother.

Polish Patriots.

A reform party calling itself the Patriots also emerged in Poland, which had been shocked by the loss of a third of its territory in the First Partition of 1772. The Patriots sought to overhaul the weak commonwealth along modern western European lines and looked to King Stanislaw August Poniatowski♦ (r. 1764–1795) to lead them. A nobleman who owed his crown solely to the dubious honor of being Catherine the Great's discarded lover but who was also a favorite correspondent of the Parisian salon hostess Madame Geoffrin, Poniatowski saw in moderate reform the only chance for his country to escape the consequences of a century's misgovernment and cultural decline. Ranged against the Patriots stood most of the aristocrats and the formidable Catherine the Great, determined to uphold imperial Russian influence.

Watchful but not displeased to see Russian influence waning in Poland, Austria and Prussia allowed the reform movement to proceed. In 1788, the Patriots got their golden chance. Bogged down in war with the Ottoman Turks, Catherine could not block the summoning of a reform-minded parliament, which with King Stanislaw's aid outmaneuvered the antireform aristocrats. Amid much oratory denouncing Russian overlordship, the parliament enacted the constitution of May 3, 1791, which established a hereditary monarchy with somewhat strengthened authority, at last freed the two-house legislature from the individual veto power of every aristocrat, granted townspeople

---

♦**Yves:** eev

♦**Poniatowski:** PAWN ya TAWF skee

limited political rights, and vaguely promised future Jewish emancipation. Abolishing serfdom was hardly mentioned. Modest though they were, the Polish reforms did not endure. Catherine II could not countenance the spread of revolution into eastern Europe and within a year engineered the downfall of the Patriots and further weakened the Polish state.

Origins of the French Revolution, 1787–1789

Many French enthusiastically greeted the American experiment in republican government and supported the Dutch, Belgian, and Polish patriots. But they did not expect the United States and the Dutch Republic to provide them a model. Montesquieu and Rousseau, the leading political theorists of the Enlightenment, taught that republics suited only small countries, not big ones like France. After suffering humiliation at the hands of the British in the Seven Years' War (1756–1763), the French had regained international prestige by supporting the victorious Americans, and the monarchy had shown its eagerness to promote reforms. In 1787, for example, the French crown granted civil rights to Protestants. Yet by the late 1780s, the French monarchy faced a serious fiscal crisis caused by a mounting deficit. It soon provoked a constitutional crisis of epic proportions.

Fiscal Crisis. France's fiscal problems stemmed from its support of the Americans against the British in the American War of Independence. About half of the French national budget went to paying interest on the debt that had accumulated. In contrast to Great Britain, which had a national bank to help raise loans for the government, the French government lived off relatively short-term, high-interest loans from private sources including Swiss banks, government annuities, and advances from tax collectors.

For years the French government had been trying unsuccessfully to modernize the tax system to make it more equitable. The peasants bore the greatest burden of taxes, whereas the nobles and clergy were largely exempt. Tax collection was also far from systematic: private contractors collected many taxes and pocketed a large share of the proceeds. With the growing support of public

Queen Marie-Antoinette
Painted in 1789 by Marie-Louise-Elizabeth Vigée-Lebrun, this portrait of the French queen shows her with her three children. Her eldest son Louis died in 1789. When he died, her second son, also called Louis, became heir to the throne. Known to supporters of the monarch as Louis XVII, he died in prison in 1795 and never ruled. Vigée-Lebrun fled France in 1789 and only returned in 1805. *Réunion des Musées Nationaux/Art Resource, NY. Photo: J. Schormanns Arnaudet.*

opinion, the bond and annuity holders from the middle and upper classes now demanded a clearer system of fiscal accountability. Declaring bankruptcy, as many rulers had in the past, was no longer an option.

In a monarchy the ruler's character is always crucial. Louis XVI (r. 1774–1792) was the model of a virtuous husband and father, but he took a limited view of his responsibilities in this time of crisis. Many complained that he showed more interest in hunting or in his hobby of making locks than in the problems of government. His wife, Marie-Antoinette, was blond, beautiful, and much criticized for her extravagant taste in clothes, elaborate hairdos, and supposed indifference to popular misery. "The Austrian bitch," as underground writers called her, had been the target of an increasingly nasty pamphlet campaign in the 1780s. By 1789, the queen had become an object of popular hatred; when confronted by the inability of the poor to buy bread, she was mistakenly reported to have replied, "Let them eat cake." The king's ineffectiveness and the queen's growing unpopularity helped undermine the monarchy as an institution.

Faced with a mounting deficit, in 1787 Louis submitted a package of reforms to the Assembly of Notables, a group of handpicked nobles, clergymen, and officials. When this group refused to cooperate, the king presented his proposals for a more uniform land tax to his old rival the parlement of Paris. When it too refused, he ordered the parlement judges into exile in the provinces. Overnight, the judges (members of the nobility because of the offices they held) became popular heroes for resisting the king's "tyranny"; in reality, however, the judges, like the notables, wanted reform only on their own terms. Louis finally gave in to demands that he call a meeting of the Estates General,♦ which had last met 175 years before.

The Estates General. The calling of the Estates General electrified public opinion. Who would determine the fate of the nation? The **Estates General** was a body of deputies from the three estates, or orders, of France. The deputies in the First Estate represented some 100,000 clergy of the Catholic church, which owned about 10 percent of the land and collected a 10 percent tax (the tithe) on peasants. The deputies of the Second Estate represented the nobility, about 400,000 men and women who owned about 25 percent of the land, enjoyed many tax exemptions, and collected seigneurial dues and rents from their peasant tenants. The deputies of the Third Estate represented everyone else, at least 95 percent of the nation. In 1614, at the last meeting of the Estates General, each order had voted separately, and either the clergy or the nobility could therefore veto any decision of the Third Estate. Before the elections to the Estates General in 1789, the king agreed to double the number of deputies for the Third Estate (making them equal in number to the other two combined), but he refused to order voting by individual head rather than by order. Voting by order (each order would have one vote) would conserve the traditional powers of the clergy and nobility; voting by head (each

deputy would have one vote) would give the Third Estate an advantage since many clergymen and even some nobles sympathized with the Third Estate.

As the state's censorship apparatus broke down, pamphleteers by the hundreds denounced the traditional privileges of the nobility and clergy and called for voting by head rather than by order. In the most vitriolic of all the pamphlets, *What Is the Third Estate?*, the middle-class clergyman Abbé (Abbot) Emmanuel-Joseph Sieyès♦ charged that the nobility contributed nothing at all to the nation's well-being; they were "a malignant disease which preys upon and tortures the body of a sick man." In the winter and spring of 1789, thousands of men (and a few women by proxy) held meetings to elect deputies and write down their grievances. The effect was immediate. Although educated men dominated the meetings at the regional level, the humblest peasants also voted in their villages and burst forth with complaints, especially about taxes. As one villager lamented, "The last crust

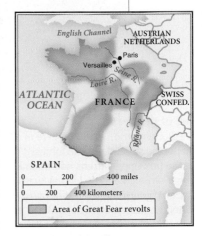

The Great Fear, 1789

of bread has been taken from us." The long series of meetings raised expectations that the Estates General would help the king solve all the nation's ills.

These new hopes soared just at the moment France experienced an increasingly rare but always dangerous food shortage. Bad weather damaged the harvest of 1788, causing bread prices to soar in many places in the spring and summer of 1789 and threatening starvation for the poorest people. A serious slump in textile production had been causing massive unemployment since 1786. Hundreds of thousands of textile workers were out of work and hungry, adding another volatile element to an already tense situation.

When some twelve hundred deputies journeyed to the king's palace of Versailles for

---

♦**Estates General:** uh STAYTS JEHN uh ruhl

♦**Emmanuel-Joseph Sieyès:** ay ma nwehl zhoh zehf syay YEHS

Fall of the Bastille

The Bastille prison is shown here in all its imposing grandeur. The moment depicted is that of the surrender of the fortress's governor, Bernard René de Launay. Because so many of the besieging citizens had been killed (only one of the defenders died), popular anger ran high and de Launay was to be the sacrificial victim. As the hastily formed citizens' guard marched him off to city hall, huge crowds taunted and spat at him. When he lashed out at one of the men nearest him, he was immediately stabbed and shot. A pastry cook cut off the governor's head, which was promptly displayed as a trophy on a pike held high above the crowd. Royal authority had been successfully challenged and even humiliated. *Château de Versailles, France/Giraudon/Bridgeman Art Library.*

the Third Estate to carry through a constitutional revolution.

July 14, 1789: The Fall of the Bastille. At first Louis appeared to agree to the new National Assembly, but he also ordered thousands of soldiers to march to Paris. The deputies who supported the Assembly feared a plot by the king and high-ranking nobles to arrest them and disperse the Assembly. "Everyone is convinced that the approach of the troops covers some violent design," one deputy wrote home. Their fears were confirmed when on July 11 the king fired Jacques Necker, the Swiss Protestant finance minister and the one high official regarded as sympathetic to the deputies' cause.

The popular reaction in Paris to Necker's dismissal and the threat of military force changed the course of the French Revolution. When the news spread, the common people in Paris began to arm themselves and attack places where either grain or arms were thought to be stored (Map 20.1). A deputy in Versailles reported home: "Today all of the evils overwhelm France, and we are between despotism, carnage, and famine." On July 14, 1789, an armed crowd marched on the Bastille, a fortified prison that symbolized royal authority. After a chaotic battle in which a hundred armed citizens died, the prison officials surrendered. The angry crowd killed the governor of the prison and flaunted his head on a pike.

The fall of the Bastille (an event now commemorated as the French national holiday) set an important precedent. The common people showed themselves willing to intervene violently at a crucial political moment (see The Third Estate Awakens). All over France, food riots turned into local revolts. The officials in one city wrote of their plight: "Yesterday afternoon [July 19] more than seven or eight thousand people, men

the opening of the Estates General in May 1789, many readers avidly followed the developments in newspapers that sprouted overnight. Although most nobles insisted on voting by order, the deputies of the Third Estate refused to proceed on that basis. After six weeks of stalemate, on June 17, 1789, the deputies of the Third Estate took unilateral action and declared themselves and whoever would join them the National Assembly, in which each deputy would vote as an individual. Two days later the clergy voted by a narrow margin to join them. Tensions rose. Denied access to their meeting hall on June 20, the deputies met on a nearby tennis court and swore an oath not to disband until they had given France a constitution that reflected their newly declared authority. This "tennis court oath" expressed the determination of

MAP 20.1 Revolutionary Paris, 1789

The French Revolution began with the fall of the Bastille prison on July 14, 1789. The huge fortified prison was located on the eastern side of the city in a neighborhood of working people. Before attacking the Bastille, crowds had torn down many of the customs booths located in the wall of the Farmers General (the private company in charge of tax collection), and taken the arms stored in the Hôtel des Invalides, a veterans' hospital on the western side of the city where the upper classes lived. In other words, the crowds had roamed throughout the city.

The Third Estate Awakens

This print, produced after the fall of the Bastille (note the heads on pikes outside the prison), shows a clergyman (First Estate) and a noble (Second Estate) alarmed by the awakening of the commoners (Third Estate). The Third Estate breaks the chains of oppression and arms itself to battle for its rights. In what ways does this print draw attention to the social conflicts that lay behind the political struggles in the Estates General? **For more help analyzing this image**, see the visual activity for this chapter in the Online Study Guide at **bedfordstmartins.com/hunt**. *Musée Carnavalet/Photo Bulloz.*

MAJOR EVENTS OF THE FRENCH REVOLUTION

1789

May 5	The Estates General opens at Versailles
June 17	The Third Estate decides to call itself the National Assembly
June 20	"Tennis court oath" shows determination of deputies to carry out a constitutional revolution
July 14	Fall of the Bastille
August 4	Night session of the National Assembly abolishes "feudalism"
August 26	National Assembly passes Declaration of the Rights of Man and Citizen
October 5–6	Women march to Versailles and join with men in bringing the royal family back to Paris

1790

July 12	Civil Constitution of the Clergy

1791

June 20	Louis and Marie-Antoinette attempt to flee in disguise and are captured at Varennes

1792

April 20	Declaration of war on Austria
August 10	Insurrection in Paris and attack on Tuileries palace lead to suspension of the king
September 2–6	Murder of prisoners in "September massacres" in Paris
September 22	Establishment of the republic

1793

January 21	Execution of Louis XVI
March 11	Beginning of uprising in the Vendée
May 31–June 2	Insurrection leading to arrest of the Girondins
July 27	Robespierre named to the Committee of Public Safety
September 29	Convention establishes General Maximum on prices and wages
October 16	Execution of Marie-Antoinette

1794

February 4	Slavery abolished in the French colonies
March 13–24	Arrest, trial, and executions of so-called ultrarevolutionaries
March 30–April 5	Arrest, trial, and executions of Danton and his followers
July 27	"The Ninth of Thermidor" arrest of Robespierre and his supporters (executed July 28–29)

1795

October 26	Directory government takes office
April 1796– October 1797	Succession of Italian victories by Bonaparte
May 1798– October 1799	Bonaparte in Egypt and Middle East

1799

November 9	Bonaparte's coup of 18 Brumaire

and women, assembled in front of the two gates to the city hall....We were forced to negotiate with them and to promise to give them wheat...and to reduce the price of bread." Local governments were forced out of power and replaced by committees of "patriots" loyal to the revolutionary cause. To restore order, the patriots relied on newly formed National Guard units composed of civilians. The king's government began to crumble. One of Louis XVI's brothers and many other leading aristocrats fled into exile. In Paris, the marquis de Lafayette, a hero of the American War of Independence and a noble deputy in the National Assembly, became commander of the new National Guard. The Revolution thus had its first heroes, its first victims, and its first enemies.

Review: In what ways did the beginning of the French Revolution resemble the other revolutions of 1787–1789?

❖ From Monarchy to Republic, 1789–1793

Until July 1789, the French Revolution followed a course much like that of the protest movements in the Low Countries. Unlike the Dutch and Belgian uprisings, however, the French Revolution did not come to a quick end. The French revolutionaries first tried to establish a constitutional monarchy based on the Enlightenment principles of human rights and rational government. This effort failed when the king attempted to raise a counter-revolutionary army. When war broke out in 1792, new tensions culminated in a second revolution on August 10, 1792, that deposed the king and established a republic in which all power rested in an elected legislature.

The Revolution of Rights and Reason

Before drafting a constitution, the deputies of the National Assembly had to confront growing violence in the countryside. Peasants made up 80 percent of the French population but owned only about 50 percent of the land. Most could barely make ends meet but still had to pay taxes to the state, the tithe to the Catholic church, and a host of seigneurial dues to their lords, whether for using the lords' mills to grind wheat or to ensure their ability to give their land as inheritance to their children. Peasants greeted the news of events in 1789 with a mixture of hope and anxiety. As food shortages spread, they feared that the beggars and vagrants crowding the roads might be part of an aristocratic plot to starve the people by burning crops or barns. In some places, the **Great Fear** (the term used by historians to describe this rural panic) turned into peasant attacks on aristocrats or on seigneurial records of peasants' dues kept in the lord's château. Peasants now refused to pay seigneurial dues to their lords, and the persistence of peasant violence raised alarms about the potential for a general peasant insurrection.

"The End of Feudalism."   In response to peasant unrest, the National Assembly decided to make sweeping changes. On the night of August 4, 1789, noble deputies announced their willingness to give up their tax exemptions and seigneurial dues. By the end of the night, amid wild enthusiasm, dozens of deputies had come to the podium to relinquish the tax exemptions of their own professional groups, towns, or provinces. The National Assembly decreed the abolition of what it called "the feudal regime"—that is, it freed the few remaining serfs and eliminated all special privileges in matters of taxation, including all seigneurial dues on land. (A few days later the deputies insisted on financial compensation for some of these dues, but most peasants refused to pay.) Peasants had achieved their goals. The Assembly also mandated equality of opportunity in access to official posts. Talent, rather than birth, was to be the key to success. Enlightenment principles were beginning to become law.

The Declaration of the Rights of Man and Citizen.   Three weeks later, the deputies drew up the **Declaration of the Rights of Man and Citizen** as a preamble to the Constitution. In words reminiscent of the American Declaration of Independence, whose author, Thomas Jefferson, was in Paris at the time, it proclaimed, "Men are born and remain free and equal in rights." The Declaration granted freedom of religion, freedom of the press, equality of taxation, and equality before the law. It established the principle of national sovereignty: since "all sovereignty rests essentially in the nation," the king derived his authority henceforth from the nation rather than from tradition or divine right.

By pronouncing all "men" free and equal, the Declaration immediately created new dilemmas. Did women have equal rights with men? What about free blacks in the colonies? How could slavery be justified if all men were born free? Did religious toleration of Protestants and Jews include equal political rights? Women never received the right to vote during the French Revolution, though Protestant and Jewish men did. Women were theoretically citizens under civil law but without the right to full political participation. (See "The Rights of Minorities," on page 758.)

Some women did not accept their exclusion, viewing it as a betrayal of the promised new order. In addition to joining demonstrations, such as the march to Versailles in

The Rights of Minorities

When the National Assembly passed the Declaration of the Rights of Man and Citizen on August 26, 1789, it opened the way to discussion of the rights of various groups, from actors (considered ineligible for voting under the monarchy because they impersonated other people as part of their profession) to women, free blacks, mulattoes, and slaves. A nobleman, Count Stanislas de Clermont Tonnerre, gave a speech on December 23, 1789, in which he advocated giving full political rights to actors, executioners, Protestants, and Jews (he did not mention women, free blacks, mulattoes, or slaves).

Sirs, in the declaration that you believed you should put at the head of the French constitution you have established, consecrated, the rights of man and citizen. In the constitutional work that you have decreed relative to the organization of the municipalities, a work accepted by the King, you have fixed the conditions of eligibility that can be required of citizens. It would seem, Sirs, that there is nothing else left to do and that prejudices should be silent in the face of the language of the law; but an honorable member has explained to us that the *non-Catholics* of some provinces still experience harassment based on former laws, and seeing them excluded from the elections and public posts, another honorable member has protested against the effect of prejudice that persecutes some professions. This prejudice, these laws, force you to make your position clear. I have the honor to present you with the draft of a decree, and it is this draft that I defend here. I establish in it the principle that professions and religious creed can never become reasons for ineligibility. . . .

Every creed has only one test to pass in regard to the social body: it has only one examination to which it must submit, that of its morals. It is here that the adversaries of the Jewish people attack me. This people, they say, is not sociable. They are commanded to loan at usurious rates; they cannot be joined with us either in marriage or by the bonds of social interchange; our food is forbidden to them; our tables prohibited; our armies will never have Jews serving in the defense of the fatherland. The worst of these reproaches is unjust; the others are only specious. Usury is not commanded by their laws; loans at interest are forbidden between them and permitted with foreigners. . . .

But, they say to me, the Jews have their own judges and laws. I respond that is your fault and you should not allow it. We must refuse everything to the Jews as a nation and accord everything to Jews as individuals. We must withdraw recognition from their judges; they should only have our judges. We must refuse legal protection to the maintenance of the so-called laws of their Judaic organization; they should not be allowed to form in the state either a political body or an order. They must be citizens individually. But, some will say to me, they do not want to be citizens. Well then! If they do not want to be citizens, they should say so, and then, we should banish them. It is repugnant to have in the state an association of non-citizens, and a nation within the nation. . . . In short, Sirs, the presumed status of every man resident in a country is to be a citizen.

Source: *Archives parlementaires*, 10 (Paris, 1878): 754–57. Translation by Lynn Hunt.

October 1789, women wrote petitions, published tracts, and organized political clubs to demand more participation (see A Women's Club, opposite). In her Declaration of the Rights of Women of 1791, Olympe de Gouges♦ (1748–1793) played on the language of the official Declaration to make the

♦**de Gouges:** duh GOOJ

point that women should also be included. In Article I, she announced, "Woman is born free and lives equal to man in her rights." She also insisted that since "woman has the right to mount the scaffold," she must "equally have the right to mount the rostrum." De Gouges linked her complaints to a program of social reform in which women would have equal rights to property and public office and equal responsibilities in taxes and criminal punishment.

The Constitution and the Church. Unresponsive to calls for women's equality, the National Assembly turned to preparing France's first written constitution. The deputies gave voting rights only to white men who passed a test of wealth. The Constitution defined them as the "active citizens"; all others were "passive." Despite these limitations, France became a constitutional monarchy in which the king served as the leading state functionary. A one-house legislature was responsible for making laws. The king could hold up enactment of laws but could not veto them absolutely. The deputies abolished all the old administrative divisions of the provinces and replaced them with a national system of eighty-three *départements* (literally "departments") with identical administrative and legal structures (Map 20.2 on page 760). All officials were elected; no offices could be bought or sold. The deputies also abolished the old taxes and replaced them with new ones that were supposed to be uniformly levied. The National Assembly had difficulty collecting taxes, however, because many people had expected a substantial cut in the tax rate. The new administrative system survived, nonetheless, and the departments are still the basic units of the French state today.

When the deputies turned to reforming the Catholic church, they created enduring conflicts. Motivated partly by the ongoing financial crisis, the National Assembly confiscated all the church's property and promised to pay clerical salaries in return. A Civil Constitution of the Clergy passed in July 1790 set pay scales for the clergy and provided that the voters elect their own parish priests and bishops just as they elected other officials. The impounded property served as a guarantee for the new paper money, called assignats,♦

♦**assignats:** a seen YAH

A Women's Club

In this gouache by the Lesueur brothers, *The Patriotic Women's Club,* the club president urges the members to contribute funds for poor patriot families. Women's clubs focused on philanthropic work but also discussed revolutionary legislation and the debates in the legislature. The colorful but sober dress indicates that the women are middle class. *Musée de la Ville de Paris/Musée Carnavalet, Paris/ Bridgeman-Giraudon/Art Resource, NY.*

issued by the government. The assignats soon became subject to inflation because the government began to sell the church lands to the highest bidders in state auctions. The sales increased the landholdings of wealthy city dwellers and prosperous peasants but cut the ground out from under the assignats.

Convinced that monastic life encouraged idleness and a decline in the nation's population, the deputies outlawed any future monastic vows and encouraged monks and nuns to return to private life on state pensions. Many monks took the opportunity, but few nuns did. For nuns, the convent was all they knew. As the Carmelite nuns of Paris responded, "If there is true happiness on earth, we enjoy it in the shelter of the sanctuary."

Faced with resistance to these changes, in November 1790, the National Assembly required all clergy to swear an oath of loyalty to the Civil Constitution of the Clergy. Pope Pius VI in Rome condemned the constitution, and half of the French clergy refused to take the oath. The oath of allegiance permanently divided the Catholic population, which had to choose between loyalty to the old church and

MAP 20.2 Redrawing the Map of France, 1789–1791
Before 1789, France had been divided into provinces, each with its own administration. Some provinces had their own law codes. As it began its deliberations, the new National Assembly determined to install uniform administrations and laws for the entire country. Discussion of the administrative reforms began in October 1789 and was completed on February 15, 1790, when the Assembly voted to divide the provinces into eighty-three departments, with names based on their geographical characteristics: Basses-Pyrenees for the Pyrenées mountains, Haute-Marne for the Marne River, and so on. How did this redrawing of the administrative map reflect the deputies' emphasis on reason over history?

Le Déménagement du Clergé

Anticlerical Sentiments
When half of the clergy refused to sign an oath of loyalty to the Civil Constitution of the Clergy, opinion divided among the Catholics in France, who made up the vast majority of the population. Many resented the new government's confiscation of church lands and the disbanding of monastic orders. Others considered the resisting clergy suspects or even traitors. This print ("The Clergy Moving Out") shows monks, nuns, and priests being forced to move out of their dwellings. The subtitle reads, "I've lost my benefices [food and shelter given in exchange for pastoral care], nothing can compare to my unhappiness." © Gianni Dagli Orti/CORBIS.

commitment to the Revolution with its "constitutional" church. The revolutionary government lost many supporters by passing laws against the clergy who refused the oath and by forcing them into exile, deporting them forcibly, or executing them as traitors. Riots and demonstrations led by women greeted many of the oath-taking priests who showed up to replace those who refused.

The End of Monarchy

The reorganization of the Catholic church offended Louis XVI, who was reluctant to recognize the new limits on his powers. On June 20, 1791, the royal family escaped in disguise from the Tuileries palace in Paris and fled to the eastern border of France, where they hoped to gather support from Austrian emperor Leopold II, the brother of Marie-Antoinette. The plans went awry when a postmaster recognized the king from his portrait on the new French money, and the royal family was arrested at Varennes, forty miles from the Austrian Netherlands border. The National Assembly tried to depict this incident as a kidnapping, but the "flight to Varennes" touched off demonstrations in Paris against the royal family, whom some now regarded as traitors. Cartoons circulated depicting the royal family as animals being returned "to the stable."

War with Austria and Prussia. The Constitution, finally completed in 1791, provided for the immediate election of the new Legislative Assembly. In a rare act of self-denial, the deputies of the National Assembly declared themselves ineligible for the new Assembly. Those who had experienced the Revolution firsthand now departed from the scene, opening the door to men with little previous experience in national politics. The status of the king might have remained uncertain if war had not intervened, but by early 1792 everyone seemed intent on war with Austria. Louis and Marie-Antoinette hoped that war would lead to the definitive defeat of the Revolution, whereas the deputies who favored a republic believed that war would reveal the king's treachery and lead to his downfall. On April 21, 1792, Louis declared war on Austria. Prussia immediately

entered on the Austrian side. Thousands of French aristocrats, including two-thirds of the army officer corps, had already emigrated, including both the king's brothers, and they were gathering along France's eastern border in expectation of joining a counter-revolutionary army.

When fighting broke out in 1792, all the powers expected a brief and relatively contained war. Instead, it would continue despite brief interruptions for the next twenty-three years. War had an immediate radicalizing effect on French politics. When the French armies proved woefully unprepared for battle, the authority of the Legislative Assembly came under fire. In June 1792, an angry crowd invaded the hall of the Assembly in Paris and threatened the royal family. In response, Lafayette left his command on the eastern front and came to Paris to insist on punishing the demonstrators. His appearance only fueled distrust of the army commanders, which increased to a fever pitch when the Prussians crossed the border and advanced on Paris. The Prussian commander, the duke of Brunswick, issued a manifesto—the Brunswick Manifesto—announcing that Paris would be totally destroyed if the royal family suffered any violence.

The Second Revolution of August 10, 1792. The ordinary people of Paris did not passively await their fate. Known as **sans-culottes** (literally, "without breeches")—because men who worked with their hands wore long trousers rather than the knee breeches of the upper classes—they had followed every twist and turn in revolutionary fortunes. Political clubs had multiplied since the founding in 1789 of the first and most influential of them, the **Jacobin Club**, named after the former monastery in Paris where the club first met. The Jacobin Club soon became part of a national political network linking all the major towns and cities. The sans-culottes had their own clubs to express their own political interests. Every local district in Paris had its club, where men and women listened to the news of the day and discussed their options.

Faced with the threat of military retaliation and frustrated with the inaction of the Legislative Assembly, on August 10, 1792,

The Execution of King Louis XVI
Louis XVI was executed by order of the National Convention on January 21, 1793. In this print, the executioner shows the severed head to the crowd, which stands in orderly silence around the scaffold. Note the empty pedestal on the right. It had held a statue of Louis XV after whom the square was named. The revolutionaries renamed it the Square of the Revolution and later put a statue of Liberty on the pedestal. *The Art Archive/Musée Carnavalet, Paris/Dagli Orti.*

one of the queen's favorites, was hacked to pieces and her mutilated body displayed beneath the windows where the royal family was kept under guard. These "September massacres" showed the dark side of popular revolution, in which the common people demanded instant revenge on supposed enemies and conspirators.

Republican Rivals and the Execution of the King. The National Convention faced a dire situation. It needed to write a new constitution for the republic while fighting a war with external enemies and confronting increasing resistance at home. The Revolution had divided the population: for some, it had not gone far enough toward providing food, land, and retribution against enemies; for others, it had gone too far by dismantling the church and the monarchy. The French people had never known any government other than monarchy. Only half the population could read and write at even a basic level. In this situation, symbolic actions became very important. Any public sign of monarchy was at risk, and revolutionaries soon pulled down statues of kings and burned reminders of the former regime.

The fate of Louis XVI and the future direction of the republic divided the deputies elected to the National Convention. Most of the deputies were middle-class lawyers and professionals who had developed their ardent republican beliefs in the network of Jacobin Clubs. After the fall of the monarchy in August 1792, however, the Jacobins divided into two factions. The Girondins♦ (named after a department in southwestern France, the Gironde, which provided some of its leading orators) met regularly at the salon of Jeanne Roland, the wife of a minister. They resented the growing power of Parisian militants and tried to appeal to the departments outside of Paris. The Mountain (so called because its

the sans-culottes organized an insurrection and attacked the Tuileries palace, the residence of the king. The king and his family had to seek refuge in the meeting room of the Legislative Assembly, where the frightened deputies ordered new elections. They abolished the property qualifications for voting required by the constitution of 1791; the voters chose the National Convention by universal male suffrage.

When it met, the National Convention abolished the monarchy and on September 22, 1792, established the first republic in French history. The republic would answer only to the people, not to any royal authority. Lafayette and other liberal aristocrats who had supported the constitutional monarchy fled into exile. Violence soon exploded again when early in September 1792 the Prussians approached Paris. Hastily gathered mobs stormed the overflowing prisons to seek out traitors who might help the enemy. In an atmosphere of near hysteria, eleven hundred inmates were killed, including many ordinary and completely innocent people. The princess of Lamballe,

♦**Girondins:** juh RAHN dihns

deputies sat in the highest seats of the National Convention), in contrast, was closely allied with the Paris militants.

The first showdown between the Girondins and the Mountain occurred during the trial of the king in December 1792. Although the Girondins agreed that the king was guilty of treason, many of them argued for clemency, exile, or a popular referendum on his fate. After a long and difficult debate, the National Convention supported the Mountain and voted by a very narrow majority to execute the king. Louis XVI went to the guillotine♦ on January 21, 1793, sharing the fate of Charles I of England in 1649. "We have just convinced ourselves that a king is only a man," wrote one newspaper, "and that no man is above the law."

> **Review:** Why did the French Revolution turn in an increasingly radical direction after 1789?

❖ Terror and Resistance

The execution of the king did not end the new regime's problems. The continuing war required even more men and money, and the introduction of a national draft provoked massive resistance in some parts of France. In response to growing pressures, the National Convention named the Committee of Public Safety to supervise food distribution, direct the war effort, and root out counter-revolutionaries. The leader of the committee, Maximilien Robespierre,♦ wanted to go beyond these stopgap measures and create a "republic of virtue," in which the government would teach, or force, citizens to become virtuous republicans through a massive program of political reeducation. Thus began the **Terror**, in which the guillotine became the most terrifying instrument of a government that suppressed almost every form of dissent (see The Guillotine, shown here). These policies only in-

♦**guillotine:** GIH luh teen
♦**Robespierre:** roh behs PYEHR

creased divisions, which ultimately led to Robespierre's fall from power and to a dismantling of government by terror.

Robespierre and the Committee of Public Safety

The conflict between the Girondins and the Mountain did not end with the execution of Louis XVI. Militants in Paris agitated for the removal of the deputies who had proposed a referendum on the king, and in retaliation the Girondins engineered the arrest of Jean-Paul Marat, a deputy who had urged violent measures in his newspaper *The Friend of the People*. When Marat was acquitted, the Girondins set up a special commission to

The Guillotine
Before 1789 only nobles were decapitated if condemned to death; commoners were usually hanged. Equalization of the death penalty was first proposed by J. I. Guillotin, a professor of anatomy and a deputy for the Third Estate in the National Assembly. He also suggested that a mechanical device be constructed for decapitation, leading to the instrument's association with his name. The Assembly decreed decapitation as the death penalty in June 1791 and another physician, A. Louis, actually invented the guillotine. The executioner pulled up the blade by a cord and then released it. Use of the guillotine began in April 1792 and did not end until 1981, when the French government abolished the death penalty. The guillotine fascinated as much as it repelled. Reproduced in miniature, painted onto snuffboxes and china, worn as jewelry, and even serving as a toy, the guillotine became a part of popular culture. How could the guillotine be simultaneously celebrated as the people's avenger by supporters of the Revolution and vilified as the preeminent symbol of the Terror by opponents? *Musée Carnavalet/ Photo Bulloz.*

investigate the situation in Paris, ordering the arrest of various local leaders. In response, Parisian militants organized an armed demonstration and invaded the National Convention on June 2, 1793, forcing the deputies to decree the arrest of their twenty-nine Girondin colleagues. The Convention consented to the establishment of paramilitary bands called "revolutionary armies" to hunt down political suspects and hoarders of grain. The deputies also agreed to speed up the operation of special revolutionary courts.

Setting the course for government and the war increasingly fell to the twelve-member Committee of Public Safety, set up by the National Convention on April 6, 1793. When Robespierre (1758–1794) was elected to the committee three months later, he became in effect its guiding spirit and the chief spokesman of the Revolution. A lawyer from northern France known as "the incorruptible" for his stern honesty and fierce dedication to democratic ideals, Robespierre remains one of the most controversial figures in world history because of his association with the Terror. In September 1793, in response to popular pressure, the deputies of the Convention voted to "put Terror on the agenda." Robespierre took the lead in implementing this decision. Although he originally opposed the death penalty and the war, he was convinced that the emergency situation of 1793 required severe measures, including death for those, such as the Girondins, who opposed the committee's policies.

Like many other educated eighteenth-century men, Robespierre had read the classics of republicanism from the ancient Roman writers Tacitus and Plutarch to the Enlightenment thinkers Montesquieu and Rousseau. But he took them a step further. He spoke eloquently about "the theory of revolutionary government" as "the war of liberty against its enemies." He defended the people's right to democratic government, while in practice he supported many emergency measures that restricted their liberties. He personally favored a free-market economy, as did almost all middle-class deputies, but in this time of crisis he was willing to enact price controls and requisitioning. In an effort to stabilize prices, the National Convention established the General Maximum on September 29,

1793, which set limits on the prices of thirty-nine essential commodities and on wages. In a speech to the Convention, Robespierre explained the necessity of government by terror: "The first maxim of your policies must be to lead the people by reason and the people's enemies by terror. . . . Without virtue, terror is deadly; without terror, virtue is impotent." *Terror* was not an idle term; it seemed to imply that the goal of democracy justified what we now call totalitarian means, that is, the suppression of all dissent.

Through a series of desperate measures, the Committee of Public Safety set the machinery of the Terror in motion. It sent deputies out "on mission" to purge unreliable officials and organize the war effort. In the first universal draft of men in history, every unmarried man and childless widower between the ages of eighteen and twenty-five was declared eligible for conscription. Revolutionary tribunals set up in Paris and provincial centers tried political suspects. In October 1793, the Revolutionary Tribunal in Paris convicted Marie-Antoinette of treason and sent her to the guillotine. The Girondin leaders and Madame Roland were also guillotined, as was Olympe de Gouges. The government confiscated all the property of convicted traitors.

The Terror won its greatest success on the battlefield. As of April 1793, France faced war with Austria, Prussia, Great Britain, Spain, Sardinia, and the Dutch Republic—all fearful of the impact of revolutionary ideals on their own populations. The execution of Louis XVI, in particular, galvanized European governments; according to William Pitt, the British prime minister, it was "the foulest and most atrocious act the world has ever seen." To face this daunting coalition of forces, the French republic tapped a new and potent source of power—nationalist pride—in decrees mobilizing young and old alike:

> *The young men will go to battle; married men will forge arms and transport provisions; women will make tents and clothing and serve in hospitals; children will make bandages; old men will get themselves carried to public places to arouse the courage of warriors and preach hatred of kings and unity of the republic.*

Forges were set up in the parks and gardens of Paris to produce thousands of guns, and citizens everywhere helped collect saltpeter, a rock salt used to make gunpowder. By the end of 1793, the French nation in arms had stopped the advance of the allied powers, and in the summer of 1794 it invaded the Austrian Netherlands and crossed the Rhine River. The army was ready to carry the gospel of revolution and republicanism to the rest of Europe.

The Republic of Virtue, 1793–1794

The program of the Terror went beyond pragmatic measures to fight the war and internal enemies to include efforts to "republicanize everything"—in other words, to effect a cultural revolution. While censoring writings deemed counterrevolutionary, the government encouraged republican art, set up civic festivals, and in some places directly attacked the churches in a campaign known as de-Christianization. In addition to drawing up plans for a new program of elementary education, the republic set about politicizing every aspect of daily life, from the naming of babies to the measurement of space and time.

Republican Culture. Refusing to tolerate opposition, the republic left no stone unturned in its endeavor to get its message across. Songs—especially the new national anthem, "La Marseillaise"—placards, posters, pamphlets, books, engravings, paintings, sculpture, even everyday crockery, chamberpots, and playing cards conveyed revolutionary slogans and symbols. Foremost among them was the figure of Liberty (an early version of the Statue of Liberty now in New York harbor), which appeared on coins and bills, letterheads and seals, and as statues in festivals (see Representing Liberty, shown here). Hundreds of new plays were produced and old classics revised. To encourage the production of patriotic and republican works, the government sponsored state competitions for artists. Works of art were supposed to "awaken the public spirit and make clear how atrocious and ridiculous were the enemies of liberty and of the Republic."

At the center of this elaborate cultural campaign were the revolutionary festivals modeled on Rousseau's plans for a civic religion. The festivals first emerged in 1789

Representing Liberty

Liberty was represented by a female figure because in French the noun is feminine (*la liberté*). This painting from 1793–1794, by Jeanne-Louise Vallain, captures the usual attributes of Liberty: she is soberly seated, wearing a Roman-style toga, and holding a pike with a Roman liberty cap on top. Her Roman appearance signals that she is the representation of an abstract quality. The fact that she holds an instrument of battle suggests that women might be active participants. Liberty is holding the Declaration of the Rights of Man and Citizen as it was revised in 1793. This painting was most likely hung in a central location in the Paris Jacobin Club. *Musée de la Revolution Française, Vizille.*

with the spontaneous planting of liberty trees in villages and towns. The Festival of Federation on July 14, 1790, marked the first anniversary of the fall of the Bastille. Under the National Convention, the well-known painter Jacques-Louis David (1748–1825), who was a deputy and associate of Robespierre, took over festival planning. David aimed to destroy the mystique of monarchy and to make the republic sacred. His Festival of Unity on August 10, 1793, for example, celebrated the first anniversary of the overthrow of the monarchy. In front of the statue of Liberty built for the occasion, a bonfire consumed the crowns and scepters of royalty while a cloud of three thousand white doves rose into the sky. This was all part of preaching the "moral order of the Republic . . . that will make us a people of brothers, a people of philosophers."

De-Christianization. Some revolutionaries hoped the festival system would replace the Catholic church altogether. They initiated a campaign of **de-Christianization** that included closing churches (Protestant as well as Catholic), selling many church buildings to the highest bidder, and trying to force even those clergy who had taken the oath of loyalty to abandon their clerical vocations and marry. Great churches became storehouses for arms or grain, or their stones were sold off to contractors. The medieval statues of kings on the facade of Notre Dame cathedral were beheaded. Church bells were dismantled and church treasures melted down for government use.

In the ultimate step in de-Christianization, extremists tried to establish what they called the Cult of Reason to supplant Christianity. In Paris in the fall of 1793, a goddess of Liberty, played by an actress, presided over the Festival of Reason in Notre Dame cathedral. Local militants in other cities staged similar festivals, which alarmed deputies in the National Convention, who were wary of turning rural, devout populations against the republic. The Committee of Public Safety halted the de-Christianization campaign, and Robespierre, with David's help, tried to institute an alternative, the Cult of the Supreme Being, in June 1794. Robespierre objected to the de-Christianization campaign's atheism; he favored a Rousseau-inspired deistic religion without the supposedly superstitious trappings of Catholicism. Neither cult attracted many followers, but both show the depth of the commitment to overturning the old order and all its traditional institutions.

Politicizing Daily Life. In principle the best way to ensure the future of the republic was through the education of the young. The deputy Georges-Jacques Danton (1759–1794), Robespierre's main competitor as theorist of the Revolution, maintained that "after bread, the first need of the people is education." The National Convention voted to make primary schooling free and compulsory for both boys and girls. It took control of education away from the Catholic church and tried to set up a system of state schools at both the primary and secondary levels, but it lacked trained teachers to replace those the Catholic religious orders provided. As a result, opportunities for learning how to read and write may have diminished. In 1799, only one-fifth as many boys enrolled in the state secondary schools as had studied in church schools ten years earlier.

Although many of the ambitious republican programs failed, almost all aspects of daily life became politicized, even colors. The tricolor—the combination of red, white, and blue that was to become the flag of France— was devised in July 1789, and by 1793 everyone had to wear a cockade (a badge made of ribbons) with the colors. Using the formal forms of speech—*vous* for "you"—or the title *monsieur* or *madame* might identify someone as an aristocrat; true patriots used the informal *tu* and *citoyen*◆ or *citoyenne* ("citizen") instead. Some people changed their names or gave their children new kinds of names. Biblical and saints' names such as Jean, Pierre, Joseph, and Marie gave way to names recalling heroes of the ancient Roman republic (Brutus, Gracchus, Cornelia), revolutionary heroes, or flowers and plants. Such changes symbolized adherence to the republic and to Enlightenment ideals rather than to Catholicism.

Even the measures of time and space were revolutionized. In October 1793, the National Convention introduced a new calendar to replace the Christian one. Its bases were reason and republican principles. Year I dated from the beginning of the republic on September 22, 1792. Twelve months of exactly thirty days each received new names

---

◆*citoyen:* sih twoy en

derived from nature—for example, Pluviôse◆ (roughly equivalent to February) recalled the rain (*la pluie*) of late winter. Instead of seven-day weeks, ten-day *décades* provided only one day of rest every ten days and pointedly eliminated the Sunday of the Christian calendar. The five days left at the end of the calendar year were devoted to special festivals called *sans-culottides*.◆ The calendar remained in force for twelve years despite continuing resistance to it. More enduring was the new metric system based on units of ten that was invented to replace the hundreds of local variations in weights and measures. Other countries in Europe and throughout the world eventually adopted the metric system.

Successive revolutionary legislatures had also changed the rules of family life. The state took responsibility for all family matters away from the Catholic church: birth, death, and marriage registration now happened at city hall, not the parish church. Marriage became a civil contract and as such could be broken and thereby nullified. The new divorce law of September 1792 was the most far-reaching in Europe: a couple could divorce by mutual consent or for reasons such as insanity, abandonment, battering, or criminal conviction. Thousands of men and women took advantage of the law to dissolve unhappy marriages, even though the pope had condemned the measure. (In 1816, the government revoked the right to divorce, and not until the 1970s did French divorce laws return to the principles of the 1792 legislation.) In one of its most influential actions, the National Convention passed a series of laws that created equal inheritance among all children in the family, including girls. The father's right to favor one child, especially the oldest male, was considered aristocratic and hence antirepublican.

Resisting the Revolution

By intruding into religion, culture, and daily life, the republic inevitably provoked resistance. Shouting curses against the republic, uprooting liberty trees, carrying statues of the Virgin Mary in procession, hiding a priest who would not take the oath, singing a royalist song—all these expressed dissent with the new symbols, rituals, and policies. Resistance also took more violent forms, from riots over food shortages or religious policies to assassination and full-scale civil war.

Women's Resistance. Many women, in particular, suffered from the hard conditions of life that persisted in this time of war, and they had their own ways of voicing discontent. Long bread lines in the cities exhausted the patience of women, and police spies reported their constant grumbling, which occasionally turned into spontaneous demonstrations or riots over high prices or food shortages. Women also took the lead in protesting against changes forced on the Catholic church; they organized their fellow parishioners to refuse to hear mass offered by the "constitutional" priests, and they protected the priests who would not sign the oath of loyalty.

Other forms of resistance were more individual. One young woman, Charlotte Corday, assassinated the outspoken deputy Jean-Paul Marat in July 1793. Corday fervently supported the Girondins, and she considered it her patriotic duty to kill the deputy who, in the columns of his paper, had constantly demanded more heads and more blood. Marat was immediately eulogized as a great martyr, and Corday went to the guillotine vilified as a monster but confident that she had "avenged many innocent victims."

Rebellion and Civil War. Organized resistance broke out in many parts of France. The arrest of the Girondin deputies in June 1793 sparked insurrections in several departments. After the government retook the city of Lyon, one of the centers of the revolt, the deputy on mission ordered sixteen hundred houses demolished. Special courts sentenced almost two thousand people to death. Thereafter, the name of the city was changed to Ville Affranchie◆ (Liberated Town).

◆**Pluviôse:** PLOO vee ohs
◆**sans-culottides:** sahn ku law TEED

◆**Ville Affranchie:** veel uh FRAHNSH ee

In the Vendée region of western France, resistance turned into full-scale civil war. Between March and December 1793, peasants, artisans, and weavers joined under noble leadership to form a "Catholic and Royal Army." One rebel group explained its motives:

The Vendée Rebellion, 1793

"They [the republicans] have killed our king, chased away our priests, sold the goods of our church, eaten everything we have and now they want to take our bodies [in the draft]." The uprising took two different forms: in the Vendée itself, a counterrevolutionary army organized to fight the republic; in nearby Brittany, resistance took the form of guerrilla bands, which united to attack a target and then quickly melted into the countryside. Great Britain provided money and underground contacts for these attacks, which were almost always aimed at towns. Town officials sold church lands, enforced measures against the clergy, and supervised conscription. In many ways this was a civil war between town and country, for the townspeople were the ones who supported the Revolution and bought church lands for themselves. The peasants had gained most of what they wanted in 1789 with the abolition of seigneurial dues, and they resented the government's demands for money and manpower and actions taken against their local clergy.

For several months in 1793, the Vendée rebels stormed the largest towns in the region. Both sides committed horrible atrocities. At the small town of Machecoul, for example, the rebels massacred five hundred republicans, including administrators and National Guard members; many were tied together, shoved into freshly dug graves, and shot. By the fall, however, republican soldiers had turned back the rebels. A republican general wrote to the Committee of Public Safety claiming, "There is no more Vendée, citizens, it has perished under our free sword along with its women and children. . . . Fol-lowing the orders that you gave me I have crushed children under the feet of horses, massacred women who at least . . . will engender no more brigands."

"Infernal columns" of republican troops marched through the region to restore control, military courts ordered thousands executed, and republican soldiers massacred thousands of others. In one especially gruesome incident, the deputy Jean-Baptiste Carrier supervised the drowning of some two thousand Vendée rebels, including a number of priests. Barges loaded with prisoners were floated into the Loire River near Nantes and then sunk. Controversy still rages about the rebellion's death toll. Estimates of rebel deaths alone range from about 20,000 to 250,000 and higher. Many thousands of republican soldiers and civilians also lost their lives. Even the low estimates reveal the carnage of this catastrophic confrontation between the republic and its opponents.

The Fall of Robespierre and the End of the Terror, 1794–1799

In an atmosphere of fear of conspiracy that these outbreaks fueled, Robespierre tried simultaneously to exert the National Convention's control over popular political activities and to weed out opposition among the deputies. As a result, the Terror intensified until July 1794, when a group of deputies joined within the Convention to order the arrest and execution of Robespierre and his followers. The Convention then ordered elections and drew up a new republican constitution that gave executive power to five directors. This "Directory government" maintained power during four years of seesaw battles between royalists and former Jacobins. Ultimately it gave way to Napoleon Bonaparte.

The Revolution Devours Its Own. In the fall of 1793, the National Convention cracked down on popular clubs and societies. First to be suppressed were women's political clubs. Founded in early 1793, the Society of Revolutionary Republican Women played a very active part in sans-culottes politics. The society urged harsher measures against the republic's enemies and insisted that women have a voice in politics even if they did not have the vote. Women had set up their own clubs in many provincial towns and also attended the meetings of local men's organizations. The closing of women's clubs marked an important turning point in the Revolution. From then on the sans-culottes and their political organizations came increasingly under the thumb of the Jacobin deputies in the National Convention.

The National Convention abolished women's political clubs in order to limit agitation in the streets. As one deputy stated, women's clubs consisted of "adventuresses, knights-errant, emancipated women, amazons." The deputies called on biological arguments about natural differences between the sexes to bolster their case. As one argued, "Women are ill suited for elevated thoughts and serious meditations." In subsequent years physicians, priests, and philosophers amplified such opinions by formulating explanations for women's "natural" differences from men to justify their inferior status.

In the spring of 1794, the Committee of Public Safety moved against its critics among leaders in Paris and deputies in the National Convention itself. First a handful of "ultrarevolutionaries"—in fact a motley collection of local Parisian politicians—were arrested and executed. Next came the other side, the "indulgents," so called because they favored a moderation of the Terror. Included among them was the deputy Danton, himself once a member of the Committee of Public Safety and a friend of Robespierre, despite the striking contrast in their personalities. Danton was the Revolution's most flamboyant orator and, unlike Robespierre, a high-living, high-spending, excitable politician. At every critical turning point in national politics, his booming voice had swayed opinion in the National Convention. Now, under government pressure, the Revolutionary Tribunal convicted him and his friends of treason and sentenced them to death.

With the arrest and execution of these leaders in Paris, the prophecies of doom for the Revolution seemed about to be realized. "The Revolution," as one of the Girondin victims of 1793 had remarked, "was devouring its own children." Even after the major threats to the Committee of Public Safety's power had been eliminated, the Terror continued and even worsened. A law passed in June 1794 denied the accused the right of legal counsel, reduced the number of jurors necessary for conviction, and allowed only two judgments: acquittal or death. The category of political crimes expanded to include "slandering patriotism" and "seeking to inspire discouragement." Ordinary people risked the guillotine if they expressed any discontent. The rate of executions in Paris rose from five a day in the spring of 1794 to twenty-six a day in the summer. The political atmosphere darkened even though the military situation improved. At the end of June, the French armies decisively defeated the main Austrian army and advanced through the Austrian Netherlands to Brussels and Antwerp. The emergency measures for fighting the war were working, yet Robespierre and his inner circle had made so many enemies that they could not afford to loosen the grip of the Terror.

The Terror hardly touched many parts of France, but overall the experience was undeniably traumatic. Across the country the official Terror cost the lives of at least forty thousand French people, most of them living in the regions of major insurrections or near the borders with foreign enemies, where suspicion of collaboration ran high. As many as 300,000 people—one out of every fifty French people—went to prison as suspects between March 1793 and August 1794. The toll for the aristocracy and the clergy was especially high. Many leading nobles perished under the guillotine, and thousands emigrated. Thirty thousand to forty thousand clergy who refused the oath emigrated, at least two thousand (including many nuns) were executed, and thousands were imprisoned. The clergy were singled out in particular in the civil war zones: 135 priests were massacred at Lyon in November 1793, and 83 were shot in one day during the Vendée revolt. Yet many victims of the Terror were peasants or ordinary working people.

The final crisis of the Terror came in July 1794. Conflicts within the Committee of Public Safety and the National Convention left Robespierre isolated. On July 27, 1794 (the ninth of Thermidor, Year II, according to the revolutionary calendar), Robespierre appeared before the Convention with yet another list of deputies to be arrested. Many feared they would be named, and they shouted him down and ordered him arrested along with his followers on the committee, the president of the Revolutionary Tribunal in Paris, and the commander of the Parisian National Guard. An armed uprising led by the Paris city government failed to save Robespierre when most of the National Guard took the side of the Convention. Robespierre tried to kill himself with a pistol but only broke his jaw. The next day he and scores of followers went to the guillotine.

The Thermidorian Reaction and the Directory, 1794–1799.   The men who led the attack on Robespierre in Thermidor (July 1794) did not intend to reverse all his policies, but that happened nonetheless because of a violent backlash known as the **Thermidorian Reaction**. As most of the instruments of terror were dismantled, newspapers attacked the Robespierrists as "tigers thirsting for human blood." The new government released hundreds of suspects and arranged a temporary truce in the Vendée. It purged Jacobins from local bodies and replaced them with their opponents. It arrested some of the most notorious "terrorists" in the National Convention, such as Carrier, and put them to death. Within the year the new leaders abolished the Revolutionary Tribunal and closed the Jacobin Club in Paris. Popular demonstrations met severe repression. In southeastern France, in particular, the "White Terror" replaced the Jacobins' "Red Terror." Former officials and local Jacobin leaders were harassed, beaten, and often murdered by paramilitary bands who had tacit support from the new authorities. Those who remained in the National Convention prepared yet another constitution in 1795, setting up a two-house legislature and an executive body—the Directory, headed by five directors.

The Directory regime tenuously held on to power for four years, all the while trying to fend off challenges from the remaining Jacobins and the resurgent royalists. The puritanical atmosphere of the Terror gave way to the pursuit of pleasure—low-cut dresses of transparent materials, the reappearance of prostitutes in the streets, fancy dinner parties, and "victims' balls" where guests wore red ribbons around their necks as reminders of the guillotine. Bands of young men dressed in knee breeches and rich fabrics picked fights with known Jacobins and disrupted theater performances with loud antirevolutionary songs. All over France people banded together and petitioned to reopen churches closed during the Terror. If necessary they broke into a church to hold services with a priest who had been in hiding or a lay schoolteacher who was willing to say Mass.

Although the Terror had ended, the revolution had not. In 1794, the most democratic and most repressive phases of the Revolution both ended at once. Between 1795 and 1799, the republic endured in France, but it directed a war effort abroad that would ultimately bring to power the man who would dismantle the republic itself.

> **Review:** What factors can explain the Terror? To what extent was it simply a response to a national emergency or a reflection of deeper problems within the French Revolution?

❖ Revolution on the March

Beginning in 1792, war raged almost constantly until 1815. At one time or another, and sometimes all at once, France faced every principal power in Europe. The French republic—and later the French Empire under its supreme commander, Emperor Napoleon Bonaparte—proved an even more formidable opponent than the France of Louis XIV. New means of mobilizing and organizing soldiers enabled the French to dominate Europe for a generation. The influence of the Revolution as a political model and the threat of French military conquest combined to challenge the traditional order in Europe.

Arms and Conquests

The powers allied against France squandered their best chance to triumph in early 1793, when the French armies verged on chaos because of the emigration of noble army officers and the problems of integrating new draftees. By the end of 1793, once the new national draft had gone into effect, the French had a huge and powerful fighting force of 700,000 men. But the army still faced many problems in the field. As many as a third of the recent draftees deserted before or during battle. Uniforms fashioned out of rough cloth constricted movements, tore easily, and retained the damp of muddy battlefields, exposing the soldiers to the elements and the spread of disease. At times the soldiers were fed only moldy bread, and if their pay was late, they sometimes resorted to pillaging and looting. Generals might pay with their lives if they lost a key battle and their loyalty to the Revolution came under suspicion.

France nevertheless had one overwhelming advantage: its soldiers, drawn largely from the peasantry and the lower classes of the cities, fought for a revolution that they and their brothers and sisters had helped make. The republic was their government, and the army was in large measure theirs too; many officers had risen through the ranks by skill and talent rather than by inheriting or purchasing their positions. One young peasant boy wrote to his parents, "Either you will see me return bathed in glory, or you will have a son who is a worthy citizen of France who knows how to die for the defense of his country."

When the French armies invaded the Austrian Netherlands and crossed the Rhine in the summer of 1794, they proclaimed a war of liberation. But as they annexed more and more territory, "liberated" people in many

MAP 20.3 French Expansion, 1791–1799

The influence of the French Revolution on neighboring territories is dramatically evident in this map. The French directly annexed the papal territories in southern France in 1791, Nice and Savoy in 1792, and the Austrian Netherlands in 1795. They set up a series of sister republics in the former Dutch Republic and in various Italian states. Local people did not always welcome these changes. For example, the French made the Dutch pay a huge war indemnity, support a French occupying army of 25,000 soldiers, and give up some southern territories. One of the generals who invaded the Dutch Republic wrote, "Holland has done nothing to avoid being classed among the general order of our conquests. . . . It follows from this that there can be no reason to treat her any differently from a conquered country." The sister republics faced a future of subordination to French national interests.

places began to view them as an army of occupation (Map 20.3). Middle-class people near the northern and eastern borders of France reacted most positively to the French invasion. In the Austrian Netherlands, Mainz, Savoy, and Nice, French officers organized

Jacobin Clubs that attracted locals. The clubs petitioned for annexation to France, and French legislation was then introduced, including the abolition of seigneurial dues. Despite resistance, especially in the Austrian Netherlands, these areas remained part of France until 1815, and the legal changes were permanent. Like Louis XIV a century before, most deputies in the National Convention considered the territories annexed in 1794 within France's "natural frontiers"—the Rhine, the Alps, and the Pyrenees.

The Directory government that came to power in 1795 was torn between defending the new frontiers and launching a more aggressive policy of creating semi-independent "sister republics" wherever the armies succeeded. Aggression won out. When Prussia declared neutrality in 1795, the French armies swarmed into the Dutch Republic, abolished the stadholderate, and—with the revolutionary penchant for renaming—created the new Batavian Republic, a satellite of France. The brilliant young general Napoleon Bonaparte defeated the Austrian armies in northern Italy in 1797 and created the Cisalpine Republic. Next he overwhelmed Venice and then handed it over to the Austrians in exchange for a peace agreement that lasted less than two years. After the French attacked the Swiss cantons in 1798, they set up the Helvetic Republic and curtailed many of the Catholic church's privileges. They conquered the Papal States in 1798 and installed a Roman Republic; the pope fled to Siena.

The revolutionary wars had an immediate impact on European life at all levels of society. Thousands of men died in every country involved, with perhaps as many as 200,000 casualties in the French armies alone in 1794 and 1795. No accurate statistics documenting casualties in these wars exist, but we do know that more soldiers died in hospitals as a result of their wounds than on the battlefields. Constant warfare hampered world commerce and especially disrupted French overseas shipping. (The abolition of slavery in the French colonies in 1794 also cut off one lucrative market for the French port cities.) In contrast to the prosperous times that preceded the French Revolution, times were now hard almost everywhere, because the dislocations of internal and external commerce provoked constant shortages.

FRENCH LIBERTY.   BRITISH SLAVERY.

The English Rebuttal
In this caricature, James Gillray satirizes the French version of liberty. Gillray, a supporter of the Tories in Britain, produced thousands of political caricatures. How would you interpret the message of this print? *British Museum.*

European Reactions to Revolutionary Change

The French Revolution profoundly transformed European politics and social relations. (See "Contrasting Views," page 774.) In 1789, many had greeted events with unabashed enthusiasm. The English Unitarian minister Richard Price had exulted, "Behold, the light . . . after setting AMERICA free, reflected to FRANCE, and there kindled into a blaze that lays despotism in ashes, and warms and illuminates EUROPE." Democrats and reformers from many countries flooded to Paris to witness events firsthand. Supporters of the French Revolution in Great Britain, like the earlier reformers of the 1760s and 1770s, joined constitutional and reform societies that sprang up in many cities. The most important of these societies, the London Corresponding Society, founded in 1792, corresponded with the Paris Jacobin Club and served as a center for reform agitation in England. Pro-French feeling ran even stronger in Ireland. Catholics and Presbyterians, both excluded from the vote, came together in 1791 in the Society of United Irishmen, which eventually pressed for secession from England.

European elites became alarmed when the French abolished monarchy and nobility and encouraged popular participation in politics. The British government, for example, quickly suppressed the corresponding societies and harassed their leaders, charging that their ideas and their contacts with the French were seditious (see the illustration opposite for a negative English view). When the Society of United Irishmen timed a rebellion to coincide with an attempted French invasion in 1798, the British mercilessly repressed them, killing thirty thousand rebels. Twice as many regular British troops (seventy thousand) as fought in any of the major continental battles were required to put down the rebellion.

Those countries near France with a substantial middle class and access to newspapers and other publications generally sympathized the most with French ideas. Yet even countries close to France sometimes fiercely resisted French occupation, often in the form of banditry. Because the French offered the Jews religious toleration and civil and political rights wherever they conquered, anti-French groups sometimes attacked Jews. One German traveler reported, "It is characteristic of the region in which the bandits are based that these two nations [the French and the Jews] are hated. So crimes against them are motivated not just by a wish to rob them but also by a variety of fanaticism which is partly political and partly religious."

Many leading intellectuals in the German states, including the philosopher Immanuel Kant, initially supported the revolutionary cause, but after 1793 most of them turned against the popular violence and military aggressiveness of the Revolution. One of the greatest writers of the age, Friedrich Schiller (1759–1805), typified the turn in sentiment against revolutionary politics:

> *Freedom is only in the realm of dreams*
> *And the beautiful blooms only in song.*

The German states, still run by many separate rulers, experienced a profound artistic and intellectual revival, which eventually connected with anti-French nationalism. This renaissance included a resurgence of intellectual life in the universities, a thriving press (1,225 journals were launched in the 1780s alone), and the multiplication of Masonic lodges and literary clubs.

Not surprisingly, the areas farthest from France—Russia, the Ottoman Empire, the Balkans, Austria, Hungary, and the Scandinavian states—were generally least affected by the French Revolution. One exception was the United States, where opinion fiercely divided on the virtues of the French Revolution. Sweden was a second exception. Gustavus III (r. 1771–1792) was assassinated in Stockholm by a nobleman who claimed that "the king has violated his oath . . . and declared himself an enemy of the realm." The king's murder changed little in Sweden's power structure, however; his son Gustavus IV (r. 1792–1809) was convinced that the French Jacobins had sanctioned his father's assassination, and he insisted on avoiding "licentious liberty." Even though it was just across the border, Spain's royal government suppressed all news from France, fearing that it might ignite the spirit

CONTRASTING VIEWS

Consequences of the French Revolution

Contemporaries instantly grasped the cataclysmic significance of the French Revolution and began to argue about its lessons for their own countries. A member of the British Parliament, Edmund Burke, ignited a firestorm of controversy with his Reflections on the Revolution in France *(Document 1). He condemned the French revolutionaries for attempting to build a government on abstract reasoning rather than taking historical traditions and customs into account; his book provided a foundation for the doctrine known as conservatism, which argued for "conserving" the traditional foundations of society and avoiding the pitfalls of radical or revolutionary change. Burke's views provoked a strong response from the English political agitator Thomas Paine. Paine's pamphlet* Common Sense *(1776) helped inspire the British North American colonies to demand independence from Great Britain. In* The Rights of Man *(Document 2), written fifteen years later, Paine attacked the traditional order as fundamentally unjust and defended the idea of a revolution to uphold rights. Joseph de Maistre, an aristocratic opponent of both the Enlightenment and the French Revolution, put the conservative attack on the French Revolution into a deeply religious and absolutist framework (Document 3). In contrast, Anne-Louise-Germaine de Staël, an opponent of Napoleon and one of the most influential intellectuals of the early nineteenth century, took the view that the violence of the Revolution had been the product of generations of superstition and arbitrary rule, that is, rule by an absolutist Catholic church and monarchical government (Document 4).*

1. EDMUND BURKE, *REFLECTIONS ON THE REVOLUTION IN FRANCE* (1790)

Born in Ireland and a supporter of the American colonists in their opposition to the British Parliament, Edmund Burke (1729–1797) opposed the French Revolution. He argued the case for tradition, continuity, and gradual reform based on practical experience—what he called "a sure principle of conservation."

Can I now congratulate the same nation [France] upon its freedom? Is it because liberty in the abstract may be classed amongst the blessings of mankind, that I am seriously to felicitate a madman, who has escaped from the protecting restraint and wholesome darkness of his cell, on his restoration to the enjoyment of light and liberty? Am I to congratulate an highwayman and murderer, who has broke prison, upon the recovery of his natural rights? . . .

Government is not made in virtue of natural rights, which may and do exist in total independence of it; and exist in much greater clearness, and in a much greater degree of abstract perfection: but their abstract perfection is their practical defect. By having a right to every thing they want every thing. . . . The science of constructing a commonwealth, or renovating it, or reforming it, is, like every other experimental science, not to be taught *a priori* [based on theory rather than on experience]. Nor is it a short experience that can instruct us in that practical science; because the real effects of moral causes are not always immediate; but that which in the first instance is prejudicial may be excellent in its remoter operation; and its excellence may arise even from the ill effects it produces in the beginning. . . .

In the groves of *their* academy, at the end of every visto [vista], you see nothing but the gallows. Nothing is left which engages the affections on the part of the commonwealth. . . . To make us love our country, our country ought to be lovely.

Source: *Two Classics of the French Revolution:* Reflections on the Revolution in France (*Edmund Burke*) and The Rights of Man (*Thomas Paine*) (New York: Doubleday Anchor Books, 1973), 19, 71–74, 90–91.

2. THOMAS PAINE, *THE RIGHTS OF MAN* (1791)

In his reply to Burke, The Rights of Man, *which sold 200,000 copies in two years, Thomas Paine (1737–1809) defended the idea of reform based on* reason, advocated a concept of universal human rights, and attacked the excesses of privilege and tradition in Great Britain. Elected as a deputy to the French National Convention in 1793 in recognition of his writings in favor of the French Revolution, Paine narrowly escaped condemnation as an associate of the Girondins.

Before anything can be reasoned upon to a conclusion, certain facts, principles, or data, to reason from, must be established, admitted, or denied. Mr. Burke, with his usual outrage, abuses the *Declaration of the Rights of Man*, published by the National Assembly of France, as the basis on which the Constitution of France is built. This he calls "paltry and blurred sheets of paper about the rights of man."

Does Mr. Burke mean to deny that *man* has any rights? If he does, then he must mean that there are no such things as rights any where, and that he has none himself; for who is there in the world but man? . . .

Hitherto we have spoken only (and that but in part) of the natural rights of man. We have now to consider the civil rights of man, and to show how the one originates from the other. Man did not enter into society to become *worse* than he was before, nor to have fewer rights than he had before, but to have those rights better secured. His natural rights are the foundation of all his civil rights. . . .

A constitution is not a thing in name only, but in fact. It has not an ideal, but a real existence; and wherever it cannot be produced in a visible form, there is none. A constitution is a thing *antecedent* to a government, and a government is only the creature of a constitution. The constitution of a country is not the act of its government, but of the people constituting a government. . . .

Can then Mr. Burke produce the English Constitution? If he cannot, we may fairly conclude, that though it has been so much talked about, no such thing as a constitution exists, or ever did exist, and consequently that the people have yet a constitution to form.

Source: *Two Classics of the French Revolution*: Reflections on the Revolution in France (*Edmund Burke*) and The Rights of Man (*Thomas Paine*) (New York: Doubleday Anchor Books, 1973), 302, 305–306, 309.

3. JOSEPH DE MAISTRE, *CONSIDERATIONS ON FRANCE* (1797)

An aristocrat born in Savoy, Joseph de Maistre (1753–1821) believed in reform but he passionately opposed both the Enlightenment and the French Revolution as destructive to good order. He believed that Protestants, Jews, lawyers, journalists, and scientists all threatened the social order because they questioned the need for absolute obedience to authority in matters both religious and political. De Maistre set the foundations for reactionary conservatism, a conservatism that defended throne and altar.

This consideration especially makes me think that the French Revolution is a great epoch and that its consequences, in all kinds of ways, will be felt far beyond the time of its explosion and the limits of its birthplace. . . .

There is a satanic quality to the French Revolution that distinguishes it from everything we have ever seen or anything we are ever likely to see in the future. Recall the great assemblies, Robespierre's speech against the priesthood, the solemn apostasy [renunciation of vows] of the clergy, the desecration of objects of worship, the installation of the goddess of reason, and that multitude of extraordinary actions by which the provinces sought to outdo Paris. All this goes beyond the ordinary circle of crime and seems to belong to another world.

Source: Joseph de Maistre, *Considerations on France*, trans. Richard A. Lebrun (Cambridge: Cambridge University Press, 1994), 21, 41.

4. ANNE-LOUISE-GERMAINE DE STAËL, *CONSIDERATIONS ON THE MAIN EVENTS OF THE FRENCH REVOLUTION* (1818)

De Staël published her views long after the Revolution was over, but she had lived through the events herself. She was the daughter of Jacques Necker, Louis XVI's Swiss Protestant finance minister. Necker's dismissal in July 1789 had sparked the attack on the Bastille. De Staël published novels, literary tracts, and memoirs and became one of the

(Continued)

(Continued)

best-known writers of the nineteenth century. In her writings she defended the Enlightenment; though she opposed the violence unleashed by the Revolution, she traced it back to the excesses of monarchical government. (See her portrait on page 795.)

Once the people were freed from their harness there is no doubt that they were in a position to commit any kind of crime. But how can we explain their depravity? The government we are now supposed to miss so sorely [the former monarchy] had had plenty of time to form this guilty nation. The priests whose teaching, example, and wealth were supposed to be so good for us had supervised the childhood of the generation that broke out against them. The class that revolted in 1789 must have been accustomed to the privileges of feudal nobility which, as we are also assured, are so peculiarly agreeable to those on whom they weigh [the peasants]. How does it happen, then, that the seed of so many vices was sown under the ancient institutions?…What can we conclude from this, then?—That no people had been as unhappy for the preceding century as the French. If the Negroes of Saint-Domingue have committed even greater atrocities, it is because they had been even more greatly oppressed.

Source: Vivian Folkenflik, ed., *An Extraordinary Woman: Selected Writings of Germaine de Staël* (New York: Columbia University Press, 1987), 365–66.

QUESTIONS TO CONSIDER

1. Which aspect of the French Revolution most disturbed these commentators?
2. How would you align each of these writers on a spectrum running from extreme right to extreme left in politics?
3. How would each of these writers judge the Enlightenment that preceded the French Revolution?

of revolt. This fear was not misplaced; even in Russia, for instance, 278 outbreaks of peasant unrest occurred between 1796 and 1798. One Russian landlord complained, "This is the self-same . . . spirit of insubordination and independence, which has spread through all Europe."

Poland Extinguished, 1793–1795

The spirit of independence made the Poles and Lithuanians especially discontent, for they had already suffered a significant loss of territory and population. "I shall fight Jacobinism, and defeat it in Poland," vowed Catherine the Great in 1792. She abolished Poland's reform constitution of May 3, 1791, and easily crushed Polish resistance while Prussian and Austrian troops battled the French in the west. Fearing a pro-French Poland, Prussia joined Russia in dividing up generous new slices of Polish territory in the Second Partition of 1793 (Map 20.4).

In response, Poland's reform movement became even more pro-French. Some leaders fled abroad, including Tadeusz Kościuszko♦ (1746–1817), an officer who had been a foreign volunteer in the War of American Independence and who now escaped to Paris. In the spring of 1794, Kościuszko returned from France to lead a nationalist revolt. Cracow, Warsaw, and the old Lithuanian capital, Vilnius, responded with uprisings. Kościuszko faced an immediate, insoluble dilemma. He could win only if the peasants joined the struggle—highly unlikely unless villagers could be convinced that serfdom would end. But such a drastic step risked alienating the nobles who had started the revolt. So Kościuszko compromised. He promised a reduction of the serfs' obligations, but not freedom itself. A few peasant bands joined the insurrection, but most let their lords fight it

---

♦**Tadeusz Kościuszko:** ta DEE oosh kawsh CHUSH koh

MAP 20.4 The Second and Third Partitions of Poland, 1793 and 1795

In 1793, after Russian armies invaded Poland, Russia and Prussia agreed to another partition of Polish territories. Prussia took over territory that included 1.1 million Poles while Russia gained 3 million new inhabitants. Austria gave up any claims to Poland in exchange for help from Russia and Prussia in acquiring Bavaria. When Kościuszko's nationalist uprising failed in 1794, Russia, Prussia, and Austria agreed to a final division. Prussia absorbed an additional 900,000 Polish subjects, including those in Warsaw; Austria incorporated 1 million Poles and the city of Cracow; Russia gained another 2 million Poles. The three powers determined never to use the term *Kingdom of Poland* again. How had Poland become such a prey to the other powers?

out alone. Urban workers displayed more enthusiasm; at Warsaw, for example, a mob hanged several Russian collaborators, including an archbishop in his full regalia.

The uprising failed. Kościuszko won a few victories, but when Catherine's forces regrouped, they routed the Poles and Lithuanians. Kościuszko and other Patriot leaders languished for years in Russian and Austrian prisons. Taking no further chances, Russia, Prussia, and Austria wiped Poland completely from the map in the Third Partition of 1795. "The Polish question" would plague international relations for more than a century as Polish rebels flocked to any international upheaval that might undo the

partitions. Beyond all this maneuvering lay the unsolved problem of Polish serfdom, which isolated the nation's gentry and townspeople from the rural masses.

Revolution in the Colonies

The revolution that produced so much upheaval in continental Europe had repercussions in France's Caribbean colonies. These colonies were crucial to the French economy. Twice the size in land area of the neighboring British colonies, they also produced nearly twice as much revenue in exports. The slave population had doubled in the French colonies in the twenty years before 1789. St. Domingue♦ (present-day Haiti) was the most important French colony. Occupying the western half of the island of Hispaniola, it was inhabited by 465,000 slaves, 30,000 whites, and 28,000 free people of color, whose primary job was to apprehend runaway slaves and ensure plantation security.

Despite the efforts of a Paris club called the Friends of Blacks, most French revolutionaries did not consider slavery a pressing problem. As one deputy explained, "This regime [in the colonies] is oppressive, but it gives a livelihood to several million Frenchmen. This regime is barbarous but a still greater barbarity will result if you interfere with it without the necessary knowledge."

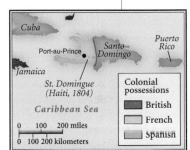

St. Domingue on the Eve of the Revolt, 1791

(See *Address to the National Assembly in Favor of the Abolition of the Slave Trade,* on page 778.)

In August 1791, however, the slaves in northern St. Domingue, inspired by the slogan "Listen to the voice of Liberty which speaks in the hearts of all," organized a large-scale revolt. To restore authority over the slaves, the Legislative Assembly in Paris granted civil and political rights to the free blacks. This action infuriated white planters and merchants, and in 1793 they signed an agreement with Great Britain, now France's

♦**St. Domingue:** sehn doh MEHNG

Address to the National Assembly in Favor of the Abolition of the Slave Trade (February 5, 1790)

Founded in 1788, the Society of the Friends of Blacks agitated for the abolition of the slave trade. Among its members were many who became leaders of the French Revolution. In this pamphlet, the Friends of Blacks denied that they wanted to abolish slavery altogether and argued only for the abolition of the slave trade. The pamphlet raised the prospect of a slave revolt, which in fact broke out in Saint Domingue in 1791. As a consequence, many planters and their allies accused the Society of fomenting the revolt.

You have declared them, these rights; you have engraved on an immortal monument that all men are born and remain free and equal in rights; you have restored to the French people these rights that despotism had for so long despoiled; . . . you have broken the chains of feudalism that still degraded a good number of our fellow citizens; you have announced the destruction of all the stigmatizing distinctions that religious or political prejudices introduced into the great family of humankind. . . .

We are not asking you to restore to French blacks those political rights which alone, nevertheless, attest to and maintain the dignity of man; we are not even asking for their liberty. No; slander, bought no doubt with the greed of the shipowners, ascribes that scheme to us and spreads it everywhere; they want to stir up everyone against us, provoke the planters and their numerous creditors, who take alarm even at gradual emancipation. They want to alarm all the French, to whom they depict the prosperity of the colonies as inseparable from the slave trade and the perpetuity of slavery.

. . . The immediate emancipation of the blacks would not only be a fatal operation for the colonies; it would even be a deadly gift for the blacks, in the state of abjection and incompetence to which cupidity has reduced them. It would be to abandon to themselves and without assistance children in the cradle or mutilated and impotent beings.

It is therefore not yet time to demand that liberty; we ask only that one cease butchering thousands of blacks regularly every year in order to take hundreds of captives; we ask that henceforth cease the prostitution, the profaning of the French name, used to authorize these thefts, these atrocious murders; we demand in a word the abolition of the slave trade. . . .

In regard to the colonists, we will demonstrate to you that if they need to recruit blacks in Africa to sustain the population of the colonies at the same level, it is because they wear out the blacks with work, whippings, and starvation; that, if they treated them with kindness and as good fathers of families, these blacks would multiply and that this population, always growing, would increase cultivation and prosperity. . . .

If some motive might on the contrary push them [the blacks] to insurrection, might it not be the indifference of the National Assembly about their lot? Might it not be the insistence on weighing them down with chains, when one consecrates everywhere this eternal axiom: *that all men are born free and equal in rights*. So then therefore there would only be fetters and gallows for the blacks while good fortune glimmers only for the whites? Have no doubt, our happy revolution must re-electrify the blacks whom vengeance and resentment have electrified for so long, and it is not with punishments that the effect of this upheaval will be repressed. From one insurrection badly pacified will twenty others be born, of which one alone can ruin the colonists forever.

Source: *Adresse à l'Assemblée Nationale, pour l'abolition de la traite des noirs.* Par la Société des Amis des Noirs de Paris (Paris, February 1790), 1–4, 10–11, 17, 19–22. Translation by Lynn Hunt.

enemy in war, declaring British sovereignty over St. Domingue. To complicate matters further, Spain, which controlled the rest of the island and had entered on Great Britain's side in the war with France, offered freedom to individual slave rebels who joined the Spanish armies as long as they agreed to maintain the slave regime for the other blacks.

The few thousand French republican troops on St. Domingue were outnumbered, and to prevent complete military disaster, the French commissioner freed all the slaves in his jurisdiction in August 1793 without permission from the government in Paris. In February 1794, the National Convention formally abolished slavery and granted full rights to all black men in the colonies. These actions had the desired effect. One of the ablest black generals allied with the Spanish, the ex-slave François Dominique Toussaint L'Ouverture◆ (1743–1803), changed sides and committed his troops to the French (see the illustration on this page). The French eventually appointed Toussaint governor of St. Domingue as a reward for his efforts.

The vicious fighting and flight of whites left St. Domingue's economy in ruins. In 1800, the plantations produced one-fifth of what they had in 1789. In the zones Toussaint controlled, army officers or government officials took over the great estates and kept all those working in agriculture under military discipline. The former slaves were bound to their estates like serfs and forced to work the plantations in exchange for an autonomous family life and the right to maintain personal garden plots.

Toussaint remained in charge until 1802, when Napoleon sent French armies to regain control of the island. They arrested Toussaint and transported him to France, where he died in prison. His arrest prompted the English poet William Wordsworth to write of him:

> There's not a breathing of the common wind
> That will forget thee; thou hast great allies;
> Thy friends are exultations, agonies,
> And love, and man's unconquerable mind.

Toussaint became a hero to abolitionists everywhere, a potent symbol of black struggles

◆**Toussaint L'Ouverture:** too san loo vehr tur

Toussaint L'Ouverture
The leader of the St. Domingue slave uprising appears in his general's uniform, sword in hand. This portrait appeared in one of the earliest histories of the revolt, Marcus Rainsford's *Historical Account of the Black Empire of Hayti* (London, 1805). Toussaint, a former slave who educated himself, fascinated many of his contemporaries in Europe as well as the New World by turning a chaotic slave rebellion into an organized and ultimately successful independence movement.
North Wind Picture Archives.

to win freedom. Napoleon attempted to restore slavery, sending Polish volunteers to do much of the grueling work, but the remaining black generals defeated his armies and in 1804 proclaimed the Republic of Haiti.

The Rise of Napoleon Bonaparte

Toussaint had followed with interest Napoleon's rise to power in France; he once wrote to Bonaparte, "From the First of the Blacks to the First of the Whites." He was not alone in his fascination, for the rise of Napoleon Bonaparte (1769–1821) is one of the most remarkable stories in Western history. It would have seemed astonishing in 1795 that the twenty-six-year-old son of a noble family from the island of Corsica off the Italian coast would within four years become the supreme ruler of France and one of the greatest military leaders in world history. In 1795, he was a penniless artillery officer, only recently released from prison as a presumed Robespierrist. Thanks to some early military successes and links to Parisian politicians, he was named commander of the French army in Italy in 1796.

Bonaparte's astounding success in the Italian campaigns of 1796–1797 launched his meteoric career. With an army of fewer than fifty thousand men, he defeated the Piedmontese and the Austrians. In quick order he established client republics dependent on his own authority; he negotiated with the Austrians himself; and he molded the army into his personal force by paying the soldiers in cash taken as tribute from the newly conquered territories. He mollified the Directory government by sending home wagonloads of great Italian masterpieces of art, which were added to Parisian museum collections (most are still there) after being paraded in victory festivals.

In 1798, the Directory set aside its plans to invade England, gave Bonaparte command of the army raised for that purpose, and sent him across the Mediterranean Sea to Egypt, away from the Parisian centers of power. The Directory government hoped that French occupation of Egypt would strike a blow at British trade by cutting the route to India and thus compensate France for its losses there years before. Once the army disembarked in Egypt, however, the British admiral Lord Horatio Nelson destroyed the French fleet while it was anchored in Aboukir Bay. In the face of determined resistance and an outbreak of the bubonic plague, Bonaparte's armies retreated from a further expedition in Syria. But the French occupation of Egypt lasted long enough for that largely Muslim country to experience the same kinds of Enlightenment-inspired legal reforms that had been introduced in Europe: the French abolished torture, introduced equality before the law, eliminated religious taxes, and proclaimed religious toleration.

Even the failures of the Egyptian campaign did not dull Bonaparte's luster. Bonaparte had taken France's leading scientists with him on the expedition, and his soldiers had discovered a slab of black basalt dating from 196 B.C.E. written in both hieroglyphic and Greek. Called the Rosetta stone after a nearby town, it enabled scholars to finally decipher the hieroglyphs used by the ancient Egyptians. When his army was pinned down after its initial successes, Bonaparte slipped out of Egypt and made his way secretly across the Mediterranean to southern France.

In October 1799, Bonaparte arrived home at just the right moment. The war in Europe was going badly. The departments of the former Austrian Netherlands had revolted against new conscription laws; deserters swelled the ranks of the rebels in western France; a royalist army had tried to take the city of Toulouse in the southwest; and many government leaders wanted to revise the Constitution of 1795. Amid increasing political instability, generals in the field had become virtually independent, and the troops felt more loyal to their units and generals than to the republic. As one army captain wrote, "In a conquering people the military spirit must prevail over other social conditions." Its victories had made the army a parallel and rival force to the state.

Disillusioned members of the government saw in Bonaparte's return an occasion to overturn the Constitution of 1795. On November 9, 1799 (18 Brumaire, Year VIII, by the revolutionary calendar), the conspirators persuaded the legislature to move out of Paris to avoid an imaginary Jacobin plot. But when Bonaparte stomped into the meeting hall the next day and demanded changes in the Constitution, he was greeted by cries of "Down with the dictator." His quick-

Bonaparte in Egypt
Antoine Jean Gros's painting *Napoleon Visiting the Victims of the Plague at Jaffa* (1804)
is meant to glorify Bonaparte's courage: he is not afraid to touch the victims of the plague.
Yet it also signals a terrible problem in Bonaparte's campaign for domination in the western Mediterranean. He has won many battles at this moment in 1799, but he is losing
the war through attrition, disease, and mounting resistance. *Réunion des Musées Nationaux/
Art Resource, NY.*

thinking brother Lucien, president of the
Council of Five Hundred (the lower house),
saved Bonaparte's coup by summoning
troops guarding the hall and claiming that
the deputies had tried to assassinate the
popular general. The soldiers ejected the
deputies, and a hastily assembled rump legislature voted to abolish the Directory and establish a new three-man executive called the
consulate.

Bonaparte became **First Consul**, a title
revived from the ancient Roman republic.

He promised to be a man above party and to
restore order to the republic. A new constitution was submitted to the voters. Millions
abstained from voting, and the government
falsified the results to give an appearance of
even greater support to the new regime. Inside France, political apathy had overtaken
the original enthusiasm for revolutionary
ideals. Altogether it was an unpromising beginning; yet within five years Bonaparte
would crown himself Napoleon I, emperor of
the French. A new order would rise from the

MAPPING THE WEST Europe in 1800
France's expansion during the revolutionary wars threatened to upset the balance of power in Europe. A century earlier the English and Dutch had allied and formed a Europe-wide coalition to check the territorial ambitions of Louis XIV. Thwarting French ambitions after 1800 would prove to be even more of a challenge to the other European powers. The Dutch had been reduced to satellite status, as had most of the Italian states. After 1800, even Austria and Prussia would suffer devastating losses to the French on the battlefield. Only a new coalition of European powers could stop France in the future.

ashes of the republic, and the French armies would recover from their reverses of 1799 to push the frontiers of French influence even farther eastward.

> **Review:** Why did some groups outside of France embrace the French Revolution while others resisted it?

Conclusion

In 1799, no one knew what course Napoleon Bonaparte would follow. Everyone sensed, however, that the political landscape in Europe had been permanently altered by the revolutionary cataclysm. Between 1789 and 1799, monarchy as a form of government had given way to a republic whose leaders were elected. Aristocracy based on rank and birth had been undermined in favor of civil equality and the promotion of merit. The people who marched in demonstrations, met in clubs, and, in the case of men, voted in national elections for the first time had insisted that government respond to them. Thousands of men had held elective office. A revolutionary government had tried to teach new values with a refashioned calendar, state festivals, and a civic religion. Its example would inspire future revolutionaries.

But the French Revolution also had its darker side. The divisions created by the Revolution within France endured in many cases until after World War II. Even now, French public-opinion surveys ask if it was right to execute the king in 1793 (most believe Louis XVI was guilty of treason but should not have been executed). The revolutionaries proclaimed human rights and democratic government as a universal goal, but they also explicitly excluded women, even though they admitted Protestant, Jewish, and eventually black men. They used the new spirit of national pride to inspire armies that conquered other peoples. Their ideals of universal education, religious toleration, and democratic participation could not prevent the institution of new forms of government terror to persecute, imprison, and kill dissidents. These paradoxes created an opening for Napoleon Bonaparte, who rushed in with his remarkable military and political skills to push France—and with it all of Europe—in new directions.

Suggested References

The Revolutionary Wave, 1787–1789

In the 1950s and 1960s, historians debated vehemently about whether the French Revolution should be considered part of a more general phenomenon of Atlantic revolutions, as R. R. Palmer argues. The most influential book on the meaning of the French Revolution is still the classic study by Tocqueville, who insisted that the Revolution continued the process of state centralization undertaken by the monarchy.

*Censer, Jack R., and Lynn Hunt. *Liberty, Equality, Fraternity: Exploring the French Revolution.* 2001. (Includes a CD-ROM with images, songs, and documents.) See also the accompanying Web site: **http://www.chnm .gmu.edu/revolution**.

Lefebvre, Georges. *The Coming of the French Revolution.* Trans. with a new preface, R. R. Palmer. 1989.

Palmer, R. R. *The Age of the Democratic Revolution: A Political History of Europe and America, 1760–1800.* Vol. 2, *The Struggle.* 1964.

Polasky, Janet L. *Revolution in Brussels, 1787–1793.* 1987.

Te Brake, Wayne. *Regents and Rebels: The Revolutionary World of an Eighteenth-Century Dutch City.* 1989.

Tocqueville, Alexis de. *The Old Regime and the French Revolution.* Trans. Stuart Gilbert. 1955. Originally published 1856.

From Monarchy to Republic, 1789–1793

From 1789 onward, commentators on the French Revolution have differed over its meaning: Was it a revolution for human rights and democracy or a dangerous experiment in implementing reason and destroying religion and tradition? Among the most important additions to the debate have been new works on women, Jews, Protestants, and slaves.

*Hunt, Lynn, ed. *The French Revolution and Human Rights: A Brief Documentary History.* 1996.

*Levy, Darline Gay, Harriet Branson Applewhite, and Mary Durham Johnson, eds. *Women in Revolutionary Paris, 1789–1795.* 1979.

Schama, Simon. *Citizens: A Chronicle of the French Revolution.* 1989.

Schechter, Ronald. *The French Revolution: The Essential Readings.* 2001.

*Two Classics of the French Revolution: Reflections on the Revolution in France (*Edmund Burke*) and* The Rights of Man (*Thomas Paine*). 1973.

*Wollstonecraft, Mary. *A Vindication of the Rights of Woman.* Ed. Miriam Brody. 1992.

Terror and Resistance

The most controversial episode in the French Revolution has not surprisingly provoked con-

---

*Primary source.

flicting interpretations. Soboul offers the Marxist interpretation, which Furet specifically opposes. Very recently interest has shifted from these broader interpretive issues back to the principal actors themselves: Robespierre, the Jacobins, and women's clubs have all attracted scholarly attention.

Desan, Suzanne. *Reclaiming the Sacred: Lay Religion and Popular Politics in Revolutionary France.* 1990.

Furet, François. *Interpreting the French Revolution.* Trans. Elborg Forster. 1981.

Godineau, Dominique. *The Women of Paris and Their French Revolution.* Trans. Katherine Streip. 1998.

Haydon, Colin, and William Doyle, eds. *Robespierre.* 1999.

Hunt, Lynn. *Politics, Culture, and Class in the French Revolution.* 1984.

Palmer, R. R. *Twelve Who Ruled: The Year of the Terror in the French Revolution.* 1989.

Soboul, Albert. *The Sans-Culottes: The Popular Movement and Revolutionary Government, 1793–1794.* Trans. Remy Inglis Hall. 1980.

Revolution on the March

In the past, controversy about the Revolution in France raged while its influence on other places was relatively neglected. This imbalance is now being redressed in studies of the colonies and the impact of the revolutionary wars on areas from Egypt to Ireland.

Beaucour, Fernand Emile, Yves Laissus, and Chantal Orgogozo. *The Discovery of Egypt.* Trans. Bambi Ballard. 1990.

Blackburn, Robin. *The Overthrow of Colonial Slavery, 1776–1848.* 1988.

Blanning, T. C. W. *The French Revolutionary Wars, 1787–1802.* 1996.

Elliot, Marianne. *Partners in Revolution: The United Irishmen and France.* 1982.

Forrest, Alan I. *The Soldiers of the French Revolution.* 1990.

Geggus, David Patrick. *Haitian Revolutionary Studies.* 2002.

Irish rebellion of 1798: **http://www.bbc.co.uk/history/timelines/ni/rebellion_1798.shtml**.

Moiret, Joseph-Marie, ed. *Memoirs of Napoleon's Egyptian Expedition, 1798–1801.* Trans. Rosemary Brindle. 2001.

CHAPTER REVIEW

IMPORTANT EVENTS

1787 Dutch Patriot revolt is stifled by Prussian invasion

1788 Beginning of resistance of Austrian Netherlands against reforms of Joseph II; opening of reform parliament in Poland

1789 French Revolution begins

1790 Internal divisions lead to collapse of resistance in Austrian Netherlands

1791 Beginning of slave revolt in St. Domingue (Haiti)

1792 Beginning of war between France and the rest of Europe; second revolution of August 10 overthrows monarchy

1793 Second Partition of Poland by Austria and Russia; Louis XVI of France executed for treason

1794 Abolition of slavery in French colonies; Robespierre's government by terror falls

1795 Third (final) Partition of Poland; France annexes the Austrian Netherlands

1797–1798 Creation of "sister republics" in Italian states and Switzerland

1799 Napoleon Bonaparte comes to power in a coup that effectively ends the French Revolution

KEY TERMS

Atlantic revolutions (749)

de-Christianization (766)

Declaration of the Rights of Man and Citizen (757)

Estates General (753)

First Consul (781)

Great Fear (757)

Jacobin Club (761)

sans-culottes (761)

Terror (763)

Thermidorian Reaction (770)

REVIEW QUESTIONS

1. In what ways did the beginning of the French Revolution resemble the other revolutions of 1787–1789?

2. Why did the French Revolution turn in an increasingly radical direction after 1789?

3. What factors can explain the Terror? To what extent was it simply a response to a national emergency or a reflection of deeper problems within the French Revolution?

4. Why did some groups outside of France embrace the French Revolution while others resisted it?

MAKING CONNECTIONS

1. Should the French Revolution be viewed as the origin of democracy or the origin of totalitarianism (a government in which no dissent is allowed)? Explain.

2. Why did the other rulers of Europe find the French Revolution so threatening?

FOR FURTHER EXPLORATION

To assess your mastery of the material in this chapter, see the Online Study Guide at **bedfordstmartins.com/hunt**.

To read additional primary-source material from this period, see Chapter 20 in *Sources of The Making of the West*, Second Edition.

Napoleon and the Revolutionary Legacy, 1800–1830

IN HER NOVEL *FRANKENSTEIN* (1818), the prototype for modern thrillers, Mary Shelley tells the story of a Swiss technological genius who creates a humanlike monster in his pursuit of scientific knowledge. The monster, "so scaring and unearthly in his ugliness," terrifies all who encounter him and ends by destroying Dr. Frankenstein's own loved ones. Despite desperate chases across deserts and frozen landscapes, Frankenstein never manages to trap the monster, who is last seen hunched over his creator's deathbed.

Frankenstein's monster can be taken as a particularly horrifying incarnation of the fears of the postrevolutionary era, but just what did Shelley intend? Did the monster represent the French Revolution, which had devoured its own children in the Terror? Shelley was the daughter of Mary Wollstonecraft, an English feminist who had defended the French Revolution and died in childbirth when Mary was born. Did the monster stand for the dangerous possibilities that might be unleashed by science and industry in the new age of industrial growth? Mary Shelley was also the wife of the romantic poet Percy Bysshe Shelley, who often wrote against the ugliness of contemporary life and celebrated nature and the "beautiful idealisms of moral excellence." Whatever the meaning—and Mary Shelley may well have intended more than one—*Frankenstein* makes the forceful point that humans cannot always control their own creations. The Enlightenment and the French Revolution had celebrated the virtues of human creativity, but Shelley shows that innovation often has a dark and uncontrollable side.

Those who witnessed Napoleon Bonaparte's stunning rise to European dominance after 1800 might have cast him as either Frankenstein or his monster. Like the scientist Frankenstein, Bonaparte created something dramatically new: the French Empire with himself as emperor. Like the former kings of France, he ruled under

---

Napoleon as Military Hero
In this painting from 1800–1801, *Napoleon Crossing the Alps at St. Bernard,* Jacques-Louis David reminds the French of Napoleon's heroic military exploits. Napoleon is a picture of calm and composure while his horse shows the fright and energy of the moment. David painted this propagandistic image shortly after one of his former students went to the guillotine on a trumped-up charge of plotting to assassinate the new French leader. The former organizer of republican festivals during the Terror had become a kind of court painter for the new regime. © *Photo RMN-Daniel Arraudet.*

his first name. This Corsican artillery officer who spoke French with an Italian accent ended the French Revolution even while maintaining some of its most important innovations. Bonaparte transformed France from a democratically elected republic to an empire with a new aristocracy based on military service. But he kept the revolutionary administration and most of its laws that ensured equal treatment of all citizens. Although he tolerated no opposition at home, he prided himself on bringing French-style changes to peoples elsewhere.

Bonaparte continued the revolutionary policy of conquest and annexation until it reached grotesque dimensions. His foreign policies made many see him as a monster hungry for dominion; he turned the sister republics of the revolutionary era into kingdoms personally ruled by his relatives, and he exacted tribute from subject peoples wherever he triumphed. Eventually resistance to the French armies and the ever-mounting costs of military glory toppled Napoleon. The powers allied against him met and agreed to restore the monarchical governments that had been overthrown by the French, shrink France back to its pre-revolutionary boundaries, and maintain this settlement against future demands for change.

Although the people of Europe longed for peace and stability in the aftermath of the Napoleonic whirlwind, they lived in a world that was deeply unsettled by two parallel revolutions: the Industrial Revolution and the French Revolution. The Industrial Revolution spread from Great Britain to the continent in the early 1800s in the form of factories and railroads. Even those who resisted the impact of the French Revolution with its Napoleonic sequel had to confront the underlying changes in social and economic structures that resulted from industrialization. These changes inevitably reinforced the legacy of the French Revolution, which included equality before the law, religious toleration, and, eventually, nationalism.

Profoundly affected by French military occupation, many peoples organized to demand ethnic and cultural autonomy, first from Napoleon and then from the restored governments after 1815. Alongside nationalism, other new ideologies such as liberalism and socialism emerged under the impact of the Industrial and French Revolutions. These offered their adherents a doctrine that explained social change and advocated political transformation. In 1830, the development of liberalism, socialism, and nationalism shocked Europe with a new round of revolutions in France, Belgium, Poland, and some of the Italian states. By then the spread of industry, the growing awareness of social problems, and aspirations for national self-determination had reinvigorated the force of the revolutionary legacy.

❖ Napoleon's Authoritarian State

When Napoleon Bonaparte came to power in 1799, his coup d'état appeared to be just the latest in a long line of upheavals in revolutionary France. Within the year, how-

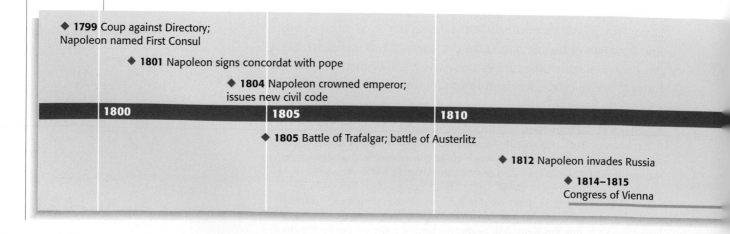

◆ **1799** Coup against Directory; Napoleon named First Consul

◆ **1801** Napoleon signs concordat with pope

◆ **1804** Napoleon crowned emperor; issues new civil code

| 1800 | 1805 | 1810 |

◆ **1805** Battle of Trafalgar; battle of Austerlitz

◆ **1812** Napoleon invades Russia

◆ **1814–1815** Congress of Vienna

ever, he had effectively ended the French Revolution and set France on a new course toward an authoritarian state. As emperor after 1804, he dreamed of European integration in the tradition of Augustus and Charlemagne, but he also mastered the details of practical administration. To achieve his goals, he compromised with the Catholic church and with exiled aristocrats willing to return to France. His most enduring accomplishment, the new Civil Code, tempered the principles of the Enlightenment and the Revolution with an insistence on the powers of fathers over children, husbands over wives, and employers over workers. His influence spread into many spheres as he personally patronized scientific inquiry and encouraged artistic styles in line with his vision of imperial greatness.

From Republic to Empire

Napoleon had no long-range plans to establish himself as emperor and conquer most of Europe. The deputies of the legislature who engineered the coup d'état of November 1799 picked him as one of three provisional **consuls** (the title drew on the ancient Roman precedent) only because he was a famous general. Napoleon immediately asserted his leadership over the other two consuls in the process of drafting another constitution—the fourth since 1789 and the third for the republic established in 1792.

The End of the Republic.   The constitution of 1799 made Napoleon the First Consul with the right to pick the Council of State,

which drew up all laws. He quickly exerted control by choosing men loyal to him. Government was no longer representative in any real sense: the new constitution eliminated direct elections for deputies and granted no independent powers to the three houses of the legislature. Napoleon and his advisers chose the legislature's members out of a small pool of "notables." Almost all men over twenty-one could vote in the plebiscite (referendum) to approve the constitution, but their only option was to choose Yes or No.

Napoleon's most urgent task was to reconcile to his regime Catholics who had been alienated by revolutionary policies. Although nominally Catholic, Napoleon held no deep religious convictions. "How can there be order in the state without religion?" he asked cynically. "When a man is dying of hunger beside another who is stuffing himself, he cannot accept this difference if there is not an authority who tells him: 'God wishes it so.'" In 1801, a concordat with Pope Pius VII (r. 1800–1823) ended a decade of church-state conflict. The pope validated all sales of church lands, and the government agreed to pay the salaries of bishops and priests who would swear loyalty to the state. Catholicism was officially recognized as the religion of "the great majority of French citizens." (The state also paid Protestant pastors' salaries.) The pope thus brought the huge French Catholic population back into the fold and Napoleon gained the pope's support for his regime.

Napoleon continued the centralization of state power that had begun under the

◆ **1815** Napoleon defeated at Waterloo, exiled to St. Helena

◆ **1818** Mary Shelley, *Frankenstein*

◆ **1824** Beethoven, *Ninth Symphony*

◆ **1830** Greece gains independence; Charles X overthrown; Louis-Phillipe installed; Manchester and Liverpool railway opens

1815	1820	1825	1830

◆ **1820** Owen, *New Moral World*; revolt against Spanish crown; Karlsbad Decrees

◆ **1825** Decembrist revolt in Russia

◆ **1832** English Reform bill; Goethe, *Faust*

absolutist monarchy of Louis XIV and resumed under the Terror. As First Consul he appointed prefects who directly supervised local affairs in every *département*, or region. He created the Bank of France to facilitate government borrowing and relied on gold and silver coinage rather than paper money. He made good use of budgets and improved tax collection, but he also frequently made ends meet by exacting tribute from the territories he conquered.

Napoleon promised order and an end to the upheavals of ten years of revolutionary turmoil, but his regime severely limited political expression. He never relied on mass executions to achieve control, but he refused to allow those who opposed him to meet in clubs, influence elections, or publish news-

Francisco de Goya, *The Colossus* (1808–1812)
The Spanish painter Goya might be imagined as capturing Frankenstein's monster or Napoleon himself as the new giant overwhelming much of Europe. Goya painted for the Spanish court before Napoleon invaded and occupied the country; after an illness left him deaf, he turned toward darkly imaginative works such as this one. *Museo del Prado, Madrid.*

papers. A decree reduced the number of newspapers in Paris from seventy-three to thirteen (and then finally to four), and the newspapers that remained became government organs. Government censors had to approve all operas and plays, and they banned "offensive" artistic works even more frequently than their royal predecessors had. The minister of police, Joseph Fouché, once a leading figure in the Terror of 1793–1794, could impose house arrest, arbitrary imprisonment, and surveillance of political dissidents. Political contest and debate shriveled to almost nothing. When a bomb attack on Napoleon's carriage failed in 1800, Fouché suppressed the evidence of a royalist plot and instead arrested hundreds of former Jacobins. More than one hundred of them were deported, and seven hundred imprisoned.

Napoleon feared the influence of fervent supporters of the republic more than that of supporters of the monarchy. In 1802, his intentions became clear: he planned to eliminate the republic. He named himself First Consul for life, and in 1804, with the pope's blessing, he crowned himself emperor. Once again, plebiscites approved his decisions, but no alternatives were offered.

Imperial Rule.   Napoleon's charismatic personality dominated the new regime. His face and name adorned coins, engravings, histories, paintings, and public monuments. His favorite painters embellished his legend by depicting him as a warrior-hero of mythic proportions even though he was short and physically unimpressive in person. Believing that "what is big is always beautiful," Napoleon embarked on ostentatious building projects that would outshine even those of Louis XIV. Government-commissioned architects built the Arc de Triomphe,♦ the Stock Exchange, fountains, and even slaughterhouses. Most of his new construction reflected his neoclassical taste for monumental buildings set in vast empty spaces.

Napoleon worked hard at establishing his reputation as an efficient administrator with broad intellectual interests: he met frequently with scientists, jurists, and artists, and stories abounded of his unflagging

♦**Arc de Triomphe:** AHRK duh tre OHNF

Napoleon's Coronation as Emperor

In *The Coronation of Napoleon and Josephine* (1805–1807), Jacques-Louis David shows Napoleon crowning his wife at the ceremony of 1804. Napoleon orchestrated the entire event and took the only active role in it: Pope Pius VII gave his blessing to the ceremony (he can be seen seated behind Napoleon), but Napoleon crowned himself. What is the significance of Napoleon crowning himself? **For more help analyzing this image**, see the visual activity for this chapter in the Online Study Guide at **bedfordstmartins.com/hunt**. *Scala/Art Resource, NY.*

energy. When not on military campaigns, he worked on state affairs, usually until 10:00 P.M., taking only a few minutes for each meal. "Authority," declared his adviser Abbé Emmanuel-Joseph Sieyès, "must come from above and confidence from below." To establish his authority, Napoleon relied on men who had served with him in the army. His chief of staff Alexandre Berthier,✦ for example, became minister of war, and the chemist Claude Berthollet,✦ who had organized the scientific part of the expedition to Egypt, became vice president of the Senate in 1804. Napoleon's bureaucracy was based on a patron-client relationship, with Napoleon as the ultimate patron. Some of Napoleon's closest associates married into his family.

Combining aristocratic and revolutionary values in a new social hierarchy that rewarded merit and talent, Napoleon personally chose as senators the nation's most illustrious generals, ministers, prefects, scientists, rich men, and former nobles. Intending to replace both the old nobility of birth and the republic's strict emphasis on equality, in 1802 he took the first step toward creating a new nobility by founding a Legion of Honor. (Members of the legion received lifetime pensions along with their titles.) Napoleon usually equated honor with military success. By 1814, the legion had thirty-two thousand members, only 5 percent of them civilians.

In 1808, Napoleon introduced a complete hierarchy of noble titles, ranging from princes down to barons and chevaliers. All Napoleonic nobles had served the state. Titles could be inherited but had to be supported by wealth—a man could not be a duke without

✦**Berthier:** behr TYAY
✦**Berthollet:** behr taw leh

Medal of the Legion of Honor
"Men are led through baubles," Napoleon once remarked, but "a little cash does not hurt." He gave this medal to members of the Legion of Honor and added a small pension. Never missing an occasion to glorify his own image, Napoleon had his portrait installed in the center of the star and garland. © *Photo Musée de L'Armée, Paris.*

a fortune of 200,000 francs, or a chevalier without 3,000 francs. To go along with their new titles, Napoleon gave his favorite generals huge fortunes, often in the form of estates in the conquered territories.

Napoleon's own family reaped the greatest benefits. He made his older brother, Joseph, ruler of the newly established kingdom of Naples in 1806, the same year he installed his younger brother Louis as king of Holland. He proclaimed his twenty-three-year-old stepson Eugène de Beauharnais viceroy of Italy in 1805 and established his sister Caroline and brother-in-law General Joachim Murat as king and queen of Naples in 1808 when he moved Joseph to the throne of Spain. Napoleon wanted to establish an imperial succession, but he lacked an heir. In thirteen years of marriage, his wife Josephine had borne no children, so in 1809 he divorced her and in 1810 married the eighteen-year-old princess Marie-Louise of Austria. The next year she gave birth to a son, to whom Napoleon immediately gave the title king of Rome.

The New Paternalism: The Civil Code

Because Napoleon shared the rewards of rule with his own family, it is perhaps not surprising that he brought a paternalist model of power to his state. Previous governments had tried to unify and standardize France's multiple legal codes, but only Napoleon successfully established a new one, partly because he personally presided over the commission that drafted the new **Civil Code**,

completed in 1804. Called the Napoleonic Code as a way of further exalting his image, it defined and assured property rights, guaranteed religious liberty, and established a uniform system of law that provided equal treatment for all adult males and affirmed the right of men to choose their professions. It also reasserted the Old Regime's patriarchal system of male domination over women and insisted on a father's control over his children, which revolutionary legislation had limited. For example, if children under age sixteen refused to follow their fathers' commands, they could be sent to prison for up to a month with no hearing of any sort. At the same time, the code required fathers to provide for their children's welfare. Napoleon himself encouraged the foundation of private charities to help indigent mothers, and one of his decrees made it easier for women to abandon their children anonymously to a government foundling hospital. Napoleon hoped that such measures would discourage abortion and infanticide, especially among the poorest classes in the fast-growing urban areas.

The code sharply curtailed women's rights in almost every aspect of public and private life. Napoleon wanted to restrict women to the private sphere of the home. One of his leading jurists remarked, "There have been many discussions on the equality and superiority of the sexes. Nothing is more useless than such disputes....Women need protection because they are weaker; men are free because they are stronger." The law obligated a husband to support his wife, but he alone controlled any property held in common; a wife could not sue in court, sell or mortgage her own property, or contract a debt without her husband's consent.

The Civil Code modified even those few revolutionary laws that had been favorable to women and in some instances denied women rights they had had under the monarchy. Divorce was still possible but severely restricted. Adultery was an acceptable grounds for divorce, but the law considered a wife's infidelity more reprehensible than a husband's. A wife could petition for divorce only if her husband brought his mistress to live in the family home. In contrast, a wife convicted of adultery could be imprisoned for up to two years. The code's framers saw these discrepancies as a way to reinforce the family and make women responsible for private virtue, while leaving public decisions to men. The French code was imitated in many European and Latin American countries and the French colony of Louisiana, where it had a similar negative effect on women's rights. Not until 1965 did French wives gain legal status equal to that of their husbands.

Napoleon took little interest in girls' education, believing that girls should spend most of their time at home learning religion, manners, and such "female occupations" as sewing and music. For boys, by contrast, the government set up a new system of lycées,♦ state-run secondary schools in which boys wore military uniforms and drumrolls signaled the beginning and end of classes. (Without the military trappings, the lycées are now coeducational and still the heart of the French educational system.)

The new paternalism extended to relations between employers and employees. The state required all workers to carry a work card attesting to their good conduct, and it prohibited all workers' organizations. The police considered workers without cards as vagrants or criminals and could send them to workhouses or prison. After 1806, arbitration boards settled labor disputes, but they took employers at their word while treating workers as minors, demanding that foremen and shop superintendents represent them. Occasionally strikes broke out, led by secret, illegal journeymen's associations, yet many employers laid off employees when times were hard, deducted fines from their wages, and dismissed them without appeal for being absent or making errors. These limitations on workers' rights won Napoleon the support of French business.

Patronage of Science and Intellectual Life

Napoleon did everything possible to promote French scientific inquiry, especially that which could serve practical ends. (See "Did You Know?," page 794.) He closely monitored the research institutes established during the Revolution, sometimes intervening personally to achieve political conformity. An impressive outpouring of new theoretical and practical scientific work rewarded the state's efforts. Experiments with balloons led to the discovery of laws about the expansion of gases, and research on fossil shells prepared the way for new theories of evolutionary change later in the nineteenth century. The surgeon Dominique-Jean Larrey developed new techniques of battlefield amputation and medical care during Napoleon's wars, winning an appointment as an officer in the Legion of Honor and becoming a baron with a pension.

Napoleon aimed to modernize French society through science, but he could not tolerate criticism. Napoleon considered most writers useless or dangerous, "good for nothing under any government." Some of the most talented French writers of the time had to live in exile. The best-known expatriate was Germaine de Staël♦ (1766–1817), known as Madame de Staël, the daughter of Louis XVI's chief minister Jacques Necker. When explaining his desire to banish her, Napoleon exclaimed, "She is a machine in motion who stirs up the salons." While exiled in the German states, Madame de Staël wrote a novel, *Corinne* (1807), whose heroine is a brilliant woman thwarted by a patriarchal system, and *On Germany* (1810), an account of the important new literary currents east of the Rhine. Her books were banned in France.

Although Napoleon restored the strong authority of state and religion in France, many royalists and Catholics still criticized him as an impious usurper. (See "Contrasting Views," page 796.) François-René de Chateaubriand (1768–1848) admired Napoleon as "the strong man who has saved us from the abyss," but he preferred monarchy. In his view, Napoleon

♦**lycées:** lee SAY

♦**Germaine de Staël:** zhehr mehn duh STAL

DID YOU KNOW?

How the Orient Became Oriental

Eugène Delacroix, *The Death of Sardanapalus* (1826–1827)
All of the exoticism, violence, and erotic imagery of the East are on view in this romantic painting that aims to recapture a moment in ancient history when the Assyrian king Sardanapalus first killed his harem before killing himself. Delacroix was presumably influenced by a play by Byron on the subject, though Delacroix's rendition is much less favorable to the king than Byron's.
© *Photo RMN/Herve Lewandowski.*

As a result of Napoleon's expedition to conquer Egypt in 1798, Europeans began to study systematically what they named the Orient (from *orins*, Latin for "rising sun"), meaning the lands east of Europe. Napoleon took with him 151 French scientific experts in everything from architecture to mineralogy. Their mission was to discover and record the natural and human history of Egypt. While some set up the Institute of Egypt in Cairo to conduct scientific experiments, others traveled with army units, collecting information and data on Egypt.

Of course, Europeans had visited the Middle East before, but they had never so rigorously studied its cultures. Although Napoleon's occupation of Egypt eventually failed, enthusiasm for so-called Orientalism spread far and wide; scholarly societies set up professorships and periodicals dedicated to Oriental studies, and before long romantic poets, novelists, and painters flocked to North Africa and the Middle East in search of new themes for their work.

Europeans viewed the Orient as exotic but also backward. In the introduction to the twenty-three-volume *Description of Egypt* published by French scholars of the Institute of Egypt between 1809 and 1828, Jean-Baptiste Fourier wrote, "Napoleon wanted to offer a useful European example to the Orient, and finally also to make the inhabitants' lives more pleasant, as well as to procure for them all the advantages of a perfect civilization." According to Fourier, "This country [Egypt], which has transmitted its knowledge to so many nations, today is plunged into barbarism." Civilization versus barbarism; advancement versus backwardness; science versus superstition: before long Europeans had set up a series of mutually reinforcing categories to distinguish their culture from that of the Orient. It is probably fair to say that Orientalism led to much new knowledge but also to many unpleasant stereotypes of non-Western peoples and cultures.

It is important to remember, moreover, that *West* and *East* are relative terms; they can be defined only in relation to each other. Americans sometimes call Japan, for instance, the Far East, following European usage, but it is closest to the western, not the eastern, half of the United States. For Japan, in fact, the United States is the "Far East."

Source: Edward W. Said, *Orientalism* (New York: Pantheon Books, 1978), quote from page 85.

Germaine de Staël
One of the most fascinating intellectuals of her time, Anne-Louise-Germaine de Staël seemed to irritate Napoleon more than any other person did. Daughter of Louis XVI's Swiss Protestant finance minister, Jacques Necker, and wife of a Swedish diplomat, Madame de Staël frequently criticized Napoleon's regime. She published best-selling novels and influential literary criticism, and whenever allowed to reside in Paris she encouraged the intellectual and political dissidents from Napoleon's regime. *Photographie Bulloz.*

had not properly understood the need to defend Christian values against the Enlightenment's excessive reliance on reason. Chateaubriand wrote his *Genius of Christianity* (1802) to draw attention to the power and mystery of faith. He warned, "It is to the vanity of knowledge that we owe almost all our misfortunes.... The learned ages have always been followed by ages of destruction."

Review: In what ways did Napoleon continue the French Revolution; in what ways did he break with it?

❖ "Europe Was at My Feet": Napoleon's Conquests

Building on innovations introduced by the republican governments before him, Napoleon revolutionized the art of war with tactics and strategy based on a highly mobile army. By 1812, he ruled an empire more extensive than any since the time of ancient Rome (Map 21.1 on page 798). Yet that empire had already begun to crumble, and with it went Napoleon's power at home. Napoleon's empire failed because it was based on a contradiction: Napoleon tried to reduce virtually all of Europe to the status of colonial dependents when Europe had long consisted of independent states. The result, inevitably, was a great upsurge in nationalist feeling that has dominated European politics to the present.

The Grand Army and Its Victories, 1800–1807

Napoleon attributed his military success "three-quarters to morale" and the rest to leadership and superiority of numbers at the point of attack. Conscription provided the large numbers: 1.3 million men ages twenty to twenty-four were drafted between 1800 and 1812, another million in 1813–1814. So many willingly served because the republic had taught them to identify the army with the nation. Military service was both a patriotic duty and a means of social mobility. The men who rose through the ranks to become officers were young, ambitious, and accustomed to the new ways of war. Consequently, the French army had higher morale than the armies of other powers, most of which rejected conscription as too democratic and continued to restrict their officer corps to the nobility. Only in 1813–1814 did French morale plummet, as the military tide turned against Napoleon.

When Napoleon came to power in 1799, desertion was rampant, and the generals competed with one another for predominance. Napoleon ended this squabbling by uniting all the armies into one Grand Army under his personal command. By 1812, he commanded 700,000 troops; while 250,000 soldiers fought in Spain, others remained garrisoned in France. In any given battle, between 70,000 and 180,000 men, not all of them French, fought for France. Life on campaign was no picnic—ordinary soldiers slept in the rain, mud, and snow and often had to forage for food—but Napoleon nonetheless inspired almost fanatical loyalty. A brilliant strategist who carefully studied the demands of war, he outmaneuvered virtually all his opponents. He fought alongside his soldiers in some sixty battles and had nineteen horses shot from under him. One opponent said that Napoleon's presence alone was worth 50,000 men.

Napoleon had a pragmatic and direct approach to strategy: he went for the main body of the opposing army and tried to crush it in a lightning campaign. He gathered the largest possible army for one great and decisive battle and then followed with a relentless pursuit to break enemy morale altogether. His military command, like his domestic role, was personal and highly centralized. He essentially served as his own

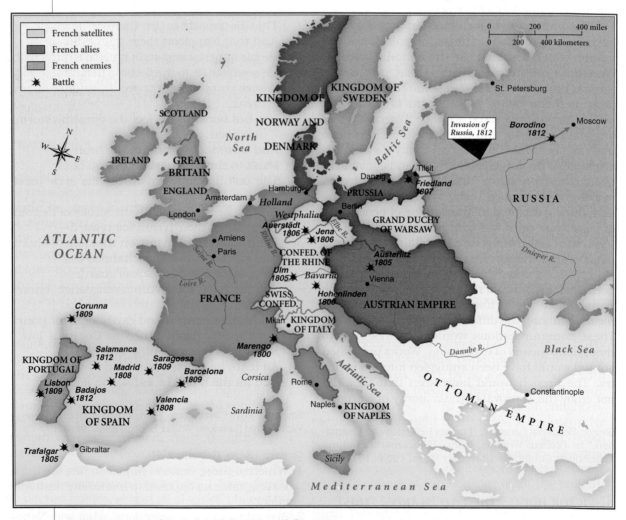

MAP 21.1 Napoleon's Empire at Its Height, 1812

In 1812, Napoleon had at least nominal control of almost all of western Europe. Even before he made his fatal mistake of invading Russia, however, his authority had been undermined in Spain and seriously weakened in the Italian and German states. His efforts to extend French power sparked resistance almost everywhere: as Napoleon insisted on French domination, local people began to think of themselves as Italian, German, or Dutch. Thus Napoleon inadvertently laid the foundations for the nineteenth-century spread of nationalism.

Following the Wars
Louis-Léopold Boilly's *Reading of the XIth and XIIth Bulletins of the Grand Army* shows ordinary
people on the home front eagerly reading Napoleon's own bulletins of the army's progress.
Collection Privée/Photographic Bulloz.

operations officer: "I alone know what I have to do," he insisted. This style worked as long as Napoleon could be on the battlefield, but he failed to train independent subordinates to take over in his absence. He also faced constant difficulties in supplying a rapidly moving army, which could not always live off the land.

One of Napoleon's greatest advantages was the lack of coordination among his enemies. Britain dominated the seas but did not want to field huge land armies. On the continent, the French republic had already set up satellites in the Netherlands and Italy, which served as a buffer against the big powers to the east, Austria, Prussia, and Russia. By maneuvering diplomatically and militarily, Napoleon could usually take these on one by one. After reorganizing the French armies in 1799, for example, Napoleon won striking victories against the Austrians at Marengo and Hohenlinden♦ in 1800, forcing them to agree to peace terms. Once the Aus-

trians had withdrawn, Britain agreed to the Treaty of Amiens in 1802, effectively ending hostilities on the continent. Napoleon considered the peace with Great Britain merely a truce, however, and it lasted only until 1803.

Napoleon used the breathing space not only to consolidate his position before taking up arms again but also to send an expeditionary force to St. Domingue to regain control of the island. Continuing resistance among the black population and an epidemic of yellow fever forced Napoleon to withdraw his troops from St. Domingue and abandon his plans to extend his

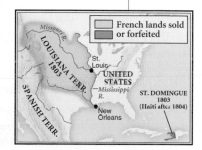

France's Retreat from America

empire to the Western Hemisphere. As part of his retreat, he sold the Louisiana Territory to the United States in 1803.

When war resumed in Europe, the British navy once more proved its superiority by

---

♦**Hohenlinden:** HOH uhn lihn duhn

blocking an attempted French invasion and by defeating the French and their Spanish allies in a huge naval battle at Trafalgar in 1805. France lost many ships; the British lost no vessels, but their renowned admiral Lord Horatio Nelson died in the battle. On land, Napoleon remained invincible. In 1805, Austria took up arms again when Napoleon demanded that it declare neutrality in the conflict with Britain. Napoleon promptly captured 25,000 Austrian soldiers at Ulm in Bavaria in 1805. After marching on to Vienna, he again trounced the Austrians, who had been joined by their new ally, Russia. The battle of Austerlitz,♦ often considered Napoleon's greatest victory, was fought on December 2, 1805, the first anniversary of his coronation.

After maintaining neutrality for a decade, Prussia now declared war on France. In 1806, the French promptly destroyed the Prussian army at Jena and Auerstadt.♦ In 1807, Napoleon defeated the Russians at Friedland. Personal negotiations between Napoleon and the young tsar Alexander I (r. 1801–1825) resulted in a humiliating settlement imposed on Prussia, which paid the price for temporary reconciliation between France and Russia; the Treaties of Tilsit turned Prussian lands west of the Elbe River into the kingdom of Westphalia♦ under Napoleon's brother Jerome, and Prussia's Polish provinces became the duchy of Warsaw. Alexander recognized Napoleon's conquests in central and western Europe and promised to help him against the British in exchange for Napoleon's support against the Turks. Neither party kept the bargain. Napoleon once again had turned the divisions among his enemies in his favor.

The Impact of French Victories

Wherever the Grand Army conquered, Napoleon's influence soon followed. By annexing some territories and setting up others as satellite kingdoms with much reduced autonomy, Napoleon attempted to colonize large parts of Europe (see Map 21.1 on

♦**Austerlitz:** AW stur lihts
♦**Auerstadt:** OW ur shteht
♦**Westphalia:** wehst FAYL yuh

page 798). But even where he did not rule directly or through his relatives, his startling string of victories forced the other powers to reconsider their own methods of rule.

Rule in the Colonized Territories. Napoleon brought the disparate German and Italian states together to rule them more effectively and to exploit their resources for his own ends. In 1803, he consolidated the tiny German states by abolishing some of them and attaching them to larger units. In July 1806, he established the Confederation of the Rhine, which soon included almost all the German states except Austria and Prussia. The Holy Roman Emperor gave up his title, held since the thirteenth century, and became simply the emperor of Austria. Napoleon established three units in Italy: the territories directly annexed to France and the satellite kingdoms of Italy and Naples. Italy had not been so unified since the Roman Empire.

Napoleon forced French-style reforms on both the annexed territories, which were ruled directly from France, and the satellite kingdoms, which were usually ruled by one or another of Napoleon's relatives but with a certain autonomy. French reforms included abolishing serfdom, eliminating seigneurial dues, introducing the Napoleonic Code, suppressing monasteries, and subordinating church to state, as well as extending civil rights to Jews and other religious minorities. The experience in the kingdom of Westphalia was typical of a French satellite. When Jerome Bonaparte and his wife, Catherine, arrived as king and queen in 1807, they relied on French experts who worked with a handpicked committee of Germans to write a constitution and install legal reforms. The Westphalian army had the first Jewish officers in the German states, and the army, administration, and judiciary were all opened to the middle classes. As time passed, however, the German subjects began to chafe under French rule. German officials enforced French decrees only halfheartedly, and the French army had to forbid its soldiers to frequent local taverns and shops because their presence often started fights.

As the example of Westphalia shows, reactions to Napoleonic innovations were mixed.

Napoleon's chosen rulers often made real improvements in roads, public works, law codes, and education. The removal of internal tariffs fostered economic growth by opening up the domestic market for goods, especially textiles. By 1814, Bologna had five hundred factories and Modena four hundred. Yet almost everyone had some cause for complaint. Republicans regretted Napoleon's conversion of the sister republics into kingdoms after his coronation. Tax increases and ever-rising conscription quotas fomented discontent as well. The annexed territories and satellite kingdoms paid half of the French war expenses.

Almost everywhere, conflicts arose between Napoleon's desire for a standardized, centralized government and local insistence on maintaining customs and traditions. Sometimes his own relatives sided with the countries they ruled. Napoleon's brother Louis, for instance, would not allow conscription in the Netherlands because the Dutch had never had compulsory military service. When Napoleon tried to introduce an economic policy banning trade with Great Britain, Louis's lax enforcement prompted the frustrated emperor to complain that "Holland [the leading province in the Netherlands] is an English province." In 1810, Napoleon annexed the satellite kingdom because his brother had become too sympathetic to Dutch interests.

Consolidation of German and Italian States, 1812

Pressure for Reform in Prussia and Russia.
Napoleon's victories forced defeated rulers to rethink their political and cultural assumptions. After the crushing defeat of Prussia in 1806 left his country much reduced in territory, Frederick William III (r. 1797–1840) appointed a reform commission, and on its recommendation he abolished serfdom and allowed nonnobles to buy and enclose land. Peasants gained their personal independence from their noble landlords, who could no longer sell them to pay gambling debts, for example, or refuse them permission to marry. Yet the lives of the former serfs remained bleak; they were left without land and their landlords no longer had to care for them in hard times. The king's advisers also overhauled the army to make the high command more efficient and to open the way to the appointment of middle-class officers. Prussia instituted these reforms to try to compete with the French, not to promote democracy. As one reformer wrote to Frederick William, "We must do from above what the French have done from below."

Reform received lip service in Russia. Tsar Alexander I had gained his throne after an aristocratic coup deposed and killed his autocratic and capricious father, Paul (r. 1796–1801), and in the early years of his reign the remorseful young ruler created Western-style ministries, lifted restrictions on importing foreign books, and founded six new universities; reform commissions studied abuses; nobles were encouraged voluntarily to free their serfs (a few actually did so); and there was even talk of drafting a constitution. But none of these efforts reached beneath the surface of Russian life, and by the second decade of his reign Alexander began to reject the Enlightenment spirit that his grandmother Catherine the Great had instilled in him.

The Continental System.
The one power always standing between Napoleon and total dominance of Europe was Great Britain. The British ruled the seas and financed anyone who would oppose Napoleon. In an effort to bankrupt this "nation of shopkeepers" by choking its trade, Napoleon inaugurated the **Continental System** in 1806. It prohibited all commerce between Great Britain and France, as well as between Great Britain and France's dependent states and allies. At first the system worked: British exports dropped by 20 percent in 1807–1808, and industrial production declined by 10 percent;

unemployment and a strike of 60,000 workers in northern England resulted. The British retaliated by confiscating merchandise on ships, even those of powers neutral in the wars, that sailed to or from ports from which the British were excluded by the Continental System.

In the midst of continuing wars, moreover, the system proved impossible to enforce, and widespread smuggling brought British goods into the European market. British industrial growth continued, despite some setbacks; calico-printing works, for example, quadrupled their production, and imports of raw cotton increased by 40 percent. At the same time, French and other continental industries benefited from the temporary protection from British competition.

Resistance to French Rule, 1807–1812. Smuggling British goods was only one way of opposing the French. Almost everywhere in Europe, resistance began as local opposition to French demands for money or draftees, but it eventually prompted a more nationalistic patriotic defense. In southern Italy, gangs of bandits harassed the French army and local officials; 33,000 Italian bandits were arrested in 1809 alone. But resistance continued via a network of secret societies, called the *carbonari* ("charcoal-burners"), which got its name from the practice of marking each new member's forehead with a charcoal mark. Throughout the nineteenth century the carbonari played a leading role in Italian nationalism. In the German states, intellectuals wrote passionate defenses of the virtues of the German nation and of the superiority of German literature.

No nations bucked under Napoleon's reins more than Spain and Portugal. In 1807, Napoleon sent 100,000 troops through Spain to invade Portugal, Great Britain's ally. The royal family fled to the Portuguese colony of Brazil, but fighting continued, aided by a

The Spanish War for Independence, 1807–1813

British army. When Napoleon got his brother Joseph named king of Spain in place of the senile Charles IV (r. 1788–1808), the Spanish clergy and nobles raised bands of peasants to fight the French occupiers. Even Napoleon's taking personal command of the French forces failed to quell the Spanish, who for six years fought a war of national independence that pinned down thousands of French soldiers. Germaine de Staël commented that Napoleon "never understood that a war might be a crusade. . . . He never reckoned with the one power that no arms could overcome—the enthusiasm of a whole people."

More than a new feeling of nationalism was aroused in Spain. Peasants hated French requisitioning of their food supplies and sought to defend their priests against French anticlericalism. Spanish nobles feared revolutionary reforms and were willing to defend the old monarchy in the person of the young Ferdinand VII, heir to Charles IV, even while Ferdinand himself was congratulating Napoleon on his victories. The Spanish Catholic church spread anti-French propaganda that equated Napoleon with heresy. As the former archbishop of Seville wrote to the archbishop of Granada in 1808, "You realize that we must not recognize as king a freemason, heretic, Lutheran, as are all the Bonapartes and the French nation." In this tense atmosphere, the Spanish peasant rebels, assisted by the British, countered every French massacre with atrocities of their own. They tortured their French prisoners (boiling one general alive) and lynched collaborators.

From Russian Winter to Final Defeat, 1812–1815

Despite opposition, Napoleon ruled over an extensive empire by 1812. He controlled more territory than any European ruler had since Roman times. Only two major European states remained fully independent—Great Britain and Russia—but once allied they would successfully challenge his dominion and draw many other states to their side. Britain sent aid to the Portuguese and Spanish rebels, while Russia once again prepared for war. Tsar Alexander I made peace with

Napoleon's Mamelukes Massacre the Spanish

In one of the paintings he produced to criticize Napoleon's occupation of Spain, *Second of May 1808 at the Puerta del Sol* (1814), Goya depicts the brutal suppression of the Spanish revolt in Madrid against Napoleon. Napoleon used Mamelukes, Egyptian soldiers descended from freed Turkish slaves. Why would the portrayal of these foreign mercenaries make the event seem even more horrifying to Spanish and European viewers? *Museo del Prado, Madrid.*

Turkey and allied himself with Great Britain and Sweden. In 1812, Napoleon invaded Russia with 250,000 horses and 600,000 men, including contingents of Italians, Poles, Swiss, Dutch, and Germans. This daring move proved to be his undoing.

Invasion of Russia, 1812. Napoleon followed his usual strategy of trying to strike quickly, but the Russian generals avoided confrontation and retreated eastward, destroying anything that might be useful to the invaders (see "An Ordinary Soldier on Campaign with Napoleon" on page 804). In September, on the road to Moscow, Napoleon finally engaged the main Russian force in the gigantic battle of Borodino (see Map 21.1 on page 798). French casualties were 30,000 men, including 47 generals; the Russians lost 45,000. The French soldiers had nothing

to celebrate around their campfires: as one soldier wrote, "Everyone . . . wept for some dead friend." Once again the Russians retreated, leaving Moscow undefended. Napoleon entered the deserted city, but the victory turned hollow because the departing Russians had set the wooden city on fire. Within a week, three-fourths of it had burned to the ground. Still Alexander refused to negotiate, and French morale plunged with worsening problems of supply. Weeks of constant marching in the dirt and heat had worn down the foot soldiers, who were dying of disease or deserting in large numbers.

In October Napoleon began his retreat; in November came the cold. Napoleon himself reported that on November 14 the temperature fell to 24 degrees Fahrenheit. A German soldier in the Grand Army described trying to cook fistfuls of raw bran with snow to make

An Ordinary Soldier on Campaign with Napoleon

Jakob Walter (1788–1864) recorded his experience as a soldier in the Napoleonic armies marching to Moscow in 1812. He wrote his account sometime after the events took place, though exactly when is not known. Walter was a German conscripted into military service from one of the many west German states controlled by Napoleon. The selection here describes the Napoleonic armies still on the offensive moving toward Moscow. But the seeds of future problems are already germinating.

On August 19, the entire army moved forward, and pursued the Russians with all speed. Four or five hours' farther up the river another battle started, but the enemy did not hold out long, and the march now led to Moshaisk [near Borodino], the so-called "Holy Valley." From Smolensk to Moshaisk the war displayed its horrible work of destruction: all the roads, fields, and woods lay as though sown with people, horses, wagons, burned villages and cities; everything looked like the complete ruin of all that lived. In particular, we saw ten dead Russians to one of our men, although every day our numbers fell off considerably. In order to pass through woods, swamps, and narrow trails, trees which formed barriers in the woods had to be removed, and wagon barricades of the enemy had to be cleared away....The march up to there, as far as it was a march, is indescribable and inconceivable for people who have not seen anything of it. The very great heat, the dust which was like a thick fog, the closed line of march in columns, and the putrid water from holes filled with dead people and cattle brought everyone close to death; and eye pains, fatigue, thirst, and hunger tormented everybody. God! How often I remembered the bread and beer which I had enjoyed at home with such an indifferent pleasure! Now, however, I must struggle, half wild, with the dead and living. How gladly would I renounce for my whole life the warm food so common at home if I only did not lack good bread and beer now! I would not wish for more all my life. But these were empty, helpless thoughts. Yes, the thought of my brothers and sisters so far away added to my pain! Wherever I looked, I saw the soldiers with dead, half-desperate faces.

Source: Marc Raeff, ed., *Jakob Walter: The Diary of a Napoleonic Foot Soldier* (New York: Doubleday, 1991), 52–53.

something like bread. For him the retreat was "the indescribable horror of all possible plagues." Within a week the Grand Army lost 30,000 horses and had to abandon most of its artillery and food supplies. Russian forces harassed the retreating army, now more pathetic than grand. By December only 100,000 troops remained, one-sixth the original number, and the retreat had turned into a rout: the Russians had captured 200,000 soldiers, including 48 generals and 3,000 other officers.

Napoleon had made a classic military mistake that would be repeated by Adolf Hitler in World War II: fighting a war on two distant fronts simultaneously. The Spanish war tied down 250,000 French troops and forced Napoleon to bully Prussia and Austria into supplying soldiers of dubious loyalty for the Moscow campaign. They deserted at the first opportunity. The fighting in Spain and Portugal also exacerbated the already substantial logistical and communications problems involved in marching to Moscow.

The End of Napoleon's Empire. Napoleon's humiliation might have been temporary if the British and Russians had not successfully organized a coalition to complete the job. Napoleon still had resources at his command; by the spring of 1813 he had replenished his army with another 250,000 men. With British financial support, Russian, Austrian, Prussian, and Swedish armies met the French outside Leipzig in October 1813 and defeated Napoleon in the Battle of the Nations. One by one, Napoleon's German allies deserted him to join the German nationalist "war of liberation." The Confederation of the Rhine dissolved, and the Dutch revolted and restored the prince of Orange. Joseph Bonaparte fled Spain, and a combined Spanish-Portuguese army under British command invaded France. In only a few months the allied powers crossed the Rhine and marched toward Paris. In March 1814, the French Senate deposed Napoleon, who abdicated when his remaining generals refused to fight. Napoleon went into exile on the island of Elba off the Italian coast. His wife, Marie-Louise, refused to accompany him. The allies restored to the throne Louis XVIII (r. 1814–1824), the brother of Louis XVI (whose son was known as Louis XVII even though he died in prison in 1795 without ever ruling).

Napoleon had one last chance to regain power because Louis XVIII lacked a solid base of support. The new king tried to steer a middle course through a charter that established a British-style monarchy with a two-house legislature and guaranteed civil rights. But he was caught between returning emigré nobles who demanded a complete restoration of their lands and powers and those who had supported either the republic or Napoleon during the previous twenty-five years. Sensing an opportunity, Napoleon escaped from Elba in early 1815 and, landing in southern France, made swift and unimpeded progress to Paris. Although he had left in ignominy, now crowds cheered him and former soldiers volunteered to serve him. The period eventually known as the Hundred Days (the length of time between Napoleon's escape and his final defeat) had begun. Louis XVIII fled across the border, waiting for help from France's enemies.

Napoleon quickly moved his reconstituted army into present-day Belgium. At first it seemed that he might succeed in separately fighting the two armies arrayed against him—a Prussian army and a joint force of Belgian, Dutch, German, and British troops led by Sir Arthur Wellesley (1769–1852), duke of Wellington. But the Prussians evaded him and on June 18, 1815, joined with Wellington at Waterloo. Completely routed, Napoleon had no choice but to abdicate again. This time the victorious allies banished him permanently to the remote island of St. Helena, far off the coast of West Africa, where he died in 1821 at the age of fifty-two.

The cost of Napoleon's rule was high: 750,000 French soldiers and 400,000 others from annexed and satellite states died between 1800 and 1815. Yet no other military figure since Alexander the Great had made such an impact on world history. (See "Contrasting Views," page 796.) His plans for a united Europe, his insistence on spreading the legal reforms of the French Revolution, his social welfare programs, and even his inadvertent awakening of national sentiment set the agenda for European history in the modern era.

Review: Why was Napoleon able to gain control over so much of Europe's territory?

❖ The "Restoration" of Europe

Even while Napoleon was making his last desperate bid for power, his enemies were meeting in the Congress of Vienna (1814–1815) to decide the fate of postrevolutionary Europe. Although interrupted by the Hundred Days, the Congress of Vienna settled the boundaries of European states, determined who would rule each nation, and established a new framework for international relations based on periodic meetings, or congresses, between the major powers. This congress system, or "concert of Europe," helped prevent another major war until the 1850s, and no conflict comparable to the Napoleonic wars would occur again until 1914.

The Congress of Vienna, 1814–1815

The Vienna settlement established a new equilibrium that relied on cooperation among the major powers while guaranteeing the

Congress of Vienna
An unknown French engraver caricatured the efforts of the diplomats at the Congress of Vienna, complaining that they used the occasion to divide the spoils of European territory. At the far left is Metternich preparing to take Venice and Lombardy (northern Italy). What elements in this engraving make it a caricature? *Historisches Museum der Stadt Wien.*

status of smaller states. The revolutionary and Napoleonic wars had produced a host of potentially divisive issues. In addition to determining the boundaries of France, the congress had to decide the fate of Napoleon's duchy of Warsaw, the German province of Saxony, the Netherlands, the states once part of the confederation of the Rhine, and various Italian territories. All had either changed hands or been created during the wars. These issues were resolved by face-to-face negotiations among representatives of the five major powers: Austria, Russia, Prussia, Britain, and France. With its aim to establish a long-lasting, negotiated peace endorsed by all parties, both winners and losers, the Congress of Vienna provided a model for the twentieth-century League of Nations and United Nations.

Austria's chief negotiator, Prince Klemens von Metternich♦ (1773–1859), took the lead in devising the settlement. A well-educated

nobleman who spoke five languages, Metternich served as a minister in the Austrian cabinet from 1809 to 1848. More than anyone else, he shaped the post-Napoleonic order. Although his penchant for womanizing made him a security risk in the eyes of the British Foreign Office (he even had an affair with Napoleon's younger sister), he worked with the British prime minister Robert Castlereagh (1769–1822) to ensure a moderate agreement that would check French aggression and yet maintain France's great-power status. Metternich and Castlereagh believed that French aggression must be contained because it had threatened the European peace since the days of Louis XIV but also that France must remain a major player precisely so that no one European power might dominate the others. In this way France could help Austria and Britain counter the ambitions of Prussia and Russia. Castlereagh hoped to make Britain the arbiter of European affairs, but he knew this could be accomplished only through adroit diplomacy because the British constitutional

♦**Klemens von Metternich:** KLAY mehnts fawn MEH tur nihk

monarchy had little in common with most of its more absolutist continental counterparts.

The task of ensuring France's status at the congress fell to Prince Charles Maurice de Talleyrand (1754–1838), an aristocrat and former bishop who had embraced the French Revolution, served as Napoleon's foreign minister, and ended as foreign minister to Louis XVIII after helping to arrange the emperor's overthrow. Informed of Talleyrand's betrayal, Napoleon called him "excrement in silk stockings." When the French army failed to oppose Napoleon's return to power in the Hundred

Days, the allies took away all territory conquered since 1790 and required France to pay an indemnity and support an army of occupation until it had paid. Talleyrand nonetheless successfully argued that the restored French monarchy could succeed only if it retained its great-power status and participated fully in the negotiations. The goal of the congress was to achieve postwar stability by establishing secure states with guaranteed borders (Map 21.2). Because the congress aimed to "restore" as many regimes as possible to their former rulers, this epoch is

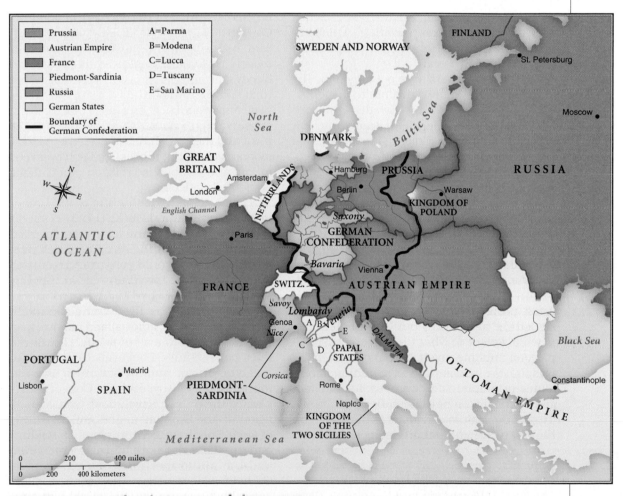

MAP 21.2 Europe after the Congress of Vienna, 1815
The Congress of Vienna forced France to return to its 1789 borders. The Austrian Netherlands and the Dutch Republic were united in a new kingdom of the Netherlands, the German states were joined in a Germanic Confederation that built upon Napoleon's Confederation of the Rhine, and Napoleon's Grand Duchy of Warsaw became the kingdom of Poland with the tsar of Russia as king. To compensate for its losses in Poland, Prussia gained territory in Saxony and on the left bank of the Rhine. Austria reclaimed the Italian provinces of Lombardy and Venetia and the Dalmatian coast.

sometimes labeled the **restoration**. Some of the returning rulers so detested French innovations that they tore French plants out of their gardens and threw French furniture out of their palaces. But simple restoration was not always feasible, and in those cases the congress rearranged territory to balance the competing interests of the great powers. Thus the congress turned the duchy of Warsaw into a new Polish kingdom but made the tsar of Russia its king. (Poland would not regain its independence until 1918.) The former Dutch Republic and the Austrian Netherlands, both annexed to France, now united as the new kingdom of the Netherlands under the restored stadholder. Austria now presided over the German Confederation, which replaced the defunct Holy Roman Empire and also included Prussia.

The lesser powers were not forgotten. The kingdom of Piedmont-Sardinia took Genoa, Nice, and part of Savoy. Sweden obtained Norway from Denmark but had to accept Russia's conquest of Finland. Finally, various international trade issues were also resolved. At the urging of Great Britain, the congress agreed to condemn in principle the slave trade, abolished by Great Britain in 1807. In reality, however, the slave trade continued in many places until the 1840s.

To impart spiritual substance to this very calculated settlement of political affairs, Tsar Alexander proposed a Holy Alliance calling upon divine assistance in upholding religion, peace, and justice. Prussia and Austria signed the agreement, but Great Britain refused to accede to what Castlereagh called "a piece of sublime mysticism and nonsense." Despite the reassertion of traditional religious principle, the congress had in fact given birth to a new diplomatic order: in the future, the legitimacy of states depended on the treaty system, not on divine right.

The Emergence of Conservatism

The French Revolution and Napoleonic domination of Europe had shown contemporaries that government could be changed overnight, that the old hierarchies could be overthrown in the name of reason, and that even Christianity could be written off or at least profoundly altered with the stroke of a pen. The

potential for rapid change raised many questions about the proper sources of authority. Kings and churches could be restored and former revolutionaries locked up or silenced, but the old order no longer commanded automatic obedience. The old order was now merely *old*, no longer "natural" and "timeless." It had been ousted once and therefore might fall again. People insisted on having reasons to believe in their "restored" governments. The political doctrine that justified the restoration was **conservatism**.

Conservatives benefited from the disillusionment that permeated Europe after 1815. In the eyes of most Europeans, Napoleon had become a tyrant who ruled in his own interests. Conservatives saw a logical progression in recent history: the Enlightenment based on reason led to the French Revolution, with its bloody guillotine and horrifying Terror, which in turn spawned the authoritarian and militaristic Napoleon. Therefore, those who espoused conservatism rejected both the Enlightenment and the French Revolution. They favored monarchies over republics, tradition over revolution, and established religion over Enlightenment skepticism.

The original British critic of the French Revolution, Edmund Burke (1729–1799), inspired many of the conservatives that followed. He had argued that the revolutionaries erred in thinking they could construct an entirely new government based on reason. Government, Burke said, had to be rooted in long experience, which evolved over generations. All change must be gradual and must respect national and historical traditions. Like Burke, later conservatives believed that religious and other major traditions were an essential foundation for any society. Conservatives blamed the French Revolution's attack on religion on the skepticism and anticlericalism of such Enlightenment thinkers as Voltaire, and they defended both hereditary monarchy and the authority of the church, whether Catholic or Protestant. The "rights of man," according to conservatives, could not stand alone as doctrine based simply on nature and reason. The community too had its rights, more important than those of any individual, and established institutions best represented those rights. The church, the state, and the patriarchal family would provide an enduring social order for everyone. Faith, sentiment, history, and tradition must fill the vacuum left by the failures of reason and excessive belief in individual rights. Across Europe these views were taken up and elaborated by government advisers, professors, and writers. Not surprisingly, they had their strongest appeal in ruling circles and guided the politics of men such as Metternich in Austria and Alexander I in Russia.

The restored monarchy in France provided a major test for conservatism because the returning Bourbons had to confront the legacy of twenty-five years of upheaval. Louis XVIII tried to ensure a measure of continuity by maintaining Napoleon's Civil Code. He also guaranteed the rights of ownership to church lands sold during the revolutionary period and created a parliament composed of a Chamber of Peers nominated by the king and a Chamber of Deputies elected by very restricted suffrage (fewer than 100,000 voters in a population of 30 million, or about 3 percent). In making these concessions, the king tried to follow a moderate course of compromise, but the Ultras (ultraroyalists) pushed for complete repudiation of the revolutionary past. When Louis returned to power after Napoleon's final defeat, armed royalist bands attacked and murdered hundreds of Bonapartists and former revolutionaries. In 1816, the Ultras insisted on abolishing divorce and set up special courts to punish opponents of the regime. When an assassin killed Louis XVIII's nephew in 1820, the Ultras demanded even more extreme measures.

The Revival of Religion

The experience of revolutionary upheaval and nearly constant warfare prompted many to renew their religious faith once peace returned. In France, the Catholic church sent missionaries to hold open-air "ceremonies of reparation" to express repentance for the outrages of revolution. In Rome, the papacy reestablished the Jesuit order, which had been disbanded during the Enlightenment. In the Italian states and Spain, governments used religious societies of laypeople to combat the influence of reformers and nationalists such as the Italian carbonari.

Revivalist movements, especially in Protestant countries, could on occasion challenge the status quo rather than supporting it. In parts of Protestant Germany and Britain, religious revival had begun in the eighteenth century with the rise of Pietism and Methodism, movements that stressed individual religious experience rather than reason as the true path to moral and social reform. The English Methodists followed John Wesley (1703–1791), who had preached an emotional, morally austere, and very personal "method" of gaining salvation. The Methodists, or Wesleyans, gradually separated from the Church of England and in the early decades of the nineteenth century attracted thousands of members in huge revival meetings that lasted for days.

Shopkeepers, artisans, agricultural laborers, miners, and workers in cottage industry, both male and female, flocked to the new denomination, even though at first Methodism seemed to emphasize conservative political views: Methodist statutes of 1792 had insisted that "none of us shall either in writing or in conversation speak lightly or irreverently of the government." In their hostility to rigid doctrine and elaborate ritual and their encouragement of popular preaching, however, the Methodists fostered a sense of democratic community and even a rudimentary sexual equality. From the beginning, women preachers traveled on horseback to preach in barns, town halls, and textile dye houses. The Methodist Sunday schools that taught thousands of poor children to read and write eventually helped create greater demands for working-class political participation.

The religious revival was not limited to Europe. In the United States, the second Great Awakening began around 1790 with huge camp meetings that brought together thousands of worshipers and scores of evangelical preachers, many of them Methodist. (The original Great Awakening took place in the 1730s and 1740s, sparked by the preaching of George Whitefield, a young English evangelist and follower of John Wesley.) Men and women danced to exhaustion, fell into trances, and spoke in tongues. During this period, Protestant sects began systematic missionary activity in other parts of the world, with British and American missionary societies taking the lead in the 1790s and early 1800s. In the British colony of India, for example, Protestant missionaries argued for the reform of Hindu customs. *Sati*◆—the burning of widows on the funeral pyres of their husbands—was abolished by the British administration of India in 1829. Missionary activity by Protestants and Catholics would become one of the arms of European imperialism and cultural influence in the nineteenth century.

> **Review:** To what extent was the old order restored by the Congress of Vienna?

❖ Forces for Social and Cultural Change

Conservatives hoped to clamp a lid on European affairs, but the lid kept threatening to fly off. Rapid urban growth and the spread of industry created new social tensions and inspired new political doctrines to explain the meaning of economic and social changes. These doctrines soon galvanized opponents of the conservative Vienna settlement. Both cutting across and drawing on the turmoil in society and politics was romanticism, a new international movement in the arts and literature that originated in reaction to the Enlightenment in the eighteenth century and dominated artistic expression in the first half of the nineteenth.

Industrial and Urban Growth in Britain

Historians today use the term *Industrial Revolution* to describe the set of changes that brought steam-driven machinery, large factories, and a new working class first to Britain, then to the rest of Europe, and eventually to the rest of the world. French and English writers of the 1820s introduced the term to capture the drama of contemporary change and to draw a parallel with the French Revolution. But we should not take the comparison too literally. Unlike the

◆ *sati:* suh TEE

French upheaval, the Industrial Revolution was not over in a decade. From Great Britain in the second half of the eighteenth century it spread slowly; even by the 1830s it had little effect on the continent outside of northern France, Belgium, and the Rhineland. Most Europeans were still peasants working in the old ways.

Factories and Workers.   Steam-driven machines first brought workers together in factories in the textile industry. By 1830, more than a million people in Britain depended on the cotton industry for employment, and cotton cloth constituted 50 percent of the country's exports. Factories quickly sprang up in urban areas, where the growing population provided a ready source of labor. The rapid expansion of the British textile industry had as its colonial corollary the destruction of the hand manufacture of textiles in India. The British put high import duties on Indian cloth entering Britain and kept such duties very low for British cloth entering India. The figures are dramatic: in 1813, the Indian city of Calcutta exported to England £2,000,000 of cotton cloth; by 1830, Calcutta was importing from England £2,000,000 of cotton cloth. When Britain abolished slavery in its Caribbean colonies in 1833, British manufacturers began to buy raw cotton in the southern United States, where slavery still flourished.

Factories drew workers from the urban population surge, which had begun in the eighteenth century and now accelerated. The reasons for urban growth are not entirely clear. The population of such new industrial cities as Manchester and Leeds increased by 40 percent in the 1820s alone. Historians long thought that factory workers came from the countryside, pushed off the land by the field enclosures of the 1700s. But recent studies have shown that the number of agricultural laborers actually increased during industrialization in Britain, suggesting that a growing birthrate created a larger population and fed workers into the new factory system.

The new workers came from several sources: families of farmers who could not provide land for all their children, soldiers demobilized after the Napoleonic wars, artisans displaced by the new machinery, and children of the earliest workers who had moved to the factory towns. A system of employment that resembled family labor on farms or in cottage industry also developed in the new factories. Entire families came to toil for a single wage, although family members performed different tasks. Workdays of twelve to seventeen hours were typical, even for children, and the work was grueling. Community ties remained important as workers migrated from rural to urban areas to join friends and family from their original villages.

As urban factories grew, their workers gradually came to constitute a new socioeconomic class with a distinctive culture and traditions. Like middle class, the term **working class** came into use for the first time in the early nineteenth century. It referred to the laborers in the new factories. In the past, workers had labored in isolated trades: water and wood carrying, gardening, laundry, and building. In contrast, factories brought working people together with machines, under close supervision by their employers. They soon developed a sense of common interests and organized societies for mutual help and political reform. From these would come the first labor unions.

Fearing displacement by machines, in 1811 and 1812 bands of handloom weavers wrecked factory machinery and burned mills in the Midlands, Yorkshire, and Lancashire. To restore order and protect industry, the government sent in an army of twelve thousand regular soldiers and made machine wrecking punishable by death. The rioters were called Luddites♦ after the fictitious figure Ned Ludd, whose signature appeared on their manifestos. (The term is still used to describe those who resist new technology.)

Other British workers focused their organizing efforts on reforming Parliament, whose members were chosen in elections dominated by the landowning elite. One reformer complained that the members of the House of Commons were nothing but "toadeaters, gamblers, public plunderers, and hirelings." Reform clubs held large open-air meetings, and ordinary people eagerly bought cheap newspapers that clamored for change. In August 1819, sixty thousand people at-

tended an illegal meeting held in St. Peter's Fields in Manchester. When the local authorities sent the cavalry to arrest the speaker, panic resulted; eleven people were killed and many hundreds injured. Punsters called it the Battle of Peterloo or the Peterloo Massacre. An alarmed government passed the Six Acts, which forbade large political meetings and restricted press criticism, suppressing the reform movement in Britain for a decade.

The Rise of the Railroad. Steam-driven engines took on a dramatic new form in the 1820s when the English engineer George Stephenson perfected an engine to pull wagons along rail tracks. (See "Taking Measure," page 812.) The idea of a railroad was not new: iron tracks had been used since the seventeenth century to haul coal from mines in wagons pulled by horses. A railroad system as a mode of transport, however, developed only after Stephenson's invention of a steam-powered locomotive. In 1830, the Liverpool and Manchester Railway line opened to the cheers of crowds and the congratulations of government officials, including the duke of Wellington, the hero of Waterloo and now prime minister. In the excitement, some of the dignitaries gathered on a parallel track. Another engine, George Stephenson's famous Rocket, approached at high speed. Most of the gentlemen scattered to safety, but former cabinet minister William Huskisson fell and was hit. In a few hours he died, the first official casualty of the newfangled railroad.

Railroads were dramatic and expensive—the most striking symbol of the new industrial age. Placed on the new tracks, steam-driven carriages could transport people and goods to the cities and link coal and iron deposits to the new factories. They gave industrialization a big push forward as every European country soon tried to set up its own railroad system. One German entrepreneur confidently predicted, "The locomotive is the hearse which will carry absolutism and feudalism to the graveyard."

The New Ideologies

Although traditional ways of life still prevailed in much of Europe, new modes of thinking about the changes in the social

♦**Luddites:** LUH dyts

TAKING MEASURE

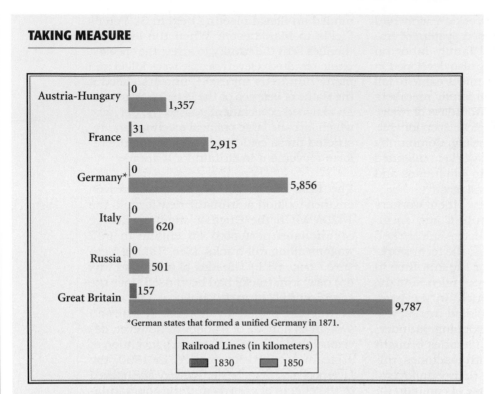

*German states that formed a unified Germany in 1871.

Railroad Lines (in kilometers)
  1830   1850

Railroad Lines, 1830–1850

Great Britain quickly extended its lead in the building of railroads. The extension of commerce and, before long, the ability to wage war would depend on the development of effective railroad networks. These statistics might be taken as predicting a realignment of power within Europe after 1850. What do the numbers say about the relative position of Germany (the German states, including Prussia but excluding Austria) and Austria-Hungary and France? *From B. R. Mitchell,* European Historical Statistics 1750–1970 *(New York: Columbia University Press, 1975), F1.*

and political order arose in direct response to what some have called the dual revolution of the French Revolution and the Industrial Revolution. The French Revolution had caused people to ask questions about the best possible form of government, and its effects had made clear that people acting together could change their political system. Similarly, the Industrial Revolution, first in Britain and then in western Europe, posed fundamental questions about changes in society and social relations: How did the new social order differ from the earlier one, which was less urban and less driven by commercial concerns? Who should control this new order? Should governments try to moderate or accelerate the pace of change? Answers to these questions about the social and political order were called ideologies. A word coined during the French Revolution, **ideology** refers to a coherent set of beliefs about the way a society's social and political order should be organized. The 1820s and 1830s were, indeed, an era of "isms" — conservatism, liberalism, nationalism, romanticism, and, newest on the scene, socialism. In the 1830s and 1840s, new political and social movements organized themselves around these ideologies.

Liberalism. As an ideology, liberalism traced its origins to the writings of John Locke in the seventeenth century and the Enlightenment philosophy of the eighteenth. The adherents of **liberalism** defined themselves in opposition to conservatives on one end of the political spectrum and revolutionaries on the other. Unlike conservatives, liberals supported the Enlightenment ideals of constitutional guarantees of personal liberty and free trade in economics, believing that greater liberty in politics and economic matters would promote social improvement and economic growth. For that reason, they also generally applauded the social and economic changes produced by the Industrial Revolution, while opposing the violence and excessive state power promoted by the French Revolution. The leaders of the rapidly expanding middle class composed of manufacturers, merchants, and professionals favored liberalism.

The foremost proponent of early-nineteenth-century liberalism was the English philosopher and jurist Jeremy Bentham (1748–1832). He called his brand of liberalism utilitarianism because he held that the best policy is the one that produces "the greatest good for the greatest number" and is thus the most useful, or utilitarian. Bentham's criticisms spared no institution; he railed against the injustices of the British parliamentary process, the abuses of the prisons and the penal code, and the educational system. In his zeal for social engineering, he proposed elaborate schemes for managing the poor and model prisons that would emphasize rehabilitation through close supervision rather than corporal punishment. British liberals like Bentham wanted government involvement, including deregulation of trade, but they shied away from any association with revolutionary violence.

Bentham and many other liberals joined the abolitionist, antislavery movement that intensified between the 1790s and 1820s. One English abolitionist put the matter in these terms: "[God] has given to us an unexampled portion of civil liberty; and we in return drag his rational creatures into a most severe and perpetual bondage." The contradiction between calling for more liberty at home and maintaining slavery in the West Indies seemed intolerable to British liberals and to many religious groups, especially the Quakers, who since the 1780s had taken the lead in forming antislavery societies in both the United States and Great Britain. Agitation by such groups as the London Society for Effecting the Abolition of the Slave Trade succeeded in gaining a first victory in 1807 when the British House of Lords voted to abolish the slave trade. Throughout the 1820s, antislavery activism expanded in the United States, Great Britain, and France because the slave trade still continued in some countries and because slavery itself had not been abolished. As one disappointed British abolitionist explained in 1830:

> We supposed that when by the abolition of the slave trade the planters could get no more slaves, they would not only treat better those whom they then had in their power, but that they would gradually find it to their advantage to emancipate them. . . . We did not sufficiently take into account the effect of unlimited power.

The abolitionists' efforts would bear fruit in 1833 when Britain abolished slavery in all its colonies.

Socialism. The newest ideology of the 1820s, **socialism**, took up where liberalism left off: socialists believed that the liberties advocated by liberals benefited only the middle class—the owners of factories and businesses, not the workers. They sought to reorganize society totally rather than to reform it piecemeal through political measures. Many were utopians who believed that ideal communities are based on cooperation rather than competition. Like Thomas More, whose book *Utopia* (1516) gave the movement its name, the utopian socialists believed that society would benefit all its members only if private property did not exist.

Socialists criticized the new industrial order for dividing society into two classes: the new middle class, or capitalists, who owned the wealth; and the working class, their downtrodden and impoverished employees. Such divisions tore the social fabric, and, as their name suggests, the socialists aimed to restore harmony and cooperation through social reorganization. Robert Owen (1771–1858), a successful Welsh-born manufacturer, founded British socialism. In 1800, he bought a cotton mill in New Lanark, Scotland, and began to set up a model factory town, where workers labored only ten hours a day (instead of seventeen, as was common) and children between the ages of five and ten attended school rather than working in the factory. Owen moved to the United States in the 1820s to put his principles once more into action in the community in Indiana he named New Harmony. The experiment collapsed after three years, a victim of internal squabbling. But out of Owen's experiments and writings, such as *The Book of the New Moral World* (1820), would come the movement for producer cooperatives (businesses owned and controlled by their workers), consumers' cooperatives (stores in which consumers owned shares), and a national trade union.

Claude Henri de Saint-Simon (1760–1825) and Charles Fourier✦ (1772–1837) were

---

✦**Fourier:** FOOR ee ay

Owen's counterparts in France. Saint-Simon was a noble who had served as an officer in the War of American Independence and lost a fortune speculating in national property during the French Revolution. Fourier traveled as a salesman for a Lyon cloth merchant. Both shared Owen's alarm about the effects of industrialization on social relations. Saint-Simon—who coined the terms *industrialism* and *industrialist* to define the new economic order and its chief animators—believed that work was the central element in the new society and that it should be controlled not by politicians but by scientists, engineers, artists, and industrialists themselves. To correct the abuses of the new industrial order, Fourier urged the establishment of utopian communities that were part garden city and part agricultural commune; all jobs would be rotated to maximize happiness. Fourier hoped that a network of small, decentralized communities would replace the state. The emancipation of women was essential to Fourier's vision of a harmonious community: "The extension of the privileges of women is the fundamental cause of all social progress." Fourier's projects sometimes included outlandish predictions; he envisioned a world in which the oceans would turn into lemonade and the population would include 37 million poets equal to Homer, 37 million mathematicians equal to Newton, and 37 million dramatists equal to Molière.

After Saint-Simon's death in 1825, some of his followers established a quasi-religious cult with elaborate rituals and a "he-pope" and "she-pope," or ruling father and mother. Saint-Simonians lived and worked together in cooperative arrangements and scandalized some by advocating free love. They set up branches in the United States and Egypt. In 1832, Saint-Simonian women founded a feminist newspaper, *The Free Woman*, asserting that "with the emancipation of woman will come the emancipation of the worker." These early utopian socialists were lonely voices. Their emphasis on community and cooperation gained more adherents after 1830.

Nationalism. Nationalists could be liberals, socialists, or even conservatives. **Nationalism** holds that all peoples derive their identities from their nations, which are defined by common language, shared cultural traditions, and sometimes religion. When such nations do not coincide with state boundaries, as they often did not in the nineteenth and twentieth centuries, nationalism can produce violence and warfare as different national groups compete for control over territory.

The French showed the power of national feeling in their revolutionary and Napoleonic wars, but they also provoked nationalism in the people they conquered. Once Napoleon and his satellite rulers departed, nationalist sentiment turned against other outside rulers—the Ottoman Turks in the Balkans, the Russians in Poland, and the Austrians in Italy. Intellectuals took the lead in demanding unity and freedom for their peoples. They collected folktales, poems, and histories and prepared grammars and dictionaries of their native languages. Students, middle-class professionals, and army officers formed secret societies to promote national independence and constitutional reform.

Nationalist aspirations were especially explosive for the Austrian Empire, which included a variety of peoples united only by their enforced allegiance to the Habsburg emperor. The empire included three main national groups: the Germans, who made up one-fourth of the population; the Magyars of Hungary (which included Transylvania and Croatia); and the Slavs, who together formed the largest group in the population but were divided into different nationalities such as Poles, Czechs, Croats, and Serbs. The empire also included Italians in Lombardy and Venetia and Romanians in Transylvania. Efforts to govern such diverse peoples preoccupied Metternich, chief minister to the weak Habsburg emperor Francis I (r. 1792–1835). Metternich's domestic policy aimed to restrain nationalist impulses, and it largely succeeded until the 1840s. He set up a secret police on the Napoleonic model that opened letters of even the highest officials. Censorship in the Italian provinces was so strict that even the works of Dante were expurgated, and Metternich announced that "the Lombards must forget that they are Italians."

In reaction, novelists, playwrights, and poets used their pens to arouse nationalist sentiment. Membership grew in secret societies such as the carbonari; before the fall of Napoleon, many had been anti-French, but now the societies turned anti-Austrian and supported political rights and national self-determination. The societies had no common program across Italy and no central organization, but they attracted tens of thousands of members, including physicians, lawyers, officers, and students.

The new Germanic Confederation set up by the Congress of Vienna had a federal assembly, but it largely functioned as a tool of Metternich's policies. The only sign of resistance came from university students, who formed nationalist student societies, or *Burschenschaften.*◆ In 1817, they held a mass rally at which they burned books they did not like, including Napoleon's Civil Code. One of their leaders, Friedrich Ludwig Jahn, spouted such xenophobic◆ (antiforeign) slogans as "If you let your daughter learn French, you might just as well train her to become a whore." Metternich was convinced that the Burschenschaften in the German states and the carbonari in Italy were linked in an international conspiracy; in 1820, when a student assassinated the playwright August Kotzebue◆ because he ridiculed the student movement, Metternich convinced the leaders of the biggest German states to pass the Karlsbad Decrees dissolving the student societies and more strictly censoring the press. No evidence for a conspiracy was found.

Tsar Alexander faced similar problems in Poland, his congress kingdom (so called because the Congress of Vienna had created it), which in 1815 was one of Europe's most liberal states. The tsar reigned in Poland as a limited monarch, having bestowed a constitution that provided for an elected parliament, a national army, and guarantees of free speech and a free press. But by 1818, Alexander had begun retracting his concessions. Polish students and military officers responded by forming secret nationalist societies to plot for change by illegal means. The government then cracked down, arresting student leaders and dismissing professors who promoted reforms. By the 1820s, Polish nationalists and the Russian imperial government were on a collision course.

Romanticism

More of an artistic movement than a true ideology, **romanticism** glorified nature, emotion, genius, and imagination. It proclaimed these as antidotes to the Enlightenment and to classicism in the arts, challenging the reliance on reason, symmetry, and cool geometric spaces. Classicism idealized models

Lord Byron
George Gordon, Lord Byron (1788–1824), lived a short, tumultuous life, wrote enduring romantic poetry, loved both women and young men, and died a heroic death fighting for Greek independence. In the midst of the Napoleonic wars, he left Britain in 1809 for a two-year trip through Spain and Portugal, Greece, Turkey, and Turkish-controlled Albania. He visited the Turkish rulers in Greece and Albania and collected souvenir costumes, such as that worn in this portrait by Thomas Philips (1813). As a result of this trip, he became passionately involved in things Greek; when the Greek rebellion broke out, he promptly joined the British Committee that gathered aid for the Greeks. He died of a fever in Greece, where he had gone to distribute funds. How would viewers have reacted to the costume Byron is wearing? *National Portrait Gallery, London.*

◆**Burschenschaften:** bur shen shaaf ten
◆**xenophobic:** zeh nuh FOH bihk
◆**Kotzebue:** KAHT suh boo

Wordsworth's Poetry

The son of a lawyer, William Wordsworth (1770–1850) studied at Cambridge University and then traveled to France during the early years of the French Revolution. He returned to England and began publishing the poetry that for many scholars marks the beginning of romanticism with its emphasis on the sublime beauties of nature. This excerpt from "Lines Composed a Few Miles above Tintern Abbey" (1798) shows the influence of his extensive walking tours through the English countryside. But the passage also captures the melancholy and nostalgia that characterized much of Romantic poetry.

And now, with gleams of half-extinguished
   thought,
With many recognitions dim and faint,
And somewhat of a sad perplexity,
The picture of the mind revives again:
While here I stand, not only with the sense
Of present pleasure, but with pleasing
   thoughts
That in this moment there is life and food
For future years. And so I dare to hope,
Though changed, no doubt, from what I was
   when first

I came among these hills; when like a roe
I bounded o'er the mountains, by the sides
Of the deep rivers, and the lonely streams,
Wherever nature led: more like a man
Flying from something that he dreads, than
   one
Who sought the thing he loved. For nature
   then
(The coarser pleasures of my boyish days,
And their glad animal movements all gone by)
To me was all in all.—I cannot paint
What then I was. The sounding cataract
Haunted me like a passion: the tall rock,
The mountain, and the deep and gloomy
   wood,
Their colours and their forms, were then to
   me
An appetite; a feeling and a love,
That had no need of a remoter charm,
By thought supplied, nor any interest
Unborrowed from the eye.—That time is past.

Source: Paul Davis, ed., *Bedford Anthology of World Literature*. Book 5: *The Nineteenth Century, 1800–1900* (Boston: Bedford/St. Martin's, 2003), 246–47.

from Roman history; romanticism turned to folklore and medieval legends. Classicism celebrated orderly, crisp lines; romantics sought out all that was wild, fevered, and disorderly. Chief among the arts of romanticism were poetry, music, and painting, which captured the deep-seated emotion characteristic of romantic expression. Romantics might take any political position, but they exerted the most political influence when they expressed nationalist feelings.

Romantic Poetry. Romantic poetry celebrated overwhelming emotion and creative imagination. George Gordon, Lord Byron (1788–1824), explained his aims in writing poetry:

*For what is Poesy but to create
From overfeeling, Good and Ill, and aim
At an external life beyond our fate,
And be the new Prometheus of new man.*

Prometheus was the mythological figure who brought fire from the Greek gods to human beings. Byron did not seek the new Prometheus among the men of industry; he sought him within his own "overfeeling," his own intense emotions. Byron became a romantic hero himself when he rushed off to act on his emotions by fighting and dying in the Greek war for independence from the Turks. An English aristocrat, Byron nonetheless claimed, "I have simplified my politics into a detestation of all existing governments."

Romantic poetry elevated the wonders of nature almost to the supernatural. In a poem that became one of the most beloved exemplars of romanticism, "Tintern Abbey" (1798), the English poet William Wordsworth (1770–1850) compared himself to a deer even while making nature seem filled with human emotions (see "Wordsworth's Poetry", opposite page). Like many poets of his time, Wordsworth greeted the French Revolution with joy; in his poem "French Revolution" (1809), he remembered his early enthusiasm: "Bliss was it in that dawn to be alive." But gradually he became disenchanted with the revolutionary experiment and celebrated British nationalism instead; in 1816, he published a poem to commemorate the "intrepid sons of Albion [England]" who died at the battle of Waterloo.

Their emphasis on authentic self-expression at times drew romantics to exotic, mystical, or even reckless experiences. Such transports drove one leading German poet to the madhouse and another to suicide. Some romantics depicted the artist as possessed by demons and obsessed with hallucinations. This more nightmarish side was captured, and perhaps criticized, by Mary Shelley in *Frankenstein*. The aged German poet Johann Wolfgang von Goethe (1749–1832) likewise denounced the extremes of romanticism, calling it "everything that is sick." In his epic poem *Faust* (1832), he seemed to warn of the same dangers Shelley portrayed in her novel. In Goethe's retelling of a sixteenth-century legend, Faust offers his soul to the devil in return for a chance to taste all human experience—from passionate love to the heights of power—in his effort to reshape nature for humanity's benefit. Faust's striving, like Frankenstein's, leaves a wake of suffering and destruction. Goethe did not make the target of his warn-

ing explicit, but the French revolutionary legacy and industrialization both seemed to be releasing Faustian energies that could turn destructive.

Romantic Painting and Music. Romanticism in painting often expressed anxiety about the coming industrial order while idealizing nature. These concerns came together in an emphasis on natural landscape. The German romantic painter Caspar David Friedrich (1774–1840) depicted scenes—often in the mountains, far from any factory—that captured the romantic fascination with the sublime power of nature (see page 818). His melancholy individual figures looked lost in the vastness of an overpowering nature. Friedrich hated the new modern world and considered industrialization a disaster. His landscapes often had religious meaning as well, as in his controversial painting *The Cross in the Mountains* (1808), which showed a Christian cross standing alone in a

William Blake, *The Circle of the Lustful* (1824)
An English romantic poet, painter, engraver, and printmaker, Blake always sought his own way. Self-taught, he began writing poetry at age twelve and apprenticed to an engraver at fourteen. His works incorporate many otherworldly attributes; they are quite literally visionary—imagining other worlds. In this engraving of hell, the figures twist and turn and are caught up in a kind of spiritual ether. Can you find elements in this engraving that reflect a criticism of Enlightenment ideals? *Blake, "The Circle of the Lustful"/ Birmingham Museums and Art Gallery.*

Caspar David Friedrich,
***Wanderer above the Sea of Fog* (1818)**
Friedrich, a German romantic painter, captured many of the themes most dear to romanticism: melancholy, isolation, and individual communion with nature. He painted trees reaching for the sky and mountains stretching into the distance. Nature to him seemed awesome, powerful, and overshadowing of human perspectives. The French sculptor David d'Angers said of Friedrich, "Here is a man who has discovered the tragedy of landscape." *Hamburg Kunsthalle, Hamburg/Bridgeman Art Library.*

mountain scene. It symbolized the steadfastness of faith but seemed to separate religion from the churches and attach it to mystical experience.

Many other artists developed similar themes. The English painter Joseph M. W. Turner (1775–1851) depicted his vision of nature in mysterious, misty seascapes, anticipating later artists by blurring the outlines of objects. The French painter Eugène Delacroix◆

◆**Delacroix:** deh luh KWAH

(1798–1863) chose contemporary as well as medieval scenes of great turbulence to emphasize light and color and break away from what he saw as "the servile copies repeated *ad nauseum* in academies of art." Critics denounced the new techniques as "painting with a drunken broom." To broaden his experience of light and color, Delacroix traveled in the 1830s to North Africa and painted many exotic scenes in Morocco and Algeria.

The towering presence of the German composer Ludwig van Beethoven (1770–1827) in early nineteenth-century music helped establish the direction for musical romanticism. His music, according to one leading German romantic, "sets in motion the lever of fear, of awe, of horror, of suffering, and awakens just that infinite longing which is the essence of Romanticism." Beethoven transformed the symphony into a connected work with recurring and evolving musical themes. Romantic symphonies conveyed the impression of growth, a metaphor for the organic process with an emphasis on the natural that was dear to the romantics. For example, Beethoven's Sixth Symphony, the *Pastoral* (1808), used a variety of instruments to represent sounds heard in the country. Beethoven's work showed remarkable diversity ranging from religious works to symphonies, sonatas, and concertos. Some of his work was explicitly political; his Ninth Symphony (1824) employed a chorus to sing the German poet Friedrich Schiller's verses in praise of universal human solidarity.

Romantic Nationalism.   If romantics had any common political thread, it was the support of nationalist aspirations, especially through the search for the historical origins of national identity. In the German states, the Austrian Empire, Russia and other Slavic lands, and Scandinavia, romantic poets and writers collected old legends and folktales that expressed a shared cultural and linguistic heritage stretching back to the Middle Ages. These collections showed that Germany, for example, had always existed even if it did not currently take the form of a single unified state. Romantic nationalism permeated *The Betrothed* (1825–1827), a novel by Alessandro Manzoni (1785–

1873) that constituted a kind of bible for Italian nationalists.

The career of Sir Walter Scott (1771–1832) incorporates many of the strands of romanticism. He translated Goethe and published Scottish ballads that he heard as a child. After achieving immediate success with his poetry, he switched to historical novels, but he also wrote a nine-volume life of Napoleon and edited historical memoirs. His novels are almost all renditions of historical events, from *Rob Roy* (1817), with its account of Scottish resistance to the English in the early eighteenth century, to *Ivanhoe* (1819), with its tales of medieval England. The influence of Scott's historical novels was immense. One contemporary critic claimed that *Ivanhoe* was more historically true than any scholarly work: "There is more history in the novels of Walter Scott than in half of the historians."

Review: In what ways did ideologies reflect the economic and social changes of the early nineteenth century?

❖ Political Challenges to the Conservative Order

In many places, discontent with the conservative Vienna settlement threatened to rise over its banks as liberals, nationalists, and socialists expressed their exasperation. The revolutionary legacy kept coming to the surface to challenge Europe's rulers. Isolated revolts threatened the hold of some conservative governments in the 1820s, but most of them were quickly bottled up. Then in 1830, successive uprisings briefly overwhelmed the established order. Across Europe, angry protesters sought constitutional guarantees of individual liberties and national unity and autonomy.

Political Revolts in the 1820s

The restoration of regimes after Napoleon's fall disappointed those who dreamed of constitutional freedoms and national independence. Revolts broke out in the 1820s in Spain and Italy, Russia, Greece (Map 21.3),

MAP 21.3 Revolutionary Movements of the 1820s

The revolts of the 1820s took place on the periphery of Europe, in Spain, Italy, Greece, Russia, and in the Spanish and Portuguese colonies of Latin America. Rebels in Spain and Russia wanted constitutional reforms. Although the Italian revolts failed, as did the uprisings in Spain and Russia, the Greek and Latin American independence movements succeeded.

Greek Independence

From 1836 to 1839 the Greek painter Panagiotis Zographos worked with his two sons on a series of scenes from the Greek struggle for independence from the Turks. Response was so favorable that one Greek general ordered lithographic reproductions for popular distribution. Nationalistic feeling could be thus encouraged even among those who were not directly touched by the struggle. Here Turkish sultan Mehmet the Conqueror, exulting over the fall of Constantinople in 1453, views a row of Greeks under the yoke, a sign of submission. *Collection, Visual Connection.*

and across the Atlantic in the Spanish and Portuguese colonies of Latin America. Most revolts failed, but those in Greece and Latin America succeeded, largely because they did not threaten the conservative order in Europe.

Uprisings in Spain and Italy. When Ferdinand VII regained the Spanish crown in 1814, he quickly restored the prerevolutionary nobility, church, and monarchy. He had foreign books and newspapers confiscated at the frontier and allowed the publication of only two newspapers. Not surprisingly, such repressive policies disturbed the middle class, especially the army officers who had encountered French ideas. Many responded by joining secret societies. In 1820, disgruntled soldiers demanded that Ferdinand proclaim his adherence to the Constitution of 1812,

which he had abolished in 1814. When the revolt spread, Ferdinand convened the *cortes*◆ (parliament), which could agree on virtually nothing. Ferdinand bided his time, and in 1823 a French army invaded and restored him to absolute power. The French acted with the consent of the other great powers, who had met to discuss the Spanish situation and agree on a course of action. The restored Spanish government tortured and executed hundreds of rebels; thousands were imprisoned or forced into exile.

Hearing of the Spanish uprising, rebellious soldiers in the kingdom of Naples joined forces with the carbonari and demanded a constitution. When a new parliament met, it too broke down over internal disagreements. The promise of reform sparked rebellion in

◆*cortes*: KAWR tays

the northern Italian kingdom of Piedmont-Sardinia, where rebels urged Charles Albert, the young heir to the Piedmont throne, to fight the Austrians for Italian unification. He vacillated; but in 1821, after the rulers of Austria, Prussia, and Russia met and agreed on intervention, the Austrians defeated the rebels in Naples and Piedmont. Liberals were arrested in many Italian states, and the pope condemned the secret societies as "at heart only devouring wolves." Despite the opposition of Great Britain, which condemned the indiscriminate suppression of revolutionary movements, Metternich convinced the other powers to agree to his muffling of the Italian opposition to Austrian rule.

The Decembrist Revolt in Russia.

Aspirations for constitutional government surfaced in Russia when Alexander I died suddenly in 1825. On the December day that the troops assembled in St. Petersburg to take an oath of loyalty to Alexander's brother Nicholas as the new tsar, rebel officers insisted that the crown belonged to another brother, Constantine, whom they hoped would be more favorable to constitutional reform. Constantine, though next in the line of succession after Alexander, had refused the crown. The soldiers nonetheless raised the cry "Long live Constantine, long live the Constitution." (Some troops apparently thought that "the Constitution" was Constantine's wife.) Soldiers loyal to Nicholas easily suppressed the Decembrists (so called after the month of their uprising), who were so outnumbered that they had no realistic chance to succeed. The subsequent trial, however, made the rebels into legendary heroes. Of their imprisonment at hard labor, the Russian poet Alexander Pushkin (1799–1837) wrote:

> The heavy-hanging chains will fall,
> The walls will crumble at a word,
> And Freedom greet you in the light,
> And brothers give you back the sword.

Pushkin would not live to see this freedom. For the next thirty years, Nicholas I (r. 1825–1855) used a new political police, the Third Section, to spy on potential opponents and stamp out rebelliousness.

Greek Independence from the Turks.

The Ottoman Turks faced growing nationalist challenges in the Balkans, but the European powers feared that supporting such opposition would encourage a rebellious spirit at home. The Serbs revolted against Turkish rule and won virtual independence by 1817. A Greek general in the Russian army, Prince Alexander Ypsilanti,◆ tried to lead a revolt against the Turks in 1820 but failed when the tsar, urged on by Metternich, disavowed him. Metternich feared rebellion even by Christians against their Turkish rulers. A second revolt, this time by Greek peasants, sparked a wave of atrocities in 1821 and 1822. The Greeks killed every Turk who did not escape; in retaliation the Turks hanged the Greek patriarch of Constantinople, and in the areas they still controlled they pillaged churches, massacred thousands of men, and sold the women into slavery.

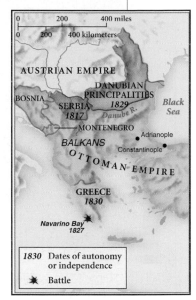

Nationalistic Movements in the Balkans, 1815–1830

Western opinion turned against the Turks; Greece, after all, was the home of Western civilization. While the great powers negotiated, Greeks and pro-Greece committees around the world sent food and military supplies; like the English poet Byron, a few enthusiastic European and American volunteers joined the Greeks. The Greeks held on until the great powers were willing to intervene. In 1827, a combined force of British, French, and Russian ships destroyed the Turkish fleet at Navarino Bay; and in 1828, Russia declared war on Turkey and advanced close to Istanbul. The Treaty of Adrianople of 1829 gave Russia a protectorate over the Danubian principalities in the Balkans and provided for a conference among representatives of Britain, Russia, and France, all of whom had broken with Austria in support of the Greeks. In 1830,

◆**Ypsilanti:** ihp suh LAN tee

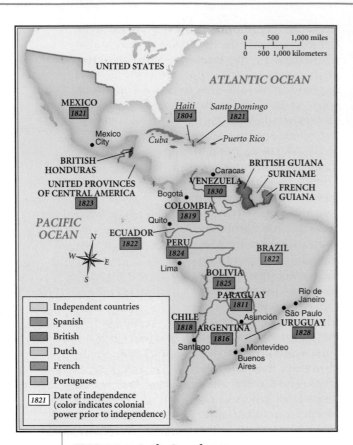

MAP 21.4 Latin American Independence, 1804–1830

Napoleon's occupation of Spain and Portugal seriously weakened those countries' hold on their Latin American colonies. Despite the restoration of the Spanish and Portuguese rulers in 1814, most of their colonies successfully broke away in a wave of rebellions between 1811 and 1830.

Simon Bolívar

Known as "the Liberator," Simon Bolívar (1783–1830) is shown in this chalk lithograph near the end of his life. He is the figure on the white horse in the front. Bolívar led the armies that gained independence from Spain in Venezuela, Colombia, Ecuador, Peru, and Bolivia. He had dreamed of creating a United States of Latin America but died of tuberculosis as factional fighting kept the various states separate from each other. *AKG-Images, London.*

Greece was declared an independent kingdom under the guarantee of the three powers; in 1833, the son of King Ludwig of Bavaria became Otto I of Greece. Nationalism, with the support of European public opinion, had made its first breach in Metternich's system.

Wars of Independence in Latin America.
Across the Atlantic, national revolts also succeeded after a series of bloody wars of independence. Taking advantage of the upheavals in Spain and Portugal that began under Napoleon, restive colonists from Mexico to Argentina rebelled. Their leader was Simon

Bolívar, son of a slave owner, who was educated in Europe on the works of Voltaire and Rousseau. Although Bolívar fancied himself a Latin American Napoleon, he had to acquiesce to the formation of a series of independent republics between 1821 and 1823, even in Bolivia, which is named after him. At the same time, Brazil (then still a monarchy) separated from Portugal (Map 21.4). The United States recognized the new states, and in 1823 President James Monroe announced his Monroe Doctrine, closing the Americas to European intervention—a prohibition that depended on British naval power and British willingness to declare neutrality. Great Britain dominated the Latin American economies, which had suffered great losses during the wars for independence.

Revolution and Reform, 1830–1832

In 1830 a new wave of liberal and nationalist revolts broke against the bulwark of conservatism. The revolts of the 1820s served as warning shots, but the earlier uprisings had been largely confined to the peripheries of Europe. Now revolution once again threatened the established order in western Europe.

The French Revolution of 1830. Louis XVIII's younger brother and successor, Charles X (r. 1824–1830), brought about his own downfall by steering the monarchy in an increasingly repressive direction. In 1825, a Law of Indemnity compensated nobles who had emigrated during the Revolution for the loss of their estates, and a Law of Sacrilege in the same year imposed the death penalty for such offenses as stealing religious objects from churches. Charles enraged liberals when he dissolved the legislature, removed many wealthy and powerful voters from the rolls, and imposed strict censorship. Spontaneous demonstrations in Paris led to fighting on July 26, 1830. After three days of street battles in which 500 citizens and 150 soldiers died, a group of moderate liberal leaders, fearing the reestablishment of a republic, agreed to give the crown to Charles X's cousin Louis-Philippe, duke of Orléans.

Charles X went into exile in England, and the new king extended political liberties and voting rights. Although the number of voting men nearly doubled, it remained minuscule—approximately 170,000 in a country of 30 million, between 5 and 6 percent. Such reforms did little for the poor and working classes, who had manned the barricades in July. Dissatisfaction with the 1830 settlement boiled over in Lyon in 1831, when a silk-workers' strike over wages turned into a rebellion that died down only when the army arrived. Revolution had broken the hold of those who wanted to restore the pre-1789 monarchy and nobility, but it had gone no further this time than installing a more liberal, constitutional monarchy.

Belgian Independence from the Dutch. The success of the July Revolution in Paris ignited the Belgians, whose country had been annexed to the kingdom of the Netherlands in 1815. Differences in traditions, language, and religion separated the largely Catholic Belgians from the Dutch. An opera about a seventeenth-century insurrection in Naples provided the spark, and students in Brussels rioted, shouting "Down with the Dutch."

The riot turned into revolt. King William of the Netherlands appealed to the great powers to intervene; after all, the Congress of Vienna had established his kingdom. But Great Britain and France opposed intervention and invited Russia, Austria, and Prussia to a conference that guaranteed Belgium independence in exchange for its neutrality in international affairs. Belgian neutrality would remain a cornerstone of European diplomacy for a century. After much maneuvering, the crown of the new kingdom of Belgium was offered to a German prince, Leopold of Saxe-Coburg, in 1831. Belgium, like France and Britain, now had a constitutional monarchy.

Revolts in Italy and Poland. The Russian tsar and the Austrian emperor would have supported intervention in Belgium had they not been preoccupied with their own revolts. Anti-Austrian uprisings erupted in a handful of Italian states, but they fizzled without the hoped-for French aid. The Polish revolt was more serious. Once again, in response to news of revolution in France, students raised the banner of rebellion, this time in Warsaw in November 1830. Polish aristocrats soon formed a provisional government. Despite some victories on the battlefield, the provisional government got no support from Britain or France and was defeated. In reprisal, Nicholas abolished the Polish constitution that Alexander had granted and ordered thousands of Poles executed or banished.

The British Reform Bill of 1832. The British had long been preoccupied with two subjects: the royal family and elections for control of Parliament. In 1820, the domestic quarrels between the new king George IV (r. 1820–1830) and his German wife, Caroline, seemed to threaten the future of the monarchy.

MAPPING THE WEST Europe in 1830

By 1830, the fragilities of the Congress of Vienna settlement had become apparent. Rebellion in Poland failed, but Belgium won its independence from the kingdom of the Netherlands, and a French revolution chased out the Bourbon ruler and installed Louis-Philippe, who promised constitutional reform. Most European rulers held on to their positions in this period of ferment, but they had to accommodate the new demands created by industrialization, desires for constitutional guarantees of rights, and growing nationalist sentiment.

When George IV came to the throne, he tried to divorce Caroline, and he refused to have her crowned queen. He hoped to use rumors of her love affairs on the continent to win his case, but the divorce trial provoked massive demonstrations in support of Caroline. Women's groups gathered thousands of signatures on petitions supporting her, and popular songs and satires portrayed George as a fat, drunken libertine. Caroline's death a few months after George's coronation ended the Queen Caroline Affair. The monarchy survived but with a tarnished reputation.

The 1820s had brought into British government new men who were open to change. Sir Robert Peel (1788–1850), the secretary for home affairs, revised the criminal code to reduce the number of crimes punishable by death and introduced a municipal police force in London, called the Bobbies after him. In 1824, the laws prohibiting labor unions were repealed, and though restrictions on strikes remained, workers could now organize themselves legally to confront their employers collectively. In 1828, the appointment of the duke of Wellington, the hero of Waterloo, as prime minister kept the Tories in power, and his government pushed through a bill in 1829 allowing Catholics to sit in Parliament and hold most public offices.

When in 1830, and again in 1831, the Whigs in Parliament proposed an extension of the right to vote, Tory diehards, principally in the House of Lords, dug in their heels and predicted that even the most modest proposals would doom civilization itself. Even though the proposed law would not grant universal male suffrage, mass demonstrations in favor of it took place in many cities. One supporter of reform described the scene: "Meetings of almost every description of persons were held in cities, towns, and parishes; by journeymen tradesmen in their clubs, and by common workmen who had no trade clubs or associations of any kind." In this "state of diseased and feverish excitement" (according to its opponents), the Reform Bill of 1832 passed, after the king threatened to create enough new peers to obtain its passage in the House of Lords.

Although the Reform Bill altered Britain's political structure in significant ways, the gains were not revolutionary. One of the bill's foremost backers, historian and member of Parliament Thomas Macaulay, explained, "I am opposed to Universal Suffrage, because I think that it would produce a destructive revolution. I support this plan, because I am sure that it is our best security against a revolution." Although the number of male voters increased by about 50 percent, only one in five Britons could now vote, and voting still depended on holding property. Nevertheless, the bill gave representation to new cities in the industrial north for the first time and set a precedent for further widening suffrage. Exclusive aristocratic politics now gave way to a mixed middle-class and aristocratic structure that would prove more responsive to the problems of a fast-growing industrial society. Those disappointed with the outcome would organize with renewed vigor in the 1830s and 1840s.

Review: Why were Austria and Russia able to thwart independence movements in Italy and Poland but not in Greece, Belgium, and Latin America?

Conclusion

The agitations and uprisings of the 1820s and early 1830s showed that the revolutionary legacy still smoldered and might erupt into flames again at any moment. Napoleon Bonaparte had kept the legacy alive by insisting on fundamental reforms wherever his armies triumphed. His imperial rule galvanized supporters and opponents alike; no one could be indifferent to his impact on European and even world affairs. The powers who eventually defeated him tried to maintain the European peace by shoring up monarchical governments and damping down aspirations for constitutional freedoms and national autonomy. They sometimes fell short. Belgium separated from the Netherlands, Greece achieved independence from the Turks, Latin American countries shook off the rule of Spain and Portugal, and the French installed a more liberal monarchy than the one envisioned by the Congress of Vienna. Yet Metternich's vision of a conservative Europe still held, and most efforts at revolt failed.

In her novel *Frankenstein*, Mary Shelley had captured some of the deepest worries of the age; human creativity might have an unpredictably destructive side in spite of every good intention. Although she did not intend her novel as a brief in support of political conservatism—she hated what Metternich stood for—she did tap into European fears about the changes taking place. The French and Industrial Revolutions promised to transform European life, for better or worse. Napoleon Bonaparte had built upon the French revolutionary legacy to reform institutions in France and elsewhere, but he also attempted to colonize much of Europe. New ideologies such as conservatism, liberalism, and socialism all took off from an analysis of the revolutionary legacy, some opposing it, others supporting parts of it. The machines of industrialization seemed to some Europeans just as horrible as Frankenstein's monster; others welcomed them as promising a brighter future. In the years to come industrialization would proceed even faster, and revolution would return to shatter the order so carefully nurtured by Metternich and his colleagues.

Suggested References

Napoleon's Authoritarian State

Much has been written about Napoleon as a military leader, but only recently has his regime within France attracted interest. Historians now emphasize the mixed quality of Napoleon's rule. He carried forward some revolutionary innovations and halted others.

*Arnold, Eric A., Jr., ed. *A Documentary Survey of Napoleonic France.* 1994.

Ellis, Geoffrey James. *Napoleon.* 1996.

Kafker, Frank A., and James M. Laux. *Napoleon and His Times: Selected Interpretations.* 1989.

Napoleon Foundation: **http://www.napoleon.org**.

Wilson-Smith, Timothy. *Napoleon and His Artists.* 1996.

Woloch, Isser. *Napoleon and His Collaborators: The Making of a Dictatorship.* 2001.

"Europe Was at My Feet": Napoleon's Conquests

Recent work shows how powerfully Napoleon's armies affected every European state. Whether annexed, allied, or simply defeated, every nation had to come to terms with this dynamo of activity.

*Brunn, Geoffrey. *Napoleon and His Empire.* 1972.

Connelly, Owen. *Napoleon's Satellite Kingdoms.* 1965.

Forrest, Alan. *Napoleon's Men: The Soldiers of the Revolution and Empire.* 2002.

Simms, Brendan. *The Impact of Napoleon: Prussian High Politics, Foreign Policy, and the Crisis of the Executive, 1797–1806.* 1997.

The "Restoration" of Europe

Diplomatic historians have shown how events in this period shaped European affairs for decades. Domestic politics have been relatively understudied, and as a consequence, Artz's book is still a good introduction.

Artz, Frederick B. *Reaction and Revolution, 1814–1832.* 1934.

---

*Primary source.

Johnson, Paul. *The Birth of the Modern: World Society, 1815–1830.* 1991.

Schroeder, Paul W. *The Transformation of European Politics, 1763–1848.* 1994.

Seward, Desmond. *Metternich: The First European.* 1991.

Forces for Social and Cultural Change

The new ideologies have been the subject of a steady stream of excellent work, ranging from individual figures such as Fourier to the antislavery movement and the origins of working-class activism. The Web site Romantic Chronology provides access to a wealth of information about every aspect of romanticism.

Beecher, Jonathan. *Charles Fourier: The Visionary and His World.* 1986.

Berlin, Sir Isaiah. *The Roots of Romanticism.* 1999.

Davis, David Brion. *The Problem of Slavery in the Age of Revolution, 1770–1823.* 1975.

*Leader, Zachary, and Ian Haywood, eds. *Romantic Period Writings, 1798–1832: An Anthology.* 1998.

Romantic Chronology: **http://english.ucsb.edu:591/rchrono**.

Thompson, E. P. *The Making of the English Working Class.* 1964.

Political Challenges to the Conservative Order

In general, the early nineteenth century is an understudied period of European history. Unsuccessful revolts attract less attention than successful ones, but even the Greek, Latin American, and Belgian independence movements need to be better integrated into European history.

Colley, Linda. *Britons: Forging the Nation, 1707–1837.* 1992.

Di Scala, Spencer. *Italy: From Revolution to Republic, 1700 to the Present.* 2nd ed. 1998.

Gallant, Thomas W. *Experiencing Dominion: Culture, Identity, and Power in the British Mediterranean.* 2002.

Spitzer, Alan B. *The French Generation of 1820.* 1987.

CHAPTER REVIEW

IMPORTANT EVENTS

1799 Coup against Directory government in France; Napoleon Bonaparte named First Consul

1801 Napoleon signs a concordat with the pope

1804 Napoleon crowned as emperor of France; issues new Civil Code

1805 British naval forces defeat the French at the battle of Trafalgar; Napoleon wins his greatest victory at the battle of Austerlitz

1812 Napoleon invades Russia

1814–1815 Congress of Vienna

1815 Napoleon defeated at Waterloo and exiled to island of St. Helena, where he dies in 1821

1818 Mary Shelley, *Frankenstein*

1820 Robert Owen, *The Book of the New Moral World*; revolt of liberal army officers against the Spanish crown; the Karlsbad Decrees abolish German student societies and tighten press censorship

1824 Ludwig van Beethoven, Ninth Symphony

1825 Russian army officers demand constitutional reform in the Decembrist Revolt

1830 The Manchester and Liverpool Railway opens in England; Greece gains its independence from Ottoman Turks; rebels overthrow Charles X of France and install Louis-Philippe

1832 English Parliament passes Reform Bill; Johann Wolfgang von Goethe, *Faust*

KEY TERMS

Civil Code (792)

conservatism (808)

consuls (789)

Continental System (801)

ideology (812)

liberalism (812)

nationalism (814)

restoration (808)

romanticism (815)

socialism (813)

working class (811)

REVIEW QUESTIONS

1. In what ways did Napoleon continue the French Revolution; in what ways did he break with it?

2. Why was Napoleon able to gain control over so much of Europe's territory?

3. To what extent was the old order restored by the Congress of Vienna?

4. In what ways did ideologies reflect the economic and social changes of the early nineteenth century?

5. Why were Austria and Russia able to thwart independence movements in Italy and Poland but not in Greece, Belgium, and Latin America?

MAKING CONNECTIONS

1. What was the long-term significance of Napoleon for Europe?

2. In what ways did Metternich succeed in holding back the tide of forces for change? In what ways did he fail? And which of those forces for change made the most difference?

FOR FURTHER EXPLORATION

To assess your mastery of the material in this chapter, see the Online Study Guide at **bedfordstmartins.com/hunt**.

To read additional primary-source material from this period, see Chapter 21 in *Sources of The Making of the West, Second Edition*.

CHAPTER 22

Industrialization, Urbanization, and Revolution,
1830–1850

IN 1830–1832 AND AGAIN in 1847–1851, devastating outbreaks of **cholera** swept across Asia and Europe, touching the United States as well in 1849–1850. Today we know that a waterborne bacterium causes cholera, but at the time no one understood the disease and everyone feared it. The usually fatal illness induced violent vomiting and diarrhea and left the skin blue, eyes sunken and dull, and hands and feet ice cold. While cholera particularly ravaged the crowded, filthy neighborhoods of rapidly growing cities, it also claimed many rural and some well-to-do victims. In Paris, 18,000 people died in the 1832 epidemic and 20,000 in that of 1849; in London, 7,000 died in each epidemic; and in Russia, the epidemic was catastrophic, claiming 250,000 victims in 1831–1832 and 1 million in 1847–1851.

Rapid industrial and urban growth in the early to mid-nineteenth century created unprecedented social problems as peasants and workers streamed into the cities. The population of London grew by 130,000 people in the 1830s alone. Berlin more than doubled between 1819 and 1849, and Paris expanded by 120,000 just between 1841 and 1846. Disease, overcrowding, prostitution, crime, and drinking all seemed to be on the increase. The lithograph, on the facing page, is one of countless that artists produced to capture the swirl of social change. A mass-produced print from inked stone, the **lithograph** played a key role in social commentary and political

---

The Threat of Cholera
In this lithograph from 1831 by the British artist Robert Seymour, Cholera appears as a kind of monster that tramples everyone in its path. Lithography (from the Greek *lithos*, "stone") was invented by a German engraver in 1798, but, like the steam engine perfected in 1776, its use spread across Europe only in the nineteenth century. In lithography, an artist uses a greasy crayon to trace an image on a flat stone; the grease attracts the ink while the blank areas repel it. The inked stone is embedded in a printing press that can produce thousands of identical images. Designed for a mass audience, nineteenth-century lithographs helped ordinary people make sense of the changes taking place around them. *Courtesy of the National Library of Medicine, Bethesda / Visual Image Presentations.*

discussion in this period. By publishing their work in daily and weekly newspapers, artists enlightened a mass audience about the social and political problems created by the startling industrial and urban growth of the 1830s and 1840s. The French artist Honoré Daumier,◆ for example, published no fewer than four thousand prints and caricatures criticizing the social inequalities exacerbated by economic development.

The shock of industrial and urban growth generated an outpouring of commentary on the need for social reforms. Painters, poets, and especially novelists joined in the chorus warning about rising tensions. Many who wrote on social issues expected middle-class women to organize their homes as a domestic haven from the heartless process of upheaval. Yet despite the emphasis on domesticity, middle-class women participated in public issues too: they set up reform societies that fought prostitution and helped poor mothers, and they agitated for temperance (abstention from alcohol) and joined the campaigns to abolish slavery. Middle-class men and women frequently denounced the lower classes' appetites for drink, tobacco, and cockfighting, but they remained largely silent when British traders received government support in forcing the Chinese to accept imports of **opium**, an addictive drug derived from the heads of poppy plants.

Social and economic changes kept the ideological pots boiling. Nationalists, liberals, socialists, and communists offered compet-

◆**Honoré Daumier:** aw naw RAY dohm YAY

ing visions of the new social order: they all agreed that change was necessary, but they disagreed about both the means and the ends of change. Their contest came to a head in 1848 when the rapid transformation of European society provided the combustible material for a new set of revolutionary outbreaks, more consuming than any since 1789. As in 1789, food shortages and constitutional crises fueled the rebellion, but now class tensions and nationalist impulses sparked outbreaks in capitals across Europe, not only in Paris. Some revolutionaries, such as Karl Marx, the theorist of communism, saw this as the beginning of a new age of class warfare. Because of internal quarrels and conflicts, however, the revolutionaries of 1848 eventually went down to defeat.

❖ The Advance of Industrialization and Urbanization

Industrialization and urbanization transformed Europe and eventually most of the world in the nineteenth and twentieth centuries. Because they are not single events but rather long-term processes that continue to the present, it is impossible to give them precise beginning and ending dates. Nevertheless, historians have shown that both processes accelerated quite suddenly in the first half of the nineteenth century and that their effects touched off loud complaints. Great Britain

◆ **1830–1832** Cholera epidemic

◆ **1830** France invades Algeria

◆ **1831** British and Foreign Temperance Society established

◆ **1832** George Sand, *Indiana*

◆ **1839** Opium War begins; invention of photography

◆ **1841** Dickens, *The Old Curiosity Shop*

1830	1835	1840

◆ **1833** British Factory Act; abolition of slavery

◆ **1834** *Zollverein* established

◆ **1835** Belgium opens first continental railway

led the way in both industrialization and urbanization, but contemporaries did not fully understand their linkage; even today, scholars debate the connection between industrial and urban growth. Rulers quickly saw the advantages in industrialization, and in the 1830s and 1840s many of them encouraged railroad construction and the mechanization of manufacturing. States exercised little control over the consequences of industrial and urban growth, and many officials, preachers, and intellectuals worried that unchecked growth would destroy traditional social relationships and create disorder. Some held out the constancy of rural life as an antidote to the ravages of industrialization and urbanization, but population growth produced new tensions in the countryside too.

Engines of Change

Great Britain had led the way in the development of factories and railroads since the late eighteenth century. In the 1830s and 1840s, industrialization spread to continental Europe, first to Belgium, northern France, and northern Italy and then eastward to Prussia, Austria, and eventually Russia. Although the new industries employed only a small percentage of workers, the working class that took shape in them immediately attracted the attention of social commentators and government officials.

Railroads and Steam. In the 1840s alone, railroad track mileage more than doubled in Great Britain, and British investment in railways jumped tenfold. The British also began to build railroads in India. Canal building waned in the 1840s: the railroad had won out. Britain's success with rail transportation led other countries to develop their own projects. Railroads grew spectacularly in the United States in the 1830s and 1840s. Belgium, newly independent in 1830, opened the first continental European railroad with state bonds backed by British capital in 1835. By 1850, France had 2,000 miles of railroad and the German states nearly twice as many; Great Britain had 6,000 miles and the United States 9,000 miles. In all, the world had 23,500 miles of track by midcentury.

Railroad building spurred both industrial development and state power (Map 22.1). Governments everywhere participated in the construction of railroads, which depended on private and state funds to pay for the massive amounts of iron, coal, heavy machinery, and human labor required to build and run them. Demand for iron products accelerated industrial development. Until the 1840s, cotton had led industrial production; between 1816 and 1840, cotton output more than quadrupled in Great Britain. But from 1830 to 1850, Britain's output of iron and coal doubled (Table 22.1). Similarly, Austrian output of iron doubled between the 1820s and the 1840s. One-third of all investment in the German states in the 1840s went into railroads.

Steam-powered engines made Britain the world leader in manufacturing. By midcentury, more than half of Britain's national income came from manufacturing and trade. The number of steamboats in Great Britain

◆ **1846** Famine in Ireland; Corn Laws repealed; insurrection in Galicia

◆ **1847** Brontë, *Jane Eyre*

◆ **1851** Crystal Palace exhibition

| 1845 | 1850 | 1855 | 1860 |

◆ **1848** Last Chartist demonstrations; Marx and Engels, *Communist Manifesto*; revolutions throughout Europe; French abolish slavery in remaining colonies; end of serfdom in Austrian Empire

The Limits of Charity

In this lithograph from 1844, Daumier shows a middle-class philanthropist refusing to give aid to a poor mother and her children. The caption below explains his refusal: "I'm sorry, my good woman, I cannot do anything for you. I am a member of the Society of Philanthropists of the Nord [a region in northern France] . . . I only give to the poor of Kamchatka!" (That is, the faraway poor rather than those at home.) Daumier spared no one in his satires, even King Louis-Philippe himself. In the early 1830s, the artist's political cartoons landed him in prison with a six-month sentence. His work always took the side of the lowly and downcast and made most fun of the high and mighty in society. His massive output of caricatures typifies an era of preoccupation with the consequences of rapid social change. *Robert D. Farber University Archives and Special Collections Department, Brandeis University Libraries. Donated by Benjamin A. and Julia M. Trustman, 1959. Forms part of the Trustman Daumier Collection.*

increased from two in 1812 to six hundred in 1840. Between 1840 and 1850, steam-engine power doubled in Great Britain and increased even more rapidly elsewhere in Europe, as those adopting British inventions strove to catch up. The power applied in German manufacturing, for example, rose from 60,000 to 360,000 hp (units horsepower) during the 1840s but still amounted to only a little more

than a quarter of the British figure. German coal and iron outputs were only 6 or 7 percent of the British outputs.

Industrialization Moves Eastward. Industrialization spread slowly east from key areas in Prussia (near Berlin), in Saxony, and in Bohemia. The Austrian Empire, with industrialization centered in Bohemia, produced more cotton cloth than either Prussia or Saxony. Cotton production in the Austrian Empire tripled between 1831 and 1845. By 1847, coal production, also concentrated in Bohemia, had increased fourfold in just over twenty years.

The advance of industrialization in eastern Europe was slow, in large part because serfdom still survived there, hindering labor mobility and tying up investment capital: as long as peasants were legally tied to the land as serfs, they could not migrate to the new factory towns, and landlords felt little incentive to invest their income in manufacturing. The problem was worst in Russia, where industrialization had hardly begun and would not take off until the end of the nineteenth century. Nevertheless, even in Russia signs of industrialization could be detected: raw cotton imports (a sign of a growing textile industry) increased sevenfold between 1831 and 1848, and the number of factories doubled along with the size of the industrial workforce.

Although Great Britain consciously strove to protect its industrial supremacy, thousands of British engineers defied laws against the export of machinery or the emigration of artisans. Only slowly, thanks to the pirating of British methods and to new technical schools, did most continental countries begin closing the gap. Belgium became the fastest-growing industrial power on the continent: between 1830 and 1844, the number of steam engines in Belgium quadrupled, and Belgians exported seven times as many steam engines as they imported. Even so, by 1850, continental Europe still lagged almost twenty years behind Great Britain in industrial development.

The Formation of the Working Class. Despite striking industrial growth, factory workers remained a minority everywhere. In the 1840s, factories in England employed only 5 percent of the workers; in France, 3 percent; in Prussia, 2 percent. Many peasants kept

MAP 22.1 Industrialization in Europe, c. 1850

Industrialization first spread in a band across northern Europe that included Great Britain, northern France, Belgium, the northern German states, the region around Milan in northern Italy, and Bohemia. Much of Scandinavia and southern and eastern Europe were left out of this first phase of industrial development. Although railroads were not the only factor in promoting industrialization, the map makes clear the interrelationship between railroad building and the development of new industrial sites of coal mining and textile production.

their options open by combining factory work with agricultural labor. From Switzerland to Russia, people worked in agriculture during the spring and summer and in manufacturing in the fall and winter. Unstable industrial wages made such arrangements essential. Some new industries idled periodically; for example, iron forges stopped for several months

when the water level in streams dropped, and blast furnaces shut down for repairs several weeks every year. In hard times, factory owners simply closed their doors until demand for their goods improved.

In addition, workers continued to toil at home in putting-out, or cottage, industries. In the 1840s, for example, two-thirds of the

TABLE 22.1 Coal Output, 1830–1850

Like the numbers for railroad mileage, these figures for coal production show the economic dominance of Great Britain throughout the period 1830–1850. As long as coal remained the essential fuel of industrialization, Britain enjoyed a clear advantage. Although it produced more coal than any other European country, rates of increase in the production of coal were comparable or even higher in other countries, showing that some countries were starting to catch up with Britain.

	Austria	Belgium	France	German States (including Prussia)	Great Britain
1830	214	*	1,863	1,800	22,800
1835	251	2,639	2,506	2,100	28,100
1840	473	3,930	3,003	3,200	34,200
1845	689	4,919	4,202	4,400	46,600
1850	877	5,821	4,434	5,100	50,200

Output of coal (in thousands of metric tons).

*Data not available.

Source: B. R. Mitchell, *European Historical Statistics, 1750–1970* (New York: Columbia University Press, 1975), D2.

manufacturing workers in Prussia and Saxony labored at home for contractors or merchants who supplied raw materials and then sold the finished goods. Women worked in the putting-out system as much as or even more than men—they plaited straw and embroidered cloth in Hungary, made pots in Denmark, fashioned lace in Great Britain and France, and spun cotton almost everywhere.

Some of the old forms of putting-out work changed during this period, even when factories did not supplant cottage industries. Tailoring, for example, which had been the province of male artisans preparing entire garments in small shops, was now farmed out to women working at home for much lower "piece rates." Even though factories employed only a small percentage of the population, they attracted much attention. Factories produced wealth without regard to the pollution they caused or the exhausted state of their workers; industry created unheard-of riches and new forms of poverty all at once. "From this foul drain the greatest stream of human industry flows out to fertilize the whole world," wrote the French aristocrat Alexis de Tocqueville after visiting the new English industrial city of Manchester in the 1830s. "From this filthy sewer pure gold flows. Here humanity attains its most complete development and its most brutish, here civilization works its miracles and civilized man is turned almost into a savage." Studies by physicians set the life expectancy of workers in Manchester at just seventeen years (partly because of high rates of infant mortality), whereas the average life expectancy in England was forty years in 1840. (See "New Sources, New Perspectives," page 836.) One American visitor in Britain in the late 1840s described how "in the manufacturing town, the fine soot or *blacks* darken the day, give white sheep the color of black sheep, discolor the human saliva, contaminate the air, poison many plants, and corrode monuments and buildings." In some parts of Europe, city leaders banned factories, hoping to insulate their towns from the effects of industrial growth.

As factory production expanded, local and national governments collected information about the workers. Investigators detailed their pitiful condition. A French physician in the eastern town of Mulhouse described the "pale, emaciated women who walk barefooted through the dirt" to reach the factory. The young children who worked in the factory appeared "clothed in rags which are greasy with the oil from the looms and frames." A report to the city government in Lille, France, in 1832 described "dark cellars" where the cotton workers lived: "the air is never renewed, it is infected; the walls are plastered with garbage." In the Prussian town of Breslau (population 111,000 in

1850), a doctor reported that in working-class districts "several persons live in one room in a single bed, or perhaps a whole family, and use the room for all domestic duties. . . . Their diet consists largely of bread and potatoes. These are clearly the two main reasons for the scrofula [a disease related to tuberculosis] which is so widespread here; the diet is also the cause of the common malformation of limbs."

Government inquiries often focused on women and children. In Great Britain, the Factory Act of 1833 outlawed the employment of children under the age of nine in textile mills (except in the lace and silk industries) and limited the workdays of children ages nine to thirteen to nine hours a day and those ages thirteen to eighteen to twelve hours. Adults worked even longer hours. When investigating commissions showed that women and young children, sometimes under age six, were hauling coal trucks through low, cramped passageways in coal mines, the British Parliament passed a Mines Act in 1842 prohibiting the employment of women and girls underground. One nine-year-old girl, Margaret Gomley, had described her typical day in the mines as beginning at 7:00 A.M. and ending at 6:00 P.M.: "I get my dinner at 12 o'clock, which is a dry muffin, and sometimes butter on, but have no time allowed to stop to eat it, I eat it while I am thrusting the load. . . . They flog us down in the pit, sometimes with their hand upon my bottom, which hurts me very much." In 1847, the Central Short Time Committee, one of Britain's many social reform organizations, successfully pressured Parliament to limit the workday of women and children to ten hours. The continental countries followed the British lead, but since most did not insist on government inspection, enforcement was lax.

Urbanization and Its Consequences

Industrial development spurred urban growth wherever factories were located in or near cities, yet cities grew even with little industry. Here, too, Great Britain led the way: half the population of England and Wales lived in towns by 1850, while in France and the German states the urban population was only about a quarter of the total. Both old and new cities teemed with growing population in the 1830s and 1840s; the population of Vienna grew by 125,000 between 1827 and 1847, and the new industrial city Manchester grew by 70,000 just in the 1830s. (See "Taking Measure," page 838.)

Massive rural emigration, rather than births to women already living in cities, accounted for this remarkable increase. Agricultural improvements had increased the food supply and hence the rural population, but the land could no longer support the people living on it. City life and new factories beckoned those faced with hunger and poverty, including emigrants from other lands: thousands of Irish emigrated to English cities, Italians went to French cities, and Poles flocked to German cities. Settlements sprang up outside the old city limits but gradually became part of the urban area. As cities grew, their medieval walls came down. At the same time, cities incorporated parks, cemeteries, zoos, and greenways, all imitations of the countryside, which itself was being industrialized by railroads and factories. "One can't even go to one's land for the slightest bit of gardening," grumbled a French citizen, annoyed by new industrial potteries in town, "without being covered with a black powder that spoils every plant that it touches."

Overcrowding and Disease. The rapid influx of people caused serious overcrowding in the cities because the housing stock expanded much more slowly than population growth. In Paris, 30,000 workers lived in lodging houses, eight or nine to a room, with no separation of the sexes. One contemporary observed: "The difficulty of finding lodgings is for the worker a constant ordeal and a perpetual cause of misery." In 1847 in St. Giles, the Irish quarter of London, 461 people lived in just twelve houses. Men, women, and children huddled together on piles of filthy rotting straw or potato peels because they had no money for fuel to keep warm.

Severe crowding worsened already dire sanitation conditions. Residents dumped refuse into streets or courtyards, and human excrement collected in cesspools under apartment houses. At midcentury, London's approximately 250,000 cesspools were emptied only once or twice a year. Water was scarce

NEW SOURCES, NEW PERSPECTIVES

Statistics and the Standard of Living of the Working Class

From the very beginning of industrialization, experts argued about whether industrialization improved or worsened the standard of living of the working class. For every claim, there was a counterclaim, and most often these claims came in the form of statistics. Some experts argued that factories offered higher-paying jobs to workers; others countered that factories took work away from artisans such as handloom weavers and left them on the verge of starvation. Supporters of industrialization maintained that factories gave women paying work; opponents insisted that factories destroyed the family by taking women away from the home. Through mass production, industrialization made goods cheaper and therefore more available; by polluting the air, it destroyed health, lowered life expectancy, and ruined the environment. Karl Marx and Friedrich Engels would give the debate even more of an edge by tying it to the ideology of communism. In 1844, Engels described to Marx his aim in writing *The Condition of the Working Class in England:* "I shall present the English with a fine bill of indictment. At the bar of world opinion I charge the English middle classes with mass murder, wholesale robbery and all the other crimes in the calendar."* The stakes of the argument were not small.

The controversy about the benefits and costs of industrialization has continued in different forms right down to the present, in part because

---

*Quoted in R. M. Hartwell et al., *The Long Debate on Poverty* (Surrey, England: Institute of Economic Affairs, 1972), 185.

it is an argument directly inspired by the ideologies—liberalism, socialism, communism—that emerged as explanations of and blueprints for economic and social change. In the 1830s and 1840s, liberals insisted that industrialization would promote greater prosperity for everyone, whereas conservatives complained that it destroyed traditional ways of life and socialists warned that it exaggerated inequality and class division. In the 1950s and 1960s, defenders of capitalist free enterprise still advanced the argument about prosperity, but now they were opposed by communists who argued that state control of production could sidestep the horrors of early capitalist exploitation. Newly developing countries looked to the history of the 1830s and 1840s for lessons about the likely impact of industrialization on their countries in the 1950s and beyond. The scholarly debates therefore attracted worldwide attention, and all sides called on statistics to make their competing cases.

Unfortunately, the statistics can be interpreted in many different ways. Did it matter more that wages for factory workers went up or that life expectancy went down? If an increase in sugar consumption in Great Britain from 207,000 tons in 1844 to 290,000 tons in 1847 meant an overall increase in the standard of living, how does that square with the hundreds of thousands of deaths in Ireland at the same time or the increasing disparity throughout Great Britain between rich and poor? Some convergence of opinion has taken place, however. Most now agree that by sometime between 1820 and 1845 (the exact date depending on the scholar), conditions

and had to be fetched daily from nearby fountains. Despite the diversion of water from provincial rivers to Paris and a tripling of the number of public fountains, Parisians had enough water for only two baths annually per person (the upper classes enjoyed more baths, of course; the lower classes, fewer). In London, private companies that supplied water turned on pumps in the poorer sections for only a few hours three days a week. In rapidly growing British industrial cities such as Manchester, one-third in Great Britain had become better than before the Industrial Revolution. And there is no doubt that the debate itself has had one major positive effect: since making one's point depends on having statistics to prove it, the debate itself has encouraged a staggering amount of research into quantitative measures of just about everything imaginable, from measures of wages and prices to rates of mortality and even average heights (height being correlated, it is thought, to economic well-being). British soldiers in the nineteenth century were taller on average than those in any other country except the United States, and people who believe that industrialization improved the standard of living are happy to seize on this as evidence for their case.

Trends in the British Nominal-Wage Gap, 1797–1851

Year	Index	Year	Index
1797	100	1827	132.4
1805	86.6	1835	134.7
1810	96.7	1851	148.3
1815	105.1		

The gap is calculated as the difference between the weighted average of nonfarm unskilled earnings (common laborers, porters, police, guards, watchmen, coal miners, and so on) and the farm-earnings rate, divided by the farm-earnings rate. Thus, it is the percentage differential by which nonfarm unskilled wages exceeded farm wages.

Source: Jeffrey G. Williamson, "Leaving the Farm to Go to the City: Did They Leave Quickly Enough?" in John A. James and Mark Thomas, *Capitalism in Context: Essays on Economic Development and Cultural Change in Honor of R. M. Hartwell* (Chicago: University of Chicago Press, 1994), 159–83; table on page 182.

One example of a recently developed statistic shows both how powerful and how debatable such sources can be. This table, adapted from a re-

cent study by Jeffrey G. Williamson, provides a simple measure—based on complex calculations—of the gap in wages between British farm and nonfarm laborers for the period 1797 to 1851. The index measures the attractiveness of nonfarm (basically city, mining, and factory) work. It shows that nonfarm wages rose faster than farm wages, but only after 1820 or so. By 1851, nonfarm wages had far outstripped those on the farm. What can we conclude? Although these data seem to support the view that the standard of living of workers improved sometime in the 1820s and continued to do so afterward, Williamson does not conclude that factory workers were better off than farmers; instead, he argues that the gap indicates that farm people did not migrate quickly enough to the city to satisfy urban labor demands. In short, he seems to consider the gap between farm and nonfarm wages to be a problem of "labor-market disequilibrium." The lesson to be learned is that all historians' conclusions depend on the questions they ask and the sources they use—and few other sources are as open to different interpretations as statistics.

QUESTIONS TO CONSIDER

1. What is a good measure of the standard of living in the first half of the nineteenth century? How would you measure the standard of living today?
2. How do you explain the initial decline in nonfarm wages relative to farm wages and the subsequent rise?
3. What are the virtues of using statistical measures to determine the standard of living? What are the defects?

FURTHER READING

Morgan, Kenneth. *The Birth of Industrial Britain: Economic Change 1750–1850*. 1999.

Thompson, Noel W. *The Real Rights of Man: Political Economies for the Working Class, 1775–1850*. 1998.

of the houses contained no latrines. Human waste ended up in the rivers that supplied drinking water. The horses that provided transportation inside the cities left droppings everywhere, and city dwellers often kept chickens, ducks, goats, pigs, geese, and even

cattle, as well as dogs and cats, in their houses. The result was a "universal atmosphere of filth and stink."

Such conditions made cities prime breeding grounds for disease; those with 50,000 people or more had twice the death rates of

TAKING MEASURE

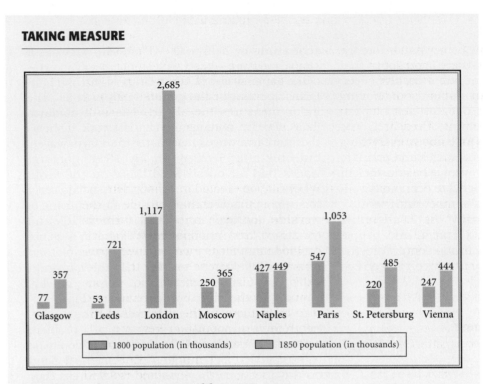

Population of Major European Cities, 1800–1850
Although London was by far the biggest city in mid-nineteenth-century Europe, it was not the fastest growing. According to these figures for population in 1800 and 1850, which city was the fastest growing? To what extent was population growth in these cities due to industrialization? What problems might have been created by especially rapid growth? *From B. R. Mitchell,* European Historical Statistics, 1750–1970 *(New York: Columbia University Press, 1975), B4.*

In Great Britain, the reports on sanitation conditions among the working class led to the passage of new public health laws.

Middle-Class Fears. Government intervention did little to ease the social tensions inspired by rapid urban growth. The middle and upper classes lived in large, well-appointed apartments or houses with more light, more air, and more water than in lower-class dwellings. But the lower classes lived nearby, sometimes in the cramped upper floors of the same apartment houses. Middle-class reformers often considered the poor to be morally degenerate because of the circumstances of urban life. In their view, overcrowding led to sexual promiscuity and illegitimacy. They depicted the lower classes

rural areas. Rumors and panic followed in the wakes of epidemics such as cholera (Map 22.2). Everywhere the downtrodden imagined conspiracies: in Paris in April 1832, a crowd of workers attacked a central hospital, believing the doctors were poisoning the poor but using cholera as a hoax to cover up the conspiracy. Eastern European peasants burned estates and killed physicians and officials. Although devastating, cholera did not kill as many people as tuberculosis, Europe's number-one deadly disease. But tuberculosis took its victims one by one and therefore had less impact on social relations.

Raging epidemics spurred a growing concern for public health. When news of the cholera outbreak in eastern Europe reached Paris in 1831, the city set up commissions in each municipal district to collect information about lower-class housing and sanitation.

as dangerously lacking in sexual self-control. A physician visiting Lille, France, in 1835 wrote of "individuals of both sexes and of very different ages lying together, most of them without nightshirts and repulsively dirty. . . . The reader will complete the picture. . . . His imagination must not recoil before any of the disgusting mysteries performed on these impure beds, in the midst of obscurity and drunkenness."

Officials collected statistics on illegitimacy that seemed to bear out these fears: one-quarter to one-half of the babies born in the big European cities in the 1830s and 1840s were illegitimate, and alarmed medical men wrote about thousands of infanticides. Between 1815 and the mid-1830s in France, 33,000 babies were abandoned at foundling hospitals every year; 27 percent of births in Paris in 1850 were illegitimate, compared with only 4 percent of rural births.

By collecting such statistics, physicians and administrators in the new public health movement hoped to promote legislation to better the living conditions for workers, but at the same time they helped stereotype workers as helpless and out of control.

Sexual disorder seemed to go hand in hand with drinking and crime. Beer halls and pubs dotted the urban landscape. By the 1830s, Hungary's twin cities of Buda and Pest had eight hundred beer and wine houses for the working classes. One London street boasted twenty-three pubs in three hundred yards. Police officials estimated that London had 70,000 thieves and 80,000 prostitutes. In many cities, nearly half the urban population lived at the level of bare subsistence, and increasing numbers depended on public welfare, charity, or criminality to make ends meet.

Everywhere reformers warned of a widening separation between rich and poor and a growing sense of hostility between the classes. The French poet Amédée Pommier wrote of "These leagues of laborers who have no work,/These far too many arms, these starving mobs." Clergy joined the chorus of physicians and humanitarians in making dire predictions. A Swiss pastor noted: "A new spirit has arisen among the workers. Their hearts seethe with hatred of the well-to-do; their eyes lust for a share of the wealth about them; their mouths speak unblushingly of a coming day of retribution." In 1848 it would seem that that day of retribution had arrived.

Agricultural Perils and Prosperity

Rising population created increased demand for food and spurred changes in life in the countryside too. Peasants and farmers planted fallow land, chopped down forests, and drained marshes to increase their farming capacity. Still, Europe's ability to feed its expanding population remained questionable: although agricultural yields increased by 30 to 50 percent in the first half of the nineteenth century, population grew by nearly 100 percent. Railroads and canals improved food distribution, but much of Europe—particularly in the east—remained isolated from markets and vulnerable to famines.

Most people still lived on the land, and the upper classes still dominated rural society. Successful businessmen bought land avidly, seeing it not only as the ticket to respectability but also as a hedge against hard times. Hardworking, crafty, or lucky commoners sometimes saved enough to purchase holdings that they had formerly rented or slowly acquired slivers of land from less fortunate neighbors. In France at midcentury, almost two million economically independent peasants tended their own small properties. But in England, southern Italy, Prussia, and eastern Europe, large landowners, usually noblemen, consolidated and expanded their estates by buying up the land of less successful nobles or peasants. As agricultural prices rose, the big landowners pushed for legislation to allow them to continue converting common land to private property.

Wringing a living from the soil under such conditions put pressure on traditional family life. For example, men often migrated seasonally to earn cash in factories or as village artisans, while their wives, sisters, and daughters did the traditional "men's work" of tending crops. The threat of subdivision of the land encouraged rudimentary forms of birth control.

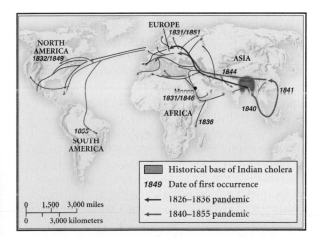

MAP 22.2 The Spread of Cholera, 1826–1855
Contemporaries did not understand the causes of the cholera epidemics in the 1830s and the 1840s in Europe. Western Europeans knew only that the disease marched progressively from east to west across Europe. Nothing seemed able to stop it. It appeared and died out for reasons that could not be grasped at the time. Nevertheless, the cholera epidemics prompted authorities in most European countries to set up public health agencies to coordinate the response and study sanitation conditions in the cities.

In France, for instance, Napoleon's Civil Code provided for an equal distribution of inheritance among all heirs; as a result, land was divided over generations into such small parcels that less than 25 percent of all French landowners could support themselves. In the past, population growth had been contained by postponing marriage (leaving fewer years for childbearing) and by high rates of death in childbirth and infant mortality. Now, as child mortality declined outside the industrial cities and people without property began marrying earlier, Europeans became more aware of birth control methods. Contraceptive techniques improved; for example, the vulcanization of rubber in the 1840s improved the reliability of condoms. When such methods failed and population increase left no options open at home, people emigrated, often to the United States. Some 800,000 Germans had moved out of central Europe by 1850, while in the 1840s famine drove tens of thousands of Irish abroad. Between 1816 and 1850, five million Europeans left their home countries for new lives overseas. When France colonized Algeria in the 1830s and 1840s, officials tried to attract settlers by emphasizing the fertility of the land; they offered the prospect of agricultural prosperity in the colony as an alternative to the rigors of industrialization and urbanization at home.

Despite all the challenges to established ways of life, rural political power remained in the hands of traditional elites. The biggest property owners dominated their tenants and sharecroppers, often demanding a greater yield without contributing to improvements that would enhance productivity. They also controlled the political assemblies and often personally selected the parish clergy and local officials. Such power not surprisingly provoked resentment. One Italian critic wrote, "Great landowner is often the synonym for great ignoramus." Nowhere did the old rural social order seem more impregnable than in Russia. Most Russian serfs remained tied to the land, and troops easily suppressed serfs' uprisings in 1831 and 1842. By midcentury, peasant emancipation remained Russia's great unresolved problem.

Review: Why were cities seen as dangerous places?

❖ Reforming the Social Order

In the 1830s and 1840s, Europeans organized to reform the social evils created by industrialization and urbanization. They acted in response to the outpouring of government reports, medical accounts, and literary and artistic depiction of new social problems. Middle-class women often took the lead in establishing new charitable organizations that tried to bring religious faith, educational uplift, and the reform of manners to the lower classes. Middle-class men and middle-class women too, expected women to soften the rigors of a rapidly changing society, but this expectation led to some confusion about women's proper role: should they devote themselves to social reform in the world or to their own domestic spaces? Many hoped to apply the same zeal for reform to the colonial peoples living in places administered by Europeans.

Cultural Responses to the Social Question

The **social question**, an expression reflecting the widely shared concern about social changes arising from industrialization and urbanization, pervaded all forms of art and literature. The dominant artistic movement of the time, romanticism, generally took a dim view of industrialization. The English-born painter Thomas Cole (1801–1848) complained in 1836: "In this age . . . a meager utilitarianism seems ready to absorb every feeling and sentiment, and what is sometimes called improvement in its march makes us fear that the bright and tender flowers of the imagination shall all be crushed beneath its iron tramp." When Cole went to the United States to paint, he depicted "primeval forests, virgin lakes and waterfalls"—that is, a landscape untouched by machinery. Yet culture itself underwent important changes as the growing capitals of Europe attracted flocks of aspiring painters and playwrights; the 1830s and 1840s witnessed an explosion in culture as the number of would-be artists increased dramatically and new technologies such as photography and lithography brought art to the masses. Many of these new intellectuals would support the revolutions of 1848.

A Romantic Poet Mourns the Fate of the Workers

When a revolt by weavers of the Prussian province of Silesia was put down by Prussian troops in June 1844, Heinrich Heine (1797–1856) wrote a poem to lament the fate of the workers. The son of a German-Jewish cloth merchant, Heine in 1831 joined the growing group of European exiles in Paris, where he lived the rest of his life. There he met Karl Marx, who published this poem, "The Silesian Weavers" (1844), in one of the reviews he edited. Heine shows little enthusiasm for German nationalism as a solution.

In gloomy eyes there wells no tear.
Grinding their teeth, they are sitting here:
Germany, your shroud's on our loom;
And in it we weave the threefold doom.
    We're weaving; we're weaving. . . .

Doomed be the king, the rich man's king,
Who would not be moved by our suffering,
Who tore the last coin out of our hands,
And let us be shot by his bloodthirsty bands—
    We're weaving; we're weaving.
Doomed be the fatherland, false name,
Where nothing thrives but disgrace and shame,
Where flowers are crushed before they unfold,
Where the worm is quickened by rot and mold—
    We're weaving; we're weaving.

Source: Frederic Ewen, ed., *The Poetry and Prose of Heinrich Heine* (New York: Citadel, 1948), 244. Translation by Aaron Kramer.

Romantic Concerns about Industrial Life. Because romanticism tended to glorify nature and reject industrial and urban growth, romantics often gave vivid expression to the problems created by rapid economic and social transformation. The English poet Elizabeth Barrett Browning, best known for her love poems, denounced child labor in "The Cry of the Children" (1843). When weavers in the Prussian province of Silesia revolted against their employers in 1844, the German poet Heinrich Heine mourned their fate in verses written from his exile in Paris (see poem above).

Architects of the period sometimes sought to recapture a preindustrial world. When the British Houses of Parliament were rebuilt after they burned down in 1834, the architect Sir Charles Barry constructed them in a Gothic style reminiscent of the Middle Ages. This medievalism was taken even further by A. W. N. Pugin,♦ who prepared the Gothic details for the Houses of Parliament. In his polemical book *Contrasts* (1836), Pugin denounced modern conditions and compared them unfavorably with those in the 1400s. To underline his view, Pugin wore medieval clothes at home.

Romantic painters specialized in landscape as a way of calling attention to the sublime wonders of nature, but sometimes even landscapes showed the power of new technologies. In *Rain, Steam, and Speed: The Great Western Railway* (1844), the leading English romantic painter, Joseph M. W. Turner (1775–1851), portrayed the struggle between the forces of nature and the means of economic growth. Turner was fascinated by steamboats: in *The Fighting "Téméraire"♦ Tugged to Her Last Berth to Be Broken Up* (1838; see the illustration on the next page), he featured the victory of steam power over more conventional sailing ships. An admirer described it as an "almost prophetic idea of smoke, soot, iron, and steam, coming to the front in all naval matters."

The Depiction of Social Conditions in Novels. The novel was the art form best suited to presenting social problems. Thanks to increased literacy, the spread of reading

♦**Pugin:** PYOO juhn

♦*Téméraire:* tch mch rair

Joseph M. W. Turner, *The Fighting "Téméraire"*
***Tugged to Her Last Berth to Be Broken Up* (1838)**
In this painting a steamer belching smoke tows a wooden sailing ship to its last berth, where it will be destroyed. Turner muses about the passing of old ways but also displays his mastery of color in the final blaze of sunset, itself another sign of the passing of time. Turner considered painting to be closely related to poetry; he was an avid reader of the romantic poets, especially Byron. How does the painting capture the clash of old and new? **For more help in analyzing this image**, see the visual activity for this chapter in the Online Study Guide at **bedfordstmartins.com/hunt**. *National Gallery, London.*

rooms and lending libraries, and serialization in newspapers and journals, novels reached a large reading public. Unlike the fiction of the eighteenth century, which had focused on individual personalities, the great novels of the 1830s and 1840s specialized in the portrayal of social life in all its varieties. Manufacturers, financiers, starving students, workers, bureaucrats, prostitutes, underworld figures, thieves, and aristocratic men and women filled the pages of works by popular writers. Pushing himself to exhaustion and a premature death to get out of debt, the French writer Honoré de Balzac (1799–1850) cranked out ninety-five novels and many short stories. He aimed to catalog the social types that could be found in French society. Many

of his characters, like himself, were driven by the desire to climb higher in the social order.

The English author Charles Dickens (1812–1870) worked with a similar frenetic energy and for much the same reasons. When his father was imprisoned for debt in 1824, the young Dickens took a job in a shoe-polish factory. In 1836, he published a series of literary sketches of daily life in London to accompany a volume of caricatures by the artist George Cruikshank. Dickens then produced a series of novels that appeared in monthly installments and attracted thousands of readers. In them, he paid close attention to the distressing effects of industrialization and urbanization. In *The Old Curiosity Shop* (1841), for example, he depicts the Black Country, the manufacturing region west and northwest of Birmingham, as a "cheerless region," a "mournful place," in which tall chimneys "made foul the melancholy air." In addition to publishing such enduring favorites as *Oliver Twist* (1838) and *A Christmas Carol* (1843), he ran charitable organizations and pressed for social reforms. For Charles Dickens, the ability to portray the problems of the poor went hand in hand with a personal commitment to reform.

Novels by women often revealed the bleaker side of women's situations. *Jane Eyre* (1847), a novel by Charlotte Brontë, describes the difficult life of an orphaned girl who becomes a governess, the only occupation open to most single middle-class women. Although in an economically weak position, Jane Eyre refuses to achieve respectability and security through marriage, the usual option for women. The French novelist George Sand (Amandine-Aurore Dupin, 1804–1876) took her social criticism a step further. She announced her independence in the 1830s by dressing like a man and smoking cigars. Like many other women writers of the time, she published her work under a male pseudonym while creating female characters who prevail in difficult circumstances through romantic love and moral idealism. Sand's novel *Indiana* (1832), about an unhappily married woman, was read all over Europe. Her notoriety—she became the lover of the Polish pianist Frédéric Chopin, among others, and threw herself into socialist politics—made the term *George Sandism* a common expression of disdain for independent women.

The Explosion of Culture. As artists became more interested in society and social relations, ordinary citizens crowded cultural

George Sand

In this lithograph by Alcide Lorentz of 1842, George Sand is shown in one of her notorious male costumes. Sand published numerous works, including novels, plays, essays, travel writing, and an autobiography. She actively participated in the revolution of 1848 in France, writing pamphlets in support of the new republic. Disillusioned by the rise to power of Louis-Napoleon Bonaparte, she withdrew to her country estate and devoted herself exclusively to her writing. *The Granger Collection.*

events. Museums opened to the public across Europe, and the middle classes began collecting art. Popular theaters in big cities drew thousands from the lower and middle classes every night; in London, for example, some 24,000 people attended eighty "penny theaters" nightly. The audience for print culture also multiplied. In the German states, for example, the production of new literary works doubled between 1830 and 1843, as did the number of periodicals and newspapers and the number of booksellers. Thirty or forty private lending libraries offered books in Berlin in the 1830s, and reading rooms in pastry shops stocked political newspapers and satirical journals. Young children and ragpickers sold cheap prints and books door to door or in taverns.

The advent of photography in 1839 provided an amazing new medium for artists. The **daguerreotype**,⬥ named after its inventor, French painter Jacques Daguerre (1787–1851), prompted one artist to claim that "from today, painting is dead." Although this prediction was highly exaggerated, photography did open up new ways of portraying reality. Visual images, whether in painting, on the stage, or in photography, heightened the public's awareness of the effects of industrialization and urbanization.

⬥**daguerreotype:** duh GEH roh type

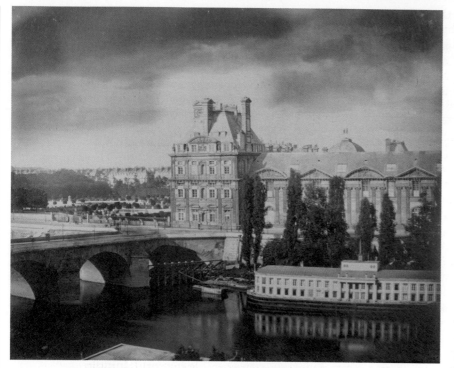

Daguerreotype of Paris
Daguerre experimented extensively with producing an image on a metal plate before he came up with a viable photographic process in 1837. In 1839, the French government bought the rights and made the process freely available. This picture of the Louvre and the Tuileries garden in Paris (c. 1850) seems almost empty of people because with the long exposure required to capture the image, moving objects did not register. The image is also reversed (as if seen in a mirror). Because of these technical problems, the early photographic process proved most suitable for portraits. *Bridgeman Art Library/ Archives Charmet.*

The number of artists and writers swelled. Estimates suggest that the number of painters and sculptors in France, the undisputed center of European art at the time, grew sixfold between 1789 and 1838. Not everyone could succeed in this hothouse atmosphere, in which writers and artists furiously competed for public attention. Their own troubles made some of them more keenly aware of the hardships faced by the poor. In one of many bitingly critical journals and booklets published in Berlin appeared the following "Lies Chronicle": "In Ipswich in England a mechanical genius has invented a stomach, whose extraordinary efficient construction is remarkable. This artificial stomach is intended for factory workers there and is adjusted so that it is fully satisfied with three lentils or peas; one potato is enough for an entire week."

The Varieties of Social Reform

Lithographs, novels, even joke booklets helped drive home the need for social reform, but religious conviction also inspired efforts to help the poor. Moral reform societies, Bible groups, Sunday schools, and temperance groups all aimed to turn the poor into respectable people. In 1844, for example, 450 different relief organizations operated in London alone. States supported these efforts by encouraging education and enforcing laws against the vagrant poor.

The Religious Impulse for Social Reform.   Religiously motivated reformers first had to overcome the perceived indifference of the working classes. Protestant and Catholic clergy complained that workers had no interest in religion; less than 10 percent of the workers in the cities attended religious services. In a report on the state of religion in England and Wales in 1851, the head of the census Horace Mann commented that "the masses of our working population . . . are *unconscious secularists*. . . . These are never, or but seldom seen in our religious congregations." To combat such indifference, British religious groups launched the Sunday school movement, which reached its zenith in the 1840s. By 1851, more than half of all working-class children ages five to fifteen were attending Sunday school, even though very few of their parents regularly went to religious services. The Sunday schools taught children how to read at a time when few working-class children could go to school during the week.

Women took a more prominent role than ever before in charitable work. Catholic religious orders, which by 1850 enrolled many more women than men, ran schools, hospitals, leper colonies, insane asylums, and old-age homes. New Catholic orders, especially for women, were established, and Catholic missionary activity overseas increased. Protestant women in Great Britain and the United States established Bible, missionary, and female reform societies by the hundreds. Chief among their concerns was prostitution, and many societies dedicated themselves to reforming "fallen women" and castigating men who visited prostitutes. As a pamphlet of the Boston Female Moral Reform Society explained, "Our mothers, our sisters, our daughters are sacrificed by the thousands every year on the altar of sin, and who are the agents in this work of destruction: Why, our fathers, our brothers, and our sons." Elizabeth Fry, an English Quaker minister, toured Europe in the 1830s helping set up institutions for female prisoners modeled on the school and manufacturing shop she had organized at Newgate Prison in London.

Catholics and Protestants alike promoted the **temperance movement**. In Ireland, England, the German states, and the United States, temperance societies organized to fight the "pestilence of hard liquor." The first societies had appeared in the United States as early as 1813, and by 1835 the American Temperance Society claimed 1.5 million members. The London-based British and Foreign Temperance Society, established in 1831, matched its American counterpart in its opposition to all alcohol. In the northern German states, temperance societies drew in the middle and working classes, Catholic as well as Protestant. Temperance advocates saw drunkenness as a sign of moral weakness and a threat to social order. Industrialists pointed to the loss of worker productivity, and efforts to promote temperance often reflected middle- and upper-class fears of the lower classes' lack of discipline. One German temperance advocate insisted, "One need not be a prophet to know that all efforts to combat the widespread and rapidly spreading pauperism will be unsuccessful as long as the common man fails to realize that the principal source of his degradation and misery is his fondness of drink." Yet temperance societies also attracted working-class people who shared the desire for respectability.

Education and Reform of the Poor.   Social reformers saw education as one of the main prospects for uplifting the poor and the working class. In addition to setting up Sunday schools, British churches founded organizations such as the National Society for the Education of the Poor in the Principles of the Established Church and the British and Foreign

The Temperance Movement

This 1847 engraving by George Cruikshank was fifth in a series of eight prints that told the story of a family ruined by drink. The caption to this engraving—"Cold misery and want destroy their youngest child: they console themselves with the bottle"—makes the artist's message clear. Alcohol only made the miserable lives of the working poor even more miserable. *Bridgeman Art Library. The Stapleton Collection.*

Bearbaiting
This colored engraving from 1821 of Charley's Theater in London shows that bearbaiting did not attract only the lower classes, as reformers often implied. Top hats were most often worn by middle-class men, who seem to be enjoying the spectacle of dogs taunting the bear as much as the working-class men present. At this time, bearbaiting, like bullbaiting, began to come under fire as cruel to animals. *Mary Evans Picture Library.*

School Society. Most of these emphasized Bible reading. More secular in intent were the Mechanics Institutes, which provided education for workers in the big cities.

In 1833, the French government passed an education law that required every town to maintain a primary school, pay a teacher, and provide free education to poor boys. As the law's author, François Guizot, argued, "Ignorance renders the masses turbulent and ferocious." Girls' schools were optional, although hundreds of women taught at the primary level, most of them in private, often religious schools. Despite these efforts, only one out of every thirty children went to school in France, many fewer than in Protestant states such as Prussia, where 75 percent of children were in primary school by 1835. Popular education remained woefully undeveloped in most of eastern Europe. Peasants were specifically excluded from the few primary schools in Russia, where Tsar Nicholas I blamed the Decembrist Revolt of 1825 on education.

Above all else, the elite sought to impose discipline and order on working people. Popular sports, especially blood sports such as cockfighting and bearbaiting, suggested a lack of control, and long-standing efforts in Great Britain to eliminate these recreations now gained momentum through organizations such as the Society for the Prevention of Cruelty to Animals. By the end of the 1830s, bullbaiting had been abandoned in Great Britain. "This useful animal," rejoiced one reformer in 1839, "is no longer tortured amidst the exulting yells of those who are a disgrace to our common form and nature." The other blood sports died out more slowly, and efforts in other countries generally lagged behind those of the British.

When private charities failed to meet the needs of the poor, governments often intervened. Great Britain sought to control the costs of public welfare by passing a new poor law in 1834, called by its critics the "Starvation Act." The law required that all able-bodied persons receiving relief be housed together in workhouses, with husbands separated from wives and parents from children. Workhouse life was designed to be as unpleasant as possible so that poor people would move on to regions of higher employment. British women from all social classes organized anti–poor law societies to protest the separation of mothers from their children in the workhouses.

Domesticity and the Subordination of Women. Many women viewed charitable work as the extension of their domestic roles: they promoted virtuous behavior and morality and thus improved society. In one widely read advice book, Englishwoman Sarah Lewis suggested in 1839 that "women may be the prime agents in the regeneration of mankind." But women's social reform activities concealed a paradox. According to the set of beliefs, or ideology, that historians call **domesticity**, women should live their lives entirely within the domestic sphere; they should devote themselves to the home. The English poet Alfred, Lord Tennyson, captured this view in a popular poem published in 1847: "Man for the field and woman for the hearth;/Man for the sword and for the needle she. . . . All else confusion." Many believed that maintaining proper and distinct roles for men and women was critically important to maintaining social order in general.

Most women had little hope of economic independence. The notion of a separate, domestic sphere for women prevented them from pursuing higher education, work in professional careers, or participation in politics through voting or holding office—all activities deemed appropriate only to men. Laws everywhere codified the subordination of women. Many countries followed the model of Napoleon's Civil Code, which classified married women as legal incompetents along with children, the insane, and criminals. In Great Britain, which had no national law code, the courts upheld the legality of a husband's complete control. For example, in 1840 a court ruled that "there can be no doubt of the general dominion which the law of England attributes to the husband over the wife." In some countries, such as France and Austria, unmarried women enjoyed some rights over property, but elsewhere laws explicitly defined them as perpetual minors under paternal control.

Distinctions between men and women were most noticeable in the privileged classes. Whereas boys attended secondary schools, most middle- and upper-class girls still received their education at home or in church schools, where they were taught to be religious, obedient, and accomplished in music and languages. As men began to wear practical clothing—long trousers and short jackets of solid, often dark colors, no makeup (previously common for aristocratic men), and simply cut hair—women continued to dress for decorative effect, now with tightly corseted waists that emphasized the differences between female and male bodies. Middle- and upper-class women had long hair that required hours of brushing and pinning up, and they wore long, cumbersome skirts. Advice books written by women detailed the tasks that such women undertook in the home: maintaining household accounts, supervising servants, and organizing social events.

Scientists reinforced stereotypes. Once considered sexually insatiable, women were now described as incapacitated by menstruation and largely uninterested in sex, an attitude that many equated with moral superiority. Thus was born the "Victorian woman," a figment of the largely male medical imagination. Physicians and scholars considered women mentally inferior. In 1839, Auguste Comte, an influential early French sociologist, wrote, "As for any functions of government, the radical inaptitude of the female sex is there yet more marked . . . and limited to the guidance of the mere family."

Some women denounced the ideology of domesticity; according to the English writer Ann Lamb, for example, "the duty of a wife *means* the obedience of a Turkish slave." Middle-class women who did not marry, however, had few options for earning a living; they often worked as governesses or ladies' companions for the well-to-do. Most lower-class women worked because of financial necessity; as the wives of peasants, workers, or shopkeepers, they had to supplement the family's meager income by working on the farm, in a factory, or in a shop. For them, domesticity might have been an ideal but rarely was it a reality. Families crammed into small spaces had no time or energy for separate spheres.

Abuses and Reforms Overseas

Like the ideal of domesticity, the ideal of colonialism often conflicted with the reality of economic interests. In the first half of the nineteenth century, those economic interests changed as European colonialism underwent a subtle but momentous transformation.

Colonialism became **imperialism**—a word coined only in the mid-nineteenth century—as Europeans turned their interest away from the plantation colonies of the Caribbean toward the new colonies in Asia and Africa. Whereas colonialism most often led to the establishment of settler colonies, direct rule by Europeans, the introduction of slave labor from Africa, and the wholesale destruction of indigenous peoples, imperialism usually meant more indirect forms of economic exploitation and political rule. Europeans still profited from their colonies, but now they also aimed to reform colonial peoples in their own image—when it did not conflict too much with their economic interests to do so.

Abolition of Slavery. Colonialism—as opposed to imperialism—rose and fell with the enslavement of black Africans. The antislavery movement spread slowly but decisively following the British withdrawal from the slave trade in 1807. The new Latin American republics abolished slavery in the 1820s and 1830s after they defeated the Spanish with armies that included many slaves. British missionary and evangelical groups condemned the conquest, enslavement, and exploitation of native African populations and successfully blocked British annexations in central and southern Africa in the 1830s. British reformers finally obtained the abolition of slavery in the British Empire in 1833. Antislavery petitions to Parliament bore 1.5 million signatures, including those of 350,000 women on one petition alone. In France, the new government of Louis-Philippe took strong measures against clandestine slave traffic, virtually ending French participation during the 1830s. Slavery was abolished in the remaining French Caribbean colonies in 1848.

Slavery did not disappear immediately just because the major European powers had given it up. The transatlantic trade in slaves actually reached its peak numbers in the early 1840s. Human bondage continued unabated in Brazil, Cuba (still a Spanish colony), and the United States. Some American reformers supported abolition, but they remained a minority. Like serfdom in Russia, slavery in the Americas involved a quagmire of economic, political, and moral problems that worsened over time.

Historians debate the causes of the end of the African slave trade and of African slavery as a form of labor in the New World. Some argue that industrialization made slavery superfluous because with steam-driven machinery free labor proved itself more productive in the long run. Yet the British textile manufacturers relied heavily on imports of cotton from the southern slave states of the United States. Others place more emphasis on the antislavery campaign itself, arguing that slavery was incompatible with the humanitarian values of a reforming era. This explanation, however, does not account for the fact that the French and Dutch governments also abolished slavery even though neither faced major public reform campaigns. Whatever the reason for abolition, slavery, and with it the old-style colonialism, was on the wane.

Economic and Political Imperialism. Despite the abolition of slavery, Britain and France had not lost interest in overseas colonies. Using the pretext of an insult to its envoy, France invaded Algeria in 1830 and after a long military campaign established political control over most of the country in the next two decades. By 1850, more than seventy thousand French, Italian, and Maltese colonists had settled there, often confiscating the lands of native peoples. The new French administration of the colony made efforts to balance native and settler interests, however, and eventually France would not only incorporate Algeria into France but also try to assimilate its native population to French culture. France also imposed a protectorate government over the South Pacific island of Tahiti.

Although the British granted Canada greater self-determination in 1839, they extended their dominion elsewhere by annexing Singapore (1819), an island off the Malay peninsula, and New Zealand (1840). They also increased their control in India through the administration of the East India Company, a private group of merchants chartered by the British crown. The British educated a native elite to take over much of the day-to-day business of administering the country and used native soldiers to augment their military control. By 1850, only one in six soldiers serving Britain in India was European.

The East India Company also tried to establish a regular trade with China in opium, a drug long known for its medicinal uses but increasingly bought in China as a recreational drug. (See "Did You Know?," page 850.) The Chinese government did its best to keep the highly addictive drug away from its people, both by forbidding Western merchants to venture outside the southern city of Guangzhou◆ (Canton) and by banning the export of precious metals and the import of opium. These measures failed. By smuggling opium into China and bribing local officials, British traders built up a flourishing market, and by the mid-1830s they were pressuring the British government to force an expanded opium trade on the Chinese. When in 1839 the Chinese authorities expelled British merchants from southern China, Britain retaliated by bombarding Chinese coastal cities. The Opium War ended in 1842, when Britain dictated to a defeated China the Treaty of Nanking, by which four more Chinese ports were opened to Europeans and the British took sovereignty over the island of Hong Kong, received a substantial war indemnity, and were assured of a continuation of the opium trade. In this case, reform took a backseat to economic interest, despite the complaints of religious groups in Britain.

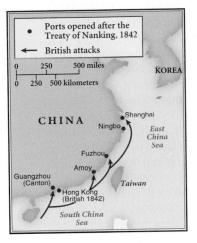

The Opium War, 1839–1842

Ports opened after the Treaty of Nanking, 1842
British attacks

0   250   500 miles
0   250   500 kilometers

KOREA

CHINA

Shanghai
Ningbo
East China Sea
Fuzhou
Amoy
Guangzhou (Canton)
Taiwan
Hong Kong (British 1842)
South China Sea

Review: How did reformers try to address the social problems created by industrialization and urbanization? In which areas did they succeed, and in which did they fail?

◆**Guangzhou:** GWAHN JOH

❖ The Ferment of Ideologies

Although reform organizations grew rapidly in the 1830s and 1840s, many Europeans found them insufficient to solve the problems created by industrialization and urbanization. They turned to movements inspired by the new political ideologies that had taken shape in the aftermath of the French Revolution. Liberals sought constitutional guarantees of rights and economic growth through free trade. Socialists developed new organizations to speak for the working classes and demand changes in the nature of work itself. But the most potent ideology—nationalism—looked past social problems to concentrate on achieving political autonomy and self-determination for groups identified by common languages and cultures rather than by class.

The Spell of Nationalism

Nationalists sought political autonomy for their ethnic group—a people linked by language and shared traditions. Although nationalism was still nascent in the first half of the nineteenth century among the peasants and workers of most countries, ethnic heritage was increasingly a major determinant of personal and political identity. Poles, Italians, Germans, Irish, and Russians all pursued nationalist goals (Map 22.3, page 852).

Polish nationalism became more self-conscious after the collapse of the revolt in 1830 against Russian domination. Ten thousand Poles, mostly noble army officers and intellectuals, fled Poland in 1830 and 1831. Most of them took up residence in western European capitals, especially Paris, where they mounted a successful public relations campaign for worldwide support. Their intellectual hero was the poet Adam Mickiewicz◆ (1798–1855), whose mystical writings portrayed the Polish exiles as martyrs of a crucified nation with an international Christian mission: "Your endeavors are for all men, not only for yourselves. You will achieve a new Christian civilization."

Mickiewicz formed the Polish Legion to fight for national restoration, but rivalries and divisions among the Polish nationalists

◆**Mickiewicz:** mihts KYAY vihch

DID YOU KNOW?

Opium Addiction in Nineteenth-Century Britain

Great Britain fought two opium wars with China (1839–1842 and 1856–1858) that drew world attention to the problem of Chinese drug addiction. In Great Britain itself, the government did not regulate or restrict opium use until 1868. Pharmacists and grocers sold pills, lozenges, enemas, vinegars, and wines prepared with opium, which came from the heads of poppy plants imported first from the Ottoman Empire and, after 1750, from India. A tincture of opium (opium dissolved in alcohol) known as laudanum was widely used as a sedative, and even children's opiates could be bought almost anywhere. Laudanum mixed with egg yolk was sold as a cure for hemorrhoids, and opiates were a popular remedy for toothache and diarrhea. Most doctors considered opium a good cure for delirium tremens, caused by alcohol abuse.

Death by overdose was a well-known phenomenon, but public opinion turned against the drug only when it became associated with abuse by the lower classes. Parliamentary inquiries in the 1830s denounced the use of opiates by working-class mothers, who gave their children Godfrey's Cordial or Street's Infant Quietness to make them sleep while they worked. Officials also worried that workers took opium and laudanum as a cheap substitute for alcohol, whose use was widely and loudly denounced by temperance societies. The concern about opiates followed from the general trend toward "reforming" lower-class behavior.

Well-known cases of addiction among writers and poets also attracted attention. The writer Thomas De Quincey stirred up controversy when he published his *Confessions of an English Opium-Eater* in 1821, but the book was reissued many times during the nineteenth century. In it, De Quincey discusses his and the romantic poet Samuel Taylor Coleridge's addiction. De Quincey calls himself the "pope" of the "true church" of opium and describes weaning himself from the drug in 1819 to escape the hallucinatory dreams that haunted him. He had terrifying nightmares of living in China in houses in which tables and sofas turned into crocodiles multiplied ten thousand times. But he relapsed and soon took bigger and bigger doses right into the 1840s. De Quincey and Coleridge were only the best-known cases of opium addiction: Lord Byron, Percy Bysshe Shelley, Elizabeth Barrett Browning, Walter Scott, and Charles Dickens all took opiates at one time or another, as did many leading doctors and preachers.

The history of opium use in the nineteenth century raises significant questions: Why did

---

prevented united action until 1846, when Polish exiles in Paris tried to launch a coordinated insurrection for Polish independence. Plans for an uprising in the Polish province of Galicia in the Austrian Empire collapsed when peasants instead revolted against their noble Polish masters. Slaughtering some two thousand aristocrats, a desperate rural population served the Austrian government's end by defusing the nationalist challenge. Class interests and national identity were not always the same.

One of those most touched by Mickiewicz's vision was Giuseppe Mazzini (1805– 1872), a fiery Italian nationalist and republican journalist. Exiled in 1831 for his opposition to Austrian rule in northern Italy, Mazzini founded Young Italy, a secret society that attracted thousands with its message that Italy would touch off a European-wide revolutionary movement. The conservative order throughout Europe felt threatened by Mazzini's charismatic leadership and conspiratorial scheming, but he lacked both European allies against Austria and widespread support among the Italian masses.

Nationalism was an especially volatile issue in the Austrian Empire because Austria

Opium Den in London (c. 1870)
This woodcut by Gustave Doré shows that opium smoking persisted in Britain at least to the 1870s. Doré was a French book illustrator who came to London in 1869–1871 and produced illustrations of the poorer neighborhoods in the city. His taste for the grotesque is apparent in the figures watching the smokers. Doré also illustrated a book of Coleridge's poetry. *Print Collection, Miriam and Ira D. Wallach Division of Arts, Prints and Photographs. New York Public Library. Astor, Lenox and Tilden Foundation/Art Resource, NY.*

British authorities condemn its use at home even while forcing opium on the Chinese? Why was lower-class use of opiates especially disturbing to officials? Why did so many writers experiment with the drug? The history of opium is a fascinating example of the West's interaction with the rest of the world: the drug was first cultivated by ancient Sumerians and passed on to the Assyrians, Babylonians, Egyptians, and then Greeks; the Portuguese brought it to Europe in the sixteenth century as part of their trade with China; and its modern derivative heroin is now the subject of worldwide smuggling and official regulation.

Sources: Virginia Berridge and Griffith Edwards, *Opium and the People: Opiate Use in Nineteenth-Century England* (New York: St. Martin's Press, 1981); Thomas De Quincey, *The Confessions of an English Opium-Eater and Other Essays* (London: Macmillan, 1924).

ruled over so many different nationalities (see Map 22.3). The 1830s and 1840s saw the spread of nationalism among Magyars, Czechs, Slovaks, Serbs, Slovenes, Croats, and Romanians, in addition to Poles and Italians, all ethnic groups within the empire. Each of these peoples produced leaders who called for a cultural revival in language, literature, and education, as well as political rights. Scholars compiled dictionaries and created standard literary languages to replace peasant dialects; writers used the rediscovered vernacular instead of Latin or German; and historians glorified the national past. During the revolutions of 1848, however, it would become evident that these different ethnic groups disliked each other as much as they disliked their Austrian masters.

Economic unification in the German states took a step forward with the foundation in 1834, under Prussian leadership, of the *Zollverein,*♦ or "customs union." Economist Friedrich List argued for external tariffs that would promote industrialization and cooperation across the boundaries of the German states so that an economically united

♦*Zollverein:* TSAWL vehr eyen

MAP 22.3 Languages of Nineteenth-Century Europe
Even this detailed map of linguistic diversity understates the number of different languages and dialects spoken in Europe. In Italy, for example, few people spoke Italian as their first language. Instead, they spoke local dialects such as Piedmontese or Ligurian, and some might speak better French than Italian if they came from the regions bordering France. How does the map underline the inherent contradictions of nationalism in Europe? What were consequences of linguistic diversity within national borders? Keep in mind that even in Spain, France, and Great Britain, linguistic diversity continued right up to the beginning of the 1900s.

Germany might compete with the rest of Europe. German nationalists sought a government uniting German-speaking peoples, but they could not agree on its boundaries. Austria was not part of the Zollverein: would the unified German state include both Prussia and the Austrian Empire? If it included Austria, what about the non-German territories of the Austrian Empire? And could the powerful and conservative kingdom of Prussia coexist in a unified German state with other, more liberal but smaller states? These questions would vex German history for decades to come.

In Russia, nationalism took the form of opposition to western ideas. Russian nationalists, or Slavophiles (lovers of the Slavs), opposed the Westernizers, who wanted Russia to follow western models of industrial development and constitutional government. The Slavophiles favored maintaining rural traditions infused by the values of the Russian Orthodox church. Only a return to Russia's basic historical principles, they argued, could protect the country against the corrosion of rationalism and materialism. Slavophiles sometimes criticized the regime, however, because they believed the state exerted too much power over the church. The conflict between Slavophiles and Westernizers continues to shape Russian cultural and intellectual life to the present day.

The most significant nationalist movement in western Europe could be found in Ireland. The Irish had struggled for centuries against English occupation, but Irish nationalists developed strong organizations only in the 1840s. In 1842, a group of writers founded the Young Ireland movement that aimed to recover Irish history and preserve the Gaelic language (spoken by at least one-third of the peasantry). Daniel O'Connell (1775–1847), a Catholic lawyer and landowner who sat in the British House of Commons, hoped to force the British Parliament to repeal the Act of Union of 1801, which had made Ireland part of Great Britain. In 1843, London newspapers reported "monster meetings" that drew crowds of as many as 300,000 people in support of repeal of the union. In response, the British government arrested O'Connell and convicted him of conspiracy. Although his sentence was overturned, O'Connell withdrew from politics, partly because of a terminal brain disease. More radical leaders, who preached insurrection against the English, replaced him.

Liberalism in Economics and Politics

Nationalism overshadowed liberalism in eastern Europe, but liberalism had a strong base in the industrializing countries of western Europe. British liberals wanted government to limit its economic role to maintaining the currency, enforcing contracts, and financing major enterprises like the military and the railroads. As historian and member of Parliament Thomas Macaulay (1800–1859) explained in 1830:

> Our rulers will best promote the improvement of the nation by strictly confining themselves to their own legitimate duties, by leaving capital to find its most lucrative course, commodities their fair price, industry and intelligence their natural reward, idleness and folly their natural punishment, by maintaining peace, by defending property, by diminishing the price of law, and by observing strict economy in every department of the State.

British liberals sought to lower or eliminate British tariffs, especially through repeal of the **Corn Laws**, which benefited landowners by preventing the import of cheap foreign grain. When landholders in the House of Commons thwarted efforts to lower grain tariffs, two Manchester cotton manufacturers set up an Anti–Corn Law League. They appealed to the middle classes against the landlords, whom they labeled "a bread-taxing oligarchy" and "blood-sucking vampires," and attracted working-class backing by promising lower food prices. The league established local branches, published newspapers and the journal *The Economist* (founded in 1843 and now one of the world's most influential periodicals), and campaigned in elections. They eventually won the support of the Tory prime minister Sir Robert Peel, whose government repealed the Corn Laws in 1846.

Liberalism had less appeal in continental Europe because industrial growth was slower and the middle classes smaller than in Britain. French liberals agitated for greater press freedoms and a broadening of the vote. Louis-Philippe's government brutally repressed working-class and republican insurrections in Lyon and Paris in the early 1830s and forced the republican opposition underground. But the French king's increasingly restrictive governments also thwarted liberals' hopes for reforms by suppressing many political organizations and reestablishing censorship.

Repression muted criticism in most other European states as well. Nevertheless, liberal reform movements grew up in pockets of industrialization in Prussia, the smaller German states, and the Austrian Empire. Some state bureaucrats, especially university-trained middle-class officials, favored economic liberalism. Hungarian count Stephen Széchenyi◆ (1791–1860) personally campaigned for the introduction of British-style changes. He introduced British agricultural techniques on his own lands, helped start up steamboat traffic on the Danube, encouraged the importation of machinery and technicians for steam-driven textile factories, and pushed the construction of Hungary's first railway line, from Budapest to Vienna.

◆**Széchenyi:** SAY chehn yih

In the 1840s, however, Széchenyi's efforts paled before those of the flamboyant Magyar nationalist Lajos Kossuth♦ (1802–1894). After spending four years in prison for sedition, Kossuth grabbed every opportunity to publicize American democracy and British political liberalism, all in a fervent nationalist spirit. In 1844, he founded the Protective Association, whose members bought only Hungarian products; to Kossuth, boycotting Austrian goods was crucial to ending "colonial dependence" on Austria. Born of a lesser landowning family without a noble title, Kossuth did not hesitate to attack "the cowardly selfishness of the landowner class."

Even in Russia, signs of liberal, even socialist, opposition appeared in the 1830s and 1840s. Small circles of young noblemen serving in the army or bureaucracy met in cities, especially Moscow, to discuss the latest Western ideas and to criticize the Russian state: "The world is undergoing a transformation, while we vegetate in our hovels of wood and clay," wrote one. Out of these groups came such future revolutionaries as Alexander Herzen (1812–1870), described by the police as "a daring free-thinker, extremely dangerous to society." Tsar Nicholas I (r. 1825–1855) banned Western liberal writings as well as all books about the United States. He sent nearly ten thousand people a year into exile in Siberia as punishment for their political activities.

Socialism and the Early Labor Movement

Socialists railed against the inequalities caused by industrialization and considered liberalism an inadequate response. They envisioned a future society in which workers would share a harmonious, cooperative, and prosperous life. Building on the theoretical and practical ideas laid out in the early nineteenth century by Count Henri de Saint-Simon, Charles Fourier, and Robert Owen, the socialists of the 1830s and 1840s hoped that economic planning and working-class organization would solve the problems caused by industrial growth, including the threat of increasingly mechanical, unfeeling social relations.

♦**Lajos Kossuth:** LAW yohsh KAW shut

Socialism and Women. Women participated actively in the socialist movements of the day, even though socialist men often shared the widespread prejudice against women's political activism. In Great Britain many women joined the Owenites and helped form cooperative societies and unions. They defended women's working-class organizations against the complaints of men in the new societies and trade unions. As one woman wrote, "Do not say the unions are only for men. . . . 'Tis a wrong impression, forced on our minds to keep us slaves!" As women became more active, Owenites agitated for women's rights, marriage reform, and popular education. Rousing speakers such as Emma Martin (1812–1851) forcefully put the case: "One great evil is the depraved and ignorant condition of woman; this evil can only be removed by Socialism." Martin's speeches often stirred turbulent opposition as clergymen urged their congregations to shout her down. Occasionally, she was jeered, chased, and even stoned by mobs, so much did her ideas and very presence challenge conventional expectations.

The French activist Flora Tristan (1801–1844) devoted herself to reconciling the interests of male and female workers. She had seen the "frightful reality" of London's poverty and made a reputation reporting on British working conditions. Tristan published a stream of books and pamphlets urging male workers to address women's unequal status, arguing that "the emancipation of male workers is *impossible* so long as women remain in a degraded state." She advocated a Universal Union of Men and Women Workers. Despite political harassment, she traveled around France speaking out for her beliefs and attempting to organize workers.

Collectivists and Communists. Even though most male socialists ignored Tristan's plea for women's participation, like her they also strove to found working-class associations. The French socialist Louis Blanc (1811–1882) explained the importance of working-class associations in *Organization of Labor* (1840), which deeply influenced the French labor movement. Similarly, Pierre-Joseph Proudhon (1809–1865) urged workers to form producers' associations so that the workers could control the work process and eliminate profits made by capitalists. His 1840 book *What Is Property?* argues that property is theft: labor alone is productive, and rent, interest, and profit unjust.

After 1840, some socialists began to call themselves **communists**, emphasizing their desire to replace private property by communal, collective ownership. The Frenchman Étienne Cabet (1788–1856) first used the word *communist*. In 1840, he published *Travels in Icaria*, a novel describing a communist utopia in which a popularly elected dictatorship efficiently organized work, reduced the workday to seven hours, and made work tasks "short, easy, and attractive."

French socialist ideas circulated throughout Europe, from Belgium and the German states to Russia. They evoked most response in areas of incipient industrialization where artisans and workers felt intensely threatened by the prospect of change. The German tailor Wilhelm Weitling (1808–1871) developed an influential variant of socialism that had deeply religious overtones. His book *Guarantees of Harmony and Freedom* (1842) argues for a communal society but also emphasizes faith as necessary to life. In his view, "Jesus, too, was a communist." Weitling made a profound impression on workers' societies in the western German states.

Out of the churning of socialist ideas of the 1840s emerged two men whose collaboration would change the definition of socialism and remake it into an ideology that would shake the world for the next 150 years. Karl Marx (1818–1883) had studied philosophy at the University of Berlin, edited a liberal newspaper until the Prussian government suppressed it, and then left for Paris, where he met Friedrich Engels (1820–1895). While working in the offices of his wealthy family's cotton manufacturing interests in Manchester, England, Engels had been shocked into writing *The Condition of the Working Class in England in 1844* (1845), a sympathetic depiction of industrial workers' dismal lives. In Paris, where German and eastern European intellectuals could pursue their political interests more freely than at home, Marx and Engels organized the Communist League, in whose name they published *The Communist Manifesto* in 1848 (see the excerpt, page 856). It eventually became the touchstone of Marxist and communist revolution all over the world. Marx and Engels embraced industrialization because they believed it would eventually bring on the proletarian revolution and lead inevitably to the abolition of exploitation, private property, and class society. Communists, the *Manifesto* declared, must aim for "the downfall of the bourgeoisie [capitalist class] and the ascendancy of the proletariat [working class], the abolition of the old society based on class conflicts and the foundation of a new society without classes and without private property."

Working-Class Organization. Socialism accompanied, and in some places incited, an upsurge in working-class organization in western Europe. British workers founded cooperative societies, local trade unions, and so-called friendly societies for mutual aid, associations that frightened the middle classes. A newspaper exclaimed in 1834, "The trade unions are, we have no doubt, the most dangerous institutions that were ever permitted to take root."

Many British workers joined in **Chartism**, which aimed to transform Britain into a democracy. In 1838, political radicals drew up the People's Charter, which demanded universal manhood suffrage, vote by secret ballot, equal electoral districts, annual elections, and the elimination of property qualifications for and the payment of stipends to members of Parliament. Chartists denounced their opponents as seeking "to keep the people in social slavery and political degradation." Many women took part by founding female political unions, setting up Chartist Sunday schools, organizing boycotts of unsympathetic shopkeepers, and joining Chartist temperance associations. Nevertheless, the People's Charter refrained from calling for woman suffrage because the movement's leaders feared that doing so would alienate potential supporters.

The Chartists organized a massive campaign during 1838 and 1839, with large public meetings, fiery speeches, and torchlight parades. Presented with petitions for the People's Charter signed by more than a million people,

Marx and Engels, *The Communist Manifesto*

Karl Marx (1818–1883) and Friedrich Engels (1820–1895) were both sons of prosperous German-Jewish families that had converted to Christianity. In the manifesto for the Communist League, they laid out many of the central principles that would guide Marxist revolution in the future: they insisted that all history is shaped by class struggle and that in future revolutions the working class would overthrow the bourgeoisie, or middle class, and replace capitalism and private property with a communist state in which all property is collectively rather than individually owned. As this selection shows, Marx and Engels always placed more emphasis on class struggle than on the state that would result from the ensuing revolution.

The history of all hitherto existing society is the history of class struggles.

Freeman and slave, patrician and plebeian, lord and serf, guild-master and journeyman, in a word, oppressor and oppressed, stood in constant opposition to one another, carried on an uninterrupted, now hidden, now open fight, a fight that each time ended, either in a revolutionary reconstitution of society at large, or in the common ruin of the contending classes. . . .

The modern bourgeois society that has sprouted from the ruins of feudal society has not done away with class antagonisms. It has but established new classes, new conditions of oppression, new forms of struggle in place of the old ones.

Our epoch, the epoch of the bourgeoisie, possesses, however, this distinctive feature: It has simplified the class antagonisms: Society as a whole is more and more splitting up into two great hostile camps, into two great classes directly facing each other: Bourgeoisie [middle class] and Proletariat [working class]. . . .

The weapons with which the bourgeoisie felled feudalism to the ground are now turned against the bourgeoisie itself.

But not only has the bourgeoisie forged the weapons that bring death to itself; it has also called into existence the men who are to wield those weapons—the modern working class—the proletarians. . . .

The essential condition for the existence, and for the sway of the bourgeois class, is the formation and augmentation of capital; the condition for capital is wage-labour. Wage-labour rests exclusively on competition between labourers. The advance of industry, whose involuntary promoter is the bourgeoisie, replaces the isolation of the labourers, due to competition, by their revolutionary combination, due to association. The development of Modern Industry, therefore, cuts from under its feet the very foundation on which the bourgeoisie produces and appropriates products. What the bourgeoisie, therefore, produces, above all, is its own gravediggers. Its fall and the victory of the proletariat are equally inevitable.

Source: Karl Marx and Friedrich Engels, *The Communist Manifesto*. Translated by Samuel Moore (New York: Penguin, 1985), 79–80, 87, 93–94.

---

the House of Commons refused to act. In response to this rebuff from middle-class liberals, the Chartists allied themselves in the 1840s with working-class strike movements in the manufacturing districts and associated with various European revolutionary movements. But at the same time they—like their British and continental allies—distanced themselves from women workers. Chartists complained that working women undermined men's manhood, taking men's jobs and turning the men into "women-men" or "eunuchs." Continuing agitation and organization prepared the way for a last wave of Chartist demonstrations in 1848.

Continental workers were less well organized because trade unions and strikes were illegal everywhere except Great Britain. Nevertheless, artisans and skilled workers in France formed mutual aid societies that provided insurance, death benefits, and education. Workers in new factories rarely organized, but artisans in the old trades, such as the silk workers of Lyon, France, created societies to resist mechanization and wage cuts.

The new workers' press, such as the Saint-Simonian *People's Beehive* (1839), spread the ideas of socialist harmony and economic reform among the working classes. In eastern and central Europe, however, socialism and labor organization—like liberalism—had less impact than in western Europe. Guild-based organizations survived in the German states, for example, but cooperative societies and workers' newspapers did not appear until 1848. Farther east, the working classes were even smaller, and labor organizing reached few people.

The New Historical Imagination

In an age of competing ideologies, every ideology offered its own reading of history. Nationalism, in particular, fostered an enthusiasm for history, because history substantiated claims for a common national identity. German nationalists, for example, avidly read such massive books as Friedrich C. Schlosser's eighteen-volume *General History for the German People* (1844–1856). In Great Britain the equally famous histories by Thomas Macaulay described the British people as "the greatest and most highly civilized people that the world ever saw." Macaulay aimed to broaden history to include everyday life as well as politics, war, and diplomacy.

History entered the lifeblood of literature and painting as well. Romanticism had given history a special glamour, opening the way for a commercially successful genre, the historical novel. Readers devoured novels like Alexandre Dumas's *The Three Musketeers* (1844), set in the reign of Louis XIII in the 1620s. Dumas, the grandson of a Haitian slave, recounts the adventures of four soldiers who valiantly serve the queen of France and foil the plots of Cardinal Richelieu. Governments appreciated the value of paintings with a historical theme in reinforcing their own legitimacy. To link himself to the growing cult of Napoleon, for example, Louis-Philippe commissioned four paintings of the emperor's victories for the new Gallery of Battles at Versailles, now transformed into a museum. This effort culminated in 1840 when the government, led by the new prime minister Adolphe Thiers♦ (himself a noted historian of the French Revolution), arranged to return Napoleon's ashes to the Invalides♦ church in Paris. Although the spectacular public funeral showed Louis-Philippe's eagerness to establish his connections to Napoleonic history, it would not succeed in its goal of stifling demands for reform.

Nationalism and the new historical imagination also influenced musical romanticism. The Polish composer and pianist Frédéric Chopin (1810–1849) became a powerful champion in the West for the cause of his native land, with music that incorporated Polish folk rhythms and melodies. Opera, long a favorite with the public, experienced an abrupt transformation about 1830. Before this time, operatic plots had generally derived from classical mythology or had been contemporary social satires; now the public demanded passionate tragedy, usually with a picturesque medieval or Renaissance setting. The operatic portrayal of heroines as tragic victims who were sexually pure, noble-minded, and emotionally vulnerable mirrored the redefinition of women's character in contemporary middle-class opinion.

Alongside the burst of interest in the political and artistic uses of history came a new trend in historical writing that valued professional training above literary skill. The foremost practitioner of this new scholarship was Leopold von Ranke (1795–1886), a professor at the University of Berlin who taught many of the leading German historians of the nineteenth century. Ranke tried to understand the past objectively, on its own terms, rather than as lessons for present-day purposes. He organized small seminars of young men for the close study of documents. His reliance on source materials instead of legend or tradition helped reshape the study of history into a discipline based on critical methods. The most immediate response to this approach came in the history of religion. In 1835, the German scholar David Friedrich Strauss published the two-volume

---

♦**Thiers:** tee EHR
♦**Invalides:** an vahl EED

MAP 22.4
The Revolutions of 1848
The attempts of rulers to hold back the forces of change collapsed suddenly in 1848 when once again the French staged a revolution that inspired many others in Europe. This time, cities all over central and eastern Europe joined in as the spirit of revolt inflamed one capital after another. Although all of these revolutions eventually failed because of social and political divisions, the sheer scale of rebellion forced rulers to reconsider their policies.

Life of Jesus, in which he argues that the Gospels were not history but only imaginative stories that reflected Jewish myths in Roman times. Widely reprinted, Strauss's book caused a storm of controversy. In the 1840s, a series of new books followed Strauss's lead; some of them ended with proclamations that Jesus never existed.

The study of geology prompted the examination of other religious doctrines. A three-volume work published in 1830–1833 by the British geologist Charles Lyell (1797–1875) with the bland title *Principles of Geology* ignited debate. Lyell argues that the earth is much older than the dating of the biblical story of creation (assumed by many to be 4004 B.C.E.). Questioning religious assumptions enraged those whose beliefs rested on biblical certainty. Under Lyell's influence, Charles Darwin (1809–1882) would begin to sketch out the essentials of his theory of evolution by natural selection. Geology, the arts, nationalist histories, and historical novels all helped foster new forms of histor-

ical sensibility. But a sense of history did nothing to quiet the storm of ideological discontent. Liberals, socialists, and nationalists all vied for public support for their answers to the political and social questions raised by industrialization, urbanization, and the demand for national self-determination.

> **Review:** Why did ideologies have such a powerful appeal in the 1830s and 1840s?

❖ The Revolutions of 1848

Food shortage, overpopulation, and unemployment helped turn ideological turmoil into revolution. In 1848, demonstrations and uprisings toppled governments, forced rulers and ministers to flee, and offered revolutionaries an opportunity to put liberal, socialist, and nationalist ideals into practice (Map 22.4). Of the major powers, only Great

The Potato Blight and Irish Famine

In this painting by Daniel McDonald, *The Discovery of the Potato Blight* (1852), a family is shown digging up its potato crop only to find that the potatoes had rotted from blight. This discovery spelled disaster for this family and thousands like it. The blight spores were airborne. After landing on potato plants, they killed the leaves, which fell to the ground. The spores were washed into the earth, where they infected the underground tubers. The crop could even look normal but still be infected.

Britain and Russia remained untouched, the former because it already had constitutional government and the latter because its autocratic government had stamped out all signs of dissent. In the end, all the revolutions failed because liberal, socialist, and nationalist movements quarreled with one another, leaving an opening for rulers and their armies to return to power.

The Hungry Forties

Beginning in 1845, crop failures across Europe caused food prices to shoot skyward. In the best of times urban workers paid 50 to 80 percent of their income for a diet consisting largely of bread; now even bread was beyond their means. An aristocrat from Silesia, a province in Prussia, described the political consequences: "As long as there was a sure, and honest livelihood, none of the Silesian weavers paid any attention to communistic agitation. . . . Despair was aroused among them by hunger."

Overpopulation hastened famine in some places, especially Ireland, where an airborne blight destroyed the staple crop, potatoes, first in 1846, and again in 1848 and 1851. Irish peasants had planted potatoes because a family of four might live off one acre of potatoes but would require at least two acres of grain. As potato cultivation increased, greater food production spurred population growth as peasants, assured of a food supply, had more children. Irish peasants often sought security in large families, trusting that their children might help work the land and care for them in old age. Thus Irish population growth surpassed that of the rest of Europe. By the 1840s, Ireland was especially vulnerable to the potato blight. Out of a population of eight million, as many as one million people died of starvation and disease. Corpses lay unburied on the sides of roads, and whole families were found dead in their cottages, half-eaten by dogs. Hundreds of thousands emigrated to England, the United States, and Canada.

Throughout Europe, famine jeopardized social peace. In age-old fashion, rumors circulated about large farmers selling to other localities or hoarding grain to drive up prices. Believing that governments should ensure fair prices that would make food accessible, crowds took over village and town streets to protest, often attacking markets or bakeries. In villages across Europe they threatened officials with retribution. "If the grain merchants do not cease to take away grains . . . we will go to your homes and cut your throats and those of the three bakers . . . and burn the whole place down." So went one threat from French villagers in the hungry winter of 1847. Although harvests improved in 1848, by then many people had lost their land or become hopelessly indebted, and they strongly resented those who had prospered from high prices.

High food prices also drove down the demand for manufactured goods, resulting in increased unemployment. Industrial workers' wages had been rising—in the German states, for example, wages rose an average of 5.5 percent in the 1830s and 10.5 percent in the 1840s—but the cost of living rose about 16 percent each decade, canceling out wage increases. Seasonal work and regular unemployment were already the norm when the crisis of the late 1840s exacerbated the uncertainties of urban life. "The most miserable class that ever sneaked its way into history" is how Friedrich Engels described underemployed and starving workers in 1847.

Another French Revolution

The specter of hunger tarnished the image of established rulers and amplified voices critical of them. Louis-Philippe's government had blocked all moves for electoral reform, and, beginning in 1847, opposition leaders in France sponsored political meetings under the cover of banquets at which they demanded liberalization of Louis-Philippe's regime. In February 1848, the banquet campaign turned into a revolution as the people of Paris took to the streets.

The February Revolution. Demonstrations began on the rainy, chilly morning of February 22, 1848. At first, the police and the army dispersed the students, workers, and the unemployed who gathered to build barricades. The next day, however, forty or fifty people died when panicky soldiers opened fire on the crowd. On February 24, faced with fifteen hundred barricades and a furious populace, Louis-Philippe abdicated and fled to England. A hastily formed provisional government declared France a republic once again. Its most noteworthy leader was Alphonse de Lamartine (1790–1869), a romantic poet, eloquent orator, and historian of the French Revolution. Lamartine's conviction that he was destined to lead the people enabled him to face down the crowds who demanded immediate responses to hunger and unemployment.

The new republican government issued liberal reforms—an end to the death penalty for political crimes, the abolition of slavery in the colonies, and freedom of the press—and agreed to introduce universal adult male suffrage despite misgivings about political participation by peasants and unemployed workers. To address the gnawing problem of unemployment, the government allowed Paris officials to organize a system of "national workshops" to provide the unemployed with construction work. When women protested their exclusion, the city set up a few workshops for women workers, albeit with wages lower than men's. To meet a mounting deficit, the provisional government then levied a 45 percent surtax on property taxes, alienating peasants and landowners.

The establishment of the republic politicized many segments of the population. Scores of newspapers and political clubs inspired grassroots democratic fervor; meeting in concert halls, theaters, and government auditoriums, clubs became a regular evening attraction for the citizenry. Women also formed clubs, published women's newspapers, and demanded representation in national politics. In a twist on domestic ideology, some argued that political activity followed naturally from motherhood. "This holy function of motherhood," one activist claimed, "gives women the right to intervene not only in all acts of civic life, but also in all acts of political life."

The June Days. Street-corner activism alarmed middle-class liberals and conservatives. To ensure its control, the republican government paid some unemployed youths to join a mobile guard with its own uniforms and barracks. Tension between the government and the workers in the national workshops rose. Soon competing groups paraded for their causes in massive demonstrations. The communist Étienne Cabet led one demonstration of 150,000 workers. Class warfare loomed like a thunderstorm on the horizon.

Faced with rising radicalism in Paris and other big cities, the voters elected a largely conservative National Assembly in April 1848; most of the deputies chosen were middle-class professionals or landowners, who favored either a restoration of the monarchy or a moderate republic. The Assembly immediately appointed a five-man executive committee to run the government and pointedly excluded known supporters of workers' rights. Suspicious of all demands for rapid change, the deputies dismissed a petition to restore divorce and voted down women's suffrage, 899 to 1. When the numbers enrolled in the national workshops in Paris rocketed from a predicted 10,000 to 110,000, the government ordered the workshops closed to new workers, and on June 21 it directed that those already enrolled move to the provinces or join the army.

The workers of Paris responded to these measures on June 23 by taking to the streets in the tens of thousands. In the June Days, as the following week came to be called, the government summoned the army, the National Guard, and the newly recruited mobile guard to fight the workers. Provincial volunteers came to help put down the workers, who had been depicted to them as lazy ruffians intent on destroying order and property. One observer breathed a sigh of relief: "The Red Republic [red being associated with demands for socialism] is lost forever; all France has joined against it. The National Guard, citizens, and peasants from the remotest parts of the country have come pouring in." The republic's army crushed the workers; more than 10,000, most of them workers, were killed or injured, 12,000 were arrested, and 4,000 eventually were convicted and deported.

The Vésuviennes, 1848
This lithograph satirizes women's political ambitions, referring to a women's club named the Vésuviennes (after the recent eruption of Mount Vesuvius in Italy). The artist implies that women have left their children at home in the care of their hapless husbands so that they can actively participate in politics. Some scholars claim that this particular club was invented by the police to ridicule women. Meetings of feminist clubs were often disrupted by men hostile to their aims. Can you compare the depiction of women in this lithograph to earlier depictions of women in the French Revolution of 1789 in Chapter 20? *Bibliothèque Nationale de France.*

Louis-Napoleon Bonaparte. When the National Assembly adopted a new constitution calling for a presidential election in which all adult men could vote, the electorate chose Louis-Napoleon Bonaparte, nephew of the dead emperor. Bonaparte got more than 5.5 million votes out of some 7.4 million cast. He had lived most of his life outside of France, and the leaders of the republic expected him to follow their tune. In uncertain times, the Bonaparte name promised something to everyone. Even many workers supported him because he had no connection with the blood-drenched June Days.

Uprising in Milan, 1848
In this painting by an unknown artist, *Fighting at the Tosa Gate*, the Milanese are setting up barricades to oppose their Austrian rulers. Whole families are involved. The flag of green, white, and red is the flag of the Cisalpine Republic of the Napoleonic period whose capital was Milan. The three colors would be incorporated into the national flag of Italy after unification. *Scala/Art Resource, NY.*

In reality, Bonaparte's election spelled the end of the Second Republic, just as his uncle had dismantled the first one established in 1792. In 1852, on the forty-eighth anniversary of Napoleon I's coronation as emperor, Louis-Napoleon declared himself Emperor Napoleon III. (Napoleon I's son died and never became Napoleon II, but Napoleon III wanted to create a sense of legitimacy and so used the Roman numeral III.) Political division and class conflict had proved fatal to the Second Republic. Although the revolution of 1848 never had a period of terror like that in 1793–1794, it nonetheless ended in similar fashion, with an authoritarian government that tried to play monarchists and republicans off against each other.

Nationalist Revolution in Italy

The Parisian uprising soon sparked other revolts. Italian nationalists hoped to unite a diverse collection of territories. When Giuseppe Verdi's opera *Macbeth* was performed in Venice in 1847, audiences leaped to their feet at the words "The fatherland has been betrayed. . . . Brothers we must hasten to save it." In January 1848, a revolt broke out in Palermo, Sicily, against the Bourbon ruler. Then came the electrify-ing news of the February Revolution in Paris. In Milan a huge nationalist demonstration quickly degenerated into battles between Austrian forces and armed demonstrators. In Venice an uprising drove out the Austrians. Peasants in the south occupied large landowners' estates. Across central Italy revolts mobilized the poor and unemployed against local rulers. Peasants demanded more land, and artisans and workers called for higher wages, restrictions on the use of machinery, and unemployment relief.

But class divisions and regional differences stood in the way of national unity. Property owners, businessmen, and professionals wanted liberal reforms and national unification under a conservative regime; intellectuals, workers, and artisans dreamed of democracy and social reforms. Some nationalists favored a loose federation; others wanted a monarchy under Charles Albert of Piedmont-Sardinia; still others urged rule by the pope; a few shared Mazzini's vision of a republic with a strong central government. Many leaders of national unification spoke Italian only as a second language; most Italians spoke regional dialects.

As king of the most powerful Italian state, Charles Albert inevitably played a central role. After some hesitation caused by fears of French intervention, he led a military campaign against Austria. It soon failed, partly because of dissension over goals and tactics among the nationalists. Although Austrian troops defeated Charles Albert in the north in the summer of 1848, democratic and nationalist forces prevailed at first in the south. In the fall the Romans drove the pope from the city and declared Rome a republic. For the next few months republican leaders, such as Mazzini and Giuseppe Garibaldi (1807–1882), congregated in Rome to organize the new republic. These efforts

The Divisions of Italy, 1848

eventually faltered when foreign powers intervened. The new president of republican France, Louis-Napoleon Bonaparte, sent an expeditionary force to secure the papal throne for Pius IX. Mazzini and Garibaldi fled. Although revolution had been defeated in Italy, the memory of the Roman republic and the commitment to unification remained, and they would soon emerge again with new force.

Revolt and Reaction in Central Europe

News of the revolution in Paris also provoked popular demonstrations in the German states. "My heart beat with joy. The monarchy had fallen. Only a little blood had been shed for such a high stake, and the great watchwords Liberty, Equality, Fraternity were again inscribed on the banner of the movement." So responded one Frankfurt woman to Louis-Philippe's overthrow. Most German rulers lost their nerve in the face of popular revolts in March 1848.

Prussia and the Frankfurt Parliament. When the Prussian army tried to push back a major demonstration in front of Berlin's royal palace on March 18, 1848, their actions provoked panic and street fighting around hastily assembled barricades. The next day the crowd paraded wagons loaded with dead bodies under King Frederick William IV's window, forcing him to salute the victims killed by his own army. In a state of near collapse, the king promised to call an assembly to draft a constitution and adopted the German nationalist flag of black, red, and gold.

The goal of German unification soon took precedence over social reform or constitutional changes within the separate states. In March and April, most of the German states agreed to elect delegates to a federal parliament at Frankfurt that would attempt to unite Germany. Local princes and even the more powerful kings of Prussia and Bavaria seemed to totter. In Bavaria, students marched to the "Marseillaise" and called for a republic. Yet the revolutionaries' weaknesses soon became apparent. The eight hundred delegates to the Frankfurt parliament had little practical political experience: "a group of old women," one socialist called

REVOLUTIONS OF 1848

1848

January Uprising in Palermo, Sicily

February Revolution in Paris; proclamation of republic

March Insurrections in Vienna, German cities, Milan, and Venice; autonomy movement in Hungary; Charles Albert of Piedmont-Sardinia declares war on Austrian Empire

May Frankfurt parliament opens

June Austrian army crushes revolutionary movement in Prague; June Days end in defeat of workers in Paris

July Austrians defeat Charles Albert and Italian forces

November Insurrection in Rome

December Francis Joseph becomes Austrian emperor; Louis-Napoleon elected president in France

1849

February Rome declared a republic

April Frederick William of Prussia rejects crown of united Germany offered by Frankfurt parliament

July Roman republic overthrown by French intervention

August Russian and Austrian armies combine to defeat Hungarian forces

them; a "Professors Parliament" was the common sneer. These delegates had no access to an army, and they dreaded the demands of the lower classes for social reforms. Unemployed artisans and workers smashed machines; peasants burned landlords' records and occasionally attacked Jewish moneylenders; women set up clubs and newspapers to demand their emancipation from "perfumed slavery."

The advantage lay with the princes, who retained legal authority and control over the armed forces. The most powerful German states, Prussia and Austria, expected to determine whether and how Germany should unite. While the Frankfurt parliament laboriously prepared a liberal constitution for a united Germany—one that denied self-determination to Czechs, Poles, and Danes within its proposed German borders—the Prussian king Frederick William IV (r. 1840–1860) recovered his confidence. First his army crushed the revolution in Berlin in the fall of 1848. Prussian troops then intervened to help other local rulers put down the last wave of democratic and nationalist insurrections in the spring of 1849. When the Frankfurt parliament finally concluded its work, offering the emperorship of a constitutional, federal Germany to the king of Prussia, Frederick William contemptuously refused this "crown from the gutter."

Ethnic Divisions in the Austrian Empire. By the summer of 1848, the Austrian Empire, too, had reached the verge of complete collapse. Just as Italians were driving the Austrians out of their lands in northern Italy and Magyar nationalists were demanding political autonomy for Hungary, on March 13, 1848, in Vienna, a student-led demonstration for political reform turned into rioting, looting, and machine-breaking. Metternich resigned, escaping to England in disguise. Emperor Ferdinand promised a constitution, an elected parliament, and the end of censorship. The beleaguered authorities in Vienna could not refuse Magyar demands for home rule, and Széchenyi and Kossuth both became ministers in the new Hungarian government. The Magyars were the largest ethnic group in Hungary but still did not make up 50 percent of the population, which included Romanians, Slovaks, Croats, and Slovenes who preferred Austrian rule to domination by local Magyars.

The ethnic divisions in Hungary foreshadowed the many political and social divisions that would doom the revolutionaries. Fears of peasant insurrection prompted the Magyar nationalists around Kossuth to abolish serfdom. This measure alienated the largest noble landowners. In Prague, Czech nationalists convened a Slav congress as a counter to the Germans' Frankfurt parliament and called for a reorganization of the Austrian Empire that would recognize the rights of ethnic minorities. Such assertiveness by non-German peoples provoked German nationalists to protest on behalf of German-speaking people in areas with a Czech or Magyar majority.

Revolution of 1848 in Eastern Europe
This painting by an unknown artist shows Ana Ipatescu leading a group of Romanian revolutionaries in Transylvania in opposition to Russian rule. The Transylvanian provinces of Moldavia and
Walachia had been under Russian domination since the 1770s and occupied directly since 1829.
In April 1848, local landowners began to organize meetings. Paris-educated nationalists spear-
headed the movement, which demanded the end of Russian control and various legal and political reforms. By August, the movement had split between those who wanted independence only
and those who pushed for the end of serfdom and for universal manhood suffrage. In response,
the Russians invaded Moldavia and the Turks moved into Walachia. By October, the uprising was
over. Russia and Turkey agreed to control the provinces jointly. *The Art Archive.*

The Austrian government slowly took advantage of these divisions. To quell peas-ant discontent and appease liberal reformers, it abolished all remaining peasant obliga-tions to the nobility in March 1848. Rejoicing country folk soon lost interest in the revolu-tion. Class conflicts flared in Vienna, where the middle classes had little sympathy for the starving artisans and workers. The new Hun-garian government alienated the other na-tionalities when it imposed the Magyar language on them. Similar divisions sapped national unity in the Polish and Czech lands of the empire.

Military force finally broke up the revo-lutionary movements. The first blow fell in Prague in June 1848; General Prince Alfred von Windischgrätz,♦ the military governor, bombarded the city into submission when a demonstration led to violence (including the shooting death of his wife, watching from a window). After another uprising in Vienna a few months later, Windischgrätz marched seventy thousand soldiers into the capital and set up direct military rule. In December the Austrian monarchy came back to life when the eighteen-year-old Francis Joseph (r. 1848–1916), unencumbered by promises extracted by the revolutionaries from his now feeble uncle Ferdinand, assumed the

---

♦**Windischgrätz:** vihn dihsh GREHTS

imperial crown after intervention by leading court officials. In the spring of 1849, General Count Joseph Radetsky defeated the last Italian challenges to Austrian power in northern Italy, and his army moved east, joining with Croats and Serbs to take on the Hungarian rebels. The Austrian army teamed up with Tsar Nicholas I, who marched into Hungary with more than 300,000 Russian troops. Hungary was put under brutal martial law. Széchenyi went mad, and Kossuth found refuge in the United States. Social conflicts and ethnic divisions weakened the revolutionary movements from the inside and gave the Austrian government the opening it needed to restore its position.

Aftermath to 1848

Although the revolutionaries of 1848 failed to achieve most of their goals, their efforts left a profound mark on the political and social landscape. Between 1848 and 1851, the French served a kind of republican apprenticeship that prepared the population for another, more lasting republic after 1870. No French government could henceforth rule without extensive popular consultation. In Italy, the failure of unification did not stop the spread of nationalist ideas and the rooting of demands for democratic participation. In the German states, the revolutionaries of 1848 turned nationalism from an idea of professors and writers into a popular enthusiasm and even practical reality. The initiation of artisans, workers, and journeymen into democratic clubs increased political awareness in the lower classes and helped prepare them for broader political participation. Almost all the German states had a constitution and a parliament after 1850. The spectacular failures of 1848 thus hid some important underlying successes.

The absence of revolution in 1848 was just as significant as its presence. No revolution occurred in Great Britain, the Netherlands, or Belgium, three places where industrialization and urbanization had developed most rapidly. In Great Britain the prospects for revolution actually seemed quite good: the Chartist movement took inspiration from the European revolutions in 1848 and mounted several gigantic demonstrations to force Parliament into granting all adult males the vote. But Parliament refused and no uprising occurred, in part because the government had already proved its responsiveness. The middle classes in Britain had been co-opted into the established order by the Reform Bill of 1832, and the working classes had won parliamentary regulation of children's and women's work.

The other notable exception to revolution among the great powers was Russia, where Tsar Nicholas I maintained a tight grip through police surveillance and censorship. The Russian schools, limited to the upper classes, taught Nicholas's three most cherished principles: autocracy (the unlimited power of the tsar), orthodoxy (obedience to the church in religion and morality), and nationality (devotion to Russian traditions). These provided no space for political dissent. Social conditions also fostered political passivity: serfdom continued in force and the slow rate of industrial and urban growth created little discontent.

For all the differences between countries, some developments touched them all. European states continued to expand their bureaucracies. For example, in 1750 the Russian government employed approximately 10,500 functionaries; a century later it needed almost 114,000. In Great Britain a swelling army of civil servants produced parliamentary studies on industrialization, foreign trade, and colonial profits, while new agencies such as the British urban police forces (ten thousand strong in the 1840s) intruded increasingly in ordinary people's lives. States wanted to take children out of the fields and factories where they worked with their families and educate them. In some German cities the police reported people who cleared snow off their roofs after the permitted hour or smoked in the street. A few governments even prescribed the length of sermons.

Although much had changed, the aristocracy remained the dominant power almost everywhere. As army officers, aristocrats put down revolutionary forces. As landlords, they continued to dominate the rural scene and control parliamentary bodies. They also held many official positions in the state bureaucracies. One Italian princess explained, "There are doubtless men capable of leading the nation . . . but their names are unknown to the people, whereas those of noble families . . .

The Crystal Palace, 1851

George Baxter's lithograph (above) shows the exterior of the main building for the Exhibition of the Works of Industry of All Nations in London. It was designed by Sir Joseph Paxton to gigantic dimensions: 1,848 feet long by 456 feet wide; 135 feet high; 772,784 square feet of ground floor area covering no less than 18 acres. The second view, a lithograph by Peter Mabuse, offers a view of one of the colonial displays at the exhibition. The tented room and ivory carved throne are meant to recall India, Britain's premier colony. In a sermon given at the opening of the exhibition, Reverend George Clayton attributed Britain's national greatness to its colonial presence: *"Great she [Britain] truly is—great in her trade and commerce—great in her laws and constitution—great in her freedom, both civil and religious—great in the power, the character, and the virtues of her queen . . . great in the resources of her wealth, in the number and extent of her colonial possessions—great in the multitude of her subjects—great in the moral and Christian bearing of a large proportion of her people—great in the cultivation of the mind and morals of the rising population of her inhabitants—great in the distribution of her Bibles, in her mission to the heathen, in the emancipation of the slave, and in the circulation of her countless tracts for the instruction of universal man." Top: Maidstone Museum and Art Gallery, Kent, UK/ Bridgeman Art Library. At right: From Dickinson's Comprehensive Pictures, The Stapleton Collection / Bridgeman Art Library.*

are in every memory." Aristocrats kept their authority by adapting to change: they entered the bureaucracy and professions, turned their estates into moneymaking enterprises, and learned how to invest shrewdly.

The reassertion of conservative rule hardened gender definitions. Women everywhere had participated in the revolutions, especially in the Italian states, where they joined armies in the tens of thousands and applied household skills toward making bandages, clothing, and food. Schoolgirls in Prague had thrown desks and chairs out of windows and helped build students' barricades. Many

MAPPING THE WEST Europe in 1850

This map of population growth between 1800 and 1850 reveals important trends that would not otherwise be evident. Although population growth correlated for the most part with industrialization, population also grew in more agricultural regions such as East Prussia, Poland, and Ireland. Ireland's rapid population growth does not appear on this map because by 1850 more than a million people had died or emigrated because of the famine of 1846–1851. Compare this map to Map 22.1: Which areas experienced both industrialization and population increase?

women in Paris had supported the new republic and seized the occasion of greater political openness to demand women's rights, only to experience isolation as their claims were denied by most republican men. Men in the revolutions of 1848 almost always defined universal suffrage as a male right. When workingmen gained the vote and women did not, the notion of separate spheres penetrated even into working-class life: political participation became one more way to distinguish masculinity from femininity. As conservatives returned to power, all signs of women's political activism disappeared. The French feminist movement, the most advanced in Europe, fell apart after the June

Days when the increasingly conservative republican government forbade women to form political clubs and arrested and imprisoned two of the most outspoken women leaders for their socialist activities.

In May 1851, Europe's most important female monarch presided over a midcentury celebration of peace and industrial growth that helped dampen the still-smoldering fires of revolutionary passion. Queen Victoria (r. 1837–1901), who herself promoted the notion of domesticity as women's sphere, opened the international Exhibition of the Works of Industry of All Nations in London on May 1. A monument of modern iron and glass architecture had been built to house the display; the building was more than a third of a mile long and so tall that it was built over the trees of its Hyde Park site. Soon people referred to it as the Crystal Palace; its nine hundred tons of glass created an aura of fantasy, and the abundant goods from all nations inspired satisfaction and pride. One German visitor described it as "this miracle which has so suddenly appeared to dazzle the inhabitants of our globe." In the place of revolutionary fervor, the Crystal Palace offered a government-sponsored spectacle of what industry, hard work, and technological imagination could produce.

> **Review:** Why did the revolutions of 1848 fail?

Conclusion

Many of the six million people who visited the Crystal Palace display had not forgotten the specter of cholera, fears of overpopulation, popular resentments, and political upheavals that had been so prominent in the 1830s and 1840s. Even though industrial growth brought railroads, cheaper clothing, and access to exhibitions like the Crystal Palace, it also brought in its train urban overcrowding and miserable working conditions. The Crystal Palace presented the rosy view, but the housing shortages, inadequacy of water supplies, and recurrent epidemic diseases had not disappeared. Social reform organizations still drew attention to prosti-

tution, child abandonment, alcohol abuse, and other problems associated with burgeoning cities.

Although the revolutions of 1848 brought to the surface the profound tensions within a European society in transition toward industrialization and modernization, they did not definitively resolve those tensions. Industrialization and urbanization continued, workers developed more extensive organizations, and liberals and socialists fought over the pace of reform. The revolutions produced their most striking impact negatively rather than positively: confronted with the menace of revolution, elites now sought alternatives that would be less threatening to the established order and still permit some change. This search for alternatives became immediately evident in the question of national unification in Germany and Italy. National unification would hereafter depend on what the Prussian leader Otto von Bismarck would call "blood and iron," and not on speeches and parliamentary resolutions.

Suggested References

The Advance of Industrialization and Urbanization

The spread of industrialization has elicited much more historical interest than the process of urbanization because the analysis of industrialization occupied a central role in Marxism.

Hobsbawm, E. J. *The Age of Revolution, 1789–1848.* 1996.

Kudlick, Catherine J. *Cholera in Post-Revolutionary Paris: A Cultural History.* 1996.

Mokyr, Joel, ed. *The British Industrial Revolution: An Economic Perspective.* 2nd ed. 1999.

Pinkney, David H. *Decisive Years in France, 1840–1847.* 1986.

*Pollard, S., and C. Holmes. *Documents of European Economic History.* Vol. 1, *The Process of Industrialization, 1750–1870.* 1968.

Spartacus Internet Encyclopedia, British History 1700–1950: http://www.spartacus.schoolnet .co.uk/Britain.html.

*Primary source.

Reforming the Social Order

Although romanticism remains a focus of interest for cultural historians, the history of women and the origins of feminism have also attracted attention in recent years. The Web site Gallica, produced by the National Library of France, offers a wealth of imagery and information on French cultural history.

Davidoff, Leonore, and Catherine Hall. *Family Fortunes: Men and Women of the English Middle Class, 1780–1850.* 1987.

The Dickens Project: **http://humwww.ucsc .edu/dickens/index.html**.

Gallica: Images and Texts from Nineteenth-Century French-Speaking Culture: **http:// gallica.bnf.fr**.

Kerr, David S. *Caricature and French Political Culture, 1830–1848.* 2000.

*Murray, Janet Horowitz. *Strong-Minded Women and Other Lost Voices from Nineteenth-Century England.* 1982.

Rendall, Jane. *The Origins of Modern Feminism: Women in Britain, France, and the United States, 1780–1860.* 1990.

Townsend, Mary Lee. *Forbidden Laughter: Popular Humor and the Limits of Repression in Nineteenth-Century Prussia.* 1992.

The Ferment of Ideologies

Ideologies are too often studied in an exclusively national context, so broader generalizations are difficult. The important exception to this national focus is the wide-ranging study by Anderson.

Anderson, Benedict. *Imagined Communities: Reflections on the Origin and Spread of Nationalism.* 1983.

Clark, Anna. *The Struggle for the Breeches: Gender and the Making of the British Working Class.* 1995.

*Mather, F. C., ed. *Chartism and Society: An Anthology of Documents.* 1980.

Sewell, William H., Jr. *Work and Revolution in France: The Language of Labor from the Old Regime to 1848.* 1980.

Taylor, Barbara. *Eve and the New Jerusalem: Socialism and Feminism in the Nineteenth Century.* 1983.

The Revolutions of 1848

Interest in the revolutions of 1848 has revived of late, perhaps because the recent upsurge of ethnic violence in the Balkans has prompted scholars to look again at this critical period.

Dowe, Dieter, ed. *Europe in 1848: Revolution and Reform.* Trans. David Higgins. 2001.

Evans, Robert, and Hartmut Pogge von Strandmann, eds. *The Revolutions in Europe, 1848–1849.* 2000.

Lincoln, W. Bruce. *Nicholas I: Emperor and Autocrat of All the Russias.* 1978.

O'Grada, Cormac. *The Great Irish Famine.* 1989.

Sperber, Jonathan. *The European Revolutions, 1848–1851.* 1994.

*Walker, Mack. *Metternich's Europe.* 1968.

––––––––––

*Primary source.

CHAPTER REVIEW

IMPORTANT EVENTS

1830–1832 Cholera epidemic sweeps across Europe

1830 France invades and begins conquest of Algeria

1831 British and Foreign Temperance Society established

1832 George Sand, *Indiana*

1833 Factory Act regulates work of children in Great Britain; abolition of slavery in the British Empire

1834 German *Zollverein* ("customs union") established under Prussian leadership

1835 Belgium opens first continental railway built with state funds

1839 Beginning of Opium War between Britain and China; invention of photography

1841 Charles Dickens, *The Old Curiosity Shop*

1846 Famine strikes Ireland; Corn Laws repealed in England; peasant insurrection in Austrian province of Galicia

1847 Charlotte Brontë, *Jane Eyre*

1848 Revolutions of 1848 throughout Europe; last great wave of Chartist demonstrations in Britain; Karl Marx and Friedrich Engels, *The Communist Manifesto*; abolition of slavery in French colonies; end of serfdom in Austrian Empire

1851 Crystal Palace exhibition in London

KEY TERMS

Chartism (855)

cholera (829)

communists (855)

Corn Laws (853)

daguerreotype (843)

domesticity (847)

imperialism (848)

lithograph (829)

opium (830)

social question (840)

temperance movement (845)

REVIEW QUESTIONS

1. Why were cities seen as dangerous places?
2. How did reformers try to address the social problems created by industrialization and urbanization? In which areas did they succeed, and in which did they fail?

3. Why did ideologies have such a powerful appeal in the 1830s and 1840s?
4. Why did the revolutions of 1848 fail?

MAKING CONNECTIONS

1. Which of the ideologies of this period had the greatest impact on political events? How can you explain this?
2. In what ways might industrialization be considered a force for peaceful change rather than a revolution? (Hint: Think about the situation in Great Britain.)

FOR FURTHER EXPLORATION

To assess your mastery of the material in this chapter, see the Online Study Guide at bedfordstmartins.com/hunt.

To read additional primary-source material from this period, see Chapter 22 in *Sources of The Making of the West*, Second Edition.

CHAPTER 23

Politics and Culture of the Nation-State, c. 1850–1870

IN 1859, THE NAME "VERDI" suddenly appeared scrawled on walls across the disunited cities of the Italian peninsula. The graffiti seemed to celebrate the composer Giuseppe Verdi, whose operas thrilled crowds of Europeans. Verdi was a hero among Italians, however, for his stories of downtrodden groups struggling against tyrannical government seemed to refer specifically to their plight. As his operatic choruses thundered out calls to rebellion in the name of the nation, Italian audiences were sure that Verdi meant for them to throw off Austrian and papal rule and unite in a new version of the ancient Roman Empire. Yet the graffiti was doubly political: A call to arms in the days before mass media, VERDI also formed an acronym for *Vittorio Emmanuele Re* ("king") *d'Italia*, and in 1859 it summoned Italians to unite immediately under Victor Emmanuel II, king of Sardinia and Piedmont—the one Italian leader with a nationalist, modernizing profile. The graffiti did its work, and the very next year Italy united as a result of warfare, popular uprisings, and hard bargaining by political realists.

In the wake of the failed revolutions of 1848, European statesmen and the politically conscious public increasingly rejected the politics of idealism in favor of **Realpolitik** ◆—a politics of tough-minded realism aimed at strengthening the state and tightening social order. Claiming to distrust the romanticism and high-minded ideologies of the revolutionaries and hoping to control nationalism and other movements for reform, Realpolitikers believed in playing power

◆**Realpolitik:** ray AHL poh lih teek
◆*Aïda:* ah EE duh

Aïda ◆ Poster

Aïda (1871), Giuseppe Verdi's opera of human passion and state power among people of different nations, became a staple of Western culture, bringing people across Europe into a common cultural orbit. Written to celebrate the opening of the Suez Canal, *Aïda* also celebrated the improvement of Europe's access to Asian resources provided by the new waterway. As the poster shows, the opera ushered in a wave of Egyptomania in which Egyptian styles and objects were of great interest in the West. What images from Egypt were popular in Western culture in the nineteenth century? What do you think the images shown here represented for Europeans? *Madeline Grimoldi.*

politics and even using violence to attain their goals. Two particularly skilled practitioners of Realpolitik, the Italian Camillo di Cavour and the Prussian Otto von Bismarck, succeeded in unifying Italy and Germany, respectively, not by consensus but by war and diplomacy. Most leading figures of the decades 1850–1870, enmeshed like Verdi's operatic heroes in violent political maneuverings, advanced state power by harnessing the forces of nationalism and liberalism that had led to earlier romantic revolts. Their achievements changed the face of Europe.

Nation building was the order of the day, and it occurred in a variety of ways during these momentous decades. Continued economic development was crucial, as was a growing sense of national identity and common purpose forged by both culture and government policy. As productivity and wealth increased, governments took vigorous steps to improve the urban environment, monitor public health, and promote national sentiment. State support for cultural developments ranging from public schools to public health programs helped establish a common fund of knowledge and even shared political beliefs. Authoritarian leaders such as Bismarck and the new French emperor Napoleon III believed that a better quality of life would not only calm revolutionary impulses and build state power but also keep political liberals at bay.

Shared culture built a sense of shared identity. Reading novels, attending art exhibitions, keeping up-to-date at the newly fashionable world's fairs, and attending theater and opera gave ordinary people a stronger sense not only of being French or German or British but also of being European. The public consumed cultural works that increasingly rejected romanticism, featuring instead harsher, more realistic aspects of everyday life. Artists painted nudes in shockingly blunt ways, eliminating romantic hues and poses. Verdi's celebrated opera *La Traviata* showed a frolicking courtesan menacing a middle-class family. The Russian author Leo Tolstoy depicted the bleak life of soldiers in the Crimean◆ War, which erupted in 1853 between the Russian and Ottoman Empires, while his countryman Fyodor Dostoevsky◆ wrote of ordinary people turning to crime in urban neighborhoods.

Advocates of Realpolitik cared less for the costs than for the outcomes of state building. Advancing state power entailed stamping out resistance to global expansion. At home, Realpolitikers uprooted neighborhoods to construct public buildings, roads, and parks. The process of nation building was often brutal, bringing war, arrests, protests, and outright civil war—all of these the centerpieces of Verdi's operas as well. As the wars of German unification drew to a close in 1871, an uprising of Parisians threw the new terms of national and industrial growth into question as citizens challenged the central government's intrusion into everyday life and its failure to count

◆**Crimean:** kry MEE uhn
◆**Dostoevsky:** dahs tuh YEHF skee

◆ **1850s–1860s** Positivism, Darwinism become influential

◆ **1850s–1870s** Realism emerges in the arts

◆ **1853–1856** Crimean War

◆ **1861–1865** U.S. Civil War

| 1850 | 1855 | 1860 |

◆ **1857** British-led forces surpress Indian Rebellion

◆ **1861** Italian unification; abolition of serfdom in Russia the costs. For the most part, the powerful Western state did not take shape automatically. Instead, its growth occasioned warfare, dislocation, new inroads on the lives of people around the world, shrewd policy, and heated debate. The Realpolitik approach to nation building that produced all of these outcomes also created a general climate of modern opinion that valued realism and hard facts.

❖ The End of the Concert of Europe

The revolutions of 1848 had weakened the concert of Europe, driving out its architect Klemens von Metternich and allowing the forces of nationalism to flourish. It became more difficult for countries to control their competing ambitions and act together. In addition, the dreaded resurgence of Bonapartism in the person of Napoleon III added to the volatility in international politics as France sought to reassert itself. One of Napoleon's targets was Russia, formerly a mainstay of the concert of Europe. Taking advantage of Russia's continuing drive to expand, France helped engineer the Crimean War. The war took a huge toll in human life and weakened Russia and Austria. Not only did Russia's defeat lead to substantial reforms in the country, but it also made way for a massive shift in the distribution of European power.

Napoleon III and the Quest for French Glory

Louis-Napoleon Bonaparte (Napoleon III) encouraged the resurgence of French grandeur and the cult of his famous uncle as part of nation building. "There are certain men who are born to serve as a means for the march of the human race," he wrote. "I consider myself to be one of these." Napoleon III acted as Europe's schoolmaster, showing its leaders how to combine economic liberalism and nationalism with authoritarian rule. Cafés where men might discuss politics were closed, and a rubber-stamp legislature (the Corps législatif) reduced representative government to a facade. Imperial style replaced republican rituals (see the illustration on the next page). Napoleon's opulent court dazzled the public, and the emperor (like his namesake) cultivated a masculine image of strength and majesty by wearing military uniforms and by conspicuously maintaining mistresses. Napoleon's wife, Empress Eugénie,◆ however, followed middle-class conventions such as separate spheres for men and women by serving as a devoted mother to her only son and supporting many volunteer charities. The authoritarian, apparently old-fashioned order imposed by Napoleon satisfied the many peasants who opposed urban radicalism as they went to the polls.

Yet Napoleon III was simultaneously a modernizer, and he promoted a strong economy, public works programs, and jobs,

---

◆**Eugénie:** oo jay NEE

◆ **1867** Second Reform Bill in England; Austro-Hungarian monarchy

◆ **1868** Meiji Restoration begins in Japan

| 1865 | 1870 | 1875 | 1880 |

◆ **1869–1871** Women's colleges founded at Cambridge University

◆ **1870–1871** Franco-Prussian War

◆ **1871** German Empire proclaimed; Paris Commune

Napoleon III and Eugénie Receive the Siamese Ambassadors, 1864
At a splendid gathering of their court, the emperor Napoleon III, his consort Eugénie, and their son and heir greet ambassadors from Siam, whose exoticism and servility before the imperial family are the centerpiece of this depiction by Jean-Léon Gerome. Amid the grandeur of the Napoleonic dynasty, the West towers above the East. How might a middle-class French grocer react to this scene? *Bridgeman-Giraudon/Art Resource, NY.*

which lured the middle and working classes away from radical politics. International trade fairs, artistic expositions, and the magnificent rebuilding of Paris helped sustain French prosperity as Europe recovered from the hard times of the late 1840s. Empress Eugénie wore lavish gowns, encouraging French silk production and keeping Paris at the center of the lucrative fashion trade. The regime also reached a free-trade agreement with Britain and backed the establishment of innovative investment banks. Such new institutions led the way in financing railroad expansion, and railway mileage increased fivefold during Napoleon III's reign. During the economic downturn of the late 1850s, he wooed support by allowing working-class organizations to form and introducing democratic features into his governing methods. Although some historians have judged Napoleon III to be enigmatic and shifty because of these abrupt changes, his maneuvers were pragmatic responses to the fluid conditions.

On the international scene, Napoleon III's main goals were to overcome the contain-ment of France imposed by the Congress of Vienna, realign continental politics to benefit France, and acquire international glory like a true Bonaparte. To realign European politics, Napoleon pitted France first against Russia in the Crimean War, then against Austria in the War of Italian Unification, and finally against Prussia in the Franco-Prussian War of 1870. Beyond Europe, Napoleon's army continued to enforce French rule in Algeria and Southeast Asia and tried to install Habsburg emperor Francis Joseph's brother Maximilian as ruler of Mexico and ultimately of all Central America—an assault that brought on rebellion and Maximilian's execution in 1867. Napoleon's foreign policy transformed relations among the great powers by causing a breakdown in the international system of peaceful diplomacy established at the Congress of Vienna. While his encouragement of projects like the Suez Canal to connect the Mediterranean and the Red Seas proved visionary, this push for worldwide influence eventually destroyed him: the French overthrew him after Prussia easily defeated his army in 1870.

The Crimean War, 1853–1856: Turning Point in European Affairs

Napoleon first flexed his diplomatic muscle in the Crimean War (1853–1856), which began as a conflict between the Russian and Ottoman Empires but ended as a war with long-lasting consequences for much of Europe. While professing to uphold the concert of Europe, Russia continued to build state power by making further inroads into Asia and the Middle East. In particular, Tsar Nicholas I wanted to absorb much of the Ottoman Empire, fast becoming known as "the sick man of Europe" because of its disintegrating authority. Napoleon III maneuvered Nicholas to be more aggressive in his expansionism, and amid this increasing belligerence war erupted in October 1853 between the two eastern empires (Map 23.1). The war disrupted the united Austrian and Russian front that kept France—and Napoleon III—in check.

The war drew in other states, because behind it lay the question of Europe's balance of power. To protect its Mediterranean routes to East Asia, Britain prodded the Ottomans to stand up to Russia. The Austrian government still resented its dependence on Russia in putting down Hungarian revolutionaries in 1849 and felt threatened by continuing Russian expansion into the Balkans. This anxiety helped Napoleon III gain a promise of Austrian neutrality during the war, thus fracturing the conservative Russian-Austrian coalition that had quashed French ambitions since 1815. In the fall of 1853, the Russians blasted the wooden Turkish ships to bits at the Ottoman port of Sinope♦ on the Black Sea; in 1854, France and Great Britain, enemies in war for more than a century, declared war on Russia to defend the Ottoman Empire's sovereignty and territories.

Faced with attacking the massive Russian Empire, the allies settled for limited military goals focused on capturing the Russian naval base at Sevastopol on the Black Sea in the Crimea. Even so, the Crimean War was spectacularly bloody. British and French troops landed in the Crimea in September 1854 and waged a long siege of the fortified city,

MAP 23.1 The Crimean War, 1853–1856
The most destructive war in Europe between the Napoleonic Wars and World War I, the Crimean War drew attention to the conflicting ambitions around territories of the declining Ottoman Empire. Importantly for state building in these decades, the war fractured the alliance of conservative forces from the Congress of Vienna, allowing Italy and Germany to come into being as unified states and permitting Napoleon III to pursue his ambitions for France. Why were Britain and France interested in so distant an area as the Crimea? What were Russia's interests?

but it fell only after a year of savage and costly combat. Generals on both sides demonstrated their incompetence, and governments failed to provide combatants with even minimal supplies, sanitation, or medical care. Hospitals had no beds, no dishes, and no water. As a result, the war claimed a massive toll. Of the three-quarters of a million deaths, more than two-thirds were from disease and starvation.

In the midst of this unfolding catastrophe, Alexander II (r. 1855–1881) ascended the Russian throne following the death of his father, Nicholas I. With casualties mounting, the new tsar asked for peace. As a result of the Peace of Paris, signed in March 1856, Russia lost the right to base its navy in the Straits of Dardanelles and the Black Sea, which were declared neutral waters. Moldavia and Walachia♦ (which soon merged to form

♦**Sinope:** suh NOH pee

♦**Walachia:** wah LAY kee uh

Romania) became autonomous Turkish provinces under the victors' protection.

Some historians have called the Crimean War one of the most senseless conflicts in modern history because competing claims in southeastern Europe could have been settled by diplomacy had it not been for Napoleon III's driving ambition to disrupt the peace. Yet the war was full of consequence. New technologies were introduced into warfare: the railroad, shell-firing cannon, breech-loading rifles, and steam-powered ships. The relationship of the home front to the battlefront was beginning to change with the use of the telegraph and increased press coverage. Home audiences received news from the Crimean front lines more rapidly and in more detail than ever before. Reports of incompe-

tence, poor sanitation, and the huge death toll outraged the public, inspiring a few to go to the front to help. Florence Nightingale became the best known of these sojourners: she seized the moment to escape the confines of middle-class domesticity by organizing a battlefield nursing service to care for the British sick and wounded. (See The Mission of Mercy, below.) Through her tough-minded organization of nursing units, she not only improved the sanitary conditions of the troops both during and after the war but also pioneered nursing as a profession. (See the excerpt on Mrs. Seacole opposite.)

More immediately, the war accomplished Napoleon III's goal of severing the alliance between the Habsburgs and Russia, the two conservative powers on which the Congress

The Mission of Mercy
Florence Nightingale organized British health-care services during the Crimean War, inspiring a committed cadre of women volunteers to leave domestic life for the battlefront. As disease took its heavy toll, Nightingale introduced sanitary measures into the care of the wounded and sick, dramatically reducing the death rate. Jerry Barrett's romantic portrayal of her greeting the wounded at Scutari hardly captures the strenuous and tough-minded efforts involved in her work. Why would the artist portray the exacting, industrious Nightingale as a romantic, ladylike heroine? *National Portrait Gallery, London.*

Mrs. Seacole: The *Other* Florence Nightingale

Another highly skilled medical worker besides Florence Nightingale made an impact on the battle-fields in Crimea. Mary Seacole (1805–1881), daughter of a free black Jamaican woman and a Scottish army officer, had learned about medicine from her mother and from doctors who passed through Kingston, staying at the family's boardinghouse. In addition to a gift for healing, Mrs. Seacole (as she was always called) had a passion for travel—to Europe, the United States, and Panama—which she supported by tending other travelers. When the Crimean War broke out, she chafed—like Nightingale herself—to be at the battlefront. Arriving in Crimea in 1855, Mrs. Seacole saved many desperately ill soldiers who lacked all medical care.

[Sick soldiers] could and did get at my store sick-comforts and nourishing food, which the heads of the medical staff would sometimes find it difficult to procure. These reasons, with the additional one that I was very familiar with the diseases which they suffered most from and successful in their treatment (I say this in no spirit of vanity), were quite sufficient to account for the numbers who came daily to the British Hotel for medical treatment.

That the officers were glad of me as a doctress and nurse may be easily understood. When a poor fellow lay sickening in his cheerless hut and sent down to me, he knew very well that I should not ride up in answer to his message empty-handed. And although I did not hesitate to charge him with the value of the necessaries I took him, still he was thankful enough to be able to *purchase* them. When we lie ill at home surrounded with comfort, we never think of feeling any special gratitude for the sick-room delicacies which we accept as a consequence of our illness; but the poor officer lying ill and weary in his crazy hut, dependent for the merest necessaries of existence upon a clumsy, ignorant soldier-cook, who would almost prefer eating his meat raw to having the troubles of cooking it (our English soldiers are bad campaigners), often finds his greatest troubles in the want of those little delicacies with which a weak stomach must be humoured into retaining nourishment.

Source: Mary Grant Seacole, *Wonderful Adventures of Mrs. Seacole in Many Lands* (New York: Oxford University Press, 1988), 125–26.

of Vienna peace settlement had rested since 1815. It thus ended Austria's and Russia's grip on European affairs and undermined their ability to contain the forces of liberalism and nationalism. Russia's catastrophic defeat thereby forced the authoritarian state to embark on a long-overdue renovation of the empire.

Spirit of Reform in Russia

Defeat in the Crimean War not only thwarted Russia's territorial ambition but also forced the country onto the path of reform. Hundreds of peasant insurrections had erupted during the decade before the Crimean War. Serf defiance ranged from malingering while at forced labor to boycotting vodka to protest its heavy taxation. "Our own and neighboring households were gripped with fear," one aristocrat reported, because everyone expected "a serf uprising at any minute." Although economic development spread in parts of eastern Europe, the Russian economy stagnated compared with that of western Europe. Old-fashioned farming techniques led to depleted soil and food shortages, and the nobility was often contemptuous of ordinary people's suffering. Works of art such as *A Hunter's Sketches* (1852), by novelist Ivan Turgenev,◆ contributed to a spirit of reform with their sympathetic portrayals of serfs

◆**Turgenev:** tur GAYN yuhf

and frank depiction of brutal masters. A Russian translation of Harriet Beecher Stowe's antislavery novel *Uncle Tom's Cabin* (1852) also struck a responsive chord. When Russia lost the Crimean War, the educated public, including some government officials, found the poor performance of serf-conscripted armies a disgrace and the system of serf labor an intolerable liability.

Emancipation of the Serfs. Confronted with the need for change, Alexander proved more flexible than his father, Nicholas I. Well educated and more widely traveled, Alexander ushered in what came to be known as the age of Great Reforms, granting Russians new rights from above as a way of ensuring that violent action from below would not force change. The most dramatic reform was the emancipation of almost fifty million serfs beginning in 1861. By the terms of emancipation, communities of former serfs, headed by male village elders, received grants of land. The community itself, traditionally called a **mir**,♦ had full power to allocate this land among individuals and to direct their economic activity. Thus, although emancipation partially laid the groundwork for a modern labor force in Russia, communal landowning and decision making prevented unlimited mobility and the development of a pool of free labor.

The condition attached to these so-called land grants was that peasants were not *given* land along with their personal freedom: they were forced to "redeem" the land they farmed by paying the government through long-term loans, which in turn compensated the original landowners. The best land remained in the hands of the nobility, and most peasants ended up owning less land than they had tilled as serfs. These conditions, especially the huge burden of debt and communal regulations, blunted Russian agricultural development for decades. But idealistic reformers believed that the emancipation of the serfs, once treated by the nobility virtually as livestock, had produced miraculous results. As one of them put it, "The people are without any exaggeration transfigured from head to foot. . . . The look, the walk, the speech, everything is changed."

The state also reformed local administration, the judiciary, and the military. The government compensated the nobility for loss of peasant services and set up **zemstvos**♦—regional councils through which aristocrats could direct neglected local matters such as education, public health, and welfare. Aristocratic dominance assured that the zemstvos would remain a conservative structure, but they became a countervailing political force to the distant central government, especially as some nobles profited from the relaxation of censorship and of restrictions on travel to see how the rest of Europe was governed. Their vision broadened as they saw new ways of solving social and economic problems. Simultaneously, judicial reform gave all Russians, even former serfs, access to modern civil courts, rather than leaving them at the mercy of a landowner's version of justice or secret, blatantly preferential practices. The principle of equality of all persons before the law, regardless of social rank, was introduced in Russia for the first time. Military reform followed in 1874 when the government ended the twenty-five-year term of conscription, substituting a six-year term and attention to education, efficiency, and humane treatment of recruits. These changes improved the fitness of Russian soldiers, bringing them closer to the level of their counterparts in western Europe.

From Reform to Rebellion. Alexander's reforms assisted modernizing and market-oriented landowners in Russia just as enclosures and emancipation had done much earlier for landowners in western Europe. At the same time, the changes diminished the personal prerogatives of the nobility, leaving their authority weakened and sparking intergenerational rebellion. "An epidemic seemed to seize upon [noble] children . . . an epidemic of fleeing from the parental roof," one observer noted. Rejecting aristocratic leisure, youthful rebels from the upper class valued practical activity and sometimes identified with peasants and workers. Some formed communes where they hoped to do humble manual labor, whereas others turned to higher education, especially the sciences. Rebellious daughters of the nobility

---

♦**mir:** mihr

♦**zemstvos:** ZEHMPST vohs

flouted parental expectations by cropping their hair short, wearing black, and escaping from home through phony marriages so they could study in European universities. This repudiation of traditional society led Turgenev to label radical youth as nihilists (from the Latin for "nothing"), those who do not believe in any values whatsoever. In fact, it showed a defiant spirit percolating in Russian society.

The atmosphere of nation building also inspired resistance among Russian-dominated ethnic groups, including an uprising by aristocratic and upper-class nationalist Poles, who sought full independence for Poland in 1863. By 1864, however, Alexander II's army had regained control of the Russian section of Poland, having used reforms to buy peasant support in defeating the rebels. In the Caucasus♦ and elsewhere, Alexander responded to nationalist unrest with repression and programs of intensive **Russification**—a tactic meant to reduce the threat of future rebellion by national minorities within the empire by forcing them to adopt Russian language and culture.

In this era of the Great Reforms, the tsarist regime only partially succeeded in developing the administrative, economic, and civic institutions that buttressed the nation-state elsewhere. The tsar and his inner circle tightly held the reins of government, allowing few to share in power. Elsewhere the sense of common citizenship took shape in the nineteenth century, but in imperial Russia the persistence of autocracy and the abuse of large numbers of the population hindered the development of a shared national identity.

> **Review:** What were the main results of the Crimean War?

❖ War and Nation Building

Politicians in the German and Italian states used the opportunity provided by the weakened concert of Europe to unify their countries quickly and violently through warfare. When national disunity threatened, the United States also waged a bloody civil war to ensure its borders and smooth the way for further expansion. Historians sometimes treat the rise of powerful **nation-states** such as Italy, Germany, and the United States and an accompanying sense of national identity among their peoples as part of an inevitable process. However, millions of individuals in the Austrian Empire, Ireland, and elsewhere maintained a regional or local sense of identity rather than a national one.

Cavour, Garibaldi, and the Process of Italian Unification

Despite the failure of the revolutions of 1848 in the Italian states, the issue of Risorgimento♦ (literally meaning "rebirth," especially associated with the movement for Italian unification) continued to simmer, aided by the disintegration of diplomatic stability across Europe. This time the clear leader of the Risorgimento would be the kingdom of Piedmont-Sardinia, in the economically modernizing north of Italy. The kingdom rallied to the operas of Verdi, and its national spirit was fortified by railroads, a modern army, and the support of France against the Austrian Empire, which still dominated the peninsula.

Cavour. The architect of the new Italy was the pragmatic Camillo di Cavour (1810–1861), prime minister of the kingdom of Piedmont-Sardinia from 1852 until his death. A rebel in his youth, Cavour had conducted agricultural experiments on his aristocratic father's land. He organized steamship companies, played the stock market, and inhaled the heady air of modernization during his travels to Paris and London. Cavour promoted economic development rather than democratic uprising as the means to achieve a united Italy. As prime minister to the capricious and scheming king, Victor Emmanuel II (r. Italy 1861–1878), he helped develop a healthy Piedmontese economy, a modern army, and a liberal political climate as the foundation for Piedmont's control of the unification process (Map 23.2).

To unify Italy, however, Piedmont would have to confront Austria, which governed the provinces of Lombardy and Venetia and

---

♦**Caucasus:** KAW kuh suhs

♦**Risorgimento:** ree zawr jih MEHN toh

MAP 23.2 Unification of Italy, 1859–1870

The many states of the Italian peninsula had different languages, ways of life, and economic interests. The northern kingdom of Sardinia, which included the commercially advanced state of Piedmont, had much to gain from a unified market and a more extensive pool of labor. Although King Victor Emmanuel's and Giuseppe Garibaldi's armies brought these states together as a single country, it would take decades to construct a culturally, socially, and economically unified nation. Given that people in the new Italian nation-state did not speak a common language or share the same economic prosperity, what held them together?

northern Italy in April 1859. The cause of Piedmont now became the cause of nationalist Italians everywhere, even those who had supported romantic republicanism in 1848. Political liberals in Tuscany and other central Italian states rose up on the side of Piedmont. Using the newly built Piedmontese railroad to move troops, the French and Piedmontese armies achieved rapid victories at Solferino and Magenta. Suddenly fearing the growth of Piedmont as a potential competing force, Napoleon independently signed a peace treaty with Habsburg emperor Francis Joseph that seemed in effect to end the war. Its terms gave Lombardy but not Venetia to Piedmont, and the rest of Italy remained disunited.

Garibaldi. Napoleon had plans for controlled liberation of Lombardy and Venetia and for the continuation of a disunited Italy, but they were derailed. Support for Piedmont continued to swell inside Italy, while a financially strapped Austria stood by, unable to keep control of events in the peninsula. Ousting their rulers, citizens of Parma, Modena, Tuscany, and the Papal States (except Rome, which French troops had occupied) elected to join Piedmont. In May 1860, Giuseppe Garibaldi (1807–1882), a committed republican, inspired guerrilla fighter, and veteran of the revolutions of 1848, set sail from Genoa with a thousand red-shirted volunteers (many of them teenage boys) to liberate Sicily, where peasant revolts against landlords and the corrupt government were under way in anticipation of the Risorgimento. In the autumn of 1860, the victorious

exerted strong influence over most of the peninsula. Cavour turned for help to Napoleon III, who at a meeting in the summer of 1858 promised French assistance in exchange for the city of Nice and the region of Savoy. Napoleon III expected that France rather than Austria would influence the peninsula thereafter. Sure of French help, Cavour provoked the Austrians to invade forces of King Victor Emmanuel descending from the north and Garibaldi moving up from the south finally met in Naples. Although some of his followers still clamored for social reform and a republic, Garibaldi threw his support to the king. In 1861, the kingdom of Italy was proclaimed with Victor Emmanuel at its head.

Exhausted by a decade of overwork, Cavour died within months of leading the unification, leaving lesser men to organize the new Italy. The task ahead was enormous and complex: for instance, 90 percent of the peninsula's inhabitants did not even speak Italian but rather local languages or dialects. The political side held difficulties too: consensus among Italy's elected political leaders was often elusive once the war was over, and admirers of Cavour, such as Verdi (who had been made senator), fled the heated political scene. Economically, the wealthy commercial north and the impoverished agricultural south remained at odds over issues such as taxation and development, as they do even today. Finally, Italian borders did not yet seem complete because Venetia and Rome remained outside them, under Austrian and French control, respectively. But the legend of an Italian struggle for freedom symbolized by the figure of Garibaldi and his Red Shirts romanticized the economic and military Realpolitik that had made unification possible. Pride in the Italian nation infused many a citizen of the new country (see the illustration opposite).

Bismarck and the Realpolitik of German Unification

The most momentous act of nation building for the future of Europe and the world was the creation of a united Germany in 1871. This too was the product of Realpolitik, undertaken once the concert of Europe was smashed and the champions of the status quo defeated. Employing the old military caste to wage war, yet enjoying support from economic modernizers who saw profits in a single national market, the Prussian state brought a vast array of cities and kingdoms under its control within a single decade. From then on, Germany prospered, continuing to consolidate its economic and political

might. By the end of the nineteenth century, it would be the foremost continental power.

Bismarck's Rise to Power. The architect of the unified Germany was Otto von Bismarck (1815–1898), the Prussian minister-president. Bismarck came from a traditional Junker (Prussian landed nobility) family on his father's side; his mother's family included high-ranking bureaucrats and literati of the middle class. At university, the young Bismarck had gambled and womanized, interested only in a course on the economic foundations of politics. After failing in the civil service, he worked to modernize operations on his landholdings while leading an otherwise loutish life. His marriage

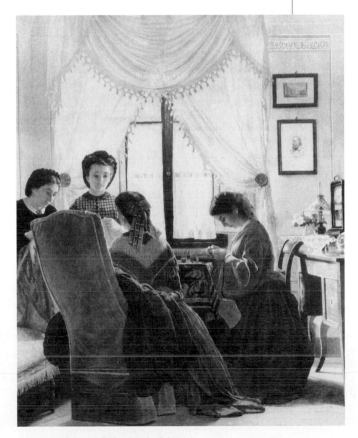

Seamstresses of the Red Shirts

Sewing uniforms and making battle flags, European women like these Italian volunteers saw themselves as contributors to the nation. Many nineteenth-century women participated in nation building as "republican mothers" by donating their domestic skills and raising the next generation of citizens to be patriotic. What advantages did the nation-state bring to women like these in the nineteenth century?

to a pious Lutheran woman worked a transformation and gave him new purpose. In the 1850s his diplomatic service to the Prussian state made him increasingly angry at the Habsburg grip on German affairs and the roadblock it created to the full flowering of Prussia. Establishing Prussia as a respected and dominant power became his cause.

In 1862, William I (king of Prussia, r. 1861–1888; German emperor, r. 1871–1888—see the illustration below) appointed Bismarck prime minister in hopes that he would quash the growing power of the liberals in the Prussian parliament. The liberals, representing the prosperous professional and business classes, had gained parliamentary strength at the expense of conservative landowners during the decades of industrial expansion. Indeed, the liberals' wealth was crucial to the Prussian state's ability to augment its power.

Desiring Prussia to be like western Europe, the liberals advocated the extension of political rights and increased civilian control of the military. William I, along with members of the traditional Prussian elite such as Bismarck, rejected the western European model. Against the liberals' will, Bismarck rammed through programs to build the army and thwart civilian control. "Germany looks not to Prussia's liberalism, but to its power," he preached. "The great questions of the day will not be settled by speeches and majority decisions—that was the great mistake of 1848 and 1849—but by iron and blood."

Prussia's Wars of Unification. After his triumph over the parliament, Bismarck led Prussia into a series of wars, against Denmark in 1864, against Austria in 1866, and, finally, against France in 1870. Using war as a political tactic, he kept the disunited German states from choosing Austrian leadership and instead united them around Prussia. Bismarck drew Austria into a joint war with Prussia against a rebellious Denmark in 1864 over its proposed incorporation of the provinces of Schleswig♦ and Holstein, with their partially German population. Their joint victory resulted in an agreement that Prussia would administer Schleswig, and Austria, Holstein. Such an arrangement stretched Austria's geographic interests far from its central European base.

Austria proved weaker than Prussia, as the Habsburg lands both lagged in economic development and suffered from a swelling national debt and the restlessness of its many national minorities. Bismarck, however, encouraged Austria's pretensions to its former grandeur and influence. He simultaneously fomented disputes over the administration of

Emperor William I of Germany, 1871
The defeat of France in the Franco-Prussian War of 1870–1871 ended with the proclamation of the king of Prussia as emperor of a unified Germany. Otto von Bismarck, who had orchestrated the wars of unification, appropriately appears in Anton von Werner's rendering as the central figure attired in heroic white. The event in the French palace of Versailles symbolized the militaristic and antagonistic side of state building, especially the Franco-German rivalry that would disastrously motivate European politics in the future. *AKG London.*

♦**Schleswig:** SHLAYS vihk

MAP 23.3 Unification of Germany, 1862–1871
In a complex series of diplomatic maneuvers, Prussian leader Otto von Bismarck welded disunited kingdoms and small states into a major continental power independent of the other dominant German dynasty, the Habsburg monarchy. Prussia's use of force against Denmark, the Habsburg Empire, and France unified Germany politically, and almost immediately that unity unleashed the new nation's economic potential. An aristocratic and agrarian elite remained firmly in power, but a rapidly growing working class would soon become a political force to be reckoned with. How did defeating its neighbors allow Prussia to create a unified nation?

Schleswig and Holstein, goading a puffed-up and confident Austria into declaring war on Prussia itself. In the summer of 1866, Austria went to war with the support of most small states in the German Confederation. Within seven weeks the modernized Prussian army, using railroads and breech-loading rifles against the outdated Austrian military, had won decisively. The smart and masterful victory allowed Bismarck to drive Austria from the German Confederation, create a North German Confederation led by Prussia, and coordinate economic and political programs (Map 23.3).

To bring the remaining German states into the rapidly developing nation, Bismarck next moved to entrap France in a war with Prussia. During the Austro-Prussian War, Bismarck had suggested to Napoleon III that his neutrality would bring France new territory,

Bismarck Tricks the Public to Get His War

By 1870 Otto von Bismarck had gained the allegiance of most of the German states (excluding Austria) by waging two successful wars and thus showing the military muscle of Prussia. Defeating France, he believed, would pull in the remaining independent German states—most notably Bavaria—and unite Germany. To this end he doctored a document sent by the Prussian king to the French ambassador over the contested issue of succession to the Spanish throne and released the edited version to the press. He knew that its newly contrived imperious tone would offend the French parliament. Realpolitik, then as now, involved manipulating the press. Here Bismarck describes his actions.

All considerations, conscious and unconscious, strengthened my opinion that war could only be avoided at the cost of the honor of Prussia and of the national confidence in her. Under this conviction I made use of the royal authorization . . . to publish the contents of the telegram; and in the presence of my two guests [General Moltke and General Roon] I reduced the telegram by striking out words, but without adding or altering anything, to the following form:

"After the news of the renunciation of the hereditary prince of Hohenzollern had been officially communicated to the imperial government of France by the royal government of Spain, the French ambassador at Ems made the further demand of his Majesty the king that he should au-

thorize him to telegraph to Paris that his Majesty the king bound himself for all future time never again to give his consent if the Hohenzollerns should renew their candidature. His Majesty the king thereupon decided not to receive the French ambassador again, and sent to tell him, through the aid-de-camp on duty, that his Majesty had nothing further to communicate to the ambassador."

The difference in the effect of the abbreviated text of the Ems telegram as compared with that produced by the original was not the result of stronger words, but of the form, which made this announcement appear decisive, while [the original] version would only have been regarded as a fragment of a negotiation still pending and to be continued at Berlin.

After I had read out the concentrated edition to my two guests, Moltke remarked: "Now it has a different ring; in its original form it sounded like a parley; now it is like a flourish of trumpets in answer to a challenge." I went on to explain: "If, in execution of his Majesty's order, I at once communicate this text, . . . not only to the newspapers, but also by telegraph to all our embassies, it will be known in Paris before midnight, and not only on account of its contents, but also on account of the manner of its distribution, will have the effect of a red rag upon the Gallic bull."

Source: Otto von Bismarck, *Memoirs* in James Harvey Robinson and Charles Beard, eds., *Readings in Modern European History* (Boston: Ginn, 1909), 2:158–59.

thus heating up nationalist sentiments for and against this expansion in both France and Germany. The atmosphere became even more charged when Spain proposed a minor Prussian prince to fill its vacant royal throne. This candidacy at once threatened the French with Prussian rulers on two of their borders and inflated Prussian pride. Bismarck used the occasion to get nationalist sentiments onto the news pages in both countries by editing a diplomatic communication (the so-called Ems telegram, named after the spa

town in which it was issued) to make it look as if the King of Prussia had insulted France over the issue of the vacant throne. Release of the revised version to journalists inflamed the French public into demanding war (see Bismarck's account above). The parliament gladly declared it on July 19, 1870, setting in motion the alliances Prussia had created with the other German states. The Prussians captured Napoleon III with his army on September 2, 1870, and the Second Empire fell two days later.

Birth of the German Empire. With Prussian forces still besieging Paris, in January 1871 in the Hall of Mirrors at Versailles, King William of Prussia was proclaimed the kaiser, or emperor, of a new, imperial Germany. The terms of the peace signed in May of that year required France to cede the rich industrial provinces of Alsace and Lorraine to Germany and to pay a multibillion-franc indemnity. Without French protection for the papacy, Rome became part of Italy. Germany was now poised to dominate continental politics.

Prussian military might served as the foundation for German state building, and a complex constitution ensured the continued political dominance of the aristocracy and monarchy—despite the growing wealth and influence of the liberal business classes. The kaiser, who remained Prussia's king, controlled the military and appointed Bismarck to the powerful position of chancellor for the Reich (empire). The German states balanced monarchical authority somewhat through the Bundesrat, a body composed of representatives from each state. The Reichstag,♦ an assembly elected by universal male suffrage, ratified all budgets but had little room to initiate bills or programs. In framing this constitutional settlement, Bismarck accorded rights such as suffrage in the belief that the masses would uphold autocracy out of their fear of "the domination of finance capital"— shorthand for "liberal power." He balanced this move, however, with an electoral system in populous and powerful Prussia in which the votes from the upper classes counted more than those from the lower. He had little to fear from liberals, who, dizzy with German military success, came to support the blend of economic progress, constitutionalism, and militaristic nationalism that Bismarck represented.

Francis Joseph and the Creation of the Austro-Hungarian Monarchy

There was no blueprint for nation building. Just as the Crimean War left Russia searching for solutions to its social and political problems, so the confrontations with Cavour and Bismarck left the Habsburg Empire de-

♦**Reichstag:** RYKS tahk

feated and at bay. At first, the Habsburg Empire emerged from the revolutions of 1848 and 1849 renewed by the ascension of Francis Joseph (r. 1848–1916), who favored absolutist rule. A tireless worker, Francis Joseph enhanced his authority through stiff, formal court ceremonies, playing to the popular fascination with the trappings of power. Though the emperor stubbornly resisted change, official standards of honesty and efficiency improved, and the government promoted local education. The German language was used by the administration and taught by the schools,

The Austro-Hungarian Monarchy, 1867

but the government respected the rights of national minorities—the Czechs and Poles, for instance—to receive education and communicate with officials in their native tongue. Above all, the government abolished most internal customs barriers, freed trade with Germany, fostered a boom in private railway construction, and attracted foreign capital. The capital city of Vienna underwent extensive rebuilding, and people found jobs as industrialization progressed, if unevenly.

In a fast-moving age, the absolutist emperor could not match Bismarck's pace in advancing modernization and the power of the state. Too much of the old regime remained as a roadblock to change, while prosperous liberals prevented measures that would strengthen the state. They resented the swarm of police informers, the virtually free hand of the Catholic church in education and in civil institutions such as marriage, and their own lack of representation in such important policy matters as taxation and finance. Thus, liberals blocked funds for modernizing the military, and there was no one to override them to bring about change.

After Prussia's victory over Francis Joseph's scaled-back armies in 1866, the most disaffected but wealthy part of the empire, Hungary, became the key to stability and even to the empire's existence. The leaders of the Hungarian agrarian elites forced the emperor to accept a **dual monarchy**—that is, one in which the Magyars had home rule over the Hungarian kingdom. This agreement restored the Hungarian parliament and gave it control of internal policy (including the right to decide how to treat Hungary's national minorities). Although the Habsburg emperor Francis Joseph was crowned king of Hungary and Austro-Hungarian foreign policy was coordinated from Vienna, the Hungarians mostly ruled themselves after 1867 and hammered out common policies such as tariffs in acrimonious negotiations with Vienna. The new political arrangement served as still another roadblock to strengthening the empire as a whole.

The dual monarchy of Austria-Hungary was designed specifically to address the Hungarian demands, but in so doing it strengthened the voices of Czechs, Slovaks, and at least half a dozen additional national groups in the Habsburg Empire wanting the same kind of self-rule. Czechs who had helped the empire advance industrially, for example, desired Hungarian-style liberties. For some of the dissatisfied ethnic groups, **Pan-Slavism**— that is, the transnational loyalty of all ethnic Slavs—became a rallying cry, as the various Slav peoples saw themselves as linked through a common heritage across national boundaries. Instead of looking toward Vienna, they turned to the largest Slavic country—Russia—as a focal point for potential unity. As the nation-state grew in strength, transnational movements like Pan-Slavism would emerge to provide alternative allegiances for those not recognized as equal citizens in their home countries. With so many competing ethnicities, the Austro-Hungarian monarchy remained a dynastic state in which people could rouse loyalty to the Habsburg dynasty but had increasing difficulty relating to one another as members of a single nation.

Political Stability through Gradual Reform in Great Britain

In contrast to the turmoil on the continent, Britain appeared the epitome of liberal progress. By the 1850s, the monarchy symbolized domestic tranquillity and propriety. Unlike their predecessors, Queen Victoria (r. 1837–1901) and her husband, Prince Albert, were considered models of morality, emblematic of British stability and middle-class virtues (see the illustration shown here). Britain's parliamentary system incorporated new ideas and steadily brought more men into the political process. Economic prosperity further fortified peaceful political reform, except for Ireland's continued suffering and thwarted demands for justice. Smooth governmental decision making was fostered by an ever-flexible party system: the Tory Party evolved into the Conservatives, who favored a more status-oriented politics but still went along with the evolving liberal consensus around economic development and representative government. The Whigs changed

Muslim Quarter and Bazaar
Nineteenth-century Europeans were a diverse people, composed of many religions, ethnicities, and ways of life. In the Balkans, many were Muslims, as this marketplace in Sarajevo, Bosnia, illustrates. The goal of finding a common cultural ground eluded the peoples of the Balkans. The Habsburg monarchy, which annexed Bosnia-Herzegovina in 1908, exerted its influence in the area to keep peoples divided and to play one against the other. *Graphische Sammlung Albertina, Wien.*

names, too, and became the Liberals. In 1867, the Conservatives, led by Benjamin Disraeli, passed the Second Reform Bill, which made a million more men eligible to vote.

Political parties supported reforms because pressure groups now influenced the party system. The Law Amendment Society and the Social Science Association, for example, lobbied for laws to improve social conditions, and women's groups advocated the Matrimonial Causes Act of 1857, which facilitated divorce, and the Married Women's Property Act of 1870, which allowed married women to own property and keep the wages they earned. Dissension over new policies was papered over by plush ceremonies that united not only critics and activists but also, and more important, different social classes.

Whereas previous monarchs' sexual infidelities had incited mobs to riot, the monarchy of Queen Victoria and Prince Albert, with its newly devised celebrations of royal marriages, anniversaries, and births, drew respectful crowds. Promoting the monarchy in this way was so successful that the term *Victorian* came to symbolize almost the entire century and could refer to anything from manners to political institutions. The aristocracy, maintaining power despite the rising wealth of liberal businessmen, built gigantic country houses in such traditional English architectural styles as Queen Anne and Georgian, still further anchoring the monarchical heritage in the modern age. Yet Britain's politicians were as devoted to Realpolitik as those in Germany, Italy, or France, especially using violence to expand their overseas empire and increasingly to control Ireland. The violence was far beyond the view of most British people, however, allowing them to imagine their nation as peaceful, advanced, and united.

Queen Victoria and Prince Albert
Mid-nineteenth-century rulers started using the new photographic technology to make themselves respectable and celebrated figures. Queen Victoria and her consort, Prince Albert, were expert publicists, often posing as an ordinary middle-class couple and the epitome of domestic order. Their photos were sold or given away on small cards called *cartes de visites*, a means used by many leaders to spread their fame. How does this presentation of Victoria and Albert differ from those of monarchs in the eighteenth century such as Catherine the Great (page 706), or Napoleon (page 786)? *The Royal Archives © Her Majesty Queen Elizabeth II.*

Civil War and Nation Building in the United States and Canada

In North America, increasing nationalism and powerful economic growth characterized the nation-building experience. The United States entered a midcentury period of upheaval with a more democratic political culture than existed in Europe. Virtually universal white male suffrage, a rambunctiously independent press, and mass political parties endorsed the accepted view that sovereignty derived from the people.

The United States continued to expand its territory to the west (Map 23.4). In 1848, victory in its war with Mexico almost doubled the size of the country: Texas was officially annexed, and large portions of California and the Southwest extended U.S. borders into formerly Mexican land. Politicians and citizens alike favored banning the native Indian peoples from these western lands. Complicating matters, however, was the question

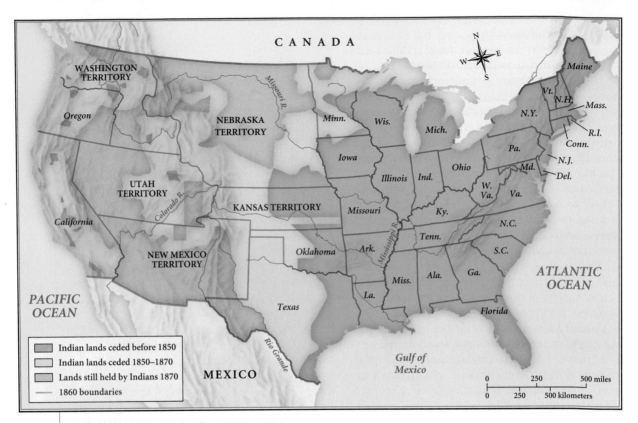

MAP 23.4   U.S. Expansion, 1850–1870
Like Russia, the United States expanded into adjacent regions to create a continental nation-state. Conquering indigenous peoples and taking over their territories, the United States differed from Russia, however, by herding native peoples into small confined spaces called reservations so that settlers could acquire thousands of square miles for farming and other enterprises. Gradually some native Americans acquired the right to vote, and the U.S. government granted full citizenship for all in 1925. What are the differences between U.S. expansion in North America and the expansion of the British in India (see page 896)?

of whether the West would be settled by free white farmers or whether southern slaveholders could bring in their slaves.

The issue polarized the country. In the North, the new Republican Party emerged to demand "free soil, free labor, free men," although few Republicans endorsed the abolitionists' demand to end slavery. With the 1860 election of Republican Abraham Lincoln to the presidency, most of the slaveholding states seceded to form the Confederate States of America. Between 1861 and 1865, the United States was torn apart by a devastating civil war.

Under Lincoln's leadership, the North fought to uphold the Union. Lincoln did not initially aim to abolish slavery, but in January 1863 his Emancipation Proclamation came into force as a wartime measure, offi-cially freeing all slaves in the Confederate states and turning the war into a fight not only for union but also for blacks' liberation from slavery. After the summer of 1863, the North's superior industrial strength and military might overpowered and physically destroyed much of the South. By April 1865, the North had prevailed, even though a Confederate sympathizer had assassinated Lincoln. Distancing the United States still further from the colonial plantation model, constitutional amendments ended slavery and promised full political rights to free African American men.

Northerners hailed their victory as the triumph of American values, but racism remained entrenched throughout the Union. By 1871, northern interest in promoting African

American political rights was waning, and southern whites began regaining control of state politics, often by organized violence and intimidation. The end of northern occupation of the South in 1877 put on hold for nearly a century the promise of rights for blacks.

The North's triumph had profound effects elsewhere in North America. It allowed the reunited United States to contribute to Napoleon III's defeat in Mexico in 1867. The United States also demanded the annexation of Canada in retribution for Britain's partiality to the Confederacy because of its dependence on cotton. To head off this threat, the British government allowed Canadians to form a united, self-governing dominion. Dominion status answered Canadian appeals for home rule and lessened domestic opposition to Britain's control of Canada.

Review: What role did warfare play in the various nineteenth-century nation-building efforts?

❖ Establishing Social Order

The age of nation building disturbed everyday life, often bringing chaos and sometimes dramatic public protest. Thus, government officials developed mechanisms to forge internal social unity and order that served to clean up or offset the violence and change by which the nation-state was expanding. Confronted with growing populations and crowded cities, governments throughout Europe intervened to guard social peace by attending to public health and safety. Many liberal theorists advocated a laissez-faire government that left social and economic life largely to private enterprise. Nevertheless, having confidence in the benefits of European institutions in general, bureaucrats and reformers paid more attention to citizens' lives and with the help of missionaries and explorers spread European influence to the farthest reaches of the globe.

Bringing Order to the Cities

European cities became the backdrop for displays of state power and national solidarity; thus, efforts to improve sanitation and control disease redounded to the state's credit. Governments focused their refurbishing efforts on their capital cities, although many noncapital cities acquired handsome parks, widened streets, and erected stately museums and massive city halls. In 1857, Francis Joseph ordered the old Viennese city walls to be replaced with concentric boulevards lined with major public buildings such as the opera house and government offices (see the illustration on the next page). Opera houses and ministries tangibly represented national wealth and power, and the broad boulevards allowed crowds to observe royal pageantry. These wider roads were also easier for troops to navigate than the twisted, narrow medieval streets that in 1848 had concealed insurrectionists in cities like Paris and Vienna—an advantage that convinced some otherwise reluctant officials to approve the expense. Impressive parks and public gardens showed the state's control of nature, while they helped order people's leisure time. Revamped European cities inspired awe among the citizens of the various nation-states and throughout their empires.

Another effect of refurbishing cities was to highlight class differences. Construction first required destruction, and officials chose to eliminate poor neighborhoods, dislocating tens of thousands of city dwellers. The new boulevards often served as boundaries marking rich and poor sections of the city. In Paris, the process of urban change was called **Haussmannization,**[*] named for the prefect Georges-Eugène Haussmann, who implemented a grand design that included eighty-five miles of new city streets, many lined with showy dwellings for the wealthy. In London, improved architectural design, including Victorian ornamentation, many believed, would blot out the ugliness of commerce and industry. Moreover, the size and spaciousness of the many new banks and insurance companies built there "help[ed] the impression of stability," as an architect put it, and this would foster social order. Civic pride would also result from urban renewal, replacing rebellion.

Yet there were problems in merely focusing on ornament and grandeur. Amid signs of economic prosperity, the devastation

---

[*]**Haussmannization:** hows muhn ih ZAY shuhn

Vienna Opera House
The era of nation building saw the construction of architectural monuments in the center of capital cities to display cultural power and to bring music, art, and science to the people. Officials directed the rebuilding of Vienna's center around imposing facades like that of the Imperial Opera House, which opened in 1869. *Hulton Archive/Getty Images.*

caused by repeated epidemics of diseases such as cholera debilitated city dwellers and gave the strong impression of social decay. Poor sanitation allowed typhoid bacteria to spread through sewage and into water supplies, infecting rich and poor alike. In 1861, Britain's Prince Albert—the beloved husband of Queen Victoria—reputedly died of typhus, commonly known as a "filth disease." Unregulated urban slaughterhouses and tanneries; heaps of animal excrement in chicken coops, pigsties, and stables; human waste alongside buildings; open cesspools; and garbage everywhere facilitated the spread of germs. The stench, diseases, and "morbid air" in cities indicated such a degree of failure, disorder, and danger that sanitation too became a government priority.

Scientific research, increasingly undertaken in public universities and hospitals, provided the means to promote public health and control disease. France's Louis Pasteur, whose three young daughters had died of typhus, advanced the germ theory of disease with its widespread sanitary application. Seeking a method to prevent wine from spoiling, Pasteur began his work in the mid-1850s by studying fermentation. He found that the growth of living organisms caused fermentation, and he suggested that certain organisms—bacteria and parasites—might be responsible for human and animal diseases. Pasteur further demonstrated that heating foods such as wine and milk to a certain temperature, a process that soon became known as pasteurization, killed these organisms and made food safe. English surgeon Joseph Lister applied the germ theory in medicine. He connected Pasteur's theory of bacteria to infection and developed antiseptics for treating wounds and preventing puerperal fever, a condition caused by the dirty hands of physicians and midwives that killed innumerable women after childbirth.

Governments undertook projects to modernize sewer and other sanitary systems—urban improvements prized by citizens, who often attributed them to national superiority. In Paris, huge underground collectors provided a watertight terminus for accumulated sewage (see Paris Sewers, below). In addition, Haussmann piped in water from uncontaminated sources in the countryside to provide each household with a secure supply. Such ventures were imitated throughout Europe: the Russian Empire's port city Riga (now in Latvia), for example, organized its first water company in 1863. Improved sanitation testified to progress and a more active role for the state. Shopkeepers agitated for paved streets to end the difficulties of transporting goods along muddy or flooded roadways. When public toilets for men became a feature of modern cities, women petitioned governments for similar facilities. On the lookout for disease and sanitary dangers, the average person became more aware of smells and the foul air that had been an accepted part of daily life for thousands of years. One citizen of a city in central Russia lamented to the Moscow newspapers that "an enormous cloud of white dust constantly over the city" injured the eyes and lungs. To show that they were becoming more "civilized," the middle and lower-middle classes bathed more regularly. Middle-class concerns for refinement and health mirrored the quest of governments for order.

Expanding the Reach of Bureaucracy

To enact new programs and build social order, governments required citizens to follow a growing catalog of regulations that reached far into the realm of everyday life. The regular censuses that Britain, France, and the United States had begun early in the nineteenth century became routine in most other countries as well. Censuses provided the state with such personal details of its citizens' lives as age, occupation, marital status, residential patterns, and fertility. Governments then used these data for a variety of en-

deavors, ranging from setting quotas for military conscription to predicting needs for new prisons. Reformers like Florence Nightingale, who gathered medical and other statistics to support sanitary reform, believed that such quantitative information made government less susceptible to corruption, special deals, and inefficiency. Decisions would be based on facts rather than on influence-peddling or ill-informed hunches. In 1860, Sweden was the first country to introduce income taxes, which opened an area of private life—one's earnings from work or investment—to government scrutiny.

To bring about their vision of social order, most governments, including those of Britain, Italy, Austria, and France, also expanded their regulation and investigation of prostitution. Venereal disease, especially syphilis, was a scourge of the era that, like typhus, infected individuals and whole families. Officials

Touring the Paris Sewers
The Paris sewers were rebuilt in Napoleon III's Second Empire as models of modern hygiene sponsored by the state. Their construction was part of the effort to eliminate smells and signs of germs from both public and private life. As society opted for hygiene, sewers became emblematic of dangerous and diseased peoples who were threats to social well-being and order. Tours of the sewer system became and remain a major tourist attraction because of the odd combination of primal sewage with modern technology. © *Collection Roger-Viollet/Getty Images.*

blamed prostitutes, not their clients, for its spread. The police picked up any suspect woman on the street, passed her to public health doctors who examined her for syphilis, and incarcerated her for mandatory treatment if she was infected. As states began monitoring prostitution and other social matters like public health and housing, they had to add new departments and agencies. In 1867, Hungary's bureaucracy handled fewer than 250,000 public welfare cases; twenty years later, it dealt with more than a million.

The middle classes recognized the potential for influential jobs in the expansion of these bureaucratic agencies and lobbied to eliminate aristocrats' stranglehold on the top positions. They argued that civil service jobs should be awarded according to talent and skill rather than political loyalty or high birth. In Britain, a civil service law passed in 1870 required competitive examinations to assure competency in government posts—an idea in the air since the West had come in contact with the Chinese examination system. Citizens thus demanded that the state itself conform to middle-class ideas of fairness, competence, and opportunity.

Schooling and Professionalizing Society

Increased emphasis on empirical knowledge and objective standards of evaluation enhanced the status of certain professions, even as it changed their nature. Growing numbers of middle-class doctors, lawyers, managers, professors, and journalists gained prestige for employing science, information, and standards in their work. Governments began to allow professional people to influence state policy and to determine rules for who would and would not be admitted to their fields. Such legislation had both positive and negative effects: groups could set high standards, but otherwise qualified people were sometimes prohibited from working because they lacked the established credentials or connections. The German medical profession, for example, was granted authority to control the licensing of physicians, which led to more rigorous university training for future doctors but also pushed midwives out of medicine and caused the arrest of healers not trained in medical school. Science, too, became

the province of the trained specialist rather than the experienced amateur; scientists were likely to be employed by universities and institutes, funded by the government, and provided with equipment and assistants. Like other members of the middle class, professors of science often interpreted their work as part of a national struggle for prestige and excellence.

Nation building required major improvements in the education of all citizens, professional or not. Bureaucrats and professionals called for radical changes in the scope, curriculum, and faculty of schools—from kindergarten to university—to make the general population more fit for citizenship and useful in furthering economic progress. Ongoing expansion of the electorate along with lower-class activism prompted one British aristocrat to say of the common people, whom he feared were gaining influence, "We must now educate our masters!" Governments also introduced compulsory schooling to reduce illiteracy rates, which were more than 65 percent in Italy and Spain in the 1870s and even higher in eastern Europe. As ordinary people were allowed to participate in government, books taught them about the responsibilities of citizenship, along with practical knowledge necessary for an industrial society.

Accomplishing this goal was not always easy. At midcentury, various religious denominations supervised schools and charged tuition, making primary education an option chosen only by prosperous or religious parents. After the 1850s many leaders felt that liberal rationalism should supplant religious fervor as a guiding principle for instruction. In 1861, an English commission on education concluded that instead of knowledge of the Bible, "the knowledge most important to a labouring man is that of the causes which regulate the amount of his wages, the hours of his work, the regularity of his employment, and the prices of what he consumes." To cohere as citizens of a nation, the young had to learn its language, literature, and history. Supplanting religion was one challenge for the secular and increasingly knowledge-based state.

Enforcing school attendance was another challenge. Though the Netherlands, Sweden, and Switzerland had functioning primary school systems before midcentury, rural parents in these and other countries did not automatically make use of the opportunity. They depended on their children to perform farm chores and often believed that young people would gain the knowledge necessary for life in the fields or the household. Urban homemakers from the lower classes needed their children to help with domestic tasks such as fetching water, disposing of waste, tending younger children, and scavenging for household necessities such as stale bread from bakers or soup from local missions. Yet even among the working poor, education, like other aspects of nation building, ultimately became a shared value and led to a craze for learning, which made traveling lecturers, public forums, reading groups, and debating societies popular among the middle and working classes.

The secondary school also expanded, reflecting the demands of both an industrial society and a bureaucratic state. In Prussia, a system of secondary schools (*Gymnasia*) offered a liberal arts curriculum that trained students for a variety of careers. In the 1860s, however, new *Realschulen*,◆ or technical schools, less prestigious at the time, emphasized math, science, and modern languages for those who would not attain a Gymnasium degree or go on to attend the university. Secondary education remained a luxury for the privileged few, however, and in some countries such as Russia it was even suspect. Authoritarian officials saw the study of modern subjects such as science as potentially subversive of the old order.

Reformers pushed to allow young women to attend more advanced and more complex courses than they had been offered in the past. In France and Russia, government leaders themselves saw that "public education has had in view only half the population—the male sex," as the Russian minister of education wrote to Tsar Alexander II in 1856. Both Napoleon III and Alexander II sponsored secondary- and university-level courses for women as part of their programs to control the modernization of society. In Britain, the founders of two women's colleges—Girton (1869) and Newnham (1871)—at Cambridge University believed that exacting standards in

women's higher education would provide an example of a modern curriculum, reward merit, and thus improve the low standards of scholarship prevalent in the men's colleges of Cambridge and Oxford. The modern need for highly competent elites thus challenged the gentlemanly ideal that education merely served to indicate social status. Nonetheless, higher education for women remained a hotly contested issue. The vast majority of people felt that knowledge of religion, sewing, deportment, and writing was adequate for women. On the other side, reformers from across the political spectrum argued that women who knew some science, history, and literature would rear their children better and prove more interesting wives.

Education also opened professional doors to women, who came to attend universities—in particular, medical schools—in Zurich and Paris in the 1860s. Despite criticism that their practicing medicine would weaken the system of separate spheres, women doctors thought that they could protect female patients' modesty better than male doctors and could bring feminine values to health care. The growing need for educated citizens also offered the opportunity for large numbers of women to enter teaching, a field once dominated by men. Hundreds of women founded nurseries, kindergartens, and primary schools based on the Enlightenment idea that developmental processes start at an early age. In Italy, these efforts coincided with the founding of a unified nation, and women there founded schools as a way to expand knowledge and teach civics lessons, thus providing a service to the fledgling state. Yet the idea of women teaching also aroused intense opposition. "I shudder at philosophic women," wrote one critic of female kindergarten teachers. Seen as radical because it enticed middle-class women out of the home, early childhood education, or the "kindergarten movement," was as controversial as most other educational reforms.

Spreading Western Order beyond the West

In an age of nation building and industrial development, colonies took on new importance, adding a political dimension, including direct rule from the homeland, to the

---

◆ *Realschulen:* ray AHL shoo lehn

economic role that global trade already played in national prosperity. After midcentury Great Britain, France, and Russia revised their colonial policies by instituting direct rule, expanding colonial bureaucracies, and in many cases providing a wider array of social and cultural services, such as schools. For instance, in the 1850s and 1860s provincial governors and local officials promoted the extension of Russian borders to gain control over nomadic tribes in central and eastern Asia. As in areas like Poland and the Ukraine, the state instituted common educational and religious policies, often enforcing the use of the Russian language and the practice of Russian orthodoxy as a means to social order.

Great Britain, the era's mightiest colonial power, made a dramatic change of course toward direct political rule during these decades. Before the 1850s, British liberals desired commercial gain from colonies, but, believing in laissez-faire, they kept political involvement in colonial affairs minimal. In India, the East India Company ruled on Britain's behalf, and many regional rulers awarded the company commercial advantages. Since the eighteenth century, the East India Company had expanded its dominion over various kingdoms on the Indian subcontinent, becoming the major tax collector for the region and building railroads throughout the countryside to make commerce and revenue collecting more efficient. As the British bureaucratic and economic presence grew, enterprising Indian merchants and financiers enhanced their wealth by dealing with the Europeans through trade and tax collection. Other local men enlisted in the British-run Indian civil service and the colonial army, which became one of the largest standing armies in the world.

In 1857, a contingent of these Indian troops, both Muslim and Hindu, violently

Indian Resistance, 1857

rebelled against the expanded British presence and the disregard it entailed for their autonomy and local beliefs. Ignoring the Hindu ban on beef and the Muslim prohibition of pork, the British forced Indian soldiers to use cartridges greased with cow and pig fat. This was not their main grievance, though. The soldiers, angered at tightening British control, stormed and conquered the old Moghul capital at Delhi and declared the independence of the Indian nation—an uprising that became known as the Indian Rebellion. Simultaneously, there erupted civil rebellions, composed both of leaders who were being displaced and the general populace who backed them. The virtually powerless emperor, Bahadur Shah, explained the rebellion as one against "the tyranny and oppression of the infidel and treacherous English." The rani ("queen") Lakshmibai,♦ widow of the ruler of the state of Jhansi♦ in central India, led a separate military revolt when the East India Company tried to take over her lands after her husband died. Brutally put down by British-led Indian forces from other regions, the Indian Rebellion of 1857 and the Jhansi revolt gave birth to Indian nationalism. (See "New Sources, New Perspectives," page 898.) They also persuaded the British government to issue the Government of India Act of 1858, which established direct British control of India.

A system of rule emerged in which close to half a million Indians governed the Asian subcontinent under the supervision of a few thousand British men. Indians also collected taxes and distributed patronage. Colonial rule meant both blatant domination and more subtle intervention in everyday life. Simultaneously, however, ordinary Indians benefited in some places from improved sanitation and medicine. Following the British attack on their cultural practices, some upper-class Indians came to reject Indian customs such as infanticide, child marriage, and *sati*—a widow's self-immolation on her husband's funeral pyre. British notions of a scientifically ordered society also proved attractive to some Indians, who sent their children to British schools for training. The unity

♦**Lakshmibai:** LAHK shmee BY
♦**Jhansi:** JAHNT see

that British rule gave to what were once small localities and princedoms with separate allegiances promoted nationalism that, paradoxically, would soon be used against them.

French political expansion was similarly a matter of push, pull, and paradox. The French government pushed to establish its dominion over Cochin◆ China (modern southern Vietnam) in the 1860s. Missionaries in the area, ambitious French naval officers stationed in Asia, and even some local peoples—as in the case of Indian merchants and financiers—urged the French government to make successive attacks in the region to establish even greater control. Like the British, the French brought improvements, such as the Mekong Delta project that increased the amount of cultivated land and spurred rapid growth in the food supply. Sanitation and public health programs proved a mixed blessing, because they led to population growth that strained other local resources. Furthermore, landowners and French imperialists siphoned off most of the profits from economic improvement. The French also undertook a cultural mission to transform cities like Saigon with signs of Western urban life such as tree-lined boulevards that emulated those of Paris. French literature, theater, and art were popular not only with colonial officials but also with upper-class Indochinese.

Strategic commercial and military advantages remained an important motivation for some European overseas ventures in this age of Realpolitik. The Crimean War had shown the great powers that the Mediterranean basin was pivotal. Napoleon III, remembering his uncle's campaign in Egypt, took an interest in building the Suez Canal, which would connect the Mediterranean with the Red Sea and the Indian Ocean and thus dramatically shorten the route from Europe to Asia. Upon completion of the work in 1869, canal mania erupted. Verdi composed the opera *Aïda*, set in ancient Egypt, and Europeans developed a craze for anything Egyptian, adopting new styles in textile design, furniture, architecture, and art.

The rest of the Mediterranean and the Ottoman Empire felt the heightened presence of the European powers. Driving into the North African hinterland, the French army occupied all of Algeria by 1870, the year in which the number of European immigrants to the region reached one-quarter million. There was also a pull: as elsewhere, French rule in Algeria was aided by the attraction of local people to European goods, technology, and institutions. Merchants and local leaders cooperated in building railroads, sought bank loans and trade from the French, and sent their children to European-style schools. Many local peoples, however, resisted the invasions by continuing to attack soldiers and settlers. Others died from European-spread diseases. By 1872, the native population in Algeria had declined by more than 20 percent from five years earlier.

Its vastness allowed China to escape complete takeover, but the Qing◆ empire was rapidly declining from its populous and prosperous peak in the eighteenth century. Traders and Christian missionaries from European countries, carrying their message of Christian salvation, made inroads for the Western powers. Directing the Christian message to a population that had almost doubled during the preceding century and now numbered about 430 million, missionaries spread Christianity in a society already destabilized by demographic growth, defeat in the Opium War, and economic pressures from European trade. These contacts with the West had helped generate the mass movement known as the Taiping◆ ("Heavenly Kingdom"). Its millions of adherents wanted an end to the ruling Qing dynasty, the elimination of foreigners, more equal treatment of women, and land reform. By the mid-1850s, the Taiping controlled half of China. The Qing regime, its dynasty threatened, promised the British and French greater influence in exchange for aid. The result was a bloody civil war that lasted until 1864 and killed some thirty to sixty million Chinese (compared with 600,000 dead in the U.S. Civil War). When peace finally came, Western governments controlled much of the Chinese customs service and had virtually unlimited access to the country.

◆**Cochin:** KOH chihn

◆**Qing:** CHIHNG
◆**Taiping:** TY PIHN

NEW SOURCES, NEW PERSPECTIVES

Photographs and Their Messages

After almost a century of experimentation, photography was invented in France and Britain in 1839, by a handful of different men working independently of one another. Photography immediately expanded people's access to visual information, and governments understood photographs to be important resources. In the Crimean War, photographers began to substitute for official illustrators and mapmakers who customarily sketched out the vistas of towns and roads, including the placement of public buildings, natural lines of defense, and fortifications necessary for army maneuvers. Among the photographers who flocked to this unrecorded region was Carol Popp de Szathmari of Budapest, who took photos of both Russian and Turkish camps. He later sold these as a popular photo album of the war. It was in the Crimean War that newspapers also began printing lithographs of wartime destruction to buildings. As in many wars, photographs of human carnage were not generally shown. An eager public bought both illustrated newspapers and albums, which strengthened their allegiance to the nation-state and its wars.

Since the Crimean War, historians have recognized the importance of photography for the data it provides about which topics were of public interest. A vast interest in Asia and the Middle East is evidenced in the thousands of extant photographs of monuments of Egypt, Turkey, and Japan taken in the second half of the nineteenth century. *Social Life of the Chinese: A Daguerreotype of Daily Life in China* was a popular album of photos published in 1868. Using photos of furniture and fashions that salesmen carried from city to city in the 1850s and 1860s, historians have been able to visualize everyday life better.

Recently, however, photography in this period has yielded new interpretations, especially about people's values. The earliest photos started inching the West toward its modern celebrity cult. Photos of renowned professors were sold right outside their classroom doors, while great poets, kings and queens, businessmen, and public figures had their likenesses taken to burnish their reputations. The British royal family was expert in image building, photographing royal weddings and affixing the photos to little cards

Japan alone in East Asia was able to escape European domination. Through Dutch traders at Nagasaki, the Japanese had become keenly aware of industrial, military, and commercial innovations of European society. By 1853, when Americans steamed into the port of Uraga and claimed to open Japan to trade, contacts with Europe had already given the Japanese not only a healthy appetite for Western goods but also knowledge of and a concern over superior Western weaponry. Trade agreements with the United States and others followed, leading to concerted effort for reform. In 1867, Japanese reformers, after a brief civil war, pressured the ruling shogun (dominant military leader), who was a descen-

dant of the Tokugawa family that had been in power for some two centuries, to abdicate. In 1868 they restored the emperor to full power. The goal of the **Meiji◆ Restoration**—as this change came to be known—was to establish Japan as a modern, technologically powerful state free from Western control. Even the word *Meiji*, chosen by the new emperor to name his reign, meant "enlightened rule," as the regime professed to combine "Western science and Eastern values" as a way of "making new"—hence, *restoration*. Oddly enough, although it adopted many Western institutions and attitudes, the Meiji Restora-

---

◆**Meiji:** MAY jee

Indian Rebellion, 1857

Photographers were on the scene at Lucknow in India to capture the destruction wrought during the Indian Rebellion. Westerners viewed the uprising as resulting from the savagery of the Asians, while the damage inflicted by the British served to remind Westerners and colonized peoples alike of the superior power of European civilization. Photography was an integral part of the advance of imperialism, recording its progress and transmitting news to the rest of the world. The photographer of this photo is even thought to have arranged the people and bones in this photo. What caption might a British newspaper editor have written for this photo in 1857? What about a South Asian journalist? *Gernsheim Collection, Harry Ransom Humanities Center/University of Texas (Austin).*

called *cartes de visites* that the public collected like today's baseball cards.

Photography allowed people to manipulate reality. Historians have recently seen the genius of Queen Isabella II of Spain, whose chaotic administration was made to look orderly by her official photographer's expert shots of tidy parts of cities and public buildings. The queen had set a publicist to work as early as 1852 to change the image of her reign. Even battlefield shots, historians have recently admitted, were often staged after the fact to reflect the public's expectations. The photograph—on the surface a portrayal of a single reality—may be open to a still wider range of interpretations.

tion ultimately inspired other regions in Asia and Africa to resist the expanding grasp of the European nation-state.

> **Review:** How did colonial expansion change in the period of nation building?

❖ The Culture of Social Order

Artists and writers of the mid-nineteenth century had complex reactions to the rising nation-state and its expanding reach. After 1848, many artists and writers expressed profound grievances, notably about political repression, economic growth, and the effect of enfranchising working-class men. Infused with commercial values and organized by officials, daily life seemed to many artists tawdry and hardly bearable. Unlike the romantics of the first half of the century, however, artists of the second half often had difficulty depicting heroic ideals. "How tired I am of the ignoble workman, the inept bourgeois, the stupid peasant, and the odious priest," wrote the French novelist Gustave Flaubert, frustrated by his inability to romanticize these figures as previous generations had done. Such disenchantment promoted the literary and artistic style called **realism**. In contrast, intellectuals proposed

AGE OF GREAT BOOKS

1851	Auguste Comte, *System of Positive Politics*
1852	Harriet Beecher Stowe, *Uncle Tom's Cabin*
1854	Charles Dickens, *Hard Times*
1857	Gustave Flaubert, *Madame Bovary*
	Charles Baudelaire, *Les Fleurs du mal*
1859	Charles Darwin, *On the Origin of Species*
	John Stuart Mill, *On Liberty*
1866	Fyodor Dostoevsky, *Crime and Punishment*
1867	Karl Marx, *Das Kapital*
1869	John Stuart Mill, *The Subjection of Women*
1871–1872	George Eliot, *Middlemarch*

scientific theories that appraised social change and even political upheaval as part of human progress. Cultural styles and intellectual ideas shared a claim to look at society with a detached eye and to depict social order starkly. It was a stark realism similar to that which statesmen applied to politics.

The Arts Confront Social Reality

The quest for national power enlisted culture in its cause. A hungry reading public devoured biographies of political leaders, past and present, and credited heroes with creating the triumphant nation-state. As the development of schooling spread literacy, all classes of readers responded to the mid-nineteenth-century novel and to an increasing number of artistic, scientific, and natural history exhibitions. Whether reading the same novels or attending musical events together, citizens came to be schooled in the common artistic style of realism and to embrace their common national heritage.

The Realist Novel. A well-financed press and commercially minded publishers produced an age of best sellers out of the craving for realism. The novels of Charles Dickens appeared in serial form in magazines and periodicals, and each installment attracted buyers eager for the latest plot twist. Dickens's characters, from contemporary English society, included starving orphans, grasping

lawyers, heartless bankers, and ruthless opportunists. *Hard Times* (1854) depicted the grinding poverty and ill health of workers, while *Bleak House* (1852) used dark humor to portray the judicial bureaucracy's intrusion into private life. The novelist George Eliot (the pseudonym of Mary Ann Evans) examined contemporary moral values and deeply probed private, "real-life" dilemmas in works like *The Mill on the Floss* (1860) and *Middlemarch* (1871–1872). Depicting rural society, high and low, Eliot allowed Britons to see one another's predicaments, wherever they lived. Eliot knew the pain of ordinary life from her own experience: she was a social outcast because she lived with a married man. Despite her fame, she was not received in polite society. These popular novels showed a hard reality and thus helped form a shared culture among people in distant parts of a nation much as state institutions did.

French writers also scorned dreams of political utopias and ideals of transcendent beauty. Gustave Flaubert's novel *Madame Bovary* (1857) tells the story of a bored doctor's wife who, full of romantic longings and eager for distraction, has one love affair after another and becomes so hopelessly indebted that she commits suicide. Serialized in a Paris journal, *Madame Bovary* scandalized French society with its frank picture of women's sexuality, but the scandal brought it a nationwide readership. The poet Charles-Pierre Baudelaire,◆ called satanic by his critics, wrote explicitly about sex; in *Les Fleurs du mal* (*Flowers of Evil*, 1857), he expressed sexual passion, described drug- and wine-induced fantasies, and spun out visions condemned as perverse. Some of his verse explicitly depicted the brown body of his mistress of African descent, expressing the colonizing mind-set of the nation-state in sexual terms. French authorities fought this violation of social convention, successfully prosecuting both Flaubert and Baudelaire on obscenity charges. At issue was social and artistic order: "Art without rules is no longer art," the prosecutor maintained.

During the era of the Great Reforms, Russian writers debated whether western European values were insidiously trans-

---

◆**Baudelaire:** bohd LEHR

forming their culture. But rather than dividing the nation, this discussion about the nature of Russian culture united people around the issue of Russianness. Adopting one viewpoint, Ivan Turgenev created a powerful novel of Russian life, *Fathers and Sons* (1862), a story of nihilistic children rejecting the older, romantic generation's spiritual values and espousing science instead. Popular in the West, Turgenev aroused anger in Russian readers for the way he criticized both romantics and the new generation of hardheaded "materialists." Expressing another point of view, Fyodor Dostoevsky in *The Possessed* (1871–1872) and other works showed the dark, ridiculous, neurotic side of nihilists, thus holding up Turgenev as a soft-headed romantic. Dostoevsky's highly intelligent characters in *Notes from Underground* (1864) and *Crime and Punishment* (1866) are personally tormented and condemned to lead absurd, even criminal lives. He used these antiheroes to emphasize spirituality and traditional Russian values but added a "realistic" spin by planting such values in ordinary people.

Painting.   Unlike writers, visual artists across Europe depended on government commissions, and government-sponsored exhibitions drew a more limited set of buyers. Prince Albert of England was an active patron of the arts, purchasing works for official collections and for himself until his death in 1861. Having artwork displayed at government-sponsored exhibitions (called salons in Paris, the center of the art world) was the best way for an artist to gain prominence and earn a living. Although officially appointed juries selected works of art to appear in the salon and then chose prize winners from among them, hundreds of thousands of people from all social classes attended.

After 1848, however, artists began rejecting romantic conventions idealizing ordinary folk or grand historic events that government purchasers continued to favor. Instead, painters like Gustave Courbet portrayed groaning laborers at backbreaking work because he believed an artist should "never permit sentiment to overthrow logic." The city, artists found, had become a visual spectacle, a setting for the destruction of old neighborhoods but also for wide new boule-

Gustave Courbet, *Wrestlers* (1850)
Courbet painted his dirty, grunting wrestlers in the realist style, which rejected the hazy romanticism of revolutionary Europe. These muscular men embodied the resort to physical struggle during the state-building decades and conveyed the art world's recognition that Realpolitik had triumphed in the governance of society. How does the realist depiction of people, as in this painting, differ from artistic depictions earlier in the nineteenth century (see page 817)? *Museum of Fine Arts, Budapest/The Bridgeman Art Library, NY.*

vards where urban residents performed as part of the cityscape. The artists' canvases showed the renovated city as a stage for individual ambition and display. *Universal Exhibition* (1867) by Édouard Manet♦ used the world's fair of 1867 as the background; figures from all social classes promenaded in the foreground, gazing at the Paris scene and watching one another to learn the new social rules of modern life. Manet also broke with romantic conventions of the nude. His *Olympia* (1865) depicted a white courtesan lying on her bed, attended by a black woman.

♦**Manet:** ma NAY

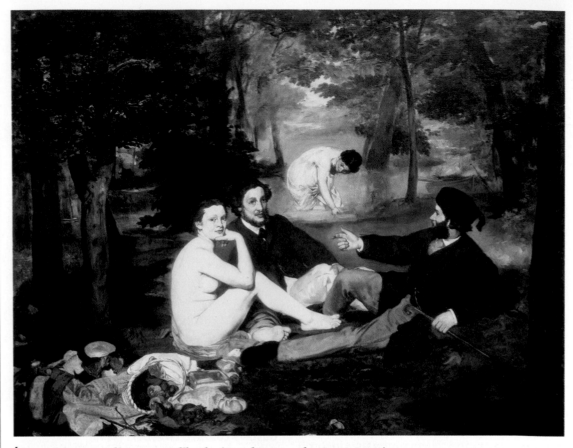

Édouard Manet, *Déjeuner sur l'herbe* **(Luncheon on the Grass, 1863)**
The leading painters of the Parisian art world rejected the highly idealized paintings of nudes and romanticized historical scenes. In Manet's portrayal of a picnic, the clothed men sitting alongside the nude and seminude women, with their garments tossed about, mocked such idealism and romanticization. Critical art like Manet's annoyed many genteel citizens in the art-viewing public. What is the difference between the female nude in this painting and the ones in the Orientalist painting in Chapter 21 (page 794)? *Bridgeman-Giraudon/Art Resource, NY.*

This disregard for the classical tradition of showing women in mythical or idealized settings was too much for the critics. "A sort of female gorilla," one wrote of *Olympia.* "Her greenish, bloodshot eyes appear to be provoking to the public," wrote another. Shocking at first, graphic portrayals that shattered comforting illusions became a feature of modern art.

Opera.   Unlike most of the visual arts, opera was commercially profitable, accessible to most classes of society, and thus effective artistically for reaching the nineteenth-century public. Verdi used musical theater to contrast noble ideals with the corrosive effects of power, love of country with the inevitable call for sacrifice and death, and the lure of passion with the need for social order. *La Traviata* (1853) stunned audiences with the tragedy of a tubercular courtesan who falls in love with a respectable middle-class man. In a series of lyrical arias, the characters express the lure of a heartfelt passion at odds with the need for stable families.

The German Richard Wagner,♦ the most flamboyant and musically innovative composer of the era, hoped to revolutionize opera by fusing music and drama to arouse the audience's fear, awe, and engagement with his vision. A gigantic cycle of four operas, *The*

♦**Wagner:** VAHG nur

Ring of the Nibelungen reshaped ancient German myths into a modern, nightmarish allegory of a world doomed by its obsessive pursuit of money and power and redeemable only through unselfish love. Wagner's operas were also influenced by the flood of philosophic and religious ideas coming from Asia—above all, Buddhism. His lovers in *Tristan and Isolde*, like characters in other operas, portray higher states of being through subduing the will and by dying in purifying flames. Wagner was a complex composer and thinker, and his opera *The Mastersingers of Nuremberg* (*Die Meistersinger*,♦ 1862–1867) was a nationalistic tribute to German culture. The piece was said to be implicitly anti-Semitic because of its rejection of influences other than German ones in the arts. Wagner's flair for publicity, self-dramatization, musical innovation, and complex national and international themes ultimately made him a major force in philosophy, politics, and the arts. By becoming a grand symbol himself, he excelled in fulfilling the nationalizing and unifying potential in all cultural works.

All of the arts, no matter how controversial, shaped the cultural attitudes of the decades 1850–1870. Favoring realism and the rising nation-state, the arts provided visions that helped unite isolated individuals into a public with a shared, if debated, cultural experience. Artists implicitly promoted nation building even as they experimented with new forms.

Religion and Secular Order

Organized religion formed one bulwark of traditional social and political order after the revolutions of 1848, but the expansion of state power set the stage for clashes over its influence. Should religion have the same hold on government and public life as in the past, thus competing with loyalty to the nation? The views were mixed and would remain so. In the 1850s, many politicians supported religious institutions and attended public church rituals because they were another source of order. Simultaneously, some nation builders, intellectuals, and economic

liberals came to reject the competing jurisdiction and religious worldview of established churches, particularly Roman Catholicism. Bismarck was one of these; he came to judge that the church impeded the growth of nationalist sentiment. He thus mounted a full-blown **Kulturkampf**♦ ("culture war") against religion. The German government expelled the Jesuits from Germany in 1872, increased state power over the clergy in Prussia in 1873, and introduced obligatory civil marriage in 1875. Bismarck had miscalculated his own ability to manipulate politics, however, for both conservatives and Catholics rebelled against policies of religious repression as part of state building. The Roman Catholic church insisted on its political influence and explicitly attacked nineteenth-century visions of progress and reform embodied in such institutions as secular public schools. Competition between church and state for power and influence heated up in the age of Realpolitik.

Catholic Reaction. The Catholic church felt assaulted by a growing rationalism that was supposed to replace religious faith and by the state building of Italy and Germany that competed for people's traditional loyalty. In addition, nation building had resulted in the extension of liberal rights to Jews, whom Christians often considered enemies. Attacking reform, Pope Pius IX issued *The Syllabus of Errors* (1864), which put the church and the pope at odds "with progress, with liberalism, and with modern civilization." In 1870, the First Vatican Council approved the dogma of papal infallibility. This teaching proclaimed that the pope, under certain circumstances, must be regarded by Catholics as speaking divinely revealed truth on issues of morality and faith. In 1878 a new pontiff, Leo XIII, began the process of reconciliation with modern politics by encouraging up-to-date scholarship in Catholic institutes and universities and by accepting aspects of democracy. Leo's ideas marked a dramatic turn, ending the Kulturkampf and fortifying beleaguered Catholics across Europe.

Religious doctrine continued to have powerful popular appeal, but the place of

---

♦*Die Meistersinger:* dee MY stur sihn gur

♦**Kulturkampf:** kul TUR kahmpf

organized religion in society at large was changing. On the one hand, church attendance declined among workers and artisans; on the other, many in the upper and middle classes and most of the peasantry remained faithful. The Orthodox church of Russia and eastern Europe with its Pan-Slavic appeal fostered nationalism among oppressed Serbs and became a rallying point. Women's spiritual beliefs became more intense, with both Roman Catholic and Russian Orthodox women's religious orders increasing in size and number; men, by contrast, were falling away from religious devotion. Many urban Jews assimilated to secular, national cultures, abandoning religious practice. The social composition of those faithful to religion had come to take a distinctly different shape from the days when it included everyone.

In 1854, the pope's announcement of the doctrine of the Immaculate Conception (stating that Mary, alone among all humans, had been born without original sin) was followed by an outburst of popular religious fervor, especially among women. In 1858, a young peasant girl, Bernadette Soubirous,◆ began having visions of the Virgin Mary at Lourdes in southern France. In these visions Mary told Bernadette to drink from the ground, at which point a spring appeared. Crowds comprised mostly of women besieged the area to be cured of ailments by the waters of Lourdes. In 1867, less than ten years later, a railroad track was laid to Lourdes to enable millions of pilgrims to visit the shrine on church-organized trips. The Catholic church thus showed that it was not passé— it could use such modern means as railroads, medical verifications of miraculous cures, and journalism to make Lourdes itself the center of a brisk commercial as well as religious culture. The cultural unity of the nation-state could be achieved by old and venerable institutions like churches, if they too followed these innovative paths to modern power.

The Challenge from Natural Science.
Almost contemporaneously with Soubirous's vision, the English naturalist Charles Darwin (1809–1882) published *On the Origin of*

◆**Soubirous:** soo bee roo

Species (1859), a challenge to the Judeo-Christian worldview that humanity was a unique creation of God. In this book and in later writings, Darwin argued that life had taken shape over countless millions of years before humans existed and that human life was but the result of this slow development, called evolution. Instead of God miraculously bringing the universe and all life into being in six days as described in Genesis, Darwin held that life developed from lower forms through a primal battle for survival and through the sexual selection of mates— processes called natural selection, which others of Darwin's contemporaries had also identified. An eminently respectable Victorian gentleman, Darwin announced that the Bible gave a "manifestly false history of the world." Darwin's theories also undermined certain liberal, secular beliefs. Enlightenment principles, for example, had glorified nature as tranquil and noble and had viewed human nature as essentially rational. The theory of natural selection, in which the fittest survive, suggested a different kind of human society, one composed of combative individuals and groups constantly at war with one another to prevail in hostile surroundings.

Darwin's findings and other innovative biological research influenced contemporary beliefs about society. Working in obscurity with pea plants in his monastery garden in the 1860s, Gregor Mendel (1822–1884) discovered the principles of heredity, from which the science of genetics later developed. Investigation into the female reproductive cycle led German scientists to discover the principle of spontaneous ovulation—the automatic release of the egg by the ovary independent of sexual intercourse. This discovery caused theorists to conclude that men had aggressive and strong sexual drives because reproduction depended on their sexual arousal. In contrast, the spontaneous and cyclical release of the egg independent of arousal indicated that women were passive and lacked sexual feeling.

Darwin also tried to use biological findings to explain social phenomena. The legal, political, and economic privilege of white European men in the nineteenth century, he maintained, naturally derived from their being more highly evolved than white women or people of color. Despite recognizing a common ancestor for all humans, Darwin held that people of color, or "lower races," were far behind whites in intelligence and civilization. As for women, "the chief distinction in the intellectual powers of the two sexes," Darwin declared, "is shewn by man's attaining to a higher eminence in whatever he takes up." A school of Social Darwinism grew out of this Darwinist thought. Social Darwinists used a distorted version of evolutionary theory to lobby for racist, sexist, and nationalist policies. Their arguments were influential in the years to come.

From Natural Science to Social Science

The spread of Darwinist ideas accelerated the search for alternatives to the religious understanding of social order as divinely ordained. Theorists and critics sought to devise hardheaded and secular explanations of how society functioned. Simultaneously, the theories of the French social philosopher Auguste Comte◆ (1798–1857), whose ideas formed the basis of a "positive science" of society and politics, inspired a host of reform organizations. **Positivism** claimed that careful study of facts would generate accurate, or "positive," laws of society. Comte's *System of Positive Politics, or Treatise on Sociology* (1851) proposed that social scientists construct knowledge of the political order as they would an understanding of the natural world, that is, according to informed secular investigation. This idea inspired people to believe they could solve the problems spawned by economic and social change. Comte also encouraged women's participation in reform because he deemed "womanly" compassion and love as equally fundamental to social harmony as was scientific public policy. Positivism led not only to women's increased social and political activism but also to the growth of the social sciences, which developed during this period, largely under the banner of positivism. Sociology, the scientific study of human society, was primary among these influential new disciplines.

◆**Auguste Comte:** oh GIHST kawnt

Darwin Ridiculed, c. 1860
Charles Darwin's theories claimed that humans evolved from animal species and rejected the long-standing explanation of a divine human origin. His scientific ideas so diverged from people's beliefs that cartoonists lampooned both the respectable Darwin and his theory. Despite the controversy, evolution withstood the test of further scientific study. What message might this cartoon have conveyed to a nineteenth-century viewer? **For more help analyzing this image,** see the visual activity for this chapter in the Online Study Guide at **bedfordstmartins.com/hunt**. *Hulton Archive/Getty Images.*

For a time, the celebrated English philosopher John Stuart Mill (1806–1873) became an enthusiast of Comte, whose theories led Mill to espouse widespread reform and mass education and to support the complete enfranchisement of women. His political treatise *On Liberty* (1859) couched his aspiration for a general social improvement in a concern that superior people not be brought down or confined by the will of the masses. Influenced by his wife, Harriet Taylor Mill, he notoriously advocated the extension of rights to women and introduced a woman suffrage bill into the House of Commons after her death. The bill's defeat prompted Mill to publish *The Subjection of Women* (1869), a work recapitulating his studies with his wife. Translated into many languages and influential in eastern Europe, Scandinavia, and the Americas, *The Subjection of Women* presented the family as maintaining an older kind of politics devoid of modern concepts of rights and freedom. Mill also proposed that the aura of women's voluntary obedience and love in marriage was necessary to mask the gross inequalities between men and women in the household. To make a woman appear "not a forced slave, but a willing one," he said, she was trained from childhood not to value her own talent and independence but to embrace "submission and yielding to the control of others." Critiquing accepted rules for men's and women's roles, *The Subjection of Women* became an internationally respected guide for a growing women's movement committed to obtaining basic rights.

The progressive side of Mill's social thought was soon lost in a flood of Social Darwinist theories. Even before *Origin of Species*, Herbert Spencer's *Social Statics* (1851) advocated the study of society but also promoted laissez-faire and unadulterated competition, claiming that the "unfit" should be allowed to perish in the name of progress. Spencer's opposition to public education, social reform, and any other attempt to soften the harshness of the struggle for existence struck a receptive chord among the middle and upper classes. The spread of his views contributed to the surge of Social Darwinism in the next decades.

These various visions of social order—all of them believed to be scientific and thus true—would become dominant in future national debates over policy in the West. The influence of Darwinism and Mill's liberalism, like that of the arts, religion, and science, would be to shape public culture, setting the subjects and terms of social and political thought.

In an age of nation building, culture often enhanced the political call for realistic, hardheaded thinking about social order.

> **Review:** What were the results of the increasing spread of the scientific method to social thought?

❖ Contesting the Growing Power of the Nation-State

By the end of the 1860s, the unchecked growth of the state and the ongoing process of economic change had led to palpable tensions in European society. New theories of work life and politics appeared to counter nationalism and capitalism—most notably those of economist and philosopher Karl Marx, who advocated socialism and international rather than national loyalties. Workers throughout the West protested the terms of work and the upheavals in everyday life caused by the expanding power of the state, as governments ripped apart cities for improvements and sent workers scurrying for new places to live. In France anger at defeat in the Franco-Prussian War and at economic hardship made these tensions erupt into a bitter, if brief, civil war. In the spring of 1871, the people of Paris, blaming the centralized state for the French surrender to the Germans, declared Paris a commune—a community of equals without bureaucrats and pompous politicians. Marx's books analyzing the growth of capitalism and national politics—as well as the Paris Commune—provided workers with a popular and politically galvanizing account of events. From the 1870s on, these two phenomena—the writings of Karl Marx and the fury of working people—renewed fear among the middle classes that both nation-state and social order might be violently destroyed.

The Rise of Marxism

Marxism arose with urbanization and the spread of industry to cities and towns across Europe. Increasingly well educated by an ambitious nation-state, urban workers frequented cafés and pubs to hear news and share with one another impressions of political and economic change. After a period of repression in the 1850s following their failed revolutions, workers' organizations slowly reemerged as a political force in the West. Like other interest groups, workers' organizations were part of a pattern of horizontal allegiances, in which people with similar backgrounds came together to shape the political process. Such allegiances replaced the old vertical allegiances that reflected not similarity and equality but the hierarchy and subordination of the old regime.

In the 1850s, governments often outlawed unions, fearing that they would challenge political order. Unions that existed in those years were thus secret, poorly coordinated, and shaped by a wide range of programs for change, including the ideas of former printer Pierre-Joseph Proudhon♦ (1809–1865). In the 1840s, Proudhon had coined the explosive saying "Property is theft," suggesting that ownership robbed propertyless people of their rightful share of the earth's benefits. He opposed the centralized state and proposed that society be organized instead around natural groupings of men in artisans' workshops. These workshops and a central bank crediting each worker for his labor would replace government and would lead to a mutualist social organization. Proudhon heartily opposed any mingling of men and women in political life; he believed the mutualist organization of men in public should be matched by the seclusion of their wives laboring at home for their husbands' comfort.

Another theory that attracted workers at the time was anarchism. Anarchists maintained that the existence of the state was the root of social injustice. According to Russian nobleman and anarchist leader Mikhail Bakhunin,♦ the slightest infringement on freedom, especially by the central state, was unacceptable. The political theory of **anarchism** thus advocated the destruction of all state power. At a London meeting in 1864, workers from Italy, Germany, Britain, and France accepted both anarchism and Proudhon's mutualism as guiding ideas for the la-

♦**Pierre-Joseph Proudhon:** pyehr zhaw ZEHF proo DAWN
♦**Mikhail Bakhunin:** myih kuh YEEL buh KOON yihn

bor movement. However, Karl Marx was a third major presence at this founding meeting of the International Workingmen's Association, and he set out to battle these two very popular, rival theories. These doctrines, Marx insisted, were emotional and wrongheaded, lacking the sound, scientific basis of his own theory, subsequently called **Marxism**. Marx's analysis, expounded most notably in *Das Kapital,* adopted the liberal idea, dating back to John Locke in the seventeenth century, that human existence was defined by the necessity of working as a way of fulfilling basic needs such as food, clothing, and shelter. *Das Kapital,* published between 1867 and 1894, was based on mathematical calculations of production and profit that would justify a Realpolitik for the working classes. Marx held that the fundamental organization of any society, including its politics and culture, derived from the relationships arising from work or production. This idea, known as materialism, meant that the foundation of a society rested on class relationships— such as those between serf and medieval lord, slave and master, or worker and capitalist. Marx called the type of class relationships that developed around work the mode of production: for instance, feudalism, slavery, or capitalism. Rejecting the liberal focus on individual rights, he emphasized the unequal class relations caused by feudal lords, slaveholders, and capitalists or the bourgeoisie— that is, those who took control of the "means of production" in the form of the capital, land, tools, or factories necessary to fulfill basic human needs. When capitalist control disappeared, a classless society of workers— that is, a socialist one—would arise.

Economic liberals expected the free market to produce balance and a harmony of interests, but Marx saw social organization and productive life not as harmonious but in conflict because of economic oppression. He believed that workers' awareness of their oppression would produce class consciousness among those in the same predicament and ultimately lead them to revolt against their exploiters. Such revolt, not reform or legislation, would be the mechanism for historical change. Capitalism would be overthrown by these workers—the **proletariat**—and the reign of socialism would ensue. Like Darwin,

Marx espoused the tough-minded theory that social conflict was necessary for progress.

Marx was never precise about what socialism would entail, except that it would involve workers' control of production in large factories. A socialist utopia meant an end to private ownership of the means of production, which would in turn end class conflict and the need for a state to prop up the propertied classes. Like many other male intellectuals at midcentury, Marx accorded little analytical importance to inequalities based on race and sex, concluding, for example, that the condition of women would automatically improve in a socialist utopia. The possibility of this socialist utopia continued to inspire many working-class men to organize unions, and some governments came to recognize an advantage in unions: they could render worker protests more predictable and more controllable. Achieving socialism also formed one source of inspiration for the Russian Revolution of 1917.

The Paris Commune versus the French State

Even as Marx's theories were taking shape, the conditions of working-class life remained harsh, and a wave of strikes erupted in the late 1860s. In France alone, 40,000 workers participated in strikes in 1869, followed by more than 85,000 in 1870. The strikers included artisans and industrial workers who felt overworked and underpaid because of the continuing pace of innovation in manufacturing. More often than not, the strikes focused on economic issues. But at times, such as in the Paris Commune, protesters questioned the system as a whole.

The bloody and bitter struggle over the Paris Commune developed using mutualist and socialist political ideas that churned to the surface in Paris as the Franco-Prussian War ended. The Haussmannization of Paris, which had displaced workers from their homes in the heart of the city, embittered many Parisians against the state. As the Prussians pressed on to Paris in 1870, the besieged Parisians demanded new republican liberties and a more balanced distribution of power between the central government and localities. By the winter of 1870–1871,

MAP 23.5 The Paris Commune, 1871
The war between the French government and the Paris Commune took place on the streets of Paris and resulted in widespread destruction of major buildings, most notably the Tuileries Palace adjacent to the Louvre. Combatants destroyed many government records in what some saw as a civil war; bitterness, like destruction of property, was great on both sides. Upon defeating the Communards, the government executed thousands of people. Why were cities like Paris key places for both advancing and protesting nation building?

the Parisian population of two million was suffering from the harsh weather and a Prussian siege that deprived them of sufficient food. As they demanded to elect their own local officials to handle the emergency (Map 23.5), the temporary republican government replacing the fallen Napoleon III sent the army into Paris in mid-March. For Parisians, this decision revealed the utter despotism of centralized government and the nation-state, and they resisted, declaring themselves a self-governing commune on March 28, 1871. Other French municipalities would do the same, in an attempt to form a decentralized state of independent, confederated units.

In the Paris Commune's two months of existence, its forty-member council, its National Guard (or citizens' army), and its many other improvised offices found themselves at cross-purposes. Trying to maintain "communal" instead of "national" values, Parisians quickly developed a wide array of political clubs, local ceremonies, and self-managed, cooperative workshops. Women workers, for example, banded together to make National Guard uniforms on a cooperative rather than a profit-making basis. Beyond liberal political equality, the Commune proposed to liberate the worker and ensure "the absolute equality of women laborers." Thus, a commune in contrast to a republic was meant to entail a social revolution that would benefit people rather than building the power of the state. But Communards often disagreed on what specific route to take to change society: mutualism, anticlericalism, feminism, international socialism, and anarchism were but a few of the proposed avenues to social justice.

In the meantime, the provisional government at Versailles struck back to reinstitute national order, as the centralized nation-state showed its power to be determined and durable. It quickly stamped out similar uprisings in other French cities. On May 21, the army entered Paris again. In a week of fighting, both Communards and the army set the city ablaze (the Communards did so to slow the progress of government troops). Both sides executed hostages, and in the wake of victory the army shot tens of thousands of citizens found on the streets. Just to be in the city meant treason: Parisian insurgents, one citizen commented, "deserved no better judge than a soldier's bullet." The Communards had fatally promoted a kind of antistate in an age of growing national power and were thus considered traitors. This reaction soon gave way to a different interpretation of the Commune as the work of the *pétroleuse*,◆ or "woman incendiary"—a case of women run mad, crowding the streets in frenzy and fury. Within a year, writers were blaming the burning of Paris on women— "shameless slatterns, half-naked women, who kindled courage and breathed life into arson." Revolutionary men often became heroes in the history books, but women in political situations were characterized as "sinister females, sweating, their clothing undone, [who] passed from man to man."

◆ *pétroleuse:* peh troh luhz

Woman Incendiary, 1871
The Paris Commune galvanized women activists, many of whom hoped to reform social conditions. During the short existence of the Commune they implemented cooperative labor-sharing programs and engaged in public political debate—something French women were legally forbidden to do. However, in the aftermath of the Commune, a disillusioned public came to fault women Communards for their political activity, crediting them with half-clothed degeneracy rather than seriousness of purpose and blaming them for the disorderliness of the Commune. Compare the depiction of the women sewing shirts for Italy (page 883) and the activists of the Commune. What message does each convey about women and politics? *The Barricade, no. 34 from* Types de la Commune *(1871). Colour litho by Lefman Bibliotheque Nationale, Paris/Lauros/Giraudon/ Bridgeman Art Library.*

Defeat in the Franco-Prussian War, the Commune, and the civil war were all horrendous blows from which the French state struggled to recover. In defeating the Commune, the state had shown its resolve, but hardheaded policies followed. Key to restoring order in France after 1870 were instilling family virtues, fortifying religion, and claiming that the Commune had resulted from

MAPPING THE WEST Europe and the Mediterranean, 1871

European nation-states consolidated their power by building unified state structures
and by developing the means for the diverse peoples within their borders to become
socially and culturally integrated. They were also rapidly expanding outside their boundaries, extending the economic and political reach of the nation-state. North Africa and
the Middle East—parts of the declining Ottoman Empire—particularly appealed to European governments because of their resources and their potential for further European
settlement. They offered a gateway to the rest of the world. Compare this map of Europe
with that from two decades earlier (page 868) to explain the progress of nation-state
building. What aspects of nation building does this map show, and what aspects do not
appear on the map?

the collapsed boundaries between the male political sphere and the female domestic sphere. Karl Marx disagreed: he portrayed the Commune as a class struggle of workers attacking upper-class interests, which were embodied in the centralized state. Executions and deportations by the thousands virtually shut down the French labor movement, while memories of the Commune kept fear of workers smoldering in middle- and upper-class hearts across Europe.

Review: Why did Marx and members of the Paris Commune object to modern social order and the expanding powers of the nation-state?

Conclusion

Throughout modern history the development of nation-states has been neither inevitable nor uniform nor peaceful. This was especially true in the nineteenth century, when ambitious politicians, resilient monarchs, and determined bureaucrats transformed very different countries into various kinds of states by a variety of methods and policies. Nation building was most dramatic in Germany and Italy, where states were unified through military force and where people of many political tendencies ultimately agreed that national unity surpassed most other causes. Compelled by military defeat to shake off centuries of tradition, the Austrian and Russian monarchs instituted reforms as a way of keeping their systems viable, but the results were different, even unique. The Habsburg Empire became a dual monarchy, an arrangement that gave the Hungarians virtual home rule and that raised the level of disunity. Russian reforms left the authoritarian monarchy intact and even protected the social and political order. In eastern Europe, the middle class was far less powerful than in western Europe, and reform came from autocratic leaders who imposed it from above to preserve the system rather than from popular agitation to democratize it.

After decades of romantic fervor, hardheaded realism in politics became a much-touted norm, often with unexpected consequences. Proponents of realism, Darwin and Marx developed theories disturbing to those who maintained an Enlightenment faith in social and political harmony. Realist novels and artworks jarred polite society, and, like the operas of Verdi, portrayed dilemmas of the times. The policies of the growing state apparatus that were meant to bring order often brought disorder, such as the destruction of entire neighborhoods and violence toward people in far-off lands. Schooling, however, taught the lower classes to be orderly citizens, and urban renewal ultimately improved cities and public health to complement nation building. Yet when the ordinary people of the Paris Commune rose up to protest the loss of French power and prestige, they also aimed to defy the trend toward state building. Their actions raised difficult questions. How far should the power of the state extend in both domestic and international affairs? Would nationalism be a force for war or for peace? As these issues ripened, the next decades saw extraordinary economic advances, and an unprecedented surge in Europe's global power.

Suggested References

The End of the Concert of Europe

Historians have often neglected the inglorious Crimean War despite its impact on European politics. Much of the best new literature focuses not only on political changes but also on the war's social impact in Russia. Worobec's book gives a searching look at Russian peasant life in this age of transition.

Edgerton, Robert B. *Death or Glory: The Legacy of the Crimean War.* 1999.

Hazareesingh, Sudhir. *From Subject to Citizen: The Second Empire and the Emergence of Modern French Democracy.* 1998.

*Seacole, Mary. *Wonderful Adventures of Mrs. Seacole in Many Lands.* 1857.

Worobec, Christine. *Peasant Russia: Family and Community in the Post-Emancipation Period.* 1991.

Wortman, Richard S. *Scenarios of Power: Myth and Ceremony in Russian Monarchy.* 2 vols. 1995–2000.

*Primary source.

War and Nation Building

Nation building has produced a varied literature ranging from biographies to studies of ceremonials and the presentation of royalty as celebrities and unifying figures. Two Web sites show the complexities of this process: Brown University's Victorian Web demonstrates the connections among royalty, politicians, religion, and culture; and Bucknell University's Russian Studies site opens to the strains of the Russian national anthem, composed in the reign of Nicholas I to foster reverence for the dynasty and homeland.

Blackbourn, David. *Fontana History of Germany, 1780–1918: The Long Nineteenth Century.* 1997.

Breuilly, John. *The Formation of the First German Nation-State, 1800–1871.* 1996.

DiScala, Spencer. *Italy: From Revolution to Republic, 1700 to the Present.* 1995.

Homans, Margaret. *Royal Representations: Queen Victoria and British Culture, 1837–1876.* 1998.

Russian Studies: **http://www.departments.bucknell .edu/Russian**.

Smith, Paul. *Disraeli: A Brief Life.* 1996.

The Victorian Web: **http://landow.stg.brown.edu/ victorian/victov.html**.

Establishing Social Order

Nation building entailed state-sponsored activities stretching from promoting education to rebuilding cities. New histories show the process of creating a sense of nationality through government management of people's environment, such that citizenship became part of everyday life. Hine and Faragher show the intersection of U.S. expansionism and nation building.

Hamm, Michael F. *Kiev: A Portrait, 1800–1917.* 1993.

Hine, Robert V., and John Mack Faragher. *The American West: A New Interpretative History.* 2001.

Hoffenberg, Peter H. *An Empire on Display: English, Indian, and Australian Exhibitions from the Crystal Palace to the Great War.* 2001.

Johanson, Christine. *Women's Struggle for Higher Education in Russia, 1855–1900.* 1987.

Jordan, David. *Transforming Paris: The Life and Labor of Baron Haussmann.* 1995.

Lebra-Chapman, Joyce. *The Rani of Jhansi: A Study in Female Heroism in India.* 1986.

Rotenberg, Robert. *Landscape and Power in Vienna.* 1995.

The Culture of Social Order

Like the biographies of politicians, the biographies of artists and intellectuals have proved crucial to understanding the period of realism and Realpolitik. They show artists, intellectuals, and scientists addressing the central issues of their day amid dramatic social change. Kaufman's book shows the connection between religious fervor, tourism, and commercial development in the West.

Bordenheimer, Rosemarie. *The Real Life of Mary Ann Evans: George Eliot, Her Letters and Fiction.* 1994.

*Darwin, Charles. *Autobiography.* 1969.

Gieson, Gerald L. *The Private Science of Louis Pasteur.* 1996.

Kaufman, Suzanne. *Lourdes and the Making of Mass Culture in Modern France.* 2004.

Mayr, Ernst. *One Long Argument: Charles Darwin and the Genesis of Modern Evolutionary Thought.* 1991.

*Turgenev, Ivan. *A Hunter's Sketches.* 1852.

Contesting the Growing Power of the Nation-State

The teachings of Karl Marx and the story of the Paris Commune haunted Europeans in the mid-nineteenth century. The following works capture the fear of the working classes that shaped middle-class thought, and they show the energy that working- and middle-class people alike put into politics in this period of nation building. Northwestern University has digitized its collection on the Siege of Paris and the Commune.

Gullickson, Gay. *Unruly Women of Paris: Images of the Commune.* 1996.

McClellan, David. *Karl Marx: His Life and Thought.* 1978.

Nord, Philip. *The Republican Moment: Struggles for Democracy in Nineteenth-Century France.* 1995.

Siege of Paris Collection, Northwestern University: **http://www.library.northwestern.edu/spec/ siege**.

CHAPTER REVIEW

IMPORTANT EVENTS

1850s–1860s	Positivism, Darwinism become influential
1850s–1870s	Realism in the arts
1853–1856	Crimean War
1857	British-led forces suppress Indian Rebellion
1861	Victor Emmanuel declared king of a unified Italy; abolition of serfdom in Russia
1861–1865	United States Civil War
1867	Second Reform Bill in England; Austro-Hungarian monarchy
1868	Meiji Restoration begins in Japan
1869–1871	Women's colleges founded at Cambridge University
1870–1871	Franco-Prussian War
1871	German Empire proclaimed at Versailles; self-governing Paris Commune established

KEY TERMS

anarchism (907)

dual monarchy (887)

Haussmannization (891)

Kulturkampf (903)

Marxism (907)

Meiji Restoration (898)

mir (880)

nation-state (881)

Pan-Slavism (888)

positivism (905)

proletariat (907)

realism (899)

Realpolitik (873)

Russification (881)

zemstvos (880)

REVIEW QUESTIONS

1. What were the main results of the Crimean War?
2. What role did warfare play in the various nineteenth-century nation-building efforts?
3. How did colonial expansion change in the period of nation building?
4. What were the results of the increasing spread of the scientific method to social thought?
5. Why did Marx and members of the Paris Commune object to modern social order and the expanding powers of the nation-state?

MAKING CONNECTIONS

1. How did realism in social thought break with Enlightenment values?
2. Why did some nation-states tend toward secularism while the kingdoms that preceded them were based on religion?
3. How was the Paris Commune related to earlier revolutions in France? How did it differ from them?

FOR FURTHER EXPLORATION

To assess your mastery of the material in this chapter, see the Online Study Guide at bedfordstmartins.com/hunt.

To read additional primary-source material from this period, see Chapter 23 in *Sources of The Making of the West*, Second Edition.

Industry, Empire, and Everyday Life, 1870–1890

BETWEEN 1870 AND 1890, MARIANNE NORTH, an unmarried Englishwoman, traveled the globe several times. The end of the nineteenth century was a time of vast migration, some of it in search of a better life, some of it for imperial conquest, and some of it, as in the case of Marianne North, in pursuit of knowledge. North was a botanical illustrator and "plant hunter," one of those avid Europeans who on their own or under government sponsorship searched the world over for plants to classify, grow, and put to commercial use. North ventured to India, North and South America, Java, Borneo, South Africa, and many other distant points setting up her easel and making scientific drawings of plants. She discovered at least five new species (officially named after her) and a new type of tree as well as collected thousands of plants to send back to botanical gardens in England. When she became too frail to travel, she organized a permanent museum in London to display her botanical drawings to the public (see the illustration on page 916). Her goal was promoting ordinary people's knowledge of the British Empire: "I want them to know," she announced, "that cocoa doesn't come from the coconut,"

Historians have aptly labeled the decades from 1870 to 1890 an era of industry and empire in the West. The Western powers were

---

Thomas Roberts, *Coming South* (1886)
The exodus of Europeans to every part of the world swelled from the middle of the nineteenth century. Most of this migration occurred for political and economic reasons, with the most beleaguered segments of the population likely to cross thousands of miles by ship to find opportunity and political freedom. In the nineteenth century employment agencies enticed male and female workers to travel to areas with labor shortages. Non-profit organizations also encouraged single women to migrate in hopes of righting the gender imbalance in most colonies. Other Western migration was temporary, like that of scientists, writers, soldiers, and missionaries. The Australian painter Thomas Roberts, who had himself migrated from London in 1869 at the age of 13, depicted these voyages on ship as so calm and boring as to test one's sanity, an atmosphere described similarly in migrants' diaries and letters. Other artists portrayed migration as tumultuous, especially at dockside, as people jostled to get on board or wept at separation—sometimes permanent—from families and loved ones. *National Gallery of Victoria, Melbourne, Australia. Gift of Col. Aubrey Gibson in Memory of John and Anne Gibson. Bridgeman Art Library.*

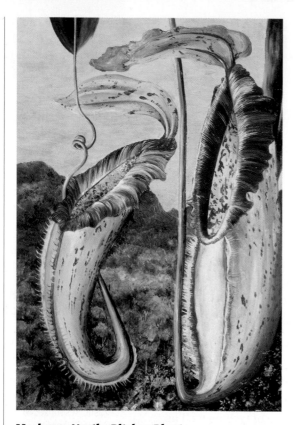

Marianne North, *Pitcher Plant*
Wealthy Europeans increasingly traveled overseas in the quest for knowledge and adventure. As the West prospered, travel and world tourism did too. An amateur artist, Marianne North initially gained an audience for her scientific drawings, reports, and specimens only because she traveled in the "best circles." Once seen, however, her canvases, like this one of a pitcher plant, were prized by scientists and curators alike. Should we consider Marianne North an imperialist? Why or why not? *Trustees of the Royal Botanic Gardens, Kew.*

rapidly expanding their empires, affecting not only politics but also industrial growth and the fabric of everyday life for Europeans. Industrial output soared in the West as industrialization spread from Britain to central and eastern Europe and new products kept appearing on the market. A growing appetite for these goods, many of them for household consumption, was partly responsible for an intensified search for raw materials around the globe. Informal educators like Marianne North made people more knowledgeable about the connections among industry, empire, and their own lives.

Those connections were tight; many Europeans benefited from the enforced labor of millions of Asians and Africans under the "new imperialism"—one name for the accelerated race for empire. The new imperialism of the late nineteenth century was merely the final gulp of global territory that Europeans had been acquiring since the late fifteenth century. They explored and took political control of the interior of Africa and worked to dominate even more of Asia until, by the beginning of the twentieth century, they claimed to control more than 80 percent of the world's surface. Control was not narrowly political: Europeans tried to stamp other continents with European-style place-names, architecture, clothing, languages, domestic customs, and other cultural features.

As Europeans forced open the globe, millions seized the opportunity to move vast distances. Some movement was temporary—migration to the colonies to serve in the colonial civil service, for instance—and some

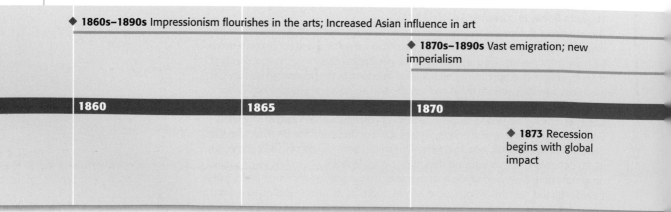

◆ **1860s–1890s** Impressionism flourishes in the arts; Increased Asian influence in art

◆ **1870s–1890s** Vast emigration; new imperialism

1860	1865	1870

◆ **1873** Recession begins with global impact

was permanent—to North and South America or Australia in search of work or personal safety. Some people simply moved to other cities or regions in Europe. Such migration changed the everyday life of both Europeans and non-Europeans; it socially dislocated tens of millions of people and brought further violence against indigenous peoples in European colonies.

The intertwined progress of industry and empire affected politics in paradoxical ways. As urban people became more educated and more united by common experiences of neighborhood and work life, they came to share political interests and make greater demands for participation in the political process. Newspapers covering political affairs expanded their sales to a growing urban population, and men from all social classes gained suffrage. Citizens took pride in their nations' conquests and their common access to a mushrooming array of colonial goods. Europe brimmed with confidence and hope, while the darker aspects of industrial and imperial progress played themselves out in distant colonies, urban slums, and declining standards of living in rural areas.

❖ The Advance of Industry

The end of the Franco-Prussian War and the Paris Commune in 1871 saw an initial burst of prosperity. Paris, Berlin, Vienna, and Rome experienced a frenzy of building, and many workers' wages increased. Industry turned

out a cornucopia of products that improved people's material well-being. Beginning in 1873, however, a series of downturns in business threatened both entrepreneurs and the working class. Businesspeople sought remedies in new technology, financial innovations, managerial techniques, and a revolutionary marketing institution—the department store. Governments played their part by changing business law and supporting the drive for global profits. The steady advance of industry and the development of a consumer economy gave rise to the service sector, laying the ground for the further transformation of work life.

Industrial Innovation

Industrial, technological, and commercial innovation together characterized nineteenth-century Europe. New products ranging from the bicycle, typewriter, and telephone to the internal combustion engine provided dizzying proof of industrial progress. Many independent tinkerers or inventor-manufacturers created new products, but sophisticated engineers also invented revolutionary technologies. For example, in 1885 the German engineer Karl Benz devised a workable gasoline engine; six years later France's Armand Peugeot◆ constructed a car and tested it by chasing a bicycle race. Electricity became more widely used after 1880, providing power to light everything from private drawing rooms to government office buildings. The Eiffel Tower, constructed

---

◆**Peugeot:** poo ZHOH

❖ **1876** Invention of the telephone

◆ **1879** Dual Alliance   ◆ **1884** Reform Act doubles British male electorate

◆ **1882** Triple Alliance formed;
Britain invades Egypt

| 1875 | 1880 | 1885 | 1890 |

◆ **1882–1884** Bismarck sponsors social welfare legislation

◆ **1884–1885** Berlin conference on African imperialism   ◆ **1889** Japan adopts constitution; Second International established

Universal Exposition of 1889
French politicians launched the Universal Exposition, or World's Fair, of 1889 in Paris to celebrate what they called the "progress resulting from one hundred years of freedom." The exposition featured the latest industrial inventions as well as musical and artistic displays from the cultures France had conquered. The greatest attraction, however, was the Eiffel Tower, constructed in two years, to much criticism. "Hideous, horrible," one Catholic leader called it, a "skeleton in stark contrast" to the city's majestic cathedrals. Nevertheless, tens of thousands flocked to ascend this masterpiece of engineering technology—the same technology Gustave Eiffel had used to provide the iron skeleton supporting the Statue of Liberty. Electric illumination and electric elevators enhanced the tower's technological impact. What were the purposes of an exposition like that of 1889? *Private Collection/Archives Charmet/Bridgeman Art Library.*

iron, and steel during the 1870s and 1880s. Production of iron increased from 11 million to 23 million tons. Even in relatively under-developed Spain, iron-ore mining unearthed a total of 6 million tons in 1890, up from 130,000 tons in 1861—an almost 5,000 percent increase. Steel output grew just as impressively in the industrial nations, increasing from 500,000 to 11 million tons in the 1870s and 1880s. Manufacturers used the metal to build the more than 100,000 locomotives that pulled trains during these years—trains that transported 2 billion people annually.

Historians used to contrast a "second" Industrial Revolution, with its concentration on heavy industrial products, to the "first" one of the eighteenth and early nineteenth centuries, in which innovations in textile making and the use of steam energy predominated. But many historians now believe that the distinction applies mainly to Britain: in countries where industrialization came later, the two stages occurred simultaneously. Numerous textile mills were installed on the continent later than in Britain, for instance, at the same time as blast furnaces were constructed. Although industrialization led to the decline of cottage production in traditional crafts like weaving, home industry—or **outwork**, defined as the process of having some aspects of industrial work done outside factories in individual homes—persisted in garment making, metalwork, and such "finishing trades" as porcelain painting and button polishing. The coexistence of home and factory enterprise continued through all the changes in manufacturing, to the present day.

Industrial innovations also transformed agriculture. Chemical fertilizers boosted crop yields, and reapers and threshers mechanized harvesting. In the 1870s, Sweden produced a cream separator, a first step toward mechanizing dairy farming. Wire fencing and barbed wire replaced wooden fencing and stone walls, both of which were labor-intensive to create. Refrigeration allowed fruits, vegetables, and meat to be transported without spoiling, thus diversifying and increasing the urban food supply. Tin from colonial trade facilitated large-scale commercial canning, which made many foods available year-round to people in the cities.

in Paris for the Universal Exposition of 1889, stood as a monument to the age's engineering wizardry; visitors rode to its summit in electric elevators (see the illustration above).

To fuel the West's explosive industrial growth, the leading industrial nations mined and produced massive quantities of coal,

Challenge to British Dominance. In the last decades of the century, Britain's rate of industrial growth slowed, as its entrepreneurs remained wedded to older, successful technologies. Although Great Britain maintained its high output of industrial goods and profited from a multitude of worldwide investments, two countries began surpassing it in research, technical education, innovation, and rate of growth: Germany and the United States.

In the aftermath of the Franco-Prussian War, Germany received the territories of Alsace and Lorraine, which had textile industries as well as rich iron deposits. Investing heavily in research, German businesses rapidly devised new industrial processes and began to mass-produce goods that other countries had originally manufactured. Germany also spent as much money on education as on its military in the 1870s and 1880s. This investment resulted in highly skilled engineers and technical workers whose productivity enabled Germany's electrical and chemical engineering capabilities to soar.

The United States began an intensive exploitation of its vast natural resources, including coal, metal ores, gold, and oil. The value of U.S. industrial goods spurted from $5 billion in 1880 to $13 billion two decades later. Whereas German accomplishments rested more on state promotion of industrial efforts, U.S. growth often involved innovative entrepreneurs, such as Andrew Carnegie in iron and steel and John D. Rockefeller in oil. The three-way industrial rivalry among Germany, the United States, and Great Britain would soon have political and diplomatic repercussions.

Areas of Slower Industrialization. With the exception of Belgium, which had been the first continental country to industrialize, other countries trailed the three industrial leaders. French industry grew steadily, but French businesses remained smaller than those in Germany and the United States. Although France had some huge mining, textile, and metallurgical establishments, many businessmen retired early to imitate the still-enviable aristocratic way of life. In Spain, Austria-Hungary, and Italy, industrial development was primarily a local phenomenon. Austria-Hungary had densely industrialized areas around Vienna and in Styria and Bohemia, but the rest of the country remained tied to traditional, unmechanized agriculture. Italy's economy continued to industrialize in the north while remaining rural and agricultural in the south. The Italian government spent more on building Rome into a grand capital than it invested in economic growth. A mere 1.4 percent of Italy's 1872 budget went to education and science, compared with 10.8 percent in Germany. The commercial use of electricity helped Scandinavians, who were poor in coal and ore, to industrialize in the last third of the nineteenth century. Sweden and Norway became leaders in the use of hydroelectric power and the development of electrical products; Denmark developed a major commercial sector in animal and dairy products. Despite these innovations, however, Scandinavia retained its mostly rural character.

Russia's road to industrialization was tortuous, slowed partly by its relatively small urban labor force. Many Russian peasants who may have wished to take advantage of the opportunities of industrialization were tied to the mir, or landed community, by the terms of the serf emancipation. Some villages sent men and women to cities, but on the condition that they return for plowing and harvesting. Nevertheless, by the 1890s, Moscow, St. Petersburg, and a few other cities had substantial working-class populations. The Russian minister of finance Sergei Witte attracted foreign capital, entrepreneurs, and engineers and used them to construct railroads, including the Trans-Siberian Railroad (1891–1916), which upon completion stretched 5,787 miles from Moscow to Vladivostok (see the illustration on the next page). The burgeoning of the railroads combined with growth in metallurgical and mining operations strengthened Russia as an industrial and military power. As in most of eastern Europe, however, the peasants bore the main burden of financing Russia's industrial growth, especially in the form of higher taxes on vodka. Thus, neither they nor the underpaid Russian workers could afford to buy the goods their country

Trans-Siberian Railroad
Begun in 1892, the Trans-Siberian railroad, the major east–west trans-portation line across the Russian Empire, took several decades to complete. From farms in western Siberia the line brought goods to markets in major cities, while in the more sparsely populated east the railroad mostly served to transport troops to secure imperial conquests and guard frontiers. The railroad also became a feature of around-the-world tourism; voyagers traveled in luxurious, if very slow, Trans-Siberian railway coaches. The infrastructure of the line, however, was cheaply built and caused incredible difficulties both in wartime and in peace-time. How did the Trans-Siberian Railroad strengthen the Russian empire? *Sovfoto.*

produced. Russia offered a prime example of the complexities of industrialization and its uneven benefits.

Facing Economic Crisis

Although innovations and business expan-sion often conveyed a sense of optimism, economic conditions were far from rosy throughout the 1870s and 1880s. Within two years of the end of the Franco-Prussian War, prosperity abruptly gave way to a severe economic depression in many industrial countries. The crisis of 1873 was followed by almost three decades of economic fluctua-tions, most alarmingly a series of sharp downturns whose severity varied from coun-try to country. People of all classes lost their jobs or businesses and faced consequences ranging from long stretches of unemploy-ment to bankruptcy. Economists of the day were stunned by the relentlessness and per-

vasiveness of the slump. Because economic ties bound industrialized western Europe to international markets, recession affected the economies of such diverse regions as Australia, South Africa, California, New-foundland, and the West Indies.

These dramatic fluctuations differed from the economic cycles that were the rule before 1850, in which failure on the land led to higher food prices and then to failure in manufacturing. Although suffering problems of its own, agriculture was no longer so dom-inant that its fate determined the welfare of other sectors of the economy. By the 1870s, industrial and financial setbacks were send-ing businesses into long-term tailspins. Innovation created new or modernized industries on an unprecedented scale, but economic disaster constantly loomed.

Economic crises were possible in a time of industrial progress because economists, industrialists, and government officials did not yet clearly understand the workings of in-dustrialized, interconnected economies. As industrialization advanced, entrepreneurs encountered fundamental problems. First, the start-up costs of new enterprises sky-rocketed. Textile mills had required relatively modest amounts of capital in comparison to factories producing steel and iron. To use the terms of modern economists, **capital-intensive industry** replaced labor-intensive industry: growth of the former required the purchase of expensive machinery, not merely the hiring of more workers. Second, the dis-tribution and consumption of goods were inadequate to sustain industrial growth. In-creased productivity in both agriculture and industry led to rapidly declining prices. Wheat, for example, dropped to one-third its 1870 price by the 1890s. Consumers, how-ever, did not always benefit from this deflation: wages were slashed and unem-ployment rose during the economic down-turns. Nor could they always afford the new goods. Industrialists had made their for-tunes by emphasizing production, not con-sumption. The series of slumps refocused entrepreneurial policy on finding ways to en-hance sales and distribution and to control markets and prices.

In response to nervous business owners and to those fearful of potential social unrest, governments took steps to foster economic prosperity. New laws spurred the development of the **limited liability corporation**, which protected investors from personal responsibility for the firm's debt. Before limited liability, businesses drew the capital they needed primarily from their own family assets, and financial backers were individually responsible for the firm's financial difficulties. In one case in England, a former partner who had failed to have his name removed from a legal document after leaving the business remained responsible to creditors when the company went bankrupt. He lost everything he owned except a watch and the equivalent of $100. The end of personal liability greatly increased investor confidence with regard to financing business ventures.

Public financing in stocks and bonds promised investors wide opportunities to gain high profits. Stock markets had existed prior to the changes in liability laws, but they had dealt mainly in government bonds and in government-sponsored enterprises such as railroads. By the end of the century, stock markets were trading heavily in industrial corporate stock owned by many individuals, and investors thus raised money from a larger pool of private capital than before. At the center of an international economy linked by telegraph, telephone, railways, and steamships, the London Stock Exchange in 1882 traded industrial shares worth £54 million, a value that surged to £443 million by 1900. The capacity to raise capital for financing industry soared.

Less personal financial liability and new sources of capital did not eliminate business difficulties, however. In another adaptive move, firms in the same industry banded together in cartels and trusts to control prices and competition. Cartels (the organization of industries into a monopoly for fixing prices) flourished particularly in German chemical, iron, coal, and electric industries. For example, the Rhenish-Westphalian Coal Syndicate, founded in 1893, eventually dominated more than 95 percent of coal production in Germany. Although business owners might continue publicly to advocate free trade, their own cartels broke with free-trade practices by restricting output and setting prices.

Trusts appeared first in the United States. In 1882, John D. Rockefeller created the Standard Oil Trust by acquiring stock from many different oil companies and placing it under the direction of trustees. The trustees then controlled so much of the companies' stock that they could set prices for the entire industry. They could even dictate to the railroads the rates for transporting the oil. Trusts and cartels also oversaw the vertical integration of industries, in which, for example, a steel company acquired mining operations in ore and coal as well as railroads to distribute its output. Such acquisitions ensured access to raw materials, lower production costs, and greater control of product distribution.

Like the establishment of cartels and trusts, government imposition of tariffs expressed declining faith in classical liberal economics. Much of Europe had adopted free trade after midcentury, but during the recessions of the 1870s, huge trade deficits—caused when imports exceed exports—soured many Europeans on the concept. A country with a trade deficit had less capital available to invest internally; thus, fewer jobs were created and the chances of social unrest increased. Farmers in many European countries were hurt when improvements in transportation made it possible to import perishable food, such as grain from the United States and Ukraine. France and Germany were particularly vulnerable to trade deficits in the last three decades of the century. In response, governments in both countries approved tariffs throughout these decades. Farmers, capitalists, and even many workers supported these taxes on imports to prevent competition from foreign goods. Governments in the West responded to calls for economic nationalism, and by the early 1890s all but Belgium, Britain, and the Netherlands had ended free trade.

Revolution in Business Practices

Industrialists tried to minimize the damage of economic downturns by revolutionizing the everyday conduct of their businesses. A generation earlier, a factory owner was directly involved in every aspect of his business and often learned to run the firm through trial and

TAKING MEASURE

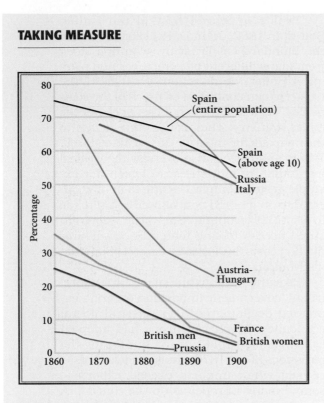

The Decline of Illiteracy

The development of mass politics and the consolidation of the nation-state depended on building a cohesive group of citizens, informed about the progress of the nation. Increasing literacy was thus a national undertaking but one with varying rates of success in different nations, ranging from low levels of illiteracy in Prussia to high levels in Austria-Hungary and Russia. Even in regions of high illiteracy, however, governments successfully encouraged people to read. In what ways does the rate of literacy reflect other developments in the countries represented above? *Theodore Hamerow, The Birth of New Europe: State and Society in the Nineteenth Century (Chapel Hill: University of North Carolina Press, 1983), 85.*

error. In the late 1800s, industrialists began to hire managers to run their increasingly complex day-to-day operations. Managers who specialized in sales and distribution, finance, and purchase of raw materials made decisions and oversaw the implementation of their policies. One German steel magnate told his managers to hire "supervisors and supervisors of supervisors to watch what our men are doing," all to the end of raising productivity.

The White-Collar Sector.
The rise of the manager was accompanied by the emer-

gence of a "white-collar" service sector. Businesses employed secretaries, file clerks, and typists to guide the flow of business information. Banks that accepted savings from the general public and that invested those funds heavily in business needed tellers and clerks; railroads, insurance companies, and government-run telegraph and telephone companies all needed armies of office workers.

Workers with mathematical skills and literacy acquired in the new public primary schools staffed this service sector, which provided in particular clean work for educated, middle-class women (see "Taking Measure," on this page). Women eventually predominated among service employees. At the beginning of the century, middle-class women still tended businesses with their husbands. In the next few decades, however, the ideology of domesticity developed to dictate that these women should not work outside the home. By the late nineteenth century, the costs of middle-class family life, especially children's education, were becoming a burden. Many middle-class people could not even afford to marry. Whether to help pay family expenses or to support themselves, both unmarried and married women of the respectable middle class increasingly took jobs. Employers, as one put it, found in the new women workers a "quickness of eye and ear, and the delicacy of touch" essential to office work. By hiring women for newly created clerical jobs, business and government contributed to a dual labor market in which certain categories of jobs were predominantly male and others were overwhelmingly female. Since women had few other employment options, businesses in the service sector saved significantly by paying women chronically low wages—much less than they would have had to pay men for the same work.

The Department Store.
Just as industrial capitalism had transformed the scale of production, the rise of consumer capitalism eventually transformed the scale of consumption. The principal institution of this change was the department store. Founded after midcentury in the largest cities, department stores gathered an impressive variety of goods in one place in imitation of the Middle

Copenhagen's Central Telephone Exchange (c. 1884)
European governments established telephone and telegraph services for individual customers late in the nineteenth century. These services were part of the rapid advance in transport and communications that characterized the modern West. Middle-class women, like these in Copenhagen's Telephone Exchange, staffed many white-collar positions that made up the new service sector. Schooling prepared more people to perform non-manual labor such as servicing telephone customers by connecting them with one another and monitoring calls or, in the case of department store clerks, selling consumer goods and calculating sales. The rise of the service economy centered in communications, banking, and consumption expanded job opportunities. *Mary Evans Picture Library.*

Eastern bazaar. Created by daring entrepreneurs such as Aristide and Marguerite Boucicaut♦ of the Bon Marché in Paris (shown on the next page) and John Wanamaker of Wanamaker's in Philadelphia, department stores eventually replaced the single-item stores that people entered knowing clearly what they wanted to purchase.

These modern palaces sought to stimulate consumer desires with luxurious fabrics, delicate laces, and richly embellished tapestries. The items spilled over railings and counters, not in the calculated order inherent in rational, middle-class ideals, but in intentional and glorious disarray. Shoppers no longer bargained over prices; instead they reacted to sales, a new marketing technique that could incite a buying frenzy. Because most men lacked the time for shopping expeditions, department stores appealed mostly to women, who came out of their domestic sphere into a new public role. Women ex-

plained their forays outside the home as necessary to enhance their home and family lives. Attractive salesgirls, another variety of service workers, were hired to inspire customers to buy. Shopping was not only an urban phenomenon: enticing mail-order catalogs from the Bon Marché or Sears, Roebuck arrived regularly in rural areas, replete with all the luxuries and household items contained in the exotic, faraway dream world of the city.

Consumerism was shaped by imperialism. Wealthy travelers like Marianne North journeyed on well-appointed oceanliners, carrying quinine, antiseptics, and other medicines as well as cameras, revolvers, and the latest in rubber goods and apparel. Coffee, tea, sugar, tobacco, cocoa, and cola from the colonies were stimulants whose consumption became more widespread. Tons of palm oil from Africa were turned into both margarine, increasing fat in the European diet, and fine soap, allowing Westerners to see themselves as cleaner and

♦**Boucicaut:** boo see KOH

The Great Staircase of the Bon Marché (c. 1880)
The Bon Marché in Paris was one of the West's premier department stores. It centralized consumption in a single large place and in so doing became the object of wonder and excitement as well as criticism. The vast array of goods caused customers to flock to these stores and gape in amazement at the luxurious displays and sheer abundance. Critics, however, charged that these stores turned sober housewives into irrational shoppers, wasteful of family resources. Instead of entering a fabric store, for example, with a clear idea of their needs, they let their fantasies run wild in a store like the Bon Marché. As a result, respectable shopkeepers with only small establishments were driven out of business as their customers defected. Consumption as a whole expanded with the birth of the department store shopper. © Snark/Art Resource, NY.

more civilized. Industry and empire jointly shaped everyday life, as a voracious desire to consume and own—whether industrial goods or colonies—took root in Western culture.

> **Review:** What economic and political factors led to the rise of the department store?

❖ The New Imperialism

In the last third of the nineteenth century, industrial demand and rampant business rivalry added fuel to the contest for territory in Africa and Asia. The new imperialism—unlike the trader-based domination of preceding centuries—brought direct European rule to many regions of these two continents.

Just as the British government took over from the East India Company trading house, other governments became directly involved in expansion. Champions of nation building came to connect industrial prosperity and imperial expansion with national identity. "Nations are not great except for the activities they undertake," declared a French advocate of huge imperial acquisitions in 1885. Conquering foreign territory appeared to heap glory on the nation-state. While the new imperialism aimed to advance Western religions and culture, the expansion of the West simultaneously increased the subjugation of local peoples, inflicting violence and radically altering their lives.

Taming the Mediterranean

European countries eyed the African and Asian shores of the Mediterranean for a primary reason, based on the old imperialism: the chance to profit through trade. Great Britain and France were especially eager to do business with Egypt, a convenient and profitable stop on the way to Asia. There, enterprising rulers had not only made Cairo into a bustling metropole but also helped boost commerce and manufacturing, the combined value of imports and exports jumping from 3.5 million Egyptian pounds in 1838 to 21 million in 1880 and to 60 million in 1913. European capital investment in the region rose, first in ventures such as the Suez Canal in the 1860s and then in the laying of thousands of miles of railroad track, the improvement of harbors, and the creation of telegraph systems. But all of these ventures cost local entrepreneurs dearly: Egyptians paid 12 percent interest rates on loans for improvements while Europeans paid 5 percent. Having invested in the

Suez Canal and in other businesses, the British and French in 1879 took over the Egyptian treasury, said to be a guarantee for their financial investments. After invading Egypt in 1882, which they claimed was necessary to put down those Egyptian nationalists who protested the takeover of the treasury, the British effectively seized control of the government as a whole. Despite heated parliamentary opposition at home, Britain forced the reshaping of the Egyptian economy from a system based on multiple crops that maintained the country's self-sufficiency to one that emphasized the production of a few crops—mainly cotton, raw silk, wheat, and rice, which were especially useful to European manufacturing. Colonial powers, local landowners, and moneylenders profited from these agricultural changes, while the bulk of the rural population barely eked out an existence.

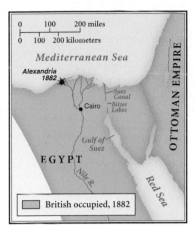

The Suez Canal and British Invasion of Egypt, 1882

As further insurance for their Mediterranean claims, the French occupied neighboring Tunisia in 1881. Businessmen from Britain, France, and Germany flooded Asia Minor, the portion of Asia at the eastern end of the Mediterranean, with cheap goods, driving artisans from their trades and into low-paid work building railroads or processing tobacco. Instead of basing wage rates on gender (as they did at home), Europeans used ethnicity and religion, paying Muslims less than Christians, and Arabs less than other ethnic groups. Such practices, as well as contact with European technology and nationalism, planted the seeds for anticolonial movements.

Scramble for Africa

Sub-Saharan Africans also felt the heavier hand of European ambition after the British takeover of the Egyptian government. Economic relations between Africans and Europeans were not new, but contact between the two continents had principally involved the trade of African slaves for European manufactured goods. The slave trade had drastically diminished by this time, and Europeans' principal objective was expanding trade in Africa's raw materials, such as palm oil, cotton, diamonds, cocoa, and rubber. Additionally, with its industrial and naval supremacy and its empire in India, Britain hoped to keep the southern and eastern coasts of Africa secure for stopover ports on the route to Asia.

Except for the French conquest of Algeria, commerce had rarely involved Europe in direct political control in Africa. Yet in the 1880s, European influence turned into direct control as one African territory after another fell to European military force (Map 24.1 on the next page). The French, Belgians, Portuguese, Italians, and Germans jockeyed to dominate peoples, land, and resources— "the magnificent cake of Africa," as King Leopold II of Belgium (r. 1865–1909) put it. Driven by insatiable greed, Leopold claimed the Congo region of central Africa, thereby initiating competition with France for that territory and inflicting on its peoples unparalleled acts of cruelty. German chancellor Otto von Bismarck, who saw colonies mostly as political bargaining chips, established German control over Cameroon and a section of East Africa. Faced with competition, the British poured millions of pounds into preserving their position by dominating the continent "from Cairo to Cape Town," as the slogan went, and the French cemented their hold on large portions of western Africa.

The scramble for Africa escalated tensions in Europe and prompted Otto von Bismarck, now the German chancellor, to call a conference of European nations at Berlin. The fourteen nations at the conference, held in a series of meetings in 1884 and 1885, decided that control of settlements along the African coast guaranteed rights to internal territory. This agreement led to the strictly linear dissection of the continent; geographers and diplomats cut across indigenous boundaries of African culture and ethnic life. The Berlin conference also banned the sale of alcohol and controlled the sale of arms to native peoples. In theory the meeting was supposed to reduce bloodshed and temper

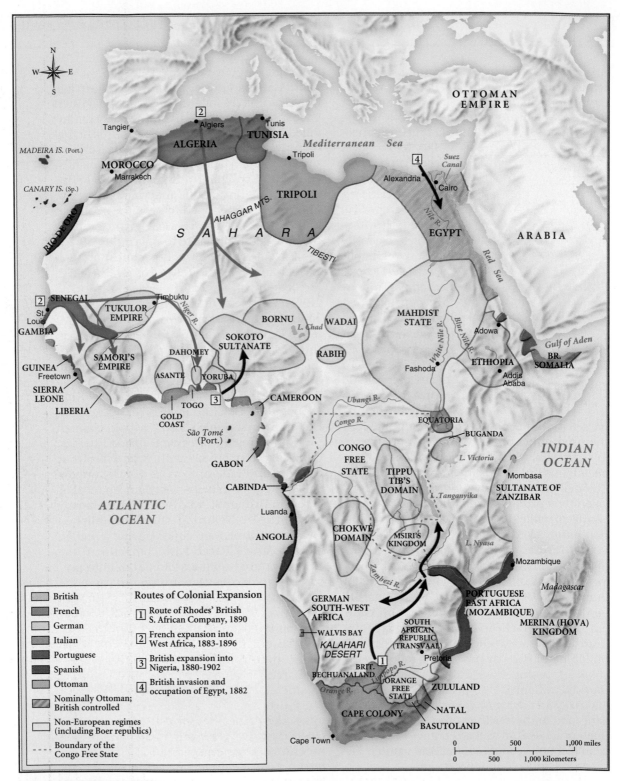

MAP 24.1 Africa, c. 1890

The "scramble for Africa" entailed a change in European trading practices, which generally had been limited to the coastline. Trying to conquer, economically penetrate, and rule the interior ultimately resulted in a map of the continent that made sense only to the imperial powers, for it divided ethnic groups and made territorial unities that had nothing to do with Africans' sense of geography or patterns of settlement. This map shows the unfolding of that process and the political and ethnic groupings to be conquered. This map doesn't yet show the partitioning of Africa that will appear in chapter 25. How do these divisions compare to national boundaries in Europe?

ambitions in Africa, but in reality European leaders were intent on maintaining and expanding their power, and savagely greedy individuals like King Leopold continued to plunder the continent and terrorize its people (as shown in the photo on this page). Journalistic reports of vast chunks of land trading hands only whetted the popular appetite for more imperialist ventures.

Technological development of powerful guns, railroads, steamships, and medicines dramatically expanded and facilitated Western domination, accelerating European penetration of all the continents after more than three centuries of exploration and trade. The gunboats that forced the Chinese to open their borders to opium played a part in forcing African ethnic groups to give up their independence. Quinine and guns were also important factors in African conquest. Before the development of medicinal quinine in the 1840s and 1850s, the deadly tropical disease malaria had threatened to decimate any European party embarking on exploration or military conquest, giving Africa the nickname "White Man's Grave." The use of quinine, extracted from cinchona bark from the Andes, to treat malaria sent death rates among missionaries, adventurers, traders, and bureaucrats plummeting.

While quinine saved white lives, technology to take lives was also advancing. Improvements to the breech-loading rifle and the development of the machine gun, or "repeater," between 1862 and the 1880s dramatically increased firepower. Europeans carried on a brisk trade selling inferior guns to Africans on the coast, while peoples of the interior still used bows and arrows. Muslim slave traders and European Christians alike crushed African resistance with blazing gunfire: "The whites did not seize their enemy as we do by the body, but thundered from afar," claimed one local African resister. "Death raged everywhere—like the death vomited forth from the tempest."

Nowhere did this destructive capacity have greater effect than in southern Africa, where farmers of European descent and immigrant prospectors, rather than military personnel, battled the Xhosa,◆ Zulu, and

The Violence of Colonization
King Leopold, ruler of the Belgian Congo, was so greedy and ruthless that his agents squeezed the last drop of rubber and other resources from local peoples. Missionaries reported such atrocities as the killing of workers whose quotas were even slightly short or the amputation of hands for the same offense. Belgian agents collected amputated hands and sent them to government officials to show Leopold that they were enforcing his kind of discipline. What attitudes allowed for such amputations, and what might have prompted the photographer to take this photo? *Anti-Slavery International.*

other African peoples for control of the frontier regions of Transvaal, Natal, the Orange Free State, Rhodesia, and the Cape Colony. Although the Dutch originally settled the area in the seventeenth century, the British had gained control by 1815. Thereafter, descendants of the Dutch, called Boers◆ (Dutch for "farmers"), were joined by British immigrants in their fight to wrest farmland and

◆**Xhosa:** KOH suh

◆**Boers:** bawrs

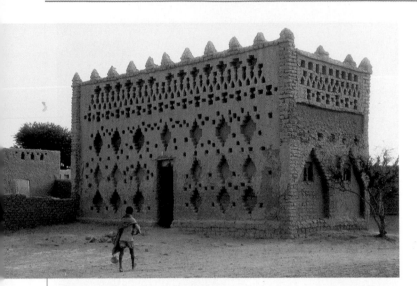

Malian Young Men's House
Europeans claimed that sub-Saharan Africans had no culture and especially no technical knowledge. Skilled road builders, textile designers, and manufacturers of weapons, Africans had also constructed intricate mosques, private dwellings, and communal buildings (such as this one for young men in Mali) long before the arrival of Europeans in the African interior. European painters, architects, and sculptors soon adapted features from African styles and even wholly modeled their designs on those of artists beyond the West. *Carollee Pelos/Jean-Louis Bourgeois.*

mineral resources from natives. British businessman and politician Cecil Rhodes (1853–1902), sent to South Africa for his health just as diamonds were being discovered in 1870, cornered the diamond market and claimed a huge amount of African territory with the help of official charters from the British government, all before he turned forty. Pushing hundreds of miles into the interior of southern Africa (a region soon to be named Rhodesia after him), Rhodes moved into gold mining too. His ambition for Britain and for himself was boundless: "I contend that we are the finest race in the world," he explained, "and that the more of the world we inhabit the better it is." Although notions of European racial superiority had been advanced before, racist attitudes now justified converting trade with Africans into conquest and political control of their lands (see "Imperialism's Popularity among the People" on the next page). Within just a few decades, Darwinism had evolved from a contribution to science to a racist justification for imperialism.

Wherever necessary to ensure profit and domination, Europeans either destroyed African economic and political systems or transformed them into instruments of their rule. A British governor of the Gold Coast put the matter succinctly in 1886: the British would "rule the country as if there were no inhabitants," as if local traditions of political and economic life did not exist. Indeed, most Europeans considered Africans barely civilized, despite the wealth local rulers and merchants accumulated in their international trade in raw materials and slaves, and despite individual Africans' accomplishments in fabric dyeing, road building, and architecture. Unlike the Chinese and Indians, whom Europeans credited with a scientific and artistic heritage, Africans were seen as valuable only for manual labor. By confiscating Africans' land, Europeans forced native peoples to work for them to earn a living and to pay the taxes they imposed. Subsistence agriculture, often performed by women and slaves, thus declined in favor of mining and farming cash crops. Standards of living dropped for Africans who lost their lands without realizing the Europeans were claiming permanent ownership. Systems of family and community unity provided support networks for Africans during this upheaval in everyday life.

Acquiring Territory in Asia

Britain justified the invasion of African countries as strategically necessary to preserve its control of India's quarter of a billion people, but in reality from the 1870s on, the expansion of European power was occurring around the world. Much of Asia, with India as the centerpiece, was integrated into Western empires.

Although half a million Indians held bureaucratic positions in India under British authority, British domination was blatant. In 1876, the British Parliament declared Queen Victoria the empress of India. British policy forced the end to indigenous production of finished goods such as cotton textiles that would compete with Britain's own manufactures. Instead the British wanted cheaper raw materials such as wheat, cotton, and jute to supply their industries. Enclaves of British civil servants, who sought prosperity and social advancement for governing the vast subcontinent, enforced segregation and an inferior status on all classes of Indians. Discriminated against but educated, the Indian elite in 1885 founded the Indian National Congress. One group among its many prosperous members accepted British liberalism in economic and social policy, but others challenged Britain's right to rule. In the next century, the Congress would develop into a mass movement.

To the east, British military forces took control of the Malay peninsula in 1874 and of the interior of Burma in 1885. In both areas, political instability often threatened secure trade. The British depended on the region's tin, oil, rice, teak, and rubber as well as its access to the numerous interior trade routes of China. The presence of British troops guaranteed the order necessary to expand railroads for more efficient export of raw materials and the development of Western systems of communication. Once secured, the relative tranquillity also allowed the British to build factories and from there to create an industrial base in China.

The British added to their holdings in Asia partly to counter Russian and French annexations. Since 1865, Russia had been absorbing the small Muslim states of central Asia, including Turkestan and provinces of Afghanistan (Map 24.2 on the next page). Besides extending into the Ottoman Empire, Russian tentacles reached Persia, India, and China, often encountering British competition. The Trans-Siberian Railroad allowed Russia to be-

British Colonialism in the Malay Peninsula and Burma, 1826–1890

Map legend:
- Annexed by British, 1826–52
- Annexed by British, 1885–86
- Annexed by British, 1890

Imperialism's Popularity among the People

Henry Stanley (1841–1904) was an unscrupulous English adventurer in Africa, who regularly killed and abused indigenous peoples to gain their land and wealth on behalf of such clients as Leopold of Belgium. Yet the press boosted sales by recounting his adventures as those of a brave and rugged soldier—an ambassador of civilized values. The celebratory tone infiltrated popular culture, as in the song below. Recounting Stanley's search for an important African leader, Emin Pasha, it brought London music hall audiences to their feet in an orgy of thunderous applause for their hero.

Oh, I went to find Emin Pasha, and started away for fun,
With a box of weeds and a bag of beads, and some tracts and a Maxim gun . . .
I went to find Emin, I did, I looked for him far and wide;
I found him right, I found him tight, and a lot of folks beside,
Away through Darkest Africa, though it cost me lots of tin,
For without a doubt I'd rind him out, when I went to find Emin!

Source: Ernest Short, *Fifty Years of Vaudeville* (New York: Eyre and Spotteswoode, 1946), 43.

gin integrating Siberia—considered a distant colony in the eighteenth and early nineteenth centuries. Hundreds of thousands of hungry peasants moved to the region and trade routes to cities in the west expanded. France meanwhile used favorable treaties backed by the threat of military action to create the Union of Indochina from the ancient states of Cambodia, Tonkin, Annam, and Cochin China in 1887 (the latter three now constitute Vietnam). Laos was added to Indochina in 1893.

To those who opposed this expansion as "spending our money on distant adventures," advocates of imperialism pointed out that, in the example of France, Europe had a

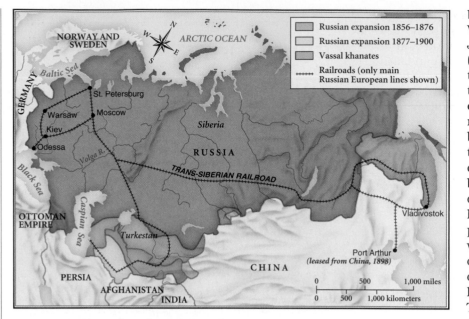

MAP 24.2 Expansion of Russia in Asia, 1865–1895
Russian administrators and military men continued enlarging Russia, bringing in Asians of many different ethnicities, ways of life, and religions. Land-hungry peasants in western Russia followed the path of expansion into Siberia and Muslim territories to the south. In some cases they drove native peoples from their lands, but in others they settled unpopulated frontier areas. As in all cases of imperial expansion, local peoples resisted any expropriation of their livelihood, while the central government tried various policies for integration. What differences do you observe about Russian expansion as opposed to British, French, American, and Dutch expansion? With whom would the Russians most likely clash?

"civilizing mission." The French thus taught some of their colonial subjects to speak French and learn French literature and history. The emphasis was always on European, not local people's culture. In Africa, an exam for students in a school run by German missionaries asked them to write on "Germany's most important mountains" and "the reign of William I and the wars he waged." The deeds of Africa's great rulers and the accomplishments of its kingdoms disappeared from the curriculum. While Europeans believed in instructing colonial subjects, they did not believe that they were equally capable of achieving great things.

Japan's Imperial Agenda

Japan escaped the new European imperialism by its rapid transformation into a modern industrial nation with its own imperial agenda. A Japanese print of the 1880s illustrates both traditional ways and the Western influence behind Japan's burgeoning power (opposite). The picture's costumed women, strolling with their parasols amid flowering cherry trees, might have been rendered centuries earlier; but a steaming locomotive in the background symbolizes change. The Japanese embraced foreign trade and industry. "All classes high and low shall unite in vigorously promoting the economy and welfare of the nation," ran one of the first pronouncements of the new Meiji regime that had come to power in 1868. The Japanese had long acquired knowledge from other countries. Unlike China, Japan endorsed Western-style modernization.

In the 1870s, Japanese government officials traveled to Europe and the United States to study technological and industrial developments. Western dress became the rule at the imperial court, and when fire destroyed Tokyo in 1872 a European planner directed the rebuilding in Western architectural style. Opposition to such changes was not tolerated, as the new central government, led by some of the old samurai, or warrior elite, crushed massive rebellions by those who resisted modernization. The Japanese adapted samurai traditions such as spiritual discipline and the drive to excel for a large, technologically modern military, filled by universal conscription. By 1894, Japan had become powerful enough to force traders to accept its terms for commerce and diplomatic relations.

The Japanese government instigated the turn toward industry. Japanese legal scholars, following German models, helped draft a constitution in 1889 that emphasized state power rather than individual rights. The state also stimulated economic development by building railroads and shipyards and establishing financial institutions. Unlike other

Modernization in Japan

Japan modernized with breathtaking speed, as this view of a railroad station demonstrates. Japan both borrowed from the West and loyally supported its own traditions. Thus, while many Japanese donned Western clothes, others remained wedded to local costumes and to native scenery such as cherry trees. In this woodcut by Ando Hiroshige II—son of an artist imitated by many in the West—the train schedule appears across the top of the depiction. How do industrial and traditional values intermingle in this woodcut? *Laurie Platt Winfrey Inc.*

The Union of Indochina, 1893

modernizing economies it kept its borrowing from Europe to a bare minimum. Then in the 1880s, when the cost of modernization had drained resources, the government auctioned off its businesses to private entrepreneurs, thereby collecting essential revenue to stabilize its finances. State support led daring innovators like Iwasaki Yataro, founder of the Mitsubishi firm, to develop heavy industries such as mining and shipping. In Japan, unlike the rest of Asia, the adaptation of Western-style enterprises became a patriotic goal. Like its Western models, Japan started intervening in Asian affairs in hopes of expanding its influence and resource base.

The Paradoxes of Imperialism

Imperialism ignited constant, sometimes heated debate because of the many paradoxes in its meaning and scope. Although it was meant to stabilize great-power status, imperialism intensified distrust in international politics. New countries vied with old ones for a share of world influence. In securing India's borders, for example, the British faced Russian expansion in Afghanistan and along the borders of China. Imperial competition even made areas of Europe, such as the Balkans, more volatile than ever as governments tried to control disputed territory of the weakening Ottoman Empire.

Politicians were at odds about the economic value of empire. The search for new markets often proved more costly than profitable to societies. Britain, for example, spent

An ABC for Baby Patriots (1899)

Pride in empire began at an early age, when learning the alphabet from this kind of book helped develop an imperial sensibility. The subject of geography became important in schools during the decades between 1870 and 1890 and helped young people know what possessions they could claim as citizens. In British schools, the young celebrated the holiday Empire Day with ceremonies and festivities emphasizing imperial power. If you were a nineteenth-century parent, how would you explain the importance of this book to your child's development? *Mary F. Ames. Reference (shelf-mark) 2523 c 24. Bodleian Library, University of Oxford.*

enormous amounts of tax revenue to maintain its empire even as its industrial base began to decline. Yet for certain businesses, colonies provided crucial markets: late in the century, French colonies bought 65 percent of France's exports of soap and 41 percent of its metallurgical exports. Imperialism provided huge numbers of jobs to people in European port cities, but—whether they benefited or not—taxpayers in all parts of a nation paid for colonial armies, increasingly costly weaponry, and administrators.

Imperialism did not always fulfill the intentions of its practitioners. Goals such as fostering national might, boosting national loyalty, and Christianizing colonized peoples often proved unattainable. Many believed that, through imperialist ventures, "a country exhibits before the world its strength or weakness as a nation," as one French politician announced. Governments worried that imperialism—because of its expense and the constant possibility of war—might weaken rather than strengthen them. Another French statesman argued that France "must keep its role as the soldier of civilization." But it was unclear whether imperialists should emphasize soldiering—that is, conflict, con-

quest, and murder of local peoples—or the exporting of culture and religion. The French tried both in Indochina, building a legacy of resistance that continued unabated until the mid-twentieth century.

Hoping to spread their religion, European missionaries ventured to newly secured areas of Africa and Asia. A woman missionary working among the Tibetans reflected a common view when she remarked that the native peoples were "going down, down into hell, and there is no one but me . . . to witness for Jesus amongst them." Europeans were confident in their religious and cultural superiority. In the judgment of many, Asians and Africans were beneath Europeans, variously characterized as lying, lazy, self-indulgent, or irrational. One English official pontificated that "accuracy is abhorrent to the Oriental mind." At the height of imperialism, such beliefs offered still another justification for conquest and dominion: the civilizing process of colonization would eventually make conquered peoples grateful for what Europe had brought them. Paradoxically, this cultural pride prompted "civilizers" such as missionaries to collaborate with the most brutal military measures to accomplish their goals.

Western scholars and travelers had long studied Asian and African languages and cultures or, like Marianne North, had sought botanical and other scientific knowledge. Yet even the best scholars' study of foreign cultures was tinged with bias. Scholars of Islam characterized Muhammad as a mere imitation of Jesus, for example. Alternatively, some Europeans—from novelists to military men—considered conquered peoples better than Europeans because they were unspoiled by civilization. "At last some local color," enthused one colonial officer, fresh from industrial cities of Europe, on seeing Constantinople. This romantic, misinformed, "orientalizing" vision of an ancient center of culture, similar to eighteenth-century condescension toward the "noble savage," had little to do with the reality of conquered peoples' lives. We see these paradoxes clearly in hindsight. At the time belief in the superiority of European ways hid many of them—above all the paradox that people who believed in national independence invaded the territory of people thousands of miles away and claimed the right to rule them.

> **Review:** What were the differences between the new imperialism and European states' earlier relationships with regions beyond the West?

❖ The Transformation of Culture and Society

Advancing industrialization and empire not only made the world an interconnected marketplace but also transformed everyday culture and society. Success in manufacturing and foreign ventures created millionaires, and the expansion of a professional middle class and development of a service sector meant that more people were affluent enough to own property, see some of the world, and provide their children a cosmopolitan education. Consumers in the West could purchase goods that poured in from around the world. Many Europeans grew healthier, partly because of improved diet and partly because of government-sponsored programs aimed at promoting the fitness necessary for citizens of imperial powers.

Industrial and imperial advance affected many working-class people in the West differently than it did the middle classes. In many cases it replaced their labor with new machinery while offering them opportunities for mobility as European societies opened up the globe. From the mid-nineteenth century on, millions migrated to the United States, Canada, Australia, Argentina, Brazil, and Siberia. In the process they imported culture. Artists captured the imperial and industrial spectacle in increasingly iconoclastic works influenced by non-Western styles. Their art, like the everyday lives of those they depicted, was transformed in the industrial, imperial crucible.

The "Best" Circles and the Expanding Middle Class

The profits from industry and empire added new members to the upper class, or "best" circles, so called at the time because of their members' wealth, education, and social status. People in the best circles often came from the aristocracy, which retained much of its power and was still widely emulated. Increasingly, however, aristocrats had to share their social position with new millionaires from the ranks of the bourgeoisie. In fact, the very distinction between aristocrat and bourgeois became blurred, as monarchs gratefully endowed millionaire industrialists and businesspeople with aristocratic titles for their contributions to national wealth. Moreover, down-at-the-heels aristocrats were only too willing to offer their children in marriage to families from the newly rich. Such arrangements brought a much-needed infusion of funds to old, established families and the cachet of an aristocratic title to upstart families. Thus, the American heiress Winaretta Singer (of Singer sewing machine fame) married Prince Edmond de Polignac of France, and Jeanette Jerome, daughter of a wealthy New York financier, married England's Lord Randolph Churchill (their son Winston later became England's prime minister). Millionaires discarded the modest ways of a century earlier to build palatial country homes and villas, engage in conspicuous displays of wealth, and wall themselves off from the poor in segregated neighborhoods. To justify

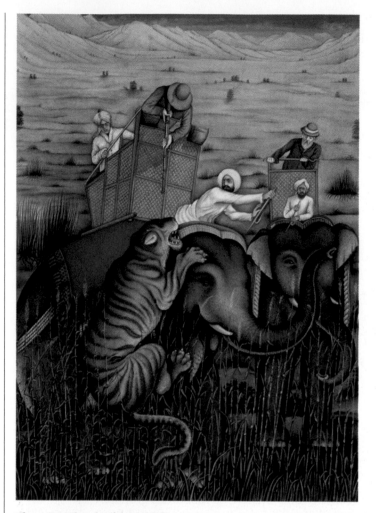

Tiger Hunting in the Punjab
Big-game hunting became the imperial sport of choice, as this Indian work of art so beautifully shows. European and American hunters took the sport over from local Asians and Africans who had previously depended on the hunt for their livelihood. Now these Asians and Africans served the Western amateurs, many of whom were in wretched physical shape and totally inexperienced in hunting big game. Nonetheless, Western manliness was coming to depend on such feats, as imperialists saw those who continued the old aristocratic fox hunt as effeminate. Though not apparent in this illustration, some Western women enjoyed hunting too. As a chivalrous gesture, men would let women issue the coup de grace, or death shot, should a tiger materialize during the hunt. © *Victoria and Albert Museum, London/Art Resource, NY.*

hunting—as reshaped by imperial contact (see the illustration on this page). Fox and bird hunting had been aristocratic pastimes in parts of Europe for centuries, but big-game hunting in Asia and Africa now became the rage. European hunters forced native Africans, who had depended on hunting for income or food and for group unity, to work as guides, porters, and domestics for European hunters instead. Mastering activities like big-game hunting or foreign games like polo demonstrated that Europeans could conquer both territory and the more intangible things like culture (see "Did You Know?" opposite). Collectors on the hunts brought exotic specimens back to Europe for zoological exhibits, natural history museums, and traveling displays, all of which flourished during this period. Stags' heads, elephant tusks, and animal skins also decorated European homes.

Members of the upper class did their best to exclude others by controlling their children's social lives. Parents of marriageable women watched them closely to preserve their chastity and to keep them from socializing with lower-class men. Upper-class men had liaisons with lower-class women—part of the double standard that saw promiscuity as normal for men and as immoral for women—but few thought of marrying them. Parents still arranged many marriages directly, but other courtships were initiated during visiting days, on which occasions prominent hostesses held an open house under rather formal conditions. Such regular social contact sometimes provided the foundation for matrimonial decisions.

Upper-class women devoted themselves to maintaining standards of etiquette and social conduct, having children, and directing staffs of servants. They took their role seriously, keeping detailed accounts of their expenditures and monitoring their children's religious and intellectual development. Their pursuit of fashion in home furnishing took on imperial motifs in these decades, featuring Persian-inspired designs in textiles, Oriental carpets, wicker furniture, and Chinese porcelains. With the importation of plants such as azaleas and rhododendrons from around the world, gardens replaced parks and lawns—another domestic element for upper-class women to oversee. Being an active consumer

their success, the wealthy often appealed to a Social Darwinist principle that their ability to accumulate money demonstrated the natural superiority of the rich over the poor.

Sport and leisure brought upper-class men together in their favorite activity—

DID YOU KNOW?

Polo and Social Class

Today's historians often see the introduction of sports by the imperial powers in colonized regions as a form of domination. By organizing teams of cricket or rugby players in West Africa, India, or the Caribbean, for instance, the British were said to be imposing Western ideas of what sports and sportsmen were on peoples with other traditions. In this interpretation, imperialists replaced local cultures with their own.

But imperialism has always been a two-way street despite great differences in power between colonizers and colonized. While playing cricket in the colonies, the British upper classes became hooked on polo, an Asian sport that imperial forces learned in India. Played on horseback, *puhluh* was a team sport that allowed a cavalry-based fighting force (both men and horses) to stay in shape during long, idle intervals. Chutneys, curries, verandahs, jodhpurs, and the game of pachisi were some of the cultural elements that the West borrowed

Anglo-Indian Polo Team
Team sports underwent rapid development during the imperial years, as spectators rooted for the success of their football team in the same spirit they rooted for their armies abroad. Some educators believed that team sports molded the male character so that men could be more effective soldiers against peoples of other races. Thus, this mixed team of polo players was uncharacteristic. In cricket, soccer, and other sports, city challenged city, nation challenged nation, and race often challenged race. How have the development and cultural exchange of sports promoted racism, nationalism, and militarism? How have they lessened racism, nationalism, and militarism? *Hulton Archive/ Getty Images.*

from India in the nineteenth century. Westerners have largely forgotten the imperial origins of polo, which seems to many people emblematic of Britain's celebrated, aristocratic way of life.

---

of fashionable clothing was time-consuming. In contrast to men's plain garments, upper-class women's elaborate costumes featured constricting corsets, long voluminous skirts, bustles, and low-cut necklines for evening wear. Upper-class women, symbols of elite leisure, tried to offset the drabness of industrial life with the rigorous practice of art and music. One Hungarian observer wrote, "The piano mania has become almost an epidemic in Budapest as well as Vienna." Some women were also quite active outside the home, engaging in religious and philanthropic activities and taking a particular interest in the welfare of lower-class women.

Below the best circles, or "upper crust," the "solid" middle class was expanding, most notably in western and central Europe. (In eastern Europe this did not happen naturally, and the Russian government often sought out foreigners to build its professional and entrepreneurial classes.) Although middle-ranked businessmen and professionals could sometimes mingle with those at the apex of society, their lives remained more modest. They employed at least one servant, to give the appearance of leisure to the middle-class woman in the home. Professional men working at home did so from the best-appointed, if not lavish, room. Middle-class domesticity substituted cleanliness and polish for upper-class conspicuous consumption. The soap and tea used in the middle-class home were becoming signs—along with hard work—of a racial superiority and higher status not accessible to the colonized peoples who actually produced those goods.

Professional Sports and Organized Leisure

As nations competed for territory and economic markets, male athletes banded together to organize team sports that eventually replaced village games. Large audiences now backed a particular team, as soccer, rugby, and cricket drew mass followings and integrated migrants as well as the lower and higher classes into a common culture. The heightened emphasis on group competition also found favor with the reading public; newspapers reported the results of all sorts of contests, including cross-country bicycle races sponsored by tire makers who wanted to prove the superiority of their product. These evolved into international events such as the Tour de France, first held in 1903. Tests of speed measured by clocks and involving the use of machines like bicycles and cars replaced older forms of competition such as cockfighting and sack racing. Competitive sports began to be seen as valuable to national strength and spirit. "The Battle of Waterloo was won on the playing fields of Eton," ran the wisdom of the day, suggesting that the games played in school could mold the strength and character of an army.

Team sports—like civilian military service—helped differentiate male and female spheres and thus promoted a social order based on distinction between the sexes. Some team sports for women emerged, such as soccer, field hockey, and rowing, but in general women were encouraged to engage in individual sports (see the illustration shown here of women bicycle racing). "Riding improves the temper, the spirits and the appetite," wrote one sportswoman. "Black shadows and morbid fancies disappear." Rejecting the idea of women's natural frailty, reformers introduced exercise and gymnastics into schools for girls, often with the idea that these would strengthen them for motherhood and thus help build the nation-state. So-called Swedish exercises for young women spread through respec-

Victorian Women's Bicycle Race
The bicycle represented freedom for millions of young people, and many credit it with changes in social customs that gradually appeared in these decades. In clubs or groups of friends, the young went off riding for miles; the bicycle was particularly liberating for young women, giving them exercise and a chance to see a bit more of the world. Their clothing changed subtly too as full skirts and abundant petticoats were soon found cumbersome and even unsafe. The bicycle also provided easier transportation for working people. *Collection of Sally Fox.*

table homes across Europe, and, as knowledge of the world developed, some women began to practice yoga.

The middle classes believed their leisure pursuits should be edifying as well as fun. Thus, mountain climbing became a popular middle-class hobby. As the editor of a Swedish publication of 1889 explained, "The passion for mountain-climbing can only be understood by those who realize that it is the step-by-step achievement of a goal which is the real pleasure of the world." Working-class people adopted middle-class habits by joining clubs for such pursuits as bicycling, touring, and hiking. Clubs that sponsored trips often had names like the Patriots or the Nationals, again associating physical fitness with national strength. The new emphasis on healthy recreation gave individuals a greater sense of individual freedom and power and thereby contributed to a developing sense of citizenship based less on constitutions and rights than on an individual nation's exercise of raw power. A farmer's son in the 1890s boasted that with a bicycle, "I was king of the road, since I was faster than a horse."

Working People's Strategies

Working people had for centuries migrated from countryside to city and from country to country to make a living. After the middle of the nineteenth century, empire and industry were powerful factors in migration. Older cities of Europe like Riga, Marseille, and Hamburg offered secure ports of entry, new industrial jobs, and opportunities for global trade, while new colonies provided land, posts for soldiers and administrators, and the possibility of unheard-of wealth in diamonds, gold, and other natural resources. City workers adapted to new conditions as industry made further inroads into the social and economic fabric.

Migration. Some Europeans followed an imperialist pattern of migration, moving well beyond their national borders to those countries where land was being taken from native peoples for white settlements (see "Contrasting Views," page 940). In parts of Europe, the land simply could not produce enough to support a rapidly expanding pop-

ulation. For example, Greek shipbuilding in ancient times had stripped the vast forests of Sicily, leaving the soil eroded and nearly worthless. By the end of the nineteenth century, hundreds of thousands of Sicilians were leaving, often temporarily, to find work in the industrial cities of northern Europe or the United States. The British Isles, especially Ireland, yielded one-third of all European emigrants between 1840 and 1920, first because of the potato famine and then because of uncertain farm tenancy and periodic economic crises. Between 1886 and 1900, half a million Swedes out of a population of 4.75 million quit their country (Figure 24.1 on the next page). Millions of rural Jews, especially from eastern Europe, left their villages for economic reasons, but Russian Jews also fled in the face of vicious anti-Semitism. Russian mobs brutally attacked Jewish communities, destroying homes and businesses and even murdering some Jews. These ritualized attacks, called pogroms, were scenes of horror. "People who saw such things never smiled anymore, no matter how long they lived," recalled one Russian Jewish woman who migrated to the United States in the early 1890s.

Commercial and imperial prosperity determined destinations. Most migrants went to North and South America, Australia, and New Zealand, as news of opportunity reached Europe. Moreover, the railroad and steamship made journeys across and out of Europe more affordable, more comfortable, and faster, even though most workers traveled in steerage, with baggage and supplies and few amenities. Once established elsewhere, migrants frequently sent money back home; the funds could be used to provide education or set up family members in small businesses, thus contributing to advancement. European farm families often received a good deal of their income from husbands or grown sons and daughters who had left. Nationalist commentators in Slovakia, Poland, Hungary, and other parts of eastern and central Europe bemoaned the loss of ethnic vigor as the young and active departed, but peasants themselves welcomed the arrival of "magic dollars" from their kin. Migrants appreciated the chance to begin anew without the deprivation and social constrictions of the old world. One settler in

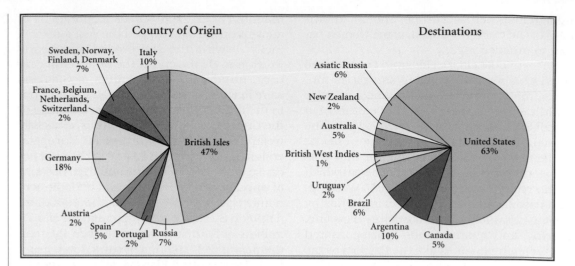

FIGURE 24.1 European Emigration, 1870–1890
The suffering caused by economic change and by political persecution motivated people from almost every European country to leave their homes for greater security elsewhere. North America attracted more than two-thirds of these migrants, many of whom followed reports of vast quantities of available land in both Canada and the United States. Both countries were known for following the rule of law and for economic opportunity in urban as well as rural areas. Which countries accounted for the largest share of emigrants and why? *Theodore Hamerow,* The Birth of New Europe: State and Society in the Nineteenth Century *(Chapel Hill: University of North Carolina Press, 1983), 169.*

the United States was relieved to escape the meager peasant meal of rye bread and herring: "God save us from . . . all that is Swedish," he wrote home sourly.

Migration out of Europe often meant the end to the old way of life. Workers immediately had to learn new languages and civic practices and to compete for jobs in growing cities where they formed the cheapest pool of labor, often in factories or sweatshops. Women who stayed at home, however, tended to associate with others like themselves, preserving traditional ways. More insulated, they might never learn the new language or put their peasant dresses away. Their children and husbands more often devalued their pasts as they were forced to build a life in schools and factories of the new world.

More common than international migration was internal migration from rural areas to European cities, accelerating the urbanization of Europe. The most urbanized countries were Great Britain and Belgium, followed by Germany, France, and the Netherlands. In Russia, only 7 percent of the population lived in cities of 10,000 or more; in Portugal the figure was 12 percent. Cities of more than

100,000 grew the most, but every urban area attracted rural people seeking employment. Migrants returned to the countryside at harvest time. Temporary migrants to the cities worked as masons, cabdrivers, or factory hands to supplement declining income from agriculture; in the winter, those remaining on the land turned to cottage industry, making bricks, pottery, sieves, shawls, lace, locks, and samovars. To maintain their status as independent artisans, handweavers sent their wives and daughters to towns to work in factories.

Adaptation to Industrial Change. Changes in technology and management practices eliminated outmoded jobs and often made the work of those who survived job cuts more difficult. Workers complained that new machinery sped up the pace of work to an unrealistic level. For example, employers at a foundry in suburban Paris required workers using new furnaces to turn out 50 percent more metal per day than they had produced using the old furnaces. Stepped-up productivity demanded much more physical exertion to tend and repair machines, often at a faster pace, but workers did not receive additional pay for their extra efforts. Workers also grumbled about the proliferation of managers; many believed that foremen, engineers, and other supervisors interfered with their work. For women, supervision sometimes brought on-the-job harassment, as in the case of female workers in a German food-canning plant who kept their jobs only in return for granting sexual favors to the male manager.

On the one hand, employers could increasingly use untrained workers, often women, and pay them less than skilled workers. On the other hand, inventions always demanded new skills for those who had to understand work processes or repair machinery. Employers began to use the concept of skill (based in the old craft traditions) to segment the labor force. They created a hierarchy of formal skill levels, although sometimes the designations were arbitrary.

Many in the urban labor force continued to do outwork at home. Every branch of industry, from metallurgy to toy manufacturing to food processing, employed women at home—and their work was essential to the family economy. They painted tin soldiers, wrapped chocolate, made cheese boxes, decorated porcelain, and polished metal. Factory owners liked the system because low piece rates made outworkers desperate for work under any conditions and thus willing to work extremely long days. A German seamstress at her new sewing machine reported that she "pedaled at a stretch from six o'clock in the morning until midnight. . . . At four o'clock I got up and did the housework and prepared meals." Owners could lay off women at home during slack times and rehire them whenever needed with little fear of organized protest.

Economic change and the periodic recurrence of hard times had uneven consequences for people's everyday lives. In the late nineteenth century, joblessness and destitution threatened. Some city workers prospered by comparison to those left behind in rural areas, though a growing number lost the steadiness of traditional artisanal work. By and large, however, the urban working class was better informed and more connected to the progress of industry and empire than their rural counterparts were.

Reform Efforts for Working-Class People

The cycle of boom and bust, the uneven prosperity of industrialism, and the upheaval of migration caused social problems that many in the middle and upper classes sought to address through reform organizations and charities. Settlement houses, clinics, and maternal and child wellness societies seemed to rise overnight in cities, quickly becoming a common sight. Young men and women, often from universities, flocked to staff these new organizations, especially the settlement houses, where the reformers took up residence in poor neighborhoods to study and help the people. Believing in the scientific approach to social problems, they thought that study would uncover the causes of social ills and point the way to solutions. One group devoted to this enterprise was the Fabian Society in London, a small organization established in 1884. Committed to a socialism based on reform and state planning rather than revolution, the Fabians helped found the Labour Party in 1893 as a way of incorporating social improvement into politics. Still other reformers were motivated by a strong religious impulse. "There is Christ's own work to be done," wrote one woman who volunteered to inspect workhouse conditions.

A Social Darwinist fear that Europeans would lack the fitness to survive in a competitive world drove philanthropists and government agencies to intervene more in the lives of working-class families. They sponsored health clinics and milk centers to provide good medical care and food for children and instructed mothers in child-care techniques, including breast-feeding—an important way, reformers maintained, to promote infant health. Some schools distributed free lunches, medicine, and clothing and inspected the health and appearance of their students. These attempts to improve urban life had their downside, however, as when government officials or private reformers deemed themselves the overseers of the working-class family and entered apartments with impunity. Such intrusions pressured poor, overworked mothers to conform to standards for their children—such as

CONTRASTING VIEWS

Experiences of Migration

In the nineteenth century millions of migrants moved thousands of miles from their homelands. The vast distances traveled and the permanent relocation of these migrants were among the issues generating a wide range of responses. Both migrants and those left behind showed acceptance and enthusiasm alternating with opposition and anger. The conflicting reactions appeared in official reports, local newspapers, poems, and very personal letters. While officials pointed with relief to the economic benefits of emigration (Document 1), people left behind were often heartbroken and destitute (Document 2). Migrants themselves had vastly differing experiences, adding to debate over migration (Documents 3 and 4).

1. THE GOVERNMENT VIEW

The preamble to the Hungarian census for 1890 was blunt and unambiguous on the subject. It saw emigration exclusively in financial terms:

Emigration has proved to be a veritable boom. The impoverished populace has been drawn off to where it has found lucrative employment; the position of those left behind, their work opportunities and standard of living, have undoubtedly improved thanks to the rise in wages, and thanks to the substantial financial aid coming into the country: sums of from 300,000 to 1,500,000 florints.

Source: Quoted in Julianna Puskas, "Consequences of Overseas Migration for the Country of Origin: The Case of Hungary," in Dirk Hoerder and Inge Blank, eds., *Roots of the Transplanted: Late 19th Century East Central and Southeastern Europe* (Boulder: East European Monographs, 1994), I:397.

2. THOSE LEFT BEHIND

Teofila Borkowska, from Warsaw, Poland, reacted to her husband's resettlement in the United States in two letters from 1893 and 1894. Stripped of a family group, Teofila had a difficult time surviving, and her husband, Wladyslaw Borkowski, never did return.

1893. Dear Husband: Up to the present I live with the Rybickis. I am not very well satisfied, perhaps because I was accustomed to live for so many years quietly, with you alone. And today you are at one end of the world and I at the other, so when I look at strange corners [surroundings], I don't know what to do from longing and regret. I comfort myself only that you won't forget me, that you will remain noble as you have been. . . . I have only the sort of friends who think that I own thousands and from time to time someone comes to me, asking me to lend her a dozen roubles.

    1894. Up to the present I thought and rejoiced that you would still come back to Warsaw, but since you write that you won't come I comply with the will of God and with your will. I shall now count the days and weeks [until you take me to America]. . . . Such a sad life! I go almost to nobody, for as long as you were in Warsaw everything was different. Formerly we had friends, and everybody was glad to see us, while now, if I go to anybody, they are afraid I need something from them and they show me beforehand a different face.

Source: Letter from Teofila Borkowska to Wladyslaw Borkowski, in William Thomas and Florian Znaniecki, *The Polish Peasant in Europe and America* (New York: Dover, 1958), July 21, 1893, April 12, 1894, II: 874–75.

finding them respectable shoes—that they could ill afford.

    To counteract the burdens facing the working-class family, some professionals began to make available birth-control infor-

mation in the belief that small families were more likely to survive the rigors of urban life. In the 1880s, Aletta Jacobs (1851–1929), a Dutch physician, opened the first birth-control clinic, which specialized in promoting

3. MIGRATION DEFENDED

In some cases emigrants were said to be unpatriotic and cowardly for leaving their homeland just to avoid hard economic times. To charges against Swedish emigrants, one journalist, Isador Kjelberg, responded with the following defense.

Patriotism? Let us not misuse so fine a word! Does patriotism consist of withholding the truth from the workingman by claiming that "things are bad in America"? I want nothing to do with such patriotism! If patriotism consists of seeking, through lies, to persuade the poorest classes to remain under the yoke, like mindless beasts, so that we others should be so much better off, then I am lacking in patriotism. I love my country, as such, but even more I love and sympathize with the human being, the worker. . . . Among those who most sternly condemn emigration are those who least value the human and civic value of the workingman. . . . They demand that he remain here. What are they prepared to give him to compensate the deprivations this requires? . . . It is only cowardly, unmanly, heartless, to let oneself become a slave under deplorable circumstances which one *can* overcome.

Source: Quoted in H. Arnold Barton, *A Folk Divided: Homeland Swedes and Swedish Americans, 1840–1940* (Carbondale: Southern Illinois University Press, 1994), 72–73.

This anonymous Swedish poem combined a political defense of migration with an economic one.

I'm bound for young America,
Farewell old Scandinavia.
I've had my fill of cold and toil,
All for the love of mother soil.
You poets with your rocks and rills
Can stay and starve—on words, no frills.
There, out west, a man breathes free,
While here one slaves, a tired bee,
Gathering honey to fill the hive
Of wise old rulers, on us they thrive.
In toil we hover before their thrones,
While they take to slumber, like lazy drones.

Drunk with our nectar they've set us afright,
But opportunity has knocked, and we'll take our flight.

Source: Quoted in ibid., 137.

4. THE PERILS OF MIGRATION

A contrasting view of emigration to the United States appeared in the following Slovak song.

My fellow countryman, Rendek from Senica, the
    son of poor parents
Went out into the wide world. In Pittsburgh he
    began to toil.
From early morning till late at night he filled
    the furnaces with coal.
Faster, faster, roared the foreman, every day. . . .
Rendek toiled harder
So as to see his wife.
But alas! He was careless
And on Saturday evening late
He received his injuries.
At home his widow waited
For the card which would never come.
I, his friend, write this song
To let you know
What a hard life we have here.

Source: Quoted in Frantisek Bielik, Horst Hogh, and Anna Stvrtecka, "Slovak Images of the New World: 'We Could Pay Off Our Debts'" in Dirk Hoerder and Inge Blank, eds., *Roots of the Transplanted: Late 19th Century East Central and Southeastern Europe* (Boulder: East European Monographs, 1994), I:388.

QUESTIONS TO CONSIDER

1. Did the vast nineteenth-century migration ultimately enrich or diminish European culture and society?
2. How would you characterize the experience of migration for families and individuals?
3. How did migration affect the national identity of both receiving countries and European countries of origin?

the new, German-invented diaphragm. Jacobs was moved to act by the plight of women in Amsterdam slums who were worn out by numerous pregnancies and whose lives, she believed, would be greatly improved by limiting their fertility. Working-class women themselves sought out these clinics, and knowledge of birth-control techniques spread by word of mouth among workers. But the churches adamantly opposed this trend, and reformers themselves were sharply divided over whether birth control was moral. Some believed that contraception would increase the sexual exploitation of women if the threat of pregnancy and its responsibilities were overcome so easily.

Reproductive issues framed another significant government reform in these decades: legislation that would "protect" women from certain kinds of work. In such cases the fear was not that families were too large but that women were not producing healthy enough children and were stealing jobs from men. Protection further divided work into jobs for men and jobs for women, which paid less. Women across Europe were barred from night work and from such "dangerous" trades as pottery making allegedly for health reasons, even though medical statistics demonstrated that women became sick on the job less often than men. But lawmakers and workingmen claimed that women's work in potteries endangered reproduction, and women who had worked in the trade were forced to find other, lower-paying jobs or remain at home. The new laws did not prevent women from holding jobs, but they made earning a living harder by limiting access to well-paying ones.

Artistic Responses to Industrial and Imperial Change

In the 1870s and 1880s, the arts explored the consequences of global expansion and economic innovation, often in the same Darwinistic and gloomy terms that fed reformers' anxieties. Despite expansion and innovation, Darwin's theory held out the possibility that strong civilizations could fail to keep up with changing conditions and could thus decay and collapse. French writer Émile Zola (1840–1902), influenced by fears of social degeneration, produced a series of novels set in industrializing France about a family plagued by alcoholism and madness. Zola's protagonists, who led violent strikes and in one case even castrated an oppressive grocer, raised real anxieties about the future of civilization. Zola had less concern for exploring character than for describing the effects of industrial society on individuals: his novel *Women's Paradise* (1883) depicts the upper-class shopper as abandoning rational,

appropriate behavior for the frenzy and "seductions" of the new department stores. Other heroines were equally upsetting because they violated still different proprieties. Norwegian playwright Henrik Ibsen (1828–1906) created the character of Nora, a woman who shocked audiences of *A Doll's House* (1879) by leaving an oppressive marriage (see excerpt opposite).

Writers envisioned a widespread deterioration that threatened all of society—men and women, aristocrats and peasants, rural folk and urbanites, workers and imperialists. Emilia Pardo Bazán (1859–1921) penned dramas of incest and murder among wealthy landowning families in rural Spain. In *The Mayor of Casterbridge* (1886), English novelist Thomas Hardy traced the path of a common man who sells his wife at a country fair and later rises to a position of power, only to find that he cannot escape his murky past. Hardy's vision was fatalistic; his characters battle forces beyond their control. Under the guise of realism Olive Schreiner's *The Story of an African Farm* (1889) finds the heroine rejecting the role of submissive wife in rural Africa. This protagonist describes the British Empire as a "dirty little world, full of confusion." Novelists addressed the burning social issues of their times in this ongoing adherence to a bleak realist style.

Industrial and imperial advances led to new design in the goods of everyday life. Country people used mass-produced textiles to design traditional-looking costumes and developed ceremonies based on a mythical past. Such customs, thought to be old and authentic, attracted city dwellers and brought tourist business to villages. So-called folk motifs caught the eye of modern urban architects and industrial designers, who turned to rural artistic styles for models of household goods, decorative objects, and clothing. In the last decades of the century, architects copied Swiss chalets and Russian country homes to achieve a rustic look capturing a bygone era. Borrowing from Persian and Indian motifs, English designers William Morris (1834–1896) and his daughter May Morris (1862–1938) designed fabrics, wallpaper, and household items based on such natural styles as the silhouettes of plants. Replacing what seemed "dead" and "ornate" styles of the early indus-

Henrik Ibsen, *A Doll's House*

Norwegian playwright Henrik Ibsen helped create the global marketplace of ideas with such scandalous plays as A Doll's House, *an 1878 work critical of traditional gender roles as this selection reveals. With women like Marianne North traveling the globe, Ibsen increasingly believed that the middle-class housewife did not develop as a full human being. His plays were performed in many countries—not only in Europe but also in Egypt, the United States, and as far away as Japan. If European artists and writers borrowed from other cultures, Europe's cultural influence also spread beyond its borders.*

HELMER. Nora, how can you be so unreasonable and ungrateful? Haven't you been happy here?

NORA. No; never. I used to think I was; but I haven't ever been happy.

HELMER. Not—not happy?

NORA. No. I've just had fun. You've always been very kind to me. But our home has never been anything but a playroom. I've been your doll-wife, just as I used to be Papa's doll-child. And the children have been my dolls. I used to think it was fun when you came in and played with me, just as they think it's fun when I go in and play games with them. That's all our marriage has been, Torvald.

HELMER. There may be a little truth in what you say, though you exaggerate and romanticize. But from now on it'll be different. Playtime is over. Now the time has come for education.

NORA. Whose education? Mine or the children's?

HELMER. Both yours and the children's, my dearest Nora.

NORA. Oh, Torvald, you're not the man to educate me into being the right wife for you.

HELMER. How can you say that?

NORA. And what about me? Am I fit to educate the children?

HELMER. Nora!

NORA. Didn't you say yourself a few minutes ago that you dare not leave them in my charge?

HELMER. In a moment of excitement. Surely you don't think I meant it seriously?

NORA. Yes. You were perfectly right. I'm not fitted to educate them. There's something else I must do first. I must educate myself. And you can't help me with that. It's something I must do by myself. That's why I'm leaving you.

HELMER (*jumps up*). What did you say?

NORA. I must stand on my own feet if I am to find out the truth about myself and about life. So I can't go on living here with you any longer.

HELMER. Nora, Nora!

NORA. I'm leaving you now, at once. Christine will put me up for tonight—

HELMER. You're out of your mind! You can't do this! I forbid you!

NORA. It's no use your trying to forbid me any more. I shall take with me nothing but what is mine. I don't want anything from you, now or ever.

HELMER. What kind of madness is this?

NORA. Tomorrow I shall go home—I mean, to where I was born. It'll be easiest for me to find some kind of a job there.

HELMER. But you're blind! You've no experience of the world—

NORA. I must try to get some, Torvald.

HELMER. But to leave your home, your husband, your children! Have you thought what people will say?

NORA. I can't help that. I only know that I must do this.

HELMER. But this is monstrous! Can you neglect your most sacred duties?

NORA. What do you call my most sacred duties?

HELMER. Do I have to tell you? Your duties towards your husband, and your children.

NORA. I have another duty which is equally sacred.

HELMER. You have not. What on earth could that be?

NORA. My duty towards myself.

Source: Henrik Ibsen, *A Doll's House* (New York: Anchor, 1966), 96–97.

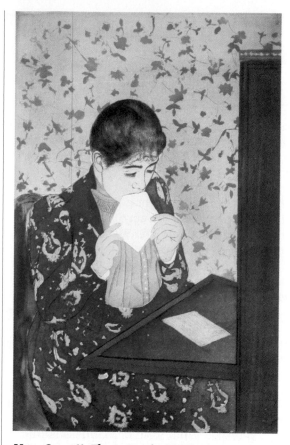

Mary Cassatt, *The Letter* (c. 1890)
Mary Cassatt, an American artist who spent much of her time in Europe, was one of the many Western artists smitten by Japanese prints. Like them, she worked to learn Japanese techniques for printmaking but she also reshaped her painting style to follow Japanese conventions in composition, perspective, and the use of color. Cassatt is known for her many depictions of Western mothers and children and of individual women. In this painting the woman herself even looks Japanese. Compare the ingredients and style of this portrait to that of Germaine de Staël on page 795. **For more help analyzing this image**, see the visual activity for this chapter in the Online Study Guide at **bedfordstmartins.com/hunt**. *The Art Institute of Chicago.*

trial years, "living flowers should inspire a living ornament," as May Morris explained. Theirs was called the "arts and crafts" style, which they hoped would build enthusiasm for handcrafted products. Industrial advance led to frequent enthusiasm for "craft" goods from an earlier age, albeit made from industrial materials and modeled on foreign designs.

By the 1870s painters felt intense competition from a popular industrial inven-

tion—the camera. Photographers could produce cheap copies of paintings and create more realistic portraits than painters could, at affordable prices. In response, painters altered their style, at times trying to make their work look as different from photographs as possible. Using thousands of dots and dabs, French painter Georges Seurat♦ (1859–1891) depicted the Parisian suburbs' newly created parks with their Sunday bicyclists and walking paths along which white-collar workers in their store-bought clothing, carrying books or newspapers, paraded like the well-to-do. Another French artist, Edgar Degas (1834–1917), focused on portraying women—from ballet dancers to laundry women—in various states of exertion and fatigue brought on by work in the fast-paced economy. He did much of his work, however, in fuzzy pastels with blurred lines that captured the mental haze of relentless physical labor while distinguishing his art from the photographic realism of the camera.

Degas and Seurat, although their styles varied, both have been characterized as avant-garde and impressionist. The term **impressionism** was first used to criticize the work of French artist Édouard Manet (1832–1883), but eventually it was used to emphasize the artist's attempt to capture a single moment by focusing on the ever-changing light and color found in ordinary scenes. Using splotches and dots, impressionists moved away from the precise realism of earlier painters; their challenge to the norm made the impressionists simultaneously avant-garde. Claude Monet (1840–1926), for example, was fascinated by the way light transformed an object, and he often portrayed the same place—a bridge or a railroad station—at different times of day. Vincent Van Gogh (1853–1890) used vibrant colors in great swirls to capture sunflowers, haystacks, and the starry evening sky. Such distortions of reality made the impressionists' visual style seem outrageous to those accustomed to realism, but others enthusiastically greeted impressionism's luminous quality. Industry contributed to the new style, as factories produced a range of pigments that allowed artists to use a wider, more intense spectrum of colors than ever before.

♦**Georges Seurat:** zhawrzh su RAH

In both composition and style, impressionists borrowed heavily from Asian art and architecture. The concept of the fleetingness of situations came from a centuries-old and well-developed Japanese concept—*mono no aware* (serenity before and sensitivity to the fleetingness of life). The color, line, and delicacy of Japanese art (which many impressionists collected) is evident, for example, in Monet's later paintings of water lilies, his studies of wisteria, and even his re-creation of a Japanese garden at his home in France as the subject for artistic study. Similarly, the American expatriate Mary Cassatt (1845–1926) used the two-dimensionality of Japanese art in *The Letter* (1890–1891) and other paintings (Cassatt, *The Letter*). Other artists, like Degas, imitated Asian art's use of wandering and conflicting lines to orchestrate space on a canvas, and Van Gogh filled the background of portraits with copies of intensely colored Japanese prints, even imitating classic Japanese woodcuts. The graphic arts and literature advanced the West's ongoing borrowing from other cultures, while responding to the changes brought about by industry and the new consumerism.

Review: How did industry and empire influence art and everyday life?

❖ The Birth of Mass Politics

Struggles for political voice, especially through the vote, accompanied imperial and economic expansion. Industrial growth and urban development strengthened networks of political communication, continuing the work of institutions such as schools, urban agencies, and government bureaucracy in producing national consciousness. As national consciousness grew among workers, western European governments continued to allow more men to vote. Even high-ranking politicians such as William Gladstone, the prime minister of Great Britain, had to campaign by railroad to win votes from a far-flung electorate. Although only men profited from electoral reform, the era's expanding franchise marked the beginning of mass politics—a hallmark of the twentieth-century West.

Without the franchise, women still participated in a range of political activism. Among the authoritarian monarchies, Germany had manhood suffrage, but in more autocratic states to the east—notably Russia and the Ottoman Empire—violence and ethnic conflict resulted from a political system that often resembled the rule imposed on colonized peoples rather than citizens.

Workers, Politics, and Protest

Workers in the 1870s–1890s coalesced politically to exert pressure on governments and businesses. Though strikes and activism were reactions to workplace hardships, they depended on community bonds forged by homemakers and neighborhood groups. With the backing of their neighbors and fellow laborers, workers in these decades built effective unions and powerful political parties—many of them based on a Marxist platform. The unions and parties acted in the public sphere to protect workers from the dizzying, often brutal pace of industrial change and to guarantee that they received a fair wage. Workers banded together at the grass roots in clubs and reading societies, yet they also aimed to unify across national boundaries. The Second International, founded in 1889, served to combat the growing nationalism that separated workers rather than binding them in a common cause.

Unions and Strikes. As the nineteenth century entered its final decades, economic uncertainties led workers to organize formal unions, which attracted the allegiance of millions. Unions demanded a say in working conditions and aimed, as one union's rule book put it, "to ensure that wages never suffer illegitimate reductions and that they always follow the rises in the price of basic commodities." Businessmen and governments viewed striking workers as insubordinate, threatening political unrest and destructive violence. Even so, strong unions appealed to some industrialists because a union could make strikes more predictable (or even prevent them), present demands more coherently, and provide a liaison for labor–management relations.

From the 1880s on, the pace of collective action for better pay, lower prices, and better working conditions accelerated. In 1888, for example, hundreds of young women who made matches, the so-called London matchgirls, struck to end the fining system, under which they could be penalized an entire day's wage for being a minute or two late to work. This system, the matchgirls maintained, helped companies reap profits of more than 20 percent. Newspapers and philanthropists picked up the strikers' story, helping them win their case. Soon thereafter, London dockworkers and gasworkers protested their precarious working conditions. Across Europe, the number of strikes and major demonstrations rose from 188 in 1888 to 289 in 1890. On May 1, 1890, for example, sixty thousand workers took to the streets of Budapest to agitate for suffrage and safer working conditions. Day laborers on Hungarian farms struck in 1891.

Housewives, who often acted in support of strikers, carried out their own protests against high food prices. In keeping with centuries of women's protest, they confiscated merchants' goods and sold them at what they considered a just price. "There should no longer be either rich or poor," argued organized Italian peasant women. "All should have bread for themselves and for their children. We should all be equal." They took other kinds of action, too: school officials or police looking for truant children met a phalanx of housewives ready to hide the children so that they could continue to help with work at home. When landlords evicted tenants, women would gather in the streets and replace household goods as fast as they were removed from the rooms of ousted families. Meeting on doorsteps or at fountains, laundries, pawnshops, and markets, women initiated rural newcomers into urban ways and developed a unity similar to that created by workers in the factory. Like strikes, political activism grew not just from the shop floor but also in neighborhoods.

Fearing threats to industrial and agricultural productivity, governments increasingly responded with force, even though most strikes were about the conditions of everyday life for workers and not about political revolution. In the face of government reaction, unions did not back down or lose their commitment to solidarity. Craft-based unions of skilled artisans, such as carpenters and printers, were the most active and cohesive, but from the mid-1880s on, a **new unionism** attracted transport workers, miners, matchgirls, and dockworkers. These new unions were nationwide groups with salaried managers who could plan massive general strikes across the trades, focusing on such common goals as the eight-hour workday, and thus paralyze an entire nation. Although small, local workers associations remained, the large unions of the industrialized countries of western Europe, like cartels and trusts, increasingly influenced business practices and society's views of workers.

Political Parties.   New political parties also engaged the masses in political life by addressing working-class issues. Workingmen helped create the Labour Party in England, the Socialist Party in France, and the Social Democratic Parties of Sweden, Hungary, Austria, and Germany—most of them inspired by Marxist theories. Germany was home to the largest socialist party in Europe after 1890. Socialist parties attracted workingmen because they promised the triumph of new male voters who could become a powerful collective force in national elections.

Those who accepted Marx's assertion that "workingmen have no country" went further, founding an international movement that could address workers' common interests across national boundaries. In 1889, some four hundred socialists from across Europe met to form the **Second International**, a federation of working-class organizations and political parties that replaced the First International, founded by Marx before the Paris Commune. This meeting adopted a Marxist revolutionary program from the start, but it also advocated suffrage where it still did not exist and better working conditions in the immediate future.

Members of the Second International determined to rid the organization of anarchists, who flourished in the less industrial parts of Europe—Russia, Italy, and Spain. In these countries anarchism got heavy support from peasants, small property owners, and agricultural day laborers, for whom the industrially based theories of Marx had less appeal. In an age of crop failures and stiff international competition in agriculture, many rural people looked to the possibility of life without the domination of large landowners and government. Many advocated extreme tactics, including physical violence and even murder. "We want to overthrow the government . . . with violence since it is by the use of violence that they force us to obey," wrote one Italian anarchist. In the 1880s, anarchists bombed stock exchanges, parliaments, and businesses. Members of the Second International felt that such random violence was counterproductive.

Workingwomen joined these parties, but in much smaller numbers than men. Not able to vote in national elections and usually responsible for housework in addition to their paying jobs, women had little time for party meetings. Furthermore, their low wages hardly allowed them to survive, much less to pay party or union dues. Many workingmen opposed their presence, fearing women would dilute the union's masculine camaraderie. Contact with women would mean "suffocation," one Russian workingman believed, and end male union members' sense of being "comrades in the revolutionary cause." Unions glorified the heroic struggles of a male proletariat against capitalism, and Marxist leaders continued to maintain that injustice to women was caused by capitalism and would disappear in the socialist society following the coming revolution. As a result, although the new political organizations encouraged women's support, they saw women's concerns about lower wages and sexual coercion in the workplace as basically unimportant.

Outside the informal ties of neighborhoods and the factory, a range of organizations forged worker solidarity through popular community activities that intertwined politics with everyday life. The gymnastics and choral societies that had once united Europeans in nationalistic fervor now served working-class goals. Songs emphasized worker freedom, progress, and eventual victory. "Out of the dark past, the light of the future shines forth brightly," went one Russian workers' song. Socialist gymnastics, bicycling, and marching societies rejected competition and prizes as middle-class preoccupations, but they valued physical fitness for what it could do to the "outer and inner organism" and for helping workers in the "struggle for existence"— a reflection of the spread of Darwinian thinking. Workers also held festivals and gigantic parades, most notably on May 1, proclaimed by the Second International as a labor holiday. Like religious processions of an earlier time, parades were rituals that fostered unity. European governments frequently prohibited such public gatherings, fearing they were tools for agitators.

Expanding Political Participation in Western Europe

Western European countries moved toward mass politics more rapidly than did countries to the east. Ordinary people everywhere in the West were becoming aware of politics through newspapers, which, combined with industrial and imperial progress, were an important nationalizing force. In western Europe in particular, people's access to newspapers and their political participation meant that politicians depended for election more on the will of the people and less on the power of small cliques.

Mass Journalism. The rise of mass journalism after 1880 gave Europeans ready access to information (and misinformation) about politics and world events. The invention of automatic typesetting and the production of newsprint from wood pulp lowered the costs of printing; the telephone allowed reporters to communicate news to their papers almost instantly. Once philosophical and literary in content, many daily newspapers emphasized the sensational, using banner headlines, dramatic pictures, and gruesome or lurid details—particularly about murders and sexual scandals—to sell papers. In the hustle and bustle of industrial society, one editor wrote, "you must strike your reader right between the eyes." A series of articles in 1885 in London's *Pall Mall Gazette* on the "white slave trade" warned the innocent not to read further. The author then proceeded to describe how young women were "snared, trapped," and otherwise forced into prostitution through sexual violation and drugs. Stories of imperial adventurers and exaggerated accounts of wasted women workers and their unborn babies similarly drew ordinary people to the mass press.

Journalism created a national community of up-to-date citizens, whether or not they could vote. Stories of crime and corruption appealed to the growing body of publicly educated, critical readers. Newspapers were meant not for quiet reflection at home or in the upper-class club but for quick reading on mass transportation and on the streets. Elites grumbled that the sensational press was itself a sign of social decay. But for up-and-coming people from the working and middle classes it provided an avenue to success. As London, Paris, Vienna, Berlin, and St. Petersburg became centers not only of politics but also of news, a number of European politicians got their start working for daily newspapers. In this context of growing political literacy, politicians in western Europe incorporated more people into the political process.

British Political Reforms. In the fall of 1879, William Gladstone (1809–1898), leader of the British Liberals, whose party was then out of power, waged an experimental campaign in northern England and in Scotland for a seat in the House of Commons. During this campaign, Gladstone spoke before thousands of workers, calling for greater self-determination in India and Africa and summoning his audiences to "honest, manful, humble effort" in the middle-class tradition of "hard work." Newspaper reports around the country highlighted his trip and, along with mass meetings, fueled public interest in politics. Queen Victoria bristled at Gladstone's speaking tour and at his attacks on her empire; she vowed that he would never again serve as prime minister. Gladstone's Liberals won, however, and he did become prime minister.

Gladstone's campaign exemplified the trend toward expanded participation in Britain's political life. The process had begun with the Reform Bill of 1832, which extended the franchise to middle-class men. The Ballot Act of 1872 made voting secret, a reform supported by those who wished to limit the influence of landlords and employers on their workers. Most significant, the **Reform Act of 1884** doubled the electorate, to around 4.5 million

men, enfranchising many urban workers and artisans and thus diminishing traditional aristocratic influence in the countryside.

As the number of British men entering political life as first-time voters increased, Liberals and Conservatives alike found it necessary to establish national political clubs as a means to gain party loyalty. These clubs competed with the insular groups of parliamentary elites who ruled through "wire-pulling," as one member of the House of Lords put it. These small cliques had heretofore determined the course of party politics. In contrast, broadly based interest groups such as unions, businessmen's associations, and national political clubs began to open up politics by appealing to many more voters.

British political reforms immediately affected Irish politics by arming disaffected tenant farmers with the secret ballot, making them less like colonized peoples than before. The political climate in Ireland was explosive mainly because of the repressive tactics of absentee landlords, many of them English and Protestant. These landlords evicted unsuccessful and prosperous tenants alike so that they could raise rents for newcomers. In 1879, opponents formed the Irish National Land League and launched fiery protests. Irish tenants elected a solid bloc of nationalist representatives to the British Parliament.

The Irish members of Parliament, voting as a group, had sufficient strength to defeat legislation proposed by either the Conservatives or the Liberals. Irish leader Charles Stewart Parnell (1846–1891) demanded British support for **home rule**—a system giving Ireland its own parliament—in return for Irish votes (see Parnell's portrait on the next page). Gladstone, who served four nonconsecutive terms as prime minister between 1868 and 1894, accommodated Parnell with bills on home rule and tenant security. But Conservatives called home rule "a conspiracy against the honor of Britain." When they were in power (1885–1886 and 1886–1892), they cracked down on Irish activism. Scandals reported in the press ultimately ended Parnell's political career. The first came late in the 1880s, when journalists at the London *Times* fabricated letters implicating Parnell in the assassination of English officials. Parnell

Charles Stewart Parnell, Irish Hero
Charles Stewart Parnell gained the support of both the moderates and the radicals working for Irish home rule. Many saw Ireland as the first of England's colonial conquests—a land that was both ruled and exploited economically like a colony. Son of a landowning Protestant and a skilled parliamentary politician, Parnell threw himself into the Irish cause by paralyzing the British Parliament's conduct of business. He was even able to topple the parliamentary leadership. In retaliation, the government used forgeries and other unsavory means to destroy Parnell; but in the end, scandal in his personal life lost him the vital support of the public. How had the means of perpetrating scandal changed since its use in the French Revolution? *Mary Evans Picture Library.*

was cleared of this charge, but in 1890 the news broke of his affair with a married woman, and he died in disgrace soon after. Following his death, Irish home rule still remained as divisive an issue as ever.

France's Third Republic.   In France, the **Third Republic** was a hotly contested political institution from its beginning in 1870 to its collapse seventy years later. It was always a question of whether it would last and whether it was worth keeping. Universal manhood suffrage already existed as a result of classical liberalism's expansion to politics, but intrigue and scandal, magnified by press coverage, threatened the functioning of popular politics. Following the Second Empire's defeat in the Franco-Prussian War, the Third Republic began shakily with monarchist political factions—Bonapartist, Orléanist, and Bourbon—struggling to control the National Assembly and to restore their respective families to power. But the republican form of government, which French supporters had been trying to solidify for almost a century, was saved when the monarchists' compromise candidate for king, the comte de Chambord, stubbornly refused to accept the tricolored flag devised in the French Revolution. Associating the tricolor with regicide, he would accept only the white flag adorned with fleur-de-lis of the Bourbons and thus lost the chance to revive the monarchy. In 1875, a new constitution created a ceremonial presidency and a premiership dependent on support from an elected Chamber of Deputies. An alliance of businessmen, shopkeepers, professionals, and rural property owners hoped the new system would prevent the kind of strong-arm politics that had ended previous republics.

Fragile constitutional compromises, menaced by a highly partisan press, kept the Third Republic on shaky ground in the midst of economic downturns, widespread corruption, and growing anti-Semitism. Support for republican government was rocked by newspaper stories about members of the Chamber of Deputies selling their votes to business interests, and the press contributed to unrest by linking economic swings to the alleged machinations of Jewish businessmen. As a result, public sentiment turned against Jews for the failures of republican government and the economy. Confidence in republican politics plummeted in 1887 when the president's son-in-law was discovered to have sold memberships in the Legion of Honor. An aborted coup by the dashing and highly popular general Georges Boulanger soon thereafter showed the fragility of the republic and thus of political liberalism. Boulanger gathered the support of those disgusted with the messiness of parliamentary politics; his own last-minute failure of will sealed the coup's failure, preserving the republic from the menace of yet another strongman.

Republican leaders attempted to coalesce citizens by fortifying civic institutions, most notably instituting compulsory and free public education in the 1880s. In public schools, secular, republican-minded teachers supplanted Catholic clergy, who often favored a restored monarchy, and a centralized curriculum featured patriotic primers and courses in French geography, literature, and history. To perpetuate a republican ethos, the government established secular public high schools for young women, seen as the educators of future citizens. Mandatory military service for men inculcated the values of national identity and pride in place of regional and rural identities. In short, it turned peasants into Frenchmen.

Political Liberalism Rejected. Although many western European leaders believed in economic liberalism, constitutionalism, and efficient government, these ideals did not always translate into universal manhood suffrage and other forms of political liberalism in the less powerful western European countries. Spain and Belgium abruptly awarded suffrage to all men in 1890 and 1893, respectively, but both governments remained monarchies. Denmark and Sweden continued to limit political participation, and reform in the Netherlands in 1887 and 1896 increased manhood suffrage to only 14 percent. An 1887 law in Italy gave the vote to all men who had a primary school education, but this affected only 14 percent of the men.

In Italy the accession of liberals to power under the constitutional monarchy had many flaws. The process of unification left a towering debt and massive pockets of discontent, including Catholic supporters of the pope and impoverished citizens in the south. Without receiving the benefits of nation building—education, urban improvements, industrial progress, and the vote—the average Italian feared the devastating effects of national taxes and the draft on the family economy. Italians were beginning to develop an unhappiness with constitutional government that would have dramatic implications.

Power Politics in Central and Eastern Europe

Germany, Austria-Hungary, and Russia diverged from the political paths taken by western European countries. These countries industrialized at varying rates—Germany rapidly and Russia far more slowly. Literacy and the development of a civic, urban culture were more advanced in Germany and Austria-Hungary than in Russia. Even Russia, however, saw the development of a modern press, although with a far smaller readership than elsewhere. Nonetheless in all three countries, agrarian political forces remained powerful, often working to block improvements in transport, sanitation, and tariff policy that would support a growing urban population.

Bismarck's Germany. Bismarck had upset the European balance of power, first by humiliating France in the Franco-Prussian War and then by creating a powerful, unified Germany, exemplified in explosive economic growth and in rapid development of every aspect of the nation-state, from transport to its thriving capital city, Berlin (Map 24.3). His goals achieved, he now desired stability and a respite from war and so turned to diplomacy. Fearing that France would soon seek revenge against the new Reich and needing peace to consolidate the nation, he pronounced Germany "satisfied," meaning that it sought no new territory. To ensure Germany's long-term security in Europe, in 1873 Bismarck forged an alliance with Austria-Hungary and Russia, called the Three Emperors' League. The three conservative powers shared a strong interest in maintaining the political status quo.

At home, Bismarck, who owned land and invested heavily in industry, joined with the liberals to create a variety of financial institutions such as a central bank to further German commerce and industry. Religious leaders mustered their forces to defeat his Kulturkampf against religious institutions, leading Bismarck to find another supposed enemy of the new regime. He stopped persecuting Catholics and turned his attention to socialists and liberals. He used unsuccessful assassination attempts on Emperor William I as a pretext to outlaw the Social Democratic Party in 1878. Simultaneously, hoping to wean the working class from socialism, between 1882 and 1884 Bismarck sponsored an accident and disability insurance program—the first of its kind in Europe and an important step in broadening the mandate of government to encompass social welfare. In 1879, he assembled a conservative Reichstag coalition that put through tariffs protecting German agriculture and industry from foreign competition but also raising the prices of consumer goods. This increased cost of basic necessities like food chipped away at industrial profits because owners had to pay their workers more. Ending his support for laissez-faire economics, Bismarck also severed his working relationship with political liberals. The agrarian conservatives, who disliked the growing power of industry and increasing urbanization, found their status enhanced by Bismarck's apparent attacks on the political force of Germany's burgeoning industrial sector.

Authoritarian Austria-Hungary.

Like Germany, Austria-Hungary frequently relied on liberal economic policies. From the 1860s, liberal businessmen succeeded in industrializing parts of the empire, and the prosperous middle classes erected conspicuously large homes, giving themselves a prominence in urban life that rivaled the aristocracy's. They persuaded the government to enact free-trade provisions in the 1870s and to search out foreign investment to build up infrastructure, such as railroads.

Yet despite such influences, Austria-Hungary remained resolutely monarchist and authoritarian. Liberals in Austria—most of them ethnic Germans—saw their influence eroded under the leadership of Count Edouard von Taaffe,♦ Austrian prime minister from 1879 to 1893. Taaffe built a coalition of

♦**von Taaffe:** fawn TAHF uh

MAP 24.3 Expansion of Berlin to 1914
"A capital city is essential for the state to act as a pivot for its culture," the German historian Heinrich von Treitschke asserted. No other capital city grew as dramatically as Berlin after German unification in 1871. Industrialists and bankers set themselves up in the new capital, while workers migrated there for jobs, swelling the population. The city was newly dotted with military monuments and with museums to show off its culture. Describe the growth of Berlin as this map conveys it. What is the virtue of a map versus a photograph of bustling Berlin?

clergy, conservatives, and Slavic parties and used its power to weaken the liberals. In Bohemia, for example, he designated Czech as an official language of the bureaucracy and school system, thus breaking the German speakers' monopoly on officeholding. Reforms outraged people at whose expense other ethnic groups received benefits, and those who won concessions, such as the Czechs, continued to clamor for even greater autonomy. In this way the government played nationalities off one another and ensured the monarchy's predominance as the central mechanism for holding competing interest groups together in an era of rapid change. Even with the success of these divide-and-rule tactics, Emperor Francis Joseph and his ministers feared the influence of the most powerful Slavic nation—Russia— on the ethnic minorities living within Austria-Hungary. Francis Joseph considered the

MAP 24.4 The Balkans, c. 1878

After midcentury, the map of the Balkans was almost constantly redrawn. This resulted in part from the weakness of the dominant Ottoman Empire, but also from the ambitions of inhabitants themselves and from great power rivalry. In tune with the growing sense of national identities based on shared culture, history, and ethnicity, various Balkan peoples sought to emphasize small-group identities rather than merging around a single dominant group such as the Serbs. Yet there was also a move by some intellectuals to transcend borders and create a southern Slav culture. How might the geography of the Balkan states and the surrounding region explain these tendencies?

government that Russia declared war on Turkey in 1877, supposedly to protect Orthodox Christians. With help from Romania and Greece, Russia defeated the Ottomans and by the Treaty of San Stefano (1878) created a large, pro-Russian Bulgaria.

The Russo-Turkish War and the ensuing treaty sparked an international uproar that almost resulted in general war. Austria-Hungary and Britain feared that an enlarged Bulgaria would become a Russian satellite that would enable the tsar to dominate the Balkans. To the Austrians this appeared the potential trigger to an uprising of its restless minorities. British prime minister Benjamin Disraeli moved warships into position against Russia in order to halt the advance of Russian influence in the eastern Mediterranean, so close to Britain's routes through the Suez Canal. The public was drawn into foreign policy: the music halls and newspapers of England echoed a new jingoism, or political sloganeering, that throbbed with sentiments of war: "we don't want to fight,/ but by Jingo if we do, /We've got the ships, /we've got the men, /we've got the money too!"

The other great powers, however, did not want a Europe-wide war, and in 1878 they attempted to revive the concert of Europe by meeting at Berlin under the auspices of Bismarck, who saw this potential war as inopportune. The Congress of Berlin rolled back the Russian victory by partitioning the large Bulgarian state that Russia had carved out of Ottoman territory and denying any part of Bulgaria full independence from the Ottomans (Map 24.4). Austria occupied (but did not annex) Bosnia and Herzegovina♦ as a way of gaining clout in

appeal of the Pan-Slavic movement dangerous to the stability of his empire.

The Balkans, where the competing forces of modernization and Ottoman decay aroused political ambition in nationalists wanting independence, became the scene of the next European struggle. Slavs in Bulgaria and Bosnia-Herzegovina revolted against Turkish rule in 1876, killing Ottoman officials. As the Ottomans slaughtered thousands of Bulgarians, two other small Balkan states, Serbia and Montenegro, rebelled against the sultan. Russian Pan-Slavic organizations sent aid to the Balkan rebels and so pressured the tsar's

---

♦**Herzegovina:** hehr tsuh goh VEE nuh

the Balkans; Serbia and Montenegro became fully independent. Nonetheless, the Balkans remained a site of political unrest and great-power rivalries.

Following the Congress of Berlin, the European powers attempted to guarantee stability through a complex series of alliances and treaties. Anxious about Balkan instability and Russian aggression, Austria-Hungary forged a defensive alliance with Germany in 1879. The **Dual Alliance**, as it was called, offered protection against Russia, whose threat to Hungarian control of its Slavic peasantry, a German diplomat wrote, "was on [the Hungarian government's] mind day and night." In 1882, Italy joined this partnership (henceforth called the Triple Alliance), largely because of Italy's imperial rivalries with France. Because tensions between Russia and Austria-Hungary remained high, Bismarck signed the Reinsurance Treaty (1887) with Russia to stifle Habsburg illusions about having a free hand in dealing with Pan-Slavism.

Unrest in Russia. Although Russia enjoyed some international success in the late nineteenth century, its internal affairs were in disarray. By 1871, the era of Great Reforms had run its course, and Russia remained almost the only European country without a constitutional government. Reform-minded youth increasingly turned to revolutionary groups for solutions to political and social problems. One such group, the Populists, wanted to rouse the debt-ridden peasantry to revolt. Other people formed tightly coordinated terrorist bands with the goal of assassinating public officials and thus forcing change. The secret police, relying on informers, rounded up hundreds of members of one of the largest groups, Land and Liberty, and subjected them to torture, show trials, and imprisonment. When in 1877 a young radical, Vera Zasulich, tried unsuccessfully to assassinate the chief of the St. Petersburg police, the people of the capital city applauded her act

Vera Zasulich
A radical activist, Vera Zasulich launched the violent phase in Russian protest when in 1877 she shot the governor-general of St. Petersburg after he ordered the beating of a political prisoner for not raising his cap to the governor. The religiously inspired daughter of a military official, Zasulich, like her two activist sisters, worked to mitigate the brutal conditions in her country. Reformers began to duplicate the violence of the government and assassinated Tsar Alexander II in 1881. *ItarTass/Sovfoto.*

and acquittal, so great was their horror at the brutal treatment of young radicals from respectable families (see the portrait of Vera Zasulich, above).

Writers added to the intense debate over Russia's future. Novelists Leo Tolstoy, author of the epic *War and Peace* (1869), and Fyodor Dostoevsky, a former radical who changed position, both opposed the revolutionaries' desire to overturn the social order; they believed that Russia above all required spiritual regeneration. Tolstoy's novel *Anna Karenina* (1877) tells the story of an impassioned, adulterous love affair, but it also weaves in the spiritual quest of Levin, a former "progressive" landowner who, like Tolstoy, eventually rejects modernization and idealizes the peasantry's tradition of stoic endurance. Dostoevsky satirized Russia's radicals in *The Possessed* (1871), a novel in which a group of revolutionaries carries out one central act: the murder of one of its own members. In Dostoevsky's view, the radicals could only act destructively and were incapable of offering any positive solution to Russia's ills.

The more radical revolutionary groups did seek to change Russia by violent action rather than by spiritual uplift. In 1881, the People's Will, a splinter group of Land and Liberty impatient with its failure to mobilize the peasantry, killed Tsar Alexander II in a bomb attack. His death, however, failed to provoke the general uprising the terrorists expected. Alexander III (r. 1881–1894), rejecting further liberal reforms, unleashed a new wave of oppression against religious and ethnic minorities and gave the police virtually unchecked power. Popular books and drawings depicted Tatars, Poles, Ukrainians, and others as horrifying, uncivilized, or utterly ridiculous—and thus always a menace to the health of Russian culture. Intensified Russification that enforced the use of the Russian language and the observance of Russian Orthodox church rituals aggravated old grievances among oppressed nationalities such as the Poles, but it also turned the once-loyal German middle and upper classes of the Baltic provinces against Russian rule, with serious long-term consequences.

The five million Russian Jews, confined to the eighteenth-century Pale of Settlement (the name for the restricted territory in which they were permitted to live), endured particularly severe oppression. Local officials instigated pogroms against Jews, whose distinctive language, dress, and isolation in ghettos made them easy targets. Government officials encouraged people to blame Jews for escalating living costs—though the true cause was the policy of making the peasantry pay for industrialization by raising taxes.

Russia: The Pale of Settlement in the Nineteenth Century

As the tsar responded to internal turmoil with even greater repression, Bismarck's delicate alliance of the three conservative powers was unraveling. A brash but deeply insecure young kaiser, William II (r. 1888–1918), mounted the German throne in 1888. William chafed under Bismarck's tutelage, and his advisers flattered the young man into thinking that his own personal talent made Bismarck a hindrance, even a rival. William dismissed Bismarck in 1890 and, because he ardently supported German nationalism, let the alliance with Russia lapse in favor of a strong relationship with the supposedly kindred Austria-Hungary. Fatefully, he had opened the door to a realignment of the great powers just as imperial rivalries were intensifying antagonisms among the European nation-states and empires.

Review: What were the major changes in political life from the 1870s to the 1890s, and which areas of Europe did they most affect?

Conclusion

The period from the 1870s to the 1890s has been called the age of industry and empire because Western society pursued both these ends in a way that rapidly transformed Europe and the world. In these decades the West appeared at the top of its form. Industrial innovation and national growth caused much of Europe to thrive and become more populous and urban. Europeans proudly spread their supposedly superior culture globally and, like Marianne North, searched out whatever other peoples and places could offer by way of knowledge, experience, and wealth. The great powers undertook a new imperialism, carving up territory and establishing direct rule over foreign peoples. As they tightened connections with the rest of the globe, Europeans felt the influence of other civilizations. In politics, reformers drew lower-class men into active citizenship by extending suffrage. Humanitarian commitment prompted the development of philanthropic agencies and promoted the development of a more activist state that worked to make citizens of imperial countries more fit.

Yet as workers struck for improved wages and conditions and the impoverished migrated to find a better life, Western society showed its fissures and divisions. While newspapers, novels, and the arts helped inform people of profound social and international changes, they also raised questions about poverty and hopelessness. By the 1890s, the advance of industry and empire was bringing unprecedented tensions to national politics, the international scene, and everyday life. Racism, anti-Semitism, and ethnic chauvinism were spreading, sanctioned in most strata of society, and the costs of empire to conquered peoples were beyond measure. Politics in the authoritarian countries was taking a more conservative turn, resisting participation and reform, while to the west democratization advanced. These differences would ultimately be of consequence for the West as a whole.

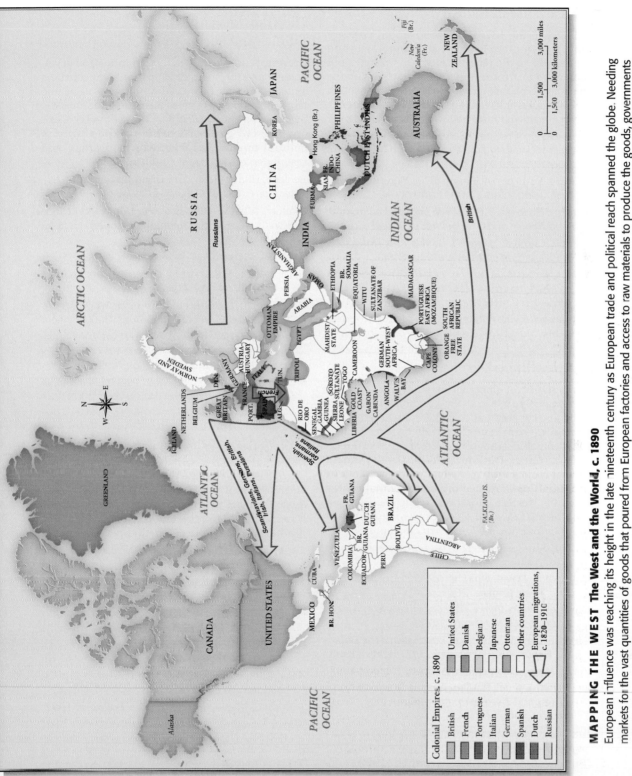

MAPPING THE WEST The West and the World, c. 1890

European influence was reaching its height in the late nineteenth century as European trade and political reach spanned the globe. Needing markets for the vast quantities of goods that poured from European factories and access to raw materials to produce the goods, governments asserted that the Western way of life should be spread to the rest of the world and that resources would be best used by Europeans. Explorations and scientific discoveries continued both to build the knowledge base of European peoples and to enhance their ability for greater conquest. Simultaneously, millions of Europeans left their homes to find a better life elsewhere. What has changed geographically in Europe's relationship with the world since the Spanish and Portuguese took colonies in the late fifteenth and early sixteenth centuries?

Suggested References

The Advance of Industry

Industry in the 1870s–1890s advanced on every front, from the development of new products and procedures to the reorganization of work life and consumption. Crouzet's sweeping new work on the creation of economic structures contrasts with other recent studies (such as Rappaport's) on the impact of consumers and taste in driving economic change.

Crossick, Geoffrey, and Serge Jaumin, eds. *Cathedrals of Consumption: The European Department Store, 1850–1939.* 1999.

Crouzet, Francois. *A History of the European Economy, 1000–2000.* 2001.

Franzoi, Barbara. *At the Very Least She Pays the Rent: Women and German Industrialization.* 1985.

Malone, Carolyn, *Women's Bodies and Dangerous Trades in England, 1880–1914.* 2003.

Marks, Steven G. *Road to Power: The Trans-Siberian Railroad and the Colonization of Asian Russia, 1850–1917.* 1991.

Rappaport, Erika. *Shopping for Pleasure: Women in the Making of London's West End.* 2000.

The New Imperialism

New studies of imperialism show not only increasing conquest and the creation of an international economy but also the cultural impulses behind it. Cannadine's book offers a readable— and debatable— interpretation of the social relations involved. The University of Pennsylvania's African studies Web site offers vivid depictions of African art and architecture, such as that confiscated for Western museums, while the Chrétien study investigates not only European imperialism in Africa but also its long-term effects.

African Studies Center: **http://www.sas.upenn.edu/African_Studies/AS.html**.

Cannadine, David. *Ornamentalism: How the British Saw Their Empire.* 2001.

Chrétien, Jean-Pierre, *The Great Lakes of Africa: 2,000 Years of History.* 2003.

Crosby, Alfred W. *Ecological Imperialism: The Biological Expansions of Europe, 900–1900.* 1993.

Ferro, Marc. *Colonization: A Global History.* 1997.

Headrick, Daniel R. *The Tools of Empire: Technology and European Imperialism in the Nineteenth Century.* 1981.

Keene, Donald. *Emperor of Japan: Meiji and His World.* 2002.

*Stanley, Sir Henry. *Autobiography.* 1909.

Wildenthal, Lora. *German Women for Empire, 1884–1945.* 2001.

The Transformation of Culture and Society

Historians have come to see that industrial development and the spread of imperialism affected the smallest details of everyday life as well as the larger phenomena of class formation and massive regional and global migration. Beckles and Stodart, and Blakely, give particularly rich portrayals of cultural mixture, exploitation, motivation, and resistance under the colonial regime.

Beckles, Hilary McD., and Brian Stodart, eds. *Liberation Cricket: West Indies Cricket Culture.* 1995.

Blakely, Allison. *Blacks in the Dutch World: The Evolution of Racial Imagery in Modern Society.* 1993.

*Bonnell, Victoria, ed. *The Russian Worker.* 1983.

Callen, Anthea. *The Art of Impressionism: Painting Technique and the Making of Modernity.* 2000.

Hoerder, Dirk. *Cultures in Contact: World Migrations in the Second Millennium.* 2002.

Maynes, Mary Jo. *Taking the Hard Road: Life Course in French and German Workers' Autobiographies in the Era of Industrialization.* 1995.

McReynolds, Louise. *Russia at Play: Leisure Activities at the End of the Tsarist Era.* 2003.

The Birth of Mass Politics

Historical study of politics in this period entails looking at both government policies and the activism based on neighborhood solidarity, the growth of unions, and the rise of the mass media. The Avalon Project at the Yale Law School provides access to major treaties and conventions, making it an excellent resource for this period.

Applegate, Celia. *A Nation of Provincials: The German Idea of Heimat.* 1990.

Avalon Project at Yale Law School: **http://www.yale.edu/lawweb/avalon/avalon.htm**.

Hoppen, K. Theodore. *Ireland since 1800: Conflict and Conformity.* 1999.

Rogger, Hans. *Jewish Policies and Right-Wing Politics in Imperial Russia.* 1986.

Ross, Ellen. *Love and Toil: Motherhood in Outcast London, 1870–1918.* 1993.

Todorova, Maria. *Imagining the Balkans.* 1997.

*Verga, Giovanni. *The House by the Medlar Tree.* 1981.

*Primary sources.

CHAPTER REVIEW

IMPORTANT EVENTS

1860s–1890s   Impressionism flourishes in the arts; absorption of Asian influences

1870s–1890s   Vast emigration from Europe continues; the new imperialism

1873   Extended economic recession begins with global impact

1876   Invention of the telephone

1879   Dual Alliance formed between Germany and Austria-Hungary

1882   Triple Alliance formed between Germany, Austria-Hungary, and Italy; Britain invades Egypt

1882–1884   Bismarck sponsors social welfare legislation

1884   British Parliament passes the Reform Act, doubling the size of the male electorate

1884–1885   European nations carve up Africa at the Berlin conference

1889   Japan adopts constitution based on European models; Socialists meet in Paris and establish the Second International

KEY TERMS

capital-intensive industry (920)

Dual Alliance (953)

home rule (948)

impressionism (944)

limited liability corporation (921)

new unionism (946)

outwork (918)

Second International (946)

Reform Act of 1884 (948)

Third Republic (949)

REVIEW QUESTIONS

1. What economic and political factors led to the rise of the department store?

2. What were the differences between the new imperialism and European states' earlier relationships with regions beyond the West?

3. How did industry and empire influence art and everyday life?

4. What were the major changes in political life from the 1870s to the 1890s, and which areas of Europe did they most affect?

MAKING CONNECTIONS

1. Compare the political and social goals of the newly enfranchised male electorate with those of people from the "best circles."

2. Describe the effects of imperialism on European politics and society as a whole.

FOR FURTHER EXPLORATION

To assess your mastery of the material in this chapter, see the Online Study Guide at **bedfordstmartins.com/hunt**.

To read additional primary-source material from this period, see Chapter 24 in *Sources of The Making of the West*, Second Edition.

Modernity and the Road to War, c. 1890–1914

IN THE FIRST DECADE OF THE TWENTIETH CENTURY, a wealthy young Russian man traveled from one country to another to find relief from neurasthenia, a common malady in those days. Its symptoms included fatigue, lack of interest in life, depression, and sometimes physical sickness. In 1910, the young man encountered Sigmund Freud, a Viennese physician whose unconventional treatment—eventually called psychoanalysis—took the form of a conversation about the patient's dreams, sexual experiences, and everyday life. Over the course of four years, Freud uncovered his patient's deeply rooted fear of castration disguised as a phobia of wolves—thus the name Wolf-Man by which he comes down to us. Often building his theories from information about colonized peoples and cultures, Freud worked his cure, as the Wolf-Man himself put it, "by bringing repressed ideas into consciousness." Freud's theories laid the groundwork for an understanding of the human psyche that has endured, with modifications and some controversy, to our own time.

The Wolf-Man was emblematic of his age. Born into a family that owned vast estates, he reflected the growing prosperity of Europeans, albeit on a grander scale than most. Simultaneously, countless individuals seemed anguished and mentally disturbed, and suicides abounded—the Wolf-Man's own sister and father died from intentional drug overdoses. European society as a whole subjected itself to agonized

---

Edvard Munch, *The Scream* (1893)

In some of his paintings Norwegian artist Edvard Munch captured the spirit of the turn of the century using delightful pastel colors to convey the leisured life of people strolling in the countryside. Impressionists similarly depicted modern life in paintings of animated conversations in outdoor cafés and gardens. But modern life at this time also had its tortured side, which Munch was equally capable of portraying. *The Scream* is taken as emblematic of the torments of modernity as the individual turns inward, beset by neuroses, self-destructive impulses, and even madness. Today some believe that *The Scream* reflects Munch's violent reaction to the earlier eruption of a volcano. While some—like the two other figures in the painting—could react calmly to whatever modern life had to offer, others like the screamer were agonized at every turn of events. It can also be suggested that the screamer, like Europe, travels the road to World War I. *National Gallery, Oslo, Norway. © Scala/Art Resource. © Copyright 2005 The Munch Museum/The Munch-Ellingsen Group/Artists Rights Society (ARS), NY.*

questioning about the family, gender relationships, empire, religion, and the consequences of technology and progress. Conflict reigned throughout Europe and the world, as an array of powers (including Japan) fought their way into even more territories and took political control. Every sign of imperial wealth brought on an apparently irrational sense of Europe's decline. British writer H. G. Wells saw in this era "humanity upon the wane . . . the sunset of mankind."

Governments expanded the male electorate during this period in the hope of making politics more harmonious and manageable. Ethnic chauvinism, anti-Semitism, and militant nationalism only increased the violence of political rhetoric, however. Women suffragists along with politically disadvantaged groups such as the Slavs and Irish demanded full rights, but the liberal ethos of tolerance receded before a wave of political assassinations and public brutality. While the great powers fought to dominate people around the world, their competition for empire fueled an arms race that threatened to turn Europe—the "most civilized" region of the world, according to its leaders—into a savage battleground.

These were just some of the conflicts associated with modernity—a term often used to describe the accelerated pace of life, the rise of mass politics, and the decline of a rural social order that were so visible in the West from the late nineteenth century on (see "Terms of History," page 962). Modernity also refers to the response of artists and intellectuals to this rapid change. The celebrated "modern" art, music, science, and philosophy of this period still resonate for their brilliant, innovative qualities. Yet these same innovations were often considered offensive at the time: cries of outrage at the new music echoed in concert halls, while educated people were utterly shocked at Freud's ideas that sexual drives motivate even the smallest children. Every advance in science and the arts simultaneously had consequences that undermined the middle-class faith in artistic and scientific progress.

When the heir to the Austro-Hungarian throne was assassinated in June 1914, few gave any thought to the global significance of the event, least of all the Wolf-Man, whose treatment with Freud was just ending and who viewed that fateful day of June 28 simply as the day he "could now leave Vienna a healthy man." Yet the assassination was the catalyst for an eruption of discord that had simmered for several decades, as the nations of Europe lurched from one diplomatic crisis to another. The consequences of the resulting disastrous war, World War I, like the insights of Freud, would shape modern life.

❖ Private Life in the Modern Age

Western ideals of a comfortable family life flourished because of Europe's improved standard of living. The prosperity brought by industrialization and empire, however, challenged traditional social norms just the way imperial and technological advance had up-

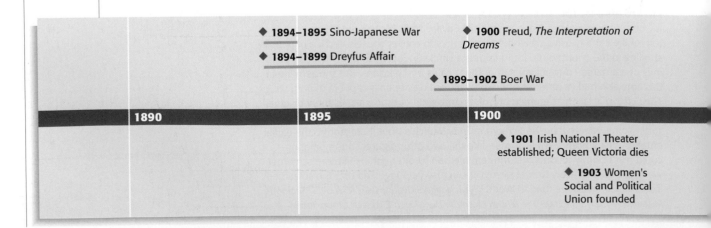

◆ **1894–1895** Sino-Japanese War

◆ **1894–1899** Dreyfus Affair

◆ **1900** Freud, *The Interpretation of Dreams*

◆ **1899–1902** Boer War

1890	1895	1900

◆ **1901** Irish National Theater established; Queen Victoria dies

◆ **1903** Women's Social and Political Union founded

set international politics and worker confidence in the economic future. A falling birthrate, a rising divorce rate, and growing activism for marriage reform provoked intense debate by the turn of the century. Some among the elites acknowledged homosexuality as a way of life, while others made it the topic of politics. Middle-class women took jobs and became active in public to such an extent that some feared the disappearance of distinct gender roles. Women's visibility in public life prompted one British songster in the late 1890s to write:

> Rock-a-bye baby, for father is near
> Mother is "biking" she never is here!
> Out in the park she's scorching all day
> Or at some meeting is talking away!

Discussions of gender roles and private life contributed to rising social tensions because they upset so many traditional ideals. They also fueled the optimism of reformers that Western society was making constant progress and becoming more rational and egalitarian. Freud and other scientists tried to study such phenomena dispassionately and eventually formulated new theories of the human personality. Public discussions of private life—especially when they became intertwined with politics—demonstrated the close connection of private and public concerns.

Population Pressure

Urgent concerns over trends in population, marriage, and sexuality clogged the agendas of politicians and reformers from the 1890s on, and they still do so in the present day. The staggering population increases of the eighteenth century had continued through the nineteenth. At the turn of the century, cities looked chaotic as population soared and changed the urban landscape by filling it with rural people and migrants—even some from other ethnicities and continents. Faced with the urban masses, often crowded into tenements and shacks, Social Darwinists warned of racial decay and Western leaders faced tense population dilemmas. Reformers, politicians, and critics of public life were seriously concerned over the quantity and quality of population.

Europe's Population Soars. Dramatic increases in the European population continued as the twentieth century opened. Germany increased in size from 41 million people in 1871 to 64 million in 1910; tiny Denmark, from 1.7 million in 1870 to 2.7 million in 1911. Such growth resulted from improvements in sanitation and public health that extended the life span and reduced infant mortality. To cope with their burgeoning populations, Berlin, Budapest, and Moscow were torn apart and rebuilt, following the lead of Vienna and Paris. The German government pulled down eighteenth-century Berlin and reconstructed the city with new roadways and mass-transport systems as the capital's population grew to over 4 million. Rebuilding to absorb population growth was not confined to capitals of the most powerful states: Balkan cities like Sofia, Belgrade, and Bucharest gained tree-lined boulevards, public buildings, and better sanitation.

◆ **1904–1905** Russo-Japanese War

◆ **1905** Revolution erupts in Russia; Duma established; Einstein, *Special Theory of Relativity*

◆ **1906** Women receive the vote in Finland

◆ **1914** Austrian archduke Ferdinand and his wife assassinated, precipitating World War I

1905	1910	1915	1920

◆ 1907 Picasso, *Les Demoiselles d' Avignon*

◆ **1908** Young Turks revolt

◆ **1911–1912** Qing dynasty overthrown; China declared a republic

TERMS OF HISTORY

Modern

The word *modernus* was introduced into Latin in the sixth century; after that, the claim to being modern occurred in many centuries and cultures. Shakespeare, for example, referred to "modern ideas" in his plays. By the second half of the nineteenth century, historians were heatedly debating where "modern" history began: with Abraham? with Charlemagne? or with the Renaissance?

Despite the many claims to being modern, the term has fastened itself most firmly around the period from the end of the nineteenth century through the first half of the twentieth. Its most specific historical use has been to describe the art, music, and dance that flourished at that time. When used in this sense, *modern* indicates a sharp break with lyrical romantic and classical music and dance and also with the conventions for representing objects in the arts. The blurred images of the impressionists and the jarring music of Arnold Schoenberg are part of modern art. The sexual rawness of *Madame Bovary* (see Chapter 23) or of Sigmund Freud's analysis of the Wolf-Man's dreams gave a further ingredient into the multifaceted meanings of the word *modern*. Sometimes this intellectual break with the cultural past is referred to as modernism.

At the end of the nineteenth century the word *modern* referred to social phenomena. Women who went to work or entered universities or began careers in the new field of social work were called modern women. They believed that by showing themselves capable and rational they could attain social progress and end restrictions placed on them. Some of them lived different lives from those women who had large families and confined themselves to the domestic sphere. This departure from tradition also made them appear modern.

In seeking an education and hoping for progress toward rationality in the law, these women were invoking a meaning of the word *modern* dating back to the Enlightenment. Progress, rational thought, and science have also been taken as the bedrock of the modern. *Modernization*—another derivative of the word *modern*—refers to the kind of scientific and technological progress that came with industrialization and the rise of commercial agriculture as they began to shape the nineteenth and twentieth centuries. Indoor plumbing, electricity, telephones, and automobiles were signs of modernity. As a result, modern artists painted teeming cities, industrial workers, world's fairs, and other scenes associated with the modernization of the late nineteenth century. In the second decade of the twentieth century, other artists started converting parts of industrial products like the toilet and the automobile into works of art.

Modern may be a popular word because it contains paradoxical meanings that make it multipurpose. While associated with the triumph of industry and rational thought at the turn of the century, cultural modernism brought a glorification of the so-called primitive and non-Western, whether in representational art, music, literature, or philosophy. The great innovative composer Richard Wagner gained inspiration from Indian philosophy, while the philosopher Friedrich Nietzsche read Asian religious and philosophical writings. Pablo Picasso derived some of his modern style from African art, while the clean lines of modern architecture—the turn away from Victorian curlicues and gaudy colors—were modeled on the pure forms of native American, African, Asian, and Middle Eastern dwellings.

Complex, paradoxical, and dense with meaning, *modern* may not always be precise enough to be useful. But its very breadth explains why *modern* remains a crucial—and debated—term of history.

In many countries the number of urban residents was surpassing that of the rural population, and the multitudes began to live their lives among strangers, getting their news from impersonal media like newspapers instead of trading stories with neighbors. Some ruling elites from the countryside protested the independence and unruliness of urban dwellers.

Alarm over the Falling Birthrate.

While the absolute size of the population was rising in much of the West, the birthrate (measured in births per thousand people) was falling because of urbanization and industrialization. The birthrate had been decreasing in France since the eighteenth century; other European countries began experiencing the decline late in the nineteenth century. The Swedish rate dropped from thirty-five births per thousand people in 1859 to twenty-four per thousand in 1911; even populous Germany went from forty births per thousand in 1875 to twenty-seven per thousand in 1913.

Rural community norms, such as postponing marriage until the late twenties when couples were too old to produce large numbers of children, broke down under rapid economic change. Urbanization released the grip of rural community decision making in reproductive matters. In an age when agriculture was also becoming industrialized, farm families needed fewer hands, and individual couples determined their own birth-control practices to limit their family's size. Abstinence was a common method, but the spread of new birth-control practices that would encompass most of the globe by the end of the twentieth century mainly accounted for modern Europe's ebbing birthrate. In cities, pamphlets and advice books for those with enough money and education spread information about coitus interruptus—the withdrawal method of preventing pregnancy. Technology also played a role in curtailing reproduction: condoms, improved after the

Large German Family
Improved medicine, hygiene, and diet at the turn of the century helped more people survive infancy and childhood. Thus, in many cases family size grew larger, as this photo from a working-class apartment suggests. Even those opposed to birth control were appalled that lower-class families were becoming larger than those of the "best circles," where family limitation was increasingly practiced. What Social Darwinist ideas could be used to describe this family? How would a birth-control activist describe it? Might these two groups have the same ideas about the family? *AKG London.*

vulcanization of rubber in the 1840s, proved fairly reliable in preventing conception, as did the German invented diaphragm. Abortions were also legion, if still legally sanctioned.

The wider use of birth control stirred controversy. Critics accused middle-class women, whose fertility was falling most rapidly, of holding a "birth strike." Anglican bishops, meeting early in the twentieth century, deplored family limitation, especially by artificial means, as "demoralizing to character and hostile to national welfare." Politicians worried about a crisis in masculinity that would detract from military strength. But U.S. president Theodore Roosevelt blamed middle-class women's selfishness for the population decline, calling it "one of the most unpleasant and unwholesome features of modern life." The "quality" of those being born worried activists and politicians: If the "best" classes had fewer children, they asked, what would society look like when peopled mostly by the "worst" classes?

Racism and nationalism shaped the debate over population. The decline in fertility, one German nationalist warned, would make the country a "conglomerate of alien peoples, above all Slavs and probably East European Jews as well." Nationalist groups promoting large, "racially fit" families sprang up in France, Germany, Britain, and elsewhere. The Social Darwinist focus on national peril in a menacing world merged the debate on gender and family issues with anxieties over class and race, inflaming the political climate. Instead of building consensus among all groups, politicians instilled fears of ethnic minorities and the poor and also placed blame on well-to-do women in order to win votes.

Reforming Marriage

Reformers focused on improving both the conditions within marriage and the quality of children born as a way of solving the problem. The fear that one's nation or "race" was being polluted by the presence of "aliens," the mentally ill, and the severely disabled was a feature of the so-called science of eugenics, a discriminatory set of beliefs about the lower classes and people of other races and ethnicities popular among wealthy, educated Europeans at the turn of the century. As a famed Italian criminologist put it, such people were not humans but "orangutans." Eugenicists favored increased fertility for "the fittest" and limitations on the fertility of "degenerates," leading even to their sterilization or elimination. Women of the "better" classes, reformers felt, would be more inclined to reproduce if the legal shackles in the traditional system of marriage were removed. Married women's wages and other property were generally made the property of the husband. Given the existing constraints of motherhood—all property legally transferred to husbands, no legal rights to their own children, little recourse and no financial resources in the event of an abusive or miserable marriage—women were reluctant to have more than two or three, if any, children. The law made both marriage and motherhood unattractive, even detrimental to women's well-being.

Reformers worked to change these conditions in order to boost the birthrate, while feminists sought to improve the lot of mothers and their children. Sweden, which made men's and women's control over property equal in marriage, allowed women to work without a husband's permission. Other countries, among them France (1884), legalized divorce and made it less complicated, and thus less costly, to obtain. There was good reason to believe that these legal changes would result in an upswing of the birthrate. Divorce would allow unhappy couples to separate and undertake new, more loving, and thus more fertile marriages. Greater financial parity in marriage was seen as a way to promote better maternal health and thus ensure higher quality children. By the early twentieth century, several countries had passed legislation that provided government subsidies for medical care and child support in order to improve motherhood among the lower classes. The concern for population lay the foundations for the welfare state—that is, one whose policies addressed the not just military defense, foreign policy, and political processes but also the social and economic well-being of its people.

The conditions of marriage, motherhood, and other aspects of women's lives varied throughout Europe; for example, women could get university degrees in Austrian universities long before they could at Oxford or Cambridge. A greater number of legal reforms occurred in western Europe, however. In much of rural eastern Europe the father's power over the extended family remained almost dictatorial. According to a survey of family life in eastern Europe in the early 1900s, fathers married off their children so young that 25 percent of women in their early forties had been pregnant more than ten times. Yet reform of everyday customs did occur, as community control gave way to individual practice in places, even though the pace of such change was slower than it was in western Europe. For instance, in some Balkan villages, a kind of extended-family system called the *zadruga,* in which all the nuclear families shared a common great house, survived from earlier times, but by the late nineteenth century individual couples developed a degree of privacy by building one-room sleeping dwellings surrounding the great house. Among the middle and upper classes of eastern Europe, many grown children were coming to believe that they had a right to select a marriage partner, not just to accept the spouse their parents chose for them on the basis of economic or social reasons.

New Women, New Men, and the Politics of Sexual Identity

Rapid social change set the stage for even bolder behaviors among some middle-class women. Adventurous women traveled the globe on their own to promote Christianity, make money, or obtain knowledge of other cultures. The increasing availability of white-collar jobs for the educated meant that more European women could afford to adopt an independent way of life. The so-called **new woman** dressed more practically, with fewer petticoats and looser corsets, biked and hiked through city streets and down country lanes, lived apart from her family in women's clubs or apartments, and supported herself (see The New Woman poster on this page). Italian educator Maria Montessori (1870–1952), for example, the first woman in Italy to earn a medical degree and the founder of an educational system that still bears her name secretly gave birth to an illegitimate child. Artists like the German painter Gabriele Münter lived openly with their lovers. The growing number of women living on their own and freely moving in public, even across the globe, disrupted accepted views of women's economic dependence and relative seclusion in the traditional middle-class family. There was protest and loud criticism: the new woman, German philosopher Friedrich Nietzsche◆ wrote, had led to the "uglification of Europe."

Not just gendered behavior but also sexual identity fueled discussion. Among books in the new field of "sexology," which studied sex scientifically from a clinical and medical point of view, *Sexual Inversion* (1894) by Havelock Ellis was popular. Ellis, a British medical doctor, postulated a new personality type—the homosexual—identifiable by such traits as effeminate behavior and attraction to the arts in males and physical passion for members of their own sex in both males and

◆**Nietzsche:** NEE chuh

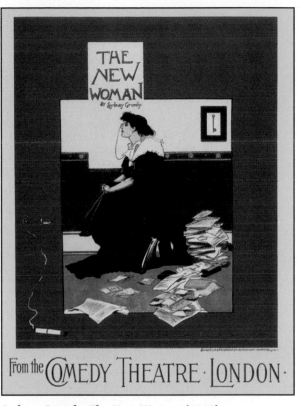

Sydney Grundy, *The New Woman* (1900)
By the opening of the twentieth century, the "new woman" had become a much-discussed phenomenon. Artists painted portraits of this independent creature, while novelists and playwrights like Henrik Ibsen and Nobel Prize winner Sigrid Undset depicted her ambition to throw off the wifely role— or at least to shape that role more to her own personality. The new woman was also well educated: she had attended a university, or wrote as a journalist, or entered professions such as law and medicine. And in this depiction, she smoked. *Colour litho by Albert Morrow. Private Collection/The Stapleton Collection/Bridgeman Art Library.*

females. Homosexuals joined the discussion, calling for recognition that they composed a legitimate and natural "third sex" and were not just people behaving sinfully. For some theorists, the third sex, which combined male and female traits, represented a higher stage in human evolution. The debate among physicians and intellectuals was part of a trend toward considering sexuality in general as a fundamental part of human identity.

The press provoked debate on the other side, presenting homosexuality as outrageous and perverse. In the spring of 1895, reporters covered the trial of Irish playwright

Oscar Wilde

The Irish-born writer Oscar Wilde symbolized the persecution experienced by homosexuals in the late nineteenth century. Tried for and convicted of having sexual relations with another man, Wilde served time in prison—a humiliation for a husband, father, acclaimed author, and witty playwright. Wilde's writings aimed to suggest that the complexities of human society made narrow moral codes harmful. *Library of Congress.*

Oscar Wilde (1854–1900), who was sentenced to two years in prison for indecency—a charge that referred to his sexual affairs with young men (see the illustration on this page). After Wilde's conviction one newspaper rejoiced, "Open the windows! Let in the fresh air!" Between 1907 and 1909, German newspapers also publicized the scandal around men in Kaiser William II's closest circle who were condemned for homosexuality and transvestitism. Amid growing concern over population and family values, the public received assurances from the government itself

that William's own family life "provides the entire country with a fine model." Sexuality thus took on patriotic overtones: the accused homosexual elite in Germany was said by journalists to be out to "emasculate our courageous master race." Although these cases paved the way for growing sexual openness in the next generations, they also showed that sexual issues were becoming regular weapons in politics.

Sciences of the Modern Self

Scientists and Social Darwinists, working during the height of European power, found cause for alarm not only in the condition of the working class but also in modern society's host of mental complaints such as fatigue and irritability. Most of these illnesses originated in the "nerves," they reasoned, which were troubled by the hectic pace and demands of urban living. Sciences of the mind such as psychology and psychoanalysis arose to treat everyone, not just the insane.

New Approaches to Mental Ailments. A rash of books in the 1890s expounded on the subject of modern nervous ailments. The most widely translated of them, *Degeneration* (1892–1893), written by Hungarian-born physician Max Nordau,♦ blamed overstimulation for both individual and national deterioration. According to Nordau, increasingly bizarre modern art, male lethargy, and female hysteria were all symptoms of overstimulation and reflected a general downturn in the human species. The standard Social Darwinist cure for such mental decline was imperial adventure, renewed virility, and increased childbearing. Medical scientists also studied the criminal, classifying typologies of the deviant mind and creating the field of criminology. They invented intelligence tests that they said could measure the capacity of the human mind more accurately than a schoolteacher could. In Russia, physiologist Ivan Pavlov (1849–1936) proposed that conditioning mental reflexes—that is, causing a subject to associate a desired response with a previously unrelated stimulus—could modify behavior. His experiments, especially his success in changing the

♦**Max Nordau:** mahks NAWR dow

behavior of a dog, were among those that formed the basis of modern psychology.

Freud and Psychoanalysis. Sigmund Freud (1856–1939) devised an approach to modern anxieties that, he claimed, avoided traditional moral evaluations of human behavior. He became convinced that the human psyche was far from rational. Dreams, he explained in *The Interpretation of Dreams* (1900), reveal a repressed part of personality—the "unconscious"—where all sorts of desires are more or less hidden. Freud also believed that the human psyche is made up of three competing parts: the ego, the part that is most in touch with external reality; the id (or libido), the part that contains instinctive drives and sexual energies; and the superego, the part that serves as the force of conscience. Freud's theory of human mental processes and his method for treating their malfunctioning came to be called **psychoanalysis**. Like Darwin's ideas, Freud's notions challenged accepted liberal belief both in a unified, rational self that acted in its own interest and, by implication, in the certainty of progress. Nonetheless, Freud placed his work squarely in the scientific tradition and announced his conclusions as resulting from observation, not religion.

Freud shocked many contemporaries by insisting that all children have sexual drives from the moment of birth, but he also believed that many of these sexual impulses have to be repressed for the individual to attain maturity and for society to remain civilized. Attaining one's adult sexual identity is always a painful process because it depends on repressing infantile urges, which include bisexuality and incest. Thus, the Wolf-Man's nightmare of white wolves outside his window symbolized his unresolved sexual feelings for members of his family. Freud claimed that certain aspects of gender roles—such as motherhood—are normal and that throughout their lives women in general achieve far less than men do. At the same time, he believed that adult gender identity results not from anatomy alone (motherhood is not the only way to be female) but from inescapable mental processing of life experiences as well. He thus made gender more complicated than simple biology would suggest. Finally, Freud's psychoanalytic theory maintained that girls and women have powerful sexual feelings, an assertion that broke with existing ideas of women's passionlessness.

The influence of psychoanalysis became pervasive in the twentieth century, offering paradoxes and representing yet another turn toward global thinking. (See "New Sources, New Perspectives," page 968.) For example, free association of ideas and interpretation of

Freud's Office
Sigmund Freud's therapy room, where his patients experienced the "talking cure," was filled with imperial trophies such as Oriental rugs and African art objects. Freud himself was fascinated by cures brought about through shamanism, trances, and other practices of non-Western medicine as well as through drug-induced mental states. In 1938, Freud fled to England to escape the Nazis. This photo shows his office in London. What impression might Freud's office have left on his patients? How might it have helped the talking cure? *Mary Evans Picture Library/Sigmund Freud copyrights.*

NEW SOURCES, NEW PERSPECTIVES

Psychohistory and Its Lessons

In the last fifty years, historians have radically changed the way they write history. In the nineteenth century, history books mostly recounted the deeds of kings and emperors, discussed royal genealogy, and listed wars and peace treaties. Determined to be factual, historians laid out the fine points of laws, charters, and treaties and they checked their sources in archives.

Much has changed since then, partly because of the rise of psychology and psychoanalysis as the twentieth century opened. Confronted with strikes, mass demonstrations, anarchist deeds, anti-Semitism, and other forms of political violence, some observers tried to explain a phenomenon they called crowd psychology. According to this view, psychic states are important factors in shaping some public events.

Not surprisingly, Sigmund Freud studied great historic figures like Leonardo da Vinci from a psychoanalytic perspective, exploring the connection between repressed childhood fantasies and later towering accomplishments. Freud also explained the outbreak of World War I as more of a psychic than a diplomatic event. He saw the war as a form of collective death wish. He subjected both individuals and entire societies to psychoanalytic probing. Few historians followed Freud's lead.

In 1957, William Langer, president of the American Historical Association, charged his fellow scholars with being foolishly backward in their methods. Unlike scientists, he claimed, historians did not try new systems or techniques such as psychoanalysis that might advance their understanding of the past. Others joined the debate, finding that traditional history sometimes attributed actions to gossipy traits such as ambition, greed, hate, and great intelligence. But what was the

"scientific" depth in such characterizations? Another criticism of history by those interested in psychology and psychoanalysis was that, if it did take human agency into account, it usually saw historical figures as acting rationally in their self-interest. Trauma, the irrational, uncontrollable drives, and unconscious motivations had no role to play in understanding historical figures.

Psychohistory was born in these discussions. A major study by psychoanalyst Erik Erikson, *Young Man Luther* (1958), announced that the Protestant Reformation originated in the childhood traumas of Martin Luther. Identity crises stemming from his relationship with his father caused Luther to search for and reject father figures, not only his own father but the pope. Erikson's book caused a stir among historians, changing the way people approached Luther and starting an entirely new school of historical thought.

Not surprisingly, some of the most compelling examples of psychohistory have focused on the lives of individuals and the development of political movements. Historians interested in psychoanalysis have tried to find in Kaiser William II's childhood answers to his rejection of Bismarck, his turn to an aggressive foreign policy, and his participation in World War I. On a collective level, analyses of Adolf Hitler's and Benito Mussolini's followers have seen mass psychic needs and traumas as motivating their blind worship of these vicious dictators. But the intense nationalism that most people in the modern world have increasingly felt for their countries has also become a phenomenon that psychohistorians examine.

Psychohistory remains controversial to this day. While its practitioners expand the field of historical explanation, its critics find that it can

dreams are mainstays in psychoanalysis derived from the African and Asian influences on Freud's thought: the "talking cure," as it was quickly labeled, gave rise to a general acceptance of talking out one's problems. As

psychoanalysis became a respected means of recovering mental health, terms such as *neurosis, unconscious,* and *libido* came into widespread use. By way of paradox, Freud attributed girls' complaints about unwanted

Kaiser William and Edward VII's Family

Psychotherapy aimed to cure the individual in good part by discussing family relationships and the fantasies built around them. Psychohistory often draws its analyses from these same relationships, as in the case of Martin Luther, for example, and his father. The royal families of Europe are ripe for such analysis because, as the photo shows, German and British monarchs (Edward VII, right; and William, second from right) were closely related; so too were the Russians, Germans, and British. These relationships raise potential questions about the outbreak of World War I as the work of complex family dynamics. *Hulton Archive/Getty Images.*

be formulaic by fitting the behavior of historical characters into Freud's schema. Other critics find that psychohistory is too imprecise and speculative because it is not based on the same kinds of hard, documentary evidence that historians have been trained to use. Nonetheless, psychohistorians have made a good case that if we are going to look at personalities, character, and relationships, we should do so in the most informed way possible. Their rationale makes psychohistory appear to be a necessity.

QUESTIONS TO CONSIDER

1. What are the advantages and disadvantages of psychohistory?
2. How would you set out to investigate the psychological reasons for the actions of William II, Emmeline Pankhurst, Marie Curie, or Gavrilo Princip? Would you look at their character, their childhood, their social background, or other parts of their lives?
3. Can we write history without talking about the emotions, mental habits, and human relationships of major figures? Should we avoid psychologizing when thinking about the past?

FURTHER READING

Binion, Rudolph. *Frau Lou: Nietzsche's Wayward Disciple.* 1968.

Erikson, Erik. *Young Man Luther: A Study in Psychoanalysis and History.* 1958.

Journal of Psychohistory.

Kohut, Thomas A. *Wilhelm II and the Germans: A Study in Leadership.* 1991.

sexual advances or abuse to fantasy caused by "penis envy," an idea that led members of the new profession of social work to believe that most instances of such abuse had not actually occurred. On the one hand, Freud was a meticulous scientist, examining symptoms, urging attention to the most minute evidence from everyday life, and demanding that sexual life be regarded with a rational rather than a religious eye. On the other hand, he was a pessimistic visionary who had abandoned the optimism of the Enlightenment and pre-Darwinian science by claiming that humans were motivated by irrational drives toward death and destruction and that these urges shaped society's collective mentality. Freud would later interpret World War I's vast devastation of humanity as bearing out his bleak conclusions.

Review: How did ideas about the self and about personal life change at the turn of the century?

❖ Modernity and the Revolt in Ideas

Although the intellectuals and artists who participated in the turmoil and triumph of turn-of-the-century society did not know it at the time, their rejection of accepted beliefs and artistic forms announced a new era. In science, theories that time is relative and that energy and mass are interchangeable rocked established truths about time, space, matter, and energy. Art and music became unrecognizable. Artists and musicians who deliberately produced shocking, lurid works were, like Freud, heavily influenced by advances in science, critical thinking, and empire. Amid contradictions such as the blending of the scientific and the irrational, and of the "West" and "non-West," intellectuals and artists helped launch the disorienting revolution in ideas and creative expression that we now identify collectively as **modernism**.

The Challenge to Positivism

Late in the nineteenth century, at the height of empire and reform efforts, many philosophers and social thinkers rejected the century-old faith that by using scientific methods one could discover enduring social laws. This belief, called positivism, had emphasized the permanent nature of fundamental laws and had motivated reformers' attempts to perfect legislation based on studies of society. Challenging positivism, the philosophers Wilhelm Dilthey (1833–1911)

in Germany and John Dewey (1859–1952) in the United States declared that because human experience is ever changing, theories and standards cannot be constant or enduring. Just as scientific theory was modified over time, so must social theories and practice react pragmatically to the immediate conditions at hand. In the same vein, German political theorist Max Weber (1864–1920) maintained that the sheer numbers involved in policymaking would often make decisive action by bureaucrats impossible—especially in times of crisis, when a charismatic leader might usurp power because of his ability to make flexible and instinctive decisions. Thus, the development of impartial forms of government such as bureaucracy carried the potential for undermining the rule of law. The turn-of-the-century thinkers, called relativists and pragmatists, influenced thinking about society throughout the twentieth century.

The most radical scholar was the German philosopher Friedrich Nietzsche (1844–1900), who called himself neither a relativist nor a pragmatist but a nihilist. Early in his career he developed the challenging distinction between the "Apollonian," or rational, side of human existence and the "Dionysian" side, with its expression of more primal urges. Nietzsche believed that people generally cling to the rational, Apollonian explanations of life because Dionysian ideas about nature, death, and love such as those found in Greek tragedy are too disturbing. Nietzsche maintained that all assertions of scientific fact and theory were mere illusions. Knowledge of nature had to be expressed in mathematical, linguistic, or artistic representation; truth thus existed only in the representation itself, for humans could never experience unfiltered knowledge of nature or reality. This aspect of Nietzsche's philosophy would lead to the late-twentieth-century school of thought called postmodernism.

Much of Nietzsche's writing consisted of aphorisms—short, disconnected statements of truth or opinion—a form that broke with the logical rigor of traditional Western philosophy. Nietzsche used aphorisms to convey the impression that his ideas were a single individual's unique perspective, not universal truths that thinkers since the Enlightenment had claimed were attainable. Influenced by a range of Asian philosophy that had filtered into Western thought, Nietzsche was convinced that late-nineteenth-century Europe was witnessing the decline of dogmatic truth, most notably in religion. In this belief, he made his announcement that "God is dead, we have killed him." Far from arousing dread, the death of God, according to Nietzsche, would give birth to a joyful quest for new "poetries of life" to replace worn-out religious and middle-class rules. Not the rule-bound bourgeois but the untethered "superman" was Nietzsche's highly influential model.

Nietzsche's thought, especially the idea of the individual as manifesting a vital life energy he called "the will to power," inspired reformers, intellectuals, and students. As a teacher, Nietzsche was so compelling that his first students thought they were hearing another Socrates. But after he contracted syphilis and became insane in the last eleven years of his life, his sister edited his diatribes against middle-class values into attacks on Jews. On her brother's death, she revised his complicated concepts of the will to power and of superman so as to appeal to nationalists and to justify violent anti-Semitism and competition for empire. Nietzsche's legacy was thus a mixed one, influencing not only the ideas of the militarist and racist right-wing political parties but also the works of avant-garde artists and thinkers.

Revolutionizing Science

While philosophers like Nietzsche questioned the ability of traditional science to provide timeless truths, scientific inquiry itself flourished and the scientific method gained authority. Technological breakthroughs and improvements in public hygiene earned science prestige in the population at large even as discoveries by pioneering researchers shook the foundations of traditional scientific certainty. In 1896,

Antoine Becquerel (1852–1908) discovered radioactivity and also suggested the mutability of elements by the rearrangement of their atoms. French chemist Marie Curie (1867–1934) and her husband, Pierre Curie (1859–1906), isolated the elements polonium and radium, which are more radioactive than the uranium Becquerel used. From these and other discoveries, scientists concluded that atoms are composed of subatomic particles moving about a core. Instead of being solid, as scientists had believed since ancient times, atoms are largely empty space and act not as a concrete substance but as an intangible electromagnetic field. German physicist Max Planck (1858–1947) announced his influential quantum theorem in 1900; it demonstrated that a flow of energy is emitted in irregular packets, not in a steady stream.

Scientists had already demonstrated that light has a uniform velocity regardless of the

Marie Curie and Her Daughter
Recipient of two Nobel Prizes, Marie Curie came from Poland to western Europe to study science. Curie's extraordinary career made her the epitome of new womanhood; her daughter Irene Joliot-Curie followed her mother into the field and also won a Nobel Prize. Both women died of leukemia caused by their exposure to radioactive materials. Today a reconstruction of the Curie laboratory as a museum contains a display of the intense radioactivity still in the scientific instruments they used a century ago. Given that other women have made important contributions to the sciences and literature, why would the Curies be so celebrated? *ACJC–Archives Curie et Joliot-Curie.*

direction it travels from the earth and that the velocity is not relative to the motion of the earth. Thus, older theories of light on which scientists had relied were no longer tenable. It was in this unsettled situation that physicist Albert Einstein (1879–1955) published his special theory of relativity. On his own, working in a Swiss patent office, he proclaimed in a 1905 paper that space and time are not absolute categories but instead vary according to the vantage point of the observer. Only the speed of light is constant. That same year he also suggested that the solution to problems in Planck's quantum theorem lay in considering light both as little packets *and* as waves. Einstein later proposed yet another blurring of two distinct physical properties, mass and energy. He expressed this equivalence in the formulation of $E = mc^2$, or energy equals mass times the square of the speed of light. In 1916, his general theory of relativity connected the force, or gravity, of an object with its mass and postulated a fourth mathematical dimension to the universe. Much more lay ahead, once Einstein's theories of energy were developed: television, nuclear power, and, within forty years, nuclear bombs.

Undercutting Newtonian physics as well as commonsense understanding, the findings of Planck, Einstein, and others were often not accepted immediately, largely because both power and time-honored beliefs were at stake. Einstein, like Planck, struggled against mainstream science and its professional institutions. Marie Curie faced such resistance from the scientific establishment that even after she became the first person ever to receive a second Nobel Prize (1911), the prestigious French Academy of Science turned down her candidacy for membership (see the illustration on page 971). Institutional recognition gradually came, however, as Max Planck institutes were established in German cities, streets across Europe were named after Marie Curie, and Einstein's name became synonymous with genius. These scientists achieved what historians call a paradigm shift—that is, in the face of understandable resistance they transformed the foundations of science and came themselves to supersede other, more accepted scientists.

Modern Art

The same conflicts between traditional values and new ideas raged in the arts, as artists distanced themselves still further from classical Western styles and from the conventions of polite society. Some modern artists tried to challenge the historic and realistic scenes still favored, for example, by the powerful German monarchy and by buyers for public museums. Modernism in the arts not only fractured traditional standards but also ushered in a proliferation of competing artistic styles and disagreement about art's relationship to society. The turn of the century was one of the most important moments in the development of Western painting.

A Variety of Styles. Some artists addressed urbanites caught up in the rush of modern life. Abandoning the soft colors of impressionism as too subtle for a dynamic industrial society, a group of Parisian artists exhibiting in 1905 combined blues, greens, reds, and oranges so intensively that they were called *fauves*, or "wild beasts." A leader of the short-lived fauvism, Henri Matisse (1869–1954) soon struck out in a new direction, targeting the expanding class of white-collar workers. Matisse dreamed of "an art . . . for every mental worker, be he businessman or writer, like an appeasing influence, like a mental soother, something like a good armchair in which to rest from physical fatigue." His colorful depictions of domestic interiors, North African scenes, and family life departed from strict realism but in fact have appealed to modern viewers up to the present in part because of their calming qualities.

French artist Paul Cézanne (1839–1906) initiated one of the most powerful and enduring trends in modern art by emphasizing structure in painting. Cézanne used rectangular daubs of paint to capture a geometric vision of dishes, fruit, drapery, and the human body. Accentuating the lines and planes found in nature, Cézanne's art, like science, was removed from the realm of people's ordinary vision. Following in Cézanne's footsteps, Spanish artist Pablo Picasso (1881–1973) developed a style called cubism. Its radical emphasis on planes and surfaces converted people into bizarre, inhuman, almost unrecognizable forms. Picasso's painting *Les Demoiselles d'Avignon* (1907), for example, depicted the bodies of the *demoiselles*, or "young ladies" (prostitutes in this case), as fragmented and angular, with their heads modeled on African masks (see the illustration on this page). Continuing along the path of impressionism and fauvism, Picasso's work showed the profound influences of African, Asian, and South American arts, but his use of these features was less decorative and more brutal than those by Matisse, for example. Like explorers, botanists, and foreign journalists, he was bringing knowledge of the empire into the imperial homeland, this time in a distinctly disturbing form.

Art as Political Criticism. Across Europe, artists mixed political criticism with the radical stylistic changes in their work. "Show the people how hideous is their actual life, and place your hands on the causes of its ugliness" was the anarchist challenge at the time. Picasso, who had spent his youth in the heart of working-class Barcelona, a hotbed of anarchist thought, aimed to replace middle-class sentimentality in art with truth about industrial society. In 1912, Picasso and French painter Georges Braque (1882–1963) devised a new kind of collage that incorporated bits of newspaper, string, and other artifacts. The effect was a canvas that appeared to be cluttered with refuse. The newspaper clippings Picasso included described battles and murders, suggesting the shallowness of Western pretensions to high civilization. In eastern and central Europe, artists criticized the growing nationalism that determined official purchases of sculpture and painting: "The whole empire is littered with monuments to soldiers and monuments to Kaiser William of the same conventional type," one German artist complained. Such groups as the Berlin Secession and the Vienna Workshop were at the forefront of producing experimental art depicting psychological states. Their joint exhibitions also featured ethnic artists, who produced work critical of the bombastic nationalism that determined official purchases of sculpture and painting.

Scandinavian and eastern European artists produced works expressing the anguished feelings many had at the time. Like the vision of Freud, their style of portraying

Pablo Picasso, *Les Demoiselles d'Avignon* (1907)
Impressionists had borrowed heavily from Asian art, but many artists in Pablo Picasso's generation leaned on Africa for inspiration. In *Les Demoiselles d'Avignon*, Picasso used the elongated, angular limbs found in African carvings, while the faces resemble African masks. The artists Amadeo Modigliani, Barbara Hepworth, and Constantin Brancusi excelled in sculpture featuring the smooth forms and lively compositions of African wooden statuary. What might be the appeal of African art to Europeans who, simultaneously, were extolling the superiority of European civilization? *Picasso, Pablo. Les Demoiselles d'Avignon. Paris (June–July 1907). Oil on canvas, 8′ X 7′8″. The Museum of Modern Art, New York. Acquired through the Lillie P. Bliss Bequest. Photograph © The Museum of Modern Art/Licensed by SCALA/Art Resource, NY © 2005 Estate of Pablo Picasso/Artists Rights Society (ARS), NY.*

inner reality—called expressionism—broke with middle-class optimism. Norwegian painter Edvard Munch (1863–1944) aimed "to make the emotional mood ring out again as happens on a gramophone." His painting *The Scream* (1893; see page 958) used twisting lines and a depiction of tortured skeletal human form to convey the horror of modern life that many artists perceived. German avant-garde artist Gabriele Münter (1877–1962) and Russian painter Wassily Kandinsky (1866–1944) opened their "Blue Rider" exhibit of "expressive" work that made use of geometric forms and striking colors. The artists of the Blue Rider group imitated the paintings of children and the mentally ill to achieve their depiction of psychological reality. Kandinsky, who employed these forms and colors to express an inner, spiritual truth, is often credited with producing the first fully abstract paintings around 1909. Shapes in these paintings no longer showed any resemblance to physical objects or reality. The expressionism of Oskar Kokoschka (1886–1980), who worked in Vienna, was even more intense, displaying ecstasy, horror, and hallucinations. As a result, his work—like that of other expressionists and cubists before World War I—was a commercial failure in an increasingly complex marketplace that featured not only museum curators but also professional dealers and art "experts." Trade in art became professionalized, as had medicine and government work before it, even as modern artists sought to shatter traditional norms.

Art Nouveau. Only one innovative style emerged an immediate commercial success: **art nouveau** ("new style") won approval from government, critics, and the masses. Creating everything from dishes and advertising posters to streetlamps and even entire buildings in this new style, designers manufactured beautiful things for the general public. As one French official said about the first version of art nouveau coins issued in 1895, "Soon even the most humble among us will be able to have a masterpiece in his pocket." Adapted from Asian design, the organic and natural elements of art nouveau were meant to offset the fragmentation of factory and office work with images depicting the unified forms of nature. The impersonality of machines was replaced by intertwined vines and flowers and the softly curving bodies of female nudes that would psychologically soothe the individual viewer—an idea that directly contrasted with Picasso's artistic vision. Gustav Klimt (1862–1918), son of a Czech goldsmith, flourished in Viennese high society because his paintings captured the psychological essence of dreamy, sensuous women. Their bodies took the shape of mosaics inspired by Turkish and Egyptian styles and were liberally dotted with gold. Art nouveau was the notable exception to the public outcries over innovations in the visual arts.

Musical Iconoclasm

"Astonish me!" was the motto of modern dance and music, both of which shocked audiences in the concert halls of Europe. American dancer Isadora Duncan (1877–1927) took Europe by storm at the turn of the century when, draped in a flowing garment, she danced barefoot in the first performance of modern dance. Drawing on sophisticated Japanese practices, hers was nonetheless called a primitive style that, as one journalist put it, "lifted from their seats people who had never left theater seats before except to get up and go home." Similarly, experimentation with forms of bodily expression animated the Russian Ballet's 1913 performance of *The Rite of Spring*, by Igor Stravinsky (1882–1971), the tale of an orgiastic dance to the death performed to ensure fertile soil and a bountiful harvest. The choreography of its star, Vaslav Nijinsky (1890–1950) created a scandal. Nijinsky and the troupe struck awkward poses and danced to rhythms intended to sound primitive. At the work's premiere in Paris, one journalist reported that "the audience began shouting its indignation. . . . Fighting actually broke out among some of the spectators." Such controversy made *The Rite of Spring* a box-office hit, although critics called its choreographer a "lunatic" and the music itself "the most discordant composition ever written."

Music had been making this turn for several decades. Having heard Asian musicians at international expositions, French composers like Claude Debussy (1862–1918) transformed their style to reflect non-European musical patterns and themes. The twentieth century opened with *Scheherazade* by Frenchman Maurice Ravel (1875–1937) and *Madame Butterfly* by the Italian composer Giacomo Puccini♦ (1858–1924), both with non-Western subject matter. Using non-Western tonalities, sound became jarring to many listeners. Austrian composer Richard Strauss (1864–1949) upset convention by using several musical keys simultaneously in his compositions. Like the fragmented representation of reality in cubism, atonality or several tonalities at once distorted familiar harmonic patterns for the audience. Strauss's operas *Salome* (1905) and *Elektra* (1909) reflected a modern fascination with violence and obsessive passion. A newspaper critic claimed that Strauss's dissonant works "spit and scratch and claw each other like enraged panthers." The Hungarian pianist Béla Bartók (1881–1945) incorporated folk melodies into his compositions in order to elevate Hungarian ethnicity above the Habsburg Empire's multinationalism. His music disturbed some audiences because of its nationalism and others because of its dissonance.

The early orchestral work of Austrian composer Arnold Schoenberg (1874–1951), who also wrote cabaret music to earn a living, shocked even Strauss. In *Theory of Harmony* (1911), Schoenberg proposed eliminating tonality altogether; a decade later he devised a new twelve-tone scale. "I am aware of having broken through all the barriers of a dated aesthetic ideal," Schoenberg wrote of his music. But new aesthetic models distanced artists like Schoenberg from their audiences, separating high from low culture even more and ending the support of many in the upper classes, who found this music not only incomprehensible but also unpleasant. The artistic elite and the social elite parted ranks. "Anarchist! Nihilist!" shouted Schoenberg's audiences, showing their contempt for modernism and bringing the language of politics into the arts.

Review: How did modernism transform the arts and the world of ideas?

♦**Giacomo Puccini:** JAH koh moh poot CHEE nee

Léon Bakst, *Nijinsky in* L'Après-Midi d'un Faune (Nijinsky in *The Afternoon of a Faun*, 1912)
Theater sets, costume designs, and performance itself resonated with the experimental climate of early-twentieth-century Europe. Léon Bakst, a Russian painter and set designer, used the art nouveau style to capture the faunlike character of ballet star Vaslav Nijinsky. Yet on the eve of World War I, Nijinsky was part of a revolution in ballet that introduced jerky, awkward, pounding movements to indicate the primal nature of dance. How is this depiction of a creative artist new? Compare it to the portrait on page 815. *Wadsworth Atheneum, Hartford. The Ella Gallup Sumner and Mary Catlin Sumner Collection Fund.*

❖ Growing Tensions in Mass Politics

Alongside modernist disturbances in intellectual life, the political atmosphere grew charged despite the advance of liberal opinions that opened the door to growing tolerance and political representation for workingmen.

Networks of communication, especially the development of journalism, enhanced the impact of expanded male suffrage in Europe, leading to the creation of mass politics. Working-class people seemed to come into their own once they had the vote: politicians had to campaign publicly and frequently to win their support. Simultaneously, however, political activists were no longer satisfied with the liberal rights sought by reformers a century earlier, and some strenuously opposed them. Militant nationalists, anti-Semites, socialists, suffragists, and others demanded changes that challenged the liberal status quo. Traditional elites, resentful of the rising middle classes and urban peoples, aimed to stem constitutional processes and the development of modern life. Mass politics soon threatened social unity, especially in central and eastern Europe, where governments often answered reformers' demands with repression.

Labor's Expanding Power

European leaders watched with dismay the rise of working-class political power late in the nineteenth century. Laboring people's growing confidence came in part from expanding educational opportunities. Workers in England, for example, avidly read works by Shakespeare and took literally his calls for political action in the cause of justice. Unions gained members among factory workers, while the Labor and Socialist Parties won seats in parliaments as men in the lower classes received the vote. In Germany, Kaiser William II had allowed antisocialist laws to lapse after dismissing Bismarck as chancellor in 1890. Through continuous grassroots organizing at the local level, the Social Democratic Party, founded by German socialists in 1875, became the largest parliamentary group in the Reichstag by 1912. Similar parties across Europe helped elect workers' representatives into parliaments, where they focused on passing legislation that benefited workers and their families.

Growing strength, especially electoral victories, raised issues for socialists. Some felt uncomfortable sitting with the upper classes in parliaments. Others worried that their participation as heads of governmental ministries would produce reform but compromise their ultimate goal of revolution. Often these deputies refused seats in the government. Between 1900 and 1904, the Second International wrestled with the issue of revisionism—that is, whether socialists should accept such incremental gains in power for laboring people rather than pushing for a violent revolution to overthrow governments. Powerful German Marxists argued that such reformism would only buttress capitalism and rule by the wealthy, who would continue to rule while throwing small crumbs to a few working-class politicians. Stormy discussions divided these German purists, who were shut out of high government positions by conservatives in the military and aristocracy, from the socialist delegates of France, England, and Belgium who had gained influential posts in their governments.

Some working-class parties were forced to operate in exile because they were utterly excluded from mass politics. The Russian government, for instance, outlawed political parties, persecuted activists, and gave the vote to only a limited number of men when it finally introduced a parliament in 1905. Thus, Russian activist V. I. Lenin (1870–1924), who would take power during the Russian Revolution of 1917, migrated to western Europe after his release from confinement to Siberia and earned a reputation among Marxists for hard-hitting journalism and political intrigue. Lenin advanced the theory that a highly disciplined socialist elite—rather than the working class as a whole—would lead a lightly industrialized Russia immediately into socialism. At a 1903 party meeting of Russian Marxists, he briefly gained the upper hand when a group of his opponents walked out of the proceedings. In the ensuing votes, Lenin's supporters eked out slim victories for control of the party. Thereafter, his faction of Bolsheviks, so named after the Russian word for "majority" (which they had temporarily formed in these successful votes), constantly struggled to suppress the Mensheviks, who had been the dominant voice in Russian Marxism until Lenin outmaneuvered them. Neither of these factions, however, had as large a constituency within Russia as the Socialist Revolutionaries, whose objective was to politicize peasants rather than industrial workers as the prelude to a populist revolution. All of these groups prepared for the revolutionary moment through study, propaganda efforts, and organizing—not through the electoral politics successfully employed elsewhere in Europe.

During this same period, anarchists, along with some trade union members known as syndicalists, kept Europe in a panic with their terrorist acts. Anarchism flourished in the less industrial parts of Europe—Russia, Italy, and Spain, where many rural people hoped for a life without the domination of large landowners and government. Members of these groups advocated extreme tactics, including physical violence and even murder. "We want to overthrow the government . . . with violence since it is by the use of violence that they force us to obey," wrote one Italian anarchist. In the 1880s, anarchists bombed stock exchanges, parliaments, and businesses; by the 1890s, they were assassinating heads of state: Spanish premier Antonio Canovas del Castillo in 1897, Empress Elizabeth of Austria-Hungary in 1898, King Umberto of Italy in 1900, and President William McKinley of the United States in 1901, to name a few famous victims. Syndicalists advocated the use of direct action, such as general strikes and sabotage, to bring industry and government under the control of labor unions by paralyzing the economy.

Whether active in representative or authoritarian countries, whether peaceful or violent, working-class organizations caused the upper and middle classes grave anxiety. Despite growing acceptance of representative institutions and despite the spread of education, many in the "best circles" still believed that they alone should hold political power. Politicians from the old landowning and military elites of eastern and central Europe were often the most adamant in their rejection of mass politics, and many of them hoped to reverse the trend toward constitutionalism, worker activism, and reform.

Rights for Women and the Battle for Suffrage

Singly or in groups, women continued to agitate for the benefits of liberalism such as the right to their wages and to parliamentary representation. In most countries women could not vote, exercise free speech, or own property if married. Laws in France, Austria, and Germany curtailed women's political activism and even made their attendance at political meetings a crime. There were many battlefields besides the one for legal rights. German women focused on widening opportunities for female education and for teaching. Their activism aimed to achieve the German cultural ideal of *Bildung*—the belief that education can build character and that individual development has public importance. In several countries, women continued to monitor the regulation of prostitution. Their goal was to prevent prostitutes from being imprisoned on suspicion of having syphilis when men with syphilis faced no such incarceration. Other women took up pacifism as their special cause. Many of them were inspired by Bertha von Süttner's popular book, *Lay Down Your Arms* (1889), which emphasized the terror inflicted on women and families by the ravages of war. (Later, von Süttner would influence Alfred Nobel to institute a peace prize and then win the prize herself in 1903.)

By the 1890s, many activists concluded that only the right to vote would correct the problems caused by male privilege that they were combating in piecemeal fashion. Thereafter, **suffragists** created major organizations involving millions of activists, paid officials, and permanent offices out of the earlier reform groups and women's clubs. Using skills gained from this organizing, British suffrage leader Millicent Garrett Fawcett (1847–1929) pressured members of Parliament for women's right to vote and participated in national and international congresses on behalf of suffrage. Across the Atlantic, American Susan B. Anthony (1820–1906) traveled across the country to speak at mass suffrage rallies, organized suffrage societies, edited a suffragist newspaper, raised money for the movement, and founded the International Woman Suffrage Association in 1904. Its leadership argued that despite men's promises to protect women in exchange for their inequality and disfranchisement, the system of male chivalry had led to exploitation and abuse. Power and privilege—no matter how couched in expressions of goodwill—worked against those without them. "So long as the subjection

Woman Suffrage in Finland

In 1906, Finnish women became the first in Europe to receive the vote in national elections when the socialist party there—usually opposed to feminism as a middle-class rather than a working-class project—supported woman suffrage. The Finnish vote elated activists in the West, now linked together by many international organizations and ties, because it showed that more than a century of lobbying for reform could lead to gains. What impact might this photograph have had on working-class women and men or middle-class women and men in other European countries? *Mary Evans Picture Library.*

of women endures, and is confirmed by law and custom, . . . women will be victimized," a leading British suffragist claimed. Other activists believed that women had attributes needed to counterbalance masculine qualities in the running of society. The characteristics that came from mothering should shape a country's destiny as much as qualities that stemmed from work in industry and trade, they asserted.

Women's rights activists were predominantly, though not exclusively, from the middle class. Not having to earn a living, they simply had more time to be activists, and a higher level of education allowed them to read the works of feminist theorists such as Harriet

Taylor and John Stuart Mill. They attended theater productions of Norwegian playwright Henrik Ibsen's jarring plays about rebellious heroines or read novels such as Sigrid Undset's *Jenny* (1911), which told the story of a woman artist deliberately choosing motherhood but not marriage. They saw feminism in part through the lens of their middle-class cultural life. But working-class women also participated, though many distrusted the middle class and believed suffrage to be less crucial than women's pressing economic concerns. Textile workers of Manchester, England, for example, put together a vigorous suffrage movement connecting the vote to improved working conditions. Although some union women participated heartily in feminist activism, socialists and suffragists usually differed over issues of class and gender.

In 1906 in Finland, suffragists achieved their first major victory when the Finnish parliament granted women the vote (see the photo on this page). But the failure of parliaments elsewhere in Europe to enact similar legislation provoked some suffragists to violence. Part of the British suffragist movement adopted a militant political style when Emmeline Pankhurst (1858–1928) and her daughters founded the Women's Social and Political Union (WSPU) in the belief that women would accomplish nothing unless they threatened men's property. Starting in 1907, members of the WSPU held parades in English cities, and in 1909 they began a campaign of violence, blowing up railroad stations, slashing works of art, and chaining themselves to the gates of Parliament. Easily disguising themselves as ordinary shoppers in the new consumer economy, they carried little hammers in their handwarming muffs to smash the plate-glass windows of department stores and shops. Parades and demonstrations made suffrage a public spectacle, and outraged men responded by attacking the marchers violently. Arrested for disturbing the peace, the marchers went on hunger strikes in prison. Like striking workers, these women were willing to use confrontational tactics to obtain rights, and like anarchists they were not afraid to damage property. As politicians continued to refuse the vote to women, militant suffragists added to the tensions of urban life.

Liberalism Modified

Governments in western Europe, where liberal institutions were seemingly well entrenched, sought to control the conflicts of the late nineteenth century with pragmatic policies that often struck at liberalism's very foundations. Some politicians and reformers ended laissez-faire trade policies by instituting protective tariffs; others decided that government needed to intervene beyond economic matters and expand social welfare legislation—another break with the liberal idea that governments should not tamper with the free development of either the economy or society. Although many programs addressed urban needs insufficiently, they added to the growing apparatus of the welfare state in which government actively promoted social well-being.

Testing Liberalism in Britain. In 1905, the British Liberal Party won a solid majority in the House of Commons and seemed determined to enact social legislation to gain working-class support. "We are keenly in sympathy with the representatives of Labour," one Liberal politician announced. "We have too few of them in the House of Commons." The government initiated a system of unemployment relief for the unemployed in the National Insurance Act of 1911 funded by new taxes on the wealthy. When the Conservatives in the House of Lords resisted the higher taxation, the Liberal government threatened to add to the number of lords and thus dilute the power and prestige of the nobility. The newcomers, unlike their recalcitrant peers, would guarantee to vote for reform. Under this threat, the lords approved the Parliament Bill of 1911, which eliminated their veto power.

Britain modified liberalism in the social arena, while the Irish question tested its commitment to such liberal values as autonomy, opportunity, and individual rights. In the 1890s, new groups formed to foster Irish culture as a way of heightening the political challenge to Britain's continuing colonization of the country. In 1901, the circle around the modernist poet William Butler Yeats (1865–1939) and the charismatic patriot and actress Maud Gonne (1866–1953) founded the Irish National Theater. Gonne took Irish politics into everyday life by opposing British efforts to woo the loyalty of the young. Every time an English monarch visited Ireland, he or she held special receptions for children. Gonne and other Irish volunteers sponsored competing events, handing out candies and other treats for patriotic youngsters. "Dublin never witnessed anything so marvelous," enthused one home rule supporter, "as the procession . . . of thirty thousand school children who refused to be bribed into parading before the Queen of England."

Speaking Gaelic instead of English, singing Gaelic songs, using Catholicism as a rallying point, and generally reconstructing an "Irish way of life," the promoters of Irish culture threw into question the educated class's preference for everything English. This cultural agenda took political shape with the founding in 1905 of Sinn Fein✦ ("We Ourselves"), a group that strove for complete Irish independence. In 1913, Parliament approved home rule for Ireland, but the outbreak of World War I prevented the legislation from taking effect and cut short dreams of independence.

Unrest in Italy. Liberal Italian nation builders, left with a towering debt from unification and with massive pockets of discontent, drifted more rapidly from liberalism's moorings. Corruption plagued Italy's constitutional monarchy, which had not yet developed either the secure parliamentary system of England or the authoritarian monarchy of Germany to guide its growth. To forge a national consensus in the 1890s, prime ministers used patriotic rhetoric, bribes to gain support from the press, and imperial adventure, culminating in a second thwarted attempt to conquer Ethiopia in 1896. Riots and strikes, followed by armed government repression, erupted, until Giovanni Giolitti (1842–1928), who served as prime minister for three terms between 1903 and 1914, adopted a policy known as *trasformismo* (from the word for "transform"), by which he used bribes, public works programs, and other benefits to localities to influence their deputies in parliament. Political opponents called Giolitti the "Minister of the Underworld" and accused him of preferring to buy the votes of local bosses rather than to spend money to develop the Italian economy. Giolitti's attempt to achieve consensus met

✦**Sinn Fein:** SHIHN FAYN

instead with unrest in the rapidly industrializing cities of Turin and Milan and in the depressed agrarian south. Urban and rural workers alike demanded change, especially of the restricted suffrage that allowed only three million of more than eight million adult men to vote. Giolitti appeased the protesters by instituting social welfare programs and, in 1912, virtually complete manhood suffrage.

Anti-Semitism, Nationalism, and Zionism in Mass Politics

In the two decades leading up to World War I, politicians used anti-Semitism and nationalism to attract support and to win elections. Amid change and complexity, they suggested that anti-Semitism and increased patriotism would easily resolve all problems. At all levels of society, many voters responded enthusiastically. They accepted that Jews were villains responsible for the perils of modern society, and they viewed the nation-state as the hero in the struggle to survive. In both republics and monarchies, anti-Semitism and nationalism played key roles in mass politics by providing a focus for the creation of a radical right increasingly committed to combating the radical left of social democracy. Adopting the imperiled nation as its theme and using the Social Darwinist category of race to identify threats to the nation, the right fundamentally changed the older notion of nationalism based on liberal ideas of constitutional rule and equality of all citizens. Liberals had hoped that voting by the masses would make politics more harmonious as parliamentary debate and compromise smoothed out class differences. The new politics shaped by right-wing leaders—usually representatives of the agrarian nobility, aristocrats who controlled the military, and highly placed clergy—dashed those hopes.

Authoritarianism in Russia.   A more traditional form of anti-Semitism existed in Russian politics. The Russian tsar Nicholas II (r. 1894–1917) confronted modern life with unswerving beliefs in orthodoxy in religion, autocracy in politics, and anti-Semitism and Russification in social policy. In this he followed the lead of his father, Alexander III, whose reign had opened in 1881 with an outbreak of

vicious pogroms against Jews. Taught as a child to hate Jews, Nicholas believed that any failure in Russian policy was the fault of the Jews. In his reign many high officials eagerly endorsed anti-Semitism to gain his favor. Pogroms became a regular feature of the Easter holiday in Russia, and he explained to his mother that in the face of such violence he would never order soldiers to "fire on Christians to protect Jews." Nicholas increasingly limited where Jews could live and how they could earn a living. Although Nicholas was crueler to Jews than parliamentary politicians of the right in France, Germany, and Austria-Hungary, there was an old-fashioned nature to his cruelty and he did not manipulate parliamentary politics via anti-Semitism. Anti-Semitism was integral to his autocracy and orthodoxy, but it was not yet a tool in modern party politics.

The Dreyfus Affair in France.   The most notorious instance of anti-Semitism in mass politics occurred in France, where the political compromise that had created the Third Republic after defeat in the Franco-Prussian War produced institutional fragility. Although an alliance of businessmen, shopkeepers, professionals, and rural property owners backed republican government, destabilizing economic downturns, widespread corruption, attempted coups, and the politics of anti-Semitism threatened political chaos at every turn. The press attributed failures of almost any kind to Jews, and despite an excellent system of primary education promoting literacy and rational thinking, the public was quick to agree. The clergy and monarchists also contributed to the belief that the republic was backed by a conspiracy of Jews.

Amid rising anti-Semitism, a Jewish captain in the French army, Alfred Dreyfus, was charged with spying for Germany in 1894. Dreyfus had attended the elite École Polytechnique in Paris and become an officer in the French military, whose upper echelons were traditionally aristocratic, Catholic, and monarchist. Dreyfus's conviction and harsh exile to Devil's Island failed to stop the espionage, but the republican government adamantly upheld his guilt. Then several newspapers received proof that the army had used perjured testimony and fabricated documents to convict Dreyfus. In 1898, the celebrated French novelist Émile Zola published an article titled *"J'accuse"*♦ (I accuse) on the front page of a Paris daily. Zola cited a list of military lies and cover-ups perpetrated by highly placed government officials to create an illusion of Dreyfus's guilt.

The article was explosive because it named the guilty parties and endorsed liberal government based on truth, tolerance, and the rule of law. "I have but one passion, that of Enlightenment," wrote Zola. His piece led to public riots, quarrels among families and friends, and denunciations of the army, eroding public confidence in the republic and in French institutions. The government finally pardoned Dreyfus in 1899, ousted from office the aristocratic and Catholic officers held responsible, and ended religious teaching orders to ensure a secular public school system that taught liberal values of tolerance. Nonetheless, the Dreyfus Affair made anti-Semitism a standard tool of politics by producing hate-filled slogans that shaped mainstream politics (see the cartoon shown here).

Nationalist and Anti-Semitic Politics in Germany. The ruling elites in Germany also used anti-Semitism as a political weapon to garner support from those who feared the consequences of Germany's sudden and overwhelming industrialization. The agrarian elites, unlike French conservatives, still controlled the highest reaches of government and influenced the kaiser's policy. But the basis of their power was rapidly eroding; agriculture, from which they drew their fortunes and social prestige, declined as a percentage of gross national product from 37 percent in the 1880s to only 25 percent early in the 1900s. As new opportunities lured rural people away from the land and as industrialists grew wealthier, the agrarian elites came to loathe industry and the working class for coming to challenge their entrenched rule. As a Berlin newspaper noted, "The agrarians' hate for cities . . . blinds them to the simplest needs and the most natural demands of the urban population." In contrast to Bismarck's astute wooing of the masses through social programs, William II's aristocracy often encouraged anti-

♦**J'accuse:** zhah KOOZ

Public Opinion in the Dreyfus Affair: "Ah! The Dirty Beast!"
The French army used forged documents and perjured testimony to convict Captain Alfred Dreyfus of espionage. In a climate of escalating anti-Semitism, the conviction of a Jew struck many in the public as yet another narrow escape for the country. Only intense detective work by pro-Dreyfus activists and lobbying by Dreyfus's family convinced republican leaders that the system of equal rights was imperiled not by Dreyfus but by the bigotry of the army and those right-wing politicians who had trumped up the case against him. What meaning is conveyed by this illustration? For what audience is it intended? *Photothèque de Musées de la Ville de Paris Toumazet.*

Semitism, both in the corridors of power and in the streets.

Conservatives and a growing radical right claimed that Jews, who made up less than 1 percent of the German population, were responsible for the disruption of traditional society and charged them with being the main beneficiaries of economic change. In the

1890s, nationalist and anti-Semitic political pressure groups flourished, spewing diatribes against Jews and "new women" but also against Social Democrats, whom they branded as internationalist, socially destructive, and unpatriotic. In the 1890s, the new Agrarian League played to the fears of small farmers by accusing Jews of causing agricultural booms and busts; it thus led other parties to imitate its hate-filled speeches against an array of groups. Expression of extremist hatreds and violent feelings of nationalism rather than rational programs to meet the problems of economic change became regular features of political campaigns. The right invented a modern politics that rejected parliamentary consensus building, relying instead on mouthing slogans and creating enemies.

Ethnic Politics in Austria-Hungary. People in the dual monarchy of Austria-Hungary also expressed their political and economic discontent using militant nationalism and anti-Semitism, but here nationalism was colored by the presence of many competing ethnic groups. Foremost among the nationalists were the Hungarians, who wanted autonomy for themselves while forcibly imposing Hungarian language and culture on all other ethnic groups in Hungary. The demands for greater Hungarian influence (or Magyarization, from Magyars, the principal ethnic group)

Principal Ethnic Groups in Austria-Hungary, c. 1900

seemed justified: Budapest was a thriving industrial city, and the export of Hungarian grain from the vast estates of the Hungarian nobility balanced the monarchy's foreign trade deficit. With vociferous nationalism and separatism mounting, the Independence Party disrupted the Hungarian parliament so regularly that it weakened the orderly functioning of the government.

Although capable of causing trouble for the empire, Hungarian nationalists, who mostly represented agrarian wealth, were vulnerable to the resistance of other nationalities and to the demands of a growing industrial proletariat. On the land, the policy of Magyarization resulted in the formation of strong political groups among the regions ethnic groups—Slovaks, Romanians, and Ruthenians. Strikes erupted to protest horrendous labor conditions, and in the fall of 1905, a hundred thousand activists demonstrated in front of the Hungarian parliament for the vote. In the face of this resistance, Hungarians intensified Magyarization, even decreeing that all tombstones be engraved in Magyar. Emperor Francis Joseph temporarily brought the Hungarian nationalists to bay by threatening to introduce universal manhood suffrage, which would allow both the Magyars' lower-class and non-Magyar opponents to vote. Although numerous nationality groups and the many Jews who settled in Budapest assimilated Magyar ways, the uncompromising and chauvinist nature of Hungarian policies toward both imperial government in Vienna and different ethnic groups within the empire made for instability throughout Austria-Hungary.

Hungarian policies changed the course of Habsburg politics by arousing other nationalists to intensify their demands for rights. Croats, Serbs, and other Slavic groups in the south organized and called for equality with the Hungarians. The central government gave more privileges to the Czechs and allowed them to increase the proportion of Czech officials in the government because growing industrial prosperity in their region gave them more influence. But every step toward recognition of Czech ethnicity provoked outrage from the traditionally dominant ethnic Germans, further straining the political fabric of the empire. When Austria-Hungary decreed in 1897 that government officials in the Czech region of the empire would have to speak Czech as well as German, the Germans rioted.

Tensions mounted as politicians in Vienna linked the growing power of Hungarian and Czech politicians to Jews. A prime instigator of the "politics of the irrational"—as historians often label this ultranationalist and anti-Semitic phenomenon—was Karl Lueger (1844–1910), whose newly formed Christian Social Party attracted members from among the aristocracy, Catholics, artisans, shopkeepers, and white-collar workers. In speeches around the city's neighborhoods, Lueger used hatred to appeal to those groups for whom modern life meant a loss of privilege and security. In 1895, he was elected mayor of Vienna after using rough language and verbal abuse against Jews and ethnic groups in his campaigns. Lueger's ethnic nationalism and anti-Semitism attracted raucous crowds and destabilized the multinational coexistence on which Austria-Hungary was based. By the turn of the century, many politicians were harping on Jewishness as a symbol in their election campaigns, calling Jews the "sucking vampire" of modernity and blaming them for the tumult of migration, social dislocation, and just about anything else people did not like. Politics became a thing not of parliaments but of the streets, bloated with racism and inflaming the atmosphere.

The Jewish Response to Anti-Liberal Politics.   The prevailing view in the West that Jews were inferior to Christians provoked varying responses from Jews themselves. Jews in western Europe had responded to increased legal tolerance by moving out of Jewish neighborhoods, intermarrying with Christians, and in some cases converting to Christianity—practices known as assimilation. Many Jews also favored the German Empire because classical German culture seemed more appealing than the Catholic ritual promoted by Austria-Hungary. By contrast, Jews in Russia and Romania were increasingly singled out for persecution, legally disadvantaged, and forced to live in ghettos. If Jews from these countries wanted refuge, the nearby cities of central and eastern Europe offered opportunity. By 1900, many Jews were prominent in cultural and economic affairs in cities across the continent, even as others were discriminated against and victimized elsewhere. Some Jews adopted the cosmo-

politan culture of Vienna or Magyar ways in Budapest; for example, despite escalating anti-Semitism, the celebrated composer Gustav Mahler (1860–1911), the budding writer Franz Kafka, and the pioneer of psychoanalysis Sigmund Freud flourished in Habsburg society.

Most Jews, however, were not so accomplished or prosperous as these cultural giants, and their migration to the United States and other countries in reaction to both pogroms and economic change filled towns and cities with poor day laborers and struggling artisans (Map 25.1). Amid this vast migration

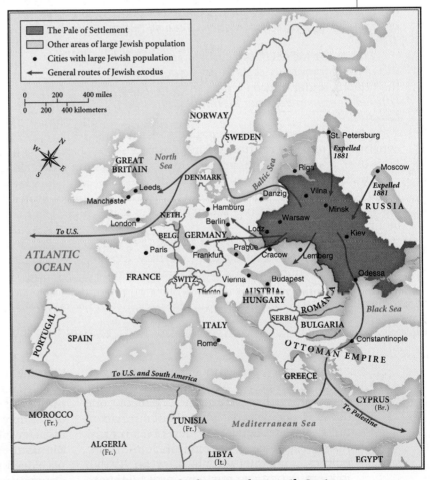

MAP 25.1 Jewish Migrations in the Late Nineteenth Century
Pogroms in eastern Europe, increasingly violent anti-Semitism across the continent, and the search for opportunity led Jews to many parts of the world. Between 1890 and 1914 some five million Jews left Russia alone. They migrated to European cities and, as Zionism progressed, to Palestine. The development of manufacturing in the United States offered a wealth of new opportunities, especially the chance to live where the rule of law was somewhat better established than in Russia. Why did the migration of Jews vary from region to region?

Leon Pinsker Calls for a Jewish State

In 1882 the Ukrainian physician Leon Pinsker published a pamphlet called Auto-Emancipation *in which he analyzed the situation of the Jews in Europe. This pamphlet convinced some in Europe—most notably Theodor Herzl—that Jews could never be assimilated to European culture no matter how many dropped their religion in favor of Christian ways. This pamphlet ultimately led to the migration of Jews to Palestine, despite Pinsker's own conviction that the Middle East was not necessarily the right place for creating a Jewish nation.*

This is the kernel of the problem, as we see it: *the Jews comprise a distinctive element among the nations under which they dwell, and as such can neither assimilate nor be readily digested by any nation. . . .*

A fear of the Jewish ghost has passed down the generations and the centuries. First a breeder of prejudice, later . . . it culminated in Judeophobia.

Judeophobia is a psychic aberration. As a psychic aberration it is hereditary, and as a disease transmitted for two thousand years it is incurable. . . .

The Jews are aliens who can have no representatives, because they have no country. Because they have none, because their home has no boundaries within which they can be entrenched, their misery too is boundless. . . .

. . . If we would have a secure home, give up our endless life of wandering and rise to the dignity of a nation in our own eyes and in the eyes of the world, we must, above all, not dream of restoring ancient Judaea. We must not attach ourselves to the place where our political life was once violently interrupted and destroyed. The goal of our present endeavors must be not the "Holy Land," but a land of our own. We need nothing but a large tract of land for our poor brothers, which shall remain our property and from which no foreign power can expel us. There we shall take with us the most sacred possessions which we have saved from the shipwreck of our former country, the *God-idea* and the *Bible.* It is these alone which have made our old fatherland the Holy Land, and not Jerusalem or the Jordan. Perhaps the Holy Land will again become ours. If so, all the better, but *first of all,* we must determine—and this is the crucial point—what country is accessible to us, and at the same time adapted to offer the Jews of all lands who must leave their homes a secure and indisputed refuge, capable of productivization. . . .

Source: Robert Chazan and Marc Lee Raphael, eds., *Modern Jewish History: A Source Reader* (New York: Schocken Books, 1974), 161, 163, 165–66, 169–71, 171–74.

and continued persecution, a spirit of Jewish nationalism arose. "Why should we be any less worthy than any other . . . people," one Jewish leader asked. "What about our nation, our language, our land?" Jews began organizing resistance to pogroms and anti-Semitic politics, and intellectuals drew on Jewish folklore, language, customs, and history to establish a national identity parallel to that of other Europeans.

In the 1880s, the Ukrainian physician Leon Pinsker (1821–1891), seeing the Jews' lack of national territory as fundamental to the persecution heaped on them, advocated the migration of Jews to Palestine (see his statement above). In 1896, Theodor Herzl (1860–1904), strongly influenced by Pinsker, published *The Jewish State,* which called not simply for migration but for the creation of a Jewish nation-state, a goal known as **Zionism**. A Hungarian-born Jew, Herzl experienced anti-Semitism firsthand as a Viennese journalist and a writer in Paris during the Dreyfus Affair. He became driven to found a Jewish state, searching Europe for financial backing, technical advice, and a political structure for the venture. His constituency should have been prosperous Jews, but many of them had assimilated and thought his ideas mad. However, with the support of poorer eastern European Jews, he succeeded in calling the first International Zionist Congress (1897), which endorsed settlement in Palestine. By 1914, some eighty-five thousand Jews had moved into Palestine.

Review: What were the points of tension in European political life at the turn of the century?

❖ European Imperialism Contested

Inflamed nationalism across the West made it difficult for nations to calm domestic politics and the traumas of modern industrial life. In 1897, the poet Rudyard Kipling (1865–1936) marked the fiftieth anniversary of Queen Victoria's reign with "Recessional," a somber poem comparing the British Empire to ancient cities whose glory had long since faded:

> Far-called our navies melt away—
> On dune and headland sinks the fire—
> Lo, all our pomp of yesterday
> Is one with Nineveh and Tyre.

Kipling's turn to pessimistic sentimentalism was apt, first because holding imperial territory was aggravating relations among the European powers and second because colonized peoples were challenging European control. Japan had become an Asian power, and nationalist movements for independence were gaining strength, a development that eventually led to new rebellions against European rule.

The Trials of Empire

After centuries of global expansion, imperial adventure soured for Britain and France as the twentieth century opened. Such newcomers as Italy and Germany had difficulty acquiring territory outside Europe, and they fought for a place at the imperial table. Increasing competition among a greater number of nations for colonies and escalating tensions between the French and British in Africa and elsewhere raised serious questions about the future of imperialism. "Where thirty years ago there existed one sensitive spot in our relations with France, or Germany, or Russia," the British economist J. A. Hobson wrote in 1902, "there are a dozen now; diplomatic strains are of almost monthly occurrence between the Powers." For their part, colonized people were fighting back with stubborn vigor.

Boer War. Accustomed to crushing resistance to their imperial ambitions, the British experienced a bloody defeat in 1895, when Cecil Rhodes, prime minister of the Cape Colony in southern Africa, directed a raid into the neighboring territory of the Transvaal. The foray was intended to stir up trouble between the Boers, descendants of early Dutch settlers, and the more recent immigrants from Britain who had come to southern Africa in search of gold and other riches. Rhodes hoped the raid would justify a British takeover of the Transvaal and the Orange Free State, which the Boers independently controlled. The Boers, however, easily routed the raiders, forcing Rhodes to resign in disgrace.

Other Europeans gloated over the British loss. Kaiser William II telegraphed his congratulations to the Transvaal president for "maintaining the independence of the country against attacks from without." Unaccustomed to defeat, the British government did not accept it easily: for the next three years it fought the **Boer War** directly against the Transvaal and the Orange Free State, causing unease and even outrage in Britain. As foreign correspondents unexpectedly flocked to South Africa, they reported on appalling bloodshed, heavy casualties, and the unfit condition of the average British soldier. Most alarmingly to those who liked to think of Britain as the most civilized country in the world, news arrived back in the capital of rampant disease and inhumane treatment of South Africans herded into a shocking and unfamiliar institution—the concentration camp, which became the graveyard of tens of thousands. Back home in England, right-minded thinkers began to see imperialism as barbarism. Britain finally annexed the area after defeating the Boers in 1902, but the cost of war in money, destruction, demoralization, and loss of life was enormous (Map 25.2).

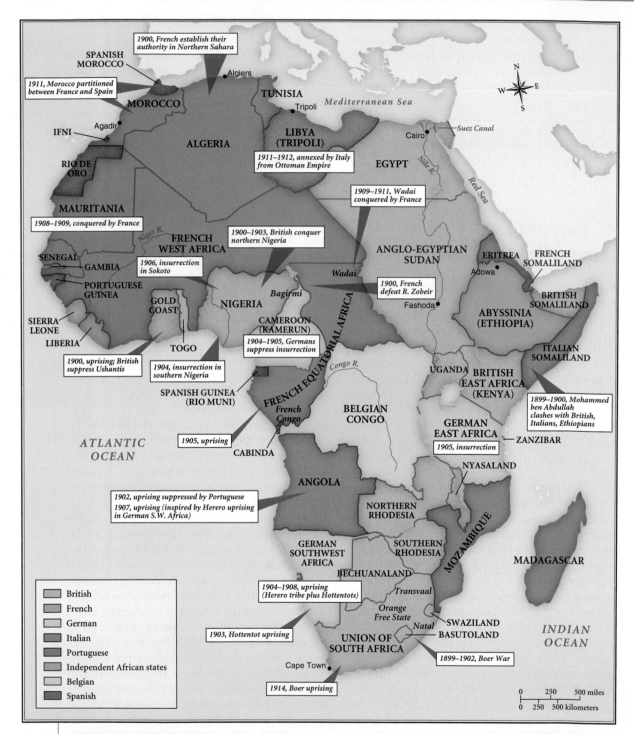

MAP 25.2 Africa in 1914

Uprisings intensified in Africa in the early twentieth century as Europeans tried both to consolidate their rule through bureaucratization and military action and to extract more wealth from the Africans. At the same time as Europeans were putting down the rebellions against their rule, a pan-African movement arose, attempting to unite Africans as one people. As in Asia and the Middle East, the more the colonial powers tried to impose their will, the greater the political forces—including the force of political ideas—that took shape against them. What impression does this map give of the status of European imperialism in Africa? Compare it to the map of Africa in chapter 24.

Newcomers Face Setbacks. Almost simultaneously, Spain lost Cuba, Puerto Rico, and the Philippines to the United States as a result of its defeat in the Spanish-American War of 1898. The United States was not a novice to imperialism. It had successfully crushed native Americans, killing many and confining survivors to reservations, and in 1898 it annexed Hawaii. Both Cuba and the Philippines had begun vigorous efforts to free themselves from Spanish rule. U.S. politicians saw their chance. Urged on by the expansionist-minded Theodore Roosevelt, then assistant secretary of the navy, and the inflammatory daily press, the United States intervened to help the independence movements. Instead of allowing the independence that victory called for, however, the U.S. government annexed Puerto Rico and Guam and bought the Philippines from Spain. Cuba was theoretically independent, but the United States monitored its activities.

War revealed the fragility of established European empires and the unpredictability of imperial fortunes. Even the triumphant United States, encouraged by Kipling to "take up the white man's burden" by bringing the benefits of Western civilization to those liberated from Spain, had to wage a bloody war against the Filipinos, who wanted independence, not another imperial ruler. Reports of American brutality in the Philippines, where some 200,000 local people were slaughtered, further disillusioned the Western public, who liked to imagine native peoples joyously welcoming the bearers of civilization.

Despite these setbacks, the emerging powers had an emotional stake in gaining colonies. In the early twentieth century, Italian public figures bragged about the Italians becoming Nietzschean supermen by conquering Africa and restoring Italy to its ancient position of world domination. After a disastrous war against Ethiopia in 1896, Italy won a costly victory over the Ottoman Empire in Libya. These wars roused Italian hopes for national grandeur only to dash them when such grandeur proved elusive or costly.

Germany likewise demanded a place at the imperial table and an end to the virtual British-French monopoly of colonial power. Foremost among the new competitors for empire, German bankers and businessmen were ensconced throughout Asia, the Middle East, and Latin America. Several centuries after other European states, Germany sent linguists, ethnographers, and museum curators to study other cultures and obtain their treasures. Despite some successes, there was no unalloyed glory. Germany, too, met humiliation and constant problems, especially in its dealings with Britain and France and with those local peoples abroad who resisted the German takeover in Africa and elsewhere. As Italy and Germany aggressively pursued new territory, the rules set for imperialism at the Congress of Berlin a generation earlier gave way to increasingly heated rivalry and nationalist fury.

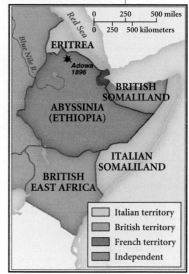

The Struggle for Ethiopia, 1896

Japan Victorious. Japan's rise as an imperial power further eroded Europeans' confident approach to imperialism. The Japanese had started building an empire by invading the Chinese island of Formosa (present-day Taiwan) in 1874 and continued by forcing trading treaties on Korea in 1876 (Map 25.3). In 1894, Japan sparked the Sino-Japanese War against China, which ended China's domination of Korea. The European powers, alarmed at Japan's victory, forced it to relinquish other gains, a move that outraged and affronted the Japanese. Japan's insecurity had risen with Russian expansion to the east and south in Asia. Pushing into eastern Asia, the Russians had built the Trans-Siberian Railroad through Manchuria, sent millions of Russian settlers eastward, and sponsored anti-Japanese groups in Korea, making the Korean peninsula appear, as a Japanese military leader put it, like "a dagger thrust at the heart of Japan." Angered by the continuing presence of Russian troops in Manchuria, the Japanese attacked tsarist forces at Port Arthur in 1904.

The conservative Russian military proved inept in the ensuing Russo-Japanese War,

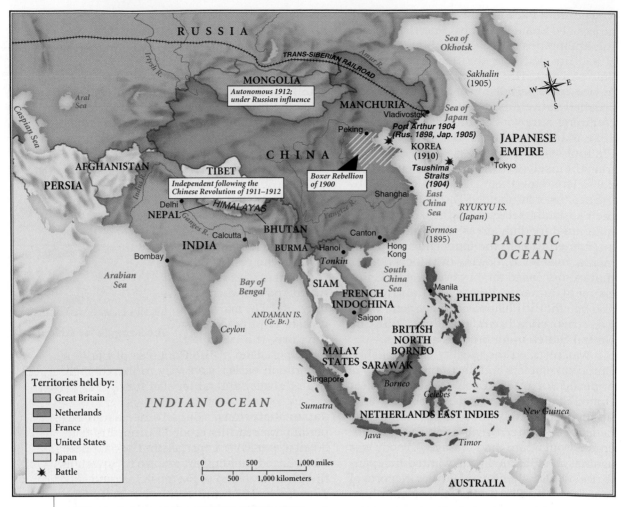

MAP 25.3 Imperialism in Asia, 1894–1914
Most of the modernizing states converged on Asia. The established imperialists came to blows in East Asia as they struggled for influence in China and as they met a formidable new rival—Japan. Simultaneously, liberation groups like the Boxers were taking shape, committed to throwing off restraints imposed by foreign powers and eliminating these interlopers altogether. Ultimately in 1911, Sun Yat-Sen overthrew the Qing dynasty that had left China unprepared to resist foreign takeover and started the country on a different course.

even though it often had better equipment or strategic advantage. In an astonishing display of poor leadership, Russia's Baltic Fleet sailed halfway around the globe only to be completely destroyed by Japan in the battle of Tsushima Straits (1905). Opening an era of Japanese domination in East Asian politics, the victory was the first by a non-European nation over a European great power in the modern age, and it gave the West an additional reason to fear the future. As one English general ominously observed of the

Russian defeat: "I have today seen the most stupendous spectacle it is possible for the mortal brain to conceive—Asia advancing, Europe falling back." Japan went on to annex Korea in 1910 and to eye other areas for colonization.

The Russian Empire Threatened

Russia, a mighty empire that had expanded southward in Asia and settled much of Siberia during the nineteenth century, concealed its weaknesses well. In reality it tottered on the brink of chaos in 1905 as revolution erupted alongside military defeat. State-sponsored industrialization in the 1890s had made the country appear modern to outside observers, and the Russification policy imitated Western-style state building by attempting to impose a unified, national culture on Russia's diverse population. Bearing the costs of industrialization and a heavy burden of post—emancipation debt, the peasantry rebelled in isolated uprisings at the turn of the century. Industrialization also produced urban unrest as Marxist and union activists incited workers to demand better conditions. In 1903, skilled workers led strikes in Baku, where Armenians and Tatars united in a demonstration that showed how urbanization and Russification could facilitate political action among the lower classes. These and other worker protests challenged the autocratic regime, which was weakened further by Japan's victory.

The Revolution of 1905. The Russian secret police hoped to stifle discontent by spying widely on citizens and by organizing its own unions staffed by police informants. In January 1905, a crowd (unaware that the priest who led them was an informant) gathered one Sunday outside the tsar's Winter Palace in St. Petersburg to march in a demonstration to make Nicholas aware of the brutal working conditions they suffered. Nicholas had often traveled the empire, displaying himself as the divinely ordained "father" of his people, and thus appealing to him seemed natural to his "children." Instead of allowing the demonstration to pass, however, troops guarding the palace shot into the trusting crowd, killing hundreds and wounding thousands. Thus began the Revolution of 1905, and news of "Bloody Sunday" spurred outraged workers to rebel.

In almost a year of turmoil across Russia, urban workers struck over wages, hours, and factory conditions and demanded political representation in the government. Delegates from revolutionary parties such as the Social Democrats and the Socialist Revolutionaries encouraged more direct blows against the central government, but workers rejected their leadership and organized their own councils, called soviets. In February, the tsar's uncle was assassinated; in June, sailors on the battleship *Potemkin* mutinied; in October, a massive railroad strike ground rail transportation to a halt and people in the Baltic States and Transcaucasia rebelled; and in November, uprisings broke out in Moscow. The tsar's Cossack troops kept killing activists across the country, but their deaths only fueled the protest.

In response to Nicholas II's absolute rule, the revolution coalesced artisans and industrial workers, peasants, professionals, and reformers in the upper classes against his support among the entrenched Russian nobility. Women joined the fray, many demanding an end to discriminatory laws such as those firing women teachers who married. Using the unrest to press their goals, liberals from the zemstvos (local councils) and the intelligentsia (a Russian word for well-educated elites) demanded political reform, in particular the replacement of autocracy with a constitutional monarchy and representative legislature. They believed that the reliance on censorship and the machinations of a secret police, characteristic of Romanov rule, relegated Russia to the ranks of the

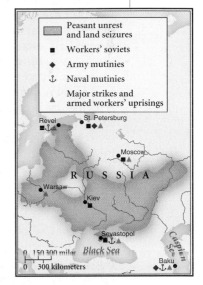

Peasant unrest and land seizures

■ Workers' soviets

◆ Army mutinies

⚓ Naval mutinies

▲ Major strikes and armed workers' uprisings

Revel · St. Petersburg

Moscow

R U S S I A

Warsaw · Kiev

Sevastopol

Black Sea

0 150 300 miles
0 300 kilometers

Baku

Caspian Sea

Russian Revolution of 1905

most backward states. Preferring a military solution, Nicholas responded with halfhearted reforms—a response that triggered more street fighting. In the words of one protester, the tsar's attitude turned "yesterday's benighted slaves into decisive warriors."

Attempts at Political Reform. Impelled by the continuing violence, the tsar created a representative body—the **Duma**. Although very few Russians could vote for representatives to the Duma, its mere existence, coupled with the right of public political debate, liberalized government and allowed people—the oppressed Jews foremost among them—to present their grievances to a responsive body.

Political parties also took shape during this time. When these newly formed constitutional parties threw their support to the reorganized government, revolutionary activity abated and the tsar's troops crushed the remaining pockets of resistance.

People soon began to wonder, however, if anything had really changed. From 1907 to 1917, the Duma convened, but twice when the tsar disliked its recommendations he sent the delegates home and forced new elections. Nicholas still considered himself the only source of authority. Prime Minister Pyotr Stolypin♦ (1863–1911), a successful administrator and landowner, was determined to eliminate the sources of discontent by ending the mir system of communal farming and taxation and canceling the land redemption payments that had burdened the peasants since their emancipation in 1861. He also made government loans available to peasants, who were then able to purchase land and to own farms outright. Although these reforms did not eradicate rural poverty, they did allow people to move to the cities in search of jobs and created a larger group of independent peasants. By 1917, some two-thirds of the peasantry had taken steps to gain title to their land, and 10 percent had acquired consolidated holdings.

Stolypin succeeded only partially in his other goal of restoring law and order. He clamped down on revolutionary organizations, executing their members by hanging them with "Stolypin neckties." The government urged more pogroms and stifled ethnic unrest by stepping up Russification. But rebels continued to assassinate government officials—four thousand were killed or wounded in 1906–1907—and Stolypin himself was assassinated in 1911. Stolypin's reforms had promoted peasant well-being, which encouraged what one historian has called a "new peasant assertiveness." The industrial workforce also grew, and another round of strikes broke out, culminating in a general strike in St. Petersburg in 1914.

Despite the creation of the Duma and other reforms, the imperial government and the conservative nobility had no solution to the ongoing social turmoil and felt little in-clination to share power. Their ineffectual response to the Revolution of 1905 would foster an even greater revolution in 1917, while ongoing domestic conflicts opened one of the roads to war.

Growing Resistance to Colonial Domination

The Japanese military victory over two important dynasties—the Qing in China and the Romanov in Russia—had domestic repercussions in both countries. Within a decade the colonies responded to the victory, further eroding the security Westerners had once found in imperialism. The Japanese victories and the ability of Russian revolutionaries to force a great European power to reform inspired nationalist-minded opponents to European imperialism. The success of a non-Western, constitutional government fed protest throughout the globe.

Boxers in China.   Uprisings began in China after its 1895 defeat by Japan forced the ruling Qing dynasty to grant more economic concessions to Western powers. Humiliated by these events, peasants organized into secret societies to restore Chinese integrity. One organization was the Society of the Righteous and Harmonious Fists (or Boxers), whose members maintained that ritual boxing would protect them from a variety of evils, including bullets. Encouraged by the Qing ruler, Dowager Empress Tz'u-hsi♦ (Cixi; 1835–1908), and desperate because of worsening economic conditions, the Boxers rebelled in 1900, massacring the missionaries and Chinese Christians to whom they attributed China's troubles. Seven of the colonial powers united to put down the Boxer Uprising and encouraged the Chinese troops in their service to ravage the areas in which the Boxers operated. Defeated once more, the Chinese were compelled to pay a huge indemnity for damages done to foreign property, to destroy many of their defensive fortifications, and to allow more extensive foreign military occupation.

The Boxer Uprising thoroughly discredited the Qing dynasty; a group of revolu-

♦**Pyotr Stolypin:** PYAW tur stuh LIH pihn

♦**Tz'u-hsi:** syoo see

tionaries finally overthrew the dynasty in 1911 and declared China a republic the next year. Their leader, Sun Yat-Sen♦ (1866–1925), who had been educated in Hawaii and Japan, used a cluster of Western ideas in his slogan "nationalism, democracy, and socialism." He shaped them with traditional Chinese values so that socialism contained the Chinese belief that all people have enough food. In sum, his movement called for freedom from the Qing dynasty, revival of the Chinese tradition of correctness in behavior between governors and the governed, modern economic reform, and a threat to European channels of trade and domination. Sun's stirring leadership and the changes brought about by China's revolution helped change the course of Western imperialism.

Nationalists in India.

In India, the Japanese victory over Russia and the Revolution of 1905 stimulated politicians to take a more radical course than that offered by the Indian National Congress. A Hindu leader, B. G. Tilak (1856–1920), fervently anti-British and less moderate than Congress reformers, preached blatant noncooperation: "We shall not give them assistance to collect revenue and keep peace. We shall not assist them in fighting beyond the frontiers or outside India with Indian blood and money." Tilak promoted Hindu customs, asserted the distinctiveness of Hindu values from British ways, and inspired violent rebellion in his followers. This brand of nationalism broke with that based on assimilating to British culture and promoting gradual change. Trying to repress Tilak, the British sponsored the Muslim League, a rival nationalist group favored for its restraint and its potential to divide Muslim nationalists from Hindus in the Congress.

The Foreign Pig Is Put to Death
The Boxers sought to fortify the Chinese government against the many powers threatening China's survival. They used brightly colored placards to spread information about their goals and about their successes in order to build wide support among the Chinese population. They felt that the presence of foreigners had caused a series of disasters including the defection of the Chinese from traditional religion, the flow of wealth from the country, and the natural disasters such as famine that seemed to be taking place with greater frequency. This depiction shows the harsh judgment of the Boxers toward foreigners and their Chinese allies—they are pigs to be killed. **For more help analyzing this image**, see the visual activity for this chapter in the Online Study Guide at **bedfordstmartins.com/hunt**. *Bridgeman Art Library.*

Faced with political activism on many fronts, however, Britain conceded the right to vote based on property ownership and to representation in ruling councils. Because the independence movement had not fully reached the masses, these small concessions temporarily maintained British power by appeasing the best-educated and most influential dissidents among the upper and middle classes. But the British hold on India was weakening.

Young Turks in the Ottoman Empire.
Revolutionary nationalism was simultaneously sapping the Ottoman Empire, which for centuries had controlled much of the Mediterranean. In the nineteenth century, several rebellions had plagued Ottoman rule, and more erupted early in the twentieth century

♦**Sun Yat-Sen:** SOON YAHT SEHN

because of growing resistance to the empire and to European influence. Just as the Habsburgs used the transnational appeal of Catholicism to quash nationalist aspirations, Sultan Abdul Hamid II (r. 1876–1909) tried to revitalize the multiethnic empire by using Islam to counteract the rising nationalism of the Serbs, Bulgarians, and Macedonians. Instead, he unwittingly provoked a burgeoning Turkish nationalism in Constantinople itself. Turkish nationalists rejected the sultan's pan-Islamic solution and built their movement on the uniqueness of their culture, history, and language, as many European ethnic groups were doing. Using the findings of Western scholarship, they first traced the history of the group they called Turks to change the word *Turk* from one of derision to one of pride. Nationalists also tried to purge their language of words from Arabic and Persian, and they popularized the folklore of rural Turkish peoples scattered across territories from eastern Europe through Asia. The events of 1904–1905 electrified these nationalists with the vision of a modern Turkey becoming "the Japan of the Middle East," as they called it. In 1908, a group of nationalists called the Young Turks took control of the government in Constantinople, which had been fatally weakened by nationalist agitation and by the empire's economic dependence on Western financiers and businessmen.

The Young Turks' triumph motivated other groups in the Middle East and the Balkans to demand an end to Ottoman domination in their regions as well. These groups adopted Western values and platforms, and some, such as the Egyptians, had strong contingents of feminist-nationalists who mobilized women to work for independence. But the Young Turks, often aided by European powers with financial and political interests in the region, brutally tried to repress the uprisings in Egypt, Syria, and the Balkans that their own success had encouraged.

The rebellions became part of the tumult shaping international relations in the decade before World War I. Empires, whether old or young, were the scene of growing resistance in the wake of Japanese, Russian, and Turkish events. In German East Africa, colonial forces countered native resistance in 1905 with a scorched-earth policy of destroying homes, livestock, food, and other resources. The Germans eventually killed more than 100,000 Africans there. The French closed the University of Hanoi, executed Indochinese intellectuals, and deported thousands of suspected nationalists merely to maintain a tenuous grip on Indochina. A French general stationed there summed up the fears of many colonial rulers in the new century: "The gravest fact of our actual political situation in Indochina is not the recent trouble in Tonkin [or] the plots undertaken against us but in the muted but growing hatred that our subjects show toward us."

Review: Why did events in overseas empires from the 1890s on prove discouraging to many Europeans back home?

❖ Roads to War

International developments simultaneously aggravated competition among the great powers and caused Western nationalism in its many varieties to swell. In the spring of 1914, U.S. president Woodrow Wilson (1856–1924) sent his trusted adviser Colonel House to Europe to assess the rising tensions among the major powers. "It is militarism run stark mad," House reported, adding that he foresaw an "awful cataclysm" ahead. Government spending on what people called the "arms race" had stimulated European economies; but arms were not stockpiled for economic growth only. As early as the mid-1890s, one socialist had called the situation a "cold war" because the hostile atmosphere made physical combat seem imminent. By 1914, the air was even more charged, with militant nationalism in the Balkan states and conflicts in domestic politics also setting the stage for war. Although historians have long debated whether World War I could have been avoided, they have never reached a consensus. Considering the feverish background of prewar change, they have had to content themselves with tracing the steps Europeans took along the road toward mass destruction.

Competing Alliances and Clashing Ambitions

As the twentieth century opened, the Triple Alliance that Bismarck had negotiated among Germany, Austria-Hungary, and Italy confronted an opposing alliance between France and Russia, created in the 1890s. The wild card in the diplomatic scenario was Great Britain, traditional enemy of France, nowhere more than in the contest for colonial power. Constant rivals in Africa, Britain and France edged to the brink of war in 1898 at Fashoda in the Sudan. The French government, however, backed away and both nations were frightened into getting along for mutual self-interest. To prevent another Fashoda, they entered into secret agreements, the first of which (1904) guaranteed British claims in Egypt and French claims in Morocco. This agreement marked the beginning of the British-French alliance called the **Entente Cordiale**. Despite the alliance, Britain's response to a European war remained in question; even French statesmen feared that their ally might remain neutral.

Germany's Imperial Demands. Germany under Kaiser William II became dissatisfied with its international status and inflamed rather than calmed the diplomatic atmosphere. Bismarck had maintained a policy of proclaiming Germany a "satisfied" nation, working to balance great-power interests, and avoiding the draining fight for colonies. To the contrary, the kaiser, emboldened by Germany's growing industrial might, strode onto the imperial stage with a big appetite for world power. Convinced of British hostility toward France, William II used the opportunity presented by the defeat of France's ally Russia to contest French claims in Morocco. A man who boasted and blustered and was easily prodded to rash actions by his advisers, William landed in Morocco in 1905, thus challenging French predominance in what became known as the First Moroccan Crisis. To resolve the situation, an international conference met in Spain in 1906, where Germany confidently expected to gain concessions and new territories. Instead the powers, now including the United States, decided to support French rule. The French

and British military, faced with German aggression in Morocco, drew closer together.

Germany found itself weak diplomatically and strong economically, a situation that made its leaders more determined to compete for territory abroad. When the French finally took over Morocco in 1911, Germany triggered the Second Moroccan Crisis by sending a gunboat to the port of Agadir and demanding concessions from the French. This time no power—not even Austria-Hungary—backed the German move. No one acknowledged this dominant country's might, nor did the constant demands for recognition encourage anyone to do so. The British and French now made binding military provisions for the deployment of their forces in case of war, thus strengthening the Entente Cordiale. Smarting from its setbacks on the world stage, Germany refocused its sights on its role on the continent and on its own alliances.

Crises in the Balkans. Germany's bold territorial claims, along with public uncertainty about the binding force of alliances, unsettled Europe, particularly the Balkans. German statesmen began envisioning the creation of a **Mitteleuropa**♦—a term that literally meant "central Europe" but that in their minds also included the Balkans and Turkey. The Habsburgs, now firmly backed by Germany, judged that expansion into the Balkans and the resulting addition of even more ethnic groups would weaken the claims of any single ethnic minority in the Dual Monarchy. Russia, however, saw itself as the protector of Slavs in the region and wanted to replace the Ottomans as the dominant Balkan power, especially after Japan had crushed its hopes for expansion to the east. Austria's swift annexation of Bosnia-Herzegovina during the Young Turk revolt in 1908 enraged not only the Russians but the Serbs as well, because these southern Slavs wanted Bosnia as part of an enlarged Serbia. The Balkans thus whetted many appetites (Map 25.4).

Even without the greedy eyes cast on the Balkans by outside powers, the situation would have been extremely complex given the tensions created by political modernity. The

---

♦**Mitteleuropa:** miht loy ROH pah

MAP 25.4 The Balkans, 1908–1914
Balkan peoples—mixed in religion, ethnicity, and political views—were successful in developing and asserting their desire for independence, especially in the First Balkan War, which claimed territory from the Ottoman Empire. Their increased autonomy sparked rivalries among them and continued to attract attention from the great powers. Three empires in particular—the Russian, Ottoman, and Austro-Hungarian—simultaneously sought greater influence for themselves in the region, which became a powderkeg of competing ambitions.

more Ottoman and Habsburg territory that included their own ethnic group—a complicated desire given the complex intermingling of ethnicities throughout the region.

In the First Balkan War, in 1912, Serbia, Bulgaria, Greece, and Montenegro joined forces to gain Macedonia and Albania from the Ottomans. The victors divided up their booty, with Bulgaria gaining the most territory, but soon they turned against one another. Serbia, Greece, and Montenegro contested Bulgarian gains in the Second Balkan War in 1913. Much to Austrian dismay, these allies won a quick victory, though Austria-Hungary managed in the peace terms to prevent Serbia from annexing parts of Albania. Grievances between the Habsburgs and the Serbs now seemed irreconcilable. Moreover, the peace conditions did not demilitarize the region, and Balkan peoples, especially angry Serbs who continued to look to Russia for help, imagined further challenges to Austria-Hungary. The Balkans had become a perilous region along whose borders both Austria-Hungary (as ruler of many Slavs) and Russia (as their protector) stationed increasing numbers of troops. The situation tempted strategists to think that a quick war there—something like Bismarck's wars—could resolve tension and uncertainty.

nineteenth century had seen the rise of nationalism and ethnicity as the basis for the unity of the nation-state, and by late in the century ethnic loyalty challenged dynastic power in the Balkans. Greece, Serbia, Bulgaria, Romania, and Montenegro emerged as autonomous states, almost all of them composed of several ethnicities as well as Orthodox Christians, Roman Catholics, and Muslims. All these states sought

The Race to Arms

In the nineteenth century, global rivalries and aspirations for national greatness made constant readiness for war seem increasingly necessary. On the seas and in foreign lands the colonial powers battled to establish control, and they developed railroad, telegraph, and telephone networks everywhere to link their conquests and to move troops as well as commercial goods. Governments began to conscript ordinary citizens for periods of two to six years into large standing armies, in contrast to smaller eighteenth-century forces that had served the more limited military goals of the time. By 1914, escalating tensions in Europe boosted the annual intake of conscripts: Germany, France, and Russia called up 250,000 or more troops each year; Austria-Hungary and Italy, about 100,000. The per capita expenditure on the military rose in all the major powers between 1890 and 1914; the proportion of national budgets devoted to defense in 1910 was lowest in Austria-Hungary at 10 percent, and highest in Germany at 45 percent.

The modernization of weaponry also transformed warfare. Swedish arms manufacturer Alfred Nobel patented dynamite and developed a kind of gunpowder that improved the accuracy of guns and produced a less clouded battlefield environment by reducing firearm smoke. Breakthroughs in the chemical industry affected long-range artillery, which by 1914 could fire on targets as far as six miles away. Such weapons as howitzers, Mauser rifles, and Hotchkiss machine guns provided improved accuracy and heavy firepower, and they were tested to great effect in the Russo-Japanese and Boer wars. These made military offensives more difficult to win than in the past because neither side could overcome such weaponry, causing military leaders to devise strategies to protect their armies from overwhelming firepower: in the Russo-Japanese War, trenches and barbed wire blanketed the front around Port Arthur. Munitions factories across Europe manufactured ever-growing stockpiles of the new weapons.

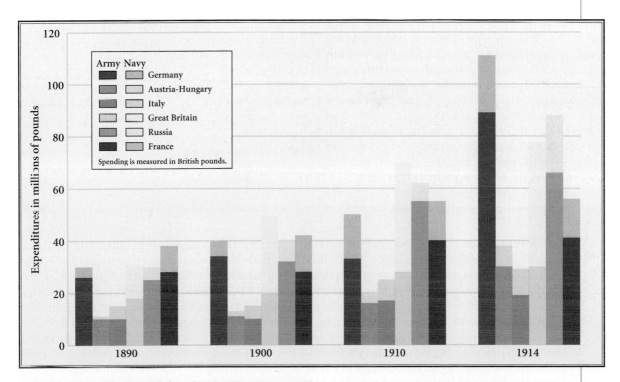

FIGURE 25.1 The Growth in Armaments, 1890–1914
The turn of the century saw the European powers engaged in a massive arms race. Several comparisons offer themselves, particularly the resources newly devoted to navies and the soaring defense spending of the Germans. Historians often ask whether better diplomacy could have prevented the outbreak of world war in 1914. The enormous military buildup, however, made some people living in the early twentieth century as well as some later historians see war as inevitable. Which countries could best afford the arms race at this time? The Hammond Atlas of the Twentieth Century *(London: Times Books, 1996), 29.*

An Historian Promotes Militant Nationalism

As the nineteenth century came to an end, competitive nationalism in preparation for war was everywhere, even in classrooms. History had developed into a "science" by this time, and historians were supposed to be neutral, basing their conclusions on solid, documentary evidence and erasing all trace of religious or national bias from their work. In the climate of military buildup, competition for empire, and a prowar spirit, the goal of dispassionate objectivity weakened. Supporting his nation was a driving force in the writing and teaching, of, among others, Heinrich von Trietschke of the University of Berlin, who delivered his lectures glorifying Germany's wars to throngs of cheering students and army officers.

The next essential function of the State is the conduct of war. The long oblivion into which this principle had fallen is a proof of how effeminate the science of government had become in civilian hands. In our century sentimentality was dissipated by Clausewitz, but a one-sided materialism arose in its place, after the fashion of the Manchester school, seeing in man a biped creature, whose destiny lies in buying cheap and selling dear. It is obvious that this idea is not compatible with war, and it is only since the last war [1870–71] that a sounder theory arose of the State and its military power.

Without war no State could be. All those we know of arose through war, and the protection of their members by armed force remains their primary and essential task. War, therefore, will endure to the end of history, as long as there is multiplicity of States. The laws of human thought and of human nature forbid any alternative, neither is one to be wished for. The blind worshipper of an eternal peace falls into the error of isolating the State, or dreams of one which is universal, which we have already seen to be at variance with reason.

Even as it is impossible to conceive of a tribunal above the State, which we have recognized as sovereign in its very essence, so it is likewise impossible to banish the idea of war from the world. It is a favourite fashion of our time to instance England as particularly ready for peace. But England is perpetually at war; there is hardly an instant in her recent history in which she has not been obliged to be fighting somewhere. The great strides which civilization makes against barbarism and unreason are only made actual by the sword.

Source: Heinrich Treitschke, *Politics*, Hans Kohn, ed., Blanche Duddale and Torben de Bille, trans. (New York: Harcourt, 1965), 37–38.

Naval construction also played a sensational role in nationalist politics. To defend against the new powerful, accurate weaponry, ships were made out of metal rather than wood after the mid-nineteenth century. In 1905, the English launched H.M.S. *Dreadnought*, a warship with unprecedented firepower and the centerpiece of the British navy's plan to construct at least seven battleships per year. Germany followed British navy building step by step and made itself a great land and sea power. Grand Admiral Alfred von Tirpitz (1849–1930) encouraged the insecure William II to view the navy as the essential ingredient in making Germany a world power and oversaw an immense buildup of the fleet. Tirpitz admired the American naval theorist Alfred Thayer Mahan (1840–1914) and planned to build naval bases as far away as the Pacific, following Mahan's conclusion that command of the seas determined international power. The German drive to build battleships further motivated Britain to ally with France in the Entente Cordiale. Britain raised its annual naval spending from $50 million in the 1870s to $130 million in 1900; Germany, from $8.75 million to $37.5 million; France, from $37 million to $62.5 million (Figure 25.1 on page 995). The Germans announced the fleet buildup as "a peaceful policy," but, like the British buildup, it led only to a hostile international climate and intense competition in weapons manufacture.

c. 1890–1914

Public relations campaigns and internal politics were important to shaping military policy (see "An Historian Promotes Militant Nationalism" on page 996). When critics of the arms race suggested a temporary "naval holiday" to stop British and German building, British officials opposed the moratorium by warning that it "would throw innumerable men on the pavement." Colonial leagues of those pushing for imperial expansion, nationalist organizations, and other patriotic groups lobbied for military spending, while enthusiasts in government publicized large navies as beneficial to international trade and domestic industry. To enlarge the German fleet, Tirpitz made sure the press connected naval buildup to the cause of national power and pride. The press accused Social Democrats, who wanted an equitable tax system more proportionate to wealth, of being unpatriotic. The Conservative Party in Great Britain, eager for more battleships, made popular the slogan "We want eight and we won't wait." The remarks of a French military leader typified the sentiments of the time, even among the public at large. When asked in 1912 about his predictions for war and peace, he responded enthusiastically, "We shall have war. I will make it. I will win it."

1914: War Erupts

June 28, 1914, began as an ordinary, even happy day not only for Freud's patient the Wolf-Man but also for the Austrian archduke Francis Ferdinand and his wife, Sophie, as they ended a state visit to Sarajevo in Bosnia. The archduke, in full military regalia, was riding in a motorcade to bid farewell to various officials when a group of young Serb nationalists threw bombs in an unsuccessful assassination attempt. The full danger did not register, and after a stop the archduke and his wife set out again. In the crowd was another nationalist, Gavrilo Princip, who for several weeks had traveled clandestinely to reach this destination, dreaming of reuniting his homeland of Bosnia-Herzegovina with Serbia and smuggling weapons with him to accomplish his end. The unprotected and unsuspecting Austrian couple became Princip's victims, as he shot both dead.

Some in the Habsburg government saw an opportunity to put down the Serbians once and for all. Evidence showed that Princip had received arms and information from Serbian officials, who directed a terrorist organization from within the government. Endorsing a quick defeat of Serbia, German statesmen and military leaders urged the Austrians to be unyielding and reiterated promises of support in case of war. The Austrians sent an ultimatum to the Serbian government, demanding public disavowals of terrorism, suppression of terrorist groups, and the participation of Austrian officials in an investigation of the crime. The ultimatum was severe. "You are setting Europe ablaze," the Russian foreign minister remarked of the Austrians' humiliating demands made on a sovereign state. Yet the Serbs were conciliatory, accepting all the terms except the presence of Austrian officials in the investigation. Kaiser William was pleased: "A great

Archduke Francis Ferdinand and His Wife in Sarajevo, June 1914
Archduke Francis Ferdinand, heir to the Austro-Hungarian monarchy, was a thorn in the side of many politicians because he did not want to favor Hungarian interests over other ethnic ones in his kingdom. His own family life was also unusual for royalty in those days in that his wife, Sophie, and he had married for love and did not like to be apart. Thus, the couple were traveling together to Bosnia in 1914 and were jointly assassinated—the immediate prelude to the outbreak of World War I. How was the assassination of the archduke and his wife related to the other factors that led to World War I? *Mary Evans Picture Library.*

MAPPING THE WEST Europe at the Outbreak of World War I, August 1914
All the powers expected a great, swift victory when war broke out. Sharing borders, many saw a chance to increase their territories; and as rivals for trade and empire, they were almost all convinced that war would bring them many advantages. But if European nations appeared well prepared and invincible at the start of the war, relatively few would survive the conflict intact. Where are the particular "hot spots" in Europe in which resentments and conflicting ambitions were centered?

moral success for Vienna! All reason for war is gone." His relief proved unfounded. Austria-Hungary, confident of German backing, used the Serbs' resistance to only one of the ultimatum's terms as the pretext for declaring war against Serbia on July 28.

Complex and ineffectual maneuvering now consumed statesmen, some of whom tried very

hard to avoid war. The tsar and the kaiser sent pleading letters to one another not to start a European war. The British foreign secretary proposed an all-European conference, but to no avail. Germany displayed firm support for Austria in hopes of convincing the French and British to shy away from the war. The failure of either to fight, German officials believed, would subsequently keep Russia from mobilizing. Additionally, German military leaders had become fixed on fighting a short, preemptive war that would provide territorial gains leading toward the goal of a Mitteleuropa; imposing martial law as part of such a war would justify arresting the leadership of the German Social Democratic Party, which threatened conservative rule.

The European press caught the war fever of the expansionist, imperialist, and other pro-war organizations, even as many governments were torn over what to do. Likewise, military leaders, especially in Germany and Austria-Hungary, promoted mobilization rather than diplomacy in the last days of July. The Austrians declared war and then ordered mobilization on July 31 without fear of a Russian attack. They did so in full confidence of German military aid, because as early as 1909 the German chief of staff Helmuth von Moltke had promised that his government would defend Austria-Hungary, believing Russia would not dare intervene. But Nicholas II ordered the Russian army to mobilize in defense of Russia's Slavic allies the Serbs. Encouraging the Austrians to attack Serbia, the German general staff mobilized on August 1. France declared war by virtue of its agreement to aid its ally Russia, and when Germany violated Belgian neutrality on its way to invade France, Britain entered the war on the side of France and Russia.

> **Review:** What were the major factors leading to the outbreak of World War I?

Conclusion

Rulers soon forgot their last-minute hesitations in the general celebration that erupted with the war. "Old heroes have reemerged from the books of legends," wrote a Viennese actor after watching the troops march off. "A mighty wonder has taken place, we have become *young*." Both sides exulted, believing in certain victory. A short conflict, people maintained, would resolve tensions ranging from the rise of the working class to political problems caused by global imperial competition. Disturbances in private life and challenges to established certainties in ideas would disappear, it was believed, in the

crucible of war. German military men saw war as an opportune moment to round up social democrats and reestablish the traditional deference of an agrarian society. Liberal government based on rights and constitutions, some believed, had simply gone too far in its production of new groups aspiring to full citizenship and political autonomy.

Even as modernity seemed to be an enemy, it had also given rise to the new technology, mass armies, and techniques of persuasion to support military buildup that moved the elites to embrace war. The arms race had stimulated militant nationalism and brought many Europeans to favor war over peace. Modernity had helped blaze the path to war: *The Rite of Spring*, the ballet that opened in Paris in 1913, had taken as its theme the ritualistic attraction of death. Facing continuing violence in politics, incomprehensibility in the arts, and problems in the industrial order, Europeans had come to believe that war would save them from the perils of modernity. The sense of decline and the worry over imperial tensions that so characterized the years before 1914 would end once and for all. "Like men longing for a thunderstorm to relieve them of the summer's sultriness," wrote one Austrian official, "so the generation of 1914 believed in the relief that war might bring." Such a possibility caused Europeans to rejoice. But tragically, their elation was short-lived. Instead of bringing the refreshment of summer rain, war opened an era of political turmoil, widespread suffering, massive human slaughter, and even greater doses of modernity.

Suggested References

Private Life in the Modern Age

Historians are engaged in serious study of the transformations of everyday life brought about by industrial and imperial advance in the early twentieth century. Women's striving for personal autonomy was expressed in dozens of novels about the "new woman," including the famous *Keys to Happiness*, now available in an English translation.

Duberman, Martin, Martha Vicinus, and George Chauncey Jr. *Hidden from History: Reclaiming the Gay and Lesbian Past.* 1989.

Gillis, John. *A World of Their Own Making: Myth, Ritual, and the Quest for Family Values.* 1996.

Roberts, Mary Louise. *Disruptive Acts: The New Woman in Fin-de-Siècle France.* 2002.

*Verbitskaya, Anastasia. *The Keys to Happiness.* 1908–1913 [trans. by Beth Holmgren and Helen Goscilo, 1999].

Walkowitz, Judith. *City of Dreadful Delight: Narratives of Sexual Danger in Late-Victorian London.* 1993.

Modernity and the Revolt in Ideas

Some of the most controversial historical writing sees the road to World War I as paved with cultural conflict. Many of the studies here suggest that new forms of art, music, dance, and philosophy were as central to the challenges Europe faced as were ethnic, economic, and international turmoil. The Web offers good cultural sites for this important period.

Art nouveau: **http://www.nga.gov/feature/nouveau/nouveau.htm**.

Eksteins, Modris. *Rites of Spring: The Great War and the Birth of the Modern Age.* 1989.

Everdell, William R. *The First Moderns: Profiles in the Origins of Twentieth-Century Thought.* 1997.

Kern, Stepen. *The Culture of Space and Time, 1880–1918.* 1983.

*Mann, Thomas. *Buddenbrooks.* 1901.

Nineteenth- and twentieth-century philosophy: **http://www.epistemelinks.com/index.asp**.

Safranski, Rüdiger. *Nietzsche: A Philosophical Biography.* 2002.

Staller, Natasha. *A Sum of Destructions: Picasso's Cultures and the Creation of Cubism.* 2001.

Growing Tensions in Mass Politics

Historians are uncovering the dramatic changes in political life and the rise of mass politics across Europe, including the development of suffragist movements. Rose shows that mass education gave the working class a foundation in the works of Shakespeare and other classical writers. Still another major phenomenon was a spreading political hatred and the rise of aggressive nationalism to replace nationalism based on constitutional values.

Burns, Michael. *Dreyfus: A Family Affair.* 1992.

Chickering, Roger. *We Men Who Feel Most German: A Cultural Study of the Pan-German League, 1886–1914.* 1984.

Dennis, David B. *Beethoven in German Politics, 1870–1989.* 1996.

Kent, Susan. *Gender and Power in Britain, 1640–1990.* 1999.

Kornberg, Jacques. *Theodor Herzl: From Assimilation to Zionism.* 1993.

* Primary source.

Lendavi, Paul. *The Hungarians: A Thousand Years of Victory in Defeat.* 2003.

Rose, Jonathan. *Intellectual Life of the British Working Class.* 2001.

European Imperialism Contested

In the midst of raucous political and social debate, the European powers faced growing resistance to their domination and increasingly serious setbacks. Many historians now judge Europe to have played a less commanding role in the rest of the world than the leading empires claimed. Imperial instability, as some studies show, paved the road to war. The fascination with the major non-Western contender—Japan—can be traced on the Japanese history Web site.

Japanese history: **http://www.csuohio.edu/history/japan/index.html**.

Gooch, John, ed. *The Boer War: Direction, Experiences, Image.* 2000.

Kansu, Aykut. *The Revolution of 1908 in Turkey.* 1997.

*Pruitt, Ida. *A Daughter of Han: The Autobiography of a Chinese Working Woman.* 1945.

Sinha, Mrinalini. *Colonial Masculinity: The "Manly Englishman" and the "Effeminate Bengali" in the Late Nineteenth Century.* 1995.

Weeks, Theodore R. *Nation and State in Late Imperial Russia: Nationalism and Russification on the Western Frontier.* 1996.

Roads to War

Why World War I broke out remains a widely debated topic. There are always newcomers to the discussion devoted to assessing the responsibility for the war's beginning, some fixing on a single country and others investigating the full range of diplomatic, military, social, and economic conditions. Trenches on the Web looks at military conditions before war erupted.

Ascher, Abraham. *The Revolution of 1905: Russia in Disarray.* 1988.

Clark, Christopher. *William II.* 2000.

Hermann, David G. *The Arming of Europe and the Making of the First World War.* 1996.

Hobson, Rolf. *Imperialism at Sea: Naval Strategic Thought, the Ideology of Sea Power, and the Tirpitz Plan, 1875–1914.* 2002.

Manning, Roberta. *The Crisis of the Old Order in Russia.* 1982.

Trenches on the Web: **http://www.trenchesontheweb.com**.

Williamson, Samuel. *Austria-Hungary and the Origins of the First World War.* 1991.

CHAPTER REVIEW

IMPORTANT EVENTS

1894–1895	Japan defeats China in the Sino-Japanese War
1894–1899	Dreyfus Affair lays bare anti-Semitism in France
1899–1902	Boer War fought between Dutch descendants and the British in South African states
1900	Sigmund Freud publishes *The Interpretation of Dreams*
1901	Irish National Theater established by Maud Gonne and William Butler Yeats; death of Queen Victoria
1903	Emmeline Pankhurst founds the Women's Social and Political Union to fight for women's suffrage in Great Britain
1904–1905	Japan defeats Russia in the Russo-Japanese War
1905	Revolution erupts in Russia; violence forces Nicholas II to establish an elected body, the Duma; Albert Einstein publishes his paper titled "Special Theory of Relativity"
1906	Women receive the vote in Finland
1907	Pablo Picasso launches cubist painting with *Les Demoiselles d'Avignon*
1908	Young Turks revolt against rule by the sultan in the Ottoman Empire
1911–1912	Revolutionaries overthrow the Qing dynasty and declare China a republic
1914	Assassination of the Austrian archduke Francis Ferdinand and his wife by a Serbian nationalist precipitates World War I

KEY TERMS

art nouveau (974)

Boer War (985)

Duma (989)

Entente Cordiale (993)

Mitteleuropa (993)

modernism (970)

new woman (965)

psychoanalysis (967)

suffragists (977)

Zionism (984)

REVIEW QUESTIONS

1. How did ideas about the self and about personal life change at the turn of the century?
2. How did modernism transform the arts and the world of ideas?
3. What were the points of tension in European political life at the turn of the century?
4. Why did events in overseas empires from the 1890s on prove discouraging to many Europeans back home?
5. What were the major factors leading to the outbreak of World War I?

MAKING CONNECTIONS

1. How did changes in society at the turn of the century affect the development of mass politics?
2. How was culture connected to the world of politics in the years 1890–1914?

FOR FURTHER EXPLORATION

To assess your mastery of the material in this chapter, see the Online Study Guide at **bedfordstmartins.com/hunt**.

To read additional primary-source material from this period, see Chapter 25 in *Sources of The Making of the West*, Second Edition.

War, Revolution, and Reconstruction, 1914–1929

JULES AMAR FOUND HIS TRUE VOCATION in World War I. A French expert on improving the efficiency of industrial work, Amar switched his focus after 1914 as hundreds of thousands of men returned from the battlefront missing body parts. Plastic surgery developed rapidly, as did the construction of masks and other devices to hide deformities. But Amar, who devised artificial limbs and appendages in these traumatic years, sought to create prostheses that would allow the wounded soldier to return to normal life by "mak[ing] up for a function lost, or greatly reduced." So he designed arms that featured hooks, magnets, and other mechanisms with which the veteran could hold a cigarette, play a violin, and, most important, work with tools such as typewriters. Mangled by the weapons of modern technological warfare, the survivors of World War I would be made whole, it was thought, by technology such as Amar's.

Amar dealt with the human tragedy of the "Great War," so named by contemporaries because of its staggering human toll—forty million wounded or killed in battle. The Great War was also what historians call a **total war**, meaning one built on full mobilization of soldiers, civilians, and the technological capacities of the nations involved. The Great War did not settle problems or restore social order as the European powers hoped it would. Instead, the war produced political cataclysm, overturning the Russian, German, Ottoman, and Austro-Hungarian empires. The crushing burden of war on the European powers accelerated the rise of the United States, while service in the war intensified the demands of colonized peoples for autonomy.

Grieving Parents
Before World War I the German artist Käthe Kollwitz gained her artistic reputation with woodcuts of handloom weavers whose livelihoods were threatened by industrialization. From 1914 on, she depicted the suffering and death that swirled around her and never with more sober force than in these two monuments to her son Peter, who had died on the western front in the first months of battle. Today one can still travel to his burial place in Vladslo, Belgium, to see this father and mother mourning their loss, like millions across Europe in those heartbreaking days. *The John Parker Picture Library. © 2005 Artists Rights Society (ARS), New York/VG Bild-Kunst, Bonn.*

For all the vast changes that the Great War ushered in, it also hastened transformations under way before it started. Nineteenth-century optimism, already tinged with a sense of decline, gave way to a more pervasive postwar cynicism. Many Westerners turned their backs on politics and attacked life with frenzied gaiety in the Roaring Twenties, snapping up new consumer goods, drinking in entertainment provided by films and radio, and enjoying personal freedoms that Victorianism had forbidden. Others found reason for hope in the new political systems the war made possible: Soviet communism and Italian fascism. Modern communication technologies such as radio gave politicians the means to promote a utopian mass politics that paradoxically was antidemocratic, militaristic, and eventually dictatorial. Already weakening during the prewar period, the gentlemanly political tone of William Gladstone's day had been devastated by total war.

Seen as a solution to the conflicts of modernity, a war that was long anticipated and even welcomed in some quarters destabilized Europe and the world far into the next decades. From statesmen to ordinary citizens, many Europeans like Amar would spend their best peacetime efforts to make war-ravaged society function normally, while others saw that task as utterly futile, given the globally transformative force of the Great War. During the 1920s, bitterness continued to haunt everyday life, while many simultaneously believed that peacetime would usher in a better society.

❖ The Great War, 1914–1918

When war erupted in August 1914, the ground had been prepared with long-standing alliances, the development of strategies for war, and the buildup of military technologies such as heavy artillery, machine guns, and the airplane. Seeing precedents in Prussia's rapid victories in the 1860s and 1870 and the swift blows that Japan dealt Russia in 1904–1905, most people felt that this would be a short, decisive conflict. But the unforeseen happened: this war would last for more than four years, and it would be a total war, mobilizing entire societies and producing the unprecedented horror that made World War I "great."

Blueprints for War

World War I pitted two sets of opponents formed roughly out of the alliances developed during the previous fifty years. On one side stood the Central Powers (Austria-Hungary and Germany), which had evolved from Bismarck's Triple Alliance, and on the other the Allies (France, Great Britain, and Russia), which had emerged as a bloc from the Entente Cordiale between France and Great Britain and the 1890s treaties between France and Russia. In 1915, Italy, originally part of the Triple Alliance, joined the Allies in hopes of postwar gain. The two sides expanded globally almost from the start: in late August 1914, Japan, eager to extend its empire into China, went over to the Allies,

◆ **1913–1915** Suffrage for women expands in Europe

◆ **1916** Easter Uprising in Ireland

◆ **1917 March** Russian Revolution
April United States enters World War I
November Bolshevik Revolution

1912	1915	1918

◆ **1918 November** World War I armistice

◆ **1919** Weimar Republic begins

◆ **1918–1922** Civil war in Russia

◆ **1914 August** World War I begins

◆ **1919–1920** Paris Peace Conference

while in the fall the Ottoman Empire united with the Central Powers against its traditional enemy, Russia (Map 26.1).

The antagonists fought with the same ferocious hunger for power, prestige, and prosperity that had inspired imperialism. Of the Central Powers, Germany aspired to a far-flung empire to be gained by annexing Russian territory and incorporating parts of Belgium, France, and Luxembourg. Some German leaders wanted to annex Austria-Hungary as well. Austria-Hungary hoped to retain its great-power status in the face of competing nationalisms within its borders. Among the Allies, Russia wanted to reassert its status as a great power and as the protector of the Slavs by adding a reunified Poland to the Russian Empire and by taking formal leadership of other Slavic peoples. The French, too, craved territory, especially the return of Alsace and Lorraine, taken from them after the Franco-Prussian War of 1870–1871, to secure its boundaries with Germany. The British sought to cement their hold on Egypt and the Suez Canal, as well as to secure the rest of their world empire. By the Treaty of London (1915), France and Britain promised Italy territory in Africa, Asia Minor, the Balkans, and elsewhere in return for joining the Allies.

The colonies provided massive assistance and were also a battleground. Some one million Africans, another one million Indians, and more than a million members of the British commonwealth countries served on the battlefronts, while the imperial powers also conscripted still uncounted numbers of colonists as forced laborers both at home and on the battlefront. For instance, a million Kenyans and Tanzanians alone are estimated to have been conscripted for portage and other menial labor in the battle for east Africa. Fighting occurred across north and sub-Saharan Africa, with colonial troops playing a major role. Reliant on Arab, African, and Indian troops, the British waged successful war on Turkey and Germany, menacing Germany's longtime interests by taking Baghdad in 1917 and also taking Palestine, Syria, and Mesopotamia. When the Russian Revolution broke out in 1917, the war moved into the Caucasus in a fight for the rich Baku oilfields, expanding the British theater of war. In sub-Saharan Africa, a vicious campaign for east Africa occurred over the course of the war, resulting not only in loss of life among the African troops used against one another on behalf of the imperialist powers but also among the civilian population whose resources were confiscated and villages burned. The Japanese seized German assets in China to enlarge their influence on the mainland permanently.

Unprecedented use of machinery also determined the course of war. In August 1914, machine guns and rifles, airplanes, battleships, submarines, and motorized transport—cars and railroads—were at the disposal of armies; new technologies like chlorine gas, tanks, and bombs would develop between 1914 and 1918. Countries differed, however, in their experience with and quantities of weapons of war. British generals who had fought fifteen years earlier in the Boer War (1899–1902) knew the destructive capacity of these weapons, while

◆ **1922** Ireland gains independence; Fascisits march on Rome under Mussolini; Eliot, *The Waste Land*; Joyce, *Ulysses*

| 1921 | 1924 | 1927 | 1930 |

◆ **1924** Lenin dies; Stalin and Trotsky contend for power

◆ **1924–1929** Economic prosperity and stability

◆ **1929 October** U.S. stock market crash

A French Regiment Leaves for the Front, August 1914
Bands played, crowds cheered, and bicyclists led the way as bayonet-equipped soldiers marched eagerly to war. The mood changed quickly as machine guns and poison chemicals brought the bravest men down. People in cities, working to provide munitions and supplies, soon felt the pinch of inflation and later many lacked food. Men returned permanently disabled, even mentally deranged from their experience. And as four major empires—Ottoman, Russian, Austro-Hungarian, and German—collapsed, the war's bright beginnings disappeared from memory. What accounts for people's high-spirited attitude as this most devastating of wars erupted? © *Collection Roger Viollet/Getty Images.*

the Germans were far more advanced in strategy and weaponry than either the Russians or the Austrians. The war itself became a lethal testing ground as both new and old weapons were used, often ineffectively. Nonetheless, officers on both sides believed in a **cult of the offensive**, in which continuous spirited attacks and high troop morale were thought to be decisive. Despite the availability of newer, more powerful war technology, an old-fashioned vision of war made many officers unwilling to abandon the more familiar sabers, lances, and bayonets. In the face of massive firepower, the cult of the offensive would cost millions of lives.

The Battlefronts

The first months of the war crushed hope of quick victory. All the major armies mobilized rapidly. The Germans were guided by

the **Schlieffen Plan**, named after its author, Alfred von Schlieffen, a former chief of the general staff. The plan essentially outlined a way to combat antagonists on two fronts by concentrating on one foe at a time. It called for a rapid and concentrated blow to the west against Russia's ally France, which would lead to that nation's defeat in six weeks, accompanied by a light holding action to the east. The western armies would

The Schlieffen Plan

then be deployed against Russia, which, it was believed, would mobilize far more slowly.

MAP 26.1 The Fronts of World War I, 1914–1918

Because the western front remained relatively stationary, devastation of land and resources was intense. All fronts, however, destroyed segments of Europe's hard-won industrial and agricultural capacity, while the immobile trenches increased military casualties whenever heavy artillery fire pounded them. Men engaged in trench warfare for so long developed an intense camaraderie based on their mutual suffering and deprivation.

The attack on France was to proceed through Belgium, whose neutrality was guaranteed by the European powers. German planners had not counted on the unexpected—resistance from Belgium and bad luck—and the other great powers were similarly unprepared for the unexpected—prolonged and devastating carnage with no hint of a victory in sight.

Indecisive Offensives: 1914–1915. The Belgian government rejected an ultimatum to allow the uncontested passage of the German

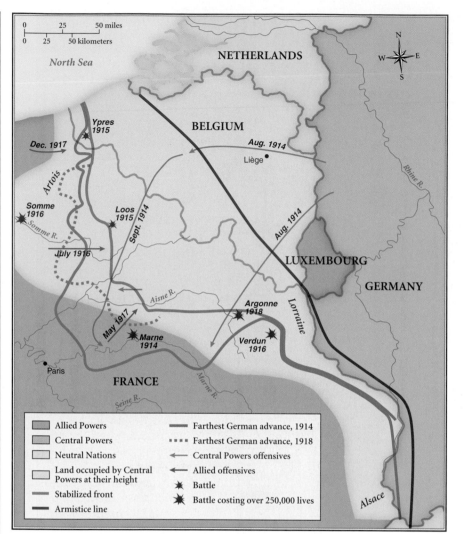

MAP 26.2 The Western Front

The western front occupied some of the richest parts of France, with long-lasting consequences. Destruction of French villages, roads, bridges, livestock, and property was the worst in Europe, while the trauma of the French people endured for generations. The effects of horrendous casualties, ever-present artillery fire, provisioning and hospital needs, and the demands of military and medical personnel changed everyone's way of life and made most people fear another war more than anything else. What different effects would trench warfare have on civilians and military personnel?

northern front. In September, the British and French armies engaged the Germans along the Marne River in France. Neither side could defeat the other, and casualties were shocking: in the first three months of war, more than 1.5 million men fell on the western front alone. Firepower with guns like the 75-millimeter howitzer that were accurate, mobile, and good at long range turned what was supposed to be an offensive war of movement into a stationary, defensive impasse along a line that stretched from the North Sea through Belgium and northern France to Switzerland (Map 26.2). Deep within parallel lines of trenches dug along this front, millions of soldiers lived in nightmarish homes.

On the eastern front, the "Russian steam-roller"—so named because of the number of men mobilized, some twelve million in all—drove far more quickly than expected into East Prussia on August 17. The Russians believed that no army could stand up to their massive numbers, no matter how ill equipped and poorly trained they were. Their success was short-lived. The Germans crushed the tsar's army in East Prussia and then turned south to Galicia.♦ Victory boosted German morale and made heroes of the military leaders Paul von Hindenburg (1847–1934) and Erich Ludendorff (1865–1937), who thereupon demanded more troops for the eastern front. Despite heartening victories, by year's end German triumphs in the east had failed to knock out the Russians and had also misdirected the Schlieffen Plan, which called for only light holding action to the east until the western front had been won.

army through the country. Thus at the beginning of August 1914, the Germans quickly reached Luxembourg and Belgium, but instead of allowing passage the Belgians offered spirited resistance. Meanwhile, the main body of French troops, tricked by German diversionary tactics, attacked the Germans in Alsace and Lorraine instead of meeting the invasion from the north. Belgian resistance slowed the German advance, allowing British and French troops to reach the

♦**Galicia:** guh LIH shee uh

War in the Skies (1914)
As the war started, modern artists saw aviators and the machines they piloted as symbols of a new age that offered humans the thrilling potential to transcend time and space. The Great War, however, featured the airplane as the new weapon in what British writer H.G. Wells called the "headlong sweep to death." Daring pilots or "aces" took the planes on reconnaissance flights, flew them over targets for bombing, and guided them in the experimental phenomenon of aerial combat, as shown in this engraving from an Italian newspaper of a French airplane shooting down a German one. Death now rained from the skies, and pilots themselves had as mixed an experience of war as did frontline soldiers. After destroying a German aircraft early in the war, one French ace announced his great joy. But later he described the experience as "horrible." And added "I remained traumatized for some time." *The Art Archive/Domenica del Corriere/Dagli Orti.*

War at sea proved equally indecisive. Confident in Britain's superior naval power, the Allies blockaded ports to prevent supplies from reaching Germany and Austria-Hungary. William II and his advisers planned a massive submarine, or U-boat (*Untersee-boot*, "underwater boat"), campaign against Allied and neutral shipping around Britain and France. In May 1915, German submarines sank the British passenger ship *Lusitania* and killed 1,198 people, including 124 Americans (Map 26.3 on the next page). Despite U.S. outrage, President Woodrow Wilson maintained a policy of neutrality; Germany, unwilling to provoke Wilson further, called off unrestricted submarine warfare. In May 1916, the navies of Germany and Britain finally clashed in the North Sea at the inconclusive battle of Jutland, which demonstrated that the German fleet could not master British seapower.

Ideas of a negotiated peace were discarded: "No peace before England is defeated and destroyed," the kaiser railed against his cousin King George V. "Only amidst the ruins of London will I forgive Georgy." French leadership called for a "war to the death." General staffs on both sides continued to prepare fierce attacks several times a year. Indecisive campaigns opened with heavy artillery pounding enemy trenches and gun emplacements. Troops then responded to the order to go "over the top" by scrambling out of their trenches and into battle, usually to be mowed down by machine-gun fire from defenders secure in their own trenches. On the western front, throughout 1915 the French assaulted the enemy in the north to drive the Germans from industrial regions, but they accomplished little, and casualties of 100,000 and more for a single campaign became commonplace. On the eastern front, Russian armies captured parts of Galicia in the spring of 1915 and lumbered toward Hungary. The Central Powers struck back in Poland later that year, bringing the front closer to Petrograd (formerly St. Petersburg), the Russian capital. The Austro-Hungarian armies routed the Serbs in 1915 and then engaged the newly mobilized Italian army.

Mounting Catastrophe: 1916. The next year was even more disastrous. To cripple French morale, the Germans launched massive assaults on the fortress at Verdun, firing as many as a million shells in a single day. Combined French and German losses totaled close to a million men. Nonetheless, the

MAP 26.3 The Russian Civil War, 1917–1922

Nationalists, aristocrats, middle-class citizens, and property-owning peasants tried to combine their interests to defeat the Bolsheviks, but they failed to create an effective political consensus. As fighting covered a broad swathe of the countryside, the result was more suffering for ordinary people, whose produce was confiscated to fight the civil war. The Western powers and Japan also sent in troops to put down this revolution that so threatened the economic and political order. How widespread was discontent with Bolshevism as expressed in the military attacks against the regime?

French held. Hoping to relieve their allies, the British unleashed an artillery pounding of German trenches in the Somme region in June 1916. In several months of battle at the Somme, 1.25 million men were killed or wounded, but the final result was stalemate. By the end of 1916, the French had absorbed more than 3.5 million casualties. To help the Allies engaged at Verdun and the Somme, the Russians struck again, driving once more into the Carpathians, recouping territory, and menacing the Habsburg Empire. Only the German army stopped the Russian advance. Amid huge losses, the Habsburg army recruited men in their mid-

fifties, and the German general staff decided it would take over Austrian military operations. The war was sapping Europe's strength and individual sovereignty.

The Soldiers' War. Had the military leaders thoroughly dominated the scene, historians judge, all armies would have been utterly demolished in nonstop offensives by the end of 1915. Yet ordinary soldiers in this war were not automatons in the face of what seemed to them suicidal orders. Some battalions went for long stretches with hardly a casualty, and these low rates stemmed from agreements among troops to avoid battles. Enemies facing each other across the trenches frequently ate their meals in peace, for example, even though the trenches were within hand-grenade reach. Throughout the war, soldiers fraternized on both fronts. They played an occasional game of soccer, shouted across the trenches, exchanged mementos, and made gestures of agreement not to fight. A British veteran of the trenches explained to a new recruit that the Germans "don't want to fight any more than we do, so there's a kind of understanding between us. Don't fire at us and we'll not fire at you." Burying enemy dead in common graves with their own fallen comrades, many ordinary soldiers came to feel more warmly toward enemies who shared the trench experience than toward civilians back home.

Newly forged bonds of male camaraderie alleviated some of the misery of trench life and aided survival. Sharing the danger of death and the deprivations of front-line experience weakened traditional class distinctions. In some cases, upper-class officers and working-class draftees became friends in that "wholly masculine way of life uncomplicated by women," as another British soldier put it. Soldiers picked lice from one another's bodies and clothes, revered section leaders who tended their blistered feet, and came to love one another, sometimes even passionately. Positive memories of this front-line community survived the war and influenced postwar politics.

Troops of colonized soldiers from Asia and Africa had different experiences, especially as they were often put in the very front ranks, where the risks were greatest. European observers noted that these soldiers suffered particularly from the rigors of a totally unfamiliar climate and strange food as well as from the ruin inflicted by Western war technology. Yet, as with class divisions, racial barriers sometimes fell, for instance, whenever a European understood enough to alleviate the distress that cold inflicted. Colonial troops' perspectives changed, too, as they saw their "masters" completely undone and "uncivilized." For when fighting did break out, trenches became a veritable hell of shelling and sniping, flying body parts, rotting cadavers, and blinding gas. Some soldiers became hysterical or succumbed to shell shock through the sheer stress and violence of battle. Alienation and cynicism rose: "It might be me tomorrow," a young British soldier wrote his mother in 1916. "Who cares?" Many had gone to war to escape ordinary life in industrial society; however, they learned, as one German put it, "that in the modern war . . . the triumph of the machine over the individual is carried to its most extreme form." They took this hard-won knowledge into battle, pulling their comrades back when an offensive seemed lost or too costly.

The Home Front

World War I took place off the battlefield too. Even before the war had reached the stage of catastrophic impasse, it had become total. Total war meant the indispensable involvement of civilians in the war industry: manufacturing the shells and machine guns, poisonous gases, bombs and airplanes, and eventually tanks that were the backbone of technological warfare. Increased production of coffins, canes, wheelchairs, and the artificial limbs devised by the likes of Jules Amar

was also a wartime necessity. Because soldiers would have utterly failed without them, civilians had to work overtime for, believe in, and sacrifice for victory. To keep the war machine operating smoothly, governments oversaw factories, transportation systems, and resources ranging from food to coal to textiles. Such tight government control would have outraged many liberals before the war but was now accepted as a necessary condition for victory.

Politics Suspended. Initially all political parties on both sides put aside their differences. Many socialists and working-class people who had formerly criticized the military buildup announced their support for the war. For decades socialist parties had preached that "the worker has no country" and that nationalism was mere ideology meant to keep workers disunited and subjected to the will of their employers. In August 1914, however, the socialist rank and file, along with most of the party leaders, became as patriotic as the rest of society. Feminists divided over whether to maintain their traditional condemnation of militarism or to support the war. Although many feminists actively opposed the conflict, the British suffrage leader Emmeline Pankhurst and her daughter Christabel were among the many activists who became militant nationalists, even changing the name of their suffrage paper to *Britannia*. Parties representing the middle classes shelved their distrust of the socialists and working classes. In the name of victory, national leaders wanted to end political division of all kinds: "I no longer recognize [political] parties," William II declared on August 4, 1914. "I recognize only Germans." The new political climate of unity was called the *Burgfriede*◆ ("domestic peace") in Germany and the *union sacrée*◆ ("sacred union") in France. Ordinary people, even those who had been at the receiving end of discrimination, came to believe that a new day of unity was dawning. One rabbi proudly echoed the kaiser: "In the German fatherland there are no longer any Christians and Jews, any believers and disbelievers, there are only Germans."

◆*Burgfriede:* burg FREE duh
◆*union sacrée:* oon yohn sah KREH

Governments Mobilize the People. Governments mobilized the home front with varying degrees of success. All countries were caught without ready replacements for their heavy losses of weapons and military equipment and soon felt the shortage of food and labor, too. War ministries set up boards to allocate labor on the home front and the battlefront and to give industrialists financial incentives to encourage productivity. In several countries, emergency measures allowed the drafting of both men and women for military or industrial service, further blurring dis-

tinctions between military and civilian life. But the Russian bureaucracy only reluctantly and ineffectively cooperated with industrialists and other groups that could aid the war effort. Desperate for factory workers, the Germans forced Belgian citizens to move to Germany, housing them in prison camps. In the face of rationing, municipal governments set up canteens and day-care centers. Rural Russia, Austria-Hungary, Bulgaria, and Serbia, where youths, women, and old men struggled to sustain farms, had no such relief programs.

Governments throughout Europe passed sedition laws that made it a crime to criticize official policies. To ensure civilian acceptance of longer working hours and shortages of consumer goods, governments created propaganda agencies to tout the war as a patriotic mission to resist villainous enemies (see the French propaganda poster on this page). British propagandists fabricated atrocities the German "Huns" supposedly committed against Belgians, and German propaganda warned that French African troops would rape German women if Germany was defeated. In Russia, Nicholas II changed the German-sounding name of St. Petersburg to the Russian Petrograd in 1914. Efforts were often clumsy: the British film *The Battle of the Somme* (1916) was so obviously sanitized of the war's horrors that soldiers in the audience roared with laughter, though civilians found it riveting. The Russians, hoping to ensure support of the many ethnicities in the empire, plastered Polish towns with posters promising national independence. It printed the Polish flag upside down, however, infuriating rather than attracting the Poles.

Playing on fears and arousing hatred, propaganda rendered a compromise peace unlikely. Nonetheless, some individuals sought to shatter the nationalist consensus supporting the war. In 1915, activists in the international women's movement met in The Hague, site of late-nineteenth-century peace conferences, in their own effort to end the war. "We can no longer endure . . . brute force as the only solution of international disputes," declared Dutch physician Aletta Jacobs. Despite their lack of success, many spent the remainder of the war urging statesmen to work out a peace settlement. In Austria-

War Propaganda, 1915
"Never Forget!" screams the headline of this French propaganda poster depicting an assaulted woman in despair. Intended to incite sentiment against the Germans, the poster suggested what German passage through neutral Belgium came to be called—the rape of Belgium. Propaganda offices for the Allies sent out reports of women attacked and children massacred as the German armies moved through Belgian territories. Why would propaganda experts use an image of a civilian woman instead of a male soldier to represent war's horrors? *Mary Evans Picture Library.*

Hungary, nationalist groups agitating for ethnic self-determination hampered the empire's war effort. The Czechs undertook a vigorous anti-Habsburg campaign at home, while exiled politicians in Paris established the Czechoslovak National Council to lobby Western governments for recognition of Czech rights. In the Balkans, Croats, Slovenes, and Serbs formed a committee to plan a South Slav state carved from Habsburg possessions and other Balkan territory. The Allies encouraged such independence movements as part of their strategy to defeat the Habsburgs.

The Civilians' War. The war upset the social order as well as the political one. In the war's early days many women had lost their jobs when luxury shops, textile factories, and other nonessential establishments closed. With men at the front, many women headed households with little support and few opportunities to work. But governments and businesses soon recognized the amount of labor it would take to wage technological war. As more and more men left for the trenches, women who had lost their jobs in nonessential businesses as well as many low-paid domestic workers took over higher-paying jobs in formerly restricted munitions and metallurgical industries. In Warsaw they drove trucks, and in London they conducted streetcars. Some young women drove ambulances and nursed the wounded near the front lines.

The press praised women's patriotism in adopted new roles, but women's assumption of men's jobs looked to many like social disorder. From the start, a steady flood of wounded and weak men returned home to women who had adapted resourcefully and taken full charge. Workingmen commonly protested that women, in the words of one metalworker, were "sending men to the slaughter." Men feared that when the war was over women would remain in the workforce, robbing men of the breadwinner role. Many people, even some women, objected to women's loss of femininity. "The feminine in me decreased more and more, and I did not know whether to be sad or glad about this," wrote one Russian nurse about adopting rough male clothing near the battlefield. But others criticized young female munitions workers for squandering their pay on

A Woman Munitions Worker in World War I, England (1917)
The transfer of tens of millions of men from the workforce to military service left a huge deficit of workers. Simultaneously, millions of women lost the support of a male wage, while they themselves were often laid off from jobs in the consumer sector that were deemed superfluous. Women thus had to work out of economic necessity during the war, and the military effort needed them in manufacturing jobs. These jobs paid salaries far beyond traditional women's jobs, which often brought accusations that extra money was making women frivolous and that their cravings were needlessly sending men to their deaths. By contrast, others applauded women's energy, patriotism, and sacrifice. Praise turned to dismay, however, when the armies began forming units of women; " 'She-Men,' who wished to be armed to the teeth," one aristocrat called them; and a letter to a London newspaper in 1915 called them "ridiculous" and insulting to the dignity of the nation. Why did gender issues remain highly debated even amid the crisis of war? ©*Hulton-Deutsch Collection / Corbis.*

ribbons and jewelry and echoed other prewar gender tensions.

Although many soldiers from different social backgrounds felt bonds of solidarity in the trenches, wartime conditions increasingly pitted civilians against one another or against the government. Workers toiled longer hours eating less, while many in the upper classes bought abundant food and fashionable clothing on the black market (outside the official system of rationing). Governments allowed many businesses high rates of profit, a step that resulted in a surge in the cost of living and thus contributed to social strife. Shortages of staples like bread, sugar, and meat grew worse across Europe, while the Germans called the brutal winter of 1916–1917 the turnip winter because turnips were often the only available food. A German roof workers' association pleaded for relief: "We can no longer go on. Our children are starving." Dredging up prewar hatred, some explained deprivation as the work of the Jews. Civilians in occupied areas and in the colonies suffered the most oppressive working conditions. The combatants deported or conscripted able-bodied people in territories they occupied. The French forcibly transported some 100,000 Vietnamese to work in France for the war effort. Africans also faced grueling forced labor along with skyrocketing taxes and prices, as the disruption of agriculture caused shortages. All such actions, like increasing class divisions, further politicized ordinary people whether in the colonies or at home in Europe.

Review: What factors contributed to making World War I a total war?

❖ Protest, Revolution, and War's End, 1917–1918

By 1917, the situation was becoming desperate for politicians, the military, and civilians alike, and discontent on the home front started shaping the course of the war. Neither patriotic slogans before the war nor propaganda during it had prepared people for wartime suffering. Cities across Europe experienced civilian revolt; soldiers mutinied, and nationalist struggles continued to plague Britain and Austria-Hungary. Soon revolution was sweeping Europe, toppling the Russian dynasty for good, and threatening the entire continent not just with war but with civil war.

War Protest

On February 1, 1917, the German government, hard-pressed by the public clamor over mounting casualties and by the military's growing control over decision making, resumed unrestricted submarine warfare.

The military made the irresistible promise to end the war in six months by cutting off imported food and military supplies to Britain and thus forcing the island nation to surrender before the United States could come to its rescue. The British responded by mining harbors and the seas and by developing the convoy system of shipping, in which a hundred or more warships and freighters traveling the seas together could drive off the submarines. The Germans' submarine gamble failed to defeat the British. Moreover, unrestricted submarine warfare brought the United States into the war in April 1917, after German U-boats had sunk several American ships.

Political opposition increased in Europe, and deteriorating living conditions sparked outright revolt by civilians. "We are living on a volcano," warned an Italian politician in the spring of 1917. High prices and food shortages plagued everyday life (Figure 26.1). Food shortages in cities of Italy, Russia, Germany, and Austria provoked riots by women who were unable to feed their families. As inflation mounted, tenants conducted rent strikes, factory hands and white-collar workers alike walked off the job, and female workers protested the skyrocketing cost of living and their fatigue from overwork. Amid protest, the new emperor of Austria-Hungary secretly asked the Allies for a negotiated peace to avoid a total collapse of his empire. In the summer of 1917, the German Reichstag made overtures for a "peace of understanding and permanent reconciliation of peoples." Woodrow Wilson further weakened civilian resolve in Germany and Austria-Hungary in January 1918 by issuing his Fourteen Points, a blueprint for a new international order that held out the promise of a nonvindictive peace settlement to war-weary citizens of the Central Powers. The Allies faced dissent too. In the spring of 1917, French soldiers mutinied against further bloody and fruitless offensives, and wartime protest in Russia turned into outright revolution.

Revolution in Russia

Of all the warring nations, Russia sustained the greatest number of casualties—7.5 million by 1917. Slaughter on the eastern front drove hundreds of thousands of peasants

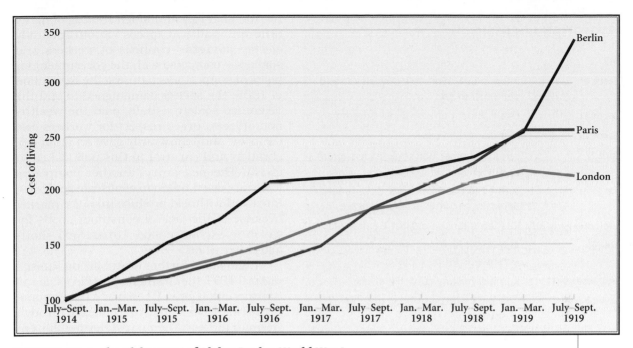

FIGURE 26.1 The Rising Cost of Living During World War I
The diversion of resources to the military resulted in a soaring cost of living for civilians. As men went to the front and as some remaining agricultural workers could find higher pay in factories, a decline in agricultural output led to scarcity and thus rising prices for food. Finally, housing came to be in short supply as resources were directed to the war effort rather than used to construct needed buildings. Even after the war, prices rose in Germany because the Allies maintained their blockade to keep the pressure on the peacemaking process. How was the pace of inflation connected to the course of the war itself? *Jay Winter and Jean-Louis Robert,* Capital Cities at War: Paris, London, Berlin, 1914–1919 *(Cambridge: Cambridge University Press, 1997), 259.*

into the Russian interior, bringing hunger, homelessness, and disease. In March 1917,* crowds of workingwomen swarmed the streets of Petrograd demanding relief from harsh conditions. As these women were turned away from stores, they fell in with other protesters commemorating International Women's Day and began looting shops for food. Factory workers and other civilians joined them. Russia's comparative economic underdevelopment overwhelmed the government's ability to provide basic necessities on the home front.

---

*Until February 1918, Russia remained on the Julian calendar, which was thirteen days behind the Gregorian calendar used by the rest of Europe. Hence, the first phase of the revolution occurred in March according to the Gregorian calendar (but February in the Julian calendar), the later phase in November using the Gregorian calendar (October according to the Julian). All dates used in this book follow the Gregorian calendar.

Many in the army, instead of remaining loyal to the tsar, were embittered by the massive casualties caused by their inferior weapons and their leaders' foolhardy tactics.

Since the Revolution of 1905 the masses had become politicized, leading to rising protest against the government's incompetence and Nicholas II's stubborn resistance to change. Unlike other heads of state, Nicholas failed to unify the bureaucracy and his peoples in a concerted wartime effort. Grigori Rasputin, a combination of holy man and charlatan, held Nicholas and his wife, Alexandra, in his thrall by claiming to control the hemophilia of their son and heir. Rasputin's disastrous influence on state matters led educated and influential leaders to withdraw their support. "Is this stupidity or treason?" one member of the Duma asked of the corrupt, impotent wartime administration. When the riots erupted in

REVOLUTION IN RUSSIA

1917

March 8	International Women's Day, strikes and demonstrations
March 12	Establishment of Provisional Government
March 15	Nicholas II abdicates
April 17	Lenin and other Bolshevik leaders return to Russia
May	Turmoil in the Provisional Government; Kerensky becomes a leading figure
Late June–early July	Russian offensive against Germany fails
Mid-July	Attempted popular uprising fails; Kerensky is Prime Minister
September 9–14	Kornilov military coup d'état fails
November 6–7	Bolshevik seizure of power on behalf of soviets
November 25	Constituent assembly elections held
1918	
January 18	Constituent assembly closed down by Bolsheviks
1918–1922	Civil war
1924	Union of Soviet Socialist Republics formally established; death of Lenin
1928–1929	Stalin takes full power

March 1917, Nicholas for once saw the reality of the situation and knew it was hopeless. He abdicated, bringing the three-hundred-year-old Romanov dynasty to an abrupt end.

The Provisional Government. Politicians from the old Duma formed a new ruling entity called the **Provisional Government**. At first hopes were high that under the Provisional Government, as one revolutionary poet put it, "our false, filthy, boring, hideous life should become a just, pure, merry, and beautiful life." Composed essentially of moderate aristocrats and members of the middle class, the Provisional Government had to pursue the war successfully, manage internal affairs better, and set government on a firm constitutional footing to establish its credibility. However, it did not rule alone, as

the Russian Revolution felt the tug of many different political forces. Spontaneously elected **soviets**—councils of workers and soldiers—competed with the government for political support. Born during the Revolution of 1905, the soviets campaigned to end the deference society usually paid the wealthy and officers, urged respect for workers and the poor, and temporarily gave an air of celebration and carnival to this political cataclysm. The peasantry, another competing force for power, began to confiscate gentry estates and withheld produce from the market because of the lack of consumer goods for which to exchange food. Urban food shortages intensified.

In hopes of further destabilizing Russia, in April 1917 the Germans provided safe rail transportation for V. I. Lenin and other prominent Bolsheviks to return from exile through German territory. Lenin had devoted his entire existence to bringing about socialism through the force of his small band of Bolsheviks, and as a political exile he had no parliamentary experience. Upon his return to Petrograd, Lenin issued the April Theses, a radical document that called for Russia to withdraw from the war, for the soviets to seize power on behalf of workers and poor peasants, and for all private land to be nationalized. The Bolsheviks aimed to supplant the Provisional Government by challenging its legitimacy with the slogans "All power to the soviets" and "Peace, land, and bread."

Time was running out for the Provisional Government, which saw a battlefield victory as the only way to ensure its position. On July 1, the Russian army attacked the Austrians in Galicia but was defeated once again. The new prime minister, the Socialist Revolutionary Aleksandr Kerensky (1881–1970), used his commanding oratory to arouse patriotism, but he lacked the political skills needed to fashion an effective wartime government. In Petrograd, groups of workers, soldiers, and sailors—many of them Bolsheviks—agitated for the soviets to replace the Provisional Government. Instead of clamping down, the Provisional Government found itself once more dependent on the people when a military coup, led by General Lavr Kornilov, broke out. Depending on its sworn enemies, the Provisional Government had shown itself once again

Lenin Addressing the Second All-Russian Congress of Soviets
In the spring of 1917, the German government craftily let Lenin and other Bolsheviks travel from
their exile in Switzerland back to the scene of the unfolding revolution in Russia. A committed
revolutionary instead of a political reformer, Lenin used his oratory and skilled maneuvering to
convince many in the soviets to follow him in overthrowing the Provisional Government, taking
Russia out of the war, and implementing his brand of communism. What impression of Lenin
and his audience does this artist hope to convey? *Novosti (London).*

impotent, failing to enact reforms, summon
a constituent assembly to plan a new permanent government, or win the war. The army
had become, as one critic put it, "a huge crowd
of tired, poorly clad, poorly fed, embittered
men"—eager for radical change.

The Bolshevik Takeover. The **Bolshevik
Revolution** took place in November 1917.
Urged on by Lenin, the Bolshevik leadership
seized power on behalf of the soviets while simultaneously asserting its own right to form
a government. When in January 1918, elections
for a constituent assembly failed to give the
Bolsheviks a plurality, the party used troops
to disrupt the assembly and took over the

government by force. They seized town and
city administrations, closing down the zemstvos (local councils) and other institutions in
the countryside where opposition support was
keen (see "Outbreak of the Russian Revolution," page 1018). In the winter of 1918–1919,
the Bolshevik government, observing Marxist
doctrine, abolished private property, nationalizing factories in order to restore production, which had fallen off precipitously. The
Provisional Government had allowed both
men and women to vote in 1917; Russia was
thus the first great power to legalize universal suffrage—a hollow privilege once the Bolsheviks limited slates to candidates from the
Communist Party.

Outbreak of the Russian Revolution

It is only clear in retrospect when a full-fledged and sustainable revolution has broken out. Here an eighteen-year-old student describes what happened when news of the St. Petersburg revolt reached Moscow in the late winter of 1917. Crowds had already formed when the young man decided to see what was happening in the streets.

In the crowd were many students who explained that a revolution had begun in St. Petersburg. The news swept through them like a breeze and created an extraordinary atmosphere. People began to embrace and kiss; strangers became close friends; some wept for joy. In five to ten minutes people seemed reborn. A pretty girl came up to me and took me by the hand, as though we had known each other for ages. Then hand-in-hand, in a warm embrace, and without asking each other's name, we proceeded toward the Krutitskie barracks. . . .

The crowd grew bigger and bigger, and somewhere in the distance one could hear the well-known refrain of a revolutionary song. By this time it was so crowded that it was quite impossible to get to one side or the other. We continued to hold hands, as though we might get lost. Slowly, barely perceptibly, the human stream moved toward the Red Gates, where I knew there was another barracks. It was the same scene there, except that the soldiers were shouting loudly, waving and greeting us. We couldn't make out what they said. Near Pokrovka we ran into a group of police officers, but instead of greeting them with good-natured jokes, thousands of voices yelled fierce, threatening cries: "Pharaohs! Your time is up! Get away for your own good!" . . . We moved slowly and could see neither the front nor the back of the crowd, for the street was blocked solid. For the first time in my life I sensed that atmosphere of joy, when everyone you meet seems close to you, your flesh and blood, when people look at one another with eyes full of love. To call it mass hypnosis is not quite right, but the mood of the crowd was transmitted from one to another like conduction, like a spontaneous burst of laughter, joy, or anger.

The majority of the crowd consisted of people who that morning had been praying for the good health of the imperial family. Now they were shouting, "Down with the Tsar!" and not disguising their joyful contempt. My companion was a good example. She showered me with questions: Where are we going? Why are we marching? Why is there a revolution? How will we manage without a tsar? It seemed like a mere holiday to her—Sunday's carnival procession, complete with mass participation. Tomorrow—Monday—humdrum working life would begin again, just as usual. Without asking a question, as though talking to herself, she suddenly said: "How good it would be if there was another revolution tomorrow!" What could I say? Tomorrow? Probably tomorrow the police would arrest us. But today there was a festival on the streets.

Source: Eduard Dune, *Notes of a Red Guard.* Translated and edited by Dianne Koenker and S. A. Smith (Champaign, Illinois, 1993), 32,34.

The Bolsheviks asked Germany for peace and agreed to the Treaty of Brest-Litovsk◆ (March 1918), which placed vast regions of the old Russian Empire under German occupation. The treaty partially realized the German ideal of a central European region, or Mitteleuropa, under German control. Because the loss of millions of square miles put Petrograd at risk, the Bolsheviks relocated the capital to Moscow and formally adopted the name Communists (taken from Karl Marx's writings) to distinguish themselves from the socialists/social democrats who had voted for the disastrous war in the first place. Lenin agreed to the catastrophic terms of the treaty not only because he had promised to bring peace to Russia but also because he believed that the rest of Europe would soon rebel against war and overthrow the capitalist order.

◆**Brest-Litovsk:** BREHST lih TAWFSK

Civil War in Russia

Resistance to Bolshevik policies, especially those that nationalized private property, mushroomed into full-fledged civil war with the pro-Bolsheviks (the "Reds") pitted against an array of antirevolutionary forces (the "Whites") (see Map 26.3, page 1010). Among the Whites, the tsarist military leadership, composed of many landlords and supporters of aristocratic rule, took to the field whatever troops it could muster. Dispossessed businessmen and the liberal intelligentsia soon lent their support. Many non-Russian nationality groups—formerly incorporated into the empire through force, Russification (which suppressed non-Russian languages and culture), and other bureaucratic efforts—fought the Bolsheviks because they saw their chance for independence. Before World War I ended, Russia's former allies, notably the United States, Britain, France, and Japan, landed troops in the country both to block the Germans and to stop Bolshevism. To compete effectively with the Bolsheviks, however, the counterrevolutionary groups desperately needed a strong leader and unified goals. Instead, the groups competed with one another: the pro-tsarist forces, for example, alienated those aspiring to nation-state status, such as the Ukrainians, Estonians, and Lithuanians. Ultimately, without a common purpose or unified command, the opponents of revolution could not win.

The civil war shaped communism. Leon Trotsky (1879–1940), Bolshevik commissar of war, built a highly disciplined army by ending democratic procedures, such as the election of officers, that had originally attracted soldiers to Bolshevism. Lenin and Trotsky introduced the policy of war communism, whereby urban workers and troops moved through the countryside, brutally confiscating grain from the peasantry to feed the army and workforce. The Cheka (secret police) set up detention camps for political opponents and black marketers and often shot them without trial. The expansion of the size and strength of the Cheka and the Red Army—the latter eventually numbered five million men—accompanied the expansion of the bureaucracy, making the government more authoritarian and undermining the promise of Marxism that revolution would bring a "withering away" of the state.

As the Bolsheviks clamped down on opposition during the bloody civil war, they organized their supporters to foster revolutionary Marxism across Europe. In March 1919, they founded the Third International, also known as the Comintern (Communist International), for the explicit purpose of replacing the Second International with a centralized organization dedicated to preaching communism. By mid-1921, the Cheka had shored up Bolshevism in Russia and the Red Army had secured the Crimea, the Caucasus, and the Muslim borderlands in central Asia. When the Japanese withdrew from Siberia in 1922, the civil war ended in central and east Asia. The Bolsheviks were now in charge of a state as multinational as the old Russian Empire had been.

The Russian Revolution, as led by the Bolsheviks, promised bold experiments in social and political leadership. But although the revolution had turned out the inept Romanovs and the privileged aristocracy, civil war turned Russia into a battlefield where disease, hunger, and death prevailed. Moreover, the brutal way the Bolsheviks came to power—by crushing opposition of all stripes—ushered in a political style and direction far different from earlier socialist hopes.

Ending the War, 1918

Having pulled Russia out of World War I, the Bolsheviks left the rest of Europe's leaders confronting a new balance of forces. Facing war protest as well, these leaders were also left fearing that communism might lie in their future.

The Central Powers made one final attempt to smash through the Allied lines using a new offensive strategy. It consisted of concentrated forces piercing single points of the enemy's relatively thin defense lines and then wreaking havoc from the rear. The Central Powers had overwhelmed the Italian army at Caporetto in the fall of 1917 with these tactics. In the spring of 1918, a similar offensive on the all-important western front ground to a bloody halt within weeks. By then the British and French had started making limited but effective use of tanks supported by airplanes. Although the first tanks were cumbersome, their ability to withstand machine-gun fire made offensive attacks possible. In the summer of 1918, the Allies, now fortified by the Americans, pushed back the Germans all along the western front and headed toward Germany. The German armies, suffering more than two million casualties between spring and summer, rapidly disintegrated.

By October 1918, the desperate German command helped create a civilian government to take over from its own dictatorial rule of the home front. It thus hoodwinked inexperienced politicians to take responsibility for the defeat and to ask for peace. Deflecting blame from the military, generals proclaimed themselves still fully capable of winning the war. Weak-willed civilians, they claimed, had dealt the military a "stab in the back" that forced a surrender. Amid this blatant political deceit, naval officers called for a final sea battle, sparking mutiny against what the sailors saw as a suicide mission. The sailors' rebellion capped years of indignities at the hands of high-ranking officers whose champagne-filled diet contrasted with the sailors' increasingly meager fare of turnips and thin soup. The sailors' revolt spread to the workers, who demonstrated in Berlin, Munich, and other major cities. The uprisings provoked Social Democratic politicians to declare a German republic in an effort to prevent revolution. On November 9, 1918, Kaiser William II fled as the Central Powers collapsed on all fronts. Since the previous winter, Austria-Hungary had kept many combat divisions at home simply to maintain civil order. At the end of October, Czechs and Slovaks had declared an independent state, and the Croatian parliament simultaneously announced Croatia's independence.

Finally, on the morning of November 11, 1918, delegates from the two sides signed an armistice. The guns fell silent on the western front six hours later. In the course of four years, European civilization had been sorely tested, if not shattered. Conservative figures put the battlefield toll at a minimum of ten million deaths and thirty million wounded, incapacitated, or eventually to die of their wounds. In every European combatant country, industrial and agricultural production had plummeted, and much of the reduced output had been put to military use. Asia, Africa, and the Americas, which depended on European trade, also felt the painful impact of Europe's declining production. From 1918 to 1919, the weakened global population suffered an influenza epidemic that left as many as one-hundred million more dead.

Besides illness, hunger, and death, the war also provoked tremendous moral questioning. Soldiers returning home in 1918 and 1919 flooded the book market with their memoirs, trying to give meaning to their experiences. Some 2,500 war poets published in Britain alone. Whereas many had begun by emphasizing heroism and glory, others were cynical and bitter by war's end. They insisted the fighting had been absolutely meaningless. Total war had drained society of resources and population and had inadvertently sown the seeds of future catastrophes.

> **Review:** Why did people revolt during World War I, and what turned revolt into outright revolution in Russia?

❖ The Search for Peace in an Era of Revolution

Amid the quest for peace, revolutionary fervor swept the continent, especially in the former empires of Germany and Austria-Hungary. In Moscow, Lenin welcomed the emperors' downfall as a phase of world revolution that would usher in an age of working-class internationalism. Until 1921, the triumph of socialism seemed plausible; many of the newly independent peoples of eastern and central Europe fervently supported socialist principles. The revolutionary mood captured workers and peasants in Germany too. In contrast, many liberal and right-wing opponents hoped for a political order based on military authority of the kind they had relied on during the war. Faced with a volatile mix of revolution and counterrevolution, diplomats from around the world arrived in Paris in January 1919 to negotiate the terms of peace, though without fully recognizing the magnitude of the changes brought about by war.

Europe in Turmoil

Urban people and returning soldiers ignited the protest that swept Europe in 1918 and 1919. In January 1919, the red flag of socialist revolution flew from the city hall in Glasgow, Scotland, while in cities of the collapsing Austro-Hungarian Monarchy workers set up councils to direct factory production and to influence politics. Many soldiers did not disband at the armistice but formed volunteer armies, making Europe ripe not for parliamentary politics but for revolution by force. Germany was politically unstable, partly because of the shock of defeat. Independent socialist groups and workers' councils vied with the dominant Social Democrats for control of the government, and workers and veterans took to the streets to demand food and back pay. Whereas in 1848 revolutionaries had marched to city hall or the king's residence, these protesters took over newspapers and telegraph offices, thus controlling the flow of information. Some were inspired by one of the most radical socialist factions, the Spartacists, led by cofounders Karl Liebknecht♦ (1871–1919) and Rosa Luxemburg (1870–1919). Unlike Lenin, the two Spartacist leaders favored political uprisings that would give workers political experience and thus eliminate the need for an all-knowing party leadership. They argued for direct worker control of institutions, but they shared Lenin's dislike for parliamentary politics.

Social Democratic leader Friedrich Ebert (1871–1925), who headed the new German government, shunned revolution and backed the creation of a parliamentary republic to replace the kaiser's rule. Splitting with his former socialist allies, he called on the German army and the Freikorps♦—a roving paramilitary band of students, demobilized soldiers, and others—to suppress the workers' councils and demonstrators. He thus appeared to endorse the idea that political differences could be settled with violence. "The enthusiasm is marvelous," wrote one young soldier. "No mercy's shown. We shoot even the wounded. . . . We were much more humane against the French in the field." Members of

♦**Liebknecht:** LEEP knehkt
♦**Freikorps:** FRY kawr

the Freikorps hunted down Luxemburg and Liebknecht and murdered them.

Protest continued even as a constituent assembly meeting in the city of Weimar in February 1919 approved a constitution and founded a parliamentary republic called the **Weimar Republic**. This time the right rebelled, for the military leadership dreamed of a restored monarchy: "As I love Germany, so I hate the Republic," wrote one officer. Facing a military coup by Freikorps officers, Ebert called for a general strike that abruptly averted a takeover of the new republic by showing the clear lack of popular support for a military regime. In so doing, the Weimar Republic had set the dangerous precedent of relying on street violence, paramilitary groups, and protests to solve political problems.

Revolutionary activism surged and was smashed. In the late winter of 1919, leftists proclaimed soviet republics—governments led by workers' councils   in Bavaria and Hungary. These soon fell before the assault of the volunteer armies and troops. The Bolsheviks tried to establish a Marxist regime in Poland in the belief that its people wanted a workers' revolution. Instead, the Poles resisted and drove the Red Army back in 1920, while the Allied powers rushed supplies and advisers to Warsaw. Though this and other revolts failed, they provided further proof that total war had loosened political and social order.

The Paris Peace Conference, 1919–1920

As political turmoil engulfed peoples from Berlin to Moscow, a peace conference opened in Paris in January 1919. Visions of communism spreading westward haunted the assembled statesmen, but the desperation of millions of war-ravaged citizens, the status of Germany, and the reconstruction of a secure Europe topped their agenda. Leaders such as French premier Georges Clemenceau had to satisfy their angry citizens who demanded revenge or, at the very least, compensation for their suffering. France had lost 1.3 million people—almost an entire generation of young men—and more than a million buildings, six thousand bridges, and thousands of miles of railroad lines and roads. Great Britain's representative, Prime

Minister David Lloyd George, caught the mood of the British public by campaigning in 1918 with such slogans as "Hang the kaiser." Italians arrived on the scene demanding the territory promised to them in the 1915 Treaty of London. Meanwhile, U.S. president Woodrow Wilson, head of the new world power that had helped achieve the Allied victory, had his own agenda. His **Fourteen Points**, on which the truce had been based, were steeped in the language of freedom and called for open diplomacy, arms reduction, an "open-minded" settlement of colonial issues, and the self-determination of peoples.

The Fourteen Points did not represent the mood of all the victors, however. Allied propaganda had made the Germans seem like inhuman monsters, and many citizens demanded a harsh peace. Moreover, some military experts feared that Germany was using the armistice only to regroup for more warfare. Indeed, Germans widely refused to admit that their army had lost the war. Eager for army support, Ebert had given returning soldiers a rousing welcome: "As you return unconquered from the field of battle, I salute you." Thus, conservative leaders among Wilson's former allies campaigned to make him look naive and deluded. "Wilson bores me with his Fourteen Points," Clemenceau complained. "Why, the good Lord himself has only ten."

Nevertheless, Wilson's Fourteen Points appealed to European moderates and persuaded Germans that the settlement would not be vindictive. His commitment to *settlement* as opposed to *surrender* contained tough-minded stipulations, for Wilson wisely recognized that Germany was still the strongest state on the continent. He merely pushed for a treaty that balanced the strengths and interests of various European powers. Economists and other specialists accompanying Wilson to Paris agreed that, harshly dealt with and humiliated, Germany might soon become vengeful and chaotic—a lethal combination that could lead to the growth of unsavory political movements.

The Peace of Paris Treaties. After six months, the statesmen and their teams of experts produced the **Peace of Paris** (1919–1920), composed of a cluster of individual treaties (Map 26.4). These treaties shocked the countries that had to accept them, and in retrospect historians see how they destabilized eastern and east-central Europe (see "Contrasting Views," page 1024). The treaties separated Austria from Hungary, reduced Hungary by almost two-thirds of its inhabitants and three-quarters of its territory, broke up the Ottoman Empire, and treated Germany severely. They replaced the Habsburg Empire with a group of small, internally divided, and relatively weak states: Czechoslovakia, Poland, and the Kingdom of the Serbs, Croats, and Slovenes, soon renamed Yugoslavia. After a century and a half of partition, Poland was reconstructed from parts of Russia, Germany, and Austria-Hungary, with one-third of its population ethnically non-Polish. The statesmen in Paris also created a Polish Corridor that connected Poland to the Baltic Sea and separated East Prussia from the rest of Germany. Austria and Hungary were both left reeling at their loss of territory and resources, while many of the new states became rivals and were for the most part politically and economically weak.

The Treaty of Versailles with Germany was the centerpiece of the Peace of Paris, however. France recovered Alsace and Lorraine, and the victors would temporarily occupy the left, or western, bank of the Rhine and the coal-bearing Saar basin. Wilson accepted his allies' expectations that Germany would pay substantial reparations for civilian damage during the war. The specific amount was set in 1921 at the crushing sum of 132 billion gold marks. Germany also had to reduce its army, almost eliminate its navy, stop manufacturing offensive weapons, and deliver a large amount of free coal each year to Belgium and France. Furthermore, it was forbidden to have an air force and had to give up its colonies. The average German saw in these terms an unmerited humiliation that was compounded by Article 231 of the treaty, which described Germany's "responsibility" for damage "imposed . . . by the aggression of Germany and her allies." The outraged German people interpreted this as a **war guilt clause**, which blamed Germany for the war and allowed the victors to collect reparations from economically viable Germany rather than from decimated Austria. War guilt made Germany an outcast in the community of nations.

MAP 26.4 Europe and the Middle East after the Peace Settlements of 1919–1920
The political landscape of central, east, and east-central Europe changed dramatically as a result of the Russian Revolution and the Peace of Paris. The Ottoman, German, Russian, and Austro-Hungarian Empires were either broken up altogether into multiple small states or territorially reduced in size. The settlement left resentments among Germans and Hungarians and created a group of weak, struggling nations in the heartland of Europe. The victorious powers took over much of the oil-rich Middle East. Why is it significant that the postwar geopolitical changes were so concentrated in one section of Europe?

The League of Nations. Besides redrawing the map of Europe, the Peace of Paris set up an organization called the **League of Nations**, whose responsibility for maintaining peace—a principle called collective security—was to replace the divisive secrecy of prewar power politics. As part of Wilson's vision, the league would guide the world toward disarmament, arbitrate its members' disputes, and monitor labor conditions around the world. Returning to prewar isolationism, the U.S. Senate, in a humiliating defeat for the president, failed to ratify the peace settlement and refused to join the league. Moreover, both

CONTRASTING VIEWS

Arguing with the Victors

The end of World War I aroused hopes around the world. The conquered expected a fair-minded treaty based on Wilson's Fourteen Points, while a variety of other peoples saw in that same document the promise of "self-determination." In particular, men living under colonial domination, such as many in Africa and the Arab states, had taken part in the conflict because the Allies had promised new rights in return for fighting this bloody and destructive war. The emir Faisal had led troops to bring about freedom and Arab unity (Document 1). Like some representatives at the Pan-African Congress, even those Africans who had not fought saw peace-making as a process that should forge a better future. Many wanted full political rights and parliamentary representation if not outright independence (Document 2).

In Paris in 1919, representatives of the victorious powers were besieged by outsiders to Western government, each making a claim for special attention to their needs or for concrete action to realize the noble rhetoric of the Fourteen Points. Feminist-pacifists wanted to ensure the pacifist cause (Document 3), while a Polish representative articulated a concern that Jews had taken too many good jobs in the new Poland (Document 4). The proposals to the peacemakers produced few results.

1. CLAIMING INDEPENDENCE FOR THE MIDDLE EAST

Arabs had hotly debated whether to join with the Allied colonizers in World War I, but promises of independence won them over. Some Arabs argued for independence of individual areas in the Middle East and for resolutions to competing claims of the Arabs and of new Jewish settlers in the region. Emir Faisal, who had commanded Arab forces in the war, presented the pan-Arab ideal.

The aim of the Arab nationalist movement is to unite the Arabs eventually into one nation. . . .

I came to Europe on behalf of my father and the Arabs of Asia to say that they are expecting the powers at the Conference not to attach undue importance to superficial differences of condition among us and not to consider them only from the low ground of existing European material interests and supposed spheres of influence. They expect the powers to think of them as one potential people, jealous of their language and liberty, and they ask that no step be taken inconsistent with the prospect of an eventual union of these areas under one sovereign government.

Source: Stephen Bonsal, *Suitors and Suppliants: The Little Nations at Versailles* (Port Washington: Kennikat Press, 1969), 32–33.

2. THE VOICE OF PAN-AFRICANISTS

African and African American leaders believed it would be opportune for them to meet in a Pan-African Congress while the Paris Peace Conference was going on. For some time an idea of a single African people had been forming among leading black intellectuals, and Pan-African meetings had taken place from the late nineteenth century on. The demands were legion, but above all the congress, by mid-February 1919, had resolved to seek better treatment from the colonial powers.

Resolved

That the Allied and Associated Powers establish a code of law for the international protection of the natives of Africa. . . .

The Negroes of the world demand that hereafter the natives of Africa and the peoples of African descent be governed according to the following principles:

1. The land: the land and its natural resources shall be held in trust for the natives and at all times they shall have effective ownership of as much land as they can profitably develop. . . .

3. Labor: slavery and corporal punishment shall be abolished and forced labor except in punishment for crime. . . .

5. The state: the natives of Africa must have the right to participate in the government as fast as their development permits, in conformity with the principle that the government exists for the natives, and not the natives for the government.

Source: Quoted in W. E. B. Du Bois, *The World and Africa* (New York: International Publishers, 1946), 11–12.

3. PACIFISTS' GOALS FOR THE PEACE PROCESS

Pacifist women were angered that the peace conference would be held in Paris instead of in a noncombatant or neutral country. Situating it where wartime hatred was at a fevered pitch, they argued, would not allow the conquered to receive a fair hearing. The continuing blockade of the Central Powers after the armistice was increasing suffering and causing deaths. Themselves meeting in neutral Switzerland, pacifist women speeded the dispatch of their resolutions to Paris when the Treaty of Versailles was announced.

The International Congress of Women regards the famine, pestilence, and unemployment extending throughout great tracts of central and eastern Europe and into Asia as a disgrace to civilization.

It therefore urges the Governments of all the Powers assembled at the Peace Conference immediately to develop the inter-allied organizations formed for purposes of war into an international organization for purposes of peace, so that the resources of the world—food, raw materials, finance, transport—shall be made available for the relief of the peoples of all countries from famine and pestilence.

To this end it urges that immediate action be taken . . . to raise the blockade.

The terms of the peace tacitly sanction secret diplomacy, deny the principles of self-determination, recognize the rights of victors to the spoils of war, and create all over Europe discords and animosities, which can only lead to future war. . . . By the financial and economic proposals a hundred million people of this generation in the heart of Europe are condemned to poverty, disease, and despair, which must result in the spread of hatred and anarchy within each nation.

Source: James Weber Linn, *Jane Addams: A Biography* (New York: Greenwood, 1968), 342–43.

4. ANTI-SEMITISM AT THE PEACE TABLE

Some of the new nations of eastern Europe were using anti-Semitism to focus their unity and independence. A Polish leader lobbied the Allies to exercise a police power in the newly independent Poland, where major problems would be rural crowding and inability to make ends meet on the land.

We have too many Jews, and those who will be allowed to remain with us must change their habits. I recognize that this will be difficult and will take time. The Jew must produce and not remain devoted exclusively to what we regard as parasitical pursuits. Unless restrictions are imposed upon them soon, all our lawyers, doctors, and small merchants will be Jews. They must turn to agriculture, and they must at least share small business and retail stores with their Polish neighbors. I readily admit that there is some basis in the Jewish contention that in days past it was difficult for them to own land or even to work the fields of others as tenants; that they were often compelled by circumstances beyond their control to gain their livelihood in ways which are hurtful to Polish economy. Under our new constitution all this will be changed, and for their own good I hope the Jews will avail themselves of their new opportunities. I say this in their own interest as well as in the interest of restored Poland.

Source: Bonsal, *Suitors and Suppliants*, 124.

QUESTIONS TO CONSIDER

1. Describe the various contending claims beyond those of the official combatant powers. Did the victorious powers heed these voices when forging the peace?

2. How were the various demands at the peace conference related to the politics and conditions of World War I?

3. Do any of the demands seem more justifiable in addressing the peacetime needs of Europe and the world?

Germany and Russia initially were excluded from the league and were thus blocked from acting in legal concert with other nations.

The covenant, or charter, of the League of Nations organized the administration of the colonies and territories of Germany and the Ottoman Empire—such as Togo, Cameroon, Syria, and Palestine—through a system of mandates. The victorious powers exercised political control over mandated territory, but local leaders retained limited authority. The league covenant justified the **mandate system** as providing governance by "advanced nations" over territories "not yet able to stand by themselves under the strenuous conditions of the modern world." However, colonized people and other people of color, who had served and fallen on the battlefield, began to challenge the claims of their European masters. They had seen how savage and degraded were these people who claimed to be racially superior, politically advanced, and leaders of global culture. "Never again will the darker people of the world occupy just the place they had before," the African American leader W. E. B. Du Bois◆ predicted in 1918. The mandate system continued the practice of apportioning the globe among European powers at a time when those powers were bankrupt and weak. Like the Peace of Paris, it aroused anger and resistance.

Economic and Diplomatic Consequences of the Peace

The financial and political settlement in the Peace of Paris had repercussions in the 1920s and beyond. Western leaders worried deeply about two intertwined issues in the aftermath of the war. The first was economic recovery and its relationship to war debts, the restoration of European trade, and German reparations. The second was ensuring that peace lasted.

Economic Dilemmas. France, the hardest hit by wartime destruction and billions of dollars in debt to the United States, estimated that Germany owed it at least $200 billion. The British, by contrast, worried about maintaining their empire and restoring trade with Germany, not about exacting huge

◆**Du Bois:** doo BOYS

reparations. Nevertheless, both France and Britain depended on some monetary redress to pay their war debts to the United States because Europe's share of world trade had plunged during the war. Germany claimed that the demand for reparations strained its government, already beset by political upheaval. But hardship was not the result of the Peace of Paris alone. The kaiser had refused to raise taxes, especially on the rich, to

Inflation in Germany (1923)
The German government resisted paying reparations by inflating the currency and slowing down the shipments of manufactured goods that were a condition of the reparations program. French troops were sent into the Ruhr manufacturing region to take goods by force, but angry workers refused to work for the occupiers. To pay the workers and service its debt, the government printed money so rapidly that inflation brought the value of the German mark from 4.2 marks to the dollar to 4.2 trillion marks to the dollar, which destroyed savings and increased resentment in Germany. As children played with worthless marks, shown in this picture, a new administration came to power in the summer, promising to resolve the currency situation and to deal with the reparations issue with practical measures, rather than futile resistance. **For more help analyzing this image**, see the visual activity for this chapter in the Online Study Guide at **bedfordstmartins.com/hunt**. *AKG Images.*

pay for the war, so the new republic had to pay reparations and to manage the staggering war debt. As an experiment in democracy, the Weimar Republic needed to woo the citizenry, not alienate it by hiking taxes. In 1921, when Germans refused to present a realistic payment scheme, the French occupied several cities in the Ruhr until a settlement was reached.

Embroiled with powers to the west, the German government deftly sought economic and diplomatic relations in eastern Europe. It reached an agreement to foster economic ties with Russia, desperate for western trade, in the Treaty of Rapallo (1922). Its relations with powers to the west, however, continued to deteriorate. In 1923, after Germany defaulted on coal deliveries, the French and Belgians sent troops into the Ruhr basin, planning to use its abundant resources to recoup their wartime expenditures. Urged on by the government, Ruhr citizens fought back, shutting down industry by staying home from work. The German government printed trillions of marks to support the workers and to pay its own war debts with practically worthless currency. Soon Germany was in the midst of a staggering inflation that demoralized its citizens and gravely threatened the international economy: at one point a single U.S. dollar cost 4.42 trillion marks, and wheelbarrows of money were required to buy a turnip. The spirit of the League of Nations demanded a resolution to this economic chaos through negotiations. The Dawes Plan (1924) and eventually the Young Plan (1929) reduced payments to the victors and restored the value of German currency. Nonetheless, the inflation had wreaked enduring psychological havoc, wiped out people's savings, and ruined those living on fixed incomes (see the photo opposite).

Ensuring Peace. A second pressing issue in addition to economic recovery involved ensuring that peace would last. Statesmen recognized that peace demanded disarmament, a return of Germany to the fold, and security for the new countries of eastern Europe. It took hard diplomatic bargaining outside the league to produce two plans in Germany's favor. At the Washington Conference in 1921, the United States, Great Britain, Japan, France, and Italy agreed to reduce their number of battleships

and to stop constructing new ones for ten years. Four years later, in 1925, the league sponsored a meeting of the great powers, including Germany, at Locarno, Switzerland. The Treaty of Locarno provided Germany with a seat in the League of Nations as of 1926. In return, Germany agreed not to violate the borders of France and Belgium and to keep the nearby Rhineland demilitarized—that is, unfortified by troops.

To the east, the door seemed open to a German attempt to regain territory lost to Poland, to form a merger with Austria, or to launch aggression against the states spun off from Austria-Hungary. To meet the threat, Czechoslovakia, Yugoslavia, and Romania formed the Little Entente in 1920–1921. This was a collective security agreement to protect themselves from their two powerful neighbors, Germany and Russia, and to guard against Hungarian expansionism. Then, between 1924 and 1927, France allied itself with the Little Entente and with Poland. The major European powers, Japan, and the United States also

The Little Entente

signed the Kellogg-Briand Pact (1928), which formally rejected international violence. The nations failed, however, to commit themselves to concrete action to prevent its outbreak.

The publicity and planning that yielded the international agreements during the 1920s sharply contrasted with old-style diplomacy, which was conducted in secret and subject to little public scrutiny or democratic influence. The development of a system of collective security and the new openness suggested a diplomatic revolution that would promote peace in international relations. Despite this promise, openness allowed diplomats of the era to feed the press reports calculated to arouse the masses. For example, much of the German populace was lashed into a nationalist frenzy by the press and opposing parties whenever Germany's diplomats, who were successfully working to undo the Treaty of Versailles by reducing reparation payments, for example, seemed to compromise. Although international meetings such as the one at Locarno appeared to promote the goal of collective security, they also exposed the diplomatic process to the nationalist press and to demagogues who could rekindle political hatreds.

Review: What were the major outcomes of the postwar peacemaking process?

❖ A Decade of Recovery: Europe in the 1920s

The 1920s were devoted to coming to terms with the cultural and political legacy of the war. The wartime spirit endured in words and phrases from the battlefield that punctuated everyday speech. Before the war the word *lousy* had meant "lice-infested," but English-speaking soldiers returning from the trenches now applied it to anything bad. Raincoats became *trenchcoats*, and terms like *bombarded* and *rank and file* entered peacetime usage. Maimed, disfigured veterans were present everywhere, and while some gained prostheses designed by Jules Amar, others without limbs were sometimes carried in baskets—hence the expression *basket case.* The veterans overflowed hospitals and mental institutions, and family life centered on their care. Society had to restore civilian government after total

war had generally strengthened military values, authoritarian government, and a controlled economy. Although contemporaries referred to the 1920s as the Roaring Twenties or the Jazz Age, the sense of cultural release masked the serious problem of restoring social stability and implementing democracy. Four autocratic governments had collapsed as a result of the war, but how newly empowered citizens would act politically remained a burning question.

Changes in the Political Landscape

The threat of revolution coexisted with a sense of democratic rebirth across Europe because of the collapse of autocratic governments and the extension of suffrage to women, widely granted at the war's end. Woman suffrage resulted in part from decades of activism; more immediately, many governments gave women the vote to reward them for their war efforts and to make revolution less tempting. In the first postwar elections, women were voted into parliaments, and the impression grew that they had also made extraordinary gains in the workplace. French men pointedly denied women the vote, insisting they would use their vote to bring back the rule of kings and priests. (Only at the end of World War II would France and Italy extend suffrage to women.) Governments continued building the welfare state by expanding payments to veterans, families with children, and workers who were unemployed or injured. New government benefits attested to a belief that more evenly distributed wealth—sometimes referred to as economic democracy—was important to social stability in postwar society.

The slow trend toward economic democracy was not easy to maintain, however, because the cycles of boom and bust that had characterized the late nineteenth century reemerged. A short postwar economic boom prompted by rebuilding war-torn areas and filling consumer needs unsatisfied during the war was followed by an economic downturn that was most severe between 1920 and 1922. Skyrocketing unemployment led some to question the effectiveness of their governments and the fairness of society. By the mid-1920s, many of the economic

WOMEN GAIN SUFFRAGE IN THE WEST	
1906	Finland
1913	Norway
1915	Denmark, Iceland
1917	Netherlands, Russia
1918	Czechoslovakia, Great Britain (limited suffrage)
1919	Germany
1920	Austria, United States
1921	Poland
1925	Hungary (limited suffrage)
1945	Italy, France
1971	Switzerland

opportunities for women had disappeared and women made up a smaller percentage of the workforce than in 1913.

Eastern Europe.   Hard times especially corroded the new republics of eastern Europe, which were unprepared for independence in the sophisticated world market. None but Czechoslovakia had a mature industrial sector, and agricultural techniques were often primitive. The development of Poland exemplified the postwar political landscape in eastern Europe. Nationalism was increasingly defined in ethnic terms, and the reunified Poland consisted of one-third Ukrainians, Belorussians, Germans, and other ethnic minorities—many of whom had grievances against the dominant Poles. Moreover, varying religious, dynastic, and cultural traditions divided the Poles, who for 150 years had been split among Austria, Germany, and Russia. Polish reunification occurred without a common currency, political structure, or language—even the railroad tracks were not a standard size.

With virtually no economic or other support from the Allies, a constitutional government nonetheless took shape in this new Poland. Under a constitution that professed equal rights for all ethnicities and religions, the new democratic government, run by the Sejm (parliament), tried to legislate the redistribution of large estates to the peasantry, but declining crop prices and overpopulation made life in the countryside difficult. Urban workers were better off than the peasantry (two-thirds of the population lived by subsistence farming) but worse off than laborers across Europe. The economic downturn brought strikes and violence in 1922–1923, and the inability of coalition parliaments to effect economic prosperity led to a coup in 1926 by strongman Jozef Pilsudski.♦ Economic hardship and strong-arm solutions went hand in hand in east-central Europe.

Central Europe.   Germany was a different case. The industrially sophisticated Weimar Republic confronted daunting challenges as it tried to make Germany democratic, even after putting down the postwar revolution. Al-

though the German economy picked up and Germany became a center of experimentation in the arts, political life remained precarious because so many people felt nostalgia for imperial glory and loathed the Treaty of Versailles's restrictions. On the surface, Weimar's political system—a bicameral parliament and a chancellor responsible to the lower house—appeared similar to the parliamentary systems in Britain and France, but extremist politicians heaped daily abuse on parliamentary politics. A wealthy newspaper and film magnate deemed anyone who cooperated with the parliamentary system "a moral cripple." Right-wing parties favored violence rather than consensus building, and nationalist thugs murdered democratic leaders and Jews.

Support for the far right came from wealthy landowners and businessmen, white-collar workers whose standard of living had dropped during the war, and members of the lower-middle

National Minorities in Postwar Poland

and middle classes hurt by inflation. Bands of disaffected youth and veterans proliferated, among them a group called the Brown Shirts, led by ex-soldier and political newcomer Adolf Hitler (1889–1945). A riveting speaker, Hitler gradually became a favorite of antigovernment political groups that used him to collect donations from the enthusiastic crowds he drew. In the wake of the Ruhr occupation of 1923, German military hero Erich Ludendorff and Hitler launched a coup d'état—or ***putsch***♦ in German—from a beer hall in Munich. Government troops suppressed the Beer Hall Putsch, but Hitler spent less than a year in jail and Ludendorff was acquitted. For conservative judges as for former aristocrats and most of the prewar bureaucrats who remained in government, such men were national heroes.

♦**Pilsudski:** pihl SOOT skee

♦***putsch:*** pooch

Western Europe. In France and Britain, parties of the right had less effect than elsewhere because parliamentary institutions were better established and the upper classes were not plotting to restore an authoritarian monarchy. In France, politicians from the conservative right and moderate left successively formed coalitions and rallied general support to rebuild war-torn regions and to force Germany to pay for the reconstruction. Hoping to stimulate population growth after the devastating loss of life, the French parliament made the distribution of birth-control information illegal and abortion a severely punished crime.

Britain encountered postwar boom and bust and continuing strife in Ireland. Ramsay MacDonald (1866–1937), elected the first Labour prime minister in 1924, represented the political ambitions of the working masses. Like other postwar British leaders, he had to swallow the paradoxical fact that although Britain had the largest world empire, many of its industries were obsolete or in poor condition. A showdown came in the ailing coal industry, where prices fell and wages plummeted once the Ruhr mines reopened and offered tough competition to British mines. On May 3, 1926, workers launched a nine-day general strike against wage cuts and dangerous conditions in the mines. The strike provoked unprecedented middle-class resistance. University students, homemakers, and businessmen shut down the strike by driving trains, working on docks, and replacing workers in other jobs. Thus, citizens from many walks of life revived the wartime spirit to defend the declining economy.

In Ireland, the British government met bloody confrontation over the continuing failure to implement home rule. Irish republicans had attacked government buildings in Dublin on Easter Monday 1916 in an effort to wrest Irish independence from Britain. Ill-prepared, their effort was easily defeated and many of them were

The Irish Free State and Ulster, 1921

executed. The severe punishment only intensified demands for home rule, and in January 1919, republican leaders announced Ireland's independence from Britain and created a separate parliament. The British government refused to recognize the parliament and sent in the Black and Tans, a volunteer army of demobilized soldiers named after the color of their uniforms. Terror reigned in Ireland, as both the pro-independence forces and the Black and Tans waged guerrilla warfare, taking hostages, blowing up buildings, and even shooting into crowds at soccer matches. By 1921, public outrage forced the British to negotiate a treaty. It reversed the Irish declaration of independence and made the Irish Free State a self-governing dominion owing allegiance to the British crown. Northern Ireland, a group of six northern counties containing a majority of Protestants, gained a separate status: it was self-governing but still had representation in the British Parliament. Incomplete independence and the rights of religious minorities remained contentious issues.

The Colonies. European powers encountered rebellion in overseas empires as well. Colonized peoples who had fought in the war expected more rights and even independence. Indeed, European politicians and military recruiters had actually promised the vote and many other reforms in exchange for support. But colonists' political activism, now enhanced by increasing education, trade, and experience with the West, mostly met a brutal response. Fearful of losing India, British forces massacred protesters at Amritsar◆ in 1919 and put down revolts against the mandate system in Egypt and Iran in the early 1920s. The Dutch jailed political leaders in Indonesia; the French punished Indochinese nationalists. For many Western governments, maintaining empires abroad was crucial to ensuring democracy at home, as any hint of declining national prestige fed antidemocratic forces.

Despite resistance, the 1920s marked the high tide of imperialism and saw a fresh burst of imperialist activity. Britain and France, enjoying new access to Germany's colonies in Africa and to the spoils of the fallen Ottoman

---

◆**Amritsar:** uhm RIHT sur

Empire in the Middle East, were at the height of their global power. Although bankrupted and shell-shocked by the war, these countries along with Holland, Belgium, Japan, and Australia took advantage of the growing profitability that enterprises around the world could bring. Middle Eastern and Indonesian oil, for instance, fueled the growing number of automobiles, airplanes, trucks, ships, and buses and heated homes. Products like hot chocolate and tropical fruit became regular items in the diet.

The balance of power among the imperial nations was changing, however. The most important change was the real competition for markets, resources, and influence with Japan. During the war, Japanese industrialization altered dramatically from the production of textiles to heavy industrial output such as shipbuilding and metallurgy. Japan's industrial development advanced because the Western powers outsourced their wartime needs for industrial goods. As Japan took shipping, financial, and other business from Britain and France, its prosperity skyrocketed and Japan began edging Britain out as the dominant power in China. The Japanese government touted its success across the region and pointed to its achievements as a sign of hope for non-Westerners. Japan's prosperity, the country's politicians claimed, would pull its neighbors from Western oppression. Strongly nationalist, the government was nonetheless accommodating toward the Western powers because it could not yet afford to compete militarily. Thus, although outraged that the Western powers at Paris had refused a nondiscrimination clause in the charter of the League of Nations, the Japanese government cooperated in the Anglo-American dominated peace, even agreeing to the settlement at the naval conference in Washington that set the ratio of English, American, and Japanese shipbuilding at 5:5:3. "Rolls Royce, Rolls Royce, Ford," a Japanese official commented bitterly.

Reconstructing the Economy

New worldwide economic competition was as big a challenge to recovery as were global political struggles. During the war the European economy had lost many of its international markets to India, Canada, Australia, Japan, and the United States. Nonetheless, the war had forced many European manufacturers to become more efficient and had expanded the demand for automotive and air transport, electrical products, and synthetic goods. The prewar pattern of mergers and cartels continued after 1918, giving rise to gigantic food-processing firms such as Nestlé in Switzerland and petroleum enterprises such as Royal Dutch Shell. Owners of these large manufacturing conglomerates wielded more financial and political power than entire small countries. By the late 1920s, Europe had overcome the wild economic swings of the immediate postwar years and was enjoying renewed economic prosperity.

Despite this growth, the United States had become the trendsetter in economic modernization. European businessmen made pilgrimages to Henry Ford's Detroit assembly line, which by 1929 produced a Ford automobile every ten seconds. Ford touted this miracle of productivity as resulting in a lower cost of living and increased purchasing power for workers. Indeed, whereas French, German, and British citizens in total had fewer than two million cars, some seventeen million cars were on U.S. streets in 1925.

Scientific management, sometimes called the science of work, also aimed to raise productivity. American efficiency expert Frederick Taylor (1856–1915) developed methods to streamline workers' tasks and motions for maximum productivity. European industrialists adopted Taylor's methods during the war and after, but they were also influenced by European psychologists who emphasized the mental aspects of productivity and the need for a balance of work and leisure activities, such as cinema and sports, for both workers and managers. In theory, increased productivity not only produced prosperity for all but also aimed to bind workers and management together, avoiding Russian-style worker revolution. In practice, streamlining did help reduce working hours in many industries, a result that encouraged union leaders to embrace modernization and the "cult of efficiency." For many workers, however, the emphasis on efficiency seemed inhuman, with restrictions on time and motion so severe that often they were allowed to use the bathroom only on a fixed schedule. "When I left the factory, it followed me," wrote one worker. "In my dreams I was a machine."

The managerial sector in industry had expanded during the war and continued to do so thereafter. Workers' initiative became devalued, with managers alone seen as creative and innovative. Managers reorganized work procedures and classified workers' skills. They categorized "female" jobs as those requiring less skill and therefore deserving of lower wages, thus adapting the old segmentation of the labor market to the new working conditions. With male workers' jobs increasingly threatened by labor-saving machinery, unions usually agreed that women should receive lower wages to keep them from competing with men for scarce high-paying jobs. Like the managerial sector, union bureaucracy had ballooned during World War I to help monitor labor's part in the war. Union bureaucrats became specialized, composed of negotiators, membership organizers, educators and propagandists, and political liaisons. Playing a key role in politics, unions could mobilize masses of people, as they demonstrated when they blocked coups against the Weimar government in the 1920s and organized the 1926 general strike in Great Britain.

Restoring Society

Postwar society met the returning millions of brutalized, incapacitated, and shell-shocked veterans with combined joy and apprehension. Many veterans harbored hostility toward civilians who had rebelled against wartime conditions, these soldiers charged, instead of patriotically enduring them. The world to which the veterans returned differed from the home they had left: the war had blurred class distinctions, giving rise to expectations that life would be fairer afterward. The massive casualties had fostered social mobility by allowing commoners to move up to the ranks of officers, positions often monopolized by the prewar aristocracy. Members of all classes had rubbed shoulders in the trenches. The enormous loss of life and the enduring wounds inspired in many a newfound sense of community. His son killed on the battlefield, author Rudyard Kipling was

among those who influenced the decision that all memorials to individual soldiers would be the same—whether the soldier was rich or poor. Wealth, he maintained, should not allow some to "proclaim their grief above other people's grief" when rich and poor had died the same death in the same cause. The identical, evenly spaced crosses of military cemeteries made all the dead equal, as did the mass "brothers' graves" at the battlefront where all ranks lay side by side in a single burial pit.

In contrast to expectations veterans often had no jobs; and some soldiers found that their wives and sweethearts had abandoned them—a wrenching betrayal for those who had risked their lives to protect the homeland. Middle-class daughters began to work outside the home; their mothers did their own housework because former servants could earn more money in factories. Women of all classes cut their hair, wore sleeker clothes, smoked, and had money of their own. In the United States this postwar version of the "new woman" was called the flapper. Patriotic when the war erupted, civilians, especially women, sometimes felt estranged from these returning warriors who had inflicted so much death and who had lived daily with filth, rats, and decaying human flesh. Civilian anxieties were often valid. Tens of thousands of German, central European, and Italian soldiers refused to disband; a few British veterans even vandalized university classrooms and assaulted women streetcar conductors and factory workers. Women who had served on the front could empathize with the soldiers' woes. But many suffragists in England, for instance, who had fought for an end to separate spheres before the war, now embraced gender segregation, so fearful were they of returning veterans.

Confronting the appeal of Bolshevism, governments tried to make civilian life as comfortable as possible to reintegrate men into society and prevent revolution. Politicians believed in the stabilizing power of traditional family values and supported social programs such as pensions, benefits for out-of-work men, and housing for veterans to alleviate their pent-up anger. The new housing—"homes for heroes," as politicians called the program—was a vast improvement over nineteenth-century working-class tenements. In Vienna,

Frankfurt, Berlin, and Stockholm, modern housing projects provided collective laundries, day-care centers, and rooms for group socializing; they featured gardens, terraces, and balconies to provide a soothing, country ambience that offset the hectic nature of industrial life. Inside, they boasted modern kitchens, indoor plumbing, central heating, and electricity. Borrowing the clean lines of East Asian and African dwellings to create a sense of modernity, domestic architects avoided ornate moldings, plasterwork, and curlicues—now seen as old-fashioned. The bungalow, a style started in India, formed the basis for early suburban developments and for the beach homes that higher productivity would allow the middle classes to enjoy.

Despite government efforts to restore traditional family values, war had dissolved many middle-class conventions, among them attempts to keep unmarried young men and women apart. Freer relationships and more open discussions of sex characterized the 1920s. Middle-class youth of both sexes visited jazz clubs and attended movies together. Revealing bathing suits, short skirts, and body-hugging

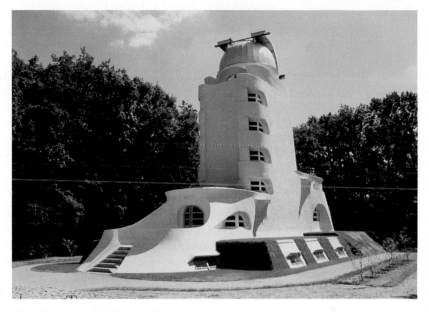

Einstein Tower (1919-1921)
While the war profoundly disillusioned many in the West, peace aroused utopian hopes for a better future, and this utopianism influenced building design. The postwar years saw the construction of modern apartment buildings with conveniences such as laundries and a spare, clean architectural style—some of these buildings were intended to be "homes for heroes." This radical break with ornate Victorian styles appears in this specially designed observatory that could also serve as a house for the celebrated physicist Albert Einstein. Its flowing lines continued the prewar trend in modern art to let forms express inner states. In this case, architect Erich Mendelsohn, who favored fantasy and utopianism in his designs at the time, shows the expressive possibilities of building materials. Design would become sparer still as the 1920s progressed. *Astrophysikalisches Institut Potsdam. Photo: Dr. J Rendtel, Potsdam, Germany.*

clothing emphasized women's sexuality, seeming to invite men and women to join together and replenish the postwar population. Still, the context for sexuality remained marriage. In 1918, British scientist Marie Stopes published the best seller *Married Love*, and in 1927, the wildly successful *Ideal Marriage: Its Physiology and Technique* by Dutch author Theodor van de Velde appeared. Both described sex in rhapsodic terms and offered precise information about birth control and sexual physiology. Changing ideas about sex were not limited to the middle and upper classes; one Viennese reformer described working-class marriage as "an erotic-comradely relationship of equals" rather than the economic partnership of past centuries. The flapper, a sexually liberated working-woman, vied with the dedicated housewife to represent the ordinary woman in the public's eyes. Meanwhile, such writers as the Briton D. H. Lawrence and the American Ernest Hemingway glorified men's sexual vigor in, respectively, *Women in Love* (1920) and *The Sun Also Rises* (1926). Mass culture's focus on heterosexuality encouraged the return to normality after the gender disorder that troubled the prewar and war years.

As images of men and women changed, people paid more attention to bodily improvement. The increasing use of toothbrushes and toothpaste, safety and electric razors, and deodorants reflected new standards for personal hygiene and grooming. For Western women, a multibillion-dollar cosmetics industry sprang up almost overnight. Women went to beauty parlors regularly to have their short hair cut, set, dyed, conditioned, straightened, or curled. They also tweezed their eyebrows, applied makeup, and even submitted to cosmetic surgery. Ordinary women painted their faces as formerly only prostitutes had done and competed in beauty contests that judged physical appearance. Instead of wanting to look plump and prosperous, people aimed to become thin and tan. The proliferation of boxers, hikers, gymnasts, and tap dancers spurred people to exercise and to participate in amateur sports. Modern industry encouraged consumers' new focus on personal health, which coincided with its need for a physically fit workforce.

As prosperity returned, people could afford to buy more consumer goods. Thanks to the gradual postwar increase in real wages, middle- and upper-class families snapped up sleek modern furniture, washing machines, and vacuum cleaners. Other modern conveniences such as electric irons and gas stoves appeared in better-off working-class households. Installment buying, popularized from the 1920s on, helped people finance these purchases. Housework became more mechanized, and family intimacy increasingly depended on machines of mass communication like radios, phonographs, and the less expensive automobiles. At the same time, these new domestic products that transformed private life brought unforeseen changes in the public world of culture and mass politics.

Review: What were the major social and economic problems facing postwar Europe, and how did leaders address them?

❖ Mass Culture and the Rise of Modern Dictators

Wartime propaganda had aimed to unite all classes against a common enemy. In the 1920s, the process of incorporating diverse groups into a homogeneous Western culture, increasingly seen as a mass culture, continued. The instruments of mass culture—primarily radio, film, and newspapers—expanded their influence in the 1920s. Whereas some intellectuals urged elites to form an experimental avant-garde that refused to cater to "the drab mass of society," others wanted to use modern media and art to reach and even control the masses. Mass media had the potential for creating an informed citizenry and thus enhancing democracy. Paradoxically, it also provided the tools for dictatorship in the troubled postwar climate. Authoritarian rulers—Benito Mussolini, Joseph Stalin, and ultimately Adolf Hitler—were thus able to control the masses in unprecedented ways.

Culture for the Masses

An array of media had received a big boost from the war. Bulletins from the battlefront had whetted the public's craving for news and real-life stories, and sales of nonfiction books soared. After years of deprivation, people were driven to achieve material success, and they devoured books that advised how to gain it. A biography of Henry Ford, telling his story of upward mobility and technological accomplishment, became a best seller in Germany. With postwar readers avidly pursuing practical knowledge, institutes and night schools became popular, and school systems promoted reading in geography, science, and history. Photographs, the radio, and movies also contributed to the formation of national culture.

In the 1920s, filmmaking changed from an experimental medium to a thriving international business in which large corporations set up theater chains and marketed films worldwide. The war years, when the U.S. film industry began to outstrip the European, gave rise to specialization: directors, producers, marketers, photographers, film editors, and many others subdivided the process. A "star" system turned film personalities into celebrities, promoted by professional publicity and royal lifestyles. Films of literary classics and political events developed people's sense of a common heritage. Thus, the British government sponsored documentaries that articulated national goals, while Bolshevik leaders also supported filmmaking, underwriting the innovative work of director Sergei Eisenstein (1898–1948). His films *Potemkin* (1925) and *Ten Days That Shook the World* (1927–1928) presented a Bolshevik view of history to Russian and international audiences.

Films incorporated familiar elements from other cultural forms to cement viewer loyalty. The piano accompaniment that went along with the action of silent films derived from music halls; comic characters, farcical plots, and slapstick humor were borrowed from street or burlesque shows and from trends in postwar living. The popular comedies of the 1920s satirized men and women who botched the job of achieving emotional intimacy or featured the flapper and made her more visible to the masses. Lavish cinema houses attracted some hundred million weekly viewers, the majority of them women. As popular films and books crossed national borders, a cosmopolitanism and global culture for an international audience flourished.

Cinematic portrayals also played to postwar fantasies and fears, even global ones. In Germany, where filmmakers used expressionist sets and costumes to make films frightening, the influential hit *The Cabinet of Doctor Caligari* (1919) depicted events in an insane asylum as horrifying symbols of state power. Popular detective and cowboy films portrayed heroes who could restore wholeness to the disordered world of murder, crime, and injustice. The plight of gangsters appealed to war veterans, who had been exposed to the cheap value of life in the modern world. English comedian, actor, and producer Charlie Chaplin (1889–1977) created the character of the Little Tramp, who won international popularity as the defeated hero, the anonymous modern man, trying to keep his dignity in a mechanical world. All of these films played in theaters internationally, reflecting the restoration of global culture. Films featured characters from around the world, especially set in the popular new areas of North Africa and the Middle East, whose deserts became a common backdrop for plays and operettas too. Sporting events like cricket and boxing became internationalized in the 1920s and 1930s as the British competed with teams from other parts of the Commonwealth. Clips from these matches were then shown as newsreels before feature films.

Film remained experimental well into the 1920s, but radio was even more so. Developed from the wireless technology of Italian inventor Guglielmo Marconi, which had been introduced at the turn of the century, radio broadcasts in the first half of the 1920s were heard by mass audiences in public halls (much like film theaters) and featured orchestras and song followed by audience discussion. The radio quickly became a relatively inexpensive consumer item, and the public concert or lecture could now penetrate the individual's private living space. Specialized programming for men (such as sports reporting) and for women (such as advice on home management) soon followed. By the 1930s, radio was available for politicians to reach the masses wherever they might be—even alone at home (see "Taking Measure," page 1036).

Cultural Debates over the Future

Cultural leaders in the 1920s either were obsessed by the horrendous experience of war or—like the modernists before the war—held high hopes for creating a fresh, utopian future that would have little relation to the past. Those haunted by the war produced bleak or violent visions, and such visions were a theme in German art especially. The sculpture and woodcuts of German artist Käthe Kollwitz (1867–1945), whose son died in the war, portrayed bereaved parents, starving children, and other heart-wrenching, antiwar images. Others, gaining connections with a wider world because of the extent of the war, thought that Europeans needed to search for answers in other cultures. Seeing Europe as decadent, some turned to the spiritual richness of Asian philosophies and religions. Some fixed on the pacifist leader for Indian independence Mohandas Gandhi,◆ and an "Asiatic fever" seemed to grip intellectuals, including influential writers like Virginia Woolf and important filmmakers like Sergei Eisenstein.

Other artists employed satire, irony, and flippancy to express postwar rage and revulsion at civilization's apparent failure. George Grosz◆ (1893–1959), stunned by the carnage like so many other German veterans, joined Dada, an artistic and literary movement that had emerged during the war. With a meaningless name, Dada produced works marked by nonsense, incongruity, and

---

◆**Mohandas Gandhi:** moh huhn DAHS GAHN dee
◆**Grosz:** gorzh

TAKING MEASURE

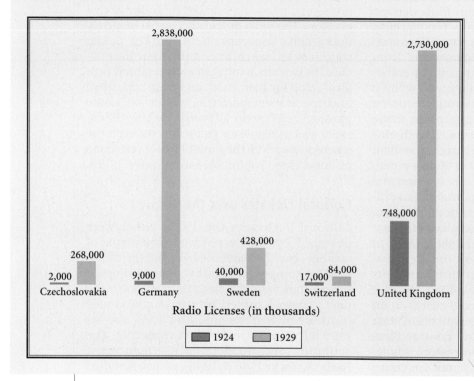

The Growth of Radio, 1924–1929
The spread of radio technology, like the earlier development of printing, advanced the cultural and political unity of citizens in a nation-state. The most industrially and commercially developed societies witnessed the most rapid diffusion of radios, which were both programmed and taxed by governments. Because of this centralized control, historians can compare the country-by-country use of radio in Europe and in much of the rest of the world. Of the five countries represented here, which experienced the most rapid spread of radio technology? Can you suggest reasons for their lead in accepting radio?

shrieking expressions of alienation. Grosz's paintings and cartoons of maimed soldiers and brutally murdered women reflected his psychic wounds and his self-proclaimed desire "to bellow back." In the postwar years, the modernist tradition of shocking audiences became more savage and often more hateful of ordinary people. Avant-garde portrayals of seediness and perversion in everyday life flourished in cabarets and theaters in the 1920s and reinforced veterans' visions of civilian decadence.

The art world itself became a battlefield, especially in defeated Germany, where it paralleled the Weimar Republic's contentious politics. Popular writers such as Ernst Jünger♦ glorified life in the trenches and called for the militarization of society to restore order. In contrast, Erich Maria Remarque cried out for an end to war in his controversial *All Quiet on the Western Front* (1928). This international best seller depicted the life shared by enemies on the battlefield,

thus aiming to dampen the national hatred stoked by wartime propaganda. Remarque's novel was part of a flood of popular, and often bitter, literature appearing on the tenth anniversary of the war's end.

Poets reflected on postwar conditions in more general terms, using styles that rejected the comforting rhymes or accessible metaphors of earlier verse. T. S. Eliot, an American-born poet who for a time worked as a banker in Britain, portrayed postwar life as petty and futile in "The Waste Land" (1922) and "The Hollow Men" (1925). The Irish nationalist poet William Butler Yeats joined Eliot in mourning the replacement of traditional society with its moral conviction and religious values by a new, superficial generation gaily dancing to jazz and engaging in promiscuous sex and vacuous conversation. Yeats's "Sailing to Byzantium" (1928), reflecting his own turn to cultures outside of Europe, starts:

That is no country for old men. The young
In one another's arms, birds in the trees
—Those dying generations . . .

♦**Jünger:** YOON gur

Both poets had an uneasy relationship with the modern world and at times advocated authoritarianism rather than democracy.

The postwar arts produced many a utopian fantasy turned upside down; dystopias of life in postrevolutionary, traumatized Europe proliferated. The bizarre expressionist stories of Franz Kafka, an employee of a large insurance company in Prague, showed the world as a vast, impersonal machine. His novels *The Trial* (1925) and *The Castle* (1926) evoked the hopeless condition of individuals caught between the cogs of society's relentlessly turning gears. His theme seemed to capture for civilian life the helplessness that soldiers had felt at the front. As an old social order collapsed in the face of political and technological innovation, other writers depicted the complex, sometimes nightmarish inner life of individuals. French author Marcel Proust,♦ in his multivolume novel *Remembrance of Things Past* (1913–1927), explored the workings of memory, the passage of time, and sexual modernity through the life of a narrator. At the beginning of the first volume, the narrator recalls a childhood obsession with his mother's absence as he tries to fall asleep at night. He witnesses progressively disturbing obsessions, such as violent sexuality and personal betrayals of love. The haunted inner life analyzed by Sigmund Freud was infiltrating fiction: for Proust, redemption lay in producing beauty from the raw material of life, not in promoting outmoded conventions of decency and morality.

Irish writer James Joyce and British writer Virginia Woolf shared Proust's vision of an interior self built on memories and sensations. Joyce's *Ulysses* (1922) and Woolf's *Mrs. Dalloway* (1925) illuminated the fast-moving inner lives of their characters in the course of a single day. In one of the most celebrated passages in *Ulysses*, a long interior monologue traces a woman's lifetime of erotic and emotional sensations. The technique of using a character's thoughts to propel a story was called stream of consciousness. For Woolf, the war had dissolved the solid society from which absorbing stories and fascinating characters were once fashioned.

♦**Proust:** proost

Otto Dix, *The Cardgame* (1920)
The Cardgame shows the human legacy of war in mutilated bodies and destroyed minds. Even though some veterans would see armed struggle as the highest expression of manhood, the artist and ex-soldier Otto Dix depicted the faces of fallen soldiers with worms crawling through them. He portrayed postwar society as being run by corrupt profiteers and filled with decrepit prostitutes and others seeking mindless pleasure. World War I had shown life to be a game of chance to be played even after one had been beaten. It was this antiwar and pessimistic spirit that caused the Nazis to hate artists like Dix and to condemn their work. *Private Collection, Konstanz. ©Erich Lessing / Art Resource, NY. ©2005 Artist Rights Society (ARS), NY / VG Bild-Kunst, Bonn.*

Her characters experience fragmented conversations, momentary sensations, and incomplete relationships. Her novel *Orlando* (1928; see page 1038) also reflected the current interest in Eastern ideas of reincarnation and the self's travels through time. In the novel, the hero Orlando lives hundreds of years and in the course of his long life is eventually transformed into a woman.

There was another side to the postwar story, one based not on the interior life of a traumatized society but on the promise of

Virginia Woolf's *Orlando* (1928)

Virginia Woolf's celebrated work featured innovations such as stream of consciousness and observations on the feelings of the modern self. She also observed changing sex roles, especially prominent after World War I, and the unequal status of women. She wrote Orlando *to show the fluidity of these roles in contrast to her contemporaries' belief in women's "eternal nature." In this witty fantasy the hero, born in the sixteenth century, wakes up mysteriously to find himself in the eighteenth century as a heroine.*

Virginia Woolf (1925) Along with Marcel Proust and James Joyce, Virginia Woolf represented the peak of literary modernism with her emphasis on interior states of mind and disjointed, dreamlike slices of reality. Woolf's novels such as Mrs. Dalloway also captured the unappreciated centrality of women, who provided an array of personal and emotional services to their families and more highly valued husbands. Woolf boldly announced that for a woman to be as creative as a man depended on her being partially relieved of the burdens of family—most notably having "a room of one's own" in which to develop that creativity.
Time Life Pictures/Getty Images.

Orlando had become a woman—there is no denying it. But in every other respect, Orlando remained precisely as he had been. The change of sex, though it altered their future, did nothing whatever to alter their identity. Their faces remained, as their portraits prove, practically the same. His memory—but in future we must for convention's sake, say "her" for "his," and "she" for "he"—her memory then, went back through all the events of her past life without encountering any obstacle. Some slight haziness there may have been, as if a few dark drops had fallen into the clear pool of memory; certain things had become a little dimmed; but that was all. The change seemed to have been accomplished painlessly and completely and in such a way that Orlando herself showed no surprise at it. Many people, taking this into account, and holding that such a change of sex is against nature, have been at great pains to prove (1) that Orlando had always been a woman, (2) that Orlando is at this moment a man. Let biologists and psychologists determine. It is enough for us to state the simple fact; Orlando was a man till the age of thirty; when he became a woman and has remained so ever since.

But let other pens treat of sex and sexuality; we quit such odious subjects as soon as we can. Orlando had now washed, and dressed herself in those Turkish coats and trousers which can be worn indifferently by either sex; and was forced to consider her position. That it was precarious and embarrassing in the extreme must be the first thought of every reader who has followed her story with sympathy. Young, noble, beautiful, she had woken to find herself in a position than which we can conceive none more delicate for a young lady of rank. We should not have blamed her had she rung the bell, screamed, or fainted. But Orlando showed no such signs of perturbation. All her actions were deliberate in the extreme, and might indeed have been thought to show tokens of premeditation. First, she carefully examined the papers on the table; took such as seemed to be written in poetry, and secreted them in her bosom; next she called her Seleuchi hound, which had never left her bed all these days, though half famished with hunger, fed and combed him; then stuck a pair of pistols in her belt. . . .

Source: Virginia Woolf, *Orlando, A Biography* (New York: Penguin, 1946), 85–86.

technology. Avant-garde artists before the war had celebrated the new, the futuristic, the utopian. Like Jules Amar crafting prostheses for shattered limbs, they were optimistic that technology could make an entire society whole after the slaughter. The aim of art, observed one of them, "is not to decorate our life but to organize it." The group of German artists called the Bauhaus◆ (after the idea of a craft association, or *Bauhütte*) created streamlined office buildings and designed functional furniture, utensils, and decorative objects, many of them inspired by forms from "untainted" East Asia and Africa. Russian artists, temporarily entranced by the Communist experiment, optimistically wrote novels about cement factories and ballets about steel—the latter an element common to artificial limbs and advanced, utopian design.

Artists fascinated by technology and machinery were drawn to the most modern of all countries—the United States. Hollywood films, glossy advertisements, and the bustling metropolis of New York tempted careworn Europeans. They loved films and pulp stories devoted to the Wild West and to the carefree modern American "girl." They were especially attracted to jazz, the improvisational music that emanated from Harlem. African American jazz musicians showed a resiliency of spirit, although Europeans could still feel superior to those of dark skin color in "primitive" costumes. Performers like Josephine Baker (1906–1976) and Louis Armstrong (1900–1971) became international sensations when they toured Europe's capital cities. Like jazz, the New York skyscraper pointed to the future. Skyscrapers rising in New York provided Europeans with a potent example of avant-garde expression that rejected a terrifying past and boldly shaped the future.

The Communist Utopia

Communism also promised a shining future and a modern, technological culture. But the Bolsheviks encountered powerful obstacles to consolidating their rule. In the early 1920s, peasant bands called Green Armies revolted against the policy of war communism that confiscated their agricultural produce. Industrial production stood at only 13 percent of its prewar output; the civil war had produced massive casualties; shortages of housing affected the entire population; and millions of refugees clogged the cities and roamed the countryside. In the early spring of 1921, workers in Petrograd and sailors at the nearby naval base at Kronstadt revolted, protesting their short rations and the privileged standard of living that Bolshevik supervisors enjoyed. They called for "soviets without Communists"—that is, a return to the early promises of the Bolsheviks for a worker state.

The government had many of the rebels shot, but the Kronstadt revolt pushed Lenin to institute reform. His New Economic Policy (NEP) returned parts of the economy to the free market, a temporary compromise with capitalist methods that allowed peasants to sell their grain freely and to profit from free trade in consumer goods. Although the state still controlled large industries and banking, the NEP encouraged people to produce, sell, and even, in the words of one leading Communist, "get rich." Consumer goods and more food to eat soon became available. Some peasants and merchants did indeed get rich, but many more remained impoverished. The rise of these wealthy "NEPmen," who bought and furnished splendid homes and who cared only about conspicuous consumption, belied the Bolshevik credo of a classless utopia.

Protest erupted within Communist ranks and prompted change. At the 1921 party congress, a group called the Worker Opposition objected to the party's usurpation of economic control from worker organizations and pointed out that the NEP was an agrarian program, not a proletarian one for workers. In response to charges of growing bureaucratization, Lenin suppressed the Worker Opposition faction and set up procedures for purging dissidents—an innovation that would become a deadly feature of Communist rule. Bolshevik leaders also tightened their grip on politics by making the Communist revolution a cultural reality that would inform people's daily lives and reshape their thoughts. Party leaders invaded the

◆**Bauhaus:** BOW hows

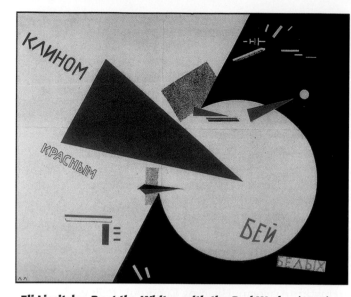

Eli Lissitsky, *Beat the Whites with the Red Wedge* (1919)
Russian artist Eli Lissitsky traveled throughout Europe to bring news of Soviet experimentation. In particular, the Soviets were taken with the new physics and their works of art surrounded the viewer with geometric forms. But abstract art was also political: in this 1919 painting, the "red wedge" uses the force of physical principles to defeat the objectively greater counterrevolutionary power of the "whites." Some revolutionary artists believed that the purity of the forms they used best represented the pure motives and high ideals of the revolutionary cause. Why might artists have moved, within a brief seventy-year period, from the realism of the 1850s and 1860s to the full abstraction of the 1920s? *David King Collection © 2005 Artists Rights Society (ARS), NY/VG Bild-Kinst, Bonn.*

countryside to set up classes in a variety of political and social subjects, and volunteers harangued the public about the importance of literacy—only 40 percent on the eve of World War I. To facilitate social equality between the sexes, as had been part of the Marxist vision of the future, the state made birth control, abortion, and divorce readily available through its agencies. As commissar for public welfare, Aleksandra Kollontai♦ (1872–1952) promoted birth-control education and the establishment of day care for children of working parents. To promote literacy, she wrote simply worded novels about love and work in the new socialist state for ordinary readers.

The bureaucracy swelled to bring modern culture to every corner of life, and *hygiene* and *efficiency* became watchwords, as

they were in the rest of Europe. Such agencies as the Zhenotdel♦ (Women's Bureau) sought to teach women about their rights under communism and about modern sanitary practices. Efficiency experts aimed to replace tsarist backwardness with technological modernity based on the American techniques of Henry Ford and Frederick Taylor. The short-lived government agency Proletkult tried to develop proletarian culture through such undertakings as workers' universities, a workers' encyclopedia, a workers' theater, and workers' publishing. Russian artists experimented with blending high art and technology in mass culture, and composers punctuated their music with the sound of train or factory whistles. The poet Vladimir Mayakovsky edited a journal advocating utilitarian art, wrote verse praising his Communist passport and essays promoting toothbrushing, and staged uproarious farces for ordinary citizens. The early days of Bolshevik rule saw interesting and enduring experiments in all of the arts and in mass culture.

As with war communism, many resisted the reshaping of culture to "modern" or "Western" standards. Bolsheviks threatened everyday customs and the distribution of power within the family. As Zhenotdel workers moved into the countryside, for example, they attempted to teach women to behave as men's equals. Peasant families were still strongly patriarchal, however, and Zhenotdel activists threatened gender relations. In Islamic regions of central Asia, incorporated from the old Russian Empire into the new Communist one, Bolsheviks urged Muslim women to remove their veils and change their way of life, but fervent Muslims often attacked both Zhenotdel workers and women who followed their advice.

In the spring of 1922, Lenin suffered a debilitating stroke, and in January 1924, amid ongoing cultural experimentation, factional fighting, and repression, the architect of the Bolshevik Revolution died. The party congress declared the day of his death a permanent holiday, changed the name of Petrograd to Leningrad, and elevated the deceased leader into a secular god. After Lenin's death, no one was allowed to criticize any-

♦**Kollontai:** kuh luhn TY

♦**Zhenotdel:** ZHEHN aht dyul

thing associated with his name, a situation that paved the way for future abuses of power by Communist leaders.

Joseph Stalin (1879–1953), who served in the powerful post of general secretary of the Communist Party, led the deification of Lenin and was chief mourner at his funeral. Stalin organized the Lenin cult, which included the public display of Lenin's embalmed corpse—still on view today. He dealt with thousands of local party officials, which gave him enormous national patronage, and in 1924 welded both Russian and non-Russian regions into the Union of Soviet Socialist Republics (USSR), which gave him a claim to executive accomplishment. Wary of Stalin's growing influence and ruthlessness, Lenin in his last will and testament had asked that "the comrades find a way to remove Stalin." Stalin, however, prevented Lenin's will from being publicized and proceeded to discredit his chief rival, Trotsky, as an unpatriotic internationalist who was unwilling to concentrate on the tough job of modernizing the Soviet Union. With the blessing of Trotsky's other rivals, Stalin had him shipped out of the country. Bringing in several hundred thousand new party members who owed their positions in government and industry to him, Stalin built a loyal base of people whose success testified to the new opportunities that the Bolsheviks had ushered in. By 1928–1929, he had achieved virtually complete control of the USSR.

Fascism on the March in Italy

The political chaos and postwar discontent in Italy brought to power Benito Mussolini (1883–1945), who, like the Bolsheviks, promised an efficient utopia. Italian anger was first aroused when the Allies at Paris refused to honor the territorial promises of the Treaty of London. Domestic unrest swelled when peasants and workers protested their economic plight, made worse by the slump of the early 1920s. Since the late nineteenth century, many Europeans had come to blame parliaments for their ills, so Italians were responsive when Mussolini, a socialist journalist who turned to the radical right, built a personal army (the Black Shirts) of veterans and the unemployed to overturn parliamentary government. In 1922, his supporters, known as Fascists, started a **march on Rome**, forcing King Victor Emmanuel III (r. 1900–1946) to make the dynamic Mussolini prime minister.

The Fascist movement flourished in the soil of poverty, social unrest, and wounded national pride. It attracted to its bands of Black Shirts many young men who felt cheated of glory by the Allies and veterans who missed the vigor of military life. The fasces,♦ an ancient Roman symbol depicting a bundle of sticks wrapped around an ax with the blade exposed, served as the movement's emblem; it represented both unity and force to Mussolini's supporters. Unlike Marxism, Fascism scoffed at coherent ideology: "Fascism is not a church," Mussolini announced upon taking power in 1922. "It is more like a training ground." **Fascism** was thus defined by its political grounding in the promotion of male violence and its opposition to the so-called antinationalist socialist movement and parliamentary rule.

Mussolini consolidated his power by making criticism of the state a criminal offense and by violently steamrolling parliamentary opposition. His Fascist bands demolished socialist newspaper offices, attacked striking workers, used their favorite tactic of forcing castor oil (which caused diarrhea) down the throats of socialists, and even murdered certain powerful opponents. Yet this brutality and the sight of the Black Shirts marching through the streets like disciplined soldiers signaled to many Italians that their country was ordered and modern. Large landowners and businessmen approved Fascist attacks on strikers, and they supported the movement financially. Their generous funding allowed Mussolini to build a large staff by hiring the unemployed and thus fostering the belief that Fascists could spark the economy when no one else could.

In addition to violence, Mussolini used mass propaganda to build support for a kind of military campaign to remake Italy. A society of extremes with severe rural poverty and thriving modern businesses such as the automobile industry, Italy welcomed the

♦**fasces:** FAS eez

Mussolini and the Black Shirts
For movements like fascism, the best society was one controlled by militarized politics that killed its critics and those of opposing political persuasions. Fascism saw parliamentary democracies as effeminate and doomed in the modern world, which would need dictators and obedient warriors to make it strong, efficient, and machinelike. Thus, in the name of promoting state power, Mussolini gained adherents both within and outside of Italy. How does this image reflect the values of Mussolini's fascism? *Farabolafoto.*

unity Mussolini promised to achieve. The mass media, addressing everyone, symbolized that unity. Peasant men huddled around radios to hear him call for a "battle of wheat" to enhance farm productivity. Peasant women, responding to his praise for maternal duty, adulated him for appearing to value womanhood. In the cities the government launched avant-garde architectural projects, designed new statues and public adornments, and used public relations promoters

to advertise its achievements. His support of literary and cultural elites turned them into supporters. The modern city became a stage set built by technology for Fascist spectacle, as modernist buildings rose to house the Fascist bureaucracy and the Party's museums. Old residential neighborhoods fell to the wrecking machines, allowing road-builders to put in broad avenues for Fascist parades. Mussolini claimed that he made the trains run on time, and this one triumph of modern technology fanned people's hopes that he could restore order out of wartime and postwar chaos.

Mussolini added a strong dose of traditional values and prejudices to his modern order. Although an atheist, he recognized the importance of Catholicism to most Italians. In 1929, the Lateran Agreement between the Italian government and the church made the Vatican a state under papal sovereignty. The government recognized the church's right to determine marriage and family doctrine and endorsed its role in education. In return, the church ended its criticism of Fascist tactics. Mussolini also introduced a "corporate" state that denied individual political rights in favor of duty to the state. Corporatist decrees in 1926 organized employers, workers, and professionals into groups or corporations that would settle grievances and determine conditions of work. These decrees outlawed independent labor unions and peasant groups, effectively ending societal and workplace activism. Mussolini drew more applause from business leaders when he announced cuts in women's wages; and then late in the 1920s he won the approval of civil servants, lawyers, and professors by banning women from those professions. Mussolini did not want women out of the workforce altogether but aimed to confine them to low-paying jobs as part of his scheme for reinvigorating men.

Mussolini's admirers were numerous across the West and included Adolf Hitler, who throughout the 1920s had been building a paramilitary group of storm troopers and a political organization called the National Socialist German Workers' Party, or Nazis. During his brief stint in jail for the Beer Hall Putsch in 1923, Hitler wrote *Mein Kampf*◆ (*My Struggle*, 1925), which articulated both a vicious anti-Semitism and a political psychology for manipulating the masses. Hitler was fascinated by the dramatic success of the Fascists' march on Rome, by Mussolini's legal accession to power, and by his ability to thwart socialists and trade unionists. But the austere conditions that had allowed Mussolini to rise to power in 1922 no longer existed in Germany.

◆*Mein Kampf:* myn KAHMPF

Although Hitler was welding the Nazi Party into a strong political instrument, the Weimar parliamentary government was actually working as the decade wore on.

> **Review:** How did the postwar cultural atmosphere encourage both beneficial innovations and the trend toward dictatorship?

Conclusion

The year 1929 was to prove just as fateful as 1914 had been. In 1914, an orgy of death had begun, leading to tens of millions of casualties, the destruction of major dynasties, and the collapse of aristocratic classes. For four years war promoted the free play of military technology, virulent nationalism, and the control of everyday life by bureaucracy. While dynasties collapsed, the centralization of power increased the scope of the nation-state. The Peace of Paris in 1919 left Germans bitterly resentful, and it formally created new states in eastern and central Europe built on principles of nationalist ethnic unity—a settlement that, given the intense intermingling of ethnicities, religions, and languages in the area, failed to guarantee a peaceful future.

War furthered the development of mass society. It leveled social classes on the battlefield and in the graveyard, standardized political thinking through wartime propaganda, and extended many political rights to women for their war effort. Peacetime turned improved techniques of wartime production toward churning out consumer goods and technological innovations like the prostheses built by Jules Amar, air transport, cinema, and radio transmission for greater numbers of people. Modernity in the arts intensified after the war, probing the nightmarish battering endured by all segments of the population.

By the end of the 1920s, the legacy of war had been to so militarize politics that strongmen had come to power in Hungary, Poland, Romania, the Soviet Union, and Italy, with Adolf Hitler waiting in the wings in Germany. Many Westerners were impressed

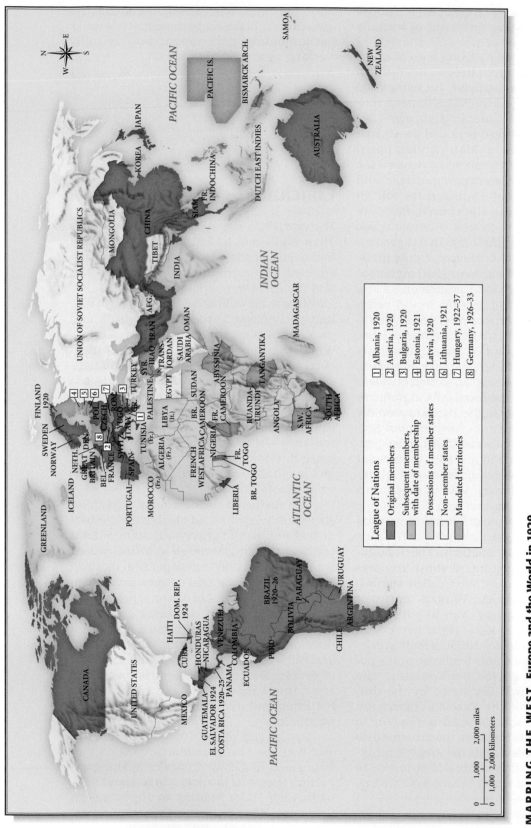

MAPPING THE WEST Europe and the World in 1929

The map reflects the partitions and nations that came into being as a result of war and revolution, while it obscures the increasing movement toward throwing off colonial rule. This was the true high point of empire: the drive for empire would diminish after 1929 except for Italy, which still craved colonies, and Japan, which continued searching for more land and resources to fuel its rapid growth. Describe the membership of the League of Nations as it existed after the war? Were there common bonds among these nations?

League of Nations

- Original members
- Subsequent members, with date of membership
- Possessions of member states
- Non-member states
- Mandated territories

1 Albania, 1920
2 Austria, 1920
3 Bulgaria, 1920
4 Estonia, 1921
5 Latvia, 1920
6 Lithuania, 1921
7 Hungary, 1922–37
8 Germany, 1926–33

by the tough, modern efficiency of the Fascists and Communists, who made parliaments and citizen rule seem out-of-date, even effeminate. Fascist and Communist commitment to violence, compared to that in the war, seemed tame. When the U.S. stock market crashed in 1929 and economic disaster circled the globe, authoritarian solutions and militarism continued to look appealing. What followed was a series of catastrophes even more devastating than World War I.

Suggested References

The Great War, 1914–1918

The most recent histories of the Great War consider its military, technological, psychic, social, and economic aspects. This vision of the war as a phenomenon occurring beyond the battlefield as well as on it characterizes the newest scholarship.

Davis, Belinda. *Home Fires Burning: Food, Politics, and Everyday Life in World War I Berlin.* 2000.

Echenberg, Myron. *Colonial Conscripts: The "Tirailleurs Sénégalais" in French West Africa, 1857–1960.* 1990.

*Hasek, Jaroslav. *The Good Soldier Schweik.* 1920.

Leed, Eric J. *No Man's Land: Combat and Identity in World War I.* 1979.

Panchasi, Roxanne. "Reconstructions: Prosthetics and the Rehabilitation of the Male Body in World War I." *Differences.* 1995.

Roshwald, Aviel, and Richard Stites, eds. *European Culture in the Great War: The Arts, Entertainment, and Propaganda, 1914–1918.* 1999.

Schmitt, Bernadotte E., and Harold C. Vederler. *The World in the Crucible, 1914–1919.* 1984.

World War I Documents Archive: http://www.lib.byu.edu/%7Erdh/wwi.

Protest, Revolution, and War's End, 1917–1918

Histories of the war's end account for the cataclysmic setting: deprivation, ongoing mass slaughter, and the eruption of revolution. Peacemaking also occurred, and that too was complex. In all, the violence of the postwar scene

has made historians call into question the idea that wars end with an armistice.

Barry, John. *The Great Influenza: The Epic Story of the Greatest Plague in History.* 2004.

Fitzpatrick, Sheila. *The Russian Revolution, 1917–1932.* 1995.

Horne, John, ed. *State, Society and Mobilization in Europe during the First World War.* 2000.

Lewis, David Levering. *W. E. B. Du Bois: The Fight for Equality and the American Century, 1919–1963.* 2000.

Smith, Leonard V., et al. *France and the Great War 1914–1918.* 2003.

Welch, David. *Germany, Propaganda, and Total War, 1914–1918: The Sins of Omission.* 2000.

The Search for Peace in an Era of Revolution

Peacemaking was a fraught process, occurring amid revolution, the flu pandemic, and starvation. Many aspired to a lasting peace and to social justice. Both dreams were to be dashed, as the story of individuals and the fate of institutions like the League of Nations show. Thompson investigates the new mandates.

Cooper, John Milton. *Breaking the Heart of the World: Woodrow Wilson and the Fight for the League of Nations.* 2001.

Marks, Sally. *The Ebbing of European Ascendency: An International History of the World.* 2002.

Thompson, Elizabeth. *Colonial Citizens: Republican Rights, Paternal Privilege, and Gender in French Syria and Lebanon.* 2000.

A Decade of Recovery: Europe in the 1920s

Two themes shape the history of the 1920s: recovery from the trauma of war and revolution and ongoing modernization of work and social life. The great technological innovations of the prewar period such as films and airplanes receive sophisticated treatment by historians for their impact on people's imagination. The radio is another phenomenon just beginning to find its historians.

Hau, Michael. *The Cult of Health and Beauty in Germany: A Social History, 1890–1930.* 2003.

Kent, Susan. *Making Peace: The Reconstruction of Gender in Postwar Britain.* 1994.

*Primary source.

Lerner, Paul. *Hysterical Men: War, Psychiatry, and the Politics of Trauma in Germany, 1890–1930.* 2003.

Nolan, Mary. *Visions of Modernity: American Business and the Modernization of Germany.* 1994.

Schwartz, Vanessa, and Leo Charney, eds. *Cinema and the Invention of Modern Life.* 1995.

Mass Culture and the Rise of Modern Dictators

Mass communications advances in cinema and radio provided new tools for the rule of modern dictators who arose from the shambles of war and revolution. Many of the most interesting recent studies look at the cultural components of the consolidation of dictatorial power, while not forgetting the violence that was a particular feature of authoritarian rule in the postwar twentieth century.

Berezin, Mabel. *Making the Fascist Self: The Political Culture of Interwar Italy.* 1997.

Harsch, Donna. *German Social Democracy and the Rise of Nazism.* 1994.

*Kollontai, Aleksandra. *Love of Worker Bees.* 1923.

Northrop, Douglas. *Veiled Empire: Gender and Power in Stalinist Central Asia.* 2004.

Sneeringer, Julia. *Winning Women's Votes: Propaganda and Politics in Weimar Germany.* 2002.

Tumarkin, Nina. *Lenin Lives! The Lenin Cult in Soviet Russia.* 1997.

---

*Primary source.

CHAPTER REVIEW

IMPORTANT EVENTS

1914 August	World War I begins
1913–1925	Suffrage for women expands in much of Europe
1916	Irish nationalists stage Easter Uprising against British rule
1917 March	Revolution in Russia overturns tsarist autocracy
1917 April	The United States enters World War I
1917 November	Bolshevik Revolution in Russia
1918 November	Armistice ends fighting of World War I revolutionary turmoil throughout Germany; the kaiser abdicates
1918–1922	Civil war in Russia
1919	The Weimar Republic established
1919–1920	Paris Peace Conference redraws the map of Europe
1922	Ireland is split in two: the independent Irish Free State in the south and British-affiliated Ulster in the north; Fascists march on Rome; Mussolini becomes Italy's prime minister; T. S. Eliot publishes "The Waste Land"; James Joyce publishes *Ulysses*
1924	Lenin dies; Stalin and Trotsky contend for power
1924–1929	Period of general economic prosperity and stability
1929 October	Stock market crash in United States

KEY TERMS

Bolshevik Revolution (1017)

cult of the offensive (1006)

Fascism (1041)

Fourteen Points (1022)

League of Nations (1023)

mandate system (1026)

march on Rome (1041)

Peace of Paris (1022)

Provisional Government (1016)

Schlieffen Plan (1006)

soviets (1016)

total war (1003)

war guilt clause (1022)

Weimar Republic (1021)

REVIEW QUESTIONS

1. What factors contributed to making World War I a total war?

2. Why did people revolt during World War I, and what turned revolt in to outright revolution in Russia?

3. What were the major outcomes of the postwar peacemaking process?

4. What were the major social and economic problems facing postwar Europe, and how did leaders address them?

5. How did the postwar cultural atmosphere encourage both beneficial innovations and the trend toward dictatorship?

MAKING CONNECTIONS

1. How was postwar mass politics shaped by the experience of war?

2. What social changes from the war carried over into the postwar years and why?

FOR FURTHER EXPLORATION

To assess your mastery of the material in this chapter, see the Online Study Guide at **bedfordstmartins.com/hunt**.

To read additional primary-source material from this period, see Chapter 26 in *Sources of The Making of the West*, Second Edition.

An Age of Catastrophes, 1929–1945

WHEN ETTY HILLESUM MOVED TO AMSTERDAM in the early 1930s to attend law school, an economic depression gripped the world. A resourceful young Dutch woman, Hillesum pieced together a living as a housekeeper and part-time language teacher. The pressures and pleasures of everyday life blinded her, however, to Adolf Hitler's spectacular rise to power in Germany on a platform demonizing her fellow Jews for the economic slump. World War II ruptured her world and woke her up. The German conquest of the Netherlands in 1940 led to direct persecution of Dutch Jews, bringing Hillesum to the shattering realization, noted in her diary: "What they are after is our total destruction." The Nazis started relocating Jews to camps in Germany and Poland. Hillesum went to work for Amsterdam's Jewish Council, which was compelled to organize the transportation of Jews to the east. Changing from self-absorbed student to heroine, she did what she could to help other Jews and meticulously recorded the deportation. "I wish I could live for a long time so that one day I may know how to explain it," she wrote. When she was taken prisoner, she smuggled out letters, bearing witness to the brutal treatment in the transit camps. Etty Hillesum never fulfilled any of her life's ambitions: she died in the Auschwitz death camp in November 1943.

The U.S. stock market crash of 1929 opened a horrific era in world history, when people, old or young like Etty Hillesum, first

---

Nazis on Parade

By the time Hitler came to power in 1933, Germany was mired in the Great Depression. Hated by Communists, Nazis, and conservatives alike, the republic had few supporters. To a nation still reeling from its defeat in World War I, the Nazis looked as if they would restore national power by defeating enemies—not the Allies but the Jews, Slavs, gypsies, and other groups both within and outside Germany's borders. Hitler took his cue from Mussolini by promising an end to democracy and tolerance. He did so in Germany and then sent his troops into the rest of Europe, including Holland, France, Poland, Czechoslovakia, and the Soviet Union. Compare the excitement of soldiers marching to war in World War I (page 1006) and the visual power of Nazi soldiers marching through the streets during the depression. **For more help analyzing this image,** see the visual activity for this chapter in the Online Study Guide at **bedfordstmartins.com/hunt**. *Hugo Jaeger/Time Life Pictures/Getty Images.*

experienced economic distress and then felt the full horror of war and genocide. During the Great Depression of the 1930s, suffering was global, intensifying social grievances throughout the world. In Europe, many people turned to military-style strongmen for solutions to economic and social ills. Chief among them, Adolf Hitler roused the German masses to pursue national greatness by scorning democratic rights and rooting out what he considered to be inferior, menacing people like Jews, Slavs, and Gypsies. Similarly authoritarian, militaristic, and fascist regimes spread to Portugal, Spain, Poland, Hungary, Japan, China, and elsewhere, trampling on representative institutions. Joseph Stalin oversaw the Soviet Union's rapid industrialization, but in the process he justified the killing of millions of citizens as necessary to Soviet growth.

The international scene was also perilous because elected leaders in the democracies reacted cautiously to the simultaneous phenomena of the depression and fascist aggression. In an age of mass media, civilian leaders appeared weak and fearful of conflict, while dictators in uniform looked bold and decisive. Only the German invasion of Poland in 1939 finally pushed the democracies to strong action, as World War II erupted in Europe. By 1941 the war had spread to the rest of the world with the United States, Great Britain, and the Soviet Union and others allied in combat against Germany, Italy, Japan, and their allies. Tens of millions would perish in this war because both technology and ideology had become more deadly than they

had been just two decades earlier. Half the dead were civilians, among them Etty Hillesum, whose only crime was being a Jew.

❖ The Great Depression

The depression triggered both by the U.S. stock market crash of 1929 and by economic developments around the world threw tens of millions out of work and brought suffering to rural and urban folk alike. The whole world felt the depression's impact as commerce and investment in industry fell off, social life and gender roles were upset, and the birthrate plummeted. From peasants in Asia to industrial workers in Germany and the United States, the lives of large segments of the global population were ravaged.

Economic Disaster Strikes

In the 1920s, U.S. corporations and banks as well as millions of individual Americans had recklessly invested their money or, more often, borrowed money to invest in the stock market, which seemed to churn out endless profits. Using easy credit, they bought shares in popular companies based on electric, automotive, and other new technologies with complete confidence in ever-rising stock prices. By the end of the decade, the Federal Reserve Bank—the nation's central bank, which controlled financial policy—tightened the availability of credit in an attempt to stabilize the market. To meet the new restrictions, brokers had to demand that their

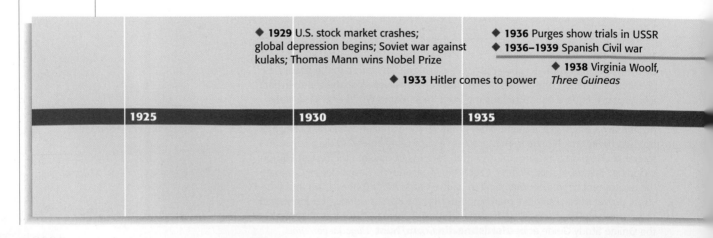

◆ **1929** U.S. stock market crashes; global depression begins; Soviet war against kulaks; Thomas Mann wins Nobel Prize

◆ **1933** Hitler comes to power

◆ **1936** Purges show trials in USSR
◆ **1936–1939** Spanish Civil war

◆ **1938** Virginia Woolf, *Three Guineas*

| 1925 | 1930 | 1935 |

clients immediately pay back the money they had borrowed to buy stock. As stocks were sold to cover the borrowed funds, the market collapsed. Between early October and mid-November 1929, the value of businesses listed on the U.S. stock market dropped from $87 billion to $30 billion. For individuals and for the economy as a whole, it was the beginning of economic catastrophe.

The crash helped bring on a global depression because the United States, a leading international creditor, had financed the economic growth of the previous five years. Suddenly strapped for credit, U.S. financiers cut back on loans and called in debts, undermining banks and industry at home and abroad. The recent U.S. lead in industrial production and the rise of Japanese manufacturing compounded the collapse in Europe. From the aging industries of Britain to the fledgling factories of eastern Europe, a decline in consumer buying and overproduction further eroded the European economy.

The Great Depression left no sector of the world economy unscathed, but government actions made the depression worse. To spur their economies, governments used standard tools such as budget cuts and high tariffs against foreign goods. Although part of accepted economic theory at the time, these policies further dampened spending and trade in the great industrial powers. By 1933, almost six million German workers, or about one-third of the workforce, were unemployed, and many others were underemployed. France had a more self-sufficient economy. Big businesses like the innovative Citroën car

manufacturer began to fail, however, and by the mid-1930s more than 800,000 French people had lost their jobs. Great Britain, with its textile, steel, and coal industries near ruin because of out-of-date techniques and foreign competition, had close to three million unemployed in 1932.

In the agricultural sector, where prices had been declining for several years because of technological innovation and abundant harvests around the world, creditors confiscated farms and equipment. With their incomes crumbling, millions of small farmers had no money to buy the chemical fertilizers and motorized machinery they needed to remain competitive, and they too went under. Eastern and southern European peasants, who had pressed for the redistribution of land after World War I, especially suffered because they could not afford to operate their newly acquired farms. In Poland, many of the 700,000 new landowners fell into debt trying to make their farms viable—a situation that was widespread across the eastern European region. Eastern European governments often ignored the farmers' plight as they poured available funds into industrialization—a policy that increased tensions in rural society.

Social Effects of the Depression

The picture of society during the Great Depression was more complex than utter ruin, however. First, the situation was not uniformly bleak. Despite the slump, modernization proceeded. Bordering English slums, one traveler in the mid-1930s noticed, were "filling stations

◆ **1939** Germany invades Poland; World War II begins

◆ **1945** Fall of Berlin; U.S. drops atomic bombs on Japan; World War II ends

◆ **1940** France falls to the German army

◆ **1940–1941** Battle of Britain

1940	1945	1950	1955

◆ **1941** Germany invades USSR; Japan attacks Pearl Harbor; U.S. enters war

◆ **1941–1945** The Holocaust

◆ **1944** Allied forces land at Normandy

Hunger Marchers in London (1934)
The interwar years were full of civilian protests against government policies. In 1934, these unemployed hunger marchers rallied in London's Trafalgar Square to oppose government cuts in
unemployment benefits during the grim years of the Great Depression. Some marchers were
impressed by the different political system in the USSR, where there was full employment during
the entire 1930s, and became committed Communists; others strove to maintain a middle-class
respectability, even when unemployed—as seen in the proper dress of these hunger strikers. Still
other kinds of politics sprang up in the streets: In Germany there were attempted coups against
the government and by the late 1920s Nazi paramilitary troops regularly marched through city
streets to show their power and their contempt for democratic politics. ©*Bettmann/Corbis.*

and factories that look like exhibition buildings, giant cinemas and dance halls and cafés,
bungalows with tiny garages, cocktail bars,
Woolworth's [and] swimming pools." Municipal and national governments continued road
construction and sanitation projects. Running water, electricity, and sewage pipes were
installed in many homes for the first time.
New factories manufactured synthetic fabrics,
electrical products such as stoves, and automobiles—all of them in demand. With government assistance, eastern European industry

developed: Romanian industrial production,
for example, increased by 55 percent between
1929 and 1939 throughout the worst of the
economic slump.

Second, the majority of Europeans and
Americans had jobs throughout the 1930s,
and people with steady employment benefited
from a drastic drop in prices. Despite the
depression, service workers, managers, and
business magnates often enjoyed considerable prosperity. Those with jobs, however, felt
the looming threat of becoming unemployed

and having to scrape, like thousands of others around them, for a bare existence. In towns with heavy industry, sometimes more than half the population was out of work. In England in the mid-1930s, close to 20 percent of the population lacked adequate food, clothing, or housing. In a 1932 school assignment, a German youth wrote: "My father has been out of work for two and a half years. He thinks that I'll never find a job." Despite the prosperity of many people, a storm cloud of fear and resentment settled over Western society.

Economic catastrophe upset social life and strained gender relations. Unemployed men sometimes stayed home all day, increasing the tension in small, overcrowded apartments. Women could often find low-paying jobs doing laundry and cleaning house for others. Men who stayed at home took over housekeeping chores, but some felt that this "women's work" demeaned their masculinity. As many women became breadwinners, albeit for low wages, men could be seen standing on street corners begging—a rearrangement of gender expectations that fueled discontent. Young men in cities faced severe unemployment. Some loitered in parks, intruding in areas usually frequented by mothers and their children and old people. As the percentage of farmworkers in the western European population decreased, rural men also faced the erosion of patriarchal authority, once central in overseeing farm labor and allocating property among heirs. Demagogues everywhere berated parliamentary politicians for their failure to stop the collapse of traditional values. The climate was thus primed for Nazi and fascist politicians who promised to restore prosperity and male dignity.

Politicians of all stripes used the continuing slide in the birthrate to stir already troubled political waters. They forecast national collapse, claiming that the declining birthrate (after a brief postwar upturn) combined with a declining economy signaled a crisis. The reason for the decline was clear: in difficult economic times, people chose to have fewer children. There was another reason too. Mandatory education and more years of required schooling, enforced more strictly after World War I, resulted in reduced income and greater expenses for parents.

Working-class children no longer brought in wages to supplement the family's income and were no longer available to help the family in other ways; instead, they cost money while they went to school. Family-planning centers opened, receiving a warm reception, and knowledge of birth control spread across the working and lower-middle classes, who continued the half-century-long trend of cutting family size.

Many politicians, however, used the population "crisis" to gain votes by igniting racism: "superior" peoples were selfishly failing to breed, they charged, while "inferior" peoples were lurking to take their place. This racism took a violent form in eastern Europe, where the rural population rose because of increased life expectancy despite an overall drop in birthrate. But increased population compounded the burdens of eastern European farm families, who faced an unprecedented struggle for survival. Throughout eastern Europe, peasant political parties blamed Jewish bankers for farm foreclosures and Jewish civil servants (of whom there were actually very few) for new taxes and inadequate relief programs. Thus, population issues along with economic misery fueled ethnic hatred, racial tensions, and anti-Semitism. Social issues inflamed the public sphere as they had before World War I.

The Great Depression beyond the West

The effects of the depression extended beyond the West, further accelerating the pace of change and spread of discontent in European empires. World War I and postwar investment had generated economic growth, a rising population, and explosive urbanization in Asia, Africa, and Latin America. Japan in particular had become a formidable industrial rival, while between 1920 and 1940, Shanghai ballooned from 1.7 million to 3.75 million residents and Calcutta from 1.8 million to 3.4 million. The depression, however, cut the demand for copper, tin, and other raw materials and for the finished products made in urban factories beyond the West. Rising agricultural productivity drove down the price of foodstuffs like rice and coffee, and this proved disastrous for people who had been forced to grow a single cash crop. However,

Gandhi Leading the Salt March (1930)

Mohandas Gandhi appealed to the masses, not just to the middle- and upper-class constituency of the Indian National Congress, which had emphasized reform and participation in government. Instead, Gandhi addressed the entire colonial system that prevented ordinary Indian people from using the country's national resources such as salt. Violating British laws, which prohibited Indians from gathering this natural product, Gandhi led the people in an act of civil disobedience—his march to the sea to harvest the salt. How might South Asians, other colonized peoples, and Europeans have reacted to this 1930 photo? © *Bettmann/Corbis.*

the economic picture was uneven in the colonies as well as in Europe. For instance, established industrial sectors of the Indian economy like textiles gained strength, with India achieving virtual independence from British cloth.

Economic distress added to smoldering grievances. During the economic crisis, colonial farmers withheld produce like cocoa from the imperial wholesalers, and strikes erupted across the colonies to restore the wages that imperial landlords and traders had cut to make up for their own economic shortfalls. Discontent ran deep. Millions of African and Asian colonial troops had fought for Britain and France in World War I, but these countries had given little back to their colonial populations. In fact, the League of Nations charter had pointedly omitted any reference to the principle of racial equality demanded by people of color at the Paris conference. Their resolve fortified by these slights, by the model of Japan's growth, and by their own industrial development, colonial peoples turned to winning independence.

India was a prime example of visibly rising anger toward colonialism. Upper-class Indians, who had organized to gain rights from Britain in the late nineteenth century, were joined in the 1930s by millions of working people, including hundreds of thousands of veterans of World War I. Mohandas Gandhi (1869–1948, called Mahatma, or "great-souled") emerged as the charismatic leader for Indian independence. Of privileged birth and trained in England as a Western-style lawyer, Gandhi embraced Hindu self-denial and rejected the elaborate trappings of British life, wearing, for example, simple clothing made of thread he had spun. He advocated **civil disobedience**—deliberately but peacefully breaking the law—which he professed to model on British suffragists' tactics and on the teachings of Jesus, Buddha, and other spiritual leaders (see the illustration on this page). Boycotting British-made goods and disobeying British laws, Gandhi aimed to end the deference Indians had traditionally shown the British. The British jailed Gandhi repeatedly and tried to split the independence movement by encouraging the Muslim League and promoting Hindu-Muslim antagonism. As in Europe itself, an inflamed atmosphere set the stage for the future.

In the Middle East, Westernizer Mustafa Kemal, or Atatürk ("first among Turks," 1881–1938), led the Turks to found an independent republic in 1923 and to craft a capitalist economy. In an effort to nationalize and modernize Turkish culture, Kemal moved the capital from Constantinople to Ankara in 1923, officially changed the ancient Greek name Constantinople to the Turkish name Istanbul in 1930, mandated Western dress for men and women, introduced the Latin alphabet, and abolished polygamy. In 1936, women received the vote and were made eligible to serve in the parliament. Persia similarly loosened the European grip on its economy, forced the negotiation of oil contracts that kept Western countries from taking the oil virtually free, updated its government, and in 1935 changed its name to Iran. In 1936, Britain agreed to end its military occupation of Egypt (though not the Suez Canal), fulfilling its promise of Egyptian self-rule granted in 1922. Subject peoples were becoming too well organized to accept colonial shackles any longer.

Pressured by rising tariffs in Europe that dampened their trade and obsessed by their own declining population, the French made fewer concessions in their colonies. Like all imperial countries, they came to depend more, not less, on what the empire could provide economically. The French also depended on the colonies for sheer numbers of people. France's trade with its colonies increased as that with Europe lagged, and the demographic surge in Asia and Africa bolstered French optimism. As one official put it, "One hundred and ten million strong, France can stand up to Germany." Like other Western-educated native leaders, Ho Chi Minh,◆ founder of the Indochinese Communist Party, contested his people's subjection, but in 1930 the French government brutally crushed the peasant uprising he led. Thus preoccupied with their empires, Britain and France fortified their troops stationed around the world and let totalitarian forces spread unchecked throughout Europe during the crisis-ridden 1930s.

> **Review:** How did the Great Depression affect society and politics?

❖ Totalitarian Triumph

Representative government collapsed in many countries under the sheer weight of social and economic crisis. After 1929, Italy's Benito Mussolini, the Soviet Union's Joseph Stalin, and Germany's Adolf Hitler were able to mobilize vast support for their violent regimes.

◆**Ho Chi Minh:** HOH CHEE MIHN

Many people admired Mussolini and Hitler for the discipline they brought to social and economic life. Eager to achieve national greatness, many citizens simply overlooked the brutal side of modern dictatorship. In an age of crisis, utopian hopes also led many to support political violence as a sign of restored power. Unity and obedience—not freedom and rights— were seen as keys to rebirth. The common use of violence has led scholars to apply the term totalitarianism to the Fascist, Nazi, and Communist regimes of the 1930s (see "Terms of History," page 1056). The term refers to highly centralized systems of government that attempt to control society and ensure conformity through a single party and police terror. Forged in the crucible of war and its aftermath, totalitarian governments broke with liberal principles of freedom and natural rights and came to wage war on their own citizens.

The Rise of Stalinism

In the 1930s, Joseph Stalin led the astonishing transformation of the USSR from a rural society into a formidable industrial power. Having taken firm control against Lenin's express wishes, Stalin ended the New Economic Policy (NEP), Lenin's temporary compromise between Marxism and capitalism, with the first of several five-year plans presented in 1929.

Transforming the Economy. Stalin's **five-year plans** outlined a program for massive increases in the output of coal, iron ore, steel, and industrial goods over successive five-year periods. Without an end to economic backwardness, Stalin warned, "the advanced countries . . . will crush us." He thus established central economic planning—a policy used on both sides in World War I and increasingly favored by economists and industrialists around the world. Between 1928 and 1940, the number of Soviet workers in industry, construction, and transport grew from 4.6 million to 12.6 million. From 1927 to 1937, production in metallurgy and machinery rose 1,400 percent. Stalin's first five-year plan helped make the USSR a leading industrial nation.

Central planning helped create a new elite of bureaucrats and industrial officials; the number of managers in heavy industry grew

TERMS OF HISTORY

Totalitarianism

Totalitarianism is a word loaded with controversy, but when first introduced in Italy, Mussolini's government adopted it as a mark of pride. In 1923, Mussolini proposed a law by which the political party that garnered the most votes would seat 75 percent of the delegates in Italy's parliament. Until then, Italy's many political parties had formed coalitions that acted together to govern. The proposed law would help Mussolini's small but powerful Fascist Party rule alone, transforming its temporary popularity into real dominance.

One journalist cried foul, claiming that this proposal would eliminate both majority rule and minority coalitions in favor of a "totalitarian" system. He was beaten to death by Mussolini's thugs. Then, in a surprising turn, the Fascists embraced the term, proclaiming the superiority of an all-encompassing state led by a virile and forward-looking party. Their model was the "total state" under conditions of "total war" when efficient military rule stamped out effeminate principles of conscience, rights, and freedom. The Nazis also picked up on the term, hailing the effective totalitarian party that could make workers and sol-diers like steel in body and in spirit. Some even pointed approvingly at the USSR's five-year plans and its use of coercion to create uniform political thinking as a "modern" kind of state power.

As refugees fled Europe in the 1930s, they contributed another ingredient to the definition of totalitarianism, a system they abhorred. Refugee intellectuals saw totalitarianism as stemming from the rational thought of the eighteenth century and the aim of the scientific revolution and the Enlightenment to dominate nature. Analogously, to their mind, the system of free trade and capitalist industrialization aimed at domination of the economy and resources. By these arguments, the Soviets were as guilty of totalitarianism as the Fascists and Nazis. As the cold war took shape in 1945, people who defended the USSR and hailed its contribution in the war to defeat Hitler and Mussolini turned against the term as a common definition for all three dictatorships. In the cold war, the United States wanted to view the Soviet system as identical to Nazism, while the USSR's defenders now envisioned the word *totalitarianism* as cold war propaganda and rejected its use. So heated became the debate over

by almost 500 percent between 1929 and 1935. Mostly party officials and technical experts, these managers dominated Soviet workers by limiting their ability to change jobs or move from place to place. Nonetheless, skilled workers as well as bureaucrats benefited substantially from the redistribution of privileges that accompanied industrialism and central planning. Compared with people working the land, both managers and workers in industry had better housing and wages, while Communist officials enjoyed additional perquisites such as country homes, food unavailable to the masses, and luxurious vacations.

Unskilled workers faced a grim plight, often with real dedication. Newcomers from the countryside were herded into barracklike dwellings, even tents, and subjected to dangerous factory conditions. Many took pride in the skills they acquired. "We mastered this profession—completely new to us—with great pleasure," a female lathe operator recalled. More often, however, workers fresh from the countryside lacked the technical education and even the tools necessary to accomplish goals prescribed by the five-year plan. Because fulfilling the plan had top priority as a measure of progress toward Communist utopia, official lying about productivity became ingrained in the economic system. Both the grim conditions and honest commitment to Communist goals turned the Soviet Union from an illiterate peasant society to an advanced industrial economy in a single decade. Intense the concept and application of *totalitarianism* as a descriptive historical term that many scholars ceased to use it.

Others, however, believe the term merits rethinking now that the cold war is over. A totalitarian state, as its definition evolved late in the twentieth century, was one that intensified government's concern with private life and individual thought, leaving no realm of existence outside the state's will. Censorship of speech, suppression of parliamentary and freely chosen representative rule, and violent elimination of disagreement were crucial ingredients of a totalitarian system. Laws regulating reproduction and family life were also central, especially those that either criminalized or enforced birth control and abortion. Hitler, Mussolini, Stalin, and later Mao Zedong of China all made state control of reproduction pivotal to their regimes. Totalitarian regimes also relied on violence to forge unity: control of military or paramilitary weaponry and modern communications technology allowed for the programming of thought and the elimination of enemies, including those who simply had different ideas. Many believe that totalitarianism can work only in a society where the state uses advanced technology and advanced communications to mold individual thought.

Nonetheless, it is important to note the vast differences among totalitarian states: the socialist economy of the Soviet Union differed from the economies of both Nazi Germany and Fascist Italy. Moreover, systems lumped under the word *totalitarian* had different intellectual roots. Nationalism was key in the rise of fascism and Nazism, whereas communism began as an international workers' movement and forced people of many ethnicities to live together. Anti-Semitism also infected totalitarian societies in varying degrees: in Italy, Jews were rarely persecuted (and frequently protected from Nazis), Stalin purged individual Jews without singling out the entire race for extermination, and Nazism had the elimination of the Jews as central to its mission.

QUESTIONS TO CONSIDER

1. What is the relationship of totalitarian states to the tradition of rights and individual freedom?
2. What are shared characteristics of totalitarian rule?
3. What was the relationship between the rise of totalitarianism and World War I?

FURTHER READING

Arendt, Hannah. *The Origins of Totalitarianism*. 1951.

Gleason, Abbott. *Totalitarianism: The Inner History of the Cold War.* 1995.

Tormey, Simon. *Making Sense of Tyranny: Interpretations of Totalitarianism.* 1995.

---

suffering was tolerated because Soviet workers believed in the ethos of "constant struggle, struggle, and struggle" to achieve a Communist society, in the words of a worker. As another put it, "Man himself is being rebuilt."

In country and city alike work was politicized. Stalin demanded more grain from peasants (who had prospered under the NEP), both to feed the urban workforce and to export as a way to finance industrialization. Peasants resisted government demands by cutting production or withholding produce from the market. Faced with such recalcitrance, Stalin announced a new revolutionary challenge: the "liquidation of the kulaks"◆

◆**kulaks:** koo LAHKS

(see "The War on Kulaks," page 1058.) The word *kulak*, which literally means "fist," was a derogatory term for prosperous peasants, but in practice it applied to anyone who opposed Stalin's plans to end independent farming. By the late 1920s, party workers were scouring villages for produce and forced villagers to identify the kulaks among them. Propaganda units instilled hatred for anyone connected with kulaks. One Russian remembered believing they were "bloodsuckers, cattle, swine, loathsome, repulsive: they had no souls; they stank." As "enemies of the state," whole families and even entire villages were robbed of their possessions, left to starve, or even murdered outright. Confiscated kulak land formed the basis of the

The War on Kulaks

Elena Trofimovna Dolgikh was born in Russia in 1910, before World War I and the Bolshevik Revolution. For her family, the war against prosperous farmers called kulaks began even before Stalin launched his first five-year plan. In response to shortages, Communists began confiscating grain and evicting peasant families as early as 1927 and 1928. In an interview given after the collapse of communism in 1989 she described the early attack on kulaks.

In our area collectivization began in '27. That's when people were labeled kulaks and dispossessed. . . . And here's what happened: First of all, they drove the kulaks from their homes. Well, they gave away our horse and the rest—cups, spoons, ladles—all of it they started to sell to people who had not been labeled kulaks. And there were people who were willing to buy those cups, spoons, and ladles. And all of our family was deported to the mountains, to some valley there. So they began to dig shelters. They weren't allowed to take anything with them—only the clothes on their backs. Everything was sold, all that "kulak" wealth. Of course, they confiscated the apiary. This happened toward winter, and that very first winter they let the bees freeze to death. When Granddaddy learned of this, he was struck dead, his heart ruptured, as they said later, because he loved the apiary, he loved the bees. There were melon fields, and everything was ruined. He and Kostia [a brother] went to some village—I don't remember the name of it—where Grandma's sister lived in the mountains. They went on foot and asked for alms. Some gave, some didn't. . . .

[My brother Serezha] was fifteen, and at some point they rounded up all the young fellows from those shelters . . . and drove them on foot 150 kilometers. . . . And it was there . . . that he worked on the construction of the coal and metallurgical complex for several years. In the winter they had to dig ditches, foundation pits, and they were only released when the project was completed, when the first blast furnace was ready to be started up. He and the others had to wear sacks used to store salt. . . . They had no bedding, nothing. They kept dying off, and their bodies were hauled away somewhere.

Source: Barbara Engel and Anastasia Posadskaya-Vanderbeck, eds., *A Revolution of Their Own: Voices of Women in Soviet History* (Boulder: Westview, 1998), 166.

kolkhoz, or collective farm, where peasants were all to live, creating a Communist agricultural system using cooperative farming, shared facilities, and modern machinery. Traditional peasant life was brought to a violent end.

Transforming Society. Once the state had politicized work life as central to the achievement of communism, economic failure took on political meaning. Such failure was legion because the inexperience of factory workers, farmers, and party officials with advanced industrialization often meant an inability to meet quotas. In the face of the murder of farmers and the experiment with collectivization, the grain harvest declined from 83 million tons in 1930 to 67 million in 1934 and Soviet citizens starved. Stalin blamed failure on "wreckers," saboteurs of communism, and he instituted **purges**—that is, state violence in the form of widespread arrests, imprisonments in labor camps, and executions—to rid society of these villains. These purges encompassed nearly all segments of society, but "bourgeois" engineers were the first group condemned for causing low productivity. Trials of prominent figures followed, beginning in 1936. When Sergei Kirov, the popular first secretary of the Leningrad Communist Party, was murdered, Stalin used his death (which he may have instigated) as the pretext to try former Bolshevik leaders in a series of "show trials"—trials based on trumped-up charges, fabricated evidence, and coerced confessions.

The government charged these Bolsheviks with conspiring to overthrow Soviet rule. Tortured and coerced to confess in court, most of those found guilty were shot. Yet there was a bizarre atmosphere of acceptance among the top leadership, who saw the purges as good for the future of socialism. Just before his execution, one Bolshevik loyalist and former editor of the party newspaper *Pravda* wrote to Stalin praising the "great and bold political idea behind the general purge" that was clearly part of the process toward democracy. "I could not hope to be left out. . . . It would be petty of me to put the fortunes of my own person on the same level as those tasks of world-historical importance, which rest above all on your shoulders."

The spirit of purge swept all levels of society, and no rung of the Soviet power structure escaped. One woman poet described the scene in towns and cities: "Great concert and lecture halls were turned into public confessionals. . . . People did penance for [everything]. . . . Beating their breasts, the 'guilty' would lament that they had 'shown political short-sightedness' and 'lack of vigilance' . . . and were full of 'rotten liberalism.'" In 1937 and 1938, military leaders were arrested and executed without public trials; some ranks were entirely wiped out. Although it appeared a suicidal massacre at a time when Hitler threatened war, thousands of high military posts became open to new talent. Stalin would not have to worry about an officer corps wedded to old ideas, as had happened in World War I. Simultaneously, the government expanded the system of prison camps, founded under Lenin, into an extensive network stretching several thousand miles from Moscow to Siberia. Called the Gulag—an acronym for the administrative arm of the government that ran the camps—the system held millions of prisoners under lethal conditions. Prisoners did every kind of work from digging canals to building apartment buildings in Moscow. Some one million died annually as a result of the harsh conditions, which included insufficient food and housing and twelve- to sixteen-hour workdays at crushing physical labor. Regular beatings and murders of prisoners rounded out Gulag life, as it became another aspect of Soviet violence.

Before the outbreak of World War II in 1939, casualties of the Soviet system far exceeded those in Nazi Germany up to that point. This bloody period of Soviet history has thus provoked intense debate among historians trying to understand the phenomenon of mass murder. Were the purges carefully planned and directed solely by Stalin, who actually watched the trials from a secret booth in the courtroom? Or were they initiated by the Communist Party's rank and file? Some historians see the purges as a clear-headed attempt on Stalin's part to eliminate barriers to total control, while others view them as the machinations of a psychopath. More recently, historians have judged the purges to result from power struggles among party officials looking for a quick route to the top. People in the lower ranks denounced their superiors to cover the way they themselves had falsified statistics, been lenient on kulaks, or lacked the proper vigilance. Still other interpretations see many denunciations and confessions as sincere expressions of workers' commitment to rooting out enemies of their proletarian utopia. Evidence shows that, in a way, the wide range of purges was a sign of social equality; no one—not even members of Stalin's family and close circle—was exempt. These debates help us attribute responsibility for the horrendous suffering and loss of life; they also add to our understanding of Communist policy in the 1930s and the nature of the Soviet regime. Even amid historical controversy regarding causes, we may be certain about the outcome: the ongoing arrests, incarcerations, and executions removed rivals to Stalin's power.

The 1930s also marked a sharp reversal of toleration in Soviet social life, as sexual freedom also retreated. Much like the rest of Europe, the USSR experienced a rapid decline in its birthrate in the 1930s. This drop, combined with the need to replace the millions of people lost since 1914, motivated Stalin to end the reproductive freedom of the early revolutionary years in order to increase the birthrate. The state restricted access to birth-control information and abortion. More lavish wedding ceremonies came back into fashion, divorces became difficult to obtain, and the state criminalized homosexuality.

N. J. Altman, *Anna Akhmatova*

This modernist painting portrays the poet Anna Akhmatova in 1914, when she was a centerpiece of literary salon life in Russia and the subject of several avant-garde portraits. In the 1930s and 1940s, Akhmatova gave poetic voice to Soviet suffering, recording in her verse ordinary people's endurance of purges, deprivation, and warfare. As she encouraged people to resist the Nazis during World War II, Stalin allowed her to revive Russian patriotism instead of socialist internationalism. What role do poets and artists play in times of suffering? Why are they considered role models when their activity is so different from other people's? *State Russian Museum, St. Petersburg/The Bridgeman Art Library. © Estate of N. J. Altman / RAO, Moscow/VAGA, NY.*

Whereas Bolsheviks had once derided the family as a "bourgeois" institution, propaganda now referred to the family unit as a "school for socialism." Yet women in rural areas made gains in literacy and received improvements in health care. Positions in the lower ranks of the party opened to women as the purges continued, and women increasingly were accepted into the professions. However, the physical and mental stress on women, particularly those in the industrial workforce, increased. After long hours in factories, workingwomen also stood in lines for scarce consumer goods and performed all household and child-care tasks under harsh conditions.

Cultural life was equally paradoxical under Stalin, for it brought an end to avant-garde experimentation. Simultaneously, modernist intellectuals continued to promote their ability to mobilize the masses by appealing to the unconscious and the emotions in their work. Stalin endorsed this role by calling artists and writers "engineers of the soul," but he controlled their output through the Union of Soviet Writers. The union assigned housing, office space, supplies, equipment, and secretarial help and even determined the types of books authors could write. In return, the "comrade artist" adhered to the official style of "socialist realism," derived from the 1920s focus on the common worker as a type of social hero. Some artists, such as the poet Anna Akhmatova (1889–1966; see the illustration on this page), refused to accept this system.

> Stars of death stood above us, and Russia,
> In her innocence, twisted in pain
> Under blood-spattered boots . . .

wrote Akhmatova in those years. Writers and artists went underground, secretly creating works that are still coming to light. Many others, including the composer Sergei Prokofiev (1891–1953), found ways to accommodate their talents to the state's demands. Prokofiev composed scores both for the delightful *Peter and the Wolf* and for Sergei Eisenstein's 1938 film *Alexander Nevsky*, a production that transparently compared Stalin to the towering medieval rulers of the Russian people. Aided by adaptable artists, workers, and bureaucrats, Stalin stood triumphant as the 1930s drew to a close. He was, as two different workers put it, "our beloved Leader" and "a god on earth."

Hitler's Rise to Power

Hitler ended German democracy. Since the early 1920s, he had tried to rouse the German masses to crush the fragile Weimar Republic. In his coup attempt of 1923, in his influential book *Mein Kampf* (My Struggle, 1925), and in his leadership of the Nazi Party, he drummed at a message of anti-Semitism and the rebirth of the German "race." When the Great Depression struck Germany, his party began to outstrip its rivals in elections, thanks in part to massive support from some big businessmen. Among these supporters, for example, was film and press mogul Alfred Hugenberg. Hugenberg's press relentlessly slammed the Weimar government, blaming it for the disastrous economy and inflaming wounded German pride over the defeat in World War I. Nazi supporters took to the streets, jousting with young Communist groups who agitated on behalf of the new Soviet experiment. Hugenberg's press always reported that Communist thugs had attacked upright Nazis, drawing sympathy and further support from the middle classes.

Parliamentary government virtually ground to a halt in the face of economic crisis and real differences over solutions, adding to the social disarray. The Reichstag, or German assembly, failed to approve emergency plans to improve the economy, as Nazi and Communist deputies disrupted its sessions and thus discredited democracy among the people. Hitler's followers made parliamentary government look even more inept by rampaging through the streets and attacking Jews, Communists, and Social Democrats. By targeting all these as a single, monolithic group of "Bolshevik" enemies, the Nazis won wide approval for confronting those who were said to have brought on the depression. Many thought it was time to replace democratic government with a bold, new leader who would take on these so-called enemies military style, without qualms or fussy legal procedures.

As a result of the depression, media publicity, and its own street tactics, Hitler's National Socialist German Workers' Party (NSDAP)—the Nazi Party—which had received little more than 2 percent of the vote in 1928, won almost 20 percent in the Reichstag elections of 1930 and more than doubled its representation in 1932. Many of Hitler's supporters, like Stalin's, were young and idealistic. In 1930, 70 percent of party members were under forty, a stark contrast to the image of Weimar politicians as aged and ineffectual. To youth, the future looked bleak, and they were full of idealism that a better world was possible if Hitler took control. Although businessmen provided substantial sums of money, every class supported the Nazis. The largest number of supporters came from the industrial working class because they had the most voters, but white-collar workers and the lower-middle class joined the party in percentages out of proportion with their numbers in the population. The years of inflation that wiped out savings left them with especially bitter memories, and they too were ready for Hitler even if he did seem a little rough around the edges.

Hitler's modern propaganda techniques helped build his appeal. Thousands of recordings of Hitler's speeches and other Nazi mementos circulated among the citizenry. Teenagers painted their fingernails with swastikas, a Buddhist symbol adopted by the Nazis,

Toys Depicting Nazis

As a totalitarian ideology, Nazism was part of everyday life. Nazi insignia decorated clothing, dishes, cigarette lighters, and even fingernails. People chose their loved ones according to Nazi rules, sent young people to Nazi clubs and organizations, and bought Nazi toys like these for their children's playtime. Nazi songs, Nazi parades and festivals, and Nazi art filled leisure hours. How important are ordinary objects in the development of political attitudes? *Imperial War Museum, London.*

and soldiers flashed metal match covers with Nazi insignia. Nazi rallies were masterpieces of political display in which Hitler mesmerized the crowds as their strong, vastly superior *Führer*, or "leader." Frenzied and inspirational, he represented neither the calculating politician nor the rational bureaucrat but "the creative element," as one poet put it. In actuality, however, Hitler viewed the masses only as tools, and he had contempt for them. In *Mein Kampf* he discussed his philosophy of how to deal with them:

> The receptivity of the great masses is very limited, their intelligence is small. In consequence of these facts, all effective propaganda must be limited to a very few points and must harp on those in slogans until the last member of the public understands what you want him to understand.

With Hitler, as with Stalin, mass politics reached terrifying and cynical proportions; Hitler's media techniques, however, were to endure, some believe to influence today's political styles.

Nazi success in the 1932 Reichstag elections was made more alarming because the Communists also did very well. The leader of one of these two parties was the logical choice as chancellor, and this fact upset conservative politicians in the government. Germany's conservative elites—from the military, industry, and the state bureaucracy—loathed and feared the Communists for their opposition to private property. They favored Hitler as a common type they believed to be easily manipulated. They invited him in January 1933 to become chancellor, and he accepted.

The Nazification of German Politics

Hitler took office amid jubilation in Berlin, as tens of thousands of Hitler's paramilitary supporters, called storm troopers, paraded through the streets with blazing torches. Millions celebrated Hitler's ascent to power. "My father went down to the cellar and brought up our best bottles of wine. . . . And my mother wept for joy," one German recalled. "Now everything will be all right," she said. Instead of being easy to manipulate, Hitler took command brutally, quickly installing himself and his party as dominant and closing down representative government with an ugly show of force.

Terror in the Nazi State. Within a month of Hitler's taking power, the elements of Nazi political domination were in place. When the Reichstag building was gutted by fire in February 1933, Nazis blamed the Communists and used the fire as the excuse for suspending civil rights, imposing censorship of the press, and prohibiting meetings of the opposition. Hitler had always claimed that all political parties except the NSDAP were his enemies. "Our opponents complain that we National Socialists, and I in particular, are intolerant and intractable," he declared. "They are right, we are intolerant! I have set myself one task, namely to sweep those parties out of Germany."

Storm troopers' political violence became a way of life. They harassed many democratic politicians into silent passivity. At the end of March, intimidated Reichstag delegates let pass the **Enabling Act**, which suspended the constitution for four years and allowed Nazi laws to take effect without parliamentary approval. Solid middle-class Germans approved the Enabling Act as a way to advance the creation of a *Volksgemeinschaft*◆ ("people's community") of like-minded, racially pure Germans—Aryans in Nazi terminology. Heinrich Himmler headed the elite Schutzstaffel (SS), an organization that protected Hitler, and he commanded the Reich's political police system. The Gestapo, or Prussian political police run by Hermann Goering, also enforced complete obedience to Nazism. These organizations had vast powers to arrest people and either execute them or imprison them in concentration camps, the first of which opened at Dachau◆ near Munich in March 1933. The Nazis filled it and later camps with political enemies like socialists, and then with Jews, homosexuals, and others said to interfere with the Volksgemeinschaft. As one Nazi leader proclaimed:

> [National socialism] does not believe that one soul is equal to another, one man equal to another. It does not believe in rights as such. It aims to create the German man of strength, its task is to protect the German people, and all . . . must be subordinate to this goal.

◆*Volksgemeinschaft:* FOHLKS geh myn shaft
◆**Dachau:** DAH kow

Hitler deliberately blurred authority in the government and party so that confusion and bitter competition reigned. He thus prevented the emergence of coalitions against him and allowed himself to arbitrate the confusion, often with violence. When Ernst Roehm, leader of the SA (storm troopers) and Hitler's longtime collaborator, called for a "second revolution" to end the corrupt influence of the old business and military elites on the Nazi leadership, Hitler ordered Roehm's assassination. The bloody Night of the Long Knives (June 30, 1934), during which hundreds of SA leaders and innocent civilians were killed, enhanced Hitler's support among conservatives. They saw that he would deal ruthlessly with those favoring a leveling out of social privilege. Nazism's terroristic politics remained as the foundation of Hitler's Third Reich, which succeeded the First Reich of Charlemagne and the Second of Bismarck and William II.

Nazi Economic and Social Programs. New economic and social programs, especially putting people back to work, were also crucial to the survival of Hitler's regime. Economic revival built popular support, strengthened military industries, and provided the basis for German expansion. The Nazi government pursued **pump priming**, that is, stimulating the economy through public works programs and other infusions of funds to the public—by building tanks and airplanes and the Autobahn, or highway system. From farms to factories, the government demanded high productivity, and unemployment declined from a peak of almost 6 million in 1932 to 1.6 million by 1936. As labor shortages began to appear in certain areas, the government conscripted single women into service as farmworkers and domestics. The Nazi Party closed down labor unions, and government managers classified jobs, determined work procedures, and set pay levels, rating women's jobs lower than men's regardless of the level of expertise required. Imitating Stalin, Hitler instituted central planning, announcing a four-year plan in 1936 with the secret aim of preparing Germany for war by 1940. His programs produced large deficits, which the spoils of future conquests were supposed to eliminate.

Hitler had unprecedented power over the workings of everyday life, including gender roles. In June 1933, a bill took effect that encouraged Aryans (those people defined as racially German) to marry and have children. The bill provided for loans to Aryan newlyweds, but only to those couples in which the wife left the workforce. The loans were forgiven on the birth of the pair's fourth child. Nazi marriage programs enforced racial ideology as well as gender ideology; women were supposed to be subordinate so men would feel tough and industrious despite military defeat and economic depression. The ideal woman gave up her job, gave birth to many children, and completely surrendered her will to that of men. She "joyfully sacrifices and fulfills her fate," as one Nazi leader explained.

Nazism impoverished culture and everyday life. Although 70 percent of households had radios by 1938, the programming broadcast was severely censored. Books like Erich Maria Remarque's *All Quiet on the Western Front* were banned, and in May 1933 a huge book-burning ceremony rid libraries of works by Jews, socialists, homosexuals, and modernist writers out of favor with the Nazis. Modern art in museums and private collections was either destroyed or confiscated, and laws took jobs from Jews and women and bestowed them on Nazi party members. In the Hitler Youth, a mandatory organization for boys and girls over age ten, children learned to report those adults they suspected of disloyalty to the regime, even their own parents. People boasted that they could leave their bicycles out at night without fear of robbery, but their world was also filled with informers—some 100,000 of them on the Nazi payroll. In general, the improved economy led many to believe that Hitler was working an economic miracle while restoring pride in Germany and the harmonious community of an imaginary past. For hundreds of thousands, if not millions, of Germans, however, Nazi rule in the 1930s brought anything but community.

Nazi Racism

The Nazis defined Jews as an inferior "race" dangerous to the superior Aryan or Germanic "race" and responsible for most of Germany's problems, including defeat in World War I and the crippling economic depression. Hitler's reasons for targeting Jews were, he insisted, modern and scientific. "National Socialism is a cool and highly reasoned approach to reality based on the greatest of scientific knowledge and its spiritual expression," he declared in a 1938 speech. Hitler attacked many ethnic and social groups, but he propelled the nineteenth-century politics of anti-Semitism to new and frightening heights. In the rhetoric of Nazism, Jews were "vermin," "abscesses," "parasites," and "Bolsheviks," whom the Germans would have to eliminate to become a true Volksgemeinschaft. By defining the Jews both as evil financiers and businessmen and as working-class Bolsheviks, Hitler fashioned an enemy for many segments of the population to hate passionately.

Nazi policy was called racial, and it led to laws against non-Aryans—a group that, like Aryans, was never defined. The word *Aryan,* which means "noble" in the ancient Asian language Sanskrit, indicated a people of great distinction who according to legend existed in distant times. Then, the legend goes, they were overtaken either by natural forces or a group of barbarians and driven from their ancient lands, ultimately reappearing as the German people. For all this legendary background, policymakers insisted that terms such as *Aryan* and *Jewish* (a religious category) were scientific racial classifications that could be determined by physical characteristics. In 1935, the government enacted the **Nuremberg Laws**, legislation that specifically deprived Jews of citizenship, defined Jewishness according to a person's ancestry, ended special consideration for Jewish war veterans, and prohibited marriage between Jews and other Germans. Whereas women defined as Aryan had increasing difficulty obtaining abortions or even birth-control information, these were readily available to the outcast groups, including Jews, Gypsies, Slavs, and mentally or physically disabled people. In the name of improving the Aryan race, doctors helped organize the T4 project, which used carbon monoxide poisoning and other means to kill large numbers of people—200,000 handicapped and elderly—late in the 1930s. The idea behind the murder of the disabled was that their condition indicated the presence of racial inferiority that endangered the Aryans. These murders pre-pared the way for even larger mass exterminations that would occur later.

Jews were forced into slave labor, evicted from their apartments, and prevented from buying most clothing and food. In 1938, a Jewish teenager, reacting to the harassment of his parents, killed a German official. In retaliation, Nazis attacked some two hundred synagogues, smashed windows of Jewish-owned stores, ransacked apartments of known or suspected Jews, and threw more than twenty thousand Jews into prisons and camps. The night of November 9–10 became known as Kristallnacht, or the Night of Broken Glass. Faced with this relentless persecution, which some historians have called a "social death," by the outbreak of World War II in 1939 more than half of Germany's 500,000 Jews had emigrated. The confiscation of emigrants' property enriched their neighbors and individual Nazis; the payment of enormous emigration fees helped finance Germany's economic revival. Identifying a group as a permanent and menacing foe was an ideological tactic used to bring unity in wartime, but it now became a political tactic to build support for Nazism in peacetime. It also brought the regime much-needed financial resources, as Jewish property was simply stolen and Jews themselves were forced to work for virtually no pay.

Review: What role did violence play in the Soviet and Nazi regimes?

❖ Democracies on the Defensive

Nazism, communism, and fascism offered bold new approaches to modern politics and new kinds of economic and social policies. These ideologies maintained that democracy was effeminate and that it wasted precious time in building consensus and practicing diplomacy. Totalitarian leaders' energetic, military style of mobilizing the masses made representative government and democratic values of the United States, France, and Great Britain appear to signal the decline of these societies. A wide range of individuals—from prominent businessmen like Henry Ford to major writers and ordinary working people—found aspects of totalitarianism appealing.

Confronting the Economic Crisis

The 1930s saw democracies on the defensive in politics and economics as they aimed to restore the well-being of citizens and defend individual rights and political processes. As the depression wore on, some governments undertook notable experiments to solve social and economic crises and still maintain democratic politics. The United States and Sweden were among the most successful in facing the double-barreled assault of economic depression and fascism. Other countries, such as France, took a zigzagging course with uneven results, especially for the cause of representative government.

The United States. In the early days of the slump, U.S. president Herbert Hoover opposed direct help to the unemployed and even ordered the army to use tanks to drive away unemployed veterans who had marched on Washington, D.C. With unemployment close to fifteen million, Franklin Delano Roosevelt (1882–1945), the wealthy, patrician governor of New York, defeated Hoover in the presidential election of 1932 on the promise of innovation. Roosevelt pushed through a torrent of legislation, some of it inspired by the central control of the economy achieved during World War I: relief for businesses, price supports for hard-pressed farmers, and public works programs for unemployed youth. The Social Security Act of 1935 set up a fund to which employers and employees contributed. It provided retirement benefits for workers, unemployment insurance, and payments to dependent

mothers, their children, and people with disabling physical conditions.

The result was to advance the trend toward the welfare state—that is, a government that guarantees a certain level of economic well-being for individuals and businesses— not only in the United States but elsewhere across the West as well. Roosevelt's "New Deal" angered businesspeople and the wealthy, who saw it as socialist. But even though the depression remained severe, Roosevelt (quickly nicknamed FDR) maintained widespread support. Like other successful politicians of the 1930s and thereafter, he was an expert at using the new mass media, especially in his series of "fireside chats" broadcast by radio to the American people (see A Fireside Chat with FDR, below). In sharp contrast to Mussolini and Hitler, however, Roosevelt aimed in his

A Fireside Chat with FDR
President Franklin Delano Roosevelt was a master of words, uttering many memorable phrases that inspired Americans during the depression and World War II. Aware of growing media power in the making and breaking of politicians, the press never showed Roosevelt's disabilities even when he used crutches or fell down. Instead, FDR became a symbol of U.S. resolve, ingenuity, and growing power. Here he addresses the nation on August 23, 1938, over a radio hookup while Eleanor Roosevelt and the president's mother, Sarah, observe. Compare the depiction of the Roosevelts as leaders to that of Mussolini on page 1042. © Hulton Archive/Getty Images.

public statements to sustain—not to denounce—faith in democratic rights and popular government. Eager to separate FDR's administration from Hoover's position, First Lady Eleanor Roosevelt rushed to greet the next group of veterans marching on Washington, and FDR himself received the delegation at the White House. The Roosevelts insisted that justice and human rights must not be surrendered in difficult times. "We Americans of today . . . are characters in the living book of democracy," FDR told a group of teenagers in 1939. "But we are also its author." Lynchings, racial violence, and harsh discrimination continued to cause enormous suffering in the United States during the Roosevelt administration, and the economy did not fully recover. But the president's media success and bold programs kept the masses committed to a democratic future.

Sweden. Sweden also developed a coherent program for solving economic and population problems. It too reconceived the government's role as central to promoting social welfare and economic democracy. Although Sweden had industrialized later than western Europe and the United States, it had a tradition of community cooperation in overcoming social and economic difficulties. Sweden succeeded in turning its economy around in the 1930s and instituted central planning and social welfare programs. It also devalued the currency to make Swedish exports more attractive on the international market. Thanks to pump-priming programs, Swedish productivity rose by 20 percent between 1929 and 1935, a time when other democracies were still experiencing decline.

Sweden addressed the population problem with government programs, but without the racist and antidemocratic coercion of totalitarianism. Alva Myrdal (1902–1986), a leading member of parliament, believed that fertility rates depended on both the economy and individual well-being. It was undemocratic, she maintained, that "the bearing of a child should mean economic distress" to those wanting children. Acting on Myrdal's advice to promote "voluntary parenthood," the government started a loan program for married couples in 1937 and introduced prenatal care, free childbirth in a hospital, a food

relief program, and subsidized housing for large families. By the end of the decade, almost 50 percent of all mothers in Sweden received government aid, most importantly in the form of a **family allowance** to help cover the costs of raising children. Long a concern of feminists and other social reformers, care of families became integral to the tasks of the modern state, which now saw itself as responsible for citizen welfare in hard times. Because all families—rural and urban, poor or prosperous—received these social benefits, there was widespread and consistent support for this experiment with developing a welfare state.

Britain and France. The most powerful democracy, the United States, had withdrawn from world leadership by refusing to participate in the League of Nations, leaving Britain and France with greater responsibility for international peace and well-being than their postwar resources could sustain. Britain was already mired in economic difficulties when the Great Depression hit. Faced with falling government revenues, Prime Minister Ramsay MacDonald, though leader of the Labour Party, reduced payments to the unemployed, and Parliament effectively denied unemployment insurance to women even though they had contributed to the unemployment fund. To protect jobs, the government imposed huge protective tariffs that actually discouraged a revival of international trade and did not relieve British misery. Only in 1933, with the economy continuing to worsen, did the government begin to take effective steps with massive programs of slum clearance, new housing construction, and health insurance for the needy. British leaders saw pump-priming methods of recovery as risky and untried, and thus they resorted to them only when all else had failed.

Depression struck later in France, but the country endured a decade of public strife in the 1930s due to severe postwar demoralization, stagnant population growth, and wage cuts. Deputies with opposing views on the economic crisis frequently came to blows in the Chamber of Deputies, and governments were voted in and out with dizzying rapidity. Parisians took to the streets to protest the government's belt-tightening policies, and right-wing paramilitary groups mushroomed, attracting the unemployed, students, and veterans to the cause of ending representative government. In February 1934, the paramilitary groups joined Communists and other outraged citizens in riots around the parliament building. "Let's string up the deputies," chanted the crowd. "And if we can't string them up, let's beat in their faces, let's reduce them to a pulp." Hundreds of demonstrators were wounded and killed, but the antirepublican right lacked both substantial support outside Paris and a leader like Hitler or Mussolini capable of unifying its various groups. As in other parts of Europe, hard times and the attractions of military dictatorship menaced democratic institutions.

Shocked into action by the force of fascism, French liberals, socialists, and Communists established an antifascist coalition known as the **Popular Front**. Until that time, such a merging of groups had been impossible in democratic countries because of Stalin's strict opposition to Communist collaboration with liberals and socialists, who disavowed Communist-style revolutions. Thus, leaders of Communist parties followed instructions not to cooperate, no matter how much they might agree that fascism had to be opposed. As fascism spread throughout Europe, however, Stalin reversed course and allowed Communists to join such efforts to protect democracy. For just over a year in 1936–1937 and again very briefly in 1938, the French Popular Front led the government, with the socialist leader Léon Blum (1872–1950) as premier. Like the American New Dealers and the Swedish Social Democrats, the Popular Front instituted long-overdue reforms. Blum extended family subsidies and welfare benefits, and he appointed women to his government (though women still were not allowed to vote). In June 1936, the government guaranteed workers two-week paid vacations, a forty-hour workweek, and the right to collective bargaining. Working people would long remember Blum as the man who improved their living standards and provided them with benefits and the right to vacations (see the illustration on this page).

During its brief life, the Popular Front offered the masses a youthful but democratic political culture. "In 1936 everyone was twenty years old," one man recalled,

Family at Normandy Beach
In the midst of the depression of the 1930s, the working classes nonetheless gained a taste of leisure when the French government under Léon Blum mandated paid vacations for all workers. As other governments followed this lead, tourism became a booming business in the West. Citizens from all walks of life traveled to see their own country, witness its geographic differences, and visit its historic monuments. How did instituting vacations promote and reflect changing political and social values? *Private Collection.*

evoking the atmosphere of idealism. Local cultural centers sprang up, and to express their opposition to fascism, citizens celebrated democratic holidays like Bastille Day with new enthusiasm. But despite this support from workers, the Popular Front governments were politically weak. Fearing for their investments, bankers and industrialists greeted Blum's appointment by sending their capital out of the country, leaving France financially strapped. "Better Hitler than Blum" was the slogan of the upper classes. Blum's government fell when it lost the left by refusing material support in the fight against fascism in Spain. As in Britain, memories of World War I caused leaders to block crucial assistance to foreign democratic forces such as the republicans in Spain and to keep the domestic military budgets small. The collapse of the antifascist Popular Front showed the difficulties that pluralistic and democratic societies faced in crisis-ridden times.

Central and Eastern Europe. Fledgling democracies in central Europe, hit hard by the depression, also fought the twin struggle for economic survival and representative government, but less successfully. In 1932, Engelbert Dollfuss came to power in Austria, dismissing the parliament and ruling briefly as a dictator. Despite his authoritarian stance, Dollfuss would not submit to the Nazis, who stormed his office and assassinated him in 1934 in an unsuccessful attempted coup. In Hungary, where outrage over the Peace of Paris remained intense, a crippled economy allowed right-wing general Gyula Gömbös♦ to take over in 1932. Gömbös reoriented his country's foreign policy toward Mussolini and Hitler. He stirred up anti-Semitism and ethnic hatreds and left considerable pro-Nazi feeling after his death in 1936. In democratic Czechoslovakia, the Slovaks, who were both poorer and less educated than the urbanized Czechs, built a strong Slovak Fascist Party. In Poland, Romania, Yugoslavia, and Bulgaria, ethnic tensions simmered and the appeal of fascism grew as the Great Depression lingered.

Cultural Visions in Hard Times

Postwar cultural leaders mobilized to meet the crisis of hard times and political menace, making films, writing novels, and producing art that captured the spirit of everyday struggle. Some empathized with the situations of factory workers, homemakers, and shopgirls straining to support themselves and their families; others looked to interpret the lives of an ever-growing number of unemployed and destitute. Artists portrayed the inhuman, regimented side of modern life. In 1931, French director René Clair's film *Give Us Liberty* related the routine of prison to work on a factory assembly line. Charlie Chaplin's film *Modern Times* (1936) showed his famous character, the Little Tramp, as a worker in a modern factory who was so molded by his monotonous job that he assumed anything he could see, even a coworker's body, needed mechanical adjustment. These sympathetic representations of the modern factory worker in hard times made Chaplin a hit even in the Soviet Union, where productions from capitalist countries were not supposed to receive such a warm welcome.

♦**Gyula Gömbös:** DYUL ah GUHM buhsh

Media sympathy poured out to victims of the economic crisis, with women portrayed alternately as the cause and as the cure for society's problems. *The Blue Angel* (1930), a German film starring Marlene Dietrich, contrasted a woman's power to the ineffectuality of an impractical professor and thus symbolized how a vital, modern woman could destroy men—and civilization. In comedies and musicals, by contrast, heroines behaved bravely, pulling their men out of the depths of despair and setting things right again. In such films as *Keep Smiling* (1938), the British comedienne Gracie Fields portrayed spunky working-class women who remained cheerful despite the challenges of living in hard times.

Ridiculed in the past, techniques of modern art became standard tools for popular culture and advertising. Graphic artists used montage, which overlaid two or more photos or parts of photos, to grab visual attention in the cultural battles of the 1930s. Some intellectuals turned away from experimentation with nonrepresentational forms as they drove home their antifascist, pacifist, or pro-worker beliefs. Popular Front writers created realistic studies of human misery and the threat of war that haunted life in the 1930s. The British writer George Orwell described his experiences among the poor of Paris and London, wrote investigative pieces about the unemployed in the north of England, and published an account of atrocities committed by both sides during the Spanish Civil War (1936–1939).

After several decades during which abstract art had often avoided giving direct political messages, art during the Great Depression and the struggle against fascism returned to affirming values—especially those of rational thought, individual rights, and the dignity of the poor. German writer Thomas Mann (1875–1955) was outraged at Hitler's ascent to power and went into exile even though he was of Christian birth. He based a series of novels on the Old Testament hero Joseph to convey the struggle between humanist values and barbarism. The fourth volume, *Joseph the Provider* (1944), eulogized Joseph's welfare state, in which the granaries were full and the rich paid taxes so the poor might live decent lives. One of the last works of English writer Virginia Woolf, *Three Guineas* (1938), rejected experimental forms such as interior monologues for a direct attack on militarism, poverty, and the oppression of women, claiming they were interconnected parts of a single, devastating ethos undermining Europe in the 1930s.

While writers rekindled moral concerns, scientists in research institutes and universities continued to point out limits to human understanding—limits that seemed at odds with the megalomaniacal pronouncements of dictators. Astronomer Edwin Hubble (1889–1953) in California determined in the early 1930s that the universe was an expanding entity. Czech mathematician Kurt Gödel (1906–1978) maintained that all mathematical systems contain some propositions that are undecidable. The German physicist Werner Heisenberg developed the uncertainty, or indeterminacy, principle in physics. Scientific observation of atomic behavior, according to this theory, actually disturbs the atom and thereby makes precise formulations impossible. Even scientists, Heisenberg asserted, had to settle for statistical probability. Limits to understanding, approximation, and probability were not concepts that military dictators welcomed, and even people in democracies had a difficult time reconciling these new ideas with the certainty of which science and technology had once boasted.

Religious leaders helped foster a spirit of resistance to dictatorship among religious people. Notable clergymen hoped for a re-Christianization of ordinary people so that they might have spiritual alternatives to fascist preachings. The Swiss theologian Karl Barth (1886–1968) encouraged opposition to the Nazis, teaching that the faithful had to take seriously scriptural justifications of resistance to oppression. In his 1931 social encyclical, a letter addressed to the world on social issues, Pope Pius XI (r. 1922–1939) condemned the failure of modern societies to provide their citizens with a decent life and supported government intervention to create better moral and material conditions. The encyclical, *Quadragesimo Anno*, seemed to some an endorsement of the heavy-handed intervention of the fascists, however. In Germany, nonetheless, German Catholics

opposed Hitler, and religious commitment inspired many other individuals to oppose the rising tide of fascism through the churches.

> **Review:** How did the democracies work to maintain their values while facing the twin challenges of economic depression and the rise of fascism?

❖ The Road to Global War

The economic crash intensified competition for wealth and influence among the major powers in the 1930s, as politicians sought to solidify their control of people and resources. External colonies were more important than ever during the depression, continuing to enrich individual investors while softening the effects in Europe. Of the British in Malaya, one businessman said, "It was impossible not to make money." Europeans who migrated to the colonies also enjoyed living sociably together away from the humdrum struggles in Europe: imperial officials and businesspeople had, according to one woman colonialist, "a very good time" full of "sunshine, servants, wonderful memories." Governments did not let up on the collection of taxes and other charges, despite hardships of the ordinary colonized person. However, no matter the wealth and self-satisfaction colonies brought, Britain and France could simply not afford to govern and protect their vast holdings should concerted challenges arise. This paradox, which continued to define imperialism, increased the tendency toward war and violence during the Great Depression.

In the context of depression and the weakened condition of the imperial leaders, contenders for empire arose. Seeking relief from economic catastrophe and a boost to their prestige, Hitler, Mussolini, and Japan's military leaders marched the world toward another catastrophic war. These leaders believed that their nations deserved to rule a far larger territory as part of their special destiny. At first, statesmen in Britain and France hoped that sanctions imposed by the League of Nations would be able to contain this new aggression. Others, believing that the powers had rushed into World War I, counseled the appeasement of Mussolini and Hitler. The

THE ROAD TO WORLD WAR II

1929   Global depression begins with U.S. stock market crash

1931   Japan invades Manchuria

1933   Hitler comes to power in Germany

1935   Italy invades Ethiopia

1936   Civil war breaks out in Spain; Hitler remilitarizes the Rhineland

1937   Japan invades China

1938   Germany annexes Austria; European leaders meet in Munich to negotiate with Hitler

1939   Germany seizes Czechoslovakia; Hitler and Stalin sign nonaggression pact; Germany invades Poland; Britain and France declare war on Germany

widespread desire for peace in the 1930s sprang from fresh and painful memories: the destruction of World War I and the economic turmoil of the Great Depression. But it left many people blind to Japanese actions in China, Hitler's outright expansionism, and the Fascist attack on the Spanish republic. So brutal were the interwar years that some historians claim that, along with World Wars I and II, they make up a single "Thirty Years' War" of the twentieth century.

A Surge in Global Imperialism

The 1930s brought the last surge of global imperialism and one that ultimately led to a thoroughly global war. As a whole, it was the most important grab for land of the century, shaping international politics down to the present because of its immense consequences. In Palestine, European Jews continued to arrive and claim the area as theirs. The numbers escalated sharply as Hitler enacted his harsh anti-Jewish policies in 1933 and as people across Europe and Asia felt the impact of the economic slump. To prevent the migration of Jews and the unemployed to their own countries, the major European states encouraged emigration to Palestine. As immigration soared, the Arabs, who even with the rapidly growing numbers of Europeans made up more than two-thirds of the population, under-

took a prolonged general strike in 1936. Nationalist politicians from the region saw in the revolt evidence of a common threat to Arabs everywhere, and pan-Arabism suddenly intensified. Japan, Germany, and Italy joined in the competition for land and resources—both close at hand and far away—to continue their economic development.

Japan's Expansionism.   Japan's military leaders chafed to control more of Asia and saw China, Russia, and the other Western powers as obstacles to the empire's prosperity and the fulfillment of its destiny. In the 1920s Japan experienced some of the turmoil that afflicted industrializing countries. Along with the development of literacy and mass politics, the country suffered from a weak monarchy in the person of Emperor Hirohito, who was barely of age. This caused a crisis of legitimacy that stimulated groups with competing ambitions to seek control of the government. Japan's military leaders developed the ideology that the military was an institution unto itself, an "emperor's army" independent of civilian control and indeed one whose well-being was separate from that of the nation. Nationalist groups encouraged these leaders to prize the military success of Japan as the basis of a new world order. By the 1930s, the young emperor and his advisers had helped reactivate emotional support for the imperial system and convince the people that Japan deserved an extensive empire (Map 27.1). Renewed military vigor was seen as key to pulling agriculture and small business from the depths of economic depression. Japan's claims to racial superiority and territorial entitlement to the lands of inferior people linked it with Germany and Italy in the 1930s, setting the stage for a powerful global alliance.

The army took the lead in making these claims a reality: in September 1931, a railroad train in the Chinese province of Manchuria blew up, and Japanese officers used the explosion, which they had actually set, as an excuse to invade the territory, set up a puppet government, and push farther into China. The public agreed with journalistic calls for aggressive expansion to restore the economy and lagging prestige, while businessmen wanted new markets and resources for their burgeoning but wounded industries. From 1931 on, Japan continued its aggression in China, not only rousing the Chinese but also angering the United States, on which it depended for natural resources and markets. Ideologically, the Japanese military leadership saw itself as fully justified in breaking the stranglehold of the status quo. "Unequal distribution of land and resources causes war," an adviser to Hirohito announced before an enthusiastic public. Advocating Asian conquest as part of Japan's "divine mission," the military extended its influence in the government. By 1936–1937, Japan was spending 47 percent of its budget on arms.

The situation in East Asia had international repercussions. Japanese military success added to the threat Japan posed to the West, as Japanese goods found even bigger markets in Asia thanks to the conquest of new regions. The League of Nations condemned the invasion of Manchuria, but it imposed no sanctions that would have put economic teeth into its condemnation. Meanwhile, the rebuff outraged the Japanese public and goaded the government to ally with Hitler and Mussolini. In 1937, Japan undertook another major attack on China, justifying its offensive as a first step toward liberating the region from Western imperialism. Hundreds of thousands of Chinese were massacred in the "Rape of Nanjing"—an atrocity so named because of the brutality toward girls and women and the grim acts of torture perpetrated by the Japanese. President Roosevelt immediately announced an embargo on U.S. export of airplane parts to Japan and later enforced stringent economic sanctions on the crucial raw materials that

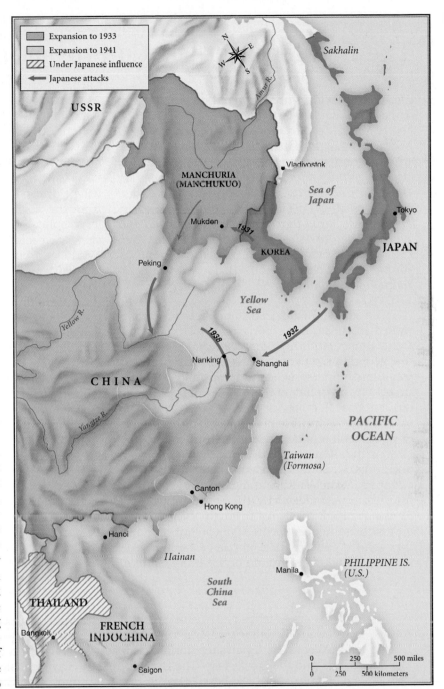

MAP 27.1 The Expansion of Japan, 1931–1941

Japanese expansion in the twentieth century approximated that of Russia and the United States in the nineteenth century: that is, it incorporated neighboring regions of Korea, Taiwan, and Manchuria with the vast area of China an inviting target. Governments of modernizing states believed that actual possession of territories was necessary for the resources, workforce, and markets they provided. But Japan's ambition fell afoul of the United States' own Pacific goals and made these two powers suddenly become deadly rivals. Why would Japan believe itself more entitled than the United States and Europe to a privileged position in the economic and political direction of East Asia?

The Greater East Asia Co-Prosperity Sphere

During the 1930s, Japan entered a new phase of imperial expansion in the Pacific, after having already taken over Korea and Formosa before World War I. To keep pace with its rapidly developing industrial and military capacities, Japan needed access to raw materials and markets blocked by the U.S. and European powers. As it invaded China and other Pacific nations, the Japanese government declared that expansion was actually a move to liberate Asians from Western imperialism and form an independent "Co-Prosperity Sphere" for the region. This secret 1942 government planning paper outlines Japan's expansion goals.

The states, their citizens, and resources, comprised in those areas pertaining to the Pacific, Central Asia, and the Indian Oceans formed into one general union are to be established as an autonomous zone of peaceful living and common prosperity on behalf of the peoples of the nations of East Asia. . . .

The above purpose presupposes the inevitable emancipation or independence of Eastern Siberia, China, Indo-China, the South Seas, Australia, and India. . . . It is intended that the unification of Japan, Manchoukuo, and China in neighborly friendship be realized by the settlement of the Sino-Japanese problems through the crushing of hostile influences in the Chinese interior, and through the construction of a new China in tune with the rapid construction of the Inner Sphere.

Aggressive American and British influences in East Asia shall be driven out of the area of Indo-China and the South Seas, and this area shall be brought into our defense sphere. The war with Britain and America shall be prosecuted for that purpose.

The Russian aggressive influence in East Asia will be driven out. Eastern Siberia shall be cut off from the Soviet regime and included in our defense sphere. For this purpose, a war with the Soviets is expected. It is considered possible that this Northern problem may break out before the general settlement of the present Sino-Japanese and the Southern problems if the situation renders this unavoidable. Next the independence of Australia, India, etc. shall gradually be brought about. For this purpose, a recurrence of war with Britain and her allies is expected. . . . Occidental individualism and materialism shall be rejected and a moral world view, the basic principle of whose morality shall be the Imperial Way, shall be established. The ultimate object to be achieved is not exploitation but co-prosperity and mutual help, not competitive conflict but mutual assistance and mild peace, not a formal view of equality but a view of order based on righteous classification, not an idea of rights but an idea of service, and not several world views but one unified world view.

Source: Ryusaku Tsunoda, Wm. Theodore de Bary, Donald Keene, *Sources of Japanese Tradition.* (New York: Columbia University Press, 1958) 802–3, 805.

---

drove Japanese industry. Nonetheless, the Western powers, including the Soviet Union, did not effectively resist Japan's territorial expansion in Asia and the Pacific (see "The Greater East Asia Co-Prosperity Sphere," above).

Germany and Italy Contest the Status Quo. Like Japanese leaders, Mussolini and Hitler called their countries have-nots and demanded a change in the status quo. Mussolini threatened "permanent conflict" to expand Italy's borders, while Hitler's agenda included breaking free from the Versailles treaty's military restrictions and gain-

ing more **Lebensraum,**♦ or living space, in which "superior" Aryans could thrive. This space would be taken from the "inferior" Slavic peoples and Bolsheviks, who would be moved to Siberia or would serve as slaves. Both dictators portrayed themselves as peace-loving men who resorted to extreme measures only to benefit their country and humanity. Their anticommunism appealed to statesmen across the West, and Hitler's anti-Semitism even found widespread support. Some thus favored accommodating these

♦**Lebensraum:** LAY buhnz rown

two dictators' demands to control more land at the expense of others.

Both leaders' moves against the international status quo were open and audacious. In the autumn of 1933, Hitler announced Germany's withdrawal from the League of Nations. In 1935, Hitler loudly rejected the clauses of the Treaty of Versailles that limited German military strength; he reintroduced military conscription and publicly started rearming, although Germany had been rearming in secret for years. Mussolini also chose 1935 to invade Ethiopia, one of the very few African states not overwhelmed by European imperialism. The attack was intended to demonstrate his regime's youth and vigor and to raise Italy's standing among the colonial powers. "The Roman legionnaires are again on the march," one soldier exulted. The poorly equipped Ethiopians resisted, but their capital, Addis Ababa, fell in the spring of 1936. The League of Nations voted to impose sanctions against Italy, but Britain and France opposed an embargo with teeth in it—one on oil—and thus kept the sanctions from being effective while also suggesting a lack of resolve to fight aggression. The fall of Ethiopia was a searing moment for many Africans, and memories of Italy's boastful assertions of African racial inferiority fortified many African national liberation movements in later years.

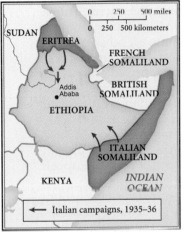

The Ethiopian War, 1935–1936

Profiting from the diversion of Italy's attack on Ethiopia, in March 1936 Hitler defiantly sent his troops into what was supposed to be a permanently demilitarized zone in the Rhineland. The inhabitants greeted the Germans with wild enthusiasm, and the French, whose security was most endangered by this action, also protested to the League of Nations instead of countering with an invasion, as they had done in the Ruhr in 1923. The British accepted the fait accompli, and the two dictators thus appeared as powerful military heroes forging, in Mussolini's muscular phrase, a "Rome–Berlin Axis." Next to them, the politicians of France and Great Britain looked timid, unfit, and defeatable.

The Spanish Civil War, 1936–1939

Spain joined the wave of authoritarianism inundating Europe, despite the country's attempts early in the 1930s to turn toward democracy. In 1931 Spanish republicans overthrew their monarchy, which for centuries had fortified the rule of large landowners and the domination of the Catholic clergy. As Spain fitfully developed an industrial capacity in cities like Barcelona and Bilbao, these ruling elites kept an impoverished peasantry in their grip, making Spain a country of economic extremes. Urban groups reacted enthusiastically to the end of the dictatorship and began debating the course of change, with Communists, socialists, anarchists, constitutionalists, and other splinter groups all holding differing views on a democratic future. For republicans, the air was electric with promise. As public debate developed, one woman recalled, people sat for hours dreaming dreams: "We saw a backward country suddenly blossoming out into a modern state. We saw peasants living like decent human beings. We saw men allowed freedom of conscience. We saw life, instead of death in Spain."

Groups on the left were so embroiled in battling one another to get their way, however, that the republic had a hard time putting in place a political program that would gain it widespread support in the countryside. Instead, they preferred symbolic acts such as releasing political prisoners and doling out coveted municipal jobs to the urban unemployed. Thus, although they wanted political and economic modernization, the Spanish republicans failed to mount a unified effort against their reactionary opponents, an especially grave failure in hard economic times. Specifically, instead of building popular loyalty and diminishing the strength of the right wing by enacting land reform, the various antimonarchist factions struggled among themselves to dominate the

0   100   200 miles
0   100   200 kilometers

Germans bomb civilians, 1937

FRANCE

Guernica

PORTUGAL

Madrid

SPAIN

Barcelona

ATLANTIC OCEAN

Surrendered March 28, 1939

Mediterranean Sea

SPANISH MOROCCO

ALGERIA

▦ Nationalist, July 1936	▦ Republican, February 1939
▦ Nationalist, October 1937	← Main Nationalist attacks
▦ Nationalist, July 1938	← Main Republican attacks
▦ Nationalist, February 1939	

MAP 27.2 The Spanish Civil War, 1936–1939
Republican and antirepublican forces bitterly fought one another to determine whether Spain would be a democracy or an authoritarian state. Germany and Italy sent military assistance to the rebels, notably airplanes to experiment with bombing civilians, while volunteers from around the world arrived to fight for the losing cause of the republic. Defeating these ill-organized groups, General Francisco Franco instituted a pro-fascist government that sent many to jail and into exile.

new government. In 1936, pro-republican forces temporarily banded together in a Popular Front coalition to win elections and prevent the republic from collapsing under the weight of internal squabbling and growing monarchist opposition. With the Popular Front victory, euphoria swept the country and unemployment abated.

In response, the forces of the right drew closer together, making use of their considerable wealth to undermine the government. In 1936, a group of army officers staged an uprising against the republican government in Madrid. The rebellious officers soon found a determined leader, General Francisco Franco (1892–1975), who was able to both unify the right and make use of its greater resources. The rebels, who now comprised monarchists, landowners, the clergy, and the fascist Falange

Party, soon had the help of fascists in other parts of Europe. Committed citizens—male and female—took up arms and formed volunteer units of republican fighters to meet the grave military challenge. In their minds, citizen armies symbolized republicanism, while professional troops followed the aristocratic rebels. As civil war gripped the country, the republicans generally held Madrid, Barcelona, and other commercial and industrial areas. The rebels found most support in the agricultural west and south (Map 27.2).

The struggle became a rehearsal for World War II when Hitler and Mussolini sent military personnel in support of Franco, gaining the opportunity to test new weapons and to practice the terror bombing of civilians. In 1937, German planes attacked the town of Guernica,♦ mowing down civilians in the streets. This gratuitous slaughter inspired Pablo Picasso's memorial mural to the dead, *Guernica* (1937), in which the intense suffering is starkly displayed in monochromatic grays and whites to capture a sense of moral decay as well as physical death. The Spanish republican government appealed everywhere for assistance, but only the Soviet Union answered (see the illustration on the facing page). Stalin withdrew his troops and tanks in 1938 as government ranks floundered, however. Britain and France refused to provide aid despite the outpouring of popular support for the cause of democracy. Instead, a few thousand volunteers from a variety of countries—including many students, journalists, and artists—fought for the republic. With Hitler and Mussolini on a rampage in Europe, "Spain was the place to stop fascism," these volunteers believed. The conflict was bitter and bloody, with widespread atrocities committed on both sides. But the splinter groups and random armies with which the Republic defended itself could not hold, while the aid Franco received ultimately proved decisive. His troops defeated the republicans in 1939, bringing another victory to the cause of authoritarianism in Europe. Franco dealt his defeated enemies a harsh peace: tens of thousands fled his government's brutal revenge while critics found themselves jailed and worse.

♦**Guernica:** gehr NEE kah

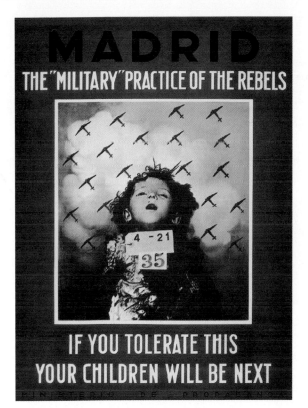

MADRID

THE "MILITARY" PRACTICE OF THE REBELS

**IF YOU TOLERATE THIS
YOUR CHILDREN WILL BE NEXT**

The Spanish Republic Appeals for Aid
The government of the Spanish Republic sent out modern advertising and propaganda to attract support from the remaining democracies—especially Great Britain and France. Antiwar sentiment remained high among the British and French, however. Thus, despite the horrifying and deliberate bombing of civilians by Franco's German allies, aid for the republic failed to arrive. What are the modernist techniques used in this propaganda photo? *Imperial War Museum, London.*

Hitler's Conquest of Central Europe, 1938–1939

The fall of central Europe that ultimately led to World War II began with Hitler's annexation of Austria in 1938. Many Austrians had actually wished for such a merger, or *Anschluss,* after the Paris peace settlement stripped them of their empire. So Hitler's troops simply entered Austria, and the enthusiasm of Nazi sympathizers among the Austrians made the Anschluss appear to support the Wilsonian idea of self-determination. The annexation began the so-called unification of Aryan peoples into one greater German nation and marked the first step in taking over

the resources of central and eastern Europe. Austria was declared a German province, the Ostmark, and Hitler's thugs ruled once-cosmopolitan Vienna. An observer later commented on the scene:

> University professors were obliged to scrub the streets with their naked hands, pious white-bearded Jews were dragged into the synagogue by hooting youths and forced to do knee-exercises and to shout "Heil Hitler" in chorus.

Nazis also generated support in Austria by solving the intractable problem of unemployment—especially among the young and out-of-work rural migrants to the cities. Factories sprang up overnight, mostly to foster rearmament, and new "Hitler housing" was of a quality that suggested the dignity of workers as propounded by the Nazis. "We were given work!" Austrians continued to say long afterward, defending their embrace of the Third Reich. It eliminated some of the pain Austrians had suffered when their empire had been reduced to a small country after World War I.

The Anschluss enhanced the image of German omnipotence, allowing Hitler to turn rapidly to Czechoslovakia and its rich resources. Overpowering this democracy did not appear as simple a task as seizing Austria, however. Czechoslovakia had a large army and formidable border defenses and armament factories, and most Czech citizens were prepared to fight for their country. However, Hitler gambled correctly that the other Western powers would not interfere, especially as the Nazi propaganda machine poured tremendous abuse on Czechoslovakia for allegedly persecuting its German minority. By October 1, 1938, Hitler warned, Czechoslovakia would have to grant autonomy (amounting to Nazi rule) to the German-populated border region, the Sudetenland, or face German invasion.

As the October deadline approached, the British prime minister Neville Chamberlain, the French premier Edouard Daladier, and Mussolini met with Hitler and agreed not to oppose Germany's claim to the Sudetenland. The strategy of preventing a war by making concessions for legitimate grievances (in this case, the alleged affront to Germans in the Peace of Paris) was called **appeasement**. At the time it was widely seen as a positive act,

MAP 27.3 The Growth of Nazi Germany, 1933–1939

German expansion was rapid and surprising, as Hitler's forces and Nazi diplomacy achieved the annexation of the new states of central and eastern Europe. Although committed to defending the sovereignty of these states through the League of Nations, French and British diplomats were more concerned with satisfying Hitler in the mistaken belief that doing so would prevent his claiming more of Europe. In the process, Hitler acquired the human and material resources of adjacent countries to support his Third Reich. What is the relationship between the expansion of Germany in the 1930s and the Peace of Paris after World War I?

and the agreement between Germany and Great Britain prompted Chamberlain to announce that he had secured "peace in our time." Stalin, excluded from the Munich deliberations, learned from the conference that the democracies were not going to fight to protect eastern Europe. Having portrayed himself as a man of peace, Hitler waited until March 1939 to invade the rest of Czechoslovakia (Map 27.3). Britain and France responded to that act by promising military support to Poland, Romania, Greece, and Turkey in case of Nazi invasion. In May 1939, Hitler and Mussolini countered this agreement by signing a pledge of offensive and defensive support called the Pact of Steel.

Some historians have sharply criticized the Munich Pact because it bought Hitler time to build his army and seemed to give him the green light for further aggression. They believe that a confrontation might have stopped Hitler and that even if war had resulted, the democracies would have triumphed at less cost than they later did. According to this view, each military move by Germany, Italy, and Japan should have been met with stiff opposition, and the Soviet Union should have been made a partner to this resistance. Others counter that appeasement provided France and Britain precious time to beef up their own armies, which the Munich crisis caused them to begin doing. The Munich Pact and the surrounding public debate about Nazi aggression also helped prepare citizens in the democracies for the possibility of another war. Finally, there were those at the time who believed that Germany deserved to have Czechoslovakia— so unfairly had the Peace of Paris treated the defeated great power.

Hitler's audacity knew no bounds. To the astonishment of public opinion in the West, on August 23, 1939, Germany and the USSR signed a nonaggression agreement. The **Nazi-Soviet Pact** provided that if one country became embroiled in war, the other country would remain neutral. Moreover, the two dictators secretly agreed to divide Poland and the Baltic States—Latvia, Estonia, and Lithuania—at some future date. The Nazi-Soviet Pact ensured that, should war come, the democracies would be fighting a Germany that feared no attack on its eastern borders. The pact also benefited the USSR. Despite Hitler's many threats to wipe the Bolsheviks off the face of the earth, Stalin needed extra time to reconstitute his officer corps destroyed in the purges. In the belief that Great Britain and perhaps even France would not fight because his aggression had met no resistance so far, Hitler now moved to enlarge his empire further and aimed his forces at Poland. The contest for territory and resources was set to become another world war.

Review: How did the aggression of Japan, Germany, and Italy create the conditions for global war?

❖ World War II, 1939–1945

The global catastrophe that quickly came to be called the Second World War opened when Hitler launched an all-out attack on Poland on September 1, 1939. In contrast to 1914, no jubilation in Berlin accompanied the invasion; when Britain and France declared war two days later, the mood in those capitals was similarly grim. Although Japan, Italy, and the United States did not join the battle immediately, their eventual participation spread the fighting throughout the world. By the time World War II ended in 1945, many Europeans were starving; much of the continent lay in ruins; and unparalleled atrocities, including technological genocide, had killed six million Jews and six million Slavs, gypsies, homosexuals, and other civilian enemies of fascism.

The German Onslaught

German ground forces quickly defeated the ill-equipped Polish troops by launching an overpowering **Blitzkrieg**❖ ("lightning war"), in which they concentrated airplanes, tanks, and motorized infantry to encircle Polish defenders and capture the capital, Warsaw, with overwhelming speed. Allowing the army to conserve supplies, Blitzkrieg assured Germans at home that the human costs of gaining Lebensraum would be low. On September 17, 1939, the Soviets invaded Poland from the east to make their own conquest. By the end of the month, the Polish army was in shambles and the victors had divided the country according to the Nazi-Soviet Pact. Hitler sold the war within the Reich as one of self-defense, especially from what propagandists called the "warlike menace" of world Jewry.

Hitler ordered an attack on France for November 1939, but his generals, who feared that Germany was ill prepared for total war, convinced him to postpone the offensive until the spring of 1940. In April 1940, the Blitzkrieg crushed Denmark and Norway; the battles of Belgium, the Netherlands, and France followed in May and June. On June 5, Mussolini, eyeing future spoils for Italy, invaded France from

❖**Blitzkrieg:** BLIHTS kreeg

the southeast. The French defense and its British allies could not withstand the German onslaught. Trapped on the beaches of Dunkirk in northern France, 370,000 British and French soldiers were rescued in a heroic effort by an improvised fleet of naval ships, fishing boats, and pleasure craft. A dejected French government surrendered on June 22, 1940, leaving Germany to rule the northern half of the country, including Paris. In the south, named Vichy◆ France after the spa town where the government sat, the reactionary and aged World War I hero Henri Philippe Pétain was allowed to govern. Stalin used the diversion in western Europe to annex the Baltic States of Estonia, Latvia, and Lithuania.

Britain now stood alone. Blaming Germany's rapid victories on his policy of appeasement, the British swept Chamberlain out of office and installed as prime minister Winston Churchill, an early advocate of resistance to Hitler. After Hitler ordered the bombardment of Britain in the summer of 1940, Churchill rallied the nation by radio—now in millions of British homes—to protect the ideals of liberty with their "blood, toil, tears, and sweat." In the battle of Britain—or Blitz, as the British called it—the German Luftwaffe (air force) bombed public buildings and monuments, harbors and weapons depots, and industry. Using the wealth of their colonies, the British poured resources into antiaircraft weapons, its highly successful code-detecting group called Ultra, and development of its advantage in radar. At year's end, the British air industry was outproducing that of the Germans by 50 percent.

By the fall of 1940, German air losses forced Hitler to abandon his plan for a naval invasion of Britain. Forcing Hungary, Romania, and Bulgaria to join with him, Hitler gained access to more food and oil. He then made his fatal decision to attack what he called the

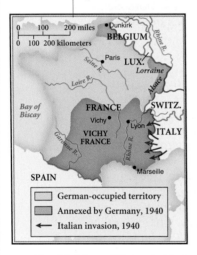

The Division of France, 1940

◆**Vichy:** VIH shee

"center of judeobolshevism"—the Soviet Union. In June 1941, the German army crossed the Soviet border, as Hitler broke the Nazi-Soviet Pact and promised to "raze Moscow and Leningrad to the ground." Deployed along a two-thousand-mile front, three million German and other Axis troops quickly penetrated Soviet lines. Stalin initially disappeared for several days but then rallied to direct the defense. By July, however, the German army had rolled to within two hundred miles of Moscow. Using a strategy of rapid encirclement, German troops had killed, captured, or wounded more than half the 4.5 million Soviet soldiers defending the borders.

Amid success, Hitler blundered. Considering himself a military genius and the Slavic people inferior, he proposed attacking Leningrad, the Baltic States, and the Ukraine simultaneously, whereas his generals wanted to concentrate on Moscow. Following this cumbersome strategy lost precious time, and driven by Stalin, local party members, and rising patriotic resolve, the Soviet people fought back. The onset of winter turned Nazi soldiers to frostbitten wretches because Hitler had feared that equipping his army for Russian conditions would suggest that a prolonged campaign lay in store—the scenario that did in fact materialize. Keeping civilians focused on victory and enjoying abundance so that they would not rebel against war thus brought additional suffering on the battlefront. Yet Hitler remained so convinced of imminent victory in the USSR that he switched German production from making tanks and artillery to making battleships and airplanes. Consequently, Germany's ill-supplied armies succumbed to the weather, disease, and ultimately a shortage of equipment. As the war became worldwide, Germany faced another obstacle: fighting a global war from a strictly European base and with far less familiarity of a global terrain than its enemies had. What it did have was an inflated and poorly calculated view of its own might.

War Expands: The Pacific and Beyond

As the German army stalled in the Soviet Union, an all-out dramatic attack ignited war in the Pacific. The outbreak of war in Europe had intensified U.S.-Japanese competition, as Japan had taken control of parts of the British Empire, bullied the Dutch in Indonesia, and invaded French Indochina to procure raw materials for its industrial and military expansion. The militarist Japanese government decided that it should settle matters with the West once and for all. In December 1941, Japanese planes bombed American naval and air bases at Pearl Harbor in Hawaii and then decimated a fleet of airplanes in the Philippines. Roosevelt summoned the U.S. Congress to declare war on Japan. By the spring of 1942, the Japanese had conquered Guam, the Philippines, Malaya, Burma, Indonesia, Singapore, and much of the southwestern Pacific. Like Hitler's expansionist drive, the Japanese victories strengthened the military's ideology that the empire was fulfilling its destiny. "The era of democracy is finished," the foreign minister announced confidently, despite Japan's dependence on the United States for trade, raw materials, technology, and loans. Officials marketed Emperor Hirohito to the region as the pan-Asian monarch who would lead the liberation and promote the well-being of Asians everywhere.

Germany quickly joined its Japanese ally and declared war on the United States—an appropriate enemy, Hitler proclaimed, as it was "half Judaized and the other half Negrified." Mussolini followed suit. The United States was not initially prepared for a prolonged struggle, partly because isolationist sentiment remained strong: its armed forces numbered only 1.6 million, and no plan existed for producing the necessary guns, tanks, and airplanes. Also working against war preparedness was ambivalence toward the Soviet Union even in the face of Hitler's attack, and Stalin himself reciprocated the mistrust. Yet despite the odds against such cooperation, Hitler's four enemies came together in the Grand Alliance of Great Britain, the Free French (an exile government led by General Charles de Gaulle and based in London), the Soviet Union, and the United States. Given the urgency of war and the partners' competing interests, the Grand Alliance and the larger coalition with twenty other countries—known collectively as the Allies—had much internal strife to overcome in their struggle against the Axis powers—Germany,

Italy, and Japan. Yet in the long run, the Allies had a distinct advantage. Their potential for war in terms of manpower and resources was vast. The extensive terrain they controlled gave them access to more goods from around the world, and these allowed them to survive the war. The globalization of the war brought into play Britain's traditional naval strength and its leaders' and troops' experience in combat on many continents. In the face of these advantages, the irrational ideology of the Axis powers only added to the problems of waging effective war.

The War against Civilians

Everyone was a target in World War II, and the war killed far more civilians than soldiers. The Axis and the Allies alike bombed cities simply to destroy civilian will to resist—a debatable tactic that seemed to inspire defiance rather than surrender. Allied firebombing of Dresden and Tokyo were but two instances that killed tens of thousands of civilians, but Axis attacks far outweighed these. The British people, not British soldiers, were the target of the battle of Britain, and as the German army swept through eastern Europe, it slaughtered Jews, Communists, Slavs, and others Nazi ideology deemed "racial inferiors" and enemies. In Poland, the SS murdered hundreds of thousands of Polish citizens or relocated them in forced labor camps. As land and homes were confiscated, they were given to "racially pure" Germans from other central European countries and from Germany. Literate people were the most vulnerable, because Hitler, like Stalin, saw them as the foundation of a civil society that he was determined to destroy. A ploy of the Nazis was to test captured people's reading skills, suggesting that those who could read would be given clerical jobs while those who could not would be relegated to hard labor. Those who could read, however, were lined up and shot. Because many in the German army initially rebelled at this inhuman mission, special Gestapo forces took up the charge of herding their victims into woods, to ravines, or even against town walls where they would be shot en masse. The Japanese did the same in China, southeast Asia, and on the islands in the Pacific. The number of civilians murdered in China alone is said to be at least 2.5 million, with untold millions murdered elsewhere.

The Holocaust. The extermination of Jews during the war became a special focus of Nazi murderers. Herded into urban ghettos, stripped of their possessions, and living on minimal rations, eastern European Jews died of starvation and disease—the Nazis' initial plan for reducing the Jewish population. There was also direct murder. Around Soviet towns, Jews were usually shot in pits, some of which they had been forced to dig themselves. After shedding their clothes and putting them in ordered piles for later Nazi use, ten thousand or more at a time were killed, often with the help of anti-Semitic villagers. However, the "Final Solution"—the Nazis' diabolical plan to exterminate all of Europe's Jews systematically—was not yet fully under way.

A bureaucratically organized and efficient technological system for rounding up Jews and transporting them to extermination sites had, however, taken shape by the fall of 1941. On the eve of war in 1939, Hitler had predicted "the destruction of the Jewish race in Europe." Although no clear order written by Hitler exists, his responsibility for it is clear: he discussed the Final Solution's progress, issued oral directives for it, and from the beginning made lethal anti-Semitism a basis for Nazism. Modern social and legal science and technology, managed by efficient scientists, doctors, lawyers, and government workers also made the Holocaust work. Six camps in Poland were developed specifically for the purposes of mass murder, though some, like Auschwitz-Birkenau,◆ served as both extermination and labor camp (Map 27.4). Using techniques developed in the T4 project that killed disabled and elderly people from 1939 on, the camp at Chelmno first gassed Christian Poles and Soviet prisoners of war. Specially designed crematoria for the mass burning of corpses started functioning in 1943. By then, Auschwitz had the capacity to burn 1.7 million bodies per year. About 60 percent of new arrivals—particularly children, women,

---

◆**Auschwitz-Birkenau:** OWSH vihts BIHR kuh now

MAP 27.4 Concentration Camps and Extermination Sites in Europe
This map shows the major extermination sites and concentration camps in Europe, but the entire continent was dotted with thousands of lesser camps to which the victims of Nazism were transported. Some of these lesser camps were merely way stations on the path to ultimate extermination. In focusing on the major camps historians often lose sight of the ways in which evidence of deportation and extermination blanketed Europe.

and old people—were selected directly for murder in the gas chambers; the other 40 percent labored until, utterly used up, they too were sent to their deaths.

Death and Life in the Camps. Extermination camps received their victims from across the continent. In the ghettos in various European cities, councils of Jewish leaders, such as the one in Amsterdam where Etty Hillesum worked, were ordered to determine those to be "resettled in the east." For weakened, poorly armed ghetto inhabitants, open resistance meant certain death. When Jews rose up against their Nazi captors in Warsaw in 1943, they were mercilessly butchered (see Persecution of Warsaw Jews, page 1081). For all their bluster, the Nazis took pains to cloak their true purposes in the extermination camps in order to prevent up-

Persecution of Warsaw Jews
Hitler was determined to exterminate Jews, Slavs, Gypsies, homosexuals, and others he deemed
"undesirable"; he often enlisted community leaders to cooperate in deportation and even executions. In the 1930s, people fled Germany; later, more fled the countries the Nazis conquered. In
the city of Warsaw, where Jews were crowded into the ghetto and deprived of food and fuel, the
Jewish uprising brought massive retaliation. How is this picture an example of World War II as a
total war? © *Bettmann/Corbis.*

risings and disorder. Bands played when
trainloads of victims arrived; some were given
postcards with reassuring messages to mail
home. Survivors later noted that the purpose of the camps was so unthinkable that
potential victims could not begin to imagine
that they were to be killed en masse. Those
not chosen for immediate murder had their
heads shaved, were showered and disin-
fected, and were then given prison garments—many of them used and so thin that
they offered no protection against winter
cold and rain. So began life in "a living hell,"
as one survivor wrote.

The camps were scenes of struggle for life
in the face of torture and death. Instead of
the minimum of two thousand calories
needed to sustain adult life, overworked inmates usually received less than five hundred
calories per day, leaving them vulnerable to
typhus and other diseases that swept
through the camps. Surviving prisoners
sometimes went mad, as did many of the

guards. In the name of advancing "racial science," doctors performed unbelievably cruel
medical experiments and operations with no
anesthesia on pregnant women, twins, and
other innocent people. The brutality of the
camp guards and the harshness of the living
conditions failed to crush everyone's spirit,
though: prisoners forged new friendships
that helped in the struggle for survival, and
women especially observed religious holidays, celebrated birthdays, and re-created
other sustaining aspects of domestic life.
Thanks to those sharing a bread ration and
doing him favors, wrote the Auschwitz survivor Primo Levi, "I managed not to forget that
I myself was a man." In the end, six million
Jews, the vast majority from eastern Europe,
along with an estimated five to six million
gypsies, homosexuals, and Slavs, and countless others were murdered in the Nazi geno-
cidal fury. What has stayed vivid in human
memory is the planned, bureaucratic organization of this vast and unspeakable crime

NEW SOURCES, NEW PERSPECTIVES

Museums and Memory

Historical monuments and museums that house historical artifacts have in recent years received unprecedented attention. Both of these institutions are testimonials to historical events because they provide records of those events and show that people were deeply moved by them. Monuments to World War I keep the memory of the Great War alive in villages and cities, while Holocaust museums are found in dozens of countries, many far from the region where the Holocaust took place.

But is the impression conveyed by a tragic photo or the memory of an event the same as its history? Historians wrestle with this question and for the most part regard photographs and oral testimony as legitimate kinds of evidence. However, many judge such institutions as Holocaust museums as only partially about the history of the Holocaust. Instead, a Holocaust museum tells a great deal about the nation or group that builds it. It tells about the "memory" that the nation or group wants average people to have of the Holocaust.

Holocaust memorials have had a complicated development that is instructive to historians. Some Holocaust memory sites sprang up spontaneously in concentration camps as memorials constructed by survivors themselves. Stones, writings, plaques, flowers and plants, and other objects were used to testify to what had happened in the camp. In many cases, these initial memorials were replaced when local and national governments stepped in to take over the site, sometimes waiting years between destroying the spon-

Holocaust Memorial Museum
Designed to evoke a sense of awe at the unprecedented sufferin[g] caused by the mass murder of the Jews, the Holocaust Memoria[l] Museum in Washington, D.C., displays pictures of thousands o[f] Germany's victims. Other museums around the world focus on different aspects of Hitler's policy of extermination, emphasizin[g] the many nationalities of his victims or the variety of reasons fo[r] their slaughter. *Johnson/Getty Images.*

perpetrated by apparently civilized humans. (See "New Sources, New Perspectives," above.)

Societies at War

Even more than World War I, World War II depended on industrial productivity geared totally toward war and mass killings. The Axis countries remained at a disadvantage throughout the war despite their initial conquests. Although the war accelerated eco-

nomic production by some 300 percent between 1940 and 1944 in all belligerent countries, the Allies produced more than three times Axis output in 1943 (Figure 27.1). Even while some of its lands were occupied and many of its cities besieged, the Soviet Union increased its production of weapons. Both Japan and Germany made the most of their lower capacity, notably in the strategy of Blitzkrieg. Hitler had to avoid imposing wartime austerity because he had come to taneous memorials and replacing them with an official one. The concentration camp at Dachau, near Munich, fell into disrepair until a group of survivors, including many Catholic clergy, demanded that the camp be made into a permanent museum and memorial, with the crematorium and other grisly features preserved. Although townspeople and local government resisted, Dachau and its crematorium became one of the most visited camps and indeed came to symbolize the Holocaust in all its horror. Yet Dachau was not primarily an extermination site for Jews, Slavs, and Gypsies but rather a grim concentration camp where Hitler put political prisoners, many of them Catholic clergy. It is so often visited because it is on the tourist route, close to a beautiful city. Indeed, among the plaques in this on-site museum, one invites visitors to tour the other cultural institutions and scenery of the area while another asks them to remember that vast numbers of those interned were Polish and Catholic. All of these factors in the politics of memories—official and unofficial, competing and contested—need to be taken into account by historians.

In the case of Holocaust museums, official memories can clash with memories of actual survivors who, for instance, do not like what is often the most aesthetic or avant-grade in terms of art and architecture. They generally reject abstract art, feeling that a more realistic depiction of their suffering seems most important. As for architectural design, the American Holocaust Museum was redone so that it would not look grimly out of place but would instead fit in with the tranquil style of the central museum mall in Washington, D.C., and thus be another nice tourist attraction. His-

torians question the way certain objects like shoes or eyeglasses are displayed to create a certain memory effect. They note that costume designers puff up prison uniforms to make them look more lifelike and to stir people emotionally.

Holocaust museums have offered a powerful, vivid, and emotionally charged experience of history. In contrast, historians pride themselves on eliminating emotions and biases in ascertaining facts, calculating cause and effect, and reaching historical judgments. Though each provides an important representation of the past, the relationship between memory and history remains fraught with questions—and never more so than in the case of the Holocaust.

QUESTIONS TO CONSIDER

1. What is the difference between a historical textbook and a historical monument?
2. Do you trust a history book more than you trust a museum? How do people compare and evaluate the presentation of the past in either one?
3. Why do museums and public exhibitions of art and artifacts arouse more debate than do history books?

FURTHER READING

Gillis, John R. *Commemorations: The Politics of National Identity.* 1994.

Sherman, Daniel J., and Irit Rogoff, eds. *Museum Culture: Histories, Discourses, Spectacles.* 1994.

Young, James Edward. *The Texture of Memory: Holocaust Memorials and Meaning.* 1993.

power promising to end economic suffering, not increase it. The use of millions of slave laborers and resources from occupied areas helped, but neither Japan nor Germany took the resources and morale of its enemies into full account.

Allied governments were overwhelmingly successful in generating civilian participation, especially among women. In the Axis countries, where government policy particularly exalted motherhood and kept women from

the best-paying jobs, officials began to realize that women were desperately needed in offices and factories. Even changing the propaganda to emphasize the need for everyone to take a job did not convince women that they should take the low-paid work offered them. In contrast, Soviet women constituted more than half the workforce by war's end. They dug massive antitank trenches around Moscow and other threatened cities, and 800,000 volunteered for the military, even

	1939	1940	1941	1942	1943	1944	1945
Aircraft							
Great Britain	7,940	15,049	20,094	23,672	26,263	26,461	12,070
United States	5,856	12,804	26,277	47,826	85,998	96,318	49,761
USSR	10,382	10,565	15,735	25,436	34,900	40,300	20,900
Germany	8,295	10,247	11,776	15,409	24,807	39,807	7,540
Japan	4,467	4,768	5,088	8,861	16,693	28,180	11,066
Major Vessels							
Great Britain	57	148	236	239	224	188	64
United States	—	—	544	1,854	2,654	2,247	1,513
USSR	—	33	62	19	13	23	11
Germany (U-boats only)	15	40	196	244	270	189	0
Japan	21	30	49	68	122	248	51
Tanks							
Great Britain	969	1,399	4,841	8,611	7,476	5,000	2,100
United States	—	c. 400	4,052	24,997	29,497	17,565	11,968
USSR	2,950	2,794	6,590	24,446	24,089	28,963	15,400
Germany	c. 1,300	2,200	5,200	9,200	17,300	22,100	4,400
Japan	c. 200	1,023	1,024	1,191	790	401	142

FIGURE 27.1 Weapons Production of the Major Powers, 1939–1945
World War II devoured people and weapons, necessitating dramatic changes in the workforce and everyday life. Because agricultural production was often hit hard by invading forces, people lived on reduced rations. Raw materials were channeled into the manufacture of weapons, and it was the real difference in productivity that spelled victory for the Allies: Germany and Japan were outproduced in almost every category. While the Allies filled their factories with women workers, German policies keeping women from well-paid industrial work could not be turned around effectively enough in wartime to boost production. What comparisons can you make among the combatants' weapons production over the course of the war? *From* The Hammond Atlas of the Twentieth Century *(London: Times Books, 1996), 103.*

support. Films depicted aviation heroes and infantrymen as well as the workingwomen and wives left behind. Filmmakers also featured stories of military heroes of myth and history—not only out of patriotism but also because government agencies monitored filmmaking and only allocated supplies to films they liked. In the United States, military leaders loaned authentic props only if they could censor the scripts.

Between 1939 and 1945, governments organized many aspects of everyday life, a necessity because resources had to be shifted away from civilians and consumption toward soldiers and military production. Bureaucrats regulated the production and distribution of food, clothing, and household products, all of which were rationed and generally of lower quality than before the war. They gave hints for meals without meat, sugar, fat, and other staples and urged women and children to embrace deprivation so that their fighting men would have more. In most countries it was simply taken for granted that civilians would not receive what they needed to survive in good health. Among the great powers, Soviet children and old people were at the greatest risk; an adolescent alive during the siege of Leningrad would most likely be among the one million residents of the city who starved to death. Governments hired more economists, statisticians, and other specialists to influence civilian thought and behavior and to streamline consumer needs. With governments standardizing such items as food, clothing, and entertainment, World War II furthered the development of mass society.

On both sides, propaganda and government policies promoted racial thinking. Since the early 1930s, the German government had

serving as pilots. As the Germans invaded, Soviet citizens moved entire factories eastward and the government came to encourage religious fervor for the Russian Orthodox church to motivate not only the Russians but also those minorities on the borderlands who were coming into contact with Nazis and even going over to their side.

Even more than in World War I, propaganda saturated society in movie theaters and on the radio. People were glued to their radios for war news, but much of it was tightly controlled. The totalitarian powers often withheld news of defeats and large numbers of casualties in order to keep civilian drawn ugly caricatures of Jews, Slavs, and gypsies. Similarly, Allied propaganda during the war depicted Germans as sadists and perverts and the "Japs" as uncivilized, insectlike fanatics. The U.S. government forced citizens of Japanese origin into concentration or internment camps. In the Soviet Union, Muslims and minority ethnic groups were uprooted and relocated as potential Nazi collaborators. Simultaneously colonized peoples were drawn into the war through conscription into the armies and forced labor. Some two million Indian men served the Allied cause, as did several hundred thousand Africans. As the Japanese swept through the Pacific and parts of East Asia, they too conscripted local men into their army. Both sides bombarded colonized societies with propaganda, as radio stations and newspapers proliferated during the war. Ironically, the propaganda and the policies of forced labor politicized colonized peoples to seek postwar liberation. The war brought about great changes—private and public, emotional and physical.

From Resistance to Allied Victory

Armies ultimately defeated the Axis powers, but civilian resistance in Nazi-occupied areas also contributed to the Allied triumph. Resistance to fascism began early in the war. Having escaped France in 1940, General Charles de Gaulle from his haven in London directed the Free French government and its forces—a mixed organization of troops of colonized Asians and Africans, soldiers who had escaped via Dunkirk, and volunteers from other occupied countries. Other resisters in occupied Europe fought in Communist-dominated groups, some of which gathered information to aid the Allied invasion of the continent. Rural groups called partisans, or the *maquis*, not only planned assassinations of traitors and German officers but also bombed bridges, rail lines, and military facilities. Although the Catholic church supported Mussolini in Italy and en-

dorsed the Croatian slaughter of a million Serbs by the Nazi puppet government, Catholic and Protestant clergy and their parishioners were among those who set up resistance networks, often hiding Jews and political suspects. Unlike the Serbs and Croats of Yugoslavia, the Polish resistance was unified against the Nazis. The spirit of resistance produced renowned heroes such as Swedish diplomat Raoul Wallenberg, whose dealings with Nazi officials saved thousands of Hungarian Jews.

People also fought back through everyday activities. Homemakers circulated newsletters urging demonstrations at prisons where civilians were detained and in marketplaces where food was rationed. In central Europe, hikers smuggled Jews and others over dangerous mountain passes. Danish villagers created vast escape networks, and countless thousands across Europe volunteered to be part of local escape routes. Resisters played on stereotypes of femininity: women often carried weapons to assassination sites in the correct belief that Nazis would rarely suspect or search them; they also seduced and murdered enemy officers. "Naturally the Germans didn't think that a woman could have carried a bomb," explained one Italian resister, "so this became the woman's task." Resistance underscored the importance of the liberal ideal of individual political action and courage in the face of the totalitarian state's monopoly of power.

A gray area of resistance, less visible and sometimes open to question, existed in

Hidden Revolver

Resistance to Nazism took many forms, from the concerted uprising in Warsaw to small acts of protest to assassinations of Nazi officers and collaborators. In a militarized state with informers everywhere, retaliation against Nazis sparked human ingenuity, whether in obtaining enough food or killing the enemy. Weapons were hidden in baby carriages, under clothing, or in books—as in this example from the Dutch resistance. How can everyday life serve as a form of resistance in wartime? *Erich Lessing/Art Resource, NY.*

the fascist countries. Couples in Germany and Italy limited family size in defiance of pro-birth policies. German teenagers danced the forbidden American jitterbug, thus defying the Nazis and forcing the police to monitor their groups. Historians question still another incident of resistance in Germany. In July 1944, a group of German military officers, fearing their country's military humiliation, made another of several attempts to assassinate Hitler. Only wounded but shaken, Hitler mercilessly tortured and killed hundreds of conspirators, opponents, and innocent friends and family members, imprisoning still others as well. Some ask whether this attempt came too late in the war to count as resistance. However, as a noted scholar points out, some five million Germans alone, and millions more of other nationalities, lost their lives in the last nine months of the war. Had Hitler died even as late as the summer of 1944, the relief to humanity would have been considerable.

The Axis Crushed in Europe.   Amid civilian resistance, Allied forces started tightening a noose around the Axis in mid-1942 (Map 27.5), and Allied victory began to look certain by 1943. Nonetheless, Hitler and his minions continued to promote an unrealistic expectation of German victory, announcing, for example, that the United States was "a big bluff." A major turning point came in August 1942, when the German army began a siege on Stalingrad, a city whose capture would give Germany access to Soviet oil and cut Soviet access to its own interior. Months of ferocious house-to-house fighting ended when the Soviet army captured the ninety thousand German survivors in February 1943. Meanwhile, the British army in North Africa held against German troops under German field marshal Erwin Rommel, an adept practitioner of the new kind of mobile warfare. Although Rommel let his tanks improvise creatively, moving hundreds of miles from supply lines, he could not overcome the Allies' access to secret German communication codes. This access ultimately helped the Allies successfully capture Morocco and Algeria in the fall of 1942. After driving Rommel out of Africa, the Allies landed in Sicily in July 1943, provoking a German in-

vasion during which they took over the war effort from the Italians. A slow, bitter fight for the Italian peninsula followed, lasting until April 1945, when Allied forces finally triumphed. After Italy's liberation, partisans shot Mussolini and his mistress and hanged their dead bodies for public display.

The victory at Stalingrad marked the beginning of the costly Soviet drive westward, during which the Soviets bore the brunt of the Nazi war machine. From the air, Britain and the United States pounded German cities with strategic bombing aimed at demoralizing ordinary Germans and destroying war industries. But it was an invasion from the west that Stalin needed, and on June 6, 1944, known as D-Day, the combined Allied forces under the command of U.S. general Dwight Eisenhower attacked the heavily fortified French beaches of Normandy and then fought their way through the German-held territory of western France. In late July, Allied forces broke through German defenses and a month later helped liberate Paris, where rebellion had erupted against the Nazis. The Soviets meanwhile took the Baltic States and entered Poland, pausing only to resupply while craftily allowing the Germans to put down a spontaneous uprising of the Polish resistance in August 1944. German elimination of the Polish resistance allowed the Soviets a freer hand in eastern Europe after the war. Facing more than twice as many troops as on the western front, the Soviet army took Bulgaria and entered Romania at the end of August, and then faced fierce German fighting in Hungary during the winter of 1944–1945. British, Canadian, U.S., and other Allied forces were simultaneously fighting their way

MAP 27.5 World War II in Europe and Africa ▶
World War II inflicted massive loss of life and destruction of property on civilians, armies, and all the infrastructure—including factories, equipment, and agriculture—needed to wage total war. Thus, the war swept the European continent as well as areas in Africa colonized by or allied with the major powers. Ultimately the Allies crushed the Axis by moving from east, west, and south to inflict a total defeat. What indications are there on the map that this war would be hard on civilians?

Legend:
- Axis powers and their allies
- Axis-held, early November 1942
- Allied powers and their allies
- Neutral nations
- Greater Germany, 1942
- Axis offensives
- Allied offensives
- ★ Major battle

400 miles
400 kilometers
0 200
0 200

N E S W

USSR

Caspian Sea

Besieged Aug. 21, 1942–Jan. 31, 1943

Stalingrad

Meeting of Roosevelt, Churchill, and Stalin, Nov.–Dec. 1943

Tehran

IRAN

IRAQ

SAUDI ARABIA

Volga R.

Don R.

Germans repulsed Dec. 1941

Moscow

Kursk July 1943

Besieged Sept. 1941–Jan. 1944

Leningrad

June 1941

Aug. 1943

Mar. 1944

Ukraine

Bessarabia

Danube R.

Yalta

Black Sea

TURKEY

SYRIA (Fr.)

LEBANON

PALESTINE (Br.)

TRANS-JORDAN (Br.)

Alexandria

EGYPT (Br.)

El Alamein Oct.–Nov. 1942

Nov. 1942

FINLAND

ESTONIA

LATVIA

LITHUANIA

Sept. 1944

July 1944

June 1941

East Prussia

Baltic Sea

SWEDEN

NORWAY

Danzig

Warsaw

POLAND

Slovakia

Oder R.

HUNGARY

Dec. 1944

ROMANIA

BULGARIA

April 1941

YUGOSLAVIA

ALBANIA (It.)

GREECE

May 1941

Crete (Gr.)

Rhodes (It.)

Mediterranean Sea

LIBYA (It.)

Cyprus (Br.)

April 1940

Surrendered May 8, 1945

Berlin

Potsdam April 1945

Elbe R.

GERMANY

DENMARK

North Sea

SWITZ.

Adriatic Sea

ITALY

Rome

Monte Cassino May 1944

Salerno Sept. 1943

Liberated June 4, 1944

Tunis

July 1943

Siciy

Sardinia

Corsica

May 1940

Rhine R.

NETH.

BELG.

LUX.

Dunkirk

Paris

FRANCE

VICHY FRANCE

Aug. 1944

June 1940

Kasserine Pass Feb. 1943

TUNISIA (Fr.)

FRENCH NORTH AFRICA

Battle of Britain, 1940

London

GREAT BRITAIN

N. IRELAND

IRELAND

Liberated Aug. 25, 1944

Normandy invasion, D-Day June 6, 1944

Battle of the Bulge Dec. 16, 1944– Jan. 31, 1945

ATLANTIC OCEAN

SPAIN

PORTUGAL

SP. MOROCCO

MOROCCO (Fr.)

ALGERIA (Fr.)

Nov. 1942

Under Vichy government 1940–42 Joined Allies Nov., 1942

Battle of Leningrad
In the face of Nazi invasion, Soviet citizens reacted heroically, moving entire factories to the interior of the country and building fortifications. Nowhere was their resolve so tested as in Leningrad (St. Petersburg), where two million are estimated to have died during a Nazi siege lasting more than two years. Before the invasion of Normandy in 1944, the people of the USSR bore the brunt of Nazi military might in Hitler's attempt to defeat "judeo-bolshevism." How does this picture of citizen defense of Leningrad differ from illustrations of Nazi power? How could the Nazis have been defeated in such events as this siege? *Sovfoto.*

eastward to join the Soviets in squeezing the Third Reich to its final defeat.

As the Allies advanced, Hitler decided that Germans were proving themselves unworthy of his greatness and deserved to perish in a cataclysmic conflagration. He thus refused to surrender and thereby spare Germans further death and destruction from the continued massive bombing. As the Soviet army took Berlin, Hitler committed suicide with his wife, Eva Braun. Although many soldiers remained committed to the Third Reich, Germany finally surrendered on May 8, 1945.

The Atomic Bomb and the Defeat of Japan. The United States and its allies had followed a "Europe first" strategy for conducting the war. They had nonetheless pursued the Japanese in the Pacific relentlessly. In 1940 and 1941, Japan had ousted the Europeans from many colonial holdings in Asia, but the Allies turned the tide in 1942 despite their diminished forces, by destroying some of Japan's formidable naval power in battles at Midway Island and Guadalcanal (Map 27.6). Unlike the United States, Japan lacked the capacity to recoup losses of ships or of manpower, while the Allies had not only their own productive power but also

access to matériel manufactured in Australia, India, and elsewhere around the world. The Allies stormed one Pacific island after another, gaining more bases from which to cut off the import of supplies and to launch bombers toward Japan itself. Short of men and weapons, the Japanese military resorted to kamikaze tactics, in which pilots deliberately crashed their planes into American ships, killing themselves in the process. In response, the Allies stepped up their bombing of major cities, killing more than 100,000 civilians in their spring 1945 firebombing of Tokyo. The Japanese leadership still ruled out surrender.

Meanwhile a U.S.-based international team of more than 100,000 workers, including scientists, technicians, and other staff, had developed the atomic bomb. The Japanese practice of dying almost to the man rather than surrendering caused Allied military leaders to calculate that defeating Japan might cost the lives of hundreds of thousands of Allied soldiers (and even more Japanese). On August 6 and 9, 1945, the U.S. government thus unleashed its new atomic weapons on Hiroshima and Nagasaki, respectively, killing 140,000 people instantly; tens of thousands later died from burns, wounds, and other afflictions (see Hiroshima Victim, page 1090).

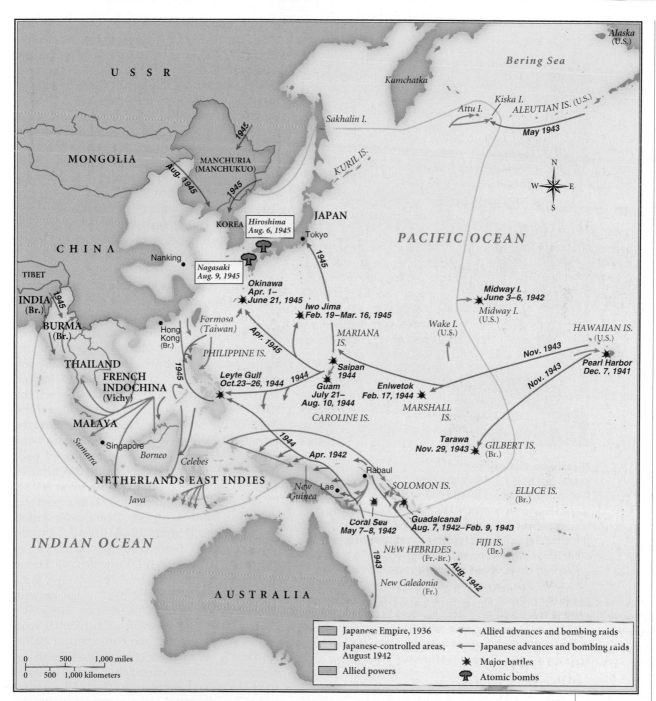

MAP 27.6 World War II in the Pacific

As in Europe, the early days of World War II gave the advantage to the Axis power Japan as it took the offensive in conquering islands in the Pacific and territories in Asia—many of them colonies of European states. Britain countered by mobilizing a vast Indian army, while the United States, after the disastrous losses at Pearl Harbor and in the Philippines, gradually gained the upper hand by costly assaults, island by island. The Japanese strategy of fighting to the last person instead of surrendering when a loss was in sight was one factor in President Truman's decision to drop the atomic bomb in August 1945. How does the war in the Pacific look different from the war in Europe and North Africa?

Hiroshima Victim
On August 6 and 9, 1945, the United States dropped the first atomic weapons on Hiroshima and Nagasaki, respectively, killing tens of thousands of Japanese instantly and leaving tens of thousands more to die of their injuries and the aftereffects. A few days later Japan surrendered, but controversy has swirled around the decision to drop the bomb ever since. Some see it as a racist act, no atomic weapons having been dropped on Germany, while others see it as a justified act of warfare in a conflict that threatened to cost countless more casualties because of Japan's policy of no surrender. What might have been the reaction at the time to such a photo in Japan, China, the United States, and Europe? *Tokyo/Fuji/Sumiko Kurita/Gamma.*

Although hardliners in the Japanese military wanted to continue the war, on August 14, 1945, Japan surrendered.

An Uneasy Postwar Settlement

Envisioning a postwar settlement had been a major priority throughout the war, and the Allies had held critical meetings during the hostilities not only to plan strategy but also to set the terms for the postwar order. Unlike World War I, however, there would be neither a celebrated peace conference nor a definitive, formal agreement among all the Allies about the final resolution. Yet peace and recovery were more important than ever, as Europe lay in ruins and as tens of millions starved, wandering the continent in search of food, shelter, and security from the armies that occupied virtually every country. Because the victorious Allies distrusted one another in varying degrees, with the United States and the Soviet Union on the brink of another struggle for supremacy, the future for most Europeans looked grim.

Wartime Agreements about the Peace. Wartime agreements among members of the Grand Alliance about the future reflected their ongoing differences, and these hard-won agreements would come to rouse intense postwar debate. In 1941, Roosevelt and Churchill forged the Atlantic Charter, which condemned aggression, reaffirmed the ideal of collective security, and endorsed the right of all people to choose their governments. Not only did the Allies come to focus on these points, but so did colonized peoples to whom, Churchill said, the charter was not meant to apply. In October 1944, Churchill and Stalin agreed on the postwar distribution of territories. The Soviet Union would control Romania and Bulgaria, Britain would control Greece, and they would jointly oversee Hungary and Yugoslavia. These agreements went against Roosevelt's faith in collective security, self-determination, and open doors in trade. In February 1945, the "Big Three"—Roosevelt, Churchill, and Stalin—met in the Crimean town of Yalta. Roosevelt advocated the institution of an organization to be called the United Nations to replace the League of Nations as a global peace mechanism and supported future Soviet influence in Korea, Manchuria, and the Sakhalin♦ and Kurile Islands. The last meeting of the Allied leaders took place at Potsdam, Germany, in the summer of 1945, where they agreed to give the Soviets control of eastern Poland, to cede a large stretch of

♦**Sakhalin:** SAH kuh leen

eastern Germany to Poland, and to adopt a temporary four-way occupation of Germany that included France as one of the supervising powers. Yet as victory unfolded, the Allies scrambled to outmaneuver one another.

The War's Grim Legacy. The Great Depression had inflicted global suffering, while the Second World War left an estimated 100 million dead, more than fifty million refugees without homes, and one of the most tragic moral legacies in human history. Thus, making peace proved a prolonged and bitter process—and one that was hardly over in 1945. Forced into armies or into labor camps for war production, colonial peoples were in

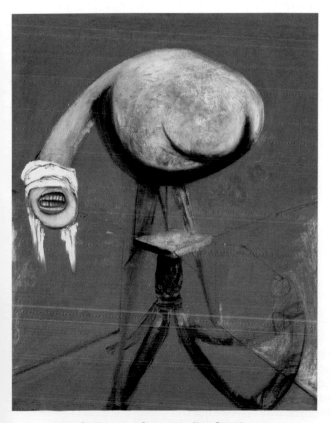

Francis Bacon, *Three Studies for Figures at Base of Crucifixion* (c. 1944)
At the end of the war, English artist Francis Bacon depicted the traditional Western subject of the crucifixion, but in a way that converted the human figure into a grotesque monster. His figures often reflect horror, disgust, and real debasement and thus seem to describe the human condition at the end of World War II and the Holocaust. *Tate Gallery, London/Art Resource, NY.*

full rebellion or close to it. For a second time in three decades, they had seen their imperial masters killing one another, slaughtered by the very technology that was supposed to make European civilization superior. Deference to Europe was virtually finished, with independence a matter of time.

Western values at home were imperiled as well. Rational, democratic Europe had succumbed to continuous wartime values, and it was this Europe that George Orwell captured in his novel *1984* (1949). Poor food and worn clothing, grimy streets and dwellings, people prematurely aged and careworn—all characterized both London of the 1940s and Orwell's fictional state, Oceania. Orwell had worked for the wartime Ministry of Information (called the Ministry of Truth in the novel) and churned out doctored news for wartime audiences. Information and truth hardly mattered: words had taken on sanitized meaning during the war as *disengagement* replaced *retreat*, *battle fatigue* substituted for *insanity*, and *liberating* a country could mean invading it and slaughtering its civilians. Millions rejoiced at the demise of Nazi evil in 1945, but Orwell saw as part of war's legacy the end of prosperity, the deadening of creativity, and the intrusion of big government into everyday life. For Orwell, bureaucratic domination depended on the perpetuation of conflict, and fresh conflict was indeed brewing in the race for Berlin and Japan even before the war ended. As Allied powers competed for territory, a new struggle called the cold war was taking root.

Review: What were the major consequences of World War II?

Conclusion

The Great Depression brought massive social dislocation and fear. It provided a setting in which dictators thrived because they promised to restore national greatness and bring economic prosperity. Enticed by the mass media, people turned away from representative institutions and toward dynamic, if brutal, leaders. Memories of World War I permitted Hitler and Mussolini to menace

Percent of population killed

- Over 10%
- 5–10%
- 1–5%
- Under 1%

- ■ Military dead
- ▲ Civilian dead (does not include 12 million death camp victims)
- ✳ City substantially damaged

FINLAND ■ 79,047

NORWAY ■ 4,780

SWEDEN

Leningrad

ESTONIA

LATVIA

North Sea

GREAT BRITAIN ■ 271,311 ▲ 60,595

IRELAND

DENMARK ■ 4,339

Baltic Sea

Königsberg

LITHUANIA

USSR ■ 14,500,000 Over 7,000,000

Coventry

London

Rotterdam

Düsseldorf

NETH. ■ 15,700 ▲ 236,300

Hamburg

Bremen

Hanover

Berlin

Dortmund

Warsaw

POLAND ■ 850,000 (169,822 as Allies) 5,778,000

Kiev

BELG. ■ 9,561 ▲ 73,000

Caen

Cologne

GERMANY ■ 2,850,000 ▲ 2,300,000

Dresden

Frankfurt

Würzburg

CZECHOSLOVAKIA ■ 6,683 310,000

FRANCE ■ 210,671 ▲ 173,260

SWITZ.

Munich

AUSTRIA ■ 380,000 145,000

HUNGARY ■ ▲ 750,000

ROMANIA ■ 519,822 465,000

Ploesti

Milan

Genoa

Bologna

YUGOSLAVIA ■ 1,700,000

Black Sea

SPAIN ■ 4,500 (For Axis) 7,500 (For Allies) ■▲ 10,000 (in concentration camps)

Corsica

ITALY ■ 279,820 ▲ 17,400 (as Allies)

BULGARIA ■ 18,500 ▲ 1,500

Sardinia

GREECE ■ 16,357 155,300

0   200   400 miles
0   200   400 kilometers

MAPPING THE WEST Europe at War's End, 1945

While all of Europe was severely shocked during the age of catastrophe, wartime damage left scars that would last for decades. Major German cities were bombed to bits, while the Soviet Union suffered an unimaginable toll of well over twenty million deaths due to the war alone. In addition to the vast civilian and military losses shown on this map, historians estimate that no less than twelve million people were murdered in the Nazi death camps. Everything from politics to family life needed rebuilding. The chaos fueled postwar tensions stemming both from the quest to punish those held responsible for such suffering and from the superpowers' determination to gain the political allegiance of recovering countries in the cold war. Explain the relative difference in loss of life in Eastern Europe and Western Europe. *From* The Hammond Atlas of the Twentieth Century *(London: Times Books, 1996), 102.*

Europe unimpeded throughout the 1930s. When a coalition formed to stop them, it was an uneasy one among the imperial powers France and Britain, the Stalinist Soviet Union, and the industrial giant the United States. World War II ended European dominance. Its economies were shattered, its population was reduced, its colonies were on the verge of independence, and its peoples were starving and homeless.

The costs of a bloody war—one waged against civilians as much as armies—taught the victorious powers different lessons. The United States, Britain, and France were convinced that a minimum of citizen well-being was necessary to prevent a recurrence of fascism. Soviet citizens hoped that their lives would become easier and more open. The devastation of the USSR's population and resources, however, made Stalin increasingly obsessed with national security and reparations. Britain and France confronted the final eclipse of their imperial might, underscoring Orwell's insight that the war had transformed society irrevocably. The militarization of society and the deliberate murder of millions of innocent citizens like Etty Hillesum were a permanent blight on the European legacy. Nonetheless, backed by vast arsenals of sophisticated weaponry, the competing visions of former Allies regarding how to deal with Germany and eastern Europe led the United States and the Soviet Union to threaten one another—and the world—with yet another war.

Suggested References

The Great Depression

Historians look to the depression as a complex event with economic, social, and cultural consequences, but in addition they see its impact as yet another indication of the tightening of global economic connections. To follow some of the political implications for European empires, see in particular Columbia University's South Asia Web site, which explores Gandhi's economic resistance to British colonialism.

Balderston, Theo, ed. *The World Economy and National Economics in the Interwar Slump.* 2003.

Evans, Richard J., and Dick Geary. *The German Unemployed: Experiences and Consequences of Mass Unemployment from the Weimar Republic to the Third Reich.* 1987.

Roszkowski, Wojciech. *Landowners in Poland, 1918–1939.* 1991.

Rothermund, Dietmar. *The Global Impact of the Great Depression, 1929–1939.* 1996.

South Asia and Gandhi: http://www.columbia.edu/cu/libraries/indiv/area/sarai.

Totalitarian Triumph

The vicious dictators Stalin, Hitler, and Mussolini are among the most popular subjects for historians and readers alike. Recent histories study their mobilization of art and the media and consider people's complex participation in totalitarian regimes. Studies like those of Gellately and Stolzfus, Kaplan, and Engel and Posadskaya-Vanderbeck have provided us with fascinating if grim insights into studies of everyday life.

Ben-Ghiat, Ruth. *Fascist Modernities: Italy, 1922–1945.* 2001.

Burleigh, Michael. *The Third Reich: A New History.* 2000.

*Engel, Barbara Alpern, and Anastasia Posadskaya-Vanderbeck, eds. *A Revolution of Their Own: Voices of Women in Soviet History.* 1998.

Fritzsche, Peter. *Germans into Nazis.* 1998.

Gellately, Robert, and Nathan Stolzfus, eds. *Social Outsiders in Nazi Germany.* 2001.

Kaplan, Marion. *Between Dignity and Despair: Jewish Life in Nazi Germany.* 1998.

Viola, Lynn, ed. *Contending with Stalinism: Soviet Power and Popular Resistance in the 1930s.* 2003.

Democracies on the Defensive

The democracies attacked the depression from a variety of perspectives ranging from state policy to film and the arts, yet another indication of how complex politics can be. Further departure from liberal policies, whether in trade or in the development of the activist welfare state, also have attracted historical study.

Kalvemark, Ann-Sofie. *More Children or Better Quality? Aspects of Swedish Population Policy.* 1980.

Kennedy, David M. *Freedom from Fear: The American People in Depression and War, 1929–1945.* 1999.

Lavin, Maud, et al. *Montage and Modern Life, 1919–1942.* 1992.

Rearick, Charles. *The French in Love and War: Popular Culture in the Era of the World Wars.* 1997.

Richards, Jeffrey, ed. *The Unknown 1930s: An Alternative History of the British Cinema, 1929–39.* 1998.

*Primary source.

The Road to Global War

The road to war encircled the globe, involving countries seemingly peripheral to the struggles among the antagonists. The perennial question for many historians is whether Hitler could have been stopped, but with globalization there is new attention to the beginnings of war beyond the West as a prelude to decolonization.

Bix, Herbert P. *Hirohito and the Making of Modern Japan.* 2000.

Crozier, Andrew. *The Causes of the Second World War.* 1997.

Knight, Patricia. *The Spanish Civil War.* 1991.

*Mangini González, Shirley. *Memories of Resistance: Women's Voices from the Spanish Civil War.* 1995.

Watt, D. Cameron. *How War Came: The Immediate Causes of the Second World War.* 1989.

World War II, 1939–1945

In a vast literature historians have charted the war's innumerable and global horrors, with issues of the Holocaust, industrial killing, and the nature of racial thinking drawing particular attention. The U.S. Holocaust Memorial Museum provides online exhibits giving the history of the Holocaust in different locations. While looking at the social aspects of war, historians have intensely debated the development of the cold war within the "hot" war.

Beevor, Anthony. *The Fall of Berlin 1945.* 2002.

Browning, Christopher. *The Origins of the Final Solution: The Evolution of Nazi Jewish Policy, September 1939–March 1942.* 2004.

*Dawidowicz, Lucy S. *A Holocaust Reader.* 1976.

Dower, John W. *War without Mercy: Race and Power in the Pacific War.* 1986.

Holocaust Museum: http://usholocaustmuseum .org.

James, Harold. *The Deutsche Bank and the Nazi Economic War Against the Jews: The Expropriation of Jewish-Owned Property.* 2001.

Miner, Steven Merritt. *Stalin's Holy War: Religion, Nationalism, and Alliance Politics, 1941–1945.* 2003.

Rhodes, Richard. *The Making of the Atomic Bomb.* 1986.

Slaughter, Jane. *Women in the Italian Resistance, 1943–1945.* 1997.

Weinberg, Gerhard. *A World at Arms: A Global History of World War II.* 1994.

---

*Primary source.

CHAPTER REVIEW

IMPORTANT EVENTS

1929	The U.S. stock market crashes; global depression begins; Soviet leadership initiates war against prosperous farmers, the kulaks; German Thomas Mann wins the Nobel Prize for literature
1933	Hitler comes to power in Germany
1936	Show trials begin in the USSR; Stalin purges top Communist Party officials and military leaders; the Spanish Civil War begins
1938	Virginia Woolf publishes *Three Guineas*
1939	Germany invades Poland; World War II begins; the Spanish Civil War ends
1940	France falls to the German army
1940–1941	The British air force fends off German attacks in the battle of Britain
1941	Germany invades the Soviet Union; Japan attacks Pearl Harbor; the United States enters the war
1941–1945	The Holocaust
1944	Allied forces land at Normandy, France
1945	The fall of Berlin; United States drops atomic bombs on Hiroshima and Nagasaki; World War II ends

KEY TERMS

appeasement (1075)

Blitzkrieg (1077)

civil disobedience (1054)

Enabling Act (1062)

family allowance (1066)

five-year plans (1056)

Lebensraum (1072)

Nazi-Soviet Pact (1077)

Nuremberg Laws (1064)

Popular Front (1067)

pump priming (1063)

purges (1058)

REVIEW QUESTIONS

1. How did the Great Depression affect society and politics?
2. What role did violence play in the Soviet and Nazi regimes?
3. How did the democracies work to maintain their values while facing the twin challenges of economic depression and the rise of fascism?
4. How did the aggression of Japan, Germany, and Italy create the conditions for global war?
5. What were the major consequences of World War II?

MAKING CONNECTIONS

1. Compare fascist ideas of the individual with the idea of individual rights that drove the American and French revolutions.
2. What are the major differences between World War I and World War II?

FOR FURTHER EXPLORATION

To assess your mastery of the material in this chapter, see the Online Study Guide at **bedfordstmartins.com/hunt**.

To read additional primary-source material from this period, see Chapter 27 in *Sources of The Making of the West*, Second Edition.

Remaking Europe in the Shadow of Cold War,
C. 1945–1965

AFTER THE UNITED STATES DROPPED two atomic bombs on Japan in 1945, the Union of Soviet Socialist Republics raced to catch up with its rival in atomic weaponry. In late August 1949, the Soviet Union detonated its own atomic bomb. Two days after President Harry S Truman announced the news of this test, Billy Graham, a young Baptist preacher, based his sermon at a revival meeting on the fearsome event. Graham warned that U.S. officials believed "we have only five to ten years and our civilization will be ended." He announced that Russia had aimed bombs to strike New York, Chicago, and Los Angeles, where the revival was taking place. "Time is desperately short....Prepare to meet thy God," he warned. People flocked to hear Graham talk about the end of the world, launching the evangelist's astonishing career of spiritual and political influence in the United States and around the globe.

Graham's message—"We don't know how soon, but we do know this, that right now the grace of God can still save a poor lost sinner"—captured the extremes of postwar sentiment in an atomic age. On the one hand, the global postwar situation was tragic. One hundred million people had died; Europe and Japan were prostrate, and their people starving; evidence of genocide and other inhumanity was everywhere; the menace of nuclear annihilation loomed. It was to this menace that Graham referred. The old international order was gone, replaced by the rivalry of the United States and the Soviet Union for control of a devastated Europe, whose political and

---

The Atomic Age
The atomic bombs dropped on Hiroshima and Nagasaki in 1945 were followed by several decades of increasingly powerful detonations for testing purposes. The Soviet Union practiced underground testing, while the United States carried out above-ground tests in the Pacific region. Protests against testing developed in the 1950s, many of them citing the hazards of radioactivity and the growing threat of nuclear annihilation. Simultaneously, nuclear power was converted to peacetime use, notably serving both as a source of energy and as a therapy for cancer. What feelings might pictures of nuclear mushroom clouds have aroused in citizens in Europe, the Soviet Union, and the United States? © *Corbis*

economic systems had collapsed. The nuclear arsenals of these two superpowers—a term coined in 1947—grew massively in the 1950s, but they were enemies who did not fight outright. Thus, their terrifying rivalry was called the **cold war**. The cold war divided the West and caused acute anxiety, even for someone like Graham from the victorious and wealthy United States.

On the other hand, the defeat of Nazism inspired an upsurge of hope, a revival of religious feeling like Graham's, and a new commitment to humanitarian goals. Heroic effort had defeated fascism, and that defeat raised hopes that a new age would begin. Atomic science promised advances in medicine, and nuclear energy was trumpeted as a replacement for coal and oil. The creation of the United Nations heralded an era of international cooperation. Around the globe, colonial peoples won independence from European masters, while in the United States the civil rights movement gained new momentum. The welfare state expanded, and by the end of the 1950s economic rebirth, stimulated in part by the cold war, had made much of Europe more prosperous than ever before. An "economic miracle" had occurred, and, unbelievably, just a decade after the war Europeans were beginning to enjoy the highest standard of living they had ever known.

Extremes of hope and fear infused the atomic age, as society, culture, and the international order were all transformed. Gone was the definition of a West comprising Europe and its cultural offshoots such as the United States and an East comprising Asian countries like India, China, and Japan. During the cold war, the word *West* came to stand for the United States and its client countries in western Europe, while *East* meant the Soviet Union and its tightly controlled bloc in eastern Europe. Still another terminology arose in the 1950s, one that divided the globe into the first world, or capitalist bloc of countries; the second world, or socialist bloc; and the **third world**, or countries emerging from imperial domination. As the world's people redefined themselves politically and culturally, the superpowers took the world to the brink of nuclear disaster when the United States discovered Soviet missile sites on the island of Cuba. From the dropping of the atomic bomb on Japan in 1945 to the Cuban missile crisis of 1962, Graham's dread that "we are moving madly toward destruction" gripped much of the world, albeit in the midst of prosperity and Europe's rebirth.

❖ World Politics Transformed

World War II ended the global leadership of Europe. Many countries lay in ruins by the summer of 1945, and conditions would deteriorate before they got better. Though victorious, bombed and bankrupt Britain could not feed its people. In contrast, the United States, whose territory was virtually untouched in the war, emerged as the world's sole economic giant, and the Soviet Union, despite suffering immense destruction, retained formidable military might. Having occupied Europe as part of the victorious alliance against Nazism

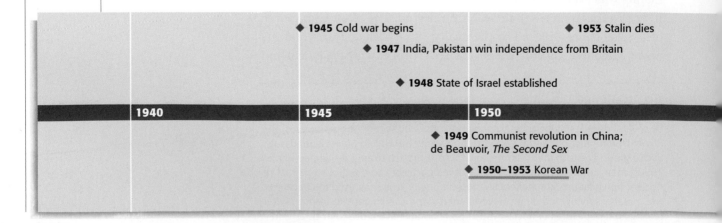

◆ **1945** Cold war begins

◆ **1953** Stalin dies

◆ **1947** India, Pakistan win independence from Britain

◆ **1948** State of Israel established

1940	1945	1950

◆ **1949** Communist revolution in China; de Beauvoir, *The Second Sex*

◆ **1950–1953** Korean War

and fascism, the two superpowers used Germany—at the heart of the continent and its politics—to divide Europe in two. By the late 1940s, the USSR imposed Communist rule throughout most of Eastern Europe and in the 1950s quashed rebellions against its dominance there. Western Europeans found themselves at least partially constricted by the very U.S. economic power that helped them rebuild, as the United States maintained air bases and nuclear weapons sites on their soil. The age of bipolar world politics had begun, with Europe as its testing ground.

Europe Prostrate

In contrast to World War I, when devastation was limited to the front lines around the trenches, armies in World War II had fought a war of movement and massive air strikes that leveled thousands of square miles of territory. Across the continent, whole cities were clogged with rubble; homeless survivors wandered the streets. In Sicily and on the Rhine River, almost no bridge remained standing; in the Soviet Union, seventy thousand villages and more than a thousand cities lay in shambles. Everywhere people were suffering. In the Netherlands, the severity of Nazi occupation left the Dutch population close to death, relieved only by a U.S. airlift of food. In Britain, basic commodities were difficult to obtain, and many died in the bitterly cold winter of 1946–1947 because of a shortage of fuel. Italian bakers sold bread by the slice. When Allied troops passed through German towns, the famished inhabitants lined the roads in hopes that someone would toss them something to eat. "To see the children fighting for food," one British soldier noted, "was like watching animals being fed in a zoo." There was social disarray, even chaos, at the war's end but no mass uprisings as after World War I. Until the late 1940s, people were too exhausted by the struggle for bare survival.

The tens of millions of refugees suffered the most. Many had been inmates of prisons and death camps, and, weakened and ill, they were now released into a world where resources were slim and old ways of living destroyed. Others, especially some twelve million ethnic Germans, fled westward to escape the victorious but destructive Red Army as it inflicted a grim occupation on eastern Europe. Native Germans in the western occupied zones viewed refugees as competitors for food and work and often provided a cold welcome. Many refugees ultimately found homes in countries that experienced little or no war damage, such as Denmark, Sweden, Canada, and Australia. Following the exodus of refugees from the east, western Europe became one of the world's most densely populated regions (Map 28.1). The USSR lobbied hard for the repatriation of several million Soviet prisoners of war and forced laborers, and the Allies transported the majority of the Russian refugees back to the Soviet Union. "Contaminated" by Western ideas, according to Soviet leaders, they faced execution until the Allies slowed the process, leaving hundreds of thousands of Soviets to join the ocean of refugees in western Europe.

◆ **1962** Cuban missile crisis

◆ **1954** *Brown* v. *Board of Education*; French defeat at Dien Bien Phu

◆ **1956** Suez Canal nationalized; Hungarian uprising

| 1955 | 1960 | 1965 | 1970 |

◆ **1957** Pasternak, *Doctor Zhivago*; *Sputnik* launched; EEC established

◆ **1958** Fifth Republic begins in France

Legend:

Lost by Germany to Poland, 1945
Territory gained by Soviet Union
Allied occupation of Germany and Austria, 1945–55
Lost by Italy to Yugoslavia, 1945
Lost by Romania to Bulgaria, 1940–47

Zones of occupation
American
British
French
Soviet
Jointly occupied cities

Refugee movements and repatriated armed forces
Germans
Finns
Baltic peoples
Russians
Poles
Czechs
People settled by the International Refugee Organization

◀ **MAP 28.1 The Impact of World War II on Europe**
European governments, many of them struggling to provide food and other necessities for their populations, found themselves responsible for hundreds of thousands, if not millions, of new refugees. Simultaneously, millions of prisoners of war, servicemen, and slave laborers were returned to the Soviet Union, many of them by force. This situation unfolded amid political instability and even violence. How would you describe the movement of refugees and soldiers in Europe conveyed by this map? What impact did this movement have on political and social life?

Survivors of the concentration camps also discovered that their suffering had not ended with Germany's defeat. Many returned diseased and disoriented, while others often had no home to return to, as property had been confiscated and entire communities destroyed. Moreover, anti-Semitism—official policy under the Nazis—lingered in popular attitudes. In the summer of 1946, a vicious crowd in Kielce,◆ Poland, rioted against 250 returning Jewish survivors, killing at least 40. Elsewhere in eastern Europe, such violence was common. Meanwhile, some officials across Europe even denied that unprecedented atrocities had been committed and wanted to refuse Jews any help. Survivors crammed into the port cities of Italy and other Mediterranean countries, eventually to escape Europe for Palestine, where Zionists had been settling for half a century. Unwilling or unable to help Hitler's most abused victims, many European countries had simply lost the capacity for moral and economic leadership.

New Superpowers: The United States and the Soviet Union

Only two powerful countries were left in 1945: the United States and the Soviet Union. The United States was now the richest country in the world. Its industrial output had increased by a remarkable 15 percent annually between 1940 and 1944, a rate of growth that was reflected in workers' wages. By 1947, the United States controlled almost two-thirds of the world's gold bullion. It also

◆ **Kielce:** kee EHLT say

controlled more than half of the commercial shipping, up from almost one-fifth of the total in the 1930s. With continued spending on industrial and military research adding prosperity to victory, a confident mood swept the United States at the end of the war. Casting aside the post–World War I policy of nonintervention, Americans embraced their position as global leaders. Many had learned about the world while tracking the war's progress; hundreds of thousands of soldiers, government officials, and relief workers had direct experience of Europe, Africa, and Asia. Although some feared a postwar depression and many shared Billy Graham's worries about nuclear annihilation, a wave of suburban housing development and consumer spending kept the economy buoyant. Temporarily reversing the trend toward a lower birthrate that had existed for most of the century, a baby boom exploded from the late 1940s through the early 1960s in response to the economic abundance.

The Soviets also emerged from the war with a well-justified sense of accomplishment. Withstanding horrendous losses, they had resisted the most massive onslaught ever launched against a nation. Instead of the international isolation dealt Russia after World War I, Soviet leadership expected equality in decision making with the United States, and indeed many Europeans and Americans had great respect for the Soviet contribution to Hitler's defeat. Ordinary Soviet citizens believed that a victory that had cost the USSR some 25 million lives would bring improvement in their everyday conditions and a continuation of the war's relatively relaxed politics. Rumors spread among the peasants that the collective farms would be disbanded and returned to them as individual property now that the war was won and agriculture modernized. "Life will become pleasant," one writer prophesied. "There will be much coming and going, and a lot of contacts with the West." The Stalinist goals of industrialization and defense against Nazism had been won, and thus many Soviets expected an end to decades of hardship, even an end to censorship and repressive government.

Stalin took a different view and moved ruthlessly to reassert control. In 1946, his new five-year plan set increased production goals and mandated more stringent collectivization of agriculture. For him, rapid recovery meant more work, not less, and more order, not greater freedom. Stalin cut back the army by two-thirds to beef up the labor force and also turned his attention to the low birthrate, a result of wartime male casualties and women's long, arduous working days, which discouraged them from adding child care to their already heavy responsibilities. He introduced an intense propaganda campaign emphasizing that women should hold down jobs and also fulfill their "true nature" by producing many children. A crackdown on freedom took place, and a new round of purges began in which people were told that enemies among them were threatening the state. Jews were especially targeted, and in 1953 the government announced that doctors—most of them Jews—had long been assassinating Soviet leaders, murdering newborns and patients in hospitals, and plotting to poison water supplies. Hysteria gripped the nation, as people feared for their lives. "I am a simple worker and not an anti-Semite," one Moscow resident wrote, "but I say…it's time to clean these people out." In these ways, Stalinism was reborn and an atmosphere developed that was ripe for cold war.

Origins of the Cold War

In the immediate postwar years, the United States and the Soviet Union launched a cold war that would afflict the world for more than four decades. No peace treaty officially ended the conflict with Germany as a written record of contest and compromise or of things gone wrong, as in the Peace of Paris of 1919–1920. As a result, the origins of the cold war remain a matter of debate, with historians faulting both sides for starting this fearsome rivalry (see "New Sources, New Perspectives," page 1104). Some point to consistent U.S., British, and French hostility to the Soviets that began as far back as the Bolshevik Revolution of 1917 and continued through the Depression and World War II. These powers opposed the Communists' abolition of private property and Russia's withdrawal from World War I. Others stress

Stalin's aggressive policies, notably the Nazi-Soviet alliance in 1939 and his quick claims on the Baltic States and Polish territory when World War II broke out. In this view, other countries naturally feared a Soviet expansionism that knew no limits.

During the war, suspicion ran deep and the Grand Alliance was always a troubled one. Stalin felt that Churchill and Roosevelt were deliberately letting the USSR bear the brunt of Hitler's onslaught on the continent as part of their anti-Communist policy. He rightly viewed Churchill in particular as interested primarily in preserving Britain's imperial power, no matter what the cost in lives of Soviet citizens. At the time, some Americans believed that dropping the atomic bomb on Japan would also frighten the Soviets from land grabs, and the new U.S. president, Harry Truman, was far tougher than Roosevelt with regard to Soviet needs. He cut off aid to the USSR almost the instant the last gun was fired, fueling Stalin's belief that the United States was aiming for his country's utter collapse. Given what Stalin interpreted as a menace from the West, especially in a revived Germany, and his own country's exhausted condition, he saw the USSR as needing not just a temporary military occupation but also a permanent "buffer zone" of European states loyal to the USSR as a safeguard. Across the Atlantic, Truman saw the Soviet occupation of eastern Europe as heralding an era of Communist takeovers around the world. By 1946, members of the U.S. State Department were describing Stalin as yet another neurotic Asian tyrant, driven to continue the centuries-old Russian thirst for world domination.

The cold war thus became a series of moves and countermoves in the shared occupation of the rich European heartland by two very different countries. In line with its geopolitical needs, the USSR repressed democratic coalition governments of liberals, socialists, Communists, and peasant parties in central and eastern Europe between 1945 and 1949. It imposed Communist rule almost immediately in Bulgaria and Romania. In Romania, Stalin cited citizen violence in 1945 as the excuse to demand an ouster of all non-Communists from the civil service and cabinet. In Poland, the Communists fixed the election results of 1945 and 1946 to create the illusion of approval for communism. Nevertheless, the Communists had to share power between 1945 and 1947 with the popular Peasant Party, which had a large constituency of rural workers and peasant landowners. The Allies protested many of these moves by the Communists as the cold war advanced.

The United States put its new interventionist spirit to work, promoting American influence. It acknowledged Soviet authority in areas it occupied but worried that Communist power would spread to western Europe. The difficult conditions of postwar life made Communist programs that promised better conditions increasingly attractive to workers, while Communist leadership in the Resistance gave the party a powerful allure. Both U.S. and British concern mounted when Communist insurgents had enough of a following to threaten the right-wing monarchy the British had installed in Greece in 1944. In March 1947, Truman reacted to the Communist threat by announcing what quickly became known as the **Truman Doctrine**, the countering of political crises with economic and military aid. The president requested $400 million in military aid for Greece and Turkey, where the Communists were also exerting pressure. Fearing that Americans would balk at backing Gr... U.S. congressmen would agree to ... gram only if Truman would "scar... out of the country," as one put it. ... thus publicized an expensive aid pro... necessary to fortify the world against a ... global Soviet conquest. The show of Ame... support convinced the Communists to ba... off, and in 1949 the Greek rebels declared ... cease-fire.

In 1947, the United States also devised the **Marshall Plan**—a program of massive economic aid to Europe—to alleviate some of the hardships that were making ordinary people in western Europe find communism attractive. "The seeds of totalitarian regimes are nurtured by misery and want," the president warned in the same speech that introduced the Truman Doctrine. Named after Secretary of State George C. Marshall, the program's direct aid would immediately improve everyday life, while the loans and other finan-

THE COLD WAR

1945–1949	USSR establishes satellite states in eastern Europe
1947	Truman Doctrine announces American commitment to contain communism; U.S. Marshall Plan provides massive aid to rebuild Europe
1948–1949	Soviet troops blockade Berlin; United States airlifts provisions to Berliners
1949	West Germany formed; Western nations form North Atlantic Treaty Organization (NATO); Soviet bloc establishes Council for Mutual Economic Assistance (COMECON); USSR tests its first nuclear weapon
1950–1953	Korean War
1950–1954	U.S. senator Joseph McCarthy leads hunt for American Communists
1953	Stalin dies
1955	USSR and Eastern bloc countries form military alliance, the Warsaw Pact
1956	Khrushchev denounces Stalin in "secret speech" to Communist Party Congress; Hungarians revolt unsuccessfully against Soviet domination
1959	Fidel Castro comes to power in Cuba
1961	... Wall erected
	... missile crisis

... the flow of inter... ...ent claimed that ...rected "against ...inst hunger, ...By the early ...t Europe ...pment, ...ts in-...cal ...rn Eu... ...ploy that c... ...ss to offer to ... ...astern and central e... ...mped down still harder on ... ...pean governments, eliminating ... ...remnants of democracy in Hungary and Poland and preventing governments in his sphere of influence from responding to the U.S. offer of assistance. For

NEW SOURCES, NEW PERSPECTIVES

Government Archives and the Truth about the Cold War

As the modern nation-state grew in the nineteenth century, historians came increasingly to rely on official government archives to answer questions arising from ideological disputes. The cold war was one such battle of charges and countercharges. Government archives have thrown light on the accusations of both sides. Participants and eyewitnesses, it is believed, are not reliable because of their bias. Instead, trained scholars, ridding themselves of bias, carefully examine government records, preserved in official repositories where tampering cannot take place.

The opening of USSR archives in the late 1980s and 1990s after the fall of Soviet communism gave answers to many cold war questions. In 1956, in the midst of superpower rivalry, Nikita Khrushchev first threw official light on the slaughter connected with Stalin's regime. In Khrushchev's partial revelation of truths, V. I. Lenin and Joseph Stalin were presented as distinctly different political beings, with Lenin an ideologue and benefactor and Stalin a creature of excess. The Soviet archives, however, revealed a more vicious Lenin, one who demanded from the start of the Bolshevik regime the kind of brutality that Khrushchev had pinned on Stalin alone. Lenin and his contemporaries started the reliance on wholesale massacre of the upper classes, peasants, dissenters, and even ordinary citizens. At the same time, the archives discredited the U.S. claim that the Soviet Union in the 1950s was out to conquer the world. Instead, scholars found both Stalin

and Khrushchev fearful of a U.S. nuclear attack and eager to come to terms. Their bluster and brinkmanship, the archives showed, often arose from a need to appear dominant to Soviet satellite states and to the new challenger for Communist leadership—the People's Republic of China.

Much official U.S. archival material still remains closed to scholars, but the Freedom of Information Act (1966, amended 1974) allows historians to press for access and at times to obtain it. Official U.S. documents have opened up debate about the dropping of the atomic bomb, with some scholars concluding that it was not merely a matter of ending the war with Japan in the most expeditious way. Instead, brandishing atomic weapons served U.S. cold war ends of scaring the Soviets. Tapes released from John F. Kennedy's administration have shown the president differing from his generals, most of whom wanted a nuclear war during the Cuban missile crisis. Kennedy, far from being the consistent cold warrior he sought to portray, pulled back from the brink.

For all that new archival evidence can reveal, reliance on this material has many pitfalls. First, one train of thought leads to the mistaken belief that if an archive contains no written evidence of an event, the event is open to question. For instance, if there is no written order from Adolf Hitler to start the Holocaust, some have argued, it means that he did not know about the event or even that it did not occur. Second, faith in archives also makes them susceptible to forg-

instance, Czechoslovakia, which by Eastern European standards had prospered under a Communist-led coalition, welcomed the Marshall Plan as the beginning of East-West reconciliation. This illusion ended, however, during a purge of non-Communist officials

that began in the autumn of 1947. By June 1948, Czechoslovakia's socialist president, Edouard Beneš,◆ had resigned and been replaced by a Communist figurehead. The pop-

◆ **Edouard Beneš:** EH doo ahrt BEH nehsh

Russian Secret Archives
The opening of archives across the former Soviet bloc had many consequences. In the former East Germany, for instance, names of secret police informers were made public and many people had their reputations utterly tarnished for their collaboration with the Communist government. The opening of the archives also exposed the cases of those convicted with trumped-up evidence (some pictured here), most of them sent to camps and to their deaths long since. The probable existence of such secret archives and concealed official information around the world has made historians and the families of victims fight for access. Simultaneously, politicians in the democracies are currently struggling to keep their archives closed, especially to scholars with training in assessing them. *ITAR-TASS/Sovfoto.*

eries and the planting of evidence, as has happened with some Russian documents of the 1990s. Finally, excessive faith in archival documents, some critics say, skews history by suggesting that the most important kind of history comes from official government sources. These critics point out that important historical evidence lies as well in sources ranging from newspapers, family account books, diaries, and personal letters to novels, paintings, and architecture, especially when many kinds of sources are used to verify one another.

QUESTIONS TO CONSIDER
1. Are archives overseen by government officials more or less likely to be biased than other sources? How can we know the extent to which they are telling the truth?
2. Make a list of the most reliable sources for discovering historical truth and provide reasons for your ranking these sources as reliable.

FURTHER READING

Andrew, Christopher, and Vasili Mitrokhin. *The Mitrokhin Archive: The KGB in Europe and the West.* 1999.
Courtois, Stephane, et al. *The Black Book of Communism: Crimes, Terror, Repression,* trans. Johnathan Murphy and Mark Kramer. 1999.
Zubok, Vladislav, and Constantine Pleshakov. *Inside the Kremlin's Cold War: From Stalin to Khrushchev.* 1996.

ulace accepted the change so passively that Communist leaders said the takeover was "like cutting butter with a knife." The Soviet Union had successfully created a buffer of satellite states in eastern Europe directed by what it called people's governments.

The only exception to the Soviet sweep in eastern Europe came in Yugoslavia, under the Communist ruler known as Tito (Josip Broz, 1892–1980). During the war, Tito led the powerful anti-Nazi Yugoslav "partisans." After the war, he drew on support from Serbs,

Croats, and Muslims to mount a Communist revolution. His revolution, however, was explicitly meant to avoid Soviet influence. Eager for Yugoslavia to develop industrially rather than simply serve Soviet needs, Tito remarked, "We study and take as an example the Soviet system, but we are developing socialism in our country in somewhat different forms." Stalin was furious; in his eyes, commitment to communism meant obedience to him. Nonetheless, Yugoslavia emerged from its Communist revolution as a culturally diverse federation of six republics and two independent provinces within Serbia. Tito's break with Stalin further fueled the purges in the USSR because the Soviet government could point to Tito as a vivid example of the treachery supposedly at work even in the depths of communist belief. Holding diverse groups of south Slavs together until his death in 1980, Tito's forceful personality and strong organization also held the Soviets at bay.

Yugoslavia after the Revolution

The Division of Germany

The cold war became most menacing when the superpowers struggled for control of Germany. The agreements reached at Yalta provided for Germany's occupation by troops divided among four zones, each of which was controlled by one of the four principal victors in World War II—the United States, the Soviet Union, Britain, and France. However, the superpowers disagreed on fundamental matters in German history. Many in the United States had come to believe that there was something inherently wrong with the character of Germans—a fatal, evil flaw responsible for two world wars and the Holocaust. After the war, the U.S. occupation forces undertook a reprogramming of German cultural attitudes by controlling the press and censoring all media in the U.S. zone to ensure that they did not express fascist or authoritarian values. In contrast, Stalin believed that Nazism was merely an extreme form of capitalism. His solution was to confiscate and redistribute the estates of wealthy Germans to ordinary people and supporters.

A second disagreement, this one over Germany's economic potential, led to that nation's partition. According to the American plan for coordinating the various segments of the German economy, surplus produce from the Soviet-occupied areas would feed urban populations in the western zones; in turn, industrial goods would be sent to the USSR. The Soviets upset this plan. Following the Grand Alliance agreement that the USSR would receive reparations from German resources, the Soviets dismantled industries and seized German equipment, shipping it all to the Soviet Union. They transported skilled workers, engineers, and scientists to the USSR to work virtually as slave laborers. The Soviets also manipulated the currency in their zone, enabling the USSR to buy German goods at unfairly low prices.

The struggle between the superpowers was escalating. The western Allies struck back by agreeing to merge their zones into a West German state. Instead of continuing to curtail German power, as wartime agreements called for, the United States began an economic buildup under the Marshall Plan to make the western zone of Germany a buffer against the Soviets. By 1948, notions of a permanently weakened Germany came to an end, as the United States enlisted many former Nazi officials as spies and bureaucrats. On July 24, 1948, Stalin retaliated by using Soviet troops to blockade Germany's capital, Berlin. Like Germany as a whole, the city had been divided into four occupation zones, even though it was located more than one hundred miles deep into the Soviet zone and was thus cut off from western territory. Expecting the United States and its allies to capitulate, the Soviets declared that Berlin was now part of their zone of occupation and refused to allow western vehicles to travel through the Soviet zone, including Berlin. The United States responded decisively, flying in millions of tons of provisions to the stricken city. During the winter of 1948–1949, the Berlin airlift—Operation Vittles, as U.S. pilots called it—even funneled in coal to warm some two million isolated Berliners (Map 28.2). Given the immense quantities of fuel and food needed to pro-

**MAP 28.2 Divided Germany
and the Berlin Airlift, 1946–1949**
Berlin, controlled by the United States, Great Britain, France,
and the Soviet Union, was deep in the Soviet zone of occupation and became a major point of contention among the
former allies. When the USSR blockaded the western half of
the city, the United States responded with a massive airlift.
To stop movement between the two zones, the USSR built a
wall in 1961 and used troops to patrol it. What reasons does
the map suggest for the attention to Berlin during the cold war?

**MAP 28.3 European NATO Members
and the Warsaw Pact in the 1950s**
The two superpowers intensified their rivalry by creating
large military alliances: NATO, formed in 1949, and
the Warsaw Pact, formed in 1955 after NATO invited
West German membership. International politics revolved around these two alliances, which faced off
in the heart of Europe. War games for the two sides
often assumed a massive war concentrated in central
Europe over control of Germany.

vision the city and the limited number of
transport planes, pilots kept the plane
engines on to achieve a rapid turnaround
that would ensure the necessary number of
flights each day. Cold war culture increasingly centered on heroic deeds enacted in
Berlin long after the end of the blockade in
May 1949, as many Westerners came to see
Berlin as the centerpiece of a moral crusade.
The divided city became the symbol of the
cold war.

Accelerating cold war tensions led to
the formation of competing military alliances (Map 28.3). The United States,
Canada, and their allies in western Europe
and Scandinavia formed the **North Atlantic
Treaty Organization (NATO)** in 1949. NATO
provided a unified military force for its
member countries. In 1955, after the United
States forced France and Britain to invite

west Germany to join NATO, the Soviet
Union retaliated by establishing with
its satellite countries the military organization commonly called the Warsaw Pact. By
that time, both the United States and the
USSR had accelerated their arms buildups.
Each had tested highly destructive hydrogen
bombs and increased its potential for anni-
hilating the enemy with nuclear weapons.
These two massive regional alliances, armed
to the teeth, formed the military muscle
for cold war politics and definitively replaced the individual might of the European
powers.

Review: What major events led to the development of the cold war between the superpowers?

❖ Political and Economic Recovery in Europe

The ideological clash between the United States and the Soviet Union served as a background to the remarkable economic and political recovery that took place in Europe even as the cold war unfolded. The first order of business on the political front was a highly charged eradication of the Nazi past and the inauguration of peacetime governments. Simultaneously, western Europe revived its democratic political structures, its individualistic culture, and its productive capabilities. Eastern Europe restlessly endured a far less prosperous and far more repressive existence under Stalinism, although even there the conditions of everyday life improved as peasant societies were forced to modernize. Some consumer goods industries and basic health services were restored. By 1960, people across the continent had escaped the poverty of the depression and war to enjoy a higher standard of living than ever before in their history. This rapid revival was even called the **economic miracle**, especially in the case of West Germany's striking prosperity. As governments took increasing responsibility for the health and well-being of citizens, the cold war era also became the age of the welfare state.

Dealing with the Nazi Past

In May 1945, Europeans lived under a complex system in which local resistance leaders, Allied armies of occupation, international relief workers, and the remnants of bureaucracies—among them Nazi sympathizers—shared jurisdiction. Amid confusion, starvation, and a thriving black market, the goals of feeding civilians, dealing with the tens of millions of refugees, purging Nazis, and setting up new governments all competed for attention. Members of governments-in-exile returned to claim their rightful share of power, but they often met up with occupying armies that covered much of the continent and were often a law unto themselves. The Soviets were especially feared for inflicting rape and robbery—abuses they justified by pointing to the twenty million and more

deaths at the hands of the Nazis. Distributing food and clothing, other armed forces tried to instill order even though there was a lively trade in food for sex among various soldiers in all armies and starving civilians. The desire for revenge against Nazis hardened with the discovery of the death camps' skeletal survivors and the remains of the millions murdered there. Swift vigilante justice by civilians released pent-up rage and aimed to punish collaborators for their complicity in genocide and occupation crimes. In France, villagers often shaved the heads of women suspected of associating with Germans and made some of them parade naked through the local streets (see the photo opposite). Members of the resistance executed tens of thousands of Nazi officers and collaborators on the spot and without trial. These became the founding acts of a reborn European political community.

Allied representatives undertook a more systematic "denazification" that ranged from forcing German civilians to view the death camps to investigating and bringing to trial suspected local collaborators. The trials conducted at Nuremberg, Germany, by the victorious Allies in the fall of 1945 used the Nazis' own documents to provide a horrifying panorama of crimes by Nazi leaders. Although international law lacked a precedent for defining genocide as a crime, the judges at Nuremberg found sufficient cause to impose death sentences on half of the twenty-four defendants, among them Hitler's closest associates, and give prison terms to the remainder. The Nuremberg trials introduced current notions of prosecution for crimes against humanity and an international politics based on demands for human rights.

Allied prosecution of Nazi and fascist leadership never succeeded completely because some of the leaders most responsible for war crimes disappeared. Furthermore, many Germans were skeptical about denazification. As women in Germany endured starvation, the menace of occupying forces, and the forced labor of clearing rubble in bombed-out cities, the belief spread among the German population that they were the main victims of the war. German civilians also interpreted the trials of Nazis as a characteristic retribution of victors rather than a

The Punishment of Collaborators

Women who had romantic involvements with Germans were called "horizontal collaborators" to suggest that they were traitorous prostitutes. With heads shaved and often stripped of their clothing, they were forced to parade through cities and towns enduring verbal and other abuse. The public shaming of these women, a vivid part of the memory of the war, served as the background for the film *Hiroshima Mon Amour,* which gripped audiences late in the 1950s. Many local collaborators of both sexes dealt with occupying troops on a daily basis, but some 80 percent of all those whose heads were shaved were women. To what should we attribute this discrepancy? *Robert Capa/Magnum Photos Inc.*

well-deserved punishment of the guilty. Soon the new West German government proclaimed that the war's real casualties were the German prisoners of war held in Soviet camps. Allied officials themselves, eager to restore government services and pursue the cold war, often came to rely on the expertise of high-ranking fascists and Nazis. The Nazi past haunted European cultural life and politics even to this day. While many were rightly horrified at the unprecedented murder and genocide, others attempted to paper over these grim truths. Political expediency led Westerners pursuing the cold war to forgive some Nazis quite easily.

Rebirth of the West

Against all political and economic odds, Europe revived at an accelerating pace in the 1950s. In western Europe, reform-minded civilian governments reflected the broad coalitions that had opposed the Axis. They conspicuously emphasized democracy to show their rejection of the totalitarian regimes that had earlier attracted so many Europeans—and with such dire consequences. Rebuilding devastated towns and cities spurred industrial recovery, while bold projects for economic cooperation like the European Common Market and the conversion of wartime technological know-how to peacetime use produced a brisk trade in consumer goods and services in western Europe by the late 1950s. Memories of the war remained vivid, but prosperity restored confidence and hope for a better future.

Democratic Politics Restored. Resistance leaders had the first claim on political office in postfascist western Europe and began asserting their rights to authority in postwar government. In France, the leader of the Free French, General Charles de Gaulle, governed briefly as chief of state, and the French approved a constitution in 1946 that established the Fourth Republic and finally granted the vote to French women. Wanting a conservative political system that would grant him more authority, de Gaulle soon resigned in favor of left-wing and centrist forces. Meanwhile, Italy replaced its constitutional monarchy with a full parliamentary system that also allowed women the vote for the first time. As in France, a resistance-based government initially took control. Then, late in 1945, the socialist and labor politicians were replaced by a coalition headed by the conservative **Christian Democrats**, descended from the traditional Catholic centrist parties of the prewar period. As in Italy, other parts of Europe saw the growing influence of Christian parties because of their participation in the resistance.

The Communist Party also attracted the vocal loyalty of a consistently large segment of the western European population. Symbol of the common citizen, the ordinary Soviet soldier was a hero to many western Europeans outside occupied Germany, as were the resistance leaders—many of them Communist until late in the war when the impending Nazi collapse lured mainline politicians to join the anti-Nazi bandwagon. People still remembered the common man's plight in the depression of the 1930s. Thus, in Britain, despite the wartime successes of Winston Churchill's Conservative Party leadership, the Labour government of Clement Attlee appeared more likely to fulfill promises to share prosperity equitably among the classes through expanded social welfare programs and the nationalization of key industries. The exceedingly hard times of the immediate postwar years only added to the voices raised for governments that would represent the millions of ordinary people who had suffered, fought, and worked incredibly hard during the war.

In West Germany, however, communism and the left in general had little appeal, so sure was the hold of the Western allies and so distasteful were the Communist takeovers going on to the east. In 1949, centrist politicians helped create a new state, the German Federal Republic, whose constitution aimed to

prevent the emergence of a dictator, to guarantee individual rights, and to build a sound economy. West Germany's first chancellor was the seventy-three-year-old Catholic anti-Communist Konrad Adenauer, who allied himself with the economist Ludwig Erhard. Committed to the free market, Erhard had stabilized the postwar German currency so that commerce could resume. The economist and the politician successfully guided Germany away from both fascism and communism and restored the representative government that Hitler had overthrown.

Paradoxically, given its leadership in the fight against fascism, the United States was the country in which individual freedom and democracy were imperiled after the war. Two events—a successful test of an atomic bomb by the Soviet Union in 1949 and the Communist revolution in China—brought to the fore Joseph McCarthy, a U.S. senator foreseeing a reelection struggle. To strengthen his following in advance of the election, McCarthy warned of a great conspiracy to overthrow the United States. As during the Soviet purges, people of all occupations including government workers, filmstars, and union leaders were called before congressional panels to confess, testify against friends, and to ask themselves whether they had ever had Communist thoughts or sympathies. The atmosphere was electric with confusion and a sense of betrayal, for only five years before the mass media had run glowing stories about Stalin and the Soviet system. During the war, Americans were told to think of Stalin as a friendly "Uncle Joe." By 1952, however, more than six million Americans had been investigated, imprisoned, or fired from their jobs. McCarthy had books like Thomas Paine's *Common Sense*, written in the eighteenth century to support the American Revolution, removed from government shelves, and he personally oversaw book burnings. Although the Senate finally voted to censure McCarthy in the winter of 1954, the assault on freedom had been devastating and anticommunism dominated political life.

Economic Rebirth.   Given the wartime destruction, the economic rebirth of western Europe was even more surprising than the revival of democracy. In the first weeks and months after the war, the job of rebuilding often involved menial physical labor that mobilized entire populations. With so many men dead, wounded, or detained as prisoners of war, German housewives, called women of the ruins, earned their living clearing rubble by hand (see the photo of women clearing rubble in Berlin). Initially governments diverted labor and capital into rebuilding infrastructure — transportation, communications, industrial capacity—and away from producing consumer goods. However, the scarcity of those goods sparked unrest and made communism politically attractive because it proclaimed less interest in the revival of big business than in the ordinary person's standard of living. In the midst of growing discontent over suffering and even starvation, the Marshall Plan boosted recovery with American dollars; food and consumer goods became more plentiful; and demand for automobiles, washing machines, and vacuum cleaners accelerated economic growth. Increased production in all sectors wiped out most unemployment. Labor-short northern Europe even arranged for "guest workers" to migrate from impoverished regions like Sicily to help rebuild cities.

The postwar recovery also featured the adaptation of wartime technology to consumer industry and the continuation of military spending. Civilian travel expanded as nations organized their own air systems based on improved airplane technology. Developed to relieve wartime shortages, synthetic goods such as nylon now became part of peacetime civilian life. Factories churned out a vast assortment of plastic products, ranging from pipes to household goods to rainwear. In the

Women Clearing Berlin
The amount of destruction caused by World War II was staggering, requiring the mobilization of the civilian population in Berlin, where women were conscripted to sort the rubble and clear it away. Scenes like this were ultimately used as propaganda in the cold war to make it seem as if the Germans were the victims rather than the perpetrators of the war. That German soldiers in the Nazi army were held in Soviet camps and were only slowly repatriated added to the image of Soviet rather than German aggression in World War II. Such depictions also made the Germans appear weak and helpless before a threatened menace, as in the photos of weak and ravaged Belgian women in World War I propaganda on page 1012. Would you describe this as a propaganda photo? Why or why not? **For more help analyzing this image**, see the visual activity for this chapter in the Online Study Guide at **bedfordstmartins.com/hunt**. *AKG Photo, London.*

climate of cold war, however, military needs remained high: governments ordered bombs, fighter planes, tanks, and missiles (Figure 28.1). They also continued to sponsor military research. The outbreak of the Korean War in 1950, and the U.S. need for manufactured goods to wage that war, further sustained economic growth in Europe. Ultimately, the cold war prevented a repeat of the 1920s, when reduced military spending threw people out of jobs and thus fed the growth of fascism.

Large and small states alike developed (or in some cases redeveloped) prosperous, modern economies. In the twelve principal countries of western Europe, the annual rate of economic growth had been 1.3 percent per inhabitant between 1870 and 1913. Between 1950 and 1973 those countries almost tripled that rate, attaining an annual rate of growth per capita of 3.8 percent. Among the larger powers, West Germany surprisingly became the economic leader by the 1960s. The smaller Scandinavian countries also achieved a notable recovery: Sweden succeeded in the development of automobile, truck, and shipbuilding industries. Finland modernized its industry in order to pay the reparations demanded by the Soviet Union for resisting its invasion; it also modernized the agricultural sector, which freed up farmers to move into factory work. Scandinavian women joined the workforce in record numbers, which also boosted economic growth and expanded prosperity.

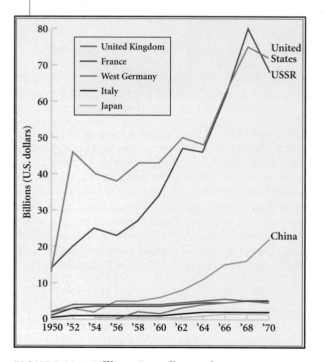

FIGURE 28.1 Military Spending and the Cold War Arms Race, 1950–1970

As soon as the war ended, the United States and the Soviet Union started a massive arms buildup that would continue into the 1980s. Because it had not suffered destruction during the war, the United States could afford spending hundreds of billions of dollars on weapons. The Soviet Union could not, and its citizens were comparatively deprived of consumer goods as a result of these expenditures. By the end of the twentieth century, the United States and Russia held vast arsenals of nuclear and other weapons and, along with France, led the way in selling arms to the rest of the world. The arms race in the early twentieth century helped produce World War I. Why has the arms buildup since World War II not produced a world war to date?

The thirty years after World War II were a golden age of European economic growth.

Birth of the Common Market. As a final ingredient in the postwar recovery, international cooperation and planning led to the creation of the Common Market and ultimately the European Union of the 1990s. The Marshall Plan demanded as a condition for assistance that recipients undertake far-reaching economic cooperation. In 1951, Italy, France, Germany, Belgium, Luxembourg, and the Netherlands formed the European Coal and Steel Community (ECSC). This organization managed joint production and prices among its members. Most important, it arranged for the abundant West German output of coal and steel to benefit all of western Europe. According to the ECSC's principal architect, Robert Schuman, the economic cooperation created by the organization would make another war "materially impossible." Simply put, the bonds of common productivity and trade would keep France and Germany from another cataclysmic war. (See "The Schuman Plan on European Unity, 1950," page 1114.)

In 1957, the six ECSC members took another major step toward regional prosperity when they signed the Treaty of Rome. The treaty provided for a more general trading partnership called the **European Economic Community (EEC)**, known popularly as the **Common Market**. The EEC reduced tariffs among the six partners and worked to develop common trade policies. It brought under one cooperative economic umbrella more than 200 million consumers and would eventually add several hundred million more. According to one of its founders, the EEC aimed to "prevent the race of nationalism, which is the true curse of the modern world." Increased cooperation produced great economic rewards for the six members, whose rates of economic growth soared. Britain pointedly refused to join the partnership at first; membership would have required that it surrender certain imperial trading rights among its Commonwealth partners such as Australia, New Zealand, and Canada. Since 1945, British statesmen had shunned the developing continental trading bloc because, as one of them put it, participation would make Britain "just another European country." Even without Britain, it

TAKING MEASURE

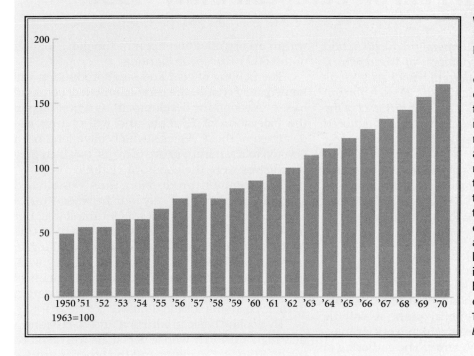

1950 '51 '52 '53 '54 '55 '56 '57 '58 '59 '60 '61 '62 '63 '64 '65 '66 '67 '68 '69 '70
1963=100

World Manufacturing Output, 1950–1970
During the long boom from the 1950s to the early 1970s, the world experienced increased industrial output, better agricultural production, and rising consumer spending. This era of prosperity resulted not only from the demand generated by the need to rebuild Europe and other areas affected by the war but also from the adaptation of war technology to peacetime uses. The General Agreement on Trade and Tariffs (GATT) was also implemented after the war, lowering tariffs and thus advancing trade. What factors were behind the conditions shown in the chart? From Hammond Atlas of the Twentieth Century *(London: Times Books, 1987), 127.*

was clear to some that the future lay with the rising prosperity of a new western Europe joined in the Common Market.

Behind the move to the Common Market stood the adoption of the economic planning and coordination by specialists employed during wartime. Called technocrats after 1945, specialists were to base decisions on expertise rather than on personal interest; those working for the Common Market were to disregard the self-interest of any one nation and thus reduce the potential for irrationality and violence in politics, both domestic and international. Administered by a commission in Brussels, the Common Market was the daily task of experts, whose functions transcended the borders of the nation-state and thus exceeded the power of elected politicians. Some critics insisted (and some still insist even today) that expert planning would diminish democracy by putting massive control in the hands of bureaucracy, not legislatures. Defenders were just as insistent that planning and cooperation would be the surest tools of prosperity and peace.

The Welfare State: Common Ground East and West

On both sides of the cold war, governments intervened forcefully to ameliorate social conditions with state-financed programs such as pensions and insurance. This system of intervention became known as the **welfare state**, indicating that states were no longer interested solely in maintaining order and augmenting their power. Veterans' pensions and programs were primary, but the welfare state had concerns beyond simply sustaining those who had sacrificed in wartime. Because the European population had declined during the war, almost all countries now desperately supported reproduction and family life with direct financial aid. Imitating the sweeping Swedish programs of the 1930s, nations expanded or created family allowances, health-care and medical benefits, and programs for pregnant women and new mothers. The French gave larger family allowances for each birth after the first; for many French families, this allowance provided as much as a third of the household income.

The Schuman Plan on European Unity (1950)

One method of reviving European productivity and well-being after the devastation of World War II was for countries to pool natural resources such as coal and steel. Robert Schuman, French foreign minister from 1948 to 1953, was an architect of the European Coal and Steel Community, instituted after the war to share resources among France, Germany, and other nations. Schuman, however, foresaw more long-term benefits, including lasting peace and the unification of all of Europe. The Schuman Plan, excerpted below, is widely viewed as a blueprint for today's European Union.

World peace can only be safeguarded if constructive efforts are made proportionate to the dangers which threaten it. . . .

Europe will not be made all at once, nor according to a single, general plan. It will be formed by taking measures which work primarily to bring about real solidarity. The gathering of the European nations requires the elimination of the age-old opposition of France and Germany. The action to be taken must first of all concern these two countries.

With this aim in view, the French Government proposes to take immediate action on one limited but decisive point. The French Government proposes that Franco-German production of coal and steel be placed under a common high authority within an organisation open to the participation of the other European nations.

The pooling of coal and steel production will immediately ensure the establishment of common bases for economic development as a first step in the federation of Europe, and will change the destinies of those regions which have long been devoted to the manufacture of arms, to which they themselves were the constant victims.

The common production thus established will make it plain that any war between France and Germany becomes not only unthinkable, but materially impossible. The establishment of this powerful entity, open to all countries willing to take part, and eventually capable of making available on equal terms the fundamental elements of industrial production, will give a real foundation to their economic unification. . . .

By pooling basic production and by creating a new high authority whose decisions will be binding on France, Germany and the other countries that may subsequently join, these proposals will lay the first concrete foundation for a European Federation which is so indispensable to the preservation of peace.

Source: U.S. Department of State Bulletin, June 12, 1959, 936–37. Reprinted in Documents on European Union, eds., A.G. Harryvan and J. van der Harst (New York: St. Martin's, 1997), 61–62.

Aspects of the welfare state reflecting gender bias worked to the detriment of women. Britain's maternity benefits and child allowances, announced in a wartime report, favored women who did not work outside the home by providing little coverage of workingwomen. The West German government passed strict legislation that forced employers to give women maternity leaves, thus discouraging them from hiring women. It also cut back or eliminated pensions and benefits to married women. In fact, West Germans bragged about removing women from the workforce, claiming that this distinguished democratic practices from Communist ones. The refusal to build day-care centers or to allow stores to remain open in the evening so that workingwomen could buy food for their families led West Germany to have among the lowest rate of female employment of any industrial country. Another result of West Germany's policies regarding women was a high rate of female poverty in old age.

By contrast, in eastern Europe and the Soviet Union, where wartime loss of life had been enormous, women worked nearly full-time and usually outnumbered men in the workforce. Like many countries of western Europe, however, child-care programs, family allowances, and maternity benefits were designed to encourage pregnancies by working women. A national health program provided medical and health services, as in most countries to the west. There were marked differences in everyday life that undermined the drive to increase population, however. The scarcity of consumer goods, the housing shortages, and the lack of household conveniences in the eastern bloc discouraged workingwomen from having large families. Because women had sole responsibility for onerous domestic duties on top of their paying jobs, their already heavy workload increased with the birth of each additional child. As a result, the birthrate in Communist states stagnated.

Across Europe welfare-state programs aimed to improve people's health. State funded medical insurance, subsidized medical care, or nationalized health-care systems covered health-care needs in most industrial nations except the United States. The combination of better material conditions and state provision of health care dramatically extended life expectancy and lowered rates of infant mortality. Contributing to the overall progress, the number of doctors and dentists more than doubled between the end of World War I and 1950, and vaccines greatly reduced the death toll from such diseases as tuberculosis, diphtheria, measles, and polio. In England, schoolchildren stood on the average an inch taller than children the same age had a decade earlier. As people lived

longer, governments began to establish programs for the elderly.

State initiatives in other areas played a role in the higher standard of living. A growing network of government-built atomic power plants brought more thorough electrification of eastern Europe and the Soviet Union. Governments legislated better conditions and more leisure time for workers. Beginning in 1955, Italian workers received twenty-eight paid holidays annually; in Sweden they received twenty-nine vacation days, a number that grew in the 1960s. Planning also helped provide a more varied diet and more abundant food, with meat, fish, eggs, cheese, milk, and fresh fruit supplementing the older grain-based foods. Housing shortages posed a daunting challenge after three decades of economic depression and destructive war. Postwar Europeans often lived with three generations sharing one or two rooms. Eastern Europeans faced the worst conditions, whereas Germans and Greeks fared better because only 20 to 25 percent of prewar housing had been lost. To rebuild, governments sponsored a postwar housing boom. New cities formed around the edges of major urban areas in both East and West. Many buildings went up slapdash, and restored towns took on an undistinguished look and a constantly deteriorating condition. Westerners labeled many Eastern-bloc apartments environmentally horrible, meaning that they were a blight on cities and towns across the Soviet landscape (see the illustration below).

Postwar Housing

The housing situation was dire in much of Europe because of the massive bombings and the destruction caused by armies on both sides crisscrossing the continent. Although financially strapped, governments poured resources into rebuilding during the immediate postwar years, but often they lacked the money for anything but minimal dwellings. This was especially the case in the Soviet Union, which faced the dual cost of repairing massive devastation and simultaneously financing the rocketry and weapons systems needed to pursue the cold war. Because of Stalin's cold war preparations, housing construction was postponed. Residential buildings, such as those in the Moscow suburbs, shown above, did not begin construction in earnest until after Stalin's death, when the living standard of ordinary people began to receive government attention. *Stan Wayman/Time Life Pictures/Getty Images.*

Recovery in the East

To create a Soviet bloc according to Stalin's prewar vision of industrialization, Communists revived the crushing methods that had served before to transform peasant economies. In eastern Europe, Stalin enforced collectivized agriculture and badly needed industrialization through the nationalization of private property. In Hungary, for example, Communists seized and reapportioned all estates over twelve hundred acres. Having gained support of the poorer peasants through this redistribution, Communists later dispossessed everyone of their prized lands and pushed them into cooperative farming. Only in Poland did a substantial number of private farms remain. The process of collectivization was brutal and slow everywhere, and rural people looked back on the 1950s as dreadful. But some among those in the countryside felt that ultimately their lives and their children's lives had improved. "Before we peasants were dirty and poor, we worked like dogs....Was that a good life? No sir, it wasn't....I was a miserable sharecropper and my son is an engineer," said one Romanian peasant. Despite modernization, government investment in agriculture was never high enough to produce the bumper crops of western Europe, and lack of motivation among farmers—even their outright hostility toward the new system—worked against the success of collective farming.

Transforming the Soviet Bloc.   An admirer of American industrial know-how, Stalin prodded all the socialist economies in his bloc to match U.S. productivity. The Soviet Union formed regional organizations like those to the west, instituting the Council for Mutual Economic Assistance (COMECON) in 1949 to coordinate economic relations among the satellite countries and Moscow. Modernization of production in the Soviet bloc opened new technical and bureaucratic careers, and modernizers in the satellite states touted the virtues of steel plants and modern transport. The terms of the COMECON relationship thwarted development of the satellite states, for the USSR was allowed to buy goods from its clients at bargain prices and sell to them at exorbitant ones. Nonethe-

less, these formerly peasant states became oriented toward technology and bureaucratically directed industrial economies. Tired of the struggles on the land, rural people moved to cities, where they received better education, health care, and ultimately jobs, albeit at the price of repression. The Roman Catholic church, which often protested the imposition of communism, was crushed as much as possible or infiltrated by government agents. Old agrarian elites, professionals, intellectuals, and other members of the middle class were discriminated against, imprisoned, or executed. Political prisoners in East German camps did hard labor in uranium and other dangerous mines.

Science and culture were the building blocks of Stalinism in the satellite countries as well as in the USSR. State-instituted programs aimed to build loyalty to the modernizing regime; thus, citizens found themselves obliged to attend adult education classes, women's groups, and public ceremonies. An intense program of Russification and de-Christianization forced students in eastern Europe to read histories of the war that ignored their own country's resistance and gave the Red Army sole credit for fighting the Nazis. They replaced national symbols with Soviet ones. For example, Hungarians had to accept a new flag with a Soviet red star beaming rays onto a hammer and sickle; the Hungarian colors were reduced to a small band on the flag. Utter historical distortion, revivified anti-Semitism, and rigid censorship resulted in what one staunchly socialist writer in the USSR characterized as "a dreary torrent of colorless, mediocre literature." Stalin also purged prominent wartime leaders to ensure obedience and conformity. Marshal Zhukov, a popular leader of the Soviet armed forces, was shipped to a distant command, while Anna Akhmatova, the great poet whose widely admired writing had emphasized perseverance and individual heroism during the war, was confined to a crowded hospital room because she refused to glorify Stalin in her postwar poetry.

The Death of Stalin.   In March 1953, amid looming troubles, Stalin died, and it soon became clear that the old ways would not hold. Political prisoners in the labor camps who had

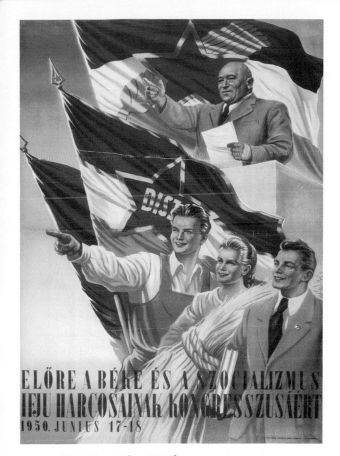

ELŐRE A BÉKE ÉS A SZOCIALIZMUS
IFJU HARCOSAINAK KONGRESSZUSÁÉRT
1950. JUNIUS 17-18

Re-creating Hungarian Youth

People across Europe focused on the well-being of young people after World War II, and in the Soviet sphere this took the form of education in Communist ways. Youth groups, such as those in the early Stalinist USSR, served this end, and vivid posters in the Soviet realist style carried inspirational messages: "Forward for the Congress of the Young Fighters of Peace and Socialism," reads this typical message to Hungarian youth in 1950. Why was the condition of youth so important a concern after World War II? Why was youth so prominent in popular culture during this period? *Magyar Nemzeti Múzeum, Budapest (Hungarian National Museum).*

started rioting late in the 1940s now pressed their demands for reform. In the spring of 1953, more than a million were released from the Gulag, or prison camp system, and returned home with horrific stories to tell. At the other end of the social order, Soviet officials enjoyed country homes, luxury goods, and plentiful food, but many of them had come to distrust Stalinism and were ready for some changes. A power struggle ensued

within the Soviet government, and protests took place across the satellites and at home. In response, the government beefed up the production of consumer goods—a policy called goulash communism because it resulted in more food for ordinary people. There was still lingering uncertainty, however, about the post-Stalin future.

In 1955, Nikita Khrushchev◆ (1894–1971), an illiterate coal miner before the revolution, outmaneuvered other rivals to emerge the undisputed leader of the Soviet Union, but he did so without the usual executions. Khrushchev listened to popular complaints in both city and countryside about conditions and continued to divert resources to consumer goods. The next year he attacked Stalinism. At a party congress, Khrushchev denounced the "cult of personality" Stalin had built about himself and announced that Stalinism did not equal socialism, thus shifting all the problems with communism onto a single individual. The "secret speech"—it was not published in the USSR but became widely known—sent tremors through Communist parties around the world and was a sensation at home. People experienced, in the words of one writer, "a holiday of the soul." Debates broke out in public, and books appeared championing the ordinary worker against the party bureaucracy. The climate of relative toleration for free expression was called the **thaw**. It was to prove an erratic and uneven Soviet policy.

In this climate of uncertainty and change, protest erupted once more in early summer 1956, when discontented Polish railroad workers struck for better wages. Popular support for their cause ushered in a more liberal Communist program. Inspired by the Polish example, Hungarians rebelled against forced collectivization in October 1956—"the golden October," they would call their uprising. As in Poland, economic issues, especially announcements of reduced wages, also sparked outbreaks of violence, but the protest soon targeted the entire Communist system. Tens of thousands of protesters filled the streets of Budapest and succeeded in returning a popular hero, Imre Nagy,◆ to power. When Nagy announced that Hungary might leave

◆ **Nikita Khrushchev:** nyih KEE tuh kroosh CHAWF
◆ **Imre Nagy:** IHM reh NAHD yuh

the Warsaw Pact, Soviet troops moved in, killing tens of thousands and causing hundreds of thousands more to flee to the West. Nagy was hanged. Crushing the Hungarian Revolution vividly displayed the limits to the thaw, but the simultaneous U.S. refusal to intervene in Hungary showed that, despite a rhetoric of liberation, the United States would not risk World War III by militarily challenging the Soviet sphere of influence.

The failure of eastern European uprisings overshadowed significant changes since Stalin's death. In the process of defeating his rivals, Khrushchev ended the Stalinist purges and reformed the courts, which came to function according to procedures instead of staging the show trials of the past. The gates of the Gulag opened further, and the secret police lost many of its arbitrary powers. A new sense of security acquired from increased productivity, military buildup, and stunning successes in aerospace development helped promote the thaw. In 1957, the Soviets successfully launched the first artificial earth satellite, *Sputnik*, and in 1961 they put the first cosmonaut, Yuri Gagarin, in orbit around the earth. The Soviets' edge in space technology shocked the Western bloc and motivated the creation of the U.S. National Aeronautics and Space Administration (NASA). Soviet successes indicated that the USSR was on the way to achieving Stalin's goal of modernization.

Nevertheless, Khrushchev alternately bullied dissidents and showed himself open to changing Soviet culture. For example, he forced Boris Pasternak to refuse the 1958 Nobel Prize in literature because his novel *Doctor Zhivago* (1957) cast doubt on the glory of the Communist revolution and affirmed the value of the individual. Yet in 1961 he allowed the publication of Aleksandr Solzhenitsyn's *One Day in the Life of Ivan Denisovitch*, a chilling account of life in the Gulag. Under the thaw, Khrushchev himself made several trips to the West and was more widely seen by the public than Stalin. More confident and more affluent, the Soviets took steps to reduce their diplomacy's paranoid style and concentrated their efforts on spreading socialism in the emerging nations of Asia, Africa, and Latin America. Despite the USSR's more relaxed posture, the cold war

advanced, as both superpowers sought influence in these new nations and continued to move the world to the nuclear brink.

> **Review:** What factors drove economic recovery in western Europe? In eastern Europe?

❖ Decolonization in a Cold War Climate

World War II dealt the final blow to the ability of European powers to maintain their vast empires, and the cold war added to opportunities for new nations to emerge with the help of the superpowers. Despite their postwar weakness, Britain, France, the Netherlands, and others futilely attempted to stamp out nationalist groups that had strengthened during the war and to reimpose their control. As before, colonized peoples had been on the front lines defending the West; and as before, they had witnessed the full barbarism of Western warfare. Excluded from victory parades and other ceremonies so that the great powers could maintain the illusion of Western supremacy, adult men in the colonies still did not receive the political rights promised them. Moreover, the successive wars had allowed local industries to develop, as the imperial powers lost their ability both to maintain their own consumer manufacturing and to stamp out local initiatives. As a result of the war, people in Asia, Africa, and the Middle East, often led by individuals steeped in Western values and experienced in military and manufacturing technology, embraced the cause of independence and often clashed with the West in bloody warfare.

The path to achieving independence—a process called **decolonization**—was paved with difficulties. In Africa, a continent whose peoples spoke more than five thousand languages, the European conquerors' creation of convenient administrative units such as Nigeria and Rhodesia had obliterated living arrangements that had relied on ethnic ties and local cultures. In addition, religion played a divisive role in independence movements. In India, Hindus and Muslims battled one another even though they shared the goal of eliminating the British. In the Middle East and North Africa, pan-Arab and pan-Islamic movements might seem to have been unifying forces. Yet many Muslims were not Arab, not all Arabs were Muslim, and Islam itself encompassed many competing beliefs and sects. Differences among religious beliefs, ethnic groups, and cultural practices—many of them invented or promoted by the colonizers to divide and rule—worked against political unity. Despite these complications, various peoples in what was coming to be called the third world succeeded in gaining

Jawaharlal Nehru, Prime Minister of India (1952)
Jawaharlal Nehru (1889-1964) led his newly independent country of India from 1947 to 1964, during its first years of freedom from British rule. Trained as a lawyer in English universities, Nehru became an adamant opponent of the British after they massacred hundreds of his countrymen at Amritsar in 1919, and the British imprisoned him during World War II. In the cold war, both sides needed to compete in order to make India an ally. However, U.S. presidents and diplomats hesitated wooing this crucial leader in part because of their suspicions about the toughness of a man who wore what appeared to them a dress along with a rose pinned to it. Nehru and his compatriots were said to be too "feminine" to be reliable in an age of robust cold-war heroes like James Bond. Nehru chose to maintain India, though a populous Asian democracy, as a neutral country. ©Bettmann/Corbis.

independence while they offered a new field for competition between the United States and the Soviet Union in the cold war.

The End of Empire in Asia

At the end of World War II, leaders in Asia began to mobilize the mass discontent that had intensified during the war and, often facing stiff resistance from white settlers, were able to drive out foreign rulers. Declining from an imperial power to a small island nation, Britain was the biggest loser. In 1947 it parted with India, whose independence it had promised in the 1930s. When the war broke out, independence was postponed and some two million Indian men were mobilized to fight in the Middle East and Asia. Local industry became an important supplier of war goods, and Indian business leaders bought out British entrepreneurs short of cash. But during this period of economic prosperity for some, food shortages created by British wartime policies drove people to overcrowded cities, and political fissures between Hindus and Muslims, long encouraged by the British, widened.

The British faced the inevitable after the war and decreed that two countries should emerge from the old colony, so great was the mistrust between the Indian National Congress and Muslim League parties. Thus, in 1947 India was created for Hindus and Pakistan—itself later divided into two parts—for Muslims. Yet during the independence year, political tensions exploded among opposing members of the two religions. Hundreds of thousands were massacred in the great shift of populations between the two nations. In 1948, a radical Hindu assassinated Gandhi, who though a Hindu himself had continued to champion religious reconciliation. Britain retained control of Hong Kong; but before two decades of the postwar era had passed, almost half a billion Asians had gained their freedom from the rule of fifty million British (see Mapping the West, page 1134).

In 1949, a Communist takeover in China brought in a government led by Mao Zedong♦ (1893–1976) that was no longer the plaything of the traditional colonial powers. Chinese

♦ **Mao Zedong:** MOW zuh DOONG

communism in the new People's Republic of China emphasized above all the welfare of the peasantry rather than the industrial proletariat and was thus distinct from Marxism and Stalinism. Mao instituted social reforms such as civil equality for women but at the same time copied Soviet collectivization, rapid industrialization, and brutal repression of the privileged classes.

The United States and the Soviet Union were deeply interested in East Asia, the United States because of the region's economic importance and the USSR because of its shared borders. Thus, the Chinese victory spurred both superpowers to increase their involvement in Asian politics. They faced off indirectly in Korea, which had been split at the thirty-eighth parallel after World War II. In 1950, the North Koreans, with the support of the Soviet Union, invaded U.S.-backed South Korea. The United States maneuvered the United Nations' Security Council into approving a "police action" against the North, and its forces quickly drove well into North Korean territory, where they were met by the Chinese army. After two and a half years of stalemate, the opposing sides finally agreed to a settlement in 1953: Korea would remain split at its prewar border, the thirty-eighth parallel. The United States lost more than fifty thousand men in the Korean War and increased its military spending from $10.9 billion in 1948 to almost $60 billion in 1953. The expansion of the cold war to Asia prompted the creation of an Asian counterpart to NATO: the Southeast Asia Treaty Organization (SEATO), established in 1954. Another side effect of the Korean War was the rapid reindustrialization of Japan to provide the United States with supplies.

The cold war spread to Indochina, where nationalists had been struggling against the

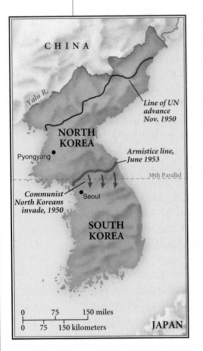

The Korean War, 1950–1953

postwar revival of French imperialism. Their leader, the European-educated Ho Chi Minh (1890–1969), preached both nationalism and socialism and built a powerful organization, the Viet Minh, to fight colonial rule. He advocated the redistribution of land held by big landowners, especially in the rich agricultural area in southern Indochina where some six thousand owners possessed more than 60 percent of the land. Viet Minh peasant guerrillas ultimately forced the technologically advanced French army, which was receiving aid from the United States, to withdraw from the country after the bloody battle of Dien Bien Phu in 1954. Later that year, the Geneva Convention carved out an independent Laos and divided Vietnam into North and South, each free from French control. The Viet Minh was ordered to retreat to an area north of the seventeenth parallel. But superpower intervention undermined the peace treaty while risking nuclear war and subjecting native peoples to the force of their military might. The United States, continuing to assist the corrupt government in the south, was acquiring a reputation as an imperialist power of the old school, and nowhere more so than in Vietnam.

Indochina, 1954

The Struggle for Identity in the Middle East

Independence struggles in the Middle East gained in force because of the world's growing need for oil and the ability of small countries to maneuver between the superpowers. As in the rest of the world after the war, Middle Eastern peoples renewed their commitment to independence and resisted attempts by the major powers to reimpose imperial control. Weakened by the war, British oil companies wanted to tighten their grip on profits, as the value of this energy source soared. But the British leaders arrogantly behaved as if they were still dominant. For example, Winston Churchill, paying a visit to Saudi Arabia during negotiations over the renewal of Britain's oil rights in the country, insisted that he be served alcohol and cigars, sneering at the Islamic prohibitions against alcohol and tobacco. The outcome was that Saudi Arabia turned to the United States, saying that the superpower could take over the oil consortium so long as Britain was kept out. The cold war also gave Middle Eastern leaders an opening to bargain with the superpowers, playing them against each other. Middle Eastern countries, mandated to Britain and France after World War I, not only gained their full independence after the war but began building their economic clout as well.

The legacy of the Holocaust, however, complicated the Middle Eastern political scene as the Western powers' commitment to secure a Jewish settlement in the Middle East further stirred up Arabs' determination not to be pushed out of their homeland. When World War II broke out, 600,000 Jewish settlers and twice as many Arabs lived, in intermittent conflict, in British-controlled Palestine. In 1947, an exhausted Britain ceded the area to the United Nations (UN) to work out a settlement between the Jews and the Arabs. In the aftermath of the Holocaust, the UN voted to partition Palestine into an Arab region and a Jewish one (Map 28.4). Conflicting claims, however, led to war, and Jewish military forces prevailed. On May 14, 1948, the state of Israel came into being. "The dream had come true," Golda Meir, the future prime minister of Israel, remembered, but "too late to save those who had perished in the Holocaust." Israel opened its gates to immigrants, driving its expansionist ambitions against those of its Arab neighbors.

One of those neighbors, Egypt, had gained its independence from Britain at the end of the war. Britain, however, retained its dominance in shipping to Asia through control of the Suez Canal, which was owned by a British-run company. In 1952, Colonel Gamal Abdel Nasser (1918–1970) became

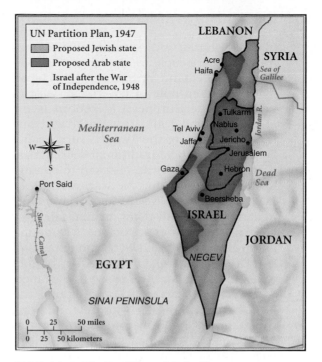

MAP 28.4 The Partition of Palestine and the Creation of Israel, 1947–1948
The creation of the Jewish state of Israel in 1948 against a backdrop of ongoing wars among Jews and indigenous Arab peoples made the Middle East a powder keg until the present day. The struggle for resources and for securing the borders of viable nation-states was at the heart of these bitter contests, threatening to pull the superpowers into a third world war. What does the position of countries on the map indicate about the likelihood that a dispute would arise in this region?

Egypt's president on a platform of economic modernization and true national independence. A prime goal was reclaiming the Suez Canal, "where 120,000 of our sons had lost their lives in digging it [by force]," he stated. In July 1956, Nasser nationalized the canal and thereby became a heroic figure to Arabs in the region. Britain, supported by Israel and France, attacked Egypt, bringing the Suez crisis to a head while the Hungarian revolt was in full swing. The British branded Nasser another Hitler and hoped that the Hungarian revolt would distract the superpowers. But American opposition, born from concerns that Egypt would turn to the USSR, made the British back down. Nasser's triumph inspired confidence that the Middle East could confront the West and win.

New Nations in Africa

In sub-Saharan Africa, nationalist leaders roused their people to challenge Europe's increasing demand for resources and labor, which resulted only in poverty for African peoples. "The European Merchant is my shepherd, and I am in want," went one African version of the Twenty-third Psalm. Disrupted in their traditional agricultural patterns, many Africans flocked to shanty-towns in cities during the war, where they kept themselves alive through scavenging, making crafts, and doing menial labor for whites. At war's end, Kwame Nkrumah◆ (1909–1972) led the diverse inhabitants of the British-controlled West African Gold Coast in Gandhian-style passive resistance. After years of arresting and jailing the protesters, the British withdrew, allowing the state of Ghana to come into being in 1957. Nigeria, the most populous African region, became independent in 1960 after the leaders of its many regional groups and political organizations reached agreement on a federal-style government. In these and other African states where the population was mostly black, independence came less violently than in mixed-race territory (Map 28.5).

The eastern coast and southern and central areas of Africa had numerous European settlers, who violently resisted independence movements. In British East Africa, where white settlers ruled in splendor and where blacks lacked both land and economic opportunity, violence erupted in the 1950s. African men formed rebel groups named the Land Freedom Army but nicknamed Mau Mau. With women serving as provisioners, messengers, and weapon stealers, Mau Mau bands, composed mostly of war veterans from the Kikuyu ethnic group, tried to recover land from whites. In 1964, Kenya gained formal independence, but only after the British had slaughtered some ten to fifteen thousand Kikuyus.

France—although eager to regain its great-power status after its humiliating defeat and occupation in World War II—easily granted certain demands for independence, such as those of Tunisia, Morocco, and West Africa, where there were fewer white settlers, more limited economic stakes, and less military involvement. Elsewhere, French struggles against independence movements were prolonged and bloody. The ultimate test of the French empire came in Algeria. When Algerian nationalists rebelled against the restoration of French rule in the final days of World War II, the French army massacred tens of thousands of protesters. The liberation movement resurfaced with ferocious intensity as the Front for National Liberation in 1954. In response, the French dug in, sending more than 400,000 troops. Neither side fought according to the rules of warfare: Algerian women, shielded by gender stereotypes, planted bombs in European cafés and carried weapons to assassination sites; the French savagely tortured Algerian Arabs. "The loss of Algeria," warned one statesman, "would be an unprecedented national disaster." Yet protests in Paris greeted reports of the army's barbarous practices against the Muslim population, while the French military and settlers in Algeria met the antiwar movement with terrorism against citizens in France. They threatened coups, set off bombs, and assassinated politicians in the name of keeping Algeria French.

France's Fourth Republic collapsed over Algeria, and Charles de Gaulle came back to power in 1958. In return for leading France out of its Algerian quagmire, de Gaulle demanded the creation of a new republican government, one with a strong president who chose the prime minister and could exercise emergency power. As his plans to decolonize Algeria unfolded, terrorism against the French government escalated. By 1962, de Gaulle had negotiated independence with the Algerian nationalists who had successfully turned world opinion against France. Hundreds of thousands of *pieds noirs*◆ ("black feet"), as the French condescendingly called Europeans in Algeria, as well as their Arab supporters fled to France. The Dutch and Belgian empires also disintegrated. Similarly, violent resistance to the reimposition of colonial rule led to the establishment of the large independent states of Indonesia and the

---

◆ **Kwame Nkrumah:** KWAH may ehn KROO mah

◆ *pieds noir:* pyay NWAR

Congo (now known as the Democratic Republic of the Congo).

As independent nations emerged from colonialism and as the continent received immigrants from former colonies, structures arose to promote international security and worldwide deliberations that included voices from the new states. Foremost among these, the **United Nations (UN)** convened for the first time in 1945. One notable change ensured it a greater chance of success than the League of Nations: both the United States and the Soviet Union were active members from the outset. The charter of the UN outlined a collective global authority that would adjudicate conflicts and provide military protection if any members were threatened by aggression. In 1955, Achmed Sukarno, who succeeded in wrenching Indonesian independence from the Dutch, sponsored the Bandung Convention of non-aligned nations to set a common policy for achieving modernization and facing the major powers. Both the UN and the meetings of emerging nations began shifting global issues away from those of the Western powers. North–south inequities and human rights nudged their way into public consciousness.

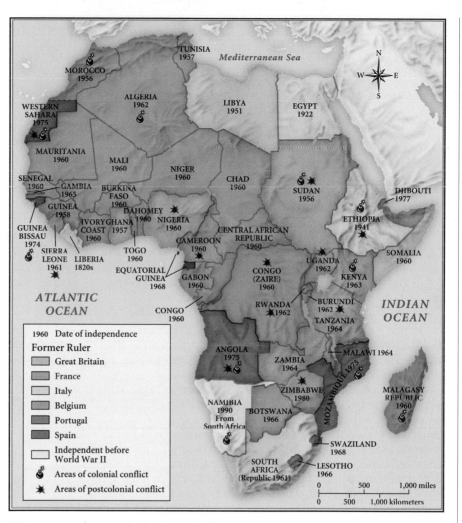

MAP 28.5 The Decolonization of Africa (1951–1990)

The liberation of Africa from European rule was an uneven process, sometimes occurring peacefully and at other times demanding armed struggle to drive out European settlers, governments, and armies. The difficult—and costly—process of nation building following liberation involved setting up state institutions, including educational and other services. Creating national unity out of many ethnicities also took work, except where the struggle against colonialism had already brought people together. To what extent did new African nations keep the borders imposed by the European imperial powers as shown in Map 25.2?

The Arrival of New Europeans

Amid the uncertainties of wars of liberation and the struggles to achieve solid economic independence, people from the former colonies began migrating to Europe—a reversal of the nineteenth century trend of migration out of Europe. The first influx of non-European newcomers came from Britain's Caribbean possessions right after the war.

Next, labor shortages in Germany, France, Switzerland, and elsewhere compelled governments to negotiate with southern European countries for temporary workers. The German situation was particularly dire because in 1950 the working age population (people between the ages of fifteen and sixty-four) was composed of 15.5 million men and 18 million women. In an ideological climate that kept women out of the workforce, the

The First "New" Europeans (1949)

World War II not only disrupted every-day life and patterns of trade in Europe, but around the globe. Some of the first people to immigrate to Europe after World War II were from the Caribbean (like these men in the photograph) and South Asia. Many arrived in Great Britain from the late 1940s onward in search of economic well-being. An expanding welfare state hired some of them to do menial work in hospitals, clinics, and construction, no matter what their qualifications. Race riots erupted, however, and immigration was so extensive that in the 1950s the British House of Commons began debating the rights of these new Europeans. While the government and businesses in western Europe needed these new laborers to rebuild after World War II, some Europeans questioned whether these workers—or their wives and children—should be allowed to become citizens. *Hulton Deutsch Collection/Corbis.*

The agreements stipulated that immigrant workers would have only temporary resident status, with a regular process of emigration back to their homeland. Turks and Algerians would arrive in Germany and France, respectively, to work for a set period of time, return home temporarily to see their families, then arrive in Europe for another period as guest workers. Initially, these workers were housed in barracks-like dormitories and few Europeans paid any attention to the quality of their lives. Instead of settling into community affairs, they created their own enclaves. They were welcomed because they took few social services, not even needing education because they came as adults. For businesspeople and policymakers alike, temporary workers made good economic sense. Virtually none of the welfare-state benefits would apply to them; often their menial work was off the books. "As they are young," one French business publication explained, "the immigrants often pay more in taxes than they receive in allowances." Most immigrants did jobs that people in the West were not likely to want: they collected garbage, built roads, held factory jobs, and cleaned homes. Although men predominated among migrant workers, women performed similar chores for less pay.

Immigrants saw Europe as a land of relatively good government, wealth, and opportunity. Others simply appreciated the conditions of everyday existence. As one Chinese immigrant to Spain put it: "If you want to be a millionaire, you must go to Singapore; if you want to be rich, you must go to Germany; but if you want good weather and an easy life, go to Spain." The advantages of living in Europe, especially the higher wages and jobs, became so overwhelming that clandestine workers began arriving. As early as the late 1960s, regularly admitted laborers formed only 12 percent of the non-European workforce and illegal workers some 88 per-

government needed immigrants. After southern European reserves proved insufficient, Germany and France turned to North African and then to sub-Saharan countries in the 1960s. During the cold war, countries in the Soviet bloc took refugees from war-torn Southeast Asia. Then, in the late 1970s, clandestine workers from Africa and Asia began entering countries like Italy that had formerly exported labor. Scandinavia received immigrants from around the world who flocked there because of reportedly greater opportunity and social programs to integrate newcomers. Immigrants from Surinam and Indonesia headed toward the Netherlands. By the 1980s, some 8 percent of the European population was foreign-born, compared to 6 percent in the United States.

cent. As empires collapsed, the composition of the European population in terms of race, religion, ethnicity, and social life began to change, becoming more multicultural and diverse than ever before in modern times. Many white Europeans looked back nostalgically on their imperial history and produced exotic films and novels about conquest and its pageantry. New nations emerged, their hopes high but their futures uncertain because of the costs of nation building and the legacy of colonial institutions and economic exploitation.

> **Review:** How did former imperial powers come to be dependent on temporary workers from the former colonies?

❖ Cultural Life on the Brink of Nuclear War

Both World War II and the cold war shaped postwar leisure and political culture. People engaged in heated debate over the responsibility for Nazism, the cause of ethnic and racial justice, and the merits of the two superpowers. During this period of intense self-scrutiny, they discussed and even fought over the course of decolonization and the Americanization that seemed to accompany the influx of U.S. dollars, consumer goods, and cultural media. Were they becoming too materialistic, like the Americans, or too intolerant like the Soviets? As Europeans examined their warlike past and the prosperity of the present, the cold war menaced hopes for peace and stability. In 1961, the USSR demanded the construction of a massive wall that physically divided the city of Berlin in half. In October 1962, the world held its breath while the leaders of the Soviet Union and the United States nearly provoked nuclear conflagration over the issue of missiles on the island of Cuba. In hindsight, the existence of extreme nuclear threat in an age of unprecedented prosperity seems utterly bewildering, but for those who lived on the precipice of global annihilation, the dangers were all too real.

Restoring "Western" Values

After the depravity and inhumanity of Nazism, cultural currents in Europe and the United States reemphasized universal values and spiritual renewal. Some, like Billy Graham, saw the churches as central to the restoration of values through an active commitment to "re-Christianizing" Europe and the United States. Their success was only partial, however, as the trend toward a more secular culture continued. In the early postwar years, people in the U.S. bloc emphasized the triumph of a Western heritage, a Western civilization, and Western values over fascism, and they characterized the war as one "to defend civilization [from] a conspiracy against man." This definition of *West* often emphasized the heritage of Greece and Rome and the rise of national governments in England, France, and western Europe as they encountered "barbaric" forces, be these nomadic tribes, Nazi armies, Communist agents, or national liberation movements in Asia and Africa. University courses in Western civilization flourished after the war to reaffirm those values. At the same time, the postwar renewal of humanitarianism pushed issues of cultural pluralism and human rights to the fore.

Holocaust and Resistance Literature. Memoirs of the death camps and tales of the resistance were compelling reading material. Rescued from the Third Reich in 1940, Nelly Sachs won the Nobel Prize in literature in 1966 for her poetry about the Holocaust. Anne Frank's *Diary of a Young Girl* (1947), the poignant record of a teenager hidden with her family in the back of an Amsterdam house, was emblematic of the survival of Western values in the face of Nazi persecution. Confronted with the small miseries of daily life and the grand evils of Nazism, Anne never stopped believing that "people are really good at heart." Governments erected permanent plaques at spots where resisters had been killed, organizations of resisters commemorated their role in winning the war, and their biographies filled magazines and bookstalls. Although resistance efforts were publicized, discussion of collaboration threatened to open old wounds. Thus, French filmmakers, for instance, avoided the subject for decades

**Jean-Paul Sartre and
Simone de Beauvoir**
The postwar period saw the rise of glossy, richly illustrated weekly magazines featuring news and pop culture. The faces of even the most complex philosophers became well known to the public, while their private lives intrigued readers. The public personae of these two existentialists, who were seen to promote the revival of human values after the nightmare of fascism, hid the twisted relationship Sartre and de Beauvoir actually had. Why did the intellectual life of Sartre, de Beauvoir, and their circle receive such media attention after World War II? Does the photo give any hints, or is it merely part of the attention itself? *Editions Gallimard.*

after the war. Many a politician with a Nazi past returned easily to the new cultural mainstream even as the stories of resistance took on mythical qualities.

Existential Philosophy.   By the end of the 1940s, **existentialism** became the rage among the cultural elites and students in universities. It explored the meaning (or lack of meaning) of human existence in a world where evil flourished. Two of its leaders, Albert Camus (1913–1960) and Jean-Paul Sartre (1905–1980), had written for the resistance during the war, although Nazi censors had allowed the production of Sartre's plays. Existentialists confronted the question of "being," given what they perceived as the absence of God and the breakdown of morality. Their answer was that being, or existing, was not the automatic process either of God's creation or of birth into the natural world. One was not born with spiritual goodness in the image of a creator, but instead one created an "authentic" existence through action and choice. Camus's novels, such as *The Stranger* (1942) and *The Plague* (1947), dissected the evils of a corrupt political order and pondered human responsibility in such situations. Sartre's writings emphasized political activism and resistance under totalitarianism. Despite the fact that they had

never confronted the enormous problems of making choices while living under fascism, young people in the 1950s found existentialism compelling and made it the most fashionable philosophy of the day.

In 1949, Simone de Beauvoir◆ (1908–1986), Sartre's lifetime companion, published the twentieth century's most important work on the condition of women, *The Second Sex.* Beauvoir believed that most women had failed to take the kind of action necessary to lead authentic lives. Instead they lived in the world of biological necessity, devoting themselves exclusively to reproduction and motherhood. Failing to create an authentic self through considered action and accomplishment, they had become its opposite—an object, or "Other." Moreover, instead of struggling to define themselves and assert their freedom, women passively accepted their own "Otherness" and lived as defined by men. Beauvoir's classic book was a smash hit, in large part because people thought Sartre had written it. Both were celebrities, for the media spread the new commitment to humane values just as it had previously spread support for Nazism and for its wartime enemies.

◆ **Simone de Beauvoir:** see MAWN duh bohv WAHR

Race and Human Rights. While Europeans debated decolonization among people of color in Africa and Asia, intellectuals spawned new theories of what their liberation would mean. The first half of the century had witnessed the rise of pan-Africanism, but it was in the 1950s and 1960s that the immensely influential Frantz Fanon (1925–1961), a black psychiatrist from the French colony of Martinique, began analyzing liberation movements. He wrote that the mental functioning of the colonized person was "traumatized" by the violence and the brutal imposition of an outside culture as the only standard of value. Ruled by guns, the colonized person knew only violence and would thus naturally decolonize by means of violence. Translated into many languages, Fanon's *Black Skin, White Masks* (1952) and *The Wretched of the Earth* (1961) posed the question of how to decolonize one's mind.

Simultaneous with decolonization, in the 1950s the commitment to the civil rights cause of such long-standing organizations as the National Association for the Advancement of Colored People (NAACP, founded 1909) intensified. African Americans had fought in the war to defeat the Nazi idea of white racial superiority; as civilians, they now hoped to advance that ideal in the United States. In 1954, the U.S. Supreme Court declared segregated education unconstitutional in *Brown v. Board of Education*, a case initiated by the NAACP. On December 1, 1955, in Montgomery, Alabama, Rosa Parks, a part-time secretary for the local branch of the NAACP, boarded a bus and took the first available seat in the so-called white section at the front. When a white man found himself without a seat, the driver screamed at Parks, "Nigger, move back." Sitting in the front violated Southern laws, which encompassed a host of inequitable, even brutal policies toward African Americans. Parks confronted that system through the studied practice of civil disobedience. She refused to move back, and her action led to a boycott of public transportation that pushed the civil rights movement into the African American community as a whole.

The culture of rights and humane values generated further organizing. A variety of civil rights groups boycotted discriminatory businesses, "sat in" at segregated facilities, and registered black voters disfranchised by local regulations. Many talented leaders emerged, foremost among them Martin Luther King Jr. (1929–1968), a Baptist pastor from Georgia whose oratorical power galvanized activists to nonviolent resistance despite brutal white retaliation. He advocated "soulforce"—Gandhi's *satyagraha,* or "holding to truth"—to counter aggression. The postwar culture of nonviolence would shape the civil rights movement for a few years. Soon, however, the voices of thinkers like Fanon would merge with those of the civil rights movement to revolutionize attitudes toward race and rights.

Rising Consumerism and Shifting Gender Norms

Government spending on reconstruction, productivity, and welfare helped prevent the kind of upheaval that had followed World War I. Nor did the same tensions prevail among men and women: men returned from World War II much less frustrated than they had been in the 1920s because of the decisive result of World War II. A rising birthrate and bustling youth culture made for an upsurge in consumer spending that edged out wartime thriftiness. So veterans had fewer worries about jobs. Nonetheless, the war affected men's roles and sense of themselves. Young men who had missed World War II adopted the rough, violent style of soldiers, and roaming gangs posed as tough military types. While Soviet youth admired aviator aces, elsewhere groups such as the "teddy boys" in England (named after their Edwardian style of dressing) and the *gamberros* ("hooligans") in Spain took their cues from pop culture in music and film.

The leader of rock-and-roll style and substance was the American singer Elvis Presley. Sporting slicked-back hair and an aviator-style jacket, Presley bucked his hips and sang sexual lyrics to screaming and devoted fans. Rock-and-roll concerts and movies galvanized youth across Europe, including the Soviet bloc, where teens demanded the production of blue jeans and leather jackets. In a German nightclub late in the 1950s, members of a rock group of Elvis fans called the

Zbigniew Cybulski, the Polish James Dean
Zbigniew Cybulski depicted a tortured young resistance fighter in the film *Ashes and Diamonds* (1958) by Andrzej Wajda. Cybulski's character is to assassinate a Communist resistance leader on what turns out to be the last day of World War II, and his human dilemma around the act is set amid the chaos in Poland at war's end. Like existentialist philosophers and other cinema directors at the time, Wajda captured the debate over human values and the interest in young heroes of the postwar era. Why would this character be attractive to audiences in eastern Europe? *Photofest.*

Quarrymen performed, yelling at and fighting with one another as part of their show. They would soon become known as the Beatles. Rebellious young American film stars like James Dean in *Rebel Without a Cause* (1955) and Marlon Brando in *The Wild One* (1953) created the beginnings of a conspicuous postwar youth culture. The rebellious and rough masculine style appeared also in literature such as James Watson's autobiography, *The Double Helix* (1968), explaining how he

and Francis Crick had discovered the structure of the gene. Portraying himself as an enthusiastic bad boy, Watson described how he had rifled people's desk drawers (among other dishonest acts) to become a scientific hero. In the revival of West German literature, Heinrich Böll published *The Clown* (1963), a novel whose young middle-class hero takes to performing as a clown and begging in a railroad station. Böll protested that West Germany's postwar goal of respectability had allowed the resurgence of precisely those groups of people who had produced Nazism. Across the Atlantic, the American "Beat" poets, who affected a dirty, bearded, and sometimes crazy appearance, like prisoners or camp survivors, critiqued traditional ideals of the upright and rational male achiever.

Both high and low culture revealed that two horrendous world wars had weakened the Enlightenment view of men as rational, responsible breadwinners. The 1953 inaugural issue of the American magazine *Playboy*, and the hundreds of magazines that came to imitate it, ushered in a startling depiction of a changed male identity. *Playboy* differed from typical pornographic magazines: along with pictures of nude women, it featured serious articles, especially on the topic of masculinity. This segment of the media presented modern man as sexually aggressive and independent of dull domestic life—just as he had been in the war. Breadwinning for a family only destroyed a man's freedom and sense of self, this new male culture claimed. The notion of men's liberty had come to include not just political and economic rights but also freedom of sexual expression outside the restrictions of the family.

In contrast, Western society promoted a postwar model for women that differed from their wartime experience. Instead of being essential workers and heads of families in the absence of their men, postwar women were made to symbolize the return to normalcy— a domestic, nonworking norm. Late in the 1940s, the fashion house of Christian Dior launched a clothing style called the "new look". It featured a pinched waist, tightly fitting bodices, and voluminous skirts. This restoration of the nineteenth-century female silhouette invited a renewal of clear gender roles. Women's magazines publicized the new look

Consumerism, Youth, and the Birth of the Generation Gap

Young people were at the cutting edge of consumerism and other aspects of Americanization and economic revival. The generation gap, so much talked about in the 1960s, was taking shape earlier because of youthful openness on matters of the body and sexuality. Not so mired in the war as their parents, the young were ready for adventure—and adults worried about the consequences. Here an Austrian working-class woman (born in 1933) who sewed for a living describes her youth around 1955.

I bought myself records, American blues and jazz, Benny Goodman and Louis Armstrong. I was happy dancing the boogie-woogie. . . .

In fashion I was always very much in opposition to my mother. First, there was craze around nylon stockings, which were very expensive, and which almost everyone bought. We wore long checked skirts, not made of sheep's wool but of a "mixed" wool that was produced out of rags. Then came a short skirt, just above the knee. When I went dancing, however, everyone wore tight, fashionable skirts. One really had to get oneself into them with a shoehorn, and one's backside stood out. I then sewed a kind of cascade on one side, and thus attired, I proudly went dancing.

At first one wore hair long. But my boss was at me so much about it that I had it cut. Then with the new permanents from America one got a totally new look which was flat in the back with a garland of curls around the rest. But fashion changed fast, at one minute such a hairdo was modern, but then one had to put a comb in to push it up higher.

My home was very nice, with a great deal of love, and because of that my parents gave me a lot of freedom although my mother was always concerned. Above everything she always worried: "What will the neighbors think?"

We only spoke about sex with our schoolmates. Certainly nothing about it came from my parents, nothing either from the school. No, one could not ask about such things . . . . Everything was taboo. And boys and girls were strictly segregated from one another in the school. I remember at carnival time a boy came to school dressed as a girl and was sent right home.

Source: Birgit Bolognese-Leuchtenmüller et al., eds., *Frauen der ersten Stunde 1945–1955*. (Vienna: Medieninhaber Europaverlag, 1985), 20–21. Translation by Bonnie G. Smith.

and urged a return to domesticity and thus normalcy. Even in the hard-pressed Soviet Union, recipes for homemade face creams passed from woman to woman and beauty parlors did a brisk business. New household products such as refrigerators and washing machines raised standards for women's accomplishment in the home by giving them the means to be "perfect" housewives.

However, new-look propaganda did not mesh with reality or even with all social norms. Dressmaking fabric was still being rationed in the late 1940s; even in the next decade, women could not get enough of it to make voluminous skirts. In Europe, where people had barely enough to eat, the underwear needed for new-look contours simply did not exist. In Spain, women were said to perform their role best by being religious and concerned with the spiritual well-being of their families. The frequent, even excessive activity known as consumerism, however, emphasized the physical beauty available through cosmetics and clothing; it urged women to buy things that would make their families look better too (see "Consumerism, Youth, and the Birth of the Generation Gap," above). European women continued to work

The New Look

Immediately after the war, the French fashion industry swung into action to devise styles for the return to normal life. Cinched, even corseted waists and voluminous skirts suggested the nineteenth century rather than the depression and war years, when some women had started regularly wearing trousers. The highly restrictive femininity was also part of the cold war, as the leisured ideal demanded by the new look for middle-class Western women contrasted with the more practical styles in the Soviet Union. Although western Europe was hard hit by the war, governments imported foreign workers to rebuild; in the USSR, in contrast, more than 90 percent of women worked to rebuild their devastated country. Why did the image of women after World War I become so modern, while the image of women after World War II became more traditional, especially in western Europe and the United States? *Liaison Agency.*

outside the home after the war; indeed, mature women and mothers were working more than ever before—especially in the Soviet bloc (Figure 28.2, opposite). The female workforce was going through a profound revolution as it gradually became less youthful and more populated by wives and mothers who would hold jobs all their lives despite being bombarded with images of nineteenth-century middle-class femininity.

The advertising business presided over the creation of cultural messages as well as over the rise of the new consumerism that accompanied recovery. Guided by marketing experts, western Europeans were imitating Americans by driving some forty million motorized vehicles, including motorbikes, cars, buses, and trucks. They drank Coca-Cola and used American detergents, toothpaste, and soap. The number of radios in homes grew steadily—for example, by 10 percent a year in Italy between 1945 and 1950—and the 1950s marked a high tide of radio influence. The development of television spread in the United States, where two-thirds of the population had sets in the early 1950s, while in Britain only one-fifth did. Only in the 1960s did television become an important consumer item for most Europeans. In the 1950s, radio was still king and consumerism a growing mass phenomenon.

The Culture of Cold War

Radio was at the center of the cold war. As superpower rivalry heated up, radio's propaganda function remained at the fore, as it had in wartime. During the late 1940s and early 1950s, the Voice of America, with its main studio in Washington, D.C., broadcast in thirty-eight languages from one hundred transmitters and provided an alternative source of news for people in eastern Europe. The Soviet counterpart broadcast in Russian around the clock but initially spent much of its wattage jamming U.S. programming. Russian programs stressed a uniform Communist culture and values; the United States, by contrast, emphasized diverse programming and promoted debate about current affairs. The contrast was meant to show commitment to socialist values versus commitment to choice and free speech.

	Member Countries of Council of Mutual Economic Assistance[1]		Member Countries of European Economic Community[2]	
	1950	1960	1950	1960
Female as % of total population	54.9	53.9	51.8	51.6
Female labor force as % of total labor force	48.5	48.7	31.1	31.4
Distribution of female labor force (%):				
Agriculture	63.3	50.0	26.1	16.8
Industry	16.9	22.6	29.3	31.3
Services	19.8	27.4	44.6	51.9

[1]Albania, Bulgaria, Czechoslovakia, East Germany, Hungary, Poland, Romania, and USSR

[2]Belgium, Denmark, France, West Germany, Ireland, Italy, Luxembourg, Netherlands, and United Kingdom

FIGURE 28.2 Women in the Workforce, 1950–1960
In contrast to the situation after World War I, women did not leave the workforce in great numbers after World War II. In fact, Europe faced labor shortages. In countries of the Soviet bloc, women vastly outnumbered men because so many men had died in the war, and the task of rebuilding demanded every available worker. In western Europe, women's workforce participation was lower, and countries like West Germany tried to keep women out of the labor pool to distinguish themselves from the Communist bloc. Note the increase in women's service-sector employment in just one decade. From *World Employment 1996–1997: National Policies in a Global Context* (Geneva: International Labour Office, 1996), 7.

Its issues and events conveyed by radio and other media, the cold war had a far-reaching emotional impact. The public heard reports of nuclear buildups; tests of emergency power facilities sent them scurrying for cover. In school, children rehearsed for nuclear war, while at home families built bomb shelters in their backyards. Books like George Orwell's *1984* (1949) were claimed by ideologues on both sides as vindicating their beliefs. Ray Bradbury's popular *Fahrenheit 451* (1953), whose title indicated the temperature at which books would burn, condemned cold war curtailment of intellectual freedom. In the USSR, official writers churned out spy stories, and espionage novels topped best-seller lists in the West. *Casino Royale* (1953), by the British author Ian Fleming, introduced James Bond, who tested his wit and physical prowess against Communist and other political villains. Soviet pilots would not take off for flights when the work of Yulian Simyonov,♦ the Russian counterpart of Ian Fleming, was playing on radio or television. Reports of Soviet -and U.S.-bloc characters—fictional or real—facing one another down became part of everyday life.

Culture as a whole came under the cold war banner. Even as Europe's major cities rebuilt their war-ravaged opera houses and museums, they could not hold back the "Americanization" they saw taking place in Europe. While many Europeans were proponents of American business practices, the Communist Party in France led a successful campaign to ban Coca-Cola for a time in the 1950s. Soviet magazines carried fashion photos touted as decently attractive in contrast to the highly sexualized garments for women to the

♦ **Yulian Simyonov:** ool ee AHN sihm YAWN uhv

Bomb Shelter

Americans expressed their fear of nuclear annihilation by building tens of thousands of individual bomb shelters. Stocked with several months' supply of canned food and other goods, the shelters were to protect a family from the nuclear blast itself and from the disorder that might follow nuclear war. The government also prepared shelters to shield top officials and to ensure the continuation of civil society despite vast casualties and massive destruction. *Bettman/Corbis.*

Barbara Hepworth, *Single Form* (1961–1964)

Like others in the West, British sculptor Barbara Hepworth was strangely buoyed by the war, hoping that it meant the dawn of a new age. Full of renewed energy, Hepworth believed that art should follow pure forms, which some called "primitive," as a way of expressing enduring values. Her twenty-one-foot abstract sculpture *Single Form,* shown here as a plaster cast, was installed at the United Nations building in New York to commemorate the life of her friend Dag Hammarskjöld, who served as secretary-general of the United Nations from 1953 until his death in 1961. *Single Form* followed the clean lines of an earlier version of the sculpture—one much loved by Hammarskjöld. "[We] depend on the pure courage of the UN," Hepworth wrote of the sculpture created to honor Hammarskjöld's life and work. *Plaster for bronze, BH325, height: 21 feet, 1961-64, Photo: Morgan-Wells, London. © Bowness, Hepworth Estate*

West. Both sides also tried to win the war by pouring vast sums of money into high culture, though the United States did it by secretly channeling government money into foundations to award fellowships to artists and writers or promote favorable journalism around the world. As leadership of the art world passed to the United States, art became part of the cold war. Abstract expressionism, practiced by American artists such as Jackson Pollock, produced nonrepresentational works by dripping, spattering, and pouring paint. Abstract expressionists spoke of the importance of the artist's self-discovery, spiritual growth, and sensations in the process of painting. "If I stretch my arms next to the rest of myself and wonder where my fingers are, that is all the space I need as a painter," commented Dutch-born Willem de Kooning on his relationship with his canvas. Said to exemplify Western freedom, such painters were given shows in Europe and awarded commissions at the secret direction of the U.S. Central Intelligence Agency.

The USSR openly promoted an official Communist culture. When a show of abstract art opened in the Soviet Union, Khrushchev yelled at the exhibition itself that it was "dog shit." Pro-Soviet critics in western Europe saw U.S.-style abstract art as "an infantile sickness" and supported socialist realist art with "human content," showing the condition of the workers and the oppressed races in the United States. In Italy, the neorealist technique was developed by filmmakers such as Roberto Rossellini in *Open City* (1945) and Vittorio De Sica in *The Bicycle Thief* (1948). Such works challenged Hollywood-style sets and costumes by using ordinary characters living in devastated, impoverished cities. By depicting stark conditions, neorealist directors conveyed their distance both from middle-class prosperity and from fascist bombast. "We are in rags? Let's show everyone our rags," said one Italian director. Many of these directors associated support for the suffering masses with the Communist cause. Seen or unseen, the cold war entered the most unsuspected aspects of cultural life.

Kennedy, Khrushchev, and the Atomic Brink

It was in this pervasive climate of cold war that John Fitzgerald Kennedy (1917–1963) became U.S. president in 1960. Kennedy represented American affluence and youth but also the nation's commitment to cold war. Kennedy's media advisers and ghostwriters recognized how perfect a match their articulate, good-looking president was to the power of television. A war hero and early fan of the fictional cold war spy James Bond, Kennedy intensified the arms race and escalated the cold war. Some of this escalation occurred over the nearby island of Cuba, where in 1959 Fidel Castro had come to power and allied his government with the Soviet Union after being rebuffed by the United States. In the spring of 1961, Kennedy, assured by the

Central Intelligence Agency (CIA) of success, launched an invasion of Cuba at the Bay of Pigs to overthrow Castro. The invasion failed miserably and humiliated the United States.

Tensions kept growing. In the summer of 1961, East German workers, supervised by police and the army, stacked bales of barbed wire across miles of the city's east–west border to begin construction of the Berlin Wall. The divided city had served as an escape route by which some three million people had fled to the West. Kennedy responded at home with a call for more weapons and an enhanced civil defense program. In October 1962, matters came to a head in the **Cuban missile crisis**, when the CIA reported the installation of Soviet medium-range missiles in Cuba (Map 28.6). Kennedy now responded forcefully, calling for

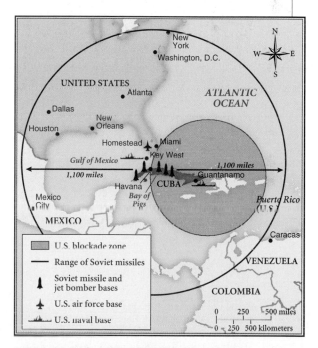

MAP 28.6 The Cuban Missile Crisis, 1962
Just off the coast of the southeastern United States, Cuba posed a threat to North American security once the Soviet Union began stocking the island with missiles. The United States reacted vigorously, insisting on the dismantling of missile sites and an end to the Soviets' supplying Cuba with further weaponry. Although his generals were prepared for nuclear war with the Soviet Union, President Kennedy refused to take this step despite his cold war stance on many other issues. Soviet premier Khrushchev similarly backed down from a military confrontation. Explain the placement of missiles in Cuba and the U.S. reaction to it.

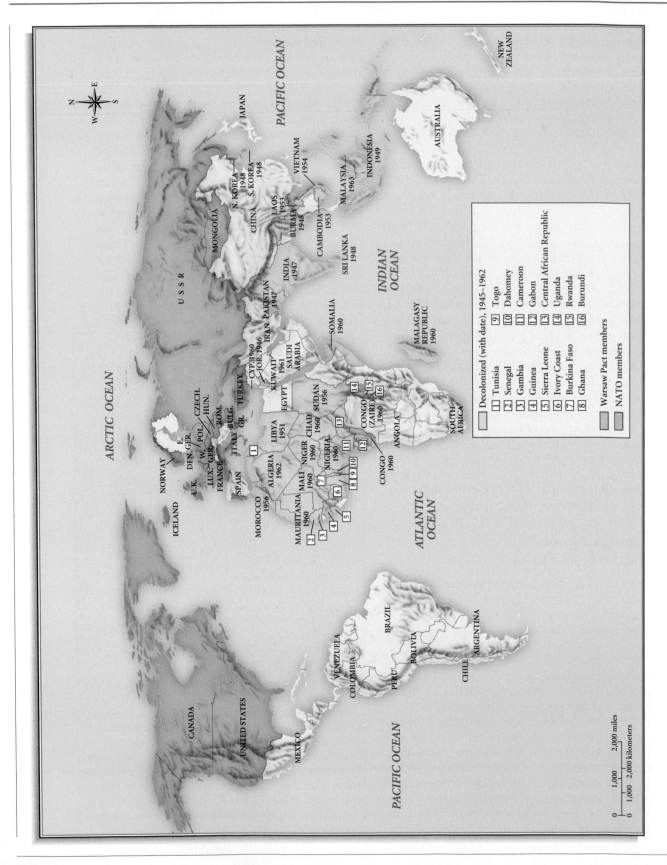

◄ **MAPPING THE WEST**
The Cold War World, c. 1960

Superpower rivalry between the United States and the Soviet Union resulted in the division of much of the industrial world into cold war alliances. Simultaneously, the superpowers vied for the allegiance of the newly decolonized countries of Asia and Africa by providing military, economic, and technological assistance. Wars such as those in Vietnam and Korea were also products of the cold war. How might this map be said to convey the idea that a first, second, and third world existed? How does this map differ from the map on page 955?

a blockade of ships headed for Cuba and threatening nuclear war if the missiles were not removed. For several days the world stood on the brink of nuclear disaster. Then, between October 25 and 27, Khrushchev and Kennedy negotiated an end to the crisis. Kennedy spent the remainder of his short life working to improve nuclear diplomacy; Khrushchev did the same. The two leaders, who had looked deeply into the nuclear future, clearly feared what they saw. In the summer of 1963, less than a year after the shock of the Cuban missile crisis, the United States and the Soviet Union signed a test-ban treaty outlawing the explosion of nuclear weapons in the atmosphere and in the seas. Backing away from the brink, the treaty held out hope that the cold war and its culture would give way to something better.

Review: How did the cold war affect everyday culture and social life?

Conclusion

World War II began the atomic age and transformed international power politics. Two superpowers, the Soviet Union and the United States, each controlling atomic arsenals, replaced the former European leadership and engaged in a menacing cold war. The cold war saturated everyday life, giving birth to cold war religion in the preachings of the Reverend Billy Graham and to a postwar revival of religious faith. In secular life, bomb shelters, spies, purges, and witch hunts kept

people thinking that war was at hand. Postwar diplomacy created a cold war division of Europe into an eastern bloc dominated by the Soviets and a freer western bloc mostly allied with the United States. It was in this grim international atmosphere that starving, homeless, and refugee people faced the task of rebuilding a devastated Europe.

Yet both halves of Europe recovered almost miraculously in little more than a decade. The east, where wartime devastation was greatest, experienced less prosperity, while in western Europe wartime technology and planning served as the basis for new consumer goods and improved health. Spurred on by aid from the United States, western Europe formed a successful Common Market that became the foundation for greater European unity. As a result of the war, Germany recovered as two countries, not one, and the weakened European powers shed their colonies. Newly independent nations emerged in Asia and Africa, opening the possibility for a more equitable distribution of global power. Often serving as pawns in the cold war, these new countries faced the problem of guaranteeing their economic future. As the West as a whole grew in prosperity, its cultural life focused paradoxically on eradicating the evils of Nazism while enjoying the new phenomenon of mass consumerism. But, like newly independent nations, the West had above all to survive the atomic rivalry of the superpowers.

Suggested References

World Politics Transformed

In the past decade, the opening of Soviet archives and closer research in American records have allowed for more informed views of the diplomacy and politics of the cold war in Europe and around the world. Although few defend Stalin, we now benefit from balanced assessments of superpower rivalry. Two Web sites on the cold war contain biographies of the main players, time lines, and miscellaneous details, while a third describes how nuclear weapons actually work and how they cause destruction.

Cold war: **http://library.thinkquest.org/ 10826.mainpage.htm**; **http://history .acusd.edu/gen/20th/coldwar0.html**; **http:// nuclearwar.org**.

Cronin, James. *The World the Cold War Made: Order, Chaos, and the Return of History*. 1996.

Eisenberg, Carolyn Woods. *Drawing the Line: The American Decision to Divide Germany, 1944–1949*. 1996.

Gaddis, John. *We Now Know: Rethinking Cold War History*. 1997.

Hogan, Michael J. *A Cross of Iron: Harry S. Truman and the Origins of the National Security State, 1945–1954*. 1998.

*Pasternak, Boris. *Doctor Zhivago*. 1958.

Zubkova, Elena. *Russia after the War: Hopes, Illusions, and Disappointments, 1945–1957*. 1998.

Political and Economic Recovery in Europe

Though painstaking and complex, recovery in its material and political forms yielded a distinctly new Europe whose characteristics historians are still uncovering. Because of the opening of the archives, historical attention has focused on charting Soviet occupation, recovery, and Communist takeover.

Herf, Jeffrey. *Divided Memory: The Nazi Past in the Two Germanies*. 1997.

Kenney, Padraic. *Rebuilding Poland: Workers and Communists, 1945–1950*. 1997.

Milward, Alan S. *The United Kingdom and the Economic Community*. 2002.

Moeller, Robert, ed. *West Germany under Construction: Politics, Society, and Culture in the Adenauer Era*. 1997.

Naimark, Norman M. *The Russians in Germany: A History of the Russian Zone of Occupation, 1945–1949*. 1995.

Taubman, William. *Khrushchev: The Man and His Era*. 2003.

Decolonization in a Cold War Climate

Novelists, philosophers, and historians debate the impact and issues of decolonization. Powerful evocations of the brutality of the process appear most often in novels such as *Cracking India*, which was made into the film *Earth*.

Connelly, Matthew. *A Diplomatic Revolution: Algeria's Quest for Independence and the Origins of the Post–Cold War Era*. 2002.

*Fanon, Frantz. *The Wretched of the Earth*. 1961.

Hargreaves, J. D. *Decolonization in Africa*. 1996.

Macey, David. *Frantz Fanon: A Biography*. 2000.

McIntyre, W. David. *British Decolonization, 1946–1997: When, Why, and How Did the British Empire Fall?* 1999.

*Sidhwa, Bapsi. *Cracking India: A Novel*. 1992.

Yergin, Daniel. *The Prize: The Epic Quest for Oil, Money, and Power*. 1991.

Cultural Life on the Brink of Nuclear War

Cold war culture, including the growth of consumerism, make the 1950s a fertile field for research, especially as new sources become available. Historians like Saunders have focused on governments' direction of high culture to the point that some artists and writers were made "stars" because of government intervention, while Engel's new work points to the lows of consumerism in the plight of the Soviet Union's women.

Bayin, Andre. *French Cinema from the Liberation to the New Wave*. 2000.

*Beauvoir, Simone de. *The Mandarins*. 1956.

Engel, Barbara Alpern. *Women in Russia, 1700–2000*. 2004.

Heineman, Elizabeth D. *What Difference Does a Husband Make? Women and Marital Status in Nazi and Postwar Germany*. 1999.

Kuisel, Richard. *Seducing the French: The Dilemma of Americanization*. 1993.

Poiger, Ute G. *Jazz, Rock, and Rebels: Cold War Politics and American Culture in a Divided Germany*. 2000.

Saunders, Frances Stonor. *Who Paid the Piper?* 1999.

Swann, Abram de. *In Care of the State: Health Care, Education, and Welfare in Europe and the United States in the Modern Era*. 1988.

*Primary source.

CHAPTER REVIEW

IMPORTANT EVENTS

1945   Cold war begins

1947   India and Pakistan win independence from Britain

1948   State of Israel established

1949   Mao Zedong leads Communist revolution in China; Simone de Beauvoir publishes *The Second Sex*

1950   Korean War begins

1953   Stalin dies; Korean War ends

1954   *Brown v. Board of Education* prohibits segregated schools in the United States; Vietnamese forces defeat the French at Dien Bien Phu

1956   Egyptian leader General Abdel Nasser nationalizes the Suez Canal; uprising in Hungary against USSR

1957   Boris Pasternak publishes *Doctor Zhivago*; USSR launches *Sputnik*; Treaty of Rome establishes the European Economic Community (Common Market)

1958   Fifth Republic begins in France

1962   The United States and USSR face off in the Cuban missile crisis

KEY TERMS

Christian Democrats (1110)

cold war (1198)

Cuban missile crisis (1133)

decolonization (1118)

economic miracle (1108)

European Economic Community (EEC or Common Market) (1112)

existentialism (1126)

Marshall Plan (1103)

North Atlantic Treaty Organization (NATO) (1107)

thaw (1117)

third world (1098)

Truman Doctrine (1103)

United Nations (UN) (1123)

welfare state (1113)

REVIEW QUESTIONS

1. What major events led to the development of the cold war between the superpowers?

2. What factors drove economic recovery in western Europe? In eastern Europe?

3. How did former imperial powers come to be dependent on temporary workers from the former colonies?

4. How did the cold war affect everyday culture and social life?

MAKING CONNECTIONS

1. What was the political climate after World War II and how did it differ from the political climate after World War I?

2. What were the relative strengths of the two European sides in the cold war?

3. How did World War II shape cultural life after the war?

4. Why did decolonization follow the war so immediately?

FOR FURTHER EXPLORATION

To assess your mastery of the material in this chapter, see the Online Study Guide at **bedfordstmartins.com/hunt**.

To read additional primary-source material from this period, see Chapter 28 in *Sources of The Making of the West*, Second Edition.

Postindustrial Society and the End of the Cold War Order, 1965–1989

IN JANUARY 1969, JAN PALACH, a twenty-one-year-old philosophy student, drove to a main square in Prague, doused his body with gasoline, and set himself ablaze. Before killing himself he left a statement in his coat—deliberately put to one side—demanding an end to Soviet-style repression in Czechoslovakia. It promised more such suicides unless the government lifted state censorship. The manifesto was signed: "Torch No. 1." Across a stunned nation, black flags were flown, close to a million people flocked to Palach's funeral, and shrines to his memory seemed to spring up overnight. In the next months, more Czech youth followed Palach's grim example and became torches for freedom.

Before his self-immolation, Jan Palach was an ordinary, well-educated citizen of the technological and postindustrial age. Having recovered from the war, the West was in the midst of still another astonishing transformation, shifting from a manufacturing economy based in heavy industry to a service economy that depended on technical knowledge in such fields as engineering, health care, and finance. This new service economy was seen as a postindustrial one. To staff it, institutions of higher education sprang up at a dizzying rate and drew in more students than ever before—among them Jan Palach. But those young people—along with women, minorities, and

---

Shrine to Jan Palach

Jan Palach was a martyr to the cause of an independent Czechoslovakia, free to pursue a non-Soviet destiny. His self-immolation on behalf of that cause roused the nation. As makeshift shrines sprang up and multiplied throughout the 1970s and 1980s, they served as common rallying points that ultimately contributed to the overthrow of Communist rule. Václav Havel, the future president of a liberated Czechoslovakia, was arrested early in the momentous year of 1989 for commemorating Palach's sacrifice at the shrine. In light of so many other deaths in the Soviet bloc, why did Jan Palach's death become so powerful a force? © Mark Gurunger/Corbis.

many other activists in the 1960s and 1970s—struck out against war and cold war, inequality and repression, and even against knowledge and technology themselves. From Czechoslovakia to the United States and around the world, protests arose against the way in which postindustrial nations in general and the superpowers in particular were directing society. Before long, countries in both the Soviet and U.S. blocs were on the verge of political revolution.

While reformers questioned the values of technological and cold war society, whole nations challenged the superpowers' monopoly of international power. An agonizing war in Vietnam sapped the resources of the United States, and China confronted the Soviet Union with increasing confidence. The oil-producing states of the Middle East formed a cartel and reduced the flow of oil to the leading industrial nations in the 1970s. The resulting price increases helped bring on a recession, throwing the future of the postindustrial order into question. Others resorted to terrorism to achieve their ends, and all the wealth and military might of the superpowers could not guarantee that they would emerge victorious in this age of increasingly global competition. An invisible erosion of Soviet legitimacy took place, and soon a reform-minded leader—Mikhail Gorbachev—directed the USSR to change course. It was too late: in 1989, the Soviet bloc collapsed, inspired by countless acts of protest, not least of them the individual heroism of Jan Palach and the other human torches.

❖ The Revolution in Technology

The protests of the 1960s and after took place in the midst of incredible technological advance. These advances steadily boosted prosperity and changed daily life in the West, where people awoke to instantaneous radio and television news, worked with computers, and used revolutionary contraceptives to control reproduction. Satellites orbiting the earth reported weather conditions, relayed telephone signals, and collected military intelligence. Smaller gadgets—electric popcorn poppers, portable radios and tape players, automatic garage door openers—made life more pleasant. The reliance of humans on machines led one philosopher to insist that people were no longer self-sufficient individuals, but rather cyborgs—that is, humans who needed machines to sustain ordinary life processes.

The Information Age: Television and Computers

Information technology catalyzed social and political change in these postindustrial decades just as innovations in textile making and the spread of railroads had in the nineteenth century. This technology's ability to transmit knowledge, culture, and political information globally appeared even more revolutionary. Mass journalism, film, and radio had begun to forge a more homogeneous society based on shared information and

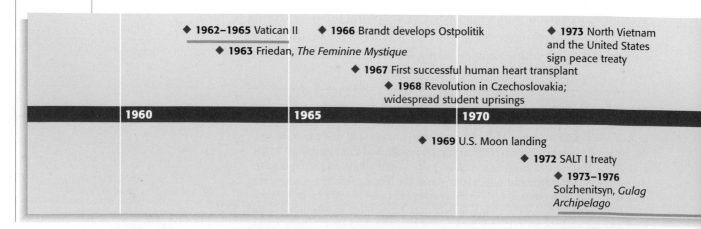

◆ **1962–1965** Vatican II   ◆ **1966** Brandt develops Ostpolitik   ◆ **1973** North Vietnam and the United States sign peace treaty

◆ **1963** Friedan, *The Feminine Mystique*

◆ **1967** First successful human heart transplant

◆ **1968** Revolution in Czechoslovakia; widespread student uprisings

1960   **1965**   **1970**

◆ **1969** U.S. Moon landing

◆ **1972** SALT I treaty

◆ **1973–1976** Solzhenitsyn, *Gulag Archipelago*

images in the first half of the twentieth century; in the last third of the century, television, computers, and telecommunications made information even more accessible and, some critics said, made culture more standardized. Once-remote villages were linked to urban capitals on the other side of the world thanks to videocassettes, satellite television, and telecommunications. Because of technology, the age of protest was also the age of communications events.

Television.   Americans embraced television in the 1950s; following the postwar recovery, it was Europe's turn. Between the mid-1950s and the mid-1970s, Europeans rapidly adopted television as a major entertainment and communications medium. In 1954, just 1 percent of French households had television; by 1974, almost 80 percent did. With the average viewer tuning in about four and a half hours a day, the audience for newspapers and theater declined. "We devote more . . . hours per year to television than [to] any other single artifact," one sociologist commented in 1969. As with radio, European governments funded television broadcasting with tax dollars and controlled TV programming to avoid what they perceived as the substandard fare offered by American commercial TV; instead they featured drama, ballet, concerts, variety shows, and news. Thus, the welfare state, in Europe at least, assumed a new obligation to fill its citizens' leisure time. It thereby gained more power to shape daily life.

With the emergence of communications satellites and video recorders in the 1960s, state-sponsored television encountered competition. Satellite technology allowed for the transmission of sports broadcasts and other programming to a worldwide audience. Feature films on videotape became readily available to television stations (although not yet to individuals) and competed with made-for-television movies and other programs. The competition increased in 1969 when the Sony Corporation introduced the first affordable color videocassette recorder to the consumer market. What statesmen and intellectuals considered the junk programming of the United States—soap operas, game shows, sitcoms—arrived dubbed in the native language, amusing a vast audience with the joys, sorrows, tensions, and aspirations of daily life. Critics charged that both state-sponsored and commercial television avoided extremes to keep sponsors happy, spoon-feeding audiences only "official" or "moderate" opinions. They complained that, although TV provided more information than had ever been available before, the resulting shared culture represented the lowest common denominator.

East and west, television exercised a powerful political and cultural influence. Even in a rural area of the Soviet Union more than 70 percent of the inhabitants watched television regularly in the late 1970s; the rest continued to prefer radio. Educational programming united the far-flung population of the USSR by broadcasting shows designed to advance Soviet culture. At the same time, with travel impossible or forbidden to many, shows about foreign lands were among the most popular—as were postcards from these

◆ **1977** First International Year of Women

◆ **1978** First test-tube baby

◆ **1978–1979** Islamic revolution in Iran

◆ **1979–1980** U.S. Hostage crisis in Iran

◆ **1985** Gorbachev becomes Soviet premier

◆ **1986** Chernobyl nuclear disaster;
Spain joins the European Community

| **1975** | **1980** | **1985** | **1990** |

◆ **1980** Solidarity resists Polish communism;
Thatcher begins dismantling the welfare state in Britain

◆ **Early 1980s** AIDS epidemic begins; rise of
the Pacific economy

◆ **1981** Reagan becomes U.S. president

◆ **1989** Revolt in
Tiananmen Square;
Communists ousted
in eastern Europe;
fall of Berlin Wall

lands, which became household decorations. Heads of state could usually preempt regular programming. In the 1960s, French president Charles de Gaulle addressed his fellow citizens frequently, employing the grandiose gestures of an imperial ruler to stir patriotism. As electoral success in western Europe increasingly depended on cultivating a successful media image, political staffs came to rely on media experts as much as they did policy experts.

Computers. Just as revolutionary, the computer reshaped work in science, defense, and ultimately industry. Computers had evolved dramatically since the first electronic

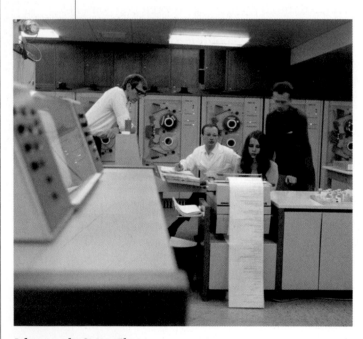

Advances in Computing

"Robotron" was the first mainframe computer in East Germany, and, like many computers in 1970, it was huge. Within a decade computing would be miniaturized because of the development of chip technology, and powerful computers would become small and lightweight. Robotron was run by a postindustrial workforce of nonmanufacturing employees, who did clean work that took more technical knowledge than muscle power. As computing became miniaturized, the ability to manipulate computers became more widespread and the postindustrial workforce itself became highly segmented among those entering data, for example, and those devising programs. Technology, like that involved in Robotron, was revolutionizing the way people worked, just as it had in the Industrial Revolution some two centuries earlier. What changes did computers like Robotron bring to modern life in the West? *AKG Images.*

ones, among them the Colossus, which the British used in 1943 to decode Nazi military and diplomatic messages. Several countries had devised these machines for processing information, all of them primitive by later standards in being gigantic, slow, noisy, and able only to decode. With growing use in civilian industry and business after the war, computing machines shrank from the size of a gymnasium in the 1940s to that of an attaché case in the mid-1980s. They also became both far less expensive and fantastically more powerful than the Colossus, thanks to the development of increasingly sophisticated digital electronic circuitry implanted on tiny silicon chips, which replaced the clumsy radio tubes used in 1940s and 1950s computers. Within a few decades, the computer could perform hundreds of millions of operations per second and the price of the integrated circuit at the heart of computer technology would fall to less than a dollar, allowing businesses and individuals access to computing ability at a reasonable cost.

Computers changed the pace and patterns of work not only by speeding up and easing tasks but also by performing many operations that workers had once done themselves. In garment making, for example, experienced workers no longer painstakingly figured out how to arrange patterns on cloth for maximum efficiency and economy. Instead, a computer specified instructions for the optimal positioning of pattern pieces, and trained workers, usually women, followed the machine's directions. By the end of the 1970s, the miniaturization of the computer had made possible a renewal of the eighteenth-century cottage industry, and in 1981 the French phone company launched a public Internet server, the Minitel—a forerunner of the World Wide Web—through which one could make reservations, perform stock transactions, and gain information. As in earlier times, people could work in the physical isolation of their homes, but technology now allowed them to be connected to a central mainframe.

Did computers transform society for the better? Whereas the Industrial Revolution had seen physical power replaced by machine capabilities, the information revolution witnessed brainpower augmented by computer technology. Many believed that computers would profoundly expand mental life, providing, in the words of one scientist, "boundless opportunities . . . to resolve the puzzles of cosmology, of life, and of the society of man." Others maintained that computers programmed people, reducing human capacity for inventiveness, problem solving, and initiative. As the 1970s closed, such predictions were still untested as the information revolution moved toward a more dramatic unfolding in the 1980s and 1990s.

The Space Age

When the Soviets launched the satellite *Sputnik* in 1957, they ignited competition with the United States that was quickly labeled the space race. John F. Kennedy became determined to beat the Soviets in space by putting a man on the moon by the end of the 1960s. The result was increasingly complex space flights that tested humans' ability to survive the process of space exploration, including weightlessness. Astronauts walked in space, endured weeks (and, later, months) in orbit, docked with other craft, fixed satellites, and carried out experiments for the military and private industry. Meanwhile, a series of unmanned rockets filled the earth's gravitational sphere with weather, television, intelligence, and other communications satellites.

In July 1969, a worldwide television audience watched as U.S. astronauts Neil Armstrong and Edwin "Buzz" Aldrin walked on the moon's surface—the climactic moment in the space race. The space race also drove Western cultural developments. Astronauts and cosmonauts were perhaps the era's most admired heroes: Yuri Gagarin, John Glenn, and Valentina Tereshkova—the first woman in space (see illustration on the next page)—topped the list. A whole new fantasy world developed. Children's toys and games revolved increasingly around space. Films such as *2001: A Space Odyssey* (1968) portrayed space explorers answering questions about life that were formerly the domain of church leaders. Likewise, in the internationally popular television series *Star Trek*, members of the starship *Enterprise*'s diverse crew wrestled with the problems of maintaining humane values against less-developed, often menacing

THE SPACE AGE

1957	Soviet Union launches the first artificial satellite, *Sputnik*
1961	Soviet cosmonaut Yuri Gagarin orbits the earth; capsule carrying Alan Shepard Jr. makes first U.S. suborbital flight
1965	United States launches first commercial communications satellite, *Intelsat I*
1969	U.S. astronauts Neil Armstrong and Edwin Aldrin walk on moon's surface
1970s–present	Soviet Union and United States individually and in collaboration with various countries perform space station maneuvers, lunar probes, and other scientific experiments
1971	Soviet Union attempts unsuccessfully to put *Salyut 1*, a space station, into orbit
1973	United States puts *Skylab*, an experimental space station, into orbit
1976	*Viking* spacecraft explores Mars
1979–1986	Spacecraft *Voyager* makes successful flybys of Jupiter, Saturn, and Uranus

civilizations. In the Eastern bloc, Polish author Stanislaw Lem's novel *Solaris* (1971) similarly portrayed space age individuals engaged in personal quests and likewise drew readers and ultimately viewers into a futuristic fantasy.

The space age grew out of cold war concerns, but it also offered the possibility of more global political cooperation. Although advances in rocket technology allowed for powerful and destructive missiles, it also promoted international efforts. From the 1960s on, U.S. spaceflights often involved the participation of other countries such as Great Britain and the Netherlands. In 1965, an international consortium headed by the United States launched the first commercial communications satellite, *Intelsat I*, and by the 1970s some 150 countries worked together at more than four hundred stations worldwide to maintain global satellite communications. Although some 50 percent of satellites were for spying purposes, the rest promoted international communication and were sustained by transnational collaboration.

Valentina Tereshkova, Russian Cosmonaut
People sent into space were heroes, representing modern values of courage, strength, and well-honed skills. Insofar as the space age was part of the cold war race for superpower superiority, the USSR held the lead during the first decade. The Soviets trained both women and men, and the 1963 flight of Valentina Tereshkova—the first woman in space—supported Soviet claims of gender equality in contrast to the all-male superstar image of the early U.S. space program. The achievements of both countries led to the launching of communications satellites that produced the globalizing communications revolution of the next decades. Does it make a difference that men and women go into space even though most analysts agree that humans are not necessary to space exploration and experimentation? *Hulton Archive/Getty Images.*

Lunar landings and experiments in space advanced pure science in the midst of space race hype. Astronomers, for example, previously dependent on remote sensing for their work, used mineral samples from the moon to calculate the age of the solar system with unprecedented precision. Unmanned spacecraft provided data on cosmic radiation, magnetic fields, and infrared sources. Although the media touted the human conquerors of space, breakthroughs in space exploration and astronomy were utterly dependent on a

range of technology, including the radiotelescope, which depicted space by receiving, measuring, and calculating nonvisible rays. These findings reinforced the so-called big bang theory of the origins of the universe, first posited in the 1930s by American astronomer Edwin Hubble and given crucial support in the 1950s by the discovery of a low level of radiation permeating the universe in all directions. Based on the earlier work of Albert Einstein and Max Planck, the big bang theory explains the development of the universe from a condition of extremely high density and temperature some ten billion years ago. Nuclei emerged when these conditions dissipated in a rapid expansion of space—the big bang.

Revolutions in Biology, Reproductive Technology, and Sexual Behavior

Sophisticated technologies extended to the life sciences, bringing dramatic new health benefits and ultimately changing reproduction itself. In 1952, scientists Francis Crick, an Englishman, and James Watson, an American, discovered the configuration of **DNA**, the material in a cell's chromosomes that carries hereditary information. Simultaneously, other scientists were working on "the pill"—an oral contraceptive for women that tapped more than a century of scientific work in the field of birth control. Still other breakthroughs lay ahead—ones that would revolutionize conception and make scientific duplication of species possible.

Understanding DNA. Crick and Watson, working from laboratories in Cambridge, England, solved the mystery of the gene and thus of biological inheritance when they demonstrated the structure of DNA. They showed how the double helix of the DNA molecule splits in cellular reproduction to form the basis of each new cell. This genetic material, biologists concluded, provides a chemical pattern for an individual organism's life. Beginning in the 1960s, genetics and the new field of molecular biology progressed rapidly. Growing understanding of nucleic acids and proteins advanced knowledge of viruses and bacteria that effectively ended the ravages of polio, tetanus, syphilis, tuberculosis, and such dangerous childhood diseases as mumps and measles in the West.

Understanding how DNA works allowed scientists both to alter the makeup of plants and to bypass natural animal reproduction in a process called cloning—obtaining the cells of an organism and dividing or reproducing them (in an exact copy) in a laboratory. In 1997 one group of researchers produced a cloned sheep named "Dolly," though the breakthrough was marred by the fact that she suffered an array of disabilities and died six years later. Cloning raised the question of whether scientists should interfere with so basic and essential a process as reproduction, and the question became more urgent when in 2002 an Italian doctor claimed to have cloned several humans—a claim disbelieved by many scientists. Similarly, the possibility of genetically altering species and even creating new ones (for instance, to control agricultural pests) led to concern about how such actions would affect the balance of nature. In 1967, Dr. Christiaan Barnard of South Africa performed the first successful heart transplant, and U.S. doctors later developed an artificial heart. Commentators debated the selection process for these scarce, reusable organs and asked whether the enormous cost of new medical technology to save a few people would be better spent on helping the many who lacked even basic medical and health care.

Transforming Reproduction.

Technology also influenced the most intimate areas of human relations—sexuality and procreation. In traditional societies, community and family norms dictated marital arrangements and sexual practices, in large part because too many or too few children threatened the crucial balance between population size and agricultural productivity. As Western societies industrialized and urbanized, however, not only did these

considerations become less urgent but the growing availability of reliable birth-control devices permitted young people to begin sexual relations earlier, with less risk of pregnancy. These trends accelerated in the 1960s as the birth-control pill, first produced in the United States and tested on women in developing areas, came on the Western market. By 1970, its use was spreading around the world. Millions also sought out voluntary surgical sterilization through tubal ligations and vasectomies. New techniques brought abortion, traditionally performed by amateurs, into the hands of medical professionals, making it a safe procedure for the first time.

Childbirth and conception itself were similarly transformed. Whereas only a small minority of Western births took place in hospitals in 1920, more than 90 percent did by 1970. Obstetricians now performed much of the work midwives had once done. As pregnancy and birth became a medical process, innovative new procedures and equipment

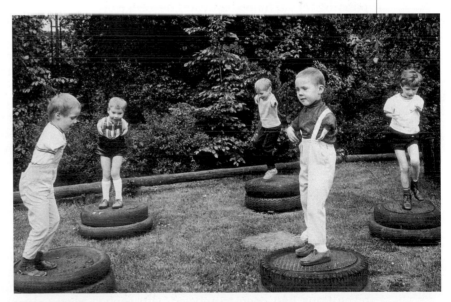

Thalidomide Children
In the last third of the twentieth century, increasingly destructive side effects of powerful medicines became apparent. Women who had taken the drug thalidomide gave birth to children with severe disabilities, and the public condemned companies selling untested products. The race to profit from scientific and technological developments sometimes ignored human well-being. Children affected by thalidomide, once they became adults, were among those who launched the disability rights movement. What questions about medicine and health care does the use of thalidomide raise? **For more help analyzing this image,** see the visual activity for this chapter in the Online Study Guide at **bedfordstmartins.com/hunt**, *Deutsche Press Agentur.*

made it possible to monitor women and fetuses throughout pregnancy, labor, and delivery. The number of medical interventions rose: cesarean births increased by 400 percent in the United States in the 1960s and 1970s, and the number of prenatal visits per patient in Czechoslovakia, for example, rose by 300 percent between 1957 and 1976. In 1978, the first "test-tube baby," Louise Brown, was born to an English couple. She had been conceived when her mother's eggs were fertilized with her father's sperm in a laboratory dish and then implanted in her mother's uterus—a complex process called **in vitro fertilization**. If a woman could not carry a child to term, the laboratory-fertilized embryo could be implanted in the uterus of a surrogate, or substitute, mother. Researchers even began working on an artificial womb to allow for reproduction entirely outside the body—from storage bank to artificial embryonic environment.

A Sexual Revolution? The globally expanding media helped spread knowledge of birth-control procedures after World War II and made public discussions of sexual matters explicit, technical, and widespread. Popular use of birth control allowed Western society to be saturated with highly sexualized music, literature, and journalism without a corresponding rise in the birthrate—evidence of the increasing separation of sexuality from reproduction. Statistical surveys showed that regular sexual activity began at an ever-younger age, and people talked more openly about sex—another component of cultural change. Finally, in a climate of increased publicity to sexuality, more open homosexual behavior became apparent, along with continued efforts to decriminalize it across the West. The Western media announced the arrival of a "sexual revolution." However, sexual revolutions had been trumpeted with each advance in birth-control technology beginning in the nineteenth century, showing once again the social and political impact of technological transformation.

> **Review:** How did the scientific advances from the 1950s and 1960s challenge established patterns of thought and social behavior?

❖ Postindustrial Society and Culture

Reshaped by soaring investments in science and the spread of technology, Western countries in the 1960s started on what has been labeled a postindustrial course (see "Terms of History," opposite). Instead of being centered on manufacturing and heavy industry, postindustrial society emphasized the distribution of services such as health care and education. The service sector was the leading force in the economy, and this meant that intellectual work, not industrial or manufacturing work, had become primary in creating jobs and profits. Moreover, all parts of society and industry interlocked, forming a system constantly in need of complex analysis. These characteristics of postindustrial society would carry over from the 1960s and 1970s into the next century; they also laid the groundwork for further globalization.

Multinational Corporations

One of the major innovations of the postindustrial era was the growing number of **multinational corporations**. These companies produced goods and services for a global market and conducted business worldwide, but unlike older kinds of international firms, they established major factories in countries other than their home base. For example, of the five hundred largest businesses in the United States in 1970, more than one hundred did over a quarter of their business abroad, with IBM operating in more than one hundred countries. Although U.S.-based corporations led the way, European and Japanese multinationals like Volkswagen, Shell, Nestlé, and Sony also had a broad global scope.

Some multinational corporations had bigger revenues than entire nations. They appeared to burst the bounds of the nation-state as they set up shop in whatever part of the world offered cheap labor. Their interests differed starkly from those of ordinary people with local or national identities. In the first years after the war, multinationals preferred European employees, who constituted a highly educated labor pool, had developed consumer habits, and eagerly sought secure

TERMS OF HISTORY

Postindustrial

In 1973, U.S. sociologist Daniel Bell's book *The Coming of Postindustrial Society* announced a momentous change in Western society. The economies of the major powers had stopped being predominantly manufacturing and had become instead postindustrial. By this, Bell meant not that there was no more industrial production of cars, household goods, and materials such as steel but rather that service industries like health care, education, and financial services had become the largest sector of the economy. Statistics from Europe and the United States bore him out.

Bell also spotted the knowledge- or information-based characteristics of postindustrial society. Decisions in individual enterprises as well as in technological society as a whole could no longer spring from hunches and small bits of information. Instead, the management of any entity depended on systems analysis, which aimed to take into account every factor pertinent to the system, be it a factory, a financial institution, or a government. Under these circumstances, those who knew how to obtain, produce, and manipulate vast quantities of knowledge could be far more important than those who could not.

The term *postindustrial* was part of a trend prevalent in these years to use the prefix *post* with an array of words, employed first in the term *postwar*. *Postwar* came to mean the period between the end of World War II and economic recovery from it, from 1945 to about 1960, even though Europe and the world still reverberated with the legacy of the Holocaust and wartime devastation for many decades. *Post*s proliferated in these years: *postmodern*, *post-Western*, *post-human*, and *post-Marxist*, to name a few of the most important uses.

The term *postmodern* arose after the various rebellions of the 1960s had challenged the rational, progressive, and technology-proud attitudes connected with the Enlightenment, the first wave of modernity. Enlightenment thinkers associated modernity with the triumph of science and Enlightenment faith that precise knowledge would yield an ever better future. In the 1960s, students and environmentalists maintained that bombs, pollution, and the rising tide of cancer—not progress—had been the major results of modernity. Over the next decades postmodernity would criticize even more aspects of the Enlightenment.

The word *post-human* also began to emerge during these decades, associated at first with the development of robots to do factory work and artificial organs and body parts to treat health conditions. Not only had machines replaced people in factories, critics observed, but ordinary people could not live without machines in their lives. The so-called virtual reality of the Internet age contributed yet another sense to the word *post-human* as people developed relationships that were purely electronic.

The word *post-Marxism* can be dated to the years before the collapse of communism when socialist countries introduced elements of the market economy. Hungary was notable in opening the road to post-Marxism economically, helping to set the stage for the collapse of communism in the 1980s and 1990s. Others maintain that post-Marxism began with the inability of the Communist system to meet the technological demands of the postindustrial age. As technology and information determined the well-being of industries, consumers, and social programs, ideology got in the way of efficiency and alienation prevented coordination and cooperation.

The emergence of a postindustrial social and economic order may well leave us wondering what will succeed it as an organizing principle for human productivity. The emergence of such concepts as *postindustrial* and *post-Marxist* suggests that theorists are seeing further change already at hand. Historians, however, counterbalance these analyses by suggesting that most proclamations of change and most visions of the future have deep roots in the past.

FURTHER READING

Bell, Daniel. *The Coming of Postindustrial Society: A Venture in Social Forecasting.* 1973.

Hayles, N. Katherine. *How We Became Posthuman: Virtual Bodies in Cybernetics, Literature, and Informatics.* 1999.

Seidman, Steven, ed. *The Postmodern Turn: New Perspectives on Social Theory.* 1994.

work. Then, beginning in the 1960s, multinationals moved more of their operations to the emerging economies of formerly colonized states to reduce labor costs, taxes, and regulations in the West. Although multinational corporations provided jobs in developing areas, profits usually enriched foreign stockholders and thus looked to some like imperialism in a new form.

Many European firms believed that they could stay competitive only by expanding, merging with other companies, or becoming partners with government in doing business. In France, for example, a massive glass conglomerate merged with a metallurgical company to form a new group specializing in all phases of construction—a wise move given the postwar building boom. European firms increased their investment in research and used international cooperation to produce major new products. This new emphasis on research was a crucial ingredient in postindustrial society. The British-French Concorde supersonic aircraft, which, beginning with its first flight in 1976, flew from London to New York in under four hours, was one result. Another venture was the Airbus, a more practical series of passenger jets inaugurated in 1972 by a consortium of European firms. Both projects attested to the strong relationship among government, business, and science as well as to the international cooperation in manufacturing among members of the Common Market (Map 29.1). The relationship allowed for successful competition with U.S.-based multinational giants. Whereas U.S. production surpassed the combined output of West Germany, Great Britain, France, Italy, and Japan in the immediate postwar years, by the mid-1970s the situation was reversed.

The New Worker

In its formative stage, industrial production had depended on workers who often labored to exhaustion, endured malnourishment, and lived in a state of poverty that sometimes led to violence. This scenario changed fundamentally in postwar Europe with the reduction of the blue-collar workforce, resource depletion in coal mines, the substitution of foreign oil for coal and of plastics for steel, the

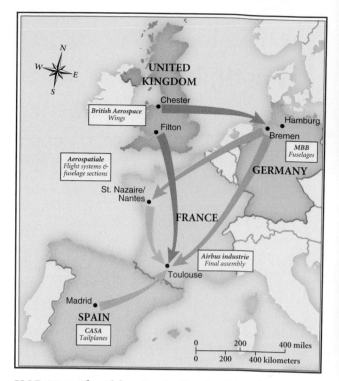

MAP 29.1 The Airbus Production System
The international consortium Airbus marked an important step in the economic and industrial integration of Europe. It also advanced the revitalization of the individual national economies by establishing new manufacturing centers away from capital cities and by modernizing older ones. Its formation presaged the international mergers and cooperative production that would characterize the late twentieth and early twenty-first centuries; today Airbus is a global enterprise with locations offering parts and service around the world, including the United States, China, and India. How does the production of the Airbus differ geographically from the early production of textiles in a nineteenth-century factory?

growth of off-shore manufacturing, and automation in industrial processes. Work in manufacturing was simply cleaner and more mechanized than ever before. Within firms, the relationship of workers to bosses shifted as management started grouping workers into teams that set their own production quotas, organized and assigned tasks, and competed with other teams to see who could produce more. As workers adopted attitudes and gained responsibilities that had once been managerial prerogatives, union membership declined.

In both the U.S. and Soviet blocs, a new kind of working class emerged, consisting of white-collar service personnel. Its rise undermined economic distinctions based on the way one worked, for those who performed service work or had managerial titles were not necessarily better paid than blue-collar workers. The ranks of service workers swelled with researchers, health-care and medical workers, technicians, planners, and government functionaries. Employment in traditional parts of the service sector—banks, insurance companies, and other financial institutions—also surged because of the vast sums of money needed to finance technology and research. Entire categories of employees such as flight attendants devoted much of their skill to the psychological well-being of customers. The consumer economy provided more jobs in restaurants and personal health,

fitness and grooming, and in hotels and tourism. By 1969, the percentage of service-sector employees had passed that of manufacturing workers in several industrial countries: 61.1 percent versus 33.7 percent in the United States; and 48.8 percent versus 41.1 percent in Sweden (see "Taking Measure," shown below).

Postindustrial work life had some different ingredients in the Soviet bloc. Late in the 1960s, Communist leaders announced a program of "advanced socialism" that included more social leveling, greater equality of salaries, and nearly complete absence of private production. The percentage of farmers remained higher in the Soviet bloc than in western Europe. A huge difference between professional occupations and those involving physical work also remained in socialist countries because of declining investment

TAKING MEASURE

United States

Japan

Average of 12 European Countries[1]

[1] Austria, Belgium, West Germany, Denmark, Spain, Finland, Greece, Ireland, Netherlands, Norway, Portugal, and Sweden

Postindustrial Occupational Structure, 1984

Striking changes occurred in the composition of the workforce in the postwar period. Agriculture continued its declining importance as a source of jobs; by the 1980s, the percentage of these workers in the most advanced industrial countries had dropped well below 10 percent. The most striking development was the expansion of the service sector, which came to employ more than half of all workers. In the United States, the agricultural and industrial (represented by production and transportation workers) sectors, which had dominated a century earlier, now offered less than a third of all jobs. What difference does it make to ordinary people that jobs in service work predominate? Yearbook of Labour Statistics *(Geneva: International Labour Office, 1992), Table 2.7.*

- ▨ Professional, technical, and related workers
- ▨ Administrative and managerial workers
- ☐ Clerical and related workers
- ▨ Sales and service workers
- ☐ Agricultural workers
- ▨ Production and transport workers, laborers
- ▨ Other

in advanced machinery and cleaner work processes. Less mobility existed between the two classifications, but much as in the U.S.-led bloc, gender also shaped the workforce into two groups, with men generally earning higher pay for better jobs and women relegated to lower pay and lesser jobs. Somewhere between 80 and 95 percent of women worked in socialist countries, mostly under these conditions.

Farm life was updated, even bureaucratized across the West. By the 1970s, one could travel for miles in Europe without seeing a farmhouse. Small landowners sold family plots to farmers engaged in agribusiness— that is, vast acreage devoted to commercial rather than peasant farming. Governments, farmers' cooperatives, and planning agencies took over decision making from the individual farmer; they set production quotas and handled an array of marketing transactions. In the 1960s, agricultural output rose an average of 3 percent per year in Greece and Spain and 2.5 percent in the Netherlands, France, and Great Britain. Genetic research that yielded pest-resistant seeds and the skyrocketing use of pesticides, fertilizers, and machinery contributed to growth. Between 1965 and 1979, the number of tractors in Germany more than tripled from 384,000 to 1,340,000.

Bureaucracy played its part too: for example, in the 1970s a French farmer, Fernande Pelletier, made a living on her hundred-acre farm in southwestern France in the new setting of international agribusiness. Advised by a government expert, Pelletier produced whatever foods might sell competitively in the Common Market. On expert advice, she switched from lamb and veal to foie gras and walnuts in order to increase her sales, and she joined with other farmers in her region to buy heavy machinery and to sell her products. Agricultural solvency required as much managerial and intellectual effort as did success in the industrial sector.

The Boom in Education and Research

Education and research were key to running postindustrial society and were the means by which nations maintained their economic and military might. In the West, common sense, hard work, and creative intuition had launched the earliest successes of the Industrial Revolution. By the late twentieth century, success in business or government demanded humanistic or technological expertise and ever-growing staffs of researchers. As one French official put it, "the accumulation of knowledge, not of wealth, . . . makes the difference" in the quest for power.

Investment in research fueled military and industrial leadership. The United States funneled more than 20 percent of its gross national product into research in the 1960s, in the process siphoning off many of Europe's leading intellectuals and technicians in a so-called brain drain. Complex systems— for example, nuclear power generation with its many components, from scientific conceptualization to plant construction to the publicly supervised disposal of radioactive waste—required intricate coordination and professional oversight. Scientists and bureaucrats frequently made more crucial decisions than did elected politicians in the realm of space programs, weapons development, and economic policy. Soviet-bloc nations proved less adept at linking their considerable achievements in science to actual applications because of bureaucratic red tape. In the 1960s, some 40 percent of Soviet-bloc scientific findings became obsolete before the government approved them for application to technology. An unseen backsliding from the superpower effectiveness and leadership had begun in the USSR.

The new criteria for success fostered unprecedented growth in education, especially in universities, scientific institutes, and other postsecondary institutions. The number of university students in Sweden rose by about 580 percent and in West Germany by 250 percent between 1950 and 1969. Great Britain established a network of polytechnic universities to encourage the technical research that traditional elite universities often scorned. France set up administrative schools for future high-level experts in administration. By the late 1970s, the Soviet Union had built its scientific establishment so rapidly that the number of its advanced researchers in the natural sciences and engineering surpassed that of the United States. Meanwhile, institutions of higher learning added courses in business and management, information technology, and systems analysis—most notably in western Europe and the United States.

In principle, education made the avenues to success more democratic by basing them on talent instead of wealth. In fact, however, societal leveling did not occur in most western European universities, and instruction often remained rigid and old-fashioned. Although eighteenth-century Europeans had pioneered educational reform, students in the 1960s reported that teachers lectured even young children, who spoke in class only to echo the teacher or to recite homework memorized the night before. At the university level, as one angry student put it, the professor was "a petty, threatened god" who puffed himself up "on the passivity and dependence of students." Such judgments would soon provoke young people to rebel against the traditional authority of teachers, officials, and parents.

A Redefined Family and a Generation Gap

Just as education changed dramatically to meet the needs of postindustrial society, the contours of the family and the nature of parent–child relationships shifted from what they had been a century earlier. Family roles were transformed, and the relationship between parents and children—long thought to be natural and unchangeable—looked different, alarmingly so to some conservatives. Even though television and media commentators delivered messages about what the family should be, technology, consumer goods, and a constant flow of guest laborers and migrants from the former colonies produced social and cultural change, including enormous variety in what households actually were. Households were now headed by a single parent, by remarried parents merging two sets of unrelated children, by unmarried couples cohabiting, or by traditionally married parents who had few—or no—children. Households of same-sex partners also became more common. At the end of the 1970s, the marriage rate in the West

had fallen by 30 percent from its 1960s level. Despite a rising divorce rate, the average marriage lasted one-third longer than it had a century earlier because of increased longevity. After almost two decades of baby boom, the birthrate dropped significantly. On average, a Belgian woman, for example, bore 2.6 children in 1960 but only 1.8 by the end of the 1970s. Although the birthrate fell, the percentage of children born outside of marriage soared.

Daily life within the family changed. Technological consumer items saturated domestic space, as radio and television often formed the basis of the household's common social life. Appliances such as dishwashers, washing machines, and clothes dryers became more affordable and more widespread, reducing (in theory) the time women had to devote to household work and raising standards of cleanliness. More women worked outside the home during these years to pay for the prolonged economic dependence of children, but working mothers still did the housework and child care almost entirely themselves.

To advance in a knowledge-based society, children did not enter the labor force until their twenties but instead attended school, thus requiring their parents' financial and emotional support. Whereas the early modern family organized labor, taught craft skills, and monitored reproductive behavior, the modern family seemed to have a primarily psychological mission. Parents were to provide emotional nurture while their children learned intellectual skills in school. They could also count on psychologists, social workers, and other social service experts to provide counseling in dealing with the stress that resulted from the emphasis on academic accomplishment. Television programs portrayed a variety of family experiences on soap operas, sitcoms, and family-oriented game shows, giving viewers an opportunity to see how other families dealt with the tensions of modern life.

Most notably, postindustrial society transformed teenagers' lives. A century earlier, teens had been full-time wage earners; now, most were students, financially dependent on their parents into their twenties. Amid the anxieties caused by this prolonged childhood, youth simultaneously gained new roles

The Beatles (1969)
"Let It Be" went the lyrics to one of the last songs of this world famous group before they disbanded to go their separate ways as performers. The Beatles represented both the aspirations of a rising generation of youth and the booming consumer culture that created the Beatles' look, sound, and message. Their records were simultaneously directed by astute marketing experts for big record companies and filled with what seemed liberating allusions to the drug culture and Asian spirituality. What was the appeal of the Beatles and the other celebrated rock stars who followed in their wake? © *Bruce McBroom/Camera Press/Retna Ltd.*

as consumers. Advertisers and industrialists saw the baby boomers as a multibillion-dollar market and wooed them with consumer items associated with rock music—records, portable radios, stereos. Replacing romantic ballads, rock music celebrated youthful rebellion against adult culture in biting, critical, and often explicitly sexual lyrics. Sex roles for the young did not change, however. Despite the popularity of a few individual women rockers, promoters focused on men, whom they depicted as heroic, surrounded by worshiping female "groupies." The new models for youth such as the Beatles were themselves the products of advanced technology and savvy marketing for mass consumption. "What's your message for American teenagers?" the Beatles were asked. "Buy some more Beatles records," they responded. But the Beatles also offered a special zest and even spirituality, derived from going to India and introducing its instruments and ideals in their songs. The mixture of high-tech music, pop-star marketing, and the youthful hysteria of fans contributed to a sense that there was a unique youth culture and a growing generation gap.

Art, Ideas, and Religion in a Technocratic Society

Cultural trends evolved with the march of consumer society and with technology itself. Like modernists in the past, a new generation of artists addressed growing consumerism and the world of space, electronics, and computers in their art. Even as colonies ripped away from the old colonial powers, their influence on the Western mind remained strong, continuing to turn musicians, scholars, and religious leaders in their direction for new ways of thinking. Conversely, many of these intellectuals enjoyed increasing international recognition and global markets—like the multinationals themselves. With the development of computers, they buttressed their prestige by employing complex statistical and other scientific methods.

The Visual Arts.   A new trend in the visual arts was called **pop art**. It featured images from everyday life and employed the glossy techniques and products of what these artists called admass, or mass advertising. "There's no reason," the group maintained of modern society's commercialism, "not to consider the world as one gigantic painting." Robert Rauschenberg, a leading U.S. practitioner, made collages from comic strips, magazine clippings, and fabric to fulfill his vision that "a picture is more like the real world when it's made out of the real world." The movement had become a financial success by the early 1960s, attracting such maverick American artists as Jasper Johns and Andy Warhol, who advanced the parody of modern commercialism. Warhol showed, for example, how the female body, the classic form that attracted nineteenth-century male art buyers, was used to sell everything mass culture had to offer in the 1960s and 1970s. He depicted Campbell's soup cans as they appeared in advertisements and sold these works as elite artistic creations.

Swedish-born artist Claes Oldenburg (b. 1929) portrayed the grotesque aspects of ordinary consumer products in *Giant Hamburger with Pickle Attached* (1962) and *Lipstick Ascending on Caterpillar Tractor* (1967). "High art" picked up not merely commercial goods but actually "low" objects such as scraps of metal, cigarette butts, dirt, and even excrement. The Swiss sculptor Jean Tinguely used rusted parts of old machines to make fountains that could move. His partner Niki de Saint-Phalle then constructed huge, gaudy figures—many of them inspired by the folk traditions of the Caribbean and Africa—to decorate them. Their colorful, mobile fountains adorned main squares in Stockholm, Montreal, Paris, and other cities (see *Fontaine Stravinsky*, below).

Niki de Saint-Phalle, *Fontaine Stravinsky* **(1983)**
Niki de Saint-Phalle's exuberant and playful art, seen in the fountains of Paris and cities around the world, captured the accessibility of pop art. Her other work drew inspiration from Caribbean and African styles and celebrated women of decolonizing countries. Living during the rebirth of activism, de Saint-Phalle lined up suspended bags of paint and machine-gunned them to create a spattered canvas—her answer to the alleged "macho" or bad-boy style of abstract expressionists like Jackson Pollock. How does the presence of such works of art change the nature of public space?
© 2005 Artists Rights Society (ARS), NY/ADAGP, Paris. Photo: Barbara Alper/Stock Boston.

To mock this mocking world of art, German artist Sigmar Polke did cartoonlike drawings of products and of those who craved them.

Music. The American composer John Cage (1912–1992) worked in a similar vein when he added sounds produced by such everyday items as combs, pieces of wood, and radio noise into his musical scores. Buddhist influence led Cage to incorporate silence in music and to compose by randomly tossing coins and then choosing notes by the corresponding numbers in the ancient Chinese *I Ching* (Book of Changes). These techniques continued the trend away from classical melody that had begun with modernism. The development widened the gulf between the composer and the larger public: many listeners simply hated such music. Other composers, called minimalists, simplified music by featuring repetition and sustained notes as well as by rejecting the "masterpiece" tradition of lush nineteenth-century symphonies and piano music. Arno Part, the famed Estonian composer, wrote minimalist pieces in the 1970s using only three or four notes in total; he called this style "starvation" music to underscore the lack of both freedom and goods in the Soviet bloc.

Some musicians stressed modern technology; they introduced tape recordings into vocal pieces and used computers and synthesizers both to compose and to perform their works. German composer Karlheinz Stockhausen introduced electronic music into classical composition in 1953; Cage also used it soon after. Influenced by his own travels, Stockhausen continued the modern style of fully exploring non-Western tonalities in such 1970s pieces as *Ceylon*. But even though this music echoed the electronic and increasingly interconnected state of human society, its concert audiences diminished because new music continued to seem dissonant and even shrill. At the same time, improved recording technology and mass marketing brought music of all varieties to a wider home audience than ever before.

Social Science. The social sciences reached the peak of their prestige during these decades, often because of their increasing use of statistical models and predictions made possible by advanced electronic computations. Sociologists and psychologists produced empirical studies that were more detailed than ever before and that purported to demonstrate rules for understanding individual, group, and societal behavior. Anthropology was among the most exciting of the social sciences, for it brought to the young university student information about societies that seemed immune to modern technology and industry. The sense of escape and adventure was more vivid than ever before, as colorful ethnographic films captured alternative lifestyles and exotic practices. While studying people who came to be called "the other," the young had their sense of freedom reinforced by the vision of going back to nature.

Simultaneously, the social sciences also undermined some of the foundations for the belief that individuals had true freedom. French anthropologist Claude Lévi-Strauss (b. 1908) developed a theory called structuralism, which insisted that all societies function within controlling structures—kinship and exchange, for example—that operate according to coercive rules similar to those of the unbreakable conventions in language. Structuralism challenged existentialism's tenet that humans could create a free existence and shook the social sciences' faith in the triumph of rationality. Lévi-Strauss's book *The Savage Mind* (1966) also demonstrated that people outside of the West had not a scientific but an improvisational style that could be extremely effective. In the 1960s and 1970s, the findings of the social sciences generally paralleled concerns that technology was creating a society of automatons and that complex managerial systems would eradicate individualism and human freedom.

Religion. Church officials and parishioners made an effort to bring religion up to date with the changing times, which tended to see merit in a variety of cultures and thus promoted toleration. Responding to what he saw as a crisis in faith caused by affluence and secularism, Pope John XXIII (r. 1958–1963) in 1962 convened the Second Vatican Council, known as **Vatican II**. The Council modernized the liturgy, democratized many church procedures, and at the last session in 1965 renounced church doctrine that condemned the Jewish people as guilty of killing Jesus. Vatican II promoted ecumenism—that is, mutual cooperation among the world's faiths. In the face of scientific advance, Pope John's successor, Paul VI (1963–1978), kept Catholic opposition to artificial birth control alive, but he also became the first pontiff to demonstrate global concerns by visiting Africa, Asia, and South America. A succession of popes, most notably Polish-born John Paul II, encouraged Catholicism in the Soviet bloc, strengthening religion as a primary focal point for anticommunism there.

In some parts of the West, there was a notable upsurge in postwar religious fervor. In the face of scientific advance, growing numbers of U.S. Protestants joined sects that stressed the literal truth of the Scripture and denied the validity of past scientific discoveries such as the age of the universe and the evolution of the species. In western Europe, however, Christian churchgoing remained at a low ebb. In the 1970s, for example, only 10 percent of the British population went to religious services—about the same number that attended live soccer matches. Most striking was the changing composition of the Western religious public. Immigration of people from former colonies and other parts of the world increased the strength of the non-Christian religions such as Islam and varieties of Hindu faiths. Cities and towns came to house mosques, Buddhist temples, and shrines to other creeds. New religious values mixed sometimes easily and sometimes tensely with both Western European Judeo-Christianity and the antireligious culture of the Soviet bloc.

Review: What major changes took place in the formation of postindustrial society?

❖ Protesting Cold War Conditions

Affluence, scientific sophistication, and military might elevated the United States and the Soviet Union to the peak of their power in the 1960s. By 1965, however, the six

nations of the Common Market had replaced the United States as the leader in worldwide trade and the marketing of new technologies and other products, and they often acted in their own self-interest across the U.S.–Soviet divide. In 1973, Britain joined the Common Market, followed by Ireland and Denmark. The market's exports now amounted to almost three times those of the United States. Communist China, along with countries in eastern Europe, contested Soviet leadership, and many decolonizing regions refused to become pliable allies to the superpowers. The struggle for Indochinese independence had never ended, and by the mid-1960s a devastating war in Vietnam was under way. At the end of the 1970s, the USSR became embroiled in an equally devastating war in Afghanistan. Another serious challenge to the cold war order also came from rising citizen discontent and from dramatic protest like that of Jan Palach. From the 1960s until 1989, people rose up against the consequences of technological development, the lack of fundamental rights, and the potential for nuclear holocaust latent in the cold war. Leaders of emerging nations in the Middle East and elsewhere struck back too, eroding industrial economies in the West and further shaking up the international political order of the cold war.

Cracks in the Cold War Order

Across the social and political spectrum there were calls for at least softening the effects of the cold war in this age of unprecedented progress and technological prowess. The new Soviet middle class of bureaucrats and managers demanded a better standard of living and a reduction in the cold war animosity that made everyday life so menacing. In western European countries, voters elected politicians in the late 1960s who promoted an increasing array of social programs designed to ensure the economic democracy of the welfare state. A significant minority shifted their votes away from the centrist Christian Democratic coalitions that supported U.S. political goals. Instead they voted for Socialist, Labor, and Social Democratic parties in hopes of shifting priorities from the cold war to ordinary people's needs during this period of rapid change. Leaders also developed new diplomatic strategies to deal with the cold war.

Germany and France. The German and French governments both made solid and highly visible changes in policy, which, though different, refused to uphold cold war. In Germany, Social Democratic politicians had enough influence to shift money from defense spending to domestic programs. Willy Brandt (1913–1992), the Socialist mayor of West Berlin, became foreign minister in 1966 and pursued an end to frigid relations with Communist East Germany. This policy, known as **Ostpolitik**, thus unsettled cold war thinking. It gave West German business leaders what they wanted: "the depoliticization of Germany's foreign trade," as one industrialist put it, and an unlocking of Soviet-bloc consumerism. West German trade with eastern Europe grew rapidly; however, it left the relatively poorer countries of the Soviet bloc strapped with mounting debt—some $45 billion annually by 1970.

To break the cold war stranglehold on international politics, French president Charles de Gaulle poured more money into French nuclear development, withdrew French forces from NATO, and signed trade treaties with the Soviet bloc. Communist China and France also drew closer. However, de Gaulle protected France's good relations with Germany to prevent further encroachments from the Soviet bloc. At home, de Gaulle's government sponsored construction of modern housing and mandated the exterior cleaning of all Parisian buildings—a massive project taking years—to wipe away more than a century of industrial grime. With his haughty and stubborn pursuit of French grandeur, de Gaulle offered the European public an alternative to submissively obeying the superpowers.

The Soviet Union. Brandt's Ostpolitik and de Gaulle's assertiveness had their echoes in Soviet-bloc reforms. Pushing de-Stalinization, the Soviet premier Nikita Khrushchev took the dangerous course of trying to reduce Communist officialdom's privileges. Khrushchev's blunders—notably his humiliation in the Cuban missile crisis, his

ineffectual schemes to improve Soviet agriculture, and his inability to patch the rift with China—were highly visible and led to his ouster in 1964. Nevertheless, the new leadership of Leonid Brezhnev♦ (1909–1982) and Alexei Kosygin♦ (1904–1980) initially continued attempts at reform, encouraging plant managers to turn a profit and allowing the production of televisions, household appliances, and cheap housing to alleviate the discontent of an increasingly better-educated and better-informed citizenry. The government also loosened restrictions to allow cultural and scientific meetings with Westerners, another move that relaxed the cold war atmosphere in the mid-1960s. The Soviet satellites in eastern Europe grasped the economic opportunity presented by Moscow's relaxed posture. Poland allowed private farmers greater freedom to make money, and Hungarian leader János Kádár introduced elements of a market system into the national economy.

In the arts, Soviet-bloc writers continued for a time to thaw the frozen monolith of socialist realism and slavish praise for the Soviet past. Ukrainian poet Yevgeny Yevtushenko exposed Soviet complicity in the Holocaust in *Babi Yar* (1961), a passionate protest against the slaughter of tens of thousands of Jews near Kiev during World War II. Challenging the celebratory nature of socialist art, East Berlin writer Christa Wolf showed a couple tragically divided by the Berlin Wall in her novel *Divided Heaven* (1965). But repression returned later in the 1960s and 1970s, however, as the Soviet government took to bulldozing outdoor art shows, thereby forcing visual artists to hold secret exhibitions in their apartments and even to turn their living spaces into a new kind of art: the installation. Installations include the arrangement of multiple components often including everyday objects in large spaces. Dissident artists' paintings depicted Soviet citizens as worn and tired in grays and other monochromatic color schemes instead of the brightly attired and heroic figures of socialist realism. For their part, writers relied on samizdat culture, a key form of dissident ac-

♦**Leonid Brezhnev:** lay oh NEED BREHZH nehf
♦**Alexei Kosygin:** uhl yihk SYAY kuh SEEG ihn

Krusikov Street (1977)

"Always forward, never backward," was what the father of Soviet Communism V. I. Lenin and subsequent leaders of the USSR demanded of Soviet citizens. All artists, writers, composers, and performers in the USSR, were supposed to follow Communist Party directives in their work, spreading such ideals as found in Lenin's slogan. Dissident artists, however, slyly undermined the Communist message, as in this depiction of Lenin and contemporary Soviets by Eric Bulatov. Despite the accepted socialist realist style of painting, the portrayal shows the leader going forward but the citizens moving in the opposite direction, which can only be called backward. This was just one dissident style among many adopted by dissident artists, who prepared the ground for a full-scale revolt against the Soviet system. It was thus with good reason that the government of the USSR mostly destroyed such works whenever they were displayed in public. *Jane Voorhees Zimmerli Art Museum, Rutgers University. The Norton and Nancy Dodge Collection of Nonconformist Art from the Soviet Union. ©Artists Rights Society (ARS), NY/ADAGP, Paris. Photo: Jack Abraham.*

tivity in which uncensored publications were reproduced by hand and passed from reader to reader, thus building a foundation for the successful resistance of the 1980s.

The United States. In the United States, other issues challenged the cold war for front-page attention. The assassination of President John F. Kennedy in November 1963 shocked the nation and the world. But only momentarily did it still escalating demands for civil rights for African Americans and other minorities. White segregationists murdered, maimed, and arrested those attempting to integrate lunch counters, register black voters, or simply march on behalf of freedom. This violent racism was a weak link in the American claim to moral superiority in the cold war, and in response to the murders and destruction, Kennedy had introduced civil

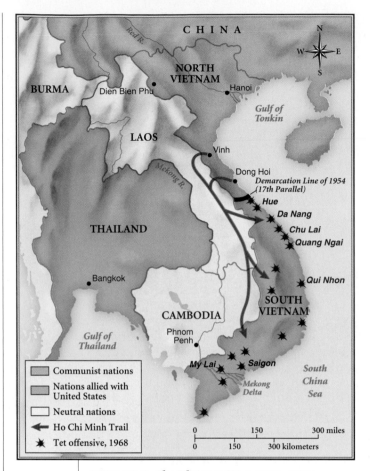

MAP 29.2 The Vietnam War, 1954–1975
The local peoples of Southeast Asia had long resisted incursions by their neighbors. They also resisted French rule from the end of the nineteenth century, never more fiercely than in the war that liberated them after World War II. Ill-prepared by comparison with the French, the Vietnamese nonetheless triumphed in the battle of Dien Bien Phu in 1954. But the Americans soon became involved, trying to stem what they saw as the tide of Communist influence behind the Vietnamese liberation movement. The ensuing war in Vietnam in the 1960s and 1970s spread into neighboring countries, making the region the scene of vast destruction. How were the Vietnamese wars after 1945 related to the struggle between Japan and the United States for resources in the region in the 1930s and in World War II? Or were these two distinct contests?

rights legislation and forced the desegregation of schools and universities. Lyndon B. Johnson (1908–1973), Kennedy's successor, steered the Civil Rights Act through Congress in 1964. This legislation forbade

segregation in public facilities and created the Equal Employment Opportunity Commission (EEOC) to fight job discrimination based on "race, color, national origin, religion, and sex." Southern conservatives had tacked on the provision against sex discrimination in the vain hope that it would doom the bill. Modeling himself on his hero Franklin Roosevelt, Johnson envisioned what he called a Great Society, in which new government programs would improve the chances of the forty million Americans living in poverty. He sponsored myriad reform programs, among them Project Head Start for disadvantaged preschool children and the Job Corps for training youth. Black novelist Ralph Ellison called Johnson "the greatest American president for the poor and the Negroes."

However, the cold war did not go away; in fact, the United States became increasingly embroiled beyond its borders in Vietnam (Map 29.2). After the Geneva settlement in 1954, the United States escalated its commitment to the corrupt and incompetent leaders in non-Communist South Vietnam. North Vietnam, China, and the Soviet Union backed the rebel Vietcong, or South Vietnamese Communists. The strength of the Vietcong seemed to grow daily, and by 1966, the United States had more than half a million soldiers in South Vietnam. Before the war ended in 1975, the United States would drop more bombs on North Vietnam than the Allies had launched on Germany and Japan combined during World War II. Early in the war, Johnson's advisers appeared on television, predicting imminent victory despite mounting U.S. casualties and the need to draft young men, many of them unwilling to go. But after decades of anticolonial struggle, the insurgents rejected a negotiated peace. Confronting growing antiwar sentiment, increasing military costs, and declining popularity, President Johnson announced in March 1968 that he would not run for president again.

The Explosion of Civic Activism

In the midst of cold war, technological transformation, and bloody conflict, a new social activism emerged. Prosperity and the rising benefits of a postindustrial, service-oriented economy made people ever more eager for peace. Students, after two decades of study, did not want to end their lives on faraway battlefields, as their fathers and grandfathers had done. Still other activists—among them minorities and women—simply wanted a fair chance at education, jobs, and political influence. Students, blacks and other minorities, Soviet-bloc citizens, women, environmentalists, and homosexuals sometimes brought their societies to the brink of revolution during what became increasingly fiery protests. Most were against the cold war order, and most wanted to share equally in postindustrial well-being.

Civil Rights. The U.S. civil rights movement expanded its bold activism, and others joined in to make demands for fair treatment. In 1965, César Chávez (1927–1993) led vulnerable Mexican American migrant workers in the California grape agribusiness to strike for better wages and working conditions. Deeply religious and ascetic, Chávez helped Hispanic Americans define their identity and struggle against deportation, inferior schooling, and discrimination.

Meanwhile, the African American civil rights movement took a dramatic turn as urban riots erupted across the United States in 1965 and subsequent summers. Frustrated and angry, many activists changed their struggle into a militant celebration of their race under the banner "Black is beautiful." The issue they faced was one they felt they had in common with decolonizing people: how to shape an identity different from that of white oppressors. Some urged a push for "black power" to reclaim rights instead of begging for them nonviolently. Separatism, not integration, became the goal of still others; small cadres of militants even took up arms, believing that, like decolonizing people elsewhere, they needed to protect themselves against the violent whites around them.

Youth Activism. The 1960s pulsated with young people's activism. As a result of the new turn in black efforts for change, white American university students who had participated in the early stages of the civil rights movement found themselves excluded from leadership positions. Many of them soon joined the swelling protest against techno-

logical change, consumerism, and the Vietnam War. European youth were also feverish for reform. In the mid-1960s, university students in Rome occupied an administration building after right-wing opponents assassinated one of their number during a protest against the 200-to-1 student–teacher ratio. In 1966, Prague students held carnival-like processions, commemorated the tenth anniversary of the 1956 Hungarian uprisings, and took to chanting, "The only good Communist is a dead one." The "situationists" in France called on students to wake up from the slumbering pace of mass society and student life by jolting individuals to action with shocking graffiti and street theater.

Throughout the 1960s, students criticized the traditional university curriculum and flaunted their own countercultural values. They questioned how studying Plato or Dante would help them after graduation. "How to Train Stuffed Geese" was French students' satirical version of the teaching methods inflicted on them. "No professors over forty" and "Don't trust anyone over thirty" were powerful slogans of the day. Long hair, communal living, and a repudiation of personal hygiene announced students' rejection of middle-class values, as did their denunciation of sexual chastity. With the widespread use of the pill, abstinence became unnecessary as a method of birth control, and students made the sexual revolution explicit and public with open promiscuity. Marijuana use became common among students, and amphetamines and barbiturates added to the drug culture, which had its own rituals, songs, and gathering places. Scorned by students, businesses nonetheless made billions of dollars not only by selling blue jeans, dolls dressed as "hippies," natural foods, and drugs but also by packaging and managing the stars of the counterculture.

The Women's Movement. Women's activism erupted across the political spectrum (see "Contrasting Views," page 1160). Working for reproductive rights, women in France helped end the ban on birth control in 1965. More politically conventional middle-class women eagerly responded to the international best seller *The Feminine Mystique*

Feminist Debates

The feminist movement of the late twentieth century provoked the most pronounced and widespread debate over gender in recorded history. Discussion often reached a heated pitch, as it did in other reform movements of the day. Hardly the single movement described by journalists, feminism had a variety of concerns, often depending on nationality, ethnicity, sexual orientation, and class. These could produce conflict among activists and serious divisions on goals and policies, as the authors of the Combahee River Statement demonstrated (Document 1). At times, concerns over issues like equal opportunity in the workplace were directed at government policies, as in the case of the Soviet worker (Document 2). Italian feminists saw all the disabilities imposed by government as characteristic of larger problems (Document 3), while Germans explicitly connected the cause of feminism to that of environmentalism (Document 4).

1. CRITICIZING FEMINISM

In the United States, black women, like several other minority groups, found themselves marginalized in both the feminist and civil rights movements. In 1977, some of them issued the Combahee River Statement.

Black, other third world, and working women have been involved in the feminist movement from its start, but both outside reactionary forces and racism and elitism within the movement itself have served to obscure our participation. . . .

Black feminist politics also have an obvious connection to movements for Black liberation, particularly those of the 1960s and 1970s. . . . It was our experience and disillusionment within these liberation movements, as well as experience on the periphery of the white male left, that led to the need to develop a politics that was antiracist, unlike those of white women, and antisexist, unlike those of Black and white men. . . .

Above all else, our politics initially sprang from the shared belief that Black women are inherently valuable, that our liberation is a necessity not as an adjunct to somebody else's but because of our need as human persons for autonomy.

Source: "The Combahee River Collective Statement" in *Feminism in Our Time: The Essential Writings, World War II to the Present*, ed. Miriam Schneir (New York: Vintage, 1994), 177–79.

2. CRITICIZING SOCIALISM

Official policy in the Soviet Union stated that socialism had brought women full equality, eliminating the need for feminism. In the 1970s, however, Russian women in clusters announced their dissatisfaction with so-called equality under socialism. Tatyana Mamonova, the editor of a collection of Russian women's writings such as this from a railroad worker, was ultimately expelled from the USSR.

It is becoming increasingly clear that the current equality means only giving women the right to perform heavy labor . . . [I]n our day the woman, still not freed from the incredible burden of the family, strains herself even harder in the service of society. The situation . . . is true not only in large cities but also in villages. On collective and state farms, women do the hardest and most exhausting work while the men are employed as administrators, agronomists, accountants, warehouse managers, or high-paid tractor and combine drivers. In other words, men do the work that is more interesting and more profitable and does not damage their health.

Source: Tatyana Mamonova, ed., *Women and Russia: Feminist Writings from the Soviet Union* (Boston: Beacon Press, 1984), 8.

3. POLICY AND PATRIARCHY

In Italy, as in the Soviet Union, feminism had an underground quality to it involving mimeographed tracts and graffiti on buildings; women formed their own bookshops and published small newspapers. But others lobbied hard to get legislation on divorce and abortion changed, while in 1976 the Feminist Movement of Rome issued this article in its paper.

Patriarchal society is based on authoritarian-exploitative relationships, and its sexuality is sadomasochistic. The values of power, of the domination of man over the other [woman], are reflected in sexuality, where historically woman is given to man for his use. . . .

The idea of woman as man's property is fundamental to her oppression and she is often the only possession that dominant men allow exploited men to keep. . . .

In other words woman is given to the (exploited) man as compensation for his lack of possessions. . . .

We denounce as the latest form of woman's oppression the idea of a "sexual revolution" where woman is forced to go from being one man's object to being everybody's object, and where sadomasochistic pornography in films, in magazines, in all the forms of mass media that brutalize and violate woman, is bandied about as a triumph of sexual liberty.

Source: "Male Sexuality—Perversion," *Movimento Femminista Romano* (1976), quoted in *Italian Feminist Thought: A Reader*, eds. Paola Bono and Sandra Kemp (Oxford: Blackwell, 1991), 68–69.

4. FEMINISM AND ENVIRONMENTALISM

"Green" feminists took a different approach, such as announced in this "Manifesto of the 'Green' Women." It was originally a 1975 speech made in West Germany in the context of men's landing on the moon and other accomplishments in space.

Man has actually landed on the moon—an admirable feat. . . . We "Green" women . . . believe that men belong to our environment. In order to rescue that environment for our children, we want to confront this man, this adventurer and moon explorer. A female cosmonaut from a so-called socialist republic doesn't justify this energy-wasting enterprise for us at a time when three-fourths of the earth's population is suffering from malnutrition.

Our inability to solve immediate problems may tempt us into escape—to the moon, into careerism, escape into ideologies, into alcohol or other drugs. But one group cannot escape completely: women, society's potential mothers, who must give birth to children, willingly or unwillingly, in this polluted world of ours.

Source: Delphine Brox-Brochot, "Manifesto of the 'Green' Women," in *German Feminism: Readings in Politics and Literature*, eds. Edith Hoshino Altbach et al. (Albany: State University of New York Press, 1984), 314.

QUESTIONS TO CONSIDER

1. Was the feminist movement of the 1960s and 1970s primarily an offshoot of other reform movements of the day, or did it have a character of its own?

2. In what ways was feminism in these decades a unified movement, and in what ways was it a set of multiple movements?

3. What issues are raised by these activists?

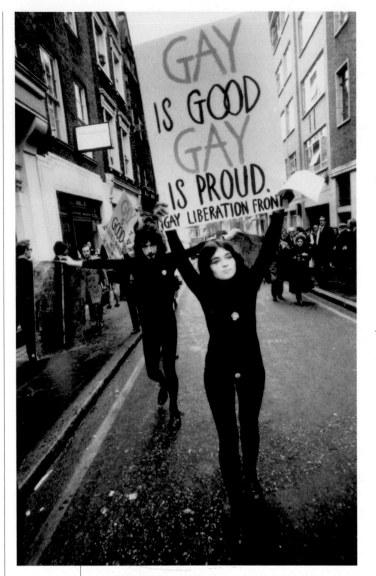

Gay Activists in London
The reformist spirit of the 1960s and 1970s changed the focus of homosexuals' activism. Instead of concentrating mostly on legal protection from criminal prosecution, gays and lesbians began affirming a special and positive identity. As other groups who had endured discrimination began making similar affirmations, "identity politics" was born. Critics charged that traditional universal values were sufficient and that homosexuals and others constituted special-interest groups. Gays, women, and ethnic or racial minorities countercharged that the universal values first put forth in the Enlightenment seemed to apply only to a privileged few. In what ways were gays' demonstrations similar to those of women, colonized people, union activists, and civil rights organizers over the past centuries? In what ways did they differ? © *Hulton Archive/Getty Images.*

(1963) by American journalist Betty Friedan. Pointing to the stagnating talents of many housewives, Friedan helped organize the National Organization for Women (NOW) in 1966 "to bring women into full participation in the mainstream of American society now." NOW advocated equal pay and a variety of other legal and economic reforms. In Sweden, women lobbied to make tasks both at home and in the workplace less gender-segregated, and in these same years a few Soviet women began speaking out against their low and unpaid work that kept the USSR running.

Those engaged in the civil rights and student movements soon realized that many of those protest organizations devalued women just as society at large did. Male activists adopted the leather-jacketed machismo style of their film and rock heroes, but women in the movements were often judged by the status of their male-protester lovers. "A woman was to 'inspire' her man," African American activist Angela Davis complained, adding that women aiming for equality supposedly "wanted to rob [male protesters] of their manhood." A speaker in Frankfurt, West Germany, interrupted a student meeting, demanding "that our problems be discussed substantively. It is no longer enough that women are occasionally allowed to say a few words."

Women also took to the streets on behalf of such issues as abortion rights or the decriminalization of gay and lesbian sexuality (see Gay Activists in London, shown here). Many flouted social conventions in their attire, language, and attitudes. Renouncing brassieres, high-heeled shoes, cosmetics, and other adornments, they spoke openly about taboo subjects such as their sexual feelings and even announced that they had resorted to illegal abortions. This brand of feminist activity was meant to shock polite society—and it did. At a Miss America contest in 1968, women protesters crowned a sheep the new beauty queen. West German women students tossed tomatoes at male protest leaders in defiance of standards for ladylike behavior. Many women of color, however, broke with feminist solidarity and spoke out against the "double jeopardy" of being "black and female." Soon there were concrete changes. In Catholic Italy, feminists won the rights to divorce, to gain access to birth-control information, and to obtain legal abortions. The demand for rights as well as for equal pay, job opportunities, and protection from rape, incest, and battering framed the major legal struggles of thousands of women's groups in the 1970s.

1968: Year of Crisis

The West seethed with protest and calls for reform finally boiled over in 1968. In January, on the first day of Tet, the Vietnamese New Year, the Vietcong and the North Vietnamese attacked more than one hundred South Vietnamese towns and American bases, inflicting heavy casualties. The Tet offensive, as it came to be called, caused many to conclude that the war might be unwinnable and gave the antiwar movement around the world crucial momentum. Meanwhile, in Czechoslovakia, a quieter movement against Soviet cold war domination had taken shape. The atmosphere in that country, as elsewhere, soon became explosive.

Violence Erupts. On April 4, 1968, Martin Luther King Jr. was assassinated by a white racist, and more than a hundred cities in the United States erupted in violence as African Americans vented their anguish and rage. Rejecting the nonviolence of King, formerly pacifist black leaders turned their rhetoric to violence: "Burn, baby, burn," chanted rioters who destroyed the grim inner cities around them. On campuses, strident confrontation over the intertwined issues of war, technology, racism, and sexism closed down classes.

Student dissent was escalating everywhere, but the most dramatic protests occurred in France. In January, students at Nanterre, outside of Paris, had gone on strike, invading administration offices to protest their inferior education and status. They called themselves a proletariat—an exploited working class—and, rejecting the Soviets, considered themselves part of a New Left. When students at the prestigious Sorbonne in Paris took to the streets in protest, police assaulted them. The Parisian middle classes reacted with unexpected sympathy to the student uprising because of their own resentment of bureaucracy. They were also horrified

at seeing the elite and brutal police force—the CRS—beating middle-class students and passersby who expressed their support.

French workers joined in: some nine million went on strike, occupying factories and calling not only for higher wages but also for participation in everyday decision making. To some, the revolt of youth and workers looked as if it might spiral into another French revolution, so unified were the expressions of political alienation. The normally decisive president Charles de Gaulle seemed paralyzed at first, but he soon sent tanks into Paris. In June, he announced a raise for workers, and businesses offered them a strengthened voice in decision making. Many citizens, having grown tired of the street violence, the destruction of so much private property, and the breakdown of services (for example, the garbage was not collected for weeks), began to sympathize with the government instead of the students. Although demonstrations continued throughout June, the student movement in France at least had been closed down. The revolutionary moment had passed.

The Prague Spring. The 1968 revolt in Prague began within the Czechoslovak Communist Party itself. In the autumn of 1967 at a party congress, Alexander Dubček,◆ head of the Slovak branch of the party, had called for more social and political openness. Attacked as an inferior Slovak by the leadership, Dubček nonetheless struck a chord among frustrated party officials, technocrats, and intellectuals: Czechoslovaks began to dream of creating a new society—one based on "socialism with a human face." Party delegates elevated Dubček to the top position, where he quickly changed the Communist style of government, ending censorship, instituting the secret ballot for party elections, and allowing

Prague Spring, 1968

◆**Dubček:** DOOB chehk

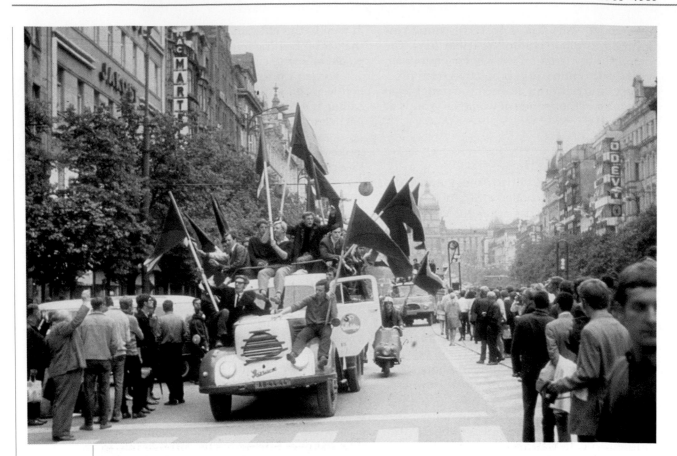

Prague Spring

When the Soviet Union and other Warsaw Pact members cracked down on the Prague Spring, they met determined citizen resistance. People refused assistance of any kind to the invaders. Indeed, despite dejection at the repression of Dubček's government, protest on a small and large scale was ongoing from then until the final fall of Communist rule two decades later. Was the citizen confrontation that occurred in Prague similar to other protests around the world, or was it unique? *Prache-Levin/Sygma.*

competing political groups to form. "Look!" one little girl in the street remarked as the new government took power. "Everyone's smiling today." The Prague Spring had begun—"an orgy of free expression," one Czech journalist called it. People bought uncensored publications, packed uncensored theater productions, and engaged in almost nonstop political debate.

Dubček faced the enormous problem of negotiating policies acceptable to the USSR, the entrenched party functionaries, and the reform-minded citizenry. Reforms were handed down with warnings about "discipline" and "wise behavior." Fearing change, the Polish, East German, and Soviet regimes threatened the reform government daily. When Dubček failed to attend a meeting of Warsaw Pact leaders, Soviet threats became intense. Finally, in August 1968, Soviet tanks rolled into Prague in a massive show of anti-revolutionary force. Citizens tried to halt the return to Communist orthodoxy by using free expression as sabotage. They painted graffiti on the tanks and confused invading troops by removing street signs. Illegal radio stations broadcast testimonials of resistance, and merchants refused to sell food or other commodities to Soviet troops. These responses could not stop the determined Soviet leadership. As it gradually removed reformers from power, Jan Palach and other university students immolated themselves, and protest of one type or another never stopped. Nonetheless, the moment of reform-minded change had passed here too.

The Superpowers Restore Order. Protest in 1968 challenged the political direction of Western societies, including superpower dominance. Yet little turned out the way reformers had hoped as governments turned to conservative solutions. In November 1968, the Soviets, for example, announced the Brezhnev Doctrine, which stated that reform movements, as a "common problem" of all socialist countries, would face swift repression. By the early 1970s, the hard-liner Brezhnev had eclipsed Kosygin's influence in the Soviet Union and freely clamped down on critics. Following the events in Czechoslovakia in 1968, Soviet dissident morale was at a low ebb. "The shock of our tanks crushing the Prague Spring . . . convinced us that the Soviet colossus was invincible," explained one pessimistic liberal. Other voices persisted, however. In 1974, Brezhnev expelled author Aleksandr Solzhenitsyn◆ from the USSR after the publication of the first volume of *Gulag Archipelago* (1973–1976) in the U.S.-led bloc. Composed from myriad biographies, firsthand reports, and other sources of information about prison camp life, Solzhenitsyn's story of the Gulag (the Soviet system of internment and forced-labor camps) documented the brutal conditions Soviet prisoners endured under Stalin and his successors. More than any other single work, the *Gulag Archipelago* disillusioned many loyal Communists around the world.

The USSR also persecuted many ordinary people who did not have Solzhenitsyn's international reputation. Soviet psychologists, complying with the government, certified the "mental illness" of people who did not play by the rules; thus, dissidents wound up as virtual prisoners in mental institutions. The crudest Soviet persecutions, however, involved anti-Semitism: Jews were subject to educational restrictions (especially in university admissions), severe job discrimination, and constant assault on their religious practice.

A commonplace accusation by Soviet officials was that Jews were "unreliable, they think only of emigrating. . . . It's madness to give them an education, because it's state money wasted." Ironically, even dissidents blamed Jews for the Bolshevik Revolution and for the terror of Stalinist collectivization. As attacks intensified in the 1970s, Soviet Jews sought to emigrate to Israel or the United States, often unsuccessfully.

By this time, the brain drain of eastern European intellectuals had become significant. The modernist composer Gyorgy Ligeti had left Hungary in 1956, after which his work was celebrated in concert halls and in such classic films as *2001: A Space Odyssey*. From exile in Paris, Czech writer Milan Kundera enthralled audiences with *The Book of Laughter and Forgetting* (1979) and *The Unbearable Lightness of Being* (1984). His novels chronicled his own descent from enthusiasm for communism to a despair characterized by bitter humor. Kundera claimed the Soviet regime in Czechoslovakia depended on making people forget. The memory of fallen leaders was ruthlessly erased from history books, for instance, and individuals papered over a grim reality through sexual promiscuity. The presence of exiles and escapees to the United States and western European capitals also eroded any lingering support for communism. As with the migration from fascist Germany and Italy in the 1930s, newcomers—from noted intellectuals to industrial workers to dancers and artisans—enriched the culture of those countries in the West that welcomed them.

In the United States the reaction against activists was different, though the impulse to restore order prevailed there too. Elected in 1968 to replace Johnson, the conservative Richard Nixon (1913–1994) promised to bring peace to Southeast Asia. In 1970, however, he ordered U.S. troops to invade Cambodia, the site of North Vietnamese bases. Campuses erupted again in protest, and on May 4 the National Guard killed four students and wounded eleven others at a demonstration at Kent State University in Ohio. Nixon called the victims "bums," and a growing reaction against the counterculture made many Americans agree with him that the guardsmen "should have fired sooner

◆**Solzhenitsyn:** suhl zhih NYEE tsihn

and longer." Mired in turmoil, the United States and North Vietnam agreed to peace in January 1973, but both sides continued to support the hostilities. In 1975, South Vietnam collapsed under a determined North Vietnamese offensive and Vietnam was forcibly reunified. The United States reeled from the defeat, having suffered loss of young lives, turbulence at home, vast military costs, and a weakening of its reputation around the world. Yet a strong current of public opinion turned against activists, born of the sense that somehow they—not the war or government corruption—had brought the United States down.

Whether burning draft cards in the United States or scribbling graffiti on public buildings in Europe, protesters had opened all leadership to question. The legacy of protesters like Jan Palach was permanent and became increasingly symbolic to those wanting political change, particularly in the Soviet bloc. As order was restored, some disappointed reformers in the West turned to open terrorism across Europe. However, new forces were also emerging from beyond the West to challenge superpower dominance and superpower policy. From the late 1960s on, the political atmosphere was volatile and the future of postindustrial prosperity uncertain.

> **Review:** What were the main issues for protesters in the 1960s, and how did governments address them?

❖ The Erosion of Superpower Mastery Ends the Cold War

The 1970s brought an era of détente♦—a lessening of cold war tensions—as mounting instability caused the United States to pull out of the Vietnam War and encouraged both superpowers to limit the nuclear arms race. Despite this relaxation in the cold war, the two powers and their allies were further chal-

♦**détente:** day TAHNT

lenged by their own internal corruption, the threat of terrorism, competition from the oil-producing states and Japan, and continuing attempts to control the world beyond their borders. An eruption of terrorist violence threw the superpowers and their allies off balance, and the oil-producing nations brought a crashing halt to postindustrial prosperity in the West. As economic hard times set in, reformers ranging from Margaret Thatcher (b. 1925) in Britain to Mikhail Gorbachev (b. 1931) in the USSR began implementing drastic new policies in the 1980s to keep the economy moving forward instead of backward. But in the Soviet bloc, postindustrial prosperity was simply unattainable under the old system. Gorbachev's reforms actually contributed to the collapse of the Soviet system and the end of the cold war in 1989.

The West, the World, and the Politics of Energy

After being tested by protest at home, the superpowers next confronted the world. In 1972, the United States pulled off a foreign policy triumph over the USSR when it opened relations with the other Communist giant—China. But it was hit hard by a Middle Eastern oil embargo that followed on the heels of that victory. As the situation in the Middle East grew ever more bloody, militants in Iran overthrew the shah—a repressive ruler allied with the United States—and then took advantage of U.S. domestic weakness by holding embassy personnel hostage. For a while, the relationship of the United States to the Middle East began to overtake the cold war as a major issue in the politics of the West and opened the future of the U.S. bloc to question.

Nixon in China.   In the midst of turmoil at home and the draining war in Vietnam, Henry Kissinger, Nixon's secretary of state and a believer—like Otto von Bismarck— in Realpolitik, decided to take advantage of the ongoing rivalry between China and the Soviets. Mao Zedong, China's Communist leader, had taken his country on a road quite different from that taken by the USSR, except for massive suffering caused by thwarted experimentation with manufacturing and agriculture. In the Cultural Revolution of the 1960s, Mao incited students to attack officials, teachers, and other authorities in order to prevent a Soviet-style bureaucracy from developing. The two Communist giants skirmished along their shared borders and in diplomatic arenas. Kissinger's efforts to forge closer ties with this other Communist power led Nixon to visit China in 1972, linking, if only tentatively, two very different great nations that both faced internal challenges. Within China, the meeting helped stop the brutality and excesses of Mao's Cultural Revolution and helped advance the careers of Chinese pragmatists interested in technology, trade, and relations with the West.

The diplomatic success also advanced détente with the Soviet Union. Fearful of the Chinese diplomatic advantage and similarly confronted by popular protest, the Soviets made their own overtures to the U.S.-led bloc. In 1972, the superpowers signed the first Strategic Arms Limitation Treaty (SALT I), which set a cap on the number of antimissile defenses each country could have. In 1975, in the Helsinki accords on human rights, the Western bloc officially acknowledged Soviet territorial gains in World War II in exchange for the Soviet bloc's guarantee of basic human rights.

Despite these successes, rising purchases of military and imported goods brought inflation and made the United States a debtor nation that owed billions to other countries. Dollars flooded the international currency markets, and in 1971, the Bretton Woods currency system, created during World War II to maintain stable international markets, collapsed. As Common Market countries united to prevent financial chaos, they forced the United States to relinquish its single-handed direction of Western economic strategy. Simultaneously, the enigmatic Nixon focused on reelection at any price. His reelection committee paid several men—caught in the act and arrested—to wiretap the telephones at Democratic Party headquarters in Washington's Watergate building. Not only had the presidential office worked to undermine free elections, but Nixon himself had attempted to cover up the truth about the Watergate break-in. Between 1968 and 1972, Nixon had forged a powerful conservative consensus, but in the summer of 1974 the Watergate scandal forced Nixon to resign in disgrace—the first U.S. president ever to do so—and profoundly weakened U.S. superpower status.

Oil and Stagflation. Amid the instability in the United States in the 1960s and 1970s, the Middle East's oil-producing nations dealt Western dominance and postindustrial prosperity still another major blow. Tensions between Israel and the Arab world provided the catalyst. On June 5, 1967, Israeli forces, responding to Palestinian guerrilla attacks, quickly seized Gaza and the Sinai peninsula from Egypt, the Golan Heights from Syria, and the West Bank from Jordan. Although Israel won a stunning victory in this action, which came to be called the Six-Day War, the Arabs' humiliation led the Arab states to try to forge a common political and economic strategy. In 1973, Egypt and Syria attacked Israel on Yom Kippur, the most holy day in the Jewish calendar, but Israel, with material assistance from the United States, stopped the assault.

Having failed militarily, the Arab nations turned decisively to economic clout. They struck at the West's weakest point—its utter dependence on Middle Eastern oil for its advanced industries and lifestyle. The Organization of Petroleum Exporting Countries **(OPEC)**, a relatively loose consortium before the Yom Kippur War, quadrupled the price of its oil and imposed an embargo, cutting off all exports of oil to the United States in retaliation for that country's support of Israel. For the first time since imperialism's heyday, the producers of raw materials—not the industrial powers controlled

Israel after the Six-Day War, 1967

the flow of commodities and set prices to their own advantage. The West was now mired in an oil crisis.

Throughout the 1970s, oil-dependent Westerners watched in astonishment as OPEC upset the balance of economic power and helped provoke a recession in the West (Figure 29.1). The oil embargo and price hike caused unemployment to rise by more than

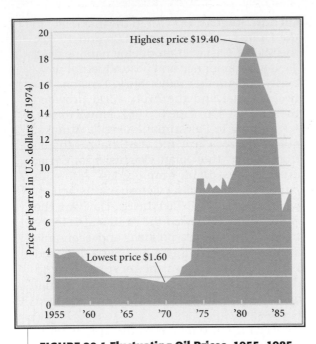

FIGURE 29.1 Fluctuating Oil Prices, 1955–1985
Colonization allowed the Western imperial powers to obtain raw materials at advantageous prices or even without paying at all. Even with decolonization, European and American firms often had such entrenched roots in newly independent economies that they were able to set the terms for trade. OPEC's oil embargo and price hikes of the 1970s were signs of change, which included the exercise of decolonized countries' control over their own resources. Not only did OPEC's action lead to a decade of painful economic downturn, but it also encouraged some European governments to improve public transportation, encourage the production of fuel-efficient cars, and impose policies that would make individual consumers cut back their dependence on oil.

50 percent in Europe and the United States and inflation to soar. By the end of 1973, the inflation rate jumped to over 8 percent in West Germany, 12 percent in France, and 20 percent in Portugal. Eastern-bloc countries, dependent on Soviet oil, fared little better because the West could no longer afford their products and the Soviets boosted the price of their own oil. Skyrocketing interest rates discouraged both industrial investment and consumer buying. With prices, unemployment, and interest rates soaring—an unusual combination of economic conditions

dubbed **stagflation**—some in the West came to realize that both energy resources and economic growth had limits. Western Europe drastically cut back on its oil dependence by undertaking conservation, enhancing public transportation, and raising the price of gasoline to encourage the development of fuel-efficient cars.

Dominance of the world by the U.S. bloc deteriorated further. In 1976, Jimmy Carter, a wealthy farmer and governor of Georgia, narrowly won the U.S. presidential election but could do little to return the economy to its pre-Vietnam and pre–oil embargo prosperity. His administration eventually faced an insurmountable crisis in the Middle East. Late in the 1970s, students, clerics, shopkeepers, and unemployed men in Iran began a religious agitation that brought to power the Islamic religious leader Ayatollah Ruhollah Khomeini.♦ Employing audiocassettes to spread his message, he called for a transformation of the country into a truly Islamic society, which meant the renunciation of the Western ways advocated by the shah, who as a result was deposed. In the autumn of 1979, revolutionary supporters of Khomeini took hostages at the American embassy in Teheran and would not release them. The paralysis of the United States in the face of Islamic militancy, along with the soaring inflation following another round of OPEC price hikes, suggested the possibility of a permanent decline of the West.

The Western Bloc Meets Challenges with Reform

As the 1980s opened, stagflation and the realignment of global economic power forced non-Communist governments in the West to put their economic houses in order. On top of the economic challenge was the growing phenomenon of **terrorism**—that is, coordinated and targeted political violence by opposition groups. The unprecedented mix of terrorism, the energy crisis, soaring unemployment, and double-digit inflation sparked the election of conservative politicians, who maintained that decades of supporting a wel-

♦**Khomeini:** koh MAY nee

The Middle East and the Politics of Oil

When Middle Eastern countries took control of the price and volume of oil they sold, Western leaders were taken aback, so thoroughly accustomed were the United States and its allies to setting the conditions of trade. OPEC leaders were lampooned in cartoons as the global economic crisis unfolded. Stagflation hit Western economies hard, while everyone came to terms with the new force of oil in international politics. What attitudes are expressed in this illustration? *Rosen-Albany Times-Union, NY/Rothco.*

"AND ANYWHERE KHALID WENT, THE LAMB WAS SURE TO GO!"

fare state were at the heart of economic problems. Across the West, tough times intensified feelings that the unemployed and new immigrants from around the world were responsible for the downturn in postindustrial progress. Nineteenth-century emphases on competitiveness, individualism, and revival of privilege for the "best circles" replaced the twentieth-century trend toward advancing economic democracy to combat totalitarianism. Postindustrial society changed political course.

Terrorism. The terrorism at the U.S. embassy in Iran was part of a trend that had actually begun in the West. In the 1970s, terrorist bands in Europe responded to the restoration of political order and the worsening economic conditions with kidnappings, bank robberies, bombings, and assassinations. Disaffected and well-to-do youth, steeped in extreme theories that said Western society was decaying, often joined these groups. Eager to bring down the Social Democratic coalition that led West Germany throughout the 1970s, the Red Army Faction assassinated prominent businessmen, judges, and other public officials. Practiced in assassinations of public figures and random shootings of pedestrians, Italy's Red Brigades kidnapped and then murdered the head of the dominant Christian Democrats in 1978.

Advocates of independence for the Basque nation in northern Spain assassinated Spanish politicians and police officers.

In Britain, nationalist and religious violence in the 1970s pitted the Catholics in Northern Ireland against the dominant Protestants. Catholics experienced job discrimination and a lack of civil rights. Demonstrators urged union with the Irish Republic, and with protest escalating, the British government sent in troops. On January 30, 1972, which became known as Bloody Sunday, British troops fired at demonstrators and killed thirteen, setting off a cycle of violence that left five hundred dead in that single year. Protestants fearful of losing their dominant position combated a reinvigorated Irish Republican Army (IRA), which carried out bombings and assassinations to achieve the union of the two Irelands in order to end

0 50 100 miles	
0 50 100 kilometers	**FRANCE**
Bilbao	San Sebastián
Basque	
	ANDORRA
SPAIN	*Catalonia*
• Madrid	Barcelona •

0 25 50 miles	*1972*
0 25 50 kilometers	*1972*
	Northern Belfast
	Ireland
	1978
1976	*1979*
IRELAND	
	• Dublin
★ Bloody Sunday, January 30, 1972	
✳ Other major incidents	

Nationalist Movements of the 1970s

Soldiers and Civilians in Northern Ireland
Separatist, civil rights, and terrorist movements made everyday life unpredictably dangerous in the last third of the twentieth century, as activists increasingly directed their violence against ordinary people. The world wars had often targeted civilians, and those leading internal struggles did so even when the declared wars were over. In Belfast, Northern Ireland, British troops fought to put down the Irish Republican Army and restore unity. Civilians were often drawn into the conflict. It was only late in the 1990s that both sides called a halt to the killing and agreed to negotiate. How did the politics of violence in the late-twentieth-century West differ from or resemble the politics of violence in the thirty years before World War I? *Brian Aris/Camera Press London.*

the oppression of Catholics (see Soldiers and Civilians in Northern Ireland, above).

Terrorists failed in their goal of overturning the existing democracies, and, sorely tried as it was, parliamentary government scored a few important successes in the 1970s. The Iberian Peninsula, suffering under dictatorship since the 1930s, regained its freedom and set out on a course of greater prosperity. The death of Spain's Francisco Franco in 1975 ended more than three decades of dictatorial rule. Franco's hand-picked successor, King Juan Carlos, surprisingly steered his nation to Western-style constitutional monarchy, facing down threatened military coups. Portugal and Greece also ousted right-wing dictators, thus paving the way for their integration into western

Europe and for substantial economic growth. Despite these democratic advances, a consensus emerged from the economic crisis, political terrorism, and failures in leadership that the West was in trouble.

Thatcher Reshapes Political Culture.
More than anyone else, Margaret Thatcher (b. 1925), the outspoken leader of Britain's Conservative Party from 1979 to 1990, reshaped the West's political and economic ideas to meet the crisis. Coming to power amid continuing economic decline, revolt in Northern Ireland, and labor unrest, the combative prime minister eschewed the politics of consensus building. Believing that only a resurgence of private enterprise could revive the sluggish British economy, Thatcher lashed

out at union leaders, Labour Party politicians, and people who received welfare-state benefits as enemies of British prosperity. Her anti-welfare-state policies struck a revolutionary chord, and she called herself "a nineteenth-century liberal" in reference to the economic individualism of that age. In her view, business leaders and entrepreneurs were the key members of society. Although immigrants often worked for the lowest wages and contributed to profits, she characterized as inferior the unemployed and those who came from Britain's former colonies, saying that neither group contributed to national wealth. Under Thatcher, even workers blamed labor leaders or newcomers for Britain's trauma.

The policies of "Thatcherism" were based on monetarist, or supply-side, theories associated most prominently with U.S. economist Milton Friedman. Monetarists contend that inflation results when government pumps money into the economy at a rate higher than a nation's economic growth rate. Thus, they advocate a tight rein on the money supply to keep prices from rising rapidly. Supply-side economists maintain that the economy as a whole flourishes when businesses grow and their prosperity "trickles down" throughout the society. To implement such theories, the British government cut income taxes on the wealthy to spur new investment, increasing sales taxes to compensate for the lost revenue. The result was an increased burden on working people, who bore the brunt of the sales tax. Thatcher also vigorously pruned government intervention in the economy: she sold publicly owned businesses and utilities such as British Airways, refused to prop up "outmoded" industries such as coal mining, and slashed education and health programs. As their influence spread through the West and the world, the package of economic policies came to be known as **neoliberalism** (see Margaret Thatcher's Economic Vision, on page 1172).

In the first three years of Thatcher's government, the British economy did not respond well to her shock treatment. The quality of universities, public transportation, highways, and hospitals deteriorated, and leading scholars and scientists left the country in a renewal of the brain drain. In addition, social unity fragmented. In 1981, blacks and Asians rioted in major cities. Thatcher's popularity sagged. She revived it by going to war with Argentina in 1982 over ownership of the Falkland Islands off the Argentinian coast. When inflation ultimately dissipated, historians and economists debated whether the change resulted from Thatcher's policies or from the lack of spending power that burdened the poor and unemployed. In any case, Thatcher's program became the standard. Britain had been one of the pioneers of the welfare state, and now it pioneered in changing course.

In Thatcher's Footsteps. In the United States, Ronald Reagan (b. 1911) followed a similar road to combat the economic crisis. Dividing citizens into the good and the bad, Reagan vowed to promote the values of the "moral majority," which included commitment

Margaret Thatcher at Conservative Party Conference (1983)
As British prime minister for more than a decade, Margaret Thatcher profoundly influenced the course of modern government by rolling back the welfare state. Thatcher was convinced and convinced others that the welfare state did not advance society and its citizens but made them lazy when it rewarded useless people with handouts. Her tenure in office encouraged other politicians, from Ronald Reagan to Helmut Kohl, to execute similar cuts in social programs. More than any other head of state during this period she set the course for domestic policy into the twenty-first century. Why was cutting social programs attractive to voters late in the twentieth century? ©*Bettmann/Corbis.*

Margaret Thatcher's Economic Vision

Margaret Thatcher, Britain's longest serving prime minister, changed Western thinking about the importance of the welfare state. Many Europeans saw the welfare state as a mainstay of democracy, which would alleviate the hardships that had turned workers toward either socialism, from Bismarck's time onward, or toward Mussolini's and Hitler's fascism, during the difficult years between the difficult interwar years. Thatcher, however, thought programs to provide healthcare, education, and housing coddled the lazy. She thought the money for such programs should be invested in private industry, to produce a profit and to encourage more investment and greater productivity. Here she outlines her thoughts on public spending to members of the Conservative Party.

. . . I and my colleagues say that to add to public spending takes away the very money and resources that industry needs to stay in business, let alone to expand. Higher public spending, far from curing unemployment, can be the very vehicle that loses jobs and causes bankruptcies in trade and commerce. That is why we warned local authorities that since rates [taxes] are frequently the biggest tax that industry now faces, increases in them can cripple local businesses. . . .

That is why I stress that if those who work in public authorities take for themselves large pay increases, they leave less to be spent on equipment and new buildings. That in turn deprives the private sector of the orders it needs, especially some of those industries in the hard pressed re-gions. Those in the public sector have a duty to those in the private sector not to take out so much in pay that they cause others' unemployment. That is why we point out that every time high wage settlements in nationalised monopolies lead to higher charges for telephones, electricity, coal, and water, they can drive companies out of business and cost other people their jobs.

If spending money like water was the answer to our country's problems, we would have no problems right now. If ever a nation has spent, spent, spent, and spent again, ours has. Today that dream is over. All of that money has got us nowhere, but it still has to come from somewhere. Those who urge us to relax the squeeze, to spend yet more money indiscriminately in the belief that it will help the unemployed and the small businessman, are not being kind or compassionate or caring. They are not the friends of the unemployed or the small business. They are asking us to do again the very things that caused the problems in the first place. . . .

I am accused of lecturing or preaching about this. I suppose it is a critic's way of saying, "Well, we know it is true, but we have to carp at something." I do not care about that. But I do care about the future of free enterprise, the jobs and exports it provides, and the independence it brings to our people.

Source: Juliet S. Thompson and Wayne C. Thompson, ed., Margaret Thatcher: Prime Minster Indomitable (Boulder: Westview, 1994), 230-31.

to Bible-based religion, dedication to work, sexual restraint, and unquestioned patriotism. Chastizing so-called spendthrift and immoral "liberals," he introduced "Reaganomics"—a program of whopping income tax cuts for the wealthy combined with massive reductions in federal spending for student loans, school lunch programs, and mass transit. Like Thatcher, Reagan believed that tax cuts would lead to investment and a reinvigo-rated economy; federal outlays for welfare programs, which he felt only encouraged bad Americans to be lazy, would generally be unnecessary thereafter.

In foreign policy, Reagan spent most of his time in office warning of the Communist threat. The longtime cold warrior labeled the Soviet Union an "evil empire" and demanded huge military budgets to counter the Soviet arms buildup of the 1970s. Reagan announced the Strategic Defense Initiative (SDI), known popularly as Star Wars, a costly plan to put lasers in space to defend the United States against a nuclear attack. The combination of tax cuts and military expansion had pushed the federal budget deficit to $200 billion by 1986.

Other western European leaders also limited welfare-state benefits in the face of stagflation, though without Thatcher's and Reagan's socially divisive rhetoric. West German leader Helmut Kohl, who took power in 1982, reduced welfare spending, froze government wages, and cut corporate taxes. By 1984, the inflation rate was only 2 percent and West Germany had acquired a 10 percent share of world trade. Unlike Thatcher, Kohl did not fan class and racial hatreds. The politics of divisiveness was particularly unwise in Germany, where terrorism on the left and on the right continued to flourish. Moreover, the legacy of Nazism loomed menacingly. When an unemployed German youth said of immigrant Turkish workers, "Let's gas 'em," the revival of Nazi language appalled many in Germany's middle class rather than gaining their support.

France took a different political path, though by 1981 stagflation had put more than 1.5 million people out of work and reduced the economic growth rate to an anemic 1.2 percent. The French elected a socialist president, François Mitterrand (1916–1996), who nationalized banks and certain industries and stimulated the economy by wage increases and social spending—the opposite of Thatcherism. New public buildings like museums and libraries arose along with new subway lines and improved public transport. Financial leaders reacted by sending capital abroad rather than investing it at home, and in Mitterrand's second term, conservatives captured the majority of seats in the assembly, which entitled them to choose the prime minister. When the conservative prime minister Jacques Chirac succeeded Mitterrand as president, he adopted neoliberal policies. Repercussions similar to those elsewhere in Europe emerged as the politically racist National Front Party won 10 percent and sometimes more of the vote with promises to deport African and Middle Eastern immigrants and cut French ties with nonwhite nations.

Revival in Smaller States. Meanwhile, a cluster of smaller states without heavy defense commitments enjoyed increasing prosperity, though many slashed away at welfare programs. In Spain, tourist dollars helped rebuild the southern cities of Grenada and Córdoba, and the country joined the Common Market in 1986. In Ireland, a surge of investment in education for high-tech jobs combined with low wage rates to attract much new business to the country in the 1990s. Prosperity and the increasingly unacceptable death toll led to a political rapprochement between Ireland and Northern Ireland in 1999. Austria prospered, too, in part by reducing government pensions and aid to business. Austrian chancellor Franz Vranitsky summed up the changed focus of government in the 1980s and 1990s: "In Austria, the shelter that the state has given to almost everyone— employee as well as entrepreneur—has led . . . a lot of people [to] think not only what they can do to solve a problem but what the state can do. . . . This needs to change." The century-long growth of the welfare state seemed to be over by the 1990s.

Almost alone, Sweden maintained a full array of social programs for everyone. The government also offered each immigrant a choice of subsidized housing in neighborhoods inhabited primarily by Swedes or primarily by people from the immigrant's native land. Such programs were expensive: the tax rate on income over $46,000 was 80 percent. Despite a highly productive workforce, Sweden dropped from fourth to fourteenth place among nations in per capita income by 1998. Although the Swedes reduced their costly dependence on foreign oil by cutting consumption in half between 1976 and 1986, their welfare state came to seem extreme to many citizens. As elsewhere, immigrants were cast as a major threat to the country: "How long will it be before our Swedish children will have to turn their faces toward Mecca?" ran one politician's campaign speech in 1993.

Collapse of Communism in the Soviet Bloc

Beginning in 1985 reform came to the Soviet Union as well, but instead of fortifying the economy, it provoked more rebellion. Within four years, communism collapsed throughout the Soviet bloc. Reform came at a time of ongoing protest by workers, artists, and intellectuals. Communications, international trade, and democratic movements were pulling apart a vast region that communism had structured for almost half a century. A deteriorating economy and a corrupt system of political and economic management prevented any kind of cure. Years of stagnant and then negative growth led to a deteriorating standard of living. After working a full day, Soviet homemakers stood in long lines to obtain basic commodities; housing and food shortages necessitated the three-generation household, in which grandparents took over tedious homemaking tasks from their working children and grandchildren. "There is no special skill to this," a seventy-three-year-old grandmother and former garbage collector remarked. "You just stand in line and wait." Even so, people often went away empty-handed as basic household supplies like soap disappeared instantly from stores. One cheap and readily available product—vodka—often formed the center of people's social lives. Alcoholism reached crisis levels, diminishing productivity and tremendously straining the nation's morale.

Mikhail Gorbachev Attempts Reform. In 1985 a new leader, Mikhail Gorbachev, unexpectedly opened an era of change. The son of peasants, Gorbachev had risen through the party ranks as an agricultural specialist and had traveled abroad to gain a firsthand glimpse of life in the West. He saw that economic stagnation had many ramifications. Ordinary people decided not to have children, and fertility fell below replacement levels throughout the Soviet bloc, except for the Muslim areas of Soviet Central Asia. The country was forced to import massive amounts of grain because 20 to 30 percent of the grain that was produced in the USSR rotted before it could be harvested or shipped to market, so great was the inefficiency of the state-directed economy. Industrial pollution, spewed out by enterprises responsible only for meeting production quotas, reached scandalous dimensions. A massive and privileged party bureaucracy hobbled innovation and failed to achieve socialism's professed goal of a decent standard of living for working people. To

match American military growth, the Soviet Union diverted 15 to 20 percent of its gross national product (more than double the U.S. proportion) to armaments, further crippling the economy's chances of raising living standards. As this combustible mix of problems heated up, a new generation was coming of age that had no memory of World War II or Stalin's purges. One Russian observer found members of the younger generation "cynical but less afraid." "They believe in nothing," a mother said of Soviet youth in 1984.

Gorbachev knew from experience and travels to western Europe that the Soviet system was woefully inadequate, and he quickly proposed several unusual programs that went hand in hand. A crucial economic reform, **perestroika** ("restructuring"), aimed to reinvigorate the Soviet economy by improving productivity, increasing the rate of capital investment, encouraging the use of up-to-date technology, and gradually introducing such market features as prices and profits. The complement to economic change was the policy of **glasnost** (usually translated as "openness" or "publicity"), which called for disseminating "wide, prompt, and frank information" and for allowing Soviet citizens new measures of free speech (see Gorbachev's statements on reform, opposite). When officials complained that glasnost threatened their status, Gorbachev replaced more than a third of the Communist Party's leadership in the first months of his administration. The pressing need for glasnost became most evident after the Chernobyl◆ catastrophe in 1986, when a nuclear reactor exploded and spewed radioactive dust into the atmosphere. Bureaucratic cover-ups delayed the spread of information about the accident, with lethal consequences for people living near the plant.

After Chernobyl, even the Communist Party and Marxism-Leninism were opened to public criticism. Party meetings suddenly included complaints about the highest leaders and their policies. Television shows adopted the outspoken methods of American investigative reporting; one program showed an interview with an executioner of political prisoners and exposed the plight of

---

◆**Chernobyl:** chur NOH buhl

Mikhail Gorbachev on Reform in the USSR

Some people—especially Westerners—have interpreted Gorbachev's reforms as noble and enlightened, opening the way to free markets and free speech. Others, especially in the Soviet Union, saw him as simply another member of the Communist establishment, hoping to prop up a rotten system. "A flatterer," one critic called him, "who can live for free in luxurious villas at our expense." For such critics Gorbachev's reforms were merely machinations by a Soviet leader hoping to boost productivity so that there would be more to siphon off. The following passage from Gorbachev's 1987 book on perestroika reveals the complex relationship between Gorbachev's program and the Communist status quo.

Perestroika is closely connected with socialism as a system. That side of the matter is being widely discussed, especially abroad, and our talk about perestroika won't be entirely clear if we don't touch upon that aspect.

Does perestroika mean that we are giving up socialism or at least some of its foundations? Some ask this question with hope, others with misgiving.

There are people in the West who would like to tell us that socialism is in a deep crisis and has brought our society to a dead end. That's how they interpret our critical analysis of the situation at the end of the seventies and beginning of the eighties. We have only one way out, they say: to adopt capitalist methods of economic management and social patterns, to drift toward capitalism.

They tell us that nothing will come of perestroika within the framework of our system. They say we should change this system and borrow from the experience of another socio-political system. To this they add that, if the Soviet Union takes this path and gives up its socialist choice, close links with the West will supposedly become possible. They go so far as to claim that the October 1917 Revolution was a mistake which almost completely cut off our country from world social progress.

To put an end to all the rumors and speculations that abound in the West about this, I would like to point out once again that we are conducting all our reforms in accordance with the socialist choice. We are looking within socialism, rather than outside it, for the answers to all the questions that arise. We assess our successes and errors alike by socialist standards. Those who hope that we shall move away from the socialist path will be greatly disappointed. Every part of our program of perestroika—and the program as a whole, for that matter—is fully based on the principle of more socialism and more democracy.

More socialism means a more dynamic pace and creative endeavor, more organization, law and order, more scientific methods and initiative in economic management, efficiency in administration, and a better and materially richer life for the people.

More socialism means more democracy, openness and collectivism in everyday life, more culture and humanism in production, social and personal relations among people, more dignity and self-respect for the individual.

More socialism means more patriotism and aspiration to noble ideals, more active civic concern about the country's internal affairs and about their positive influence on international affairs.

In other words, more of all those things which are inherent in socialism and in the theoretical precepts which characterize it as distinct socio-economic formation.

We will proceed toward better socialism rather than away from it. We are saying this honestly, without trying to fool our own people of the world. Any hopes that we will begin to build a different, non-socialist society and go over to the other camp are unrealistic and futile. Those in the West who expect us to give up socialism will be disappointed. It is high time they understood this, and, even more importantly, proceeded from that understanding in practical relation with the Soviet Union.

Source: Mikhail Gorbachev, *New Thinking for Our Country and the World* (New York: Harper & Row: 1987), 36-37.

Gorbachevs and Reagans at the Ranch
Ronald Reagan raised the temperature of the cold war with a massive arms buildup in the 1980s that caused the U.S. budget deficit to soar. When Mikhail Gorbachev came to power in the USSR, he changed course, encouraging freer speech, seeking innovation in the economy, and reducing cold war tensions. The two leaders' regular meetings helped slow down the arms race, but Gorbachev's policies also inadvertently helped bring down the Soviet system of eastern European satellites. How is this photograph related to the end of the cold war? *Ruelas, L.A. Daily News/Sygma.*

Glasnost and perestroika dramatically affected superpower relations as well. Recognizing how severely the cold war arms race was draining Soviet resources, Gorbachev almost immediately began scaling back missile production. His unilateral actions gradually won over Ronald Reagan. In 1985, the two leaders initiated a personal relationship and began defusing the cold war. "I bet the hard-liners in both our countries are bleeding when we shake hands," said the jovial Reagan at the conclusion of one meeting. In early 1989, Gorbachev at last withdrew his country's forces from the debilitating war in Afghanistan, and by the end of the year the United States started to cut back its own vast military buildup.

Rebellion in Poland.   As Gorbachev's reforms in the USSR started spiraling out of his control, they did so in an atmosphere of rising dissent across the Soviet bloc, but most notably in Poland. Already in the summer of 1980, Poles had reacted furiously to government-increased food prices by going on strike. As the protest spread, workers at the Gdańsk shipyards, led by electrician Lech Walesa and crane operator Anna Walentynowicz, created an independent labor movement called **Solidarity**. The organization soon embraced much of the adult population, including a million members of the Communist Party. Both intellectuals and the Catholic church, long in the forefront of opposition to socialist secularization, supported Solidarity workers as they occupied factories in protest against inflation, the scarcity of food, and other deteriorating conditions of everyday life. The members of Solidarity waved Polish flags and paraded giant portraits of the Virgin Mary and Pope John Paul II (b. 1920)—a Polish native.

Having achieved mass support at home and worldwide sympathy through media coverage, Solidarity leaders insisted that the

Leningrad's homeless children. Instead of publishing made-up letters praising the great Soviet state, newspapers were flooded with real ones complaining of shortages and abuse. One outraged "mother of two" protested that the cost-cutting policy of reusing syringes in hospitals was a source of AIDS. "Why should little kids have to pay for the criminal actions of our Ministry of Health?" she asked. Debate and factions arose across the political spectrum. In the fall of 1987, one of Gorbachev's erstwhile allies, Boris Yeltsin, quit the governing Politburo after denouncing perestroika as insufficient to produce real reform. Yeltsin's political daring, which in the past would have consigned him to oblivion (or Siberia), inspired others to organize in opposition to the crumbling ruling orthodoxy. By the spring of 1989, in a remarkably free balloting in Moscow's local elections, not a single Communist was chosen.

government recognize it as an independent union—a radical demand under communism. As food became scarce and prices rose, tens of thousands of women marched in the streets crying, "We're hungry!" They, too, protested working conditions, but as both workers and the only caretakers of home life, it was the scarcity of food that sent them into the streets. The Communist Party teetered on collapse, until the police and the army, with Soviet support, imposed a military government and in the winter of 1981 outlawed Solidarity. Continued efforts by reporters and dissidents, using global communications, kept Solidarity alive as a force both inside and outside of Poland. Stern and puritanical, General Wojciech Jaruzelski took over as the head of Poland's new regime in 1981, but the general could not push repression too far: he needed new loans from the U.S.-led bloc to keep the sinking Polish economy afloat. Workers, additionally, kept meeting, creating a new culture outside the official Soviet arts and newscasts. Poets read dissident verse to overflow crowds, and university professors lectured to Solidarity members on such forbidden topics as Polish resistance in World War II. Ongoing activism in Poland set the stage for communism's downfall.

The Revolutions of 1989. The year 1989 has been designated the twentieth century's annus mirabilis, or year of miracles, because of the sudden and unexpected disintegration of Communist power. Inspired by Gorbachev's visit to China's capital, Beijing, in the spring of 1989 thousands of students massed in the city's Tiananmen Square, the world's largest public square, to demand democracy. They used telex machines and e-mail to rush their messages to the international community, and they effectively conveyed their goals through the cameras that Western television trained on them. China's aged Communist leaders, while pushing economic modernization and even allowing market operations, refused to consider the introduction of democracy. As workers began joining the pro-democracy forces, the government crushed the movement and executed as many as a thousand rebels.

The protests in Tiananmen Square were galvanizing nonetheless. In June 1989, the Polish government, weakened by its own bungling of the economy and lacking Soviet support for further repression, held free parliamentary elections. Solidarity candidates overwhelmingly defeated the Communists, and in early 1990, Walesa became president, hastening Poland's rocky transition to a market economy. Gorbachev pointedly reversed the Brezhnev Doctrine, refusing to interfere in the political course of another nation. As it became evident that the Soviet Union would not intervene in Poland, the fall of communism repeated itself in country after country.

Communism collapsed first in Poland and then in Hungary because of those countries' early introduction of free-market ingredients. In Hungary, which had experimented with "market socialism" since the 1960s, even officials began to realize that political democracy had to accompany economic freedom. Citizens lobbied against ecologically unsound projects like the construction of a new dam. They encouraged boycotts of Communist holidays and on March 15, 1989, they commemorated instead the anniversary of the Hungarian uprising—the "battle of the holidays" it was called. Finally, when these popular demands for liberalization led the Parliament in the fall of 1989 to dismiss the Communist Party as the official ruling institution, people tore down Soviet and Communist symbols across the country.

The most potent symbol of a divided Europe—the Berlin Wall—stood in the midst of a divided Germany. East Germans had attempted to escape over the wall for decades, and since the early 1980s dissidents had held peace vigils in cities across East Germany. In the summer of 1989, crowds of East Germans flooded the borders of the crumbling Soviet bloc, and hundreds of thousands of protesters rallied throughout the fall against the regime. Satellite television brought them visions of postindustrial prosperity and of free and open public debate in West Germany. The crowds intensified in November, when Gorbachev, taken as a hero by many, visited the country. On November 9, an ambiguous statement from the government encouraged guards to allow free passage across the wall. Protest turned to festive holiday: West Berliners handed out bananas, a consumer good that had been in short supply in the Eastern zone, and that fruit became the unofficial symbol of a newfound liberation. As they strolled freely

Reunited Berliners Welcome the New Year.
On New Year's Eve, 1989, Berliners—and indeed supporters from around the world—celebrated the fall of the Berlin wall and the prospect of a new Germany. The exuberant crowd tore the Communist seal from the flag and then hoisted it above the Brandenburg Gate as fireworks added to the intense emotion of the moment. Disposing of the remnants of Communism lay in the future, and for many the transition would prove difficult. Rebuilding Berlin after Communism, like the rebuilding of most of eastern Europe, lasted into the twenty-first century.
Ullstein-Boening, Berlin.

in the streets, East Berliners saw firsthand the goods available in a successful postindustrial society. Soon thereafter, citizens—east and west—released years of frustration by assaulting the Berlin Wall with sledgehammers and bringing home chunks as souvenirs. The government finished the wall's complete destruction in the fall of 1990.

In Czechoslovakia, which after 1968 had been firmly restored to Soviet-style rule, people also watched the progress of glasnost expectantly. Persecuted, dissidents had nonetheless maintained their critique of Communist rule. In an open letter to the Czechoslovak Communist Party leadership, playwright Václav Havel accused Marxist-Leninist rule of making people materialist and indifferent to civic life. In 1977, Havel, along with a group of

fellow intellectuals and workers, signed Charter 77, a public protest against the regime that resulted in the arrest of the signers. In the mid-1980s these dissidents watched Gorbachev on television calling for free speech, though never mentioning reform in Czechoslovakia. Demonstrators protested in the streets for democracy, but the government cracked down by turning the police on them, arresting Havel again in January 1989 for commemorating the death of Jan Palach. The turning point came in November 1989 when Alexander Dubček, leader of the Prague Spring of 1968, addressed the crowds in Prague's Wenceslas Square with a call for the ouster of Stalinists from the government after the police had beaten students. Almost immediately, Communist leadership resigned. Capping the country's "velvet revolution," as it became known for its lack of bloodshed, the formerly Communist-dominated parliament elevated the dissident Havel to the presidency.

The world's attention now fastened on an unfolding political drama in Romania. From the mid-1960s on, Nicolae Ceaușescu◆ had ruled as the harshest dictator in Communist Europe since Stalin. In the name of modernization, he destroyed whole villages; to build up the population, he outlawed contraceptives and abortions, a restriction that led to the abandonment of tens of thousands of children. He preached the virtues of a very slim body so that he could cut rations and use the savings on his pet projects such as buying up private castles and other property. Most Romanians lived in utter poverty as Ceaușescu determined to channel almost all the country's resources into building himself an enormous palace in Bucharest. To this end, he tore down entire neighborhoods and dozens of historical buildings, and so much did he torture any opponents that the gaudy project seemed to have unanimous support. Yet in early December 1989, an opposition movement rose up and workers kept up a string of demonstrations against the dictatorial government. Most of the army rose up, too, and crushed the forces loyal to Ceaușescu. On Christmas Day, viewers watched on television as the dictator and his wife were tried by a military court and then executed. For many, the death of Ceaușescu meant that the very worst of communism was over.

Homeless Romanian Children (1995)
These children were among the many who lived without families around the railroad station in Romania's capital city, Bucharest. Nicolae Ceaușescu's regime prohibited birth control and abortion in order to increase the supply of workers while simultaneously cutting back on food rations. The redirected funds were then used on lavish homes for Ceaușescu and his family. Children were the victims of this policy, even after Ceaușescu was overthrown, as families simply abandoned children they could not support. In order to survive, the children scavenged, stole, begged, and did small tasks. They often slept on baggage carts at the railroad station (like the children in this photograph) — never losing their haunted expressions. Young children in orphanages sometimes fared better, especially if they were adopted by couples from other countries. ©*Barry Lewis/Corbis.*

Review: What factors led to the collapse of communism in the Soviet bloc?

◆**Nicolae Ceaușescu:** nee koh LY chow SHEHS koo

Conclusion

The fall of the Berlin Wall in 1989 symbolized the end of the cold war, even though the USSR still stood as a bulwark of communism. Collapse of communism in the Soviet satellites was an utter surprise, for U.S.-bloc analysts had erroneously reported throughout the 1980s that the Soviet empire was in dangerously robust health. But no one should have been unaware of dissent or economic discontent. Since the 1960s, a surge of rebellion among youth, ethnic and racial minorities, and women condemned conditions across the West, along with criticizing the threat posed by the cold war. By the early 1980s, wars in Vietnam and Afghanistan,

MAPPING THE WEST The Collapse of Communism in Europe, 1989–1990
The 1989 overthrow of the Communist party in the USSR satellite countries of Eastern Europe occurred with surprising rapidity. The transformation began in Poland when Polish voters tossed out Communist party leaders in June 1989, and then accelerated in September when thousands of East Germans fled to Hungary, Poland, and Czechoslovakia. Between October and December, communist regimes were replaced in East Germany, Czechoslovakia, Bulgaria, and Romania. Within three years the Baltic States would declare their independence, the USSR itself would dissolve, and the breakup of Yugoslavia would lead to war in the Balkans.

protests against privations in the Soviet bloc, the power of oil-producing states, and the growing political force of Islam had weakened superpower preeminence. Reformers like Margaret Thatcher, Ronald Reagan, and Mikhail Gorbachev tried with varying degrees of success to put their postindustrial and cold war houses in order. The first two were successful, while Gorbachev brought on collapse by introducing glasnost and pere-

stroika—each a policy aimed at political and economic change.

Glasnost and perestroika were supposed to bring about the high levels of postindustrial prosperity enjoyed outside the Soviet bloc. Across the West, including the USSR, an unprecedented technological development had transformed businesses, the exploration of space, and the functioning of government. It also had an enormous impact on everyday life. Work changed, as society reached a stage called postindustrial, in which the service sector predominated. New patterns of family life, new relationships among the generations, and revised standards for sexual behavior also characterized these years. But it was only in the United States and western Europe that the consumer benefits of postindustrialization had reached ordinary people, for the attainment of a thoroughgoing consumer, service, and high-tech society demanded levels of efficiency, coordination, and cooperation that had not been reached in the Soviet bloc. For the most part, the old coercion that drove rapidly industrializating economies still prevailed.

There were complaints everywhere, nonetheless, about the dramatic changes that postindustrial society entailed and, ironically, about its failure to materialize sufficiently. The protesters of the late 1960s addressed postindustrial society's stubborn problems: concentrations of bureaucratic and industrial power, social inequality, environmental degradation, even uncertainty about humankind's future. In the Soviet sphere, these protests never stopped but were never heeded until the collapse of Soviet domination of eastern Europe in 1989. Soon communism would be overturned in the USSR itself. However, the triumph of democracy in the former Soviet empire opened an era of painful adjustment, impoverishment, and violence for hundreds of millions of people. Ending the cold war, it also accelerated the process of globalization.

Suggested References

The Revolution in Technology

Wartime technological development came to have profound consequences for the peacetime lives of individuals and for society. The works listed here describe the new technologies and analyze their importance, with authors divided on whether the new developments should be feared or embraced. Fordham University's history Web site has a section on recent developments in science and technology.

Bauer, Martin W., and George Gaskell, eds. *Biotechnology: The Making of a Global Controversy*. 2002.

Fordam University, Internet Modern History Sourcebook: **http://www.fordham.edu/halsall/mod/modsbook59.html**.

Hecht, Gabrielle. *The Radiance of France: Nuclear Power and National Identity after World War II*. 1998.

Natalicchi, Giorgio. *Wiring Europe: Re-Shaping the European Telecommunications Regime*. 2001.

Singer, Edward Nathan. *The Twentieth Century Revolution in Technology*. 1998.

*Stanworth, Michelle, ed. *Reproductive Technologies: Gender, Motherhood, and Medicine*. 1987.

Postindustrial Society and Culture

Changes in the way people worked became striking in the 1960s, causing social observers to analyze the social and cultural meaning of the transformation. Many critics agree that technology's creation of a postindustrial workplace changed not only the way people worked but also how they lived in families and interacted with peers.

Evans, Christopher. *The Micro Millennium*. 1979.

Hochschild, Arlie. *The Time Bind: When Work Becomes Home and Home Becomes Work*. 1997.

Proctor, Robert. *Cancer Wars: The Politics behind What We Know and Don't Know about Causes and Trends*. 1994.

Ramet, Sabrina P., and Gordana P. Crnković, eds. *Kazaaam! Splat! Ploof! The American Impact on European Culture since 1945*. 2003.

Roulleau Berger, Laurence. *Youth and Work in the Post-Industrial City of North America and Europe*. 2003.

Sinfield, Alan. *Literature, Politics, and Culture in Post-war Britain*. 1989.

Protesting Cold War Conditions

Historians look to domestic politics, international events, and social change to capture the texture of the tumultuous 1960s. The momentous changes on so many fronts are beginning to receive synthetic treatment in books such as Suri's, which connects the move for détente with domestic protest around the world. The Martin Luther King Web site introduces visitors to the biography, speeches, sermons, and major life events of the slain civil rights leader.

*Dubček, Alexander. *Hope Dies Last: The Autobiography of Alexander Dubček*. 1993.

*Primary source.

Fink, Carole et al., eds. *1968: The World Transformed.* 1998.

*Guy-Sheftall, Beverly, ed. *Words of Fire: An Anthology of African-American Feminist Thought.* 1995.

*Lévi-Strauss, Claude. *Tristes Tropiques.* 1961.

The Martin Luther King Jr. Papers Project at Stanford University: http://www.stanford.edu/group/King.

Ross, Kristin. *May '68 and Its Afterlives.* 2003.

Suri, Jeremi. *Power and Protest: Global Revolution and the Rise of Détente.* 2003.

Varon, Jeremy. *Bringing the War Home: The Weather Underground, the Red Army Faction, and Revolutionary Violence in the Sixties and Seventies.* 2004.

The Erosion of Superpower Mastery Ends the Cold War

As the superpowers continued their standoff, historians found that myriad global changes affected their status and that protest continued at home. Many interesting Web sites explore the development of green parties over the past three decades, the most inclusive being that of the global organization with links to green parties of all continents and countries. Protest also continued in the Soviet bloc: the dissident art of the Soviet Union is striking for its deft and moving critique of life under communism. Attempts at reform succeeded in the United States and western Europe, but eastern Europe saw the surprising collapse of communism and the end of the cold war in 1989.

*Gorbachev, Mikhail. *Memoirs.* 1996.

Green Parties worldwide: http://www.greens.org.

Kligman, Gail. *The Politics of Duplicity: Controlling Reproduction in Ceauşescu's Romania.* 1998.

Laqueur, Walter. *The Age of Terrorism.* 1987.

Olson, James S., and Randy Roberts. *Where the Domino Fell: America and Vietnam, 1945–1990.* 1996.

Reiton, Earl A. *The Thatcher Revolution: Margaret Thatcher, John Major, Tony Blair, and the Transformation of Modern Britain.* 2002.

Rosenfeld, Alla, and Norton T. Dodge. *From Gulag to Glasnost: Nonconformist Art from the Soviet Union.* 1995.

Rothschild, Joseph, and Nancy M. Wingfield. *Return to Diversity: A Political History of East Central Europe.* 2000.

*Solzhenitsyn, Aleksandr Isaevich. *The Gulag Archipelago.* 1973–1976.

Sternhal, Suzanne. *Gorbachev's Reforms: De-Stalinization through Demilitarization.* 1997.

Weigel, George. *Witness to Hope: The Biography of Pope John Paul II.* 1999.

CHAPTER REVIEW

IMPORTANT EVENTS

1962–1965	Vatican II reforms Catholic ritual and dogma
1963	Betty Friedan publishes *The Feminine Mystique*
1966	Willy Brandt becomes West German foreign minister and develops Ostpolitik, a policy designed to bridge tensions between the two Germanies
1967	South Africa's Dr. Christiaan Barnard performs first successful human heart transplant
1968	Revolution in Czechoslovakia against communism; student uprisings throughout Europe and the United States
1969	U.S. astronauts walk on the moon's surface
1972	SALT I treaty between the United States and Soviet Union
1973	North Vietnam and the United States sign treaty ending war in Vietnam; OPEC raises price of oil and imposes oil embargo on the West
1973–1976	Aleksandr Solzhenitsyn publishes *Gulag Archipelago*
1977	Feminists gather in Houston to mark the first International Year of Women
1978	The first test-tube baby is born in England
1978–1979	Islamic revolution in Iran; hostages taken at U.S. embassy in Teheran
1980	An independent trade union, Solidarity, organizes resistance to Polish communism; Prime Minister Margaret Thatcher begins dismantling the welfare state in Britain
Early 1980s	AIDS epidemic strikes the West
1981	Ronald Reagan becomes U.S. president
1985	Mikhail Gorbachev comes to power in the USSR
1986	Explosion at Soviet nuclear plant at Chernobyl; Spain joins the Common Market
1989	Chinese students revolt in Tiananmen Square and government suppresses them; Communist governments ousted in eastern Europe; fall of the Berlin Wall

KEY TERMS

DNA (1144)
glasnost (1174)
in vitro fertilization (1146)
multinational corporation (1146)
neoliberalism (1171)
perestroika (1174)
pop art (1152)
OPEC (1167)
Ostpolitik (1156)
samizdat (1156)
Solidarity (1176)
stagflation (1168)
terrorism (1168)
Vatican II (1154)

REVIEW QUESTIONS

1. How did the scientific advances from the 1950s and 1960s challenge established patterns of thought and social behavior?
2. What major changes took place in the formation of postindustrial society?
3. What were the main issues for protesters in the 1960s, and how did governments address them?
4. What factors led to the collapse of communism in the Soviet bloc?

MAKING CONNECTIONS

1. What were the differences between industrial society of the late nineteenth century and postindustrial society of the late twentieth century?
2. Why were there so many protests, acts of terrorism, and uprisings across the West in the decades between 1960–1990?
3. What have been the long-term consequences of Communist rule between 1917 and 1989?

FOR FURTHER EXPLORATION

To assess your mastery of the material in this chapter, see the Online Study Guide at bedfordstmartins.com/hunt.

To read additional primary-source material from this period, see Chapter 29 in *Sources of The Making of the West*, Second Edition.

The New Globalism: Opportunities and Dilemmas,
1989 to the Present

ON JANUARY 1, 2002, PEOPLE in twelve countries of the European Union (EU) woke up to find their centuries-old national currencies gone, replaced by a single unit of money—the **euro**. The bills were all standard, designed to represent the EU's shared ideals, represented by the image of bridges. The design of the coins was different, however. One side of the coin was common, while on the other each country was, for an allotted number of coins, allowed to put a unique national symbol. Supporters of the currency pointed to the savings on currency exchanges for businesses, consumers, and international travelers, while its detractors felt that a traditional bulwark of the nation-state—a controlled, independent monetary system—would be undermined, and perhaps national integrity with it. Thus, Britain, Sweden, and Denmark refused to join the currency system despite being members of the EU. For those adopting the euro, funds for industry and commerce moved unhampered. Having the new currency in their pockets also gave psychological advantages to EU citizens. "People with the same money don't go to war with one another," a French nuclear scientist remarked. An Italian student enthused that the euro provided "a sense of belonging to a European Union and I think it's beautiful that there's this big European country."

The Euro
These new bills went into circulation on January 1, 2002, even though banks and other financial institutions began using the euro monetary unit two years earlier. The design of the euro bills and coins, like everything else in the European Union, represented compromise and unity. The bills' designer used architectural imagery of windows and bridges, suggesting openness, light, connectedness, and boundary crossing. Reflecting the compromise between Europe and individual states, the head side of the coins bears a common image, while the tail sides contain symbols chosen by individual nations within the euro zone. Europeans were generally enthusiastic about the common currency for many reasons both idealistic and practical: it allowed for more effective bargain hunting, while it also represented yet another step in ending the divisive nationalism that had plagued the history of the West. Why might some Europeans object to the euro? *Royalty Free/Corbis.*

For these people, the euro represented post–cold war opportunity—an opportunity to start the new millennium with the risks of disastrous wars perhaps permanently diminished.

The end of the cold war rivalry between the superpowers and their allies paved the way for a more intimately connected world, and the euro was just one concrete example of weakening national boundaries. The collapse of communism in Europe spread after 1989 to include Yugoslavia and then the Soviet Union itself—another major piece of the globalization puzzle. After that, the former Common Market transformed itself into the European Union and in 2004 admitted many states from the former Soviet empire in Eastern Europe. Instead of being forced to adhere to the demands of one superpower or the other, nations around the world had more opportunity to trade and interact with each other freely, and technology moved openly from region to region. Further advances in communication added to the potential for Europe-wide and global relationships; spurred by the fall of the Soviet realm, these advances paved the way for the West as a whole to enter the global age. The world was no longer divided in two with all the guarded borders and burdensome restrictions the cold war division implied. Rather, a denser web of economic and social ties bound peoples and cultures together.

The globalizing world brought challenges, opportunities, disasters, and astonishing accomplishments. Migration from eastern to western Europe accelerated in the 1990s as an unexpected consequence of the Soviet collapse. As the costs of the welfare state were cut across the West, governments increased subsidies and incentives for businesses facing global competition from the rising economic power of Japan, China, and other Asian countries. International business mergers accelerated from the 1990s on. The global age brought the vast international and national migration of tens of millions of people; an expanding global marketplace; and an accelerated cultural exchange of popular music, books, films, and television entertainment. Less hopefully, it also encompassed the international impact of lethal disasters such as AIDS, environmental degradation, genocide, and terrorism. The global age was indeed one of golden opportunities and unprecedented dilemmas.

While the end of superpower rivalry made global exchange easier, it also resulted in the dominance of a single power, the United States, in world affairs. As the United States sought to exercise global power through warfare, however, the West itself seemed to fragment. European states, more interested in peace than war, started to resist the United States just as the Soviet satellites had pulled away from the USSR. As global events progressed, new forces arose to rival those of the West, not only the economic power of the Asian and Middle Eastern countries but also the cultural might of Islam. Some observers predicted a huge "clash of civilizations" based on the total incompatibility of Western civilization and cultures beyond the West. Others, however, saw a different clash—one between a Europe reborn after decades of

◆ **1990s** Internet revolution

◆ **1990–1991** Persian Gulf War

◆ **1995** International congress of women at Beijing

◆ **1997** Economic problems for the Pacific tigers

◆ **1991** Civil war in Yugoslavia; failed coup in the Soviet Union

1985   **1990**   **1995**

◆ **1992** Soviet Union dissolves

◆ **1993** Toni Morrison wins Nobel Prize

◆ **1989** Tiananmen Square uprising; Berlin Wall falls

◆ **1994** Mandela elected in South Africa; Russia invades Chechnya; EU formed disastrous wars as a nonmilitaristic group of nations allied with other peace-seeking states confronting an imperial United States that, like Europe in the nineteenth century, was increasingly at war around the world. Instead of bringing connections and understanding, globalization in either of these scenarios could entail global holocaust.

For historians, understanding the recent past is a challenge in itself. Every day since 1989 has been filled with news, and never more so than after September 11, 2001. This news receives virtually instantaneous reporting because of global communication technology. Unlike journalists, historians do not choose from this mass the most sensational story of the moment or the one that will attract the greater readership. Rather, they are interested in judging which items from the unfiltered mass of technologically transmitted news are actually true and, of these, which will be important in the long run. Moving beyond a single U.S.-based newspaper or television station, historians want to identify social, cultural, and political events that are uniquely important or generally significant for people's everyday lives, and they need time to collect facts from more than one national tradition. They make the most reliable evaluations when phenomena are no longer "news"—that is, after a good period of time has shown their staying power and influence.

When we first started writing this book, we held our breath in the face of rapidly changing events and judged that the fall of communism and the increasing interconnectedness of the world's peoples and cultures

were the challenges not only of the moment but also of history. In this second edition we persisted in that judgment although the fall of communism and coming of globalism had brought greater perils than we had seen only five or six years earlier. Other forces, such as the Internet, had missed our notice altogether despite the fact that the system had been around for several decades. Today, almost a decade after we made our first selections of important trends, we judge the gradual unification of the entire European continent as potentially momentous. We also see the forces of terrorism and possibly a new fragmentation of the West itself into U.S. and European blocs as events with historical staying power. As an experiment in history, you might note the important events of the months in which you take this course, put your list away for several years or more, and then see if they—along with the events discussed in this chapter—stand the test of time.

❖ Soviet Collapse Releases Global Forces

Rejection of communism spread in the 1990s, turning events in unpredictable and ever more violent directions. Yugoslavia and then the Soviet Union itself fell apart. Like Hungarians and Czechs in the early-twentieth-century Habsburg Empire, nationality groups in the USSR began to demand political and cultural autonomy. The Soviet empire had held together more than one hundred ethnic

◆ **1999** Euro introduced; world population reaches six billion

◆ **2000** Putin becomes Russian president

◆ **2001** September 11 attacks on U.S.; U.S. launches war against terrorism

| 2000 | 2005 | 2010 | 2015 |

◆ **2003** U.S. invades Iraq, the West divides

◆ **2004** Ten countries join the European Union

MAP 30.1 Eastern Europe in the 1990s

In the 1990s, the countries of Eastern Europe tried to forge their own destiny free from the direction of either the Russia or the United States. The transition, as the new situation came to be called, was far from easy. Old states like Czechoslovakia fragmented and many state borders were contested. Turning definitively from Russia, the leadership of these countries began to look to Western Europe, most of them eventually opting for membership in the European Union. Compare this map to the sharp divisions between Eastern and Western Europe shown in Map 28.3. What are the most significant changes to the region in the post-cold world era?

unstable years of the early 1990s, ambitious politicians used ethnicity as their most effective political slogan, and ethnic violence became the major political tool, continuing to shape post-Communist politics into the new millennium. (Map 30.1) Alongside such human issues in post-Soviet society lay the question of who would control the massive Soviet arsenal of nuclear weapons and the further one of how global politics would shape up without cold war guidelines.

The Breakup of Yugoslavia

Ethnic nationalism came to replace communism in Yugoslavia, shaping political debate for the first time in decades. Tensions erupted in Yugoslavia in 1990 when a Serb Communist, Slobodan Milosevic, won the presidency of Serbia and began to assert Serb ascendancy instead of communism in the Yugoslav federation as a whole. Other ethnic groups in Yugoslavia resisted Milosevic's militant pro-Serb nationalism and called for secession. "Slovenians . . . have one more reason to say they are in favor of independence," warned one of them in the face of mounting Serb claims to rule the other groups. Against Milosevic's desire to maintain a centralized state, Slovenia, Croatia, and Bosnia hoped for a confederation of independent republics (Map 30.2). In the spring of 1991, first Slovenia and then Croatia seceded, but Croatia soon lost almost a quarter of its territory when the Serb-dominated Yugoslav army, eager to enforce Serbian supremacy, invaded. An even more devastat-

groups, and the five republics of Soviet Central Asia were home to fifty million Muslims. For more than a century, successive governments had attempted to instill Russian and Soviet culture, although some cultural autonomy was allowed. The policy of Russification failed to build full allegiance but instead only improvised at holding the vast multiethnic empire together. The USSR fragmented quickly. In Yugoslavia, Communist rulers had also enforced unity among religious and ethnic groups, and intermarriage among them occurred regularly. During the ing civil war engulfed Bosnia-Herzegovina, where the republic's Muslim majority tried to create a multicultural and multiethnic state. Many Bosnian Serb men formed a guerrilla army, backed by the covert military support of Milosevic's government, and gained the upper hand. A United Nations (UN) arms embargo prevented the Bosnian Muslims from equipping their forces adequately to defend themselves even as the Serbs took to massacring them.

Violence in the Balkans was relentless and unspeakable—all in the name of creating "ethnically pure" states in a region where ethnic mixture, not ethnic purity, was the norm. During the 1990s, civilians died by the tens of thousands, as Serbs under Milosevic's leadership pursued a policy they called **ethnic cleansing**—that is, genocide—against the other nationalities. They raped women to leave them pregnant with Serb babies as another form of conquest. Men and boys were taken away and murdered. Croatian forces also murdered people of other ethnicities, and each competing force took aim at the cultural heritage of its opponent. Military units on all sides destroyed libraries and museums, architectural treasures like the Mostar Bridge, and cities rich with history such as Dubrovnik. Ethnic cleansing thus entailed eliminating both actual people and all traces of their complex past. Many in the West explained violence in the Balkans as part of "age-old" blood feuds typical of a backward, almost "Asian" society. Others saw ethnic rivalry using genocide to achieve national power as a modern phenomenon practiced by a variety of politicians, including Adolf Hitler. Still others

MAP 30.2 The Former Yugoslavia, c. 2000
After a decade of destructive civil war, UN forces and UN-brokered agreements attempted to protect the civilians of the former Yugoslavia from the brutal consequences of post-Communist rule. Ambitious politicians, most notably Slobodan Milosevic, used the twentieth-century Western strategy of fostering ethnic and religious hatred as a powerful tool to build support for themselves while making those favoring peace look softhearted and unfit to rule. What issues of national identity does the breakup of Yugoslavia indicate? Have these changed since the nineteenth century?

blamed the former great powers for stirring up many of these tensions in the first place.

The civil wars in Yugoslavia shook Europeans' confidence that they had finally put an end to their heritage of slaughter. Western values were tested still further when, late in the 1990s, Serb forces, having withdrawn from Croatia, moved to attack Muslims of Albanian ethnicity living in the Yugoslav province of Kosovo. From 1997 to 1999, hundreds of thousands of Albanian Kosovars fled their homes as Serb militias and the Yugoslav army slaughtered the civilian population.

was turned over to the International Court of Justice, or World Court, in the Netherlands to be tried for crimes against humanity. In 2003, Milosevic loyalists, many of them in line to be rounded up for trial in the World Court, assassinated the new Serbian president. Across both western and eastern Europe, the language of racial, ethnic, and religious hatred was influencing political agendas, nowhere more violently than in the former Communist states.

The Soviet Union Comes Apart

Amid the ongoing genocide in the former Yugoslavia came the total collapse of the Soviet Union in 1992. A string of secessions in the 1990s and into the next century held the potential for widespread destabilization of regional and perhaps global politics. By 1990, perestroika had failed to revitalize the Soviet economy; people confronted soaring prices, the specter of unemployment, and even greater scarcity of goods than

Yugoslavia in 1990, before Destruction of the Mostar Bridge (top) and after (bottom)
In modern history the construction of a nation-state has depended on the growth of institutions such as armies and bureaucracies and the promotion of a common national culture. In an effort to dominate Bosnia and Croatia, Serbs destroyed non-Serb architecture, books, and such ancient symbols as the Mostar Bridge. Why was it important for the various factions to attack and destroy cultural objects in the breakup of Yugoslavia and successive wars? *Top: Sygma; bottom: Stephane Cardinale/Sygma.*

NATO pilots bombed the region in an attempt to drive back the army and Serb militias. Amid incredible violence and suffering, UN peacekeeping forces stepped in to enforce an interethnic truce, but people throughout the world felt that this intervention came far too late, reflecting great-power self-interest rather than a true commitment to maintaining peace and protecting human rights. Alongside the decimated independent republics of Slovenia, Bosnia, and Croatia, a new regime emerged in Serbia, and Milosevic

they had endured in the past. Although Mikhail Gorbachev announced late that year that there was "no alternative to the transition to the market [economy]," his plan was too little, too late and satisfied no one. After the Russian parliament's election of Boris Yeltsin as president of the Russian Republic over a Communist candidate in 1991, a group of eight antireform hard-liners, from the Soviet vice president to the powerful head of the Soviet secret police, or KGB, tried to overthrow the government. Holding Gorbachev under house arrest, coup leaders claimed to be rescuing the Soviet Union from the "mortal danger" posed by "extremist forces." Yeltsin, defiantly standing atop a tank outside the Russian Republic's parliament building, called for mass resistance. Hundreds of thousands of residents of Moscow and Leningrad filled the streets, and units of the army defected to protect Yeltsin's headquarters. People used fax machines and computers to coordinate internal resistance and send messages to the rest of the world. The coup was in complete disarray in the face of citizen determination not to allow a return of Stalinism, or indeed of any form of Soviet orthodoxy.

Yeltsin Defeats the Communists.   After the failed coup, the Soviet Union disintegrated. People tore down statues of Soviet heroes; Yeltsin outlawed the Communist Party newspaper, *Pravda*, and sealed the KGB's files. At the end of August 1991, the Soviet parliament suspended operations of the Communist Party itself. The Baltic States of Estonia, Latvia, and Lithuania declared their independence in September, and one republic after another followed their lead. Bloody ethnic conflicts erupted in the disintegrating Soviet world. In the Soviet republic of Tajikistan,♦ native Tajiks rioted against Armenians living there; in Azerbaijan,♦ Azeris and Armenians clashed over contested territory; and in the Baltic States, anti-Semitism revived as a political tool. The USSR finally dissolved on January 1, 1992. Twelve of the fifteen former Soviet republics banded together in a Commonwealth of Independent States (CIS), but that hardly ended the disintegration of Russian power (Map 30.3 on the next page).

The coup and the drive for dissolution of the USSR so tainted Gorbachev that he abandoned politics, leaving Yeltsin as head of the Russian state. The change to a market economy under Yeltsin introduced new problems. Plagued by corruption, the Russian economy entered an ever-deepening crisis. Yeltsin's political allies bought up national resources, stripped them of their value, and sent billions of dollars out of the country. By

♦**Tajikistan:** tah jih kih STAN
♦**Azerbaijan:** a zur by JAHN

1999, Yeltsin's own family appeared to be deeply implicated in stealing the wealth once seen as belonging to all the people. Managers, military officers, and bureaucrats took whatever goods they could lay their hands on, including weaponry, and sold it. Ethnic and religious battles continued for the entire decade of the 1990s, and the government undertook disastrous policies. In an attempt to consolidate support, Yeltsin launched military action against Muslim dissenters in the province of Chechnya, inflicting destruction and massive casualties on both sides. The political right appealed to nationalist sentiments in Russia, and ethnic hatred became a standard tool in the new multiparty politics. Political disorder was matched by social disarray as organized criminals interfered in the distribution of goods and services and assassinated legitimate entrepreneurs, legislators, and anyone who criticized them. As a result, Western powers drastically reduced the aid they were willing to supply Russia to rebuild its infrastructure. In 1998, the Russian government devalued its currency and defaulted on its loans, bringing temporary chaos to world financial markets. As the Russian parliament pursued an investigation in the business dealings of Yeltsin, his family, and his allies, Yeltsin resigned on December 31, 1999. He appointed a new protégé, Vladimir Putin, as interim president.

Vladimir Putin Takes Charge.   Putin was a little-known functionary in Russia's new security apparatus, which had evolved from the old KGB. Observers thought that in the upcoming presidential elections of spring 2000 he would garner about 1 percent of the vote. Putin surprised everyone, however; though associated with the Yeltsin family corruption, he proved himself a leader committed to legality. "Democracy," he announced, "is the dictatorship of law." The electorate voted him in, abandoning old Communist bosses, rabid nationalists, and new robber barons alike. With a solid mandate, Putin proceeded to drive from power the biggest figures in regional government, usually the henchmen of the robber barons, and he fired their associates who held high positions in the central government. Ultimately, he also sent into exile Boris Berezovsky, who

MAP 30.3 Countries of the Former Soviet Union, c. 2000
Following an agreement of December 1991, twelve of the countries of the former Soviet
Union formed the Commonwealth of Independent States (CIS). Dominated by Russia and
with Ukraine often disputing this domination, the CIS worked to bring about common
economic and military policies. As nation-states dissolved rapidly in the late twentieth
century, regional alliances and coordination were necessary to meet the political and
economic challenges of the global age. What is the relationship between the breakup of
the Soviet Union over the course of the 1990s and international events in the 1990s and
early twenty-first century?

had gained his billions of dollars from wheedling control of the Russian media and oil. Faced with a desperate situation, Putin aimed to restore "strong government" and end the influence of a "handful of billionaires with only egotistical concerns." Putin's popularity rose even more when in 2003 the government arrested yet another billionaire, the head of the Yukos Oil Company. The pillaging of the country—the source of ordinary citizens' recent suffering—was finally being punished. Yet while cleaning up the government and the economy, Putin continued the destructive war in Chechnya to quell the independence movement. Casualties, atrocities, disease, and physical devastation of the cities continued as a virtual plague on all concerned.

An Elusive Market Economy

Developing a free market and a republican government brought misery to Russia and the rest of eastern Europe. The conditions of everyday life grew increasingly dire as salaries went unpaid, food remained in short supply, and essential services disintegrated. In 1994, inflation soared at a rate of 14 percent a month in Russia, while industrial production dropped by 15 percent. People took drastic steps to stay alive. Hotel lobbies became clogged with prostitutes because women were the first people fired as governments privatized industry and cut service jobs. Unpaid soldiers sold their services to the Mafia. Ordinary citizens stood on the sidewalks of major cities selling their household possessions. Simultaneously, a pent-up demand was unleashed for items never before available. An enormous underground economy existed in goods such as automobiles stolen from people in other countries and then driven or shipped to Russia.

There were, of course, many pluses: people were able to travel freely for the first time, and the media were more open than ever before in Russian history. Some workers, many of them young and highly educated, profited from contacts with technology and business. However, their frequent emigration to more prosperous parts of the world further depleted Russia's human resources. "I knew in my heart that communism would collapse," said one ex-dissident, commenting

sadly on the exodus of youth from his country, "but it never crossed my mind that the future would look like this." At the same time, as the different republics that had once comprised the Soviet Union became independent, the hundreds of thousands of Russians who had earlier been sent there by the state as colonizers returned as refugees to put further demands on the chaotic Russian economy. Some 900,000 returned in 1993 alone. The dismantling of communism was thus more complicated and painful than anyone had imagined it would be.

The Economic Agenda. For many in the former Soviet bloc, the first priority was getting economies running again—but on new terms. Replacing a government-controlled economy with a market one could not happen naturally or automatically but rather required government planning. Given the spiraling misery, however, many opposed the introduction of new market-oriented measures. In Russia, members of collective farms fought to preserve them as a means of security in a rapidly changing world. With the farms up for sale, most collective farmers faced landlessness and starvation. The countries that experienced the most success were those in which administrators had introduced ingredients of free trade, such as allowing farmers to sell their produce on the open market or encouraging independent entrepreneurs or even government factories to deal in international trade. Countries also had to recognize that the emergence of a free market needed time—and governmental support. Hungary and Poland thus emerged from the transition with less strain, because both had favored market elements early on and had hired advisers to speed the transformation of the economy. They set up business schools and other institutions to foster modern trade and industry with comparative ease. Foreign capital arrived as well, anchoring these two countries securely to the world economy.

Elsewhere, however, the transition happened differently. The former Soviet Union itself, in the words of one critic, became simply one vast "kleptocracy" in the 1990s as the country's resources—theoretically the property of all the people—were stolen for individual gain. In this regard, one Polish adviser noted,

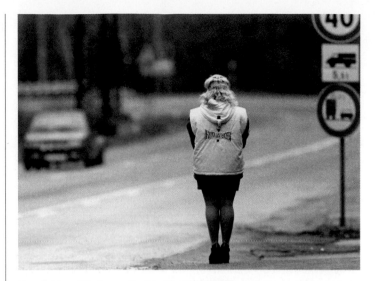

Czech Prostitute on the Border with Germany
The collapse of communism and the Soviet Union created financial disaster, particularly for women who represented more than two-thirds of all the unemployed. Communists advocated the belief that all people, regardless of gender, should work and that they should be paid equally. While this equality never worked in practice, it did provide jobs so that women could support themselves and their children. Under the free market system, women were eliminated from good jobs and given lower pay. Many resorted to prostitution, especially seeking clients from the West. The global sex industry expanded, using ads for attractive women with good skills and then forcing them into prostitution by confiscating their passports and identity papers. More casual prostitution took place on borders with more prosperous countries such as Germany, shown here. *Sean Gallup/Getty Images.*

democracy and a successful transition went hand in hand, for unless the people were represented and institutionally powerful enough to prevent it, former dictatorial leaders and administrators would operate as criminals. In the long run, the worst-case scenario involved post-Communist countries dealing with a cancerous inheritance of corruption, tax evasion, and off-the-books dealing. Moreover, because the socialist leadership had removed their economies from global developments, they had not benefited from technological change, leaving plants and personnel hopelessly out of date, even worthless. In these countries, competition and free trade meant closing plants and firing all the workers.

Talent Flees the Region. A final element in post-Soviet economic difficulties stemmed from a brain drain that plagued the region. The fall of the Soviet empire and the economic chaos that followed brought a rush of migration from eastern Europe to western Europe, often involving those with marketable skills. The countries that received the most migrants were Austria and Germany, which bordered the former Soviet satellites. Migrants left for several reasons, including the lack of jobs, the upsurge of ethnic hatreds, and the availability of higher remuneration for well-educated workers in other countries. Escaping anti-Semitism also played a role: post-Communist politicians used the cruel rallying cry of hatred of Jews to build a following, just as Hitler and many others had done so effectively in the past. Banditry and violence inflicted by organized crime added to the disadvantages of remaining in eastern Europe and helping transform the economy. Some migrants from the east, fearful of reprisals, sought political asylum.

The everyday amenities of western Europe included safe water, better housing, better roads, and at least a minimal level of social services. Although western Europe was now on a firm neoliberal course of cutting the social programs of the welfare state, in formerly Communist countries benefits had disappeared entirely. Pensions for veterans and retired workers were rarely paid, and even when paid were often worthless given the soaring inflation; day-care centers, kindergartens, and homes for the elderly closed their doors; and hospitals and health care deteriorated. Salaries of government employees plummeted. In these circumstances, the benefits of citizenship in western European countries appeared even more desirable.

Chechnya and Central Asian States: The Quest for Independence and Influence

Although Gorbachev had pulled the Soviet Union out of its disastrous war with Afghanistan, his successors opened another war to prevent the secession of oil-rich Chechnya and to provide a nationalist rallying cry to shore up domestic support for the administration. For decades, Chechens had been integrated into the bureaucracy and military. The Soviets had effectively squashed ethnic hostility of and toward Chechens, deporting those who used ethnic politics and importing peoples to regions where ethnic concentrations needed diluting. In the fall of 1991, the National Congress of the Chechen People took over the government of the region from the USSR, moving toward the same kind of independence sought by the Baltic nations and other former Soviet states. In June 1992, after the collapse of the Soviet Union, Chechen rebels got control of massive numbers of Russian weapons, including airplanes, tanks, and some forty thousand automatic weapons and machine guns.

In December 1994, the Russian government sealed the Chechen borders and invaded. A high Russian official defended the war as crucial to bolstering Yeltsin's position: "We now need a small victorious war. . . . We must raise the President's rating." Yeltsin, prompted by his advisers, announced the impossibility of negotiating with the Chechens to counteract the Russian population's opposition to the war. In 1996, the KGB assassinated the Chechen leader Dzhokhar Dudayev with a rocket as he spoke on his cell phone, but the war persisted. There was intense suffering among the Chechen themselves and retaliatory terrorist attacks in Russian cities, particularly Moscow. As the war dragged on, Chechnya's capital city of Goszny was pounded to bits, but Russian casualties mounted too—as did protest against continuing the conflict. In 2002, Chechen loyalists took hundreds of hostages in a Moscow theater; they were killed by nerve gas in a successful liberation attempt that also killed almost two hundred of the hostages. The Chechen war, which continued to unfold tragically and endlessly even as Russia was trying to create a new future, only compounded Russia's problems of establishing a sound economy and credible post-Communist government.

As the war in Chechnya continued, the newly independent states of Central Asia became enmeshed in the politics of oil and Islam, as did much of the rest of the world. Led by strong men, if not dictators, the states of Kazakhstan♦ and Uzbekistan♦ became es-

♦ **Kazakhstan:** kah zahk STAHN
♦ **Uzbekistan:** ooz BEHK uh stan

Terrorist Attack on a Moscow Bus, 1996
Terrorism became more widespread from the 1970s onward, taking many forms and espousing many causes. Although terrorists often targeted prominent individuals for kidnapping and assassination, they also engineered wider attacks on random citizens to increase the loss of life. Post-Soviet Russia experienced such attacks at the hands of breakaway Chechens, whose independence Russia violently resisted. But large-scale bombings occurred in the Paris subway, on London streets, and on Spanish railways, causing these countries to cover public wastebaskets and to train people to be vigilant about parcels in streets, public buildings, and train and subway stations. Terrorism instilled a generalized feeling of fear that the wartime targeting of civilians had become a regular threat in peacetime. © *Ivo Lorenc/Corbis Sygma.*

pecially involved in the intertwined issues of terrorism, local political factionalism, and the global economy, particularly centered on issues of oil. Uzbekistan lent its territory to various groups of anti-Western radicals for the purposes of recruiting and training militant activists. Kazakhstan had huge resources to exploit, which allowed it to play Western oil companies off against Muslim interests in the region. As in some of the other newly independent nations of the former USSR, such as Ukraine, critics of the strongmen were murdered. Democracy and human rights were not an issue: they simply did not exist.

Review: What were the major issues facing the former Soviet world in the 1990s and early 2000s?

❖ Global Opportunities Transcend the Nation-State

Although the end of the Soviet system fractured one large regional economy, it gave further impetus to European unification. The European Community was robust compared to former Soviet-bloc countries, many of which applied for membership. Europe as a whole was poised to enter a new phase—one based on further steps toward unity. This move toward unity stood in marked contrast to the wars and civil strife that plagued many other regions of the world, and the union's economic success provoked the formation of the North American Free Trade Agreement (NAFTA), which established a free-trade zone of the United States, Canada, and Mexico. As new forms of world governance and large regional blocs took shape, people debated whether the nation-state would disappear in Europe as an outmoded vestige of a bloody past.

Europe Looks Beyond the Nation-State

The peoples of Europe took immense strides in the 1990s to move their institutions beyond those of the traditional nation-state. The Common Market had opened the pathway to unified supranational policy in economic matters, and its evolution into the European Union expanded that cooperation to political and cultural matters. The nationalist function of cities diminished as major urban areas like London and Paris became packed with people from other countries, who in turn brought new ideas and attractive new customs. These trends, however, aroused resistance from those who wanted to preserve their own traditions and who felt the loss of a face-to-face, local way of life. For many, globalization posed the problem of preserving the best of global, national, and local relationships, although these might be in conflict.

From Common Market to European Union. In 1992, the twelve countries of the Common Market ended national distinctions in the spheres of business activity, border controls, and transportation, effectively closing down passport controls at most of their common borders. Citizens of the member countries carried a common burgundy-colored passport, and governments, whether municipal or national, had to treat all member nations' firms the same. In 1994, by the terms of the **Maastricht◆ Treaty**, the European Community became the **European Union (EU)**, and in 1999 a common currency—the euro—came into being, first for transactions among financial institutions and then in 2002 for general use by the public. Common policies governed everything from the number of American soap operas aired on television to pollution controls on automobiles to the health warnings on cigarette packages. The EU parliament convened regularly in Strasbourg, France, while subgroups met to negotiate further cultural, economic, and social policies. With the adoption of a common currency, an EU central bank came into being to guide interest rates and economic policy.

The EU continued to play a pacifying role in Europe. It was Greece that pushed for the admission of its traditional enemy Turkey in 2002 and 2003 despite the warnings of a former president of France that a predominantly Muslim country could never fit in with the Christian traditions of EU members. Many EU members disputed this appraisal, but Greece took the lead, having developed diplomatic ties with Turkey. "Turkey has been a great European power since the sixteenth century," Greek prime minister Costas Simitis maintained in 2003. Rejecting religious criteria to resolve political issues, Costas pointed to the common desire of Turks and other Europeans for "democratization and economic stability"—both of them fundamental tenets of the EU. Both Greece and Turkey stood to benefit by having their disputes adjudicated by the larger body of European members, principally by being able to cut that part of their defense budget used for weaponry against the other country. Like the rivalry between Germany and France, that between Turkey and Greece, it was hoped, would dissolve if bound by the strong economic and political ties of the EU.

Drawbacks to EU membership remained, however. The EU enforced no common regu-

◆**Maastricht:** MAHS trihkt

latory practices, and the common economic policies demanding cooperation among its members were not always observed. Individual governments set up hurdles and barriers for businesses, for instance obstructing transnational mergers they did not like. One government might secretly block the acquisition of a company based on its own soil no matter what the advantages to shareholders, economy, the workforce, or unified Europe's consumers. Nonetheless, countries of eastern Europe clamored to join, working hard to meet not only the EU's fiscal requirements but also those pertaining to human rights and social policy (Map 30.4 shown here). As the EU grew more powerful, nations once committed to remaining outside the euro or the EU itself scheduled referenda to rethink membership. In 2003, a draft constitution for the EU was formulated to forge an even tighter bond among member states.

East Joins West. The EU's attractions became clear to eastern Europe, as demonstrated in the case of Greece, long considered the poor relative of the other member countries. Greece joined the European Community in 1981; its per capita gross domestic product was 64 percent of the European average in 1985 and 58.5 percent in 1990. However, Greek leaders and the EU made a real effort during the 1990s to bring the country closer to EU norms. By the early twenty-first century, thanks to advice from the EU and an infusion of funds—8.3 percent of the total EU budget—Greece had reached 80 percent of the EU per capita gross domestic product. It also aimed to develop economic

MAP 30.4 The European Union in 2004

The European Union (EU) appeared to increase the economic health of its members despite the rocky start of its common currency: the euro. The EU helped end the traditional competition between its members and facilitated trade and worker migration by providing common passports and business laws, and open borders. But many critics feared a loss of cultural distinctiveness among peoples, in an age of mass communications, if the economic union turned into a political one. What advantages does the expansion of the EU provide to Europe and to the world? What are the disadvantages?

relations in the Balkan and Eastern Mediterranean.

Hoping for similar gains, the countries to the east moved toward EU membership throughout the 1990s. The collapse of the Soviet system advanced privatization of industry, as governments offered basic services for sale to the highest bidder. Often, only companies in the wealthy western countries of the EU could afford to purchase eastern European assets. For example, the Czech Republic in 2001 sold its major energy

Moscow "Hyperstore"
Daily life in the post-Soviet world was one of extremes. At first, many experienced a sudden collapse in their standard of living, which was already low because of the planned economy that diverted many resources to building cold war weapons. Within several years, entrepreneurs set up vast "hyperstores" filled with more goods than most Muscovites had ever seen before—testimony to the potential for a better life that globalization offered. Along with the unprecedented array of goods, the collapse of communism brought new dangers as well, such as bombings on public transportation and in apartment buildings, hostage-takings, and an increased mafia presence. What is the relationship, if any, between the post-communist terrorism that menaced Russians (as shown on page 1197) and the appearance of mass consumerism in their society? *Peter Blakely/CORBIS SABA.*

distributor Transgaz and eight other regional distributors for 4.1 billion euros to a German firm. Lower wages and costs of doing business in eastern Europe attracted foreign investment, which reached its peak of $20 billion in 2000. The most attractive countries for investment were Poland, the Czech Republic, Hungary, and Slovenia—the most developed state spun off from Yugoslavia. Although the economies of these four countries grew at a faster rate than elsewhere in Europe, unemployment remained high, and they still had no safety net should their economies slow. (See the excerpt from Václav Havel's speech, opposite.)

In 2002, members of the EU voted to admit ten new members, mostly from central and eastern Europe (Estonia, Latvia, Lithuania, Poland, the Czech Republic, Slovakia, Hungary, Slovenia, Malta, and Cyprus), and in May of that same year the Declaration of Rome announced an affiliation between NATO and Russia—once the enemy that spawned NATO's creation. On the eve of Poland's admission to the EU, its standard of living was 39 percent of EU standards, up from 33 percent in 1995. The Czech Republic and Hungary enjoyed 55 and 50 percent, respectively, but in all three cases these figures masked the discrepancy between the ailing countryside and thriving cities. Further, in these countries a far larger proportion of income went to purchasing food rather than leisure and other nonessentials, and on the eve of entering the EU, citizens in eastern Europe were not always happy at the prospect. "It's bad," a farmer in the Czech Republic maintained. "The European Union is already imposing various quotas and regulations on us." A retiree foresaw the cost of beer going up and added, "If I wanted to join anything in the West, I would have defected." Still others felt that having just established an independent national identity, it was premature to join yet another body that would swallow them up.

The economic life of eastern Europe had nonetheless picked up considerably by 2000. In contrast to the first bleak years of massive layoffs, soaring inflation, and unpaid salaries, in 2002 residents of Poland, Slovenia, and Estonia had purchasing power some 40 percent higher than in 1989. Latvia, Romania, and Bulgaria were at the bottom of the former Communist states. Even there, however, a greater number of residents enjoyed freezers, computers, and portable telephones. Automobile purchases were increasing by 10 to 12 percent a year, but 30 to 40 percent of the people were automatically excluded from the consuming public because they simply lacked the wherewithal to make what would be considered in western Europe basic purchases. The shopping malls that rose mostly around capital cities testified to the urban nature of the benefits of the free economy. They also showed that eastern Europe was seen as a great new market consisting of 100 million customers for superstores like the furniture giant IKEA or the electronics firm Electroworld. "When Electroworld

Václav Havel,
"Czechoslovakia Is Returning to Europe"

Czech playwright and longtime anti-Communist activist Václav Havel became the first president of his country after the Communist Party was ousted in 1989. Havel was an idealist who believed that the people of eastern Europe had gained important insights from their experience of Soviet domination. This speech provides a backdrop to the admission of eastern European countries to the European Union in 2004. Despite fears among more prosperous EU countries that the lower standard of living in eastern Europe will drag the EU down, there is also a strong sense that the EU is incomplete without them. Havel details what eastern Europeans have to offer, even to those who have long enjoyed greater freedom and prosperity.

Czechoslovakia is returning to Europe. . . . We are doing what we can so that Europe will be capable of really accepting us, its wayward children. Which means that it may open itself to us, and may begin to transform its structures—which are formally European but de facto Western European . . .

The Communist type of totalitarian system has left . . . all the nations of the Soviet Union and the other countries the Soviet Union subjugated in its time, a legacy of countless dead, an infinite spectrum of human suffering, profound economic decline, and above all enormous human humiliation. It has brought us horrors that fortunately you have not known.

At the same time, however—unintentionally, of course—it has given us something positive: a special capacity to look, from time to time, some-what further than someone who has not undergone this bitter experience. A person who cannot move and live a somewhat normal life because he is pinned under a boulder has more time to think about his hopes than someone who is not trapped that way. . . .

For this reason, the salvation of the human world lies nowhere else than in the human heart, in the human power to reflect, in human meekness and in human responsibility. . . . If we are no longer threatened by world war, or by the danger that the absurd mountains of accumulated nuclear weapons might blow up the world, this does not mean that we have definitively won. We are in fact far from the final victory. . . .

In other words, we still don't know how to put morality ahead of politics, science and economics. We are still incapable of understanding that the only genuine backbone of all our actions—if they are to be moral—is responsibility. Responsibility to something higher than my family, my country, my company, my success. Responsibility to the order of Being, where all our actions are indelibly recorded. . . .

I end where I began: history has accelerated. I believe that once again it will be the human mind that will notice this acceleration, give it a name, and transform those words into deeds.

Source: From speech delivered to the Joint Session of Congress, Washington, D.C., on February 21, 1990. Reprinted in *Vital Speeches of the Day*, March 15, 1990, 329–30.

opened in Budapest [April 2002], it provoked a riot. Two hundred thousand people crowded to get in the doors," reported one observer. A French entrepreneur, commenting on the rapid development of the superstore in the Czech Republic, called it a marvel: "In France it took thirty years to build a network of stores . . . but in the East we only needed three years to provision the entire country with them." Critics worried that eastern Europeans had fallen prey to uncontrolled materialism and frenzied shopping, a Western disease they called "Consomania."

Consumption patterns evolved over the first decades of the free market. At first, people spent money on any available product; it was, according to one eastern European businessperson, "a social act, indicating that one had joined consumer society." However, people learned to read labels and to use the superstores, where prices were lower. Because of relentless housing shortages, young adults with incomes lived with their parents, giving them significant purchasing power and making them the target of advertisers. Italian fashions, fast cars, and exotic products especially sold among the young. Joining the consumer world was a sign of belonging to a global community of those free and prosperous enough to consume.

Globalizing Cities and Fragmenting Nations

The West in the transitional period of the 1990s and early 2000s both fragmented into more nation-states and consolidated new forms—most notably the global city. These were cities whose institutions, functions, and visions were overwhelmingly global rather than regional or national. They contained stock markets, legal firms, insurance companies, financial service organizations, and other enterprises that operated across local and national borders, linking to similar enterprises in other global cities. Within these cities there came together high-level decision makers who interacted with one another primarily to set global economic policy and to enact global business. The high-powered and high-priced nature of such global business operatives made life in global cities extremely costly, driving middle managers and engineers to lower-priced living quarters in the suburbs that nonetheless provided good schools and other amenities for well-educated white-collar earners. However, living in very squalid conditions in the global cities were the very lowest paid of service providers—the maintenance, domestic, and other workers whose menial labor was essential around the clock to the needs and comfort of those at the top.

Global cities were those with the best transport or telecommunication facilities. They thus became centers for migration, whether of highly skilled or more modest workers. Paris, London, and New York were not just cosmopolitan but global, with direct and constant contact around the world. As a result citizens of other cities who took pride in

maintaining a distinctive national culture or way of life denounced them. Global cities also drew criticism for their very concentrated wealth, seen to be taken at the expense of poorer people in southern countries. The need to populate global cities with the working poor gave rise to new enterprises, such as recruiters to fill jobs for which local peoples had no taste. In other cases, however, globalization produced intentional diasporas of willing migrants, such as the estimated ninety thousand Japanese in England in the mid-1990s who staffed Japan's global businesses. Because these migrants did not aim to become citizens, they made no economic or political claims on the adopted country and were thus sometimes said to be invisible migrants. For global citizens, there were no more "traumas of exile" because they could commune with massive numbers of like-minded wanderers in their communities and partake of the multiculturalism of the cities themselves. Global cities were said to produce a "deterritorialization of identities"— meaning that many urbanites lacked both a national and a local sense of themselves, so much did they travel the world.

Ironically, as globalization took hold economically and culturally, political borders grew smaller. There were more nations in Europe in 2000 than there had been in 1945, as individual nation-states fragmented under the rising tide of ethnic distinctiveness. Despite two centuries aimed at Slavic unification and the trend toward larger nation-states, ethnic groups separated in the 1990s and early twenty-first century. In 1993, Czechoslovakia split into the Czech Republic and Slovakia (see Map 30.1 on page 1188). As noted earlier in this chapter, Yugoslavia came apart into several states and Russia fought to keep Chechnya from becoming independent as many other states of the former Soviet Union had become.

Activists launched movements for regional autonomy in places such as France, Italy, and Spain. Some Bretons and Corsicans demanded their independence from France, the latter violently attacking national officials. Basque nationalists in northern Spain continued to assassinate tourists, police, and other public servants in an effort to gain autonomy. The push for an independent northern Italy began somewhat halfheartedly, but when politicians saw its attractiveness to voters, they became adamant in their demands and the movement grew. Given the presence of global cities and fragmenting nations, new combinations of local and global identities took shape. These developments, plus the overall consolidation shown in the growth of the European Union, made the status of the nation-state uncertain.

Global Organizations

Globalization spawned the proliferation of supranational organizations, many of them regulating international finance and trade but others addressing social issues. The **World Bank** and the International Monetary Fund had been in existence for several decades, but as national economies interacted more closely, these supranational organizations gained in power and new ones such as the World Trade Organization came into being (1995). Raising money from individual governments, the International Monetary Fund made loans to developing countries but on the condition that they restructure their economies according to neoliberal principles. Other supranational organizations were charitable foundations, many of them based in Europe and the United States. Because some—the Rockefeller, Ford, and Open Society Foundations, for example—controlled so much money, **nongovernmental organizations (NGOs)** often had considerable international power. After the fall of the Soviet bloc, NGOs used their resources to shape economic and social policy and the course of political reform. Some charitable and activist NGOs, like the French-based Doctors Without Borders, gained money through global contributions and used it to provide medical attention in such places as the former Yugoslavia, where people facing war otherwise had no medical help. Small, locally based NGOs excelled at inspiring grassroots activism. All of these various organizations, both small and large, were in tune with the globalization process, and the larger ones were often criticized for exercising their power with no regard for democratic processes.

While the World Bank, World Trade Organization, and International Monetary Fund forced poorer nations to adopt free trade in exchange for loans and financial aid, the European Union and the United States enacted huge tariffs to prevent cheap goods from competing with their own products. In 2002, the U.S. government under George W. Bush, a staunch advocate of free trade, levied large tariffs on steel in order to win the votes of workers in this declining industry. The European Union threatened retaliation with its own list of U.S. goods to be taxed. The biggest threat, however, came from the financial help given to European and U.S. agribusiness by propping up prices, enacting tariffs, and providing outright subsidies—all of which artificially made them profitable in the world market even though poor countries with lower wages produced less expensive food. Tariffs and subsidized profits, it was estimated, diverted $100 billion worth of business away from poorer nations even though their goods were better bargains for consumers.

Activists began movements to attack globalization itself. In 1998, Bernard Cassen of France founded one of them, the Association for the Benefit of Citizens (or ATTAC, after its French name). The organization, which soon had adherents in forty different countries, stood against the control of globalization by the forces of high finance: "Commercial totalitarianism is not free trade." ATTAC took its major policy goal from U.S. economist and Nobel Prize winner James Tobin: to tax financial transactions (just as the purchase of household necessities were taxed) and to create with the tax a fund for people living in underdeveloped countries. Cassen sided with European integration and opposed the "balkanization" of regions and countries. Instead of obstructing globalization, ATTAC believed, countries needed to show policy alternatives. The organization held well-attended conferences to find new directions, especially to help countries hurt in the crush of global development. ATTAC was but one of several antiglobalization movements, some of which organized mass demonstrations during a variety of international economic meetings.

Review: What trends suggest that the nation-state was a declining institution at the beginning of the twenty-first century?

❖ Global Challenges and Discontents

It is now a common belief that we live in a global age, but once our historical vision widens to encompass the globe we see a picture of uneven development and much room for debate about the state of our planet and its peoples. Despite prosperity for many, the end of the cold war ushered in many challenges. First, the health of the world's peoples and their environment came under a multi-pronged attack from nuclear disaster, acid rain, and surging population. Second, economic prosperity and physical safety continued to elude great masses of people, especially in the southern half of the globe. Third, as suprastate organizations developed, transnational allegiances and religious and ethnic movements also vied for power and influence. Growing prosperity in regions outside the West gave these movements not only financing but also confidence in the idea that it was time for the West to surrender some of its power.

Pollution and Population

Whereas industrialization and a growing population had once appeared wholly positive, people in the late twentieth century became more than ever aware of their dangers and limits. Despite spreading ecological awareness, technological development continued to threaten the environment. The aftermath of the 1986 nuclear explosion at Chernobyl left thousands perishing slowly from the effects of radiation. Levels of radioactivity rose for hundreds of miles in all directions, and by the 1990s cancer rates in the region were soaring, particularly among children.

Other environmental problems were more insidious but also had devastating global effects. Fossil-fuel pollutants such as those from natural gas, coal, and oil mixed with atmospheric moisture to produce acid rain, a poisonous brew that destroyed forests in industrial areas. In eastern Europe, the unchecked use of fossil fuels ravaged forests and inflicted ailments such as chronic bronchial disease on children. In less indus-

trial areas, the world's rain forests were hacked down at an alarming rate to develop the land for cattle grazing or for cultivation of cash crops. Clearing the forests depleted the global oxygen supply and threatened the biological diversity of the entire planet. By the late 1980s, scientists determined that the use of chlorofluorocarbons (CFCs), chemicals found in aerosol and refrigeration products, had blown a hole in the earth's ozone layer, the part of the blanket of atmospheric gases that prevents harmful ultraviolet rays from reaching the planet. Simultaneously, automobile and industrial emissions of chemicals were adding to that thermal blanket. The result was **global warming**, an increase in the temperature of the earth's lower atmosphere. Changes in temperature and dramatic weather cycles of drought or drenching rain indicated that a greenhouse effect might be permanently warming the earth. Already in the 1990s the Arctic pack ice was breaking up, allowing Finland to ship oil along the once-iced-over route in 2002. Scientists predicted dire consequences: the rate of global ice melting, which had more than doubled since 1988, would raise sea levels 27 centimeters by 2100, flooding coastal areas, disturbing fragile ecosystems, and harming the fresh water supply.

Rising activism protesting unbridled industrial growth took decades to develop as an effective political force. An escapee from Nazi Germany, E. F. "Fritz" Schumacher, produced one of the bibles of the environmental movement, *Small Is Beautiful* (1973), which spelled out how technology and industrialization actually threatened the earth and its inhabitants. Behind him stood the legacy of American Rachel Carson, author of a powerful critique—*Silent Spring* (1962), which advocated the immediate rescue of rivers, forests, and the soil from the ravages of factories and chemical farming. In West Germany, environmentalism united members of older and younger generations around a political tactic called citizen initiatives, in which groups of people blocked everything from public transportation fare increases to plans for urban growth. In 1979, the Green Party was founded in West Germany and across Europe Green Party candidates came to force other politicians to voice their con-

Petra Kelly, Activist for the Green Party

Petra Kelly was a typical transnational, who had been born in Germany but who received some of her childhood education in the United States. When her younger sister died of cancer, Kelly became an environmentalist and active member of the German Green Party. Kelly, like many Greens, came to believe that environmentalism involved more than simply eliminating carcinogens in the air. The movement needed to advocate a new lifestyle in general and new forms of political participation. In the excerpt below, Kelly outlines the goals of the Green Party.

The Green Party must remain a movement for non-violent change, and, at the same time, it must use parliament to make the case for non-violence to the electorate. One of the most important tasks for a parliamentary, extra-parliamentary party is to campaign for the recognition and protection of human rights. Food, health care, work, housing, freedom of religion and belief, freedom of assembly, freedom of expression, humane treatment of prisoners—all these human rights have been formally recognized by the member states of the United Nations, and all of them continue to be abused. These rights derive from a human being's right to life. Abuse of human rights can lead to the outbreak of war. Respect for human rights can help to build peace.

The Greens demand the unconditional abolition of all weapons of mass destruction. This demand is addressed to everybody, immediately and without exception, regardless of whether or when others make the same move. The destruction of mankind is the most heinous crime against

humanity imaginable. There can be no justification for it or for any action which might cause such destruction.

The Greens seek a new life-style for the Western world, as well as in their own personal lives. They would like to see an alternative way of life without exploitation, and they aim for non-violent relationships with others and with themselves. . . . We should muster some solidarity, some friendship, in the face of our throw-away life-style. More important than material goods, is enhancing the quality of life and living in harmony with the need for the preservation of nature and cyclical renewal. This is one of the most important objectives that the Greens are working for in the new political culture.

However, there can be no future for the Greens if they go in for gaining power in the same way as the established parties. The Greens are ready to work with others if the demand that parliament should speak the language of the people is finally met. So far, parliaments have acted simply as the executive body of the bureaucracy in the ministries, especially where important proposals such as airports or nuclear power stations are concerned. . . .

We are, and I hope we will remain, half party and half local action group—we shall go on being an anti-party party. The learning process that takes place on the streets, on construction sites, at nuclear bases, must be carried into parliament.

Source: Petra Kelly, *Fighting for Hope* (Boston: South End Press, 1984), 19–21.

cern for the environment. (See "Petra Kelly, Activist for the Green Party" above.) As the horrific effects of utterly unchecked pollution in eastern Europe became known, protest mounted and solutions began to unfold.

Europeans attacked environmental problems on both the local and global levels.

Some European cities—Frankfurt, for example—developed car-free zones, and the city of Venice operated completely without the use of automobiles. In Paris, when levels of emissions reached a certain level, the use of automobiles was restricted, and when the pollution reached dangerous levels, cars were banned altogether. The Smart, a very small car using reduced amounts of fuel, became a fashionable way in Europe to reduce dependence on fossil fuels. Cities also developed bicycle lanes on major city streets. To reduce dependence on fossil fuels, some areas of Europe developed wind power to such an extent that 20 percent of the country's electricity was generated by wind. To eliminate pollution, Denmark banned the use of aluminum cans in favor of glass containers, and many cities in the West began to recycle waste materials. These were success stories, involving changing habits and dependencies, by some of the most industrialized countries in the world. Many of these countries added their signatures to the Kyoto Protocol, an international treaty fashioned in 1997 to reduce the level of emissions and other pollutants around the world. But here, as in other policies, the West was fragmenting: the United States and Russia—among the world's top polluters—rejected the treaty, making cooperation on the environment a dead issue.

Population and Disease

Nations with less-developed economies struggled with the pressing problem of surging population, while the global public health establishment confronted the spread of deadly disease. The cause of the population surge was complex. Whereas by 1995 Europe was actually experiencing negative growth (that is, more deaths than births), the less industrially developed countries accounted for 98 percent of worldwide population growth in part because the spread of Western medicine enabled people there to live much longer than before. By late 1999, the earth's population had reached six billion, with a doubling forecast for 2045 (see "Taking Measure," opposite). In nonindustrial countries, birthrates were much higher than in the West, while life expectancy rose by an average of sixteen years between 1950 and 1980. The world's sole remaining superpower did not fare particularly well by this measure of social health: by 1995, the United States had fallen from the

Windmills in the Netherlands

The oil crisis of the 1970s caused so much havoc in the world economy that many European states encouraged the development of alternate sources of energy. Surprisingly, entrepreneurs turned to an older source of power—that provided by the wind—and constructed these modern windmills that dot many coastal regions of northern Europe. Whereas windmills several centuries earlier had powered tools that ground grain, these mills generated energy that was stored and then sold to regional power companies. What made the windmill an attractive means of generating power? © Benoit Roland/ The Image Works.

top twenty in longevity for both women and men. However, life expectancy in the Soviet Union and then in its successor states was catastrophic, falling steadily from a peak of seventy years for Russian men in the mid-1970s to fifty-three in 1995 and to fifty-one at the beginning of the twenty-first century. Meanwhile, fertility rates were declining. They had been dropping in the West for decades. In the less economically developed world they also began to fall noticeably by 1995. Though birthrates in these countries were higher than in the West, some 58 percent of couples in the emerging economies were estimated to use birth control. Many took the slowdown in population increase as a heartening sign of the potential for taming calamitous growth. Migration and urbanization only added to the problems faced by nations lacking the industrial resources to care for their swelling numbers.

TAKING MEASURE

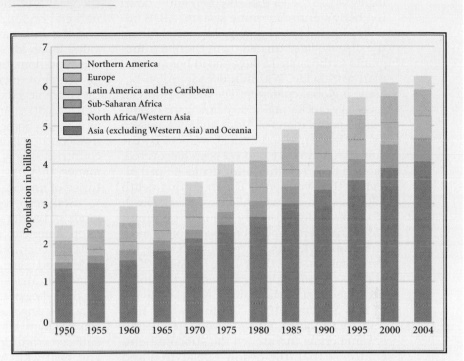

World Population Growth, 1950–2004

In the twenty-first century, a major question is whether the global environment can sustain billions of people indefinitely. In the early modern period, local communities had lived according to unwritten rules that balanced population size with the productive capacities of individual farming regions. Centuries later, the same need for balance had reached global proportions. As fertility dropped around the planet because of contraception, population continued to grow because of improved health. The political, social, and environmental results remain unclear. What are the major population issues demonstrated by this chart?

Western medicine and better health found their way into the less-developed world in the form of vaccines and drugs for diseases such as malaria and smallpox. However, half of all Africans did not benefit from basic public health facilities such as safe drinking water. Drought and poverty, along with the maneuvers of politicians in some cases, spread famine in regions like the Sudan, Somalia, and Ethiopia. Critics pointed to medical practices in the industrialized nations that focused on high-tech solutions to health problems and provided a disproportionate amount of expensive and high-tech hospital services to the upper classes. Specialists performed heart bypass surgery, transplanted organs, and treated cancer with radiation and chemotherapy, while preventive care for the masses received less attention. The poor and unemployed suffered more chronic illnesses than those who were better off, but they received less care. The distribution of health services became a hotly debated issue in the general argument about whether technological solutions could remedy global problems.

Disease, like population and technology, operated on a global terrain. In the early 1980s, both Western values and Western technological expertise were challenged by the spread of a global epidemic disease: acquired immuno-deficiency syndrome (AIDS). An incurable, highly virulent killer that effectively shuts down the body's entire immune system, AIDS initially afflicted heterosexuals in central Africa; the disease later turned up in Haitian immigrants to the United States and in homosexual men worldwide. Within a decade, AIDS became a global epidemic. The disease spread especially quickly and widely among the heterosexual populations of Africa and Asia, passed mainly by men to and through women. By the late 1990s, no cure had yet been discovered, though protease-inhibiting drugs helped alleviate the symptoms. The mounting death toll made some equate AIDS to a Black Death of the twentieth century, reinforcing prejudices and stereotypes about some of its most vulnerable victims. As millions contracted the disease—some thirty-three million in 2000 had it—treatment was often not forthcoming because most of the ill were too poor, living in sub-Saharan Africa. As the twenty-first century unfolded, an unprecedented demographic crisis threatened the subcontinent. On top of that, the deadly Ebola virus and dozens of other viruses smoldered like a global conflagration in the making. Interconnectedness via disease became all too real once again in 2003, when an unknown respiratory illness traveled the world: in the space of a month, severe acute respiratory syndrome (SARS) caused hundreds of deaths. Despite quarantines and surveillance of travelers, economic activity in Asia plunged, threatening the world economy, if only temporarily. Although it was rapidly brought under control through global medical cooperation, SARS showed the potential for medical and economic crisis in the global age.

North versus South?

During the 1980s and 1990s, world leaders tried to address the growing economic schism between the earth's northern and southern regions. Other than Australians and New Zealanders, southern peoples generally suffered lower living standards and measures of health than northerners. Recently emerging from colonial rule and economic exploitation by northerners, citizens in the southern regions could not yet count on their new governments to provide welfare services or education. Their funds generally coming from the wealth of the northern countries, international organizations like the World Bank and the International Monetary Fund provided loans for economic development, but the conditions tied to them, such as cutting government spending, led to criticism that underprivileged citizens gained no real benefit if education and health care had to be cut as a result. Some twenty-first-century leaders from both regions advocated that wealthy countries simply give southern countries the money they needed in recognition of centuries of imperial pillage.

Southern regions experienced different kinds of barriers to economic development. Latin American nations grappled with government corruption, multibillion-dollar debt, widespread crime, and grinding poverty, though some countries—prominent among them Mexico—began to strengthen theireconomies by marketing their oil and other natural resources more effectively. Sub-Saharan Africa suffered from drought, continuing famine, and civil war. In lands such as Rwanda, military rule, ideological factionalism, and ethnic antagonism encouraged under imperialism produced a lethal mixture of conflict and genocide in the 1990s. Millions perished; others were left starving and homeless due to a kleptocracy that drained resources. Although African countries began turning away from military dictatorship and toward parliamentary government, global economic advance was uneven on that continent, and in the twenty-first century the scourge of AIDS added to the weight of Africa's problems.

Emerging economies in the Southern Hemisphere as a whole continued to increase their share of the world's gross domestic product during the 1980s and 1990s, and some achieved political gains as well. In South Africa, native peoples began winning the struggle for political rights when, in 1990, the moderate government of F. W. de Klerk released political leader Nelson Mandela, imprisoned for almost three decades because of his antiapartheid activism. De Klerk followed Mandela's release with a gradual dismantling of apartheid, including the desegregation of parks and beaches. In 1993, the government agreed to a democratic constitution that granted the vote to the nonwhite majority while guaranteeing whites and other minorities civil liberties. The next year, Mandela became the country's president in a landslide victory, formalizing the institution of a multiracial democracy in which international business made strides. In India, Rajiv Gandhi, the grandson of India's first prime minister, Jawaharlal Nehru, worked for education, women's rights, and an end to bitter local rivalries, but his assassination in 1991 raised the question of whether India would continue to have the strong leadership necessary to attract investment and thus to continue modernization. That question was especially difficult to answer. India developed strong leadership in communications and other technology alongside the rise of Hindu nationalism and movements that actually obstructed, even through violence, India's global reach.

Islam Confronts the West

The Iranian hostage crisis that began in 1979 showed religion, nationalism, and the power of oil uniting to make the Middle East an arbiter of international order. The charismatic leaders of the 1980s and 1990s— Iran's Ayatollah Ruhollah Khomeini; Libya's Muammar Qaddafi;◆ Iraq's Saddam Hussein; and Osama bin Laden, leader of the al-Qaeda transnational terrorist organization— variously promoted a pan-Arabic or pan-Islamic world order that gathered increasing support. Khomeini's program—"Neither East, nor West, only the Islamic Republic"— had wide appeal. Turning from the Westernization that had flourished under the shah, his regime in Iran required women once again to cover their bodies almost totally in special clothing, restricted their access to divorce, and eliminated a range of other rights. Buoyed by the prosperity that oil had brought, Islamic revolutionaries believed these restrictions would restore the pride and Islamic identity that imperialism had stripped from Middle Eastern men. Khomeini built widespread support among the Shi'ite Muslims by proclaiming the ascendancy of the Shi'ite clergy. Even though they were numerous and even constituted the majority in parts of the Middle East, the Shi'ites had long been ruled by the Sunnis.

Power in the Middle East remained dispersed, however, and Islamic leaders did not achieve their unifying goals. Instead, war plagued the region, as Saddam Hussein of Iraq sought to make his country the dominant power and launched an attack on Iran in 1980. Hussein feared that Iraq's Shi'ite minority might be convinced by Iran's example to rebel against his regime, and he sought to channel their aggression through a patriotic crusade against the non-Arab Iranians. The United States provided Iraq with massive aid in the struggle against the power of Muslims in Iran. But eight years of combat led to stalemate and extensive loss of life on both sides. Simultaneously, the Soviet Union had become embroiled against Islam when it supported a coup by a Communist faction against the government in Afghanistan in 1979. Tens of thousands of Soviets fought in Afghanistan, using the USSR's most advanced missiles and artillery to combat a powerful group of Muslim resisters. The United States, China, Saudi Arabia, and Pakistan provided aid to this resistance movement, some of which later coalesced into the Taliban. The losing war in Afghanistan so riled the Soviet population and drained resources that the Soviet leaders withdrew the troops in 1989. Power in Afghanistan remained contested until the late 1990s when the fundamentalist Taliban movement succeeded in imposing a strict regime, creating millions of political and religious refugees.

As the USSR's empire fell apart, Saddam Hussein was the first to test the post–cold war waters. At the end of the Iran-Iraq war in 1988, Iraq staggered under a heavy debt and a lowered standard of living. Hussein viewed the annexation of neighboring Kuwait, whose 600,000 citizens enjoyed the world's highest per capita income, as a way to rebuild his economy. In 1990, he invaded the oil-rich country. Contrary to Hussein's expectations that he would be left alone, the deployment of Iraqi troops on the Saudi Arabian border galvanized a UN coalition (joined by the USSR) to stop the Iraqi invasion. A multinational force led by the United States pummeled the Iraqi army (Map 30.5, page 1208).

◆**Qaddafi:** kuh DAH fee

MAP 30.5 The Middle East, c. 2003

Tensions among states in the Middle East, especially the ongoing conflict between the Palestinians and Israelis, became more complicated in the 1990s. As Islam took center stage in politics, Middle Eastern populations divided over such issues as the extent of religious determination of state policies, the rule of religion in everyday life, and access to human rights including freedom of speech and of movement. Conflicts erupted around some of these questions because, as elsewhere, they were also vehicles for political ambition. The increasing demands of globalization in the 1990s pulled other citizens in the direction of secularization, high-tech international partnerships, and a reduction in the costly politics of violence. In 2001, however, violence escalated among Arabs and Israelis, bringing tensions in the region close to the breaking point. In 2003, the situation in the Middle East grew more uncertain and violent when the United States and Britain led an invasion in Iraq to seize its weapons of mass destruction and to overthrow the government of the dictator Saddam Hussein.

The Middle East remained in turmoil, and discontent mounted, even while efforts to resolve conflicts between the Israelis and the Palestinians continued. Peace talks broke down in 2001. As Israeli settlers began taking more Palestinian land, in the late 1990s, Palestinian suicide bombers began murdering Israeli civilians. The Israeli government retaliated with missiles, machine guns, and tanks, often killing Palestinian civilians in turn. Throughout the 1980s and 1990s, terrorists from the Middle East and North Africa planted bombs in many European cities, blew up airplanes, and bombed the Paris subway system. These attacks, causing widespread destruction and loss of life, were said to be punishment for the West's support for both Israelis and the repressive regimes in the Middle East.

On September 11, terrorism finally caught the full attention of the United States. In an unprecedented act, Muslim militants hijacked four planes in the United States and flew two of them into the World Trade Center in New York and one into the Pentagon in Virginia. The fourth plane crashed in Pennsylvania. The hijackers, all but one of whom were from Saudi Arabia, were inspired by the wealthy radical leader, Osama bin Laden, who sought to end the presence of U.S. forces in Saudi Arabia. These hijackers trained in bin Laden's terrorist camps in Afghanistan and learned to pilot planes in the United States. The loss of more than three thousand lives led the United States to declare a "war against terrorism." The administration of U.S. president George W. Bush forged a multinational coalition, which included the vital cooperation of Islamic countries such as Pakistan. The coalition enjoyed quick successes in driving out the ruling Taliban party in Afghanistan, though it failed in its major goal of capturing bin Laden.

Terrorism became one of the most frightening global challenges of the twenty-first century, and there was real cooperation in the wake of the September 11 attacks, as European countries rounded up terrorists and conducted the first successful trials of them in the spring of 2003. However, ultimately the West fragmented its efforts when the United States claimed that Iraq's Saddam Hussein had menacing weapons of mass destruction and suggested ties between Saddam Hussein and bin Laden's terrorist group. The most powerful European states, including Germany, Russia, and France, refused to back the invasion of Iraq the United States undertook in March 2003. Many people in the United States were furious. Bumper stickers appeared saying "First Iraq, Next France," and bars and pubs held regular happy hours to encourage "French bashing." Although British prime minister Tony Blair supported the U.S. effort, the separation grew wider as the United States suggested that Syria and Iran would need to

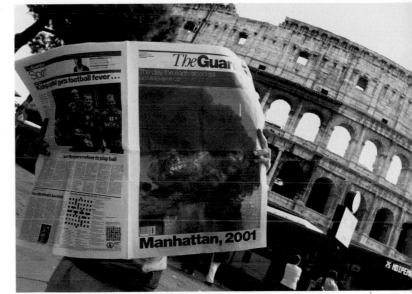

Manhattan, 2001

Europeans React to 9/11 Terror
On September 11, 2001, terrorists killed thousands of people from dozens of countries in airplane attacks on the World Trade Center in New York. Throughout the world, people expressed their shock and sorrow in vigils, and like this British tourist in Rome, they remained glued to the latest news. Terrorism, which had plagued Europeans for several decades, easily traveled the world in these days of more open borders, economic globalization, and cultural exchange, finally reaching the sole superpower left after the collapse of the Soviet Union. © *Pizzoli Alberto/Corbis Sygma.*

be invaded as well. Casualties and resistance to the U.S. occupation mounted, even as Saddam Hussein himself was captured in late 2003. Europeans in general, including the British public, accused the United States of becoming a world military dictatorship in order to preserve its only remaining value—wasteful consumerism. The United States countercharged that the Europeans were too selfish in their enjoyment of democracy and creature comforts to fund military defense of freedom under attack. There was a sense that the West was coming apart.

The Rise of the Pacific Economy

Additional evidence of weakening Western leadership came from the global diffusion of industry and technology in the last third of the twentieth century. Just as economic change in the early modern period had redirected European affairs from the Mediterranean to the Atlantic, so explosive productivity from Japan to Singapore in the 1980s and 1990s spread economic power from the Atlantic region to the Pacific. In 1982, the Asian Pacific nations accounted for 16.4 percent of global gross domestic product, a figure that had doubled since the 1960s. By 1989, the share of East Asia's world production was more than 25 percent as that of the West declined. By the mid-1990s China alone was achieving economic growth rates of 8 percent per year and more, while Japan had developed the second largest national economy after the United States, with Germany in third place.

South Korea, Taiwan, Singapore, and Hong Kong were popularly called **Pacific tigers** for the ferocity of their growth in the 1980s and 1990s. China, pursuing a policy of economic modernization and market orientation, saw phenomenal economic growth in the 1990s as well. Japan, however, had led the charge of Asian economies. Investment in high-tech consumer industries drove the Japanese economy. Thus, in 1982, Japan had 32,000 industrial robots in operation; western Europe employed only 9,000, and the United States had 7,000. In 1989, the Japanese government and private businesses invested $549 billion to modernize industrial capacity, a full $36 billion more than American public and private investment combined. Such spending paid off substantially, as buyers around the world snapped up automobiles, televisions, videocassette recorders, and computers from Japanese or other Asian Pacific companies. As the United States poured vast sums into its cold war military budget, Asian Pacific funds purchased U.S. government bonds, thus financing America's ballooning national debt. Forty years after its total defeat in World War II, Japan was bankrolling its former conqueror and its citizens had come to be the world's leading savers.

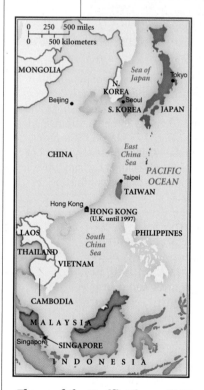

Tigers of the Pacific Rim, c. 1995

Despite rising national prosperity, individual Asian workers, particularly outside of Japan, often paid dearly for this newly created wealth. For example, women in South Korea and Taiwan labored in sweatshops to produce clothing for such U.S.-based companies as J. C. Penney and Calvin Klein. Using the lure of a low-paid and docile female workforce, governments were able to attract electronics and other industries. However, educational standards rose, along with access to birth control and other medical care for these women. Despite the persistent grip of authoritarian government, some of the Pacific tigers ranked high by UN standards for human development.

Mounting economic difficulties plagued Japan and the other Pacific tigers in the 1990s and early twenty-first century. Financial scandals and widespread corruption, which the government refused to address, destabilized the Japanese economy. The stock market plunged, as did the value of the yen. Domestic consumers cut back, and some of those interested in saving sent their money abroad for higher returns. From 1997 on, Japan's depressed economy menaced the region and the world, and little reform was in sight. A severe business crisis struck the Pacific rim as currency speculation and irresponsible and corrupt financial practices—labeled crony capitalism—first brought down the Thai currency in 1997 and then toppled politicians and industrial leaders in Indonesia, South Korea, and elsewhere in the region; by 2001, the economic downturn had spread to Europe and the United States. Europeans were slow to reduce the heavy welfare costs paid by businesses that might have restimulated investment and thus economic growth. Only China continued its expansion. Other economic leaders, notably the Japanese, vacillated amid a growing recognition that in the twenty-first century, global industrial and financial health depended on the highly developed and emerging economies outside the West as well as on the West itself.

Review: What were the most important challenges facing the West in the new millennium?

❖ Global Culture and Society in the New Millennium

As the final years of the millennium unfolded, thinkers began to debate the future, with scenarios changing as rapidly as global politics and economics did. Some saw the world's peoples rapidly absorbing Western cultural values with the adoption of the West's systems of technology, representative government, and the free market. An opposing view predicted a clash of civilizations in which increasingly incompatible religions and cultures would lead to future global strife. These thinkers believed that Islam, with more than one billion followers, would confront Western values rather than absorb them. Finally, there was the prediction of the collapse of the West itself because the United States continued to venture forth as the determining force in the world, opposed by much of Europe, which—as in the case of the Iraq invasion—suddenly refused to obey U.S. requests for cooperation in successive invasions of sovereign states.

Yet the migration that had accelerated since the 1990s, the movement of disease and climate, the information revolution, and the global sharing of culture argued against the cultural purity of any group—including the West. "Civilizations," as Nobel Prize winner Amartya Sen wrote after the terrorist attacks of September 11, "are hard to partition . . . , given the diversities within each society as well as the linkages among different countries and cultures." In the 1980s and 1990s, Western society changed even more rapidly than when it came into intense contact with the rest of the globe hundreds of years earlier. Moreover, national boundaries in the traditional European center of the West were weakening politically and economically, given the growing strength of the European Union and the simultaneous influx of migrants. Culture ignored national boundaries, as East, West, North, and South became saturated with one another's cultural products. Observers even labeled the new millennium an era of denationalization—meaning that national cultures as well as national boundaries were becoming less distinct. But there is no denying that even while

the West absorbed peoples and cultures, it continued to exercise not only economic but also cultural influence over the rest of the globe. This influence, like global military power, was also debated and contested. (See "Contrasting Views," page 1212.)

Redefining the West: The Impact of Global Migration

The global movement of people was massive in the last third of the twentieth century and into the twenty-first. Uneven economic development, political persecution, and warfare (which claimed more than 100 million victims worldwide after 1945) sent tens of millions in search of opportunity and safety. In the 1970s alone, more than 4.7 million people moved to the United States. By 2001, France had some six million Muslims within its borders and Europe as a whole had between thirty-five and fifty million. But other parts of the world were as full as the West of people from other cultures on the move. The oil-producing nations of the Middle East employed millions of foreign workers, who generally constituted one-third of the labor force. Singapore and Nigeria were also home to still further millions of foreign-born inhabitants. The ongoing violence in Africa sent Rwandans, Congolese, and others to South Africa, as its government became dominated by blacks. War in Afghanistan increased the number of refugees to Iran to close to two million in 1995, while the Iraq-Iran war and successive attacks on Iraq by the West had sent still further millions fleeing. By 2000, there were some 120 million migrants worldwide.

Migrants often earned desperately needed income for family members who remained in the native country, and in some cases they propped up the economies of entire nations. In the southern African country of Lesotho, where the soil had been ruined by overuse during colonial rule, between 40 and 50 percent of national income came from migrant workers, particularly from those who toiled in the mines of South Africa. In countries as different as Yugoslavia, Egypt, Spain, and Pakistan, money sent home from abroad constituted up to 60 percent of national income. In places where immigration was restricted, millions of people nevertheless

CONTRASTING VIEWS

The Debate over Globalization

Globalization has transformed the workings of government and industry, provoked the rise of thousands of organizations devoted to supporting and combating it, and expanded educational offerings to meet its needs. As part of the controversy over its value were hardheaded economic arguments on both sides: whereas a Harvard professor advocated the global scale of business (Document 1), two environmental scientists saw globalization as a disaster for the future of agriculture in India (Document 2). Another component of globalization— migration—aroused real opposition. According to a British newspaper editor, it led to political instability (Document 3). Rightist French politician Jean-Marie Le Pen preached "cultural diversity" for the world, by which he meant that the many peoples and cultures should be kept separate, with strict control of migration and of immigrants (Document 4).

1. GLOBALIZATION BUILDS THE ECONOMIC FUTURE

Rosabeth Moss Kanter, a renowned management consultant and professor, cited the advantages of globalization in 1994.

[G]lobalization encourages the formation of alliances and partnerships—cooperative relationships that extend each partner's global reach while each contributes its local competence. . . . Some countries require local partners in order for companies to do business there. But even where this is not required, many companies recognize the benefits of establishing alliances to combine technologies or develop market access quickly. Connection to a global network allows smaller companies to gain the purchasing power or market clout of larger ones.

Source: Rosabeth Moss Kanter, Afterword to *Global Strategies: Insights from the World's Leading Thinkers*, ed. Percy Barnevik and Rosabeth Moss Kanter (Cambridge: Harvard Business Review Books, 1994), 230.

2. DESTRUCTION OF AN AGRICULTURAL WAY OF LIFE

Scientists Vandana Shiva and Radha Holla-Bhar have protested the ways in which economic globalization has affected the environment and local farmers in their native India.

Until very recently in India, biodiversity was something held entirely in common by local communities of people. Resources and knowledge about forest or agricultural properties were freely shared. Whether it was seeds of the farm or plants of the forest, all were clearly understood to be part of the cultural, spiritual, and biological commons.

The idea that the commons could be divided up, purchased, and owned by individuals or companies for their own commercial purposes was unknown to Indian farmers until the early 1960s, when certain international conventions established "plant breeder's rights." These new "rights" allowed commercial plant breeders to take traditional indigenous varieties of seed, for example, "improve" them (often by very minor alterations of genetic structure), and then patent and commercialize them, eventually selling back the patented seeds to the communities that first provided them freely.

This globalization of the South's biodiversity commons was a windfall for northern corporations, which began a race to patent and privatize as much of this natural commons as possible, without ever paying royalties to the original breeders and farmers . . . who gathered all the knowledge about them.

The issue came to a crisis during the GATT [General Agreement on Tariffs and Trade] negotiations [1986], when the United States and other northern countries imposed their new rules of Trade-Related Intellectual Property Rights. . . . The northern countries argued that when southern farmers attempted to retain free use of their own seeds, developed by them over thousands of years, it was a form of piracy. . . .

Before GATT, Indian law excluded the private ownership of patent rights in biological materials. This helped ensure that entitlements to food and nutrition remained as broad-based as possible.

Source: Vandana Shiva and Radha Holla-Bhar, "Piracy by Patent: The Case of the Neem Tree," in *The Case against the Global Economy and for a Turn toward the Local*, ed. Jerry Mander and Edward Goldsmith (San Francisco: Sierra Club Books, 1996), 146–48.

3. THE PERILS OF GLOBAL MIGRATION

In 1995, Martin Woollacott, deputy editor of the influential British newspaper the Guardian, *found the global migration of peoples and their settlement in diasporas or communities of migrants from a different native land far from positive.*

Diasporas have many beneficial effects on both host and migrant communities, but they may also breed pathological attitudes among a small minority. Some may fight their own wars on foreign soil. Or diaspora communities can provide inadvertent cover, in their separateness from the main society, for terrorists and extremists from inside or outside who want to attack their hosts. . . . The global village can be a violent place. Its curse is that new combination of intimacy and aggression, with societies so penetrated by each other physically and culturally that awful damage can be wreaked at close quarters in a way that was not possible in the past.

Source: Martin Woollacott, "Living in the Age of Terror," *Guardian*, August 22, 1995.

4. GUARDING THE NATION FROM GLOBAL MIXTURE

In France, Jean-Marie Le Pen led a popular political party, the National Front, committed to renewed nationalism in the face of globalization. Here is an excerpt from his platform.

The French will have priority when it comes to being hired. In the event of group redundancies, they will be the first to keep their jobs. The immigrants who will be induced to going back to their country of origin will liberate numerous jobs for the French. Through the application of new protectionism, jobs will be protected against unauthorized competition from countries where wages and social protection are low. . . .

Foreigners whose resident's permit has expired and immigrant unemployed people with no more unemployment allowance rights will be repatriated to their country of origin in humane and dignified conditions. Expulsions of illegal immigrants and delinquents will be effectively upheld. French people will be given priority for social allowances, housing and jobs. Family allowances and the Minimum Revenue for Insertion (RMI) will be reserved for our compatriots, and will therefore be revalued. In order to avoid all disguised immigration the right of asylum will be strictly limited, family regrouping will be abolished and French naturalization will become more difficult.

Source: mosaique@mosaique.worldnet.net. Copyright Mosaïque, March 1995.

QUESTIONS TO CONSIDER

1. Describe and analyze the areas in which globalization seems to raise the most questions.

2. In what ways are issues around globalization centuries-old points of contention?

3. Is it possible or desirable to change the course of globalization?

4. List the benefits of globalization and assess whether the benefits outweigh the costs, some of which are presented in these documents.

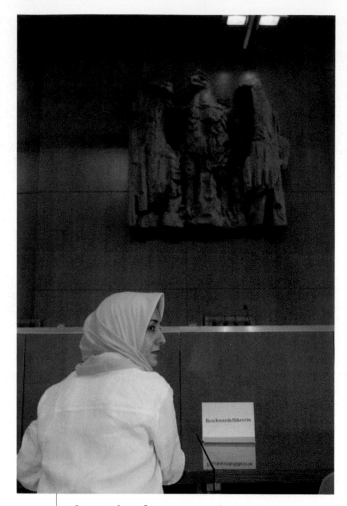

The Headscarf Controversy in Germany
For centuries people in Western countries have debated the relationship between religion and the nation-state. In particular, that debate targeted the need for religiously neutral education in order to develop citizens with impartial judgment and undivided national loyalties. In an age of global migration, the issue of religion in the schools has resurfaced, this time focusing on the headscarfs worn by many Muslim women. Critics see this religious garb in the schools as weakening the commitment to secular education. In 2004, France banned all conspicuous religious attire in schools, including headscarves, yarmulkes, and crosses. Although in 2003 Germany upheld the right of the teacher Fereshta Ludin, pictured above, to wear her headscarf while teaching on the grounds of religious freedom, it simultaneously asserted the right of children to a religiously neutral education. Such complex debates show how individual rights, born in the eighteenth and nineteenth centuries, have become open to intense questioning in the twenty-first century world. *Photo: Michael Latz/ddp, Berlin.*

successfully crossed borders: from Mexico or China into the United States; over unguarded African frontiers; and between European states. Such migrants, unprotected by law, risked exploitation and abuse of their human rights. Those at greatest risk were the eastern European and Asian prostitutes, many of whom were coerced into international sex rings that controlled their passports, wages, and lives. Foreign workers were convenient scapegoats for native peoples suffering from economic woes such as unemployment caused by downsizing. Political parties with racist programs came to life in Europe, where unemployment was a problem from the mid-1970s on. Yet the West remained a place of opportunity and hope despite all obstacles.

Among migrants to the West, women had little to say in decisions about leaving home; a patriarchal head of the household generally made such choices. Once abroad, migrant women suffered the most from unstable working conditions and usually obtained more menial, lower-paying jobs than migrant men or native Europeans. They were also more likely than men to be refused political asylum. Rape and other violence against them, even during civil war, were classified as part of everyday life, not politics. The offspring of immigrants often had a difficult time being accepted even when they were citizens of their parents' adopted land. Unemployment hit them especially hard because "whites" and native-born people received preference. They also struggled with questions of identity, sometimes feeling torn between two cultures. Young black immigrants in particular forged transnational identities, for example, when they created music combining elements of African, Caribbean, Afro-American, and European cultures. As tens of millions of people migrated in the 1980s and 1990s, belief in a national identity based on a single, unique culture was losing credibility.

Global Networks and the Economy

Rapid technological change in electronic communications also made traditional national borders appear permeable, if not obsolete, and it made the world's economy far more global than ever before. In 1969, the U.S. Department of Defense developed a computer network to carry communications in case of nuclear war. This system and others like it in universities, government, and business grew into an unregulated system of more than ten thousand networks globally. These came to be known as the Internet—shorthand for *internetworking*. By 1995, users in more than 137 countries were connected to the Internet, creating new "communities" based on business needs, shared cultural interests, or other factors that transcended common citizenship in a particular nation-state. Communicating via the Internet allowed users often to escape state regulation such as censorship. An online global marketplace emerged, offering goods and services ranging from advanced weaponry to organ transplants. While enthusiasts claimed that the Internet could promote world democracy, critics

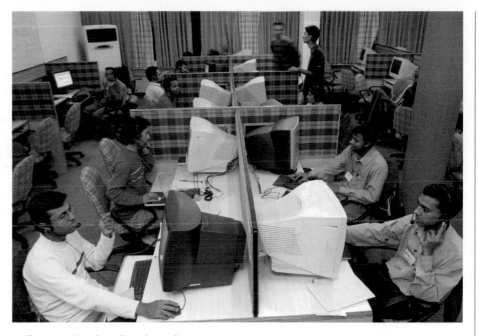

Call Center in Chandigarh, India
Modern communications now permits the outsourcing not just of manufacturing jobs, which began after World War II, but of service jobs to places like eastern Europe, Africa, and South Asia. In many countries, citizens are bi- and poly-lingual, enabling them to service customers in Europe and the United States, such as these telemarketers in India, who are calling consumers in the United States to persuade them to switch long-distance telephone plans. New Web sites like callcentersindia.com offer "one-stop shopping for Indian call centers," which includes consulting, training, and site visits for businesses that want to set up their own call centers to take advantage of the comparatively low wages and reduced benefits. What are the advantages and disadvantages of a division of labor that operates internationally? *Pablo Bartholomew/NetPhotograph.com*

charged that communications technology favored elites and disadvantaged those without computer skills. Yet these skills advanced so quickly that in 2001 countries like Estonia, Hungary, and the Czech Republic as well as Morocco, India, and the Philippines were successfully luring businesses to employ their help desk and other call-center service workers. By the early twenty-first century, three percent of India's domestic product came from the outsourcing work it did for English-speaking governments and private industries based in Europe, the United States, and the South Pacific. The Internet allowed some service industries to globalize as the manufacturing sector had done.

Globalization of the economy affected the West in complex ways. Those who worked in outsourcing enterprises were more likely

than those in domestic firms to participate in the global consumer economy, much of it for Western goods. A twenty-one-year-old Indian woman, working for a service provider in Bangalore under the English name Sharon, was able to buy a cell phone from the Finnish company Nokia and other consumer items with her salary. "As a teenager I wished for so many things," she said of her job. "Now I'm my own Santa Claus." The Irish and the eastern Europeans benefited from the booming global economy of the 1990s. Their new disposable income gave them access to luxury automobiles, CD players, and personal computers that would have been far beyond their means a decade before. The downside for ordinary Western workers was that this global revolution threatened their jobs. In Germany, where taxes for social security and other welfare-state financing comprised 42 percent of payroll costs in 2003, the incentive for business to move to countries with lower costs was strong. Here again, the West parted ways. For instance, book publishers in such places as France and Canada were enticed to outsource more of their work to pools of comparatively low-paid, highly educated editors in the United States who received fewer benefits. Thus, an editor in western Europe might now compete for work with an editor in the United States. Globalization redistributed jobs and reworked economic networks.

The Global Diffusion of Culture

Culture has long transcended political boundaries, and in fact archaeologists point to its diffusion as a constant of tens of thousands of years of human history. In the ancient world, the Romans studied the work of Greek philosophers; in the eighteenth and nineteenth centuries, Western scholars immersed themselves in Asian languages. In the postwar period, cultural exchange accelerated vastly through new forms of transportation and communication: tourism, for instance, became the largest single industry in Britain and in many other Western countries by the early 1990s. Throngs of visitors from Japan and elsewhere testified to the powerful place the West held in the world's imagination. Chinese students in Tiananmen Square in 1989 had rallied around their own representation of the Statue of Liberty (which itself was a gift from France to the United States). In Japan, businesspeople wore Western-style clothing and watched soccer, baseball, and other Western sports using English terms, but the connections flew in many directions.

Remarkable innovations in communications integrated cultures and made the earth seem a much smaller place, though possibly one with a Western flavor. Videotapes and satellite-beamed telecasts transported American television shows to Hong Kong and Japanese movies to Europe and North America. American rock music sold briskly in Russia and elsewhere in the former Soviet bloc. When more than 100,000 Czechoslo-

vakian rock fans, including President Václav Havel, attended a Rolling Stones concert in Prague in 1990, it was clear that despite half a century of supposedly insular Communist culture, Czechs and Slovaks had tuned in to the larger world. Sports stars like the Brazilian soccer player Pelé, the American basketball hero Michael Jordan, and Japanese baseball ace Ichiro Suzuki became better known to countless people than their own national leaders were. In today's world, millions of people might even, at the same moment, be spectators at a live event anywhere on the planet, whether a World Cup competition or an Academy Awards broadcast from Hollywood. With their messages conveyed around the world, even today's moral leaders—the Nobel Peace Prize winners Nelson Mandela, former president of South Africa; the Dalai Lama, the spiritual leader of Tibet; and Aung San Suu Kyi,◆ opposition leader in Burma—are global figures.

Culture from Beyond the West.   As it had done for centuries, the West continued to devour material from other cultures—whether Hong Kong films, African textiles, Indian music, or Latin American pop culture. Publishers successfully marketed the outpouring of written work by major non-Western artists and intellectuals, and Hollywood made many of their novels into internationally marketed films. Such literature won both popular and critical acclaim and exerted a strong influence on European and North American writers. The lush, exotic fantasies of Colombian-born Nobel Prize winner Gabriel García Márquez, for example, attracted a vast Western readership. His novels, including *One Hundred Years of Solitude* (1967) and *Love in the Time of Cholera* (1988), portray people of titanic ambitions and passions who endure war and all manner of personal trials. Another Nobel Prize recipient who won high regard in the West was Egyptian writer Naguib Mahfouz.◆ Having immersed himself in his youth in great Western literature, Mahfouz authored more than forty books. His celebrated *Cairo Trilogy*, written in the 1950s, describes a middle-class family—

◆**Aung San Suu Kyi:** AWN SAHN SOO CHEE
◆**Naguib Mahfouz:** nuh GEEB mahk FOOS

from its practice of Islam and seclusion of women to the business and cultural life of men in the family. British colonialism forms the trilogy's backdrop; it impassions the protagonists and shapes their lives and destinies. In the eyes of many Arab observers, Mahfouz was a safe choice for the Nobel Prize in 1988, not only because he produced a literature about the history of colonialism but also because he had adopted a European style. "He borrowed the novel from Europe; he imitated it," charged one fellow Egyptian writer. "It's not an Egyptian art form. Europeans . . . like it very much because it is their own form." The globally read Egyptian Nawal el-Saadawi was also accused of producing exotic accounts of women's oppression to appeal to Western feminists. Thus, although non-Western literature reshaped Western taste, it sometimes provoked charges of inauthenticity in its authors' homelands.

Immigrants to Europe described how the experience of Western culture felt to the transnational person. The popular writer Buchi Emecheta, in her novel *In the Ditch* (1972) and her autobiography *Head above Water* (1986), explored her experiences as a newcomer to Britain. Her *Joys of Motherhood* (1979) was an imaginary foray back in time to probe the nature of mothering under colonial rule in her native Lagos, Nigeria. While critiquing colonialism and the welfare state from a non-Western perspective, Emecheta, like many writers and politicians from less-developed countries, felt the lure of Western education and Western values. International conflict around artistic expression became dangerous. Salman Rushdie, also an immigrant to Great Britain (from India), produced the novel *The Satanic Verses* (1988), which ignited outrage among Muslims around the world because it appeared to blaspheme the prophet Muhammad. From Iran, the Ayatollah Khomeini promised both a monetary reward and salvation in the afterlife to anyone who would assassinate the writer. In a display of Western cultural unity, international leaders took bold steps to protect Rushdie until the threat was lifted a decade later.

The mainstream became fraught with conflict as groups outside the accepted circles engaged in artistic production. From within the West, novelist Toni Morrison, who in 1993

Toni Morrison Receiving the Nobel Prize
The first African American woman to receive the Nobel Prize, Toni Morrison had used her literary talent to depict the condition of blacks under slavery and after emancipation. Morrison also published cogent essays on social, racial, and gender issues in the United States. *Pressens Bild/Gamma Liaison.*

became the first African American woman to win the Nobel Prize in literature, described the nightmares, daily experiences, and dreams of the descendants of men and women who had been brought as slaves to the United States. But some parents objected to the inclusion of Morrison's work in school curricula. Critics charged that, unlike Shakespeare's universal Western truth, the writing of African Americans, Native Americans, and women represented only a partial vision, not great literature. In both the United States and western Europe, politicians on the right saw the presence of multiculturalism as a sign of deterioration similar to that brought about by racial mixing. It was an era of culture wars—much like that ushered in by the Nazis and by the cold warriors of both the USSR and United States—when strong political attacks on new kinds of thinking and writing took place.

Building Post-Soviet Culture. In the former Soviet bloc, artists and writers faced unique challenges. The collapse of the Soviet Union put literary dissidents out of business. Those who had helped bring down the Soviet regime had lost their subject matter—the critique of a tyrannical system. Tied as their work was to the drama of the Soviet empire, there was no drama left. Moreover the lack of state support meant that authors had to sell their products on the free market in countries where economic conditions were so harsh as to make books an unaffordable luxury. Additionally, there was no consensus on what the post-Communist arts should be. Was everything that had appeared under the Soviets utterly worthless because it was produced by a corrupt system? Some seemed to think so, for shortlisted novels for major prizes in the 1990s were those influenced by Buddhist and other worldwide texts and such writers as Hermann Hesse and Thomas Mann. The post-Soviet legacy was to look beyond the region itself for models to replace Communist ones.

However, in music and the other arts much energy was spent on simply absorbing all the underground arts that had been hidden since 1917. The situation was utterly astonishing as the work of literally dozens of first-rate composers, for example, emerged. They had written their classical works in private for fear that they might contain phrasings, sounds, and rhythms that would be called subversive. Meanwhile, they had often earned a living writing for films, as did Giya Kancheli, who wrote immensely popular music for more than forty films. Other work could now become even better known. Alfred Schnittke (1934–1998) produced rich compositions—dozens of operas, symphonies, chamber music pieces, concertos, and other works—that were extremely sad, punctuated with anger in loud bursts of dissonance, and set in a somber bass register. The public also discovered virtually unknown composers, such as Galina Ustvolskaya, a protégé and lover of Soviet composer Dmitry Shostakovich. Ustvolskaya lived in poverty because she refused to join the Communist cultural system; her music surfaced for the public only after the USSR collapsed, as did unknown works of classical writers like Mikhail Bulgakov (1891–1940), famous for his novel *The Master and Margarita* (published 1966–1967).

Cultural reappraisals were often the order of the day in eastern Europe, and the entire intellectual world adjusted to the novel atmosphere of artistic freedom. Old works were unearthed, and dissident writing was harshly criticized. Eastern-bloc writers who formerly found success in the West seemed less heroic—and less talented—in the wide-open post-Soviet world. Milan Kundera's work, for example, lost its luster. It was, according to one critic, merely a phenomenon of the West's prosperous book contracts, not literature but merely a "line of business." eastern European artists both reappraised their cultural past and tried to redefine the future of creativity.

U.S. Cultural Dominance. The political and economic power of the United States gave its culture an edge. U.S. success in "marketing" culture, along with the legacy of British imperialism, helped make English the dominant international language by the end of the twentieth century. Such English words as *stop*, *shopping*, *parking*, *okay*, *weekend*, and *rock* infiltrated dozens of non-English vocabularies. English became an official language of the European Union, but it functioned across Europe as the main language of such educational institutions as the Central European University in Budapest and the European University Institute in Florence. It has united the scientific community as well as guiding travelers. In the 1960s, French president de Gaulle, fearing the corruption of the French language, had banned such new words as *computer* in government documents, and his path was followed by succeeding administrations; but such a directive did not stop the influx of English into scientific, technical, diplomatic, and daily life. Nonetheless, in another sign of cultural divide, the European Union's parliament, as well as national cultural ministries, has regulated the amount of American programming on television and in cinemas.

American influence in film was dominant, making such films as *Titanic* (1997) and *The Matrix Reloaded* (2003) works that earned hundreds of millions of dollars from global audiences. American pop music and television stars filled the pages of foreign magazines because of their international appeal. Simultaneously, however, the United States itself welcomed films from around the world—whether the Chinese *Crouching Tiger, Hidden Dragon* (2000), the Mexican *Y Tu Mamá También* (2001), or the Italian *Life Is Beautiful* (1997)—the number one favorite foreign film in the United States. "Bollywood" films—happy, lavish films from the Indian movie industry—had a huge following in all Western countries, even influencing the plots of some American productions. The fastest-growing media in the United States in the twenty-first century was Spanish-language television, just one more indication that culture even in the United States was based on mixture and global exchange.

Postmodernism. Some have called the global culture of the late twentieth and early twenty-first centuries **postmodernism**, defined in part as intense stylistic mixing in the arts without a central unifying theme or privileged canon. Striking examples of postmodern art abounded in Western society, including the AT&T building in New York City, the work of architect Philip Johnson. Although the structure itself, designed in the late 1970s, looked sleek and modern, its entryway was a Roman arch, and its cloud-piercing top suggested eighteenth-century Chippendale furniture. The buildings of Johnson and other postmodernists appealed to the human past and drew from cultural styles that spanned millennia and continents without valuing one style above others. The Guggenheim Museum in Bilbao, Spain, designed by American Frank Gehry, was similarly bizarre by classical or even "modern" standards as it represented forms, materials, and perspectives that by rules of earlier decades did not belong together. Finally the postunification rebuilding of Berlin was accomplished by architects from around the world in a variety of hybrid styles.

Other intellectuals defined the postmodern in political terms as an outgrowth of the

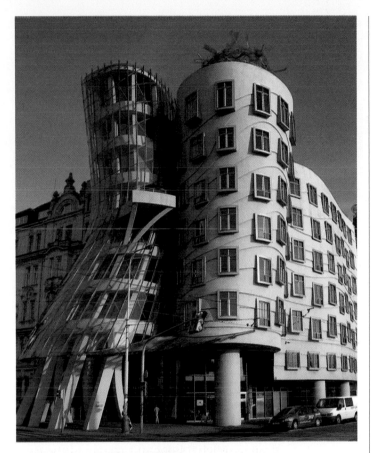

The "Dancing Building," Prague

This building—also nicknamed "Fred and Ginger" after the famed American dancers—rose in the 1990s on the site of an accidental bombing by U.S. forces in World War II. American architect Frank Gehry and Czech architect Vladimir Milunic hoped to achieve something light and pleasure-giving—a mark of postmodern style. Critics, however, felt that the building looked more like a crushed can of Coca-Cola and that it served as an ugly reminder of American militarism and consumerism. Others lamented that in the place of a good Czech building something American would arise on exactly the spot where Americans had left their destructive mark. Defenders, however, pointed to the international cooperation of the design team and the fact that its eccentric look called attention to the destruction instead of simply papering over the wartime devastation with a mere restoration of the original building. Why are cultural works such as paintings, novels, and architecture the subject of such debate in today's world? *Ben R. Hays/brhphoto.com*

demise of the eighteenth-century Enlightenment ideals of human rights, individualism, personal freedom, and their guarantor—the Western nation-state. A structure like the Bilbao Guggenheim was just an international tourist attraction that had no Spanish roots or purpose; consumption, global technology, mass communications, and international migration made citizenship, nationalism, and rights irrelevant to its meaning. It was a rootless structure, unlike the Louvre in Paris. Moreover, the end of imperialism meant an end to the white privilege behind modern civil rights as defined in the eighteenth century. The 1982 American film *Blade Runner*, for example, depicted a dangerous, densely packed, multiethnic Los Angeles patrolled by police with high-tech gear—a metropolis with no place for national or personal identity or human rights. For postmodernists of a political bent, computers had replaced the autonomous, free self and bureaucracy had rendered representative government obsolete.

A third definition of the postmodern involved investigating the "unfreedom" or irrationality that shaped human life. Thus, French psychoanalyst Jacques Lacan, whose writing deeply influenced Western literary criticism in the 1990s, maintained that people operate in an unfree, predetermined world of language. In becoming social, communicating beings, we must bow to these laws, implanted in us at birth. Another prominent French thinker, Michel Foucault, deplored the easy acceptance of such liberal ideas as the autonomous self, the progressive march of history, and the advance of freedom. For him, the sexual revolution had not been liberating at all; rather, sexuality was merely a way in which humans expressed power over one another and through which society, by allowing greater sexual expression, actually controlled individuals. Some postmodern thinkers thus questioned the West's conviction that it had achieved freedom: even in the most intimate part of human experience, people were inescapably locked in a grid of social and individual constraint.

The issues raised by postmodernism—whether in architecture, ideas, or the popular media—focused on the basic ingredients of Western identity as it had been defined over the past two hundred years. Postmodernism was part of a great enterprise of rethinking and questioning that accompanied globalization. We can point to such critical thinking—whatever its momentary conclusions—as itself a key ingredient in the making of the West.

> **Review:** What social and cultural questions has globalization raised?

Conclusion: The Making of the West Continues

Although some postmodernists have proclaimed an end to centuries of faith in progress, they themselves have worked within the modern Western tradition of constant criticism and reevaluation. Moreover, said their critics, the daunting problems of contemporary life—population explosion, resource depletion, North–South inequities, global pollution, ethnic hatred, and global terrorism—demanded, more than ever, the exercise of humanistic values and the renewal of a rational commitment to progress. Postmodernists and other philosophers countered with the question of "unintended consequences," that is, the question of whether one could begin to know the consequences of an act. Who would have predicted, for example, the human misery resulting from the fall of the Soviet empire?

The years since 1990 have proved both sides correct. The collapse of communism signaled the eclipse of an ideology that was perhaps noble in intent but deadly in practice. Events from South Africa and Northern Ireland, for example, indicated that certain long-feuding groups were wearying of conflict and groping for peace, even as other peoples took up arms against their neighbors. Yet the unintended consequences of communism's fall were bloodshed, sickness, and hardship, while the global age ushered in by the Soviet collapse has brought denationalization to many regions of the world. Instead of being advocates for peace, prosperous militants from Saudi Arabia, Egypt, Indonesia, and the Philippines have unleashed unprecedented terrorism on the world, while many in Africa and Asia also face disease and the dramatic social and economic change associated with the global age.

Western traditions of democracy, human rights, and economic equality have much to offer. Given that these were initially intended only for certain people, global debates about

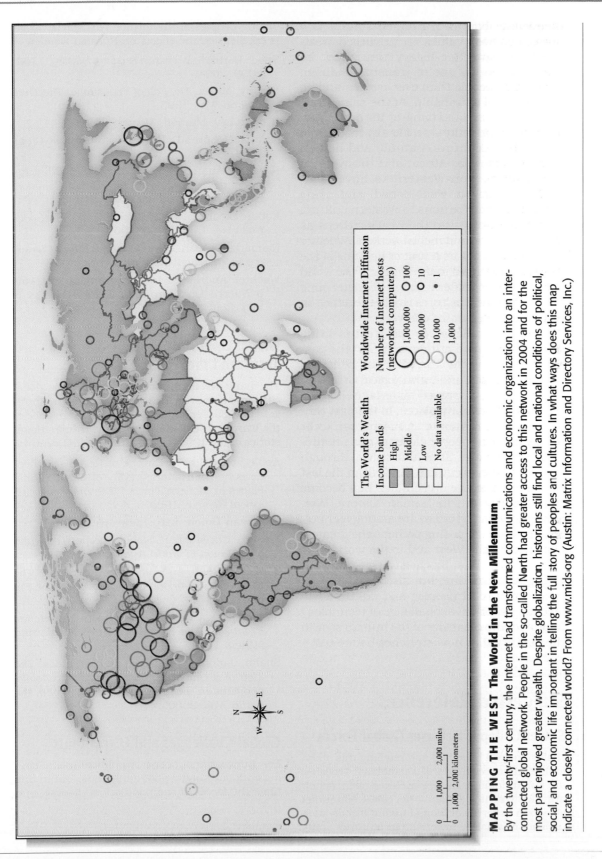

MAPPING THE WEST The World in the New Millennium

By the twenty-first century, the Internet had transformed communications and economic organization into an inter-connected global network. People in the so-called North had greater access to this network in 2004 and for the most part enjoyed greater wealth. Despite globalization, historians still find local and national conditions of political, social, and economic life important in telling the full story of peoples and cultures. In what ways does this map indicate a closely connected world? From www.mids.org (Austin: Matrix Information and Directory Services, Inc.).

The World's Wealth

Income bands

	High
	Middle
	Low
	No data available

Worldwide Internet Diffusion

Number of Internet hosts
(networked computers)

- 1,000,000
- 100,000
- 10,000
- 1,000
- 100
- 10
- 1

their value abound. The nation-state, which protected those values for privileged Westerners, is another legacy that must be rethought in an age of transnationalism, when more people than ever are demanding the dignity of citizenship. At the same time, the West faces questions of its own unity and cultural identity—an identity made from the far-flung cultural, natural, and human resources of Asia, Africa, and the Western Hemisphere. Non-Westerners have challenged, criticized, refashioned, and made enormous contributions to Western culture; they have also served the West's citizens as slaves, servants, and menial workers. Whether the West survives as a unit or not, one of the greatest challenges to the West and the world in this global millennium is to determine how peoples and cultures can live together on terms that are fair for everyone.

A final challenge to the West is living with the inventive human spirit. In the past five hundred years, the West has benefited from its scientific and technological advances. Longevity and improved material well-being have spread to many places. In the past century, communication and information technology brought people closer to one another than ever before. Simultaneously, through the use of technology the period from the last century and to the present one has become the bloodiest era in human history. War, genocide, and terrorism are among technology's hallmarks, posing perhaps the greatest challenge to the West and to the world. The making of the West has been a constantly inventive undertaking, but also a deadly one. What mixture of peoples and cultures will face the paradoxical challenge of technology to protect the creativity of the human race in the century that now stretches before us?

Suggested References

Soviet Collapse Releases Global Forces

Historians will be telling and retelling this story, for the full consequences of communism's collapse are still unfolding. As new archives open, scholars like Wachtel explain the post-Communist situation in terms of long-standing trends such as the obstacles to creating cultural unity among peoples of the former Yugoslavia. Engel is excellent on the effects on Russian women.

Engel, Barbara. *Women in Russian History, 1700–2000.* 2004.

Glenny, Misha. *The Fall of Yugoslavia: The Third Balkan War.* 1996.

*Gorbachev, Mikhail. *Memoirs.* 1996.

Jarausch, Konrad. *The Rush to German Unity.* 1994.

Kazanov, Anatoly M. *After the USSR: Ethnicity, Nationalism, and Politics in the Commonwealth of Independent States.* 1995.

Kotkin, Stephen. *Armageddon Averted: The Soviet Collapse, 1970–2000.* 2001.

Naimark, Norman. *Fires of Hatred: Ethnic Cleansing in Twentieth-Century Europe.* 2001.

Wachtel, Andrew B. *Making a Nation, Breaking a Nation: Literature and Cultural Politics in Yugoslavia.* 1998.

Global Opportunities Transcend the Nation-State

The many new institutional forms, such as global cities and rising regionalism, are outlined in Applegate and Sassen, among others. The advance of the European Union is one of the transnational stories of the 1990s and the twenty-first century.

Applegate, Celia. "A Europe of Regions: Reflections on the Historiography of Sub-National Places in Modern Times." *The American Historical Review.* 1999.

European Union: http://europa.eu.int.

Piening, Christopher. *Global Europe: The European Union in World Affairs.* 1997.

Redmond, John, and Glenda S. Rosenthal. *The Expanding European Union: Past, Present, Future.* 1998.

Sassen, Saskia. *Globalization and Its Discontents: Essays on the New Mobility of People and Money.* 1998.

Shalin, Jamal, and Michael J. Wintel, eds. *The Idea of a United Europe: Political, Economic, and Cultural Integration Since the Fall of the Berlin Wall.* 2000.

Global Challenges and Discontents

The international scene is politically challenging and, one should add, dangerous. But in this time, the forces of overpopulation, disease, and

---

*Primary source.

pollution remain potentially destructive. Huntington and Kagan give two different pictures of world events.

Bess, Michael. *The Light-Green Society: Economic and Technological Modernity in France.* 2003.

Huntington, Samuel P. *The Clash of Civilizations and the Remaking of the World Order.* 1996.

Kagan, Robert. *Of Paradise and Power: America and Europe in the New World Order.* 2003.

Morris, Benny. *Righteous Victims: A History of the Zionist-Arab Conflict, 1881–1999.* 2000.

Rashid, Ahmed. *Jihad: The Rise of Militant Islam in Central Asia.* 2002.

United Nations. *State of the World Population: People, Poverty, and Possibilities.* 2003.

Global Culture and Society in the New Millennium

The fate of cultural identity in an age of globalization engages a wide range of investigation and theorizing. In an age of migration and the Internet, people need to rethink long-standing identities and individual relationships, as Turkle, among others, suggests. Western prosperity is both enhanced and challenged by this technology. The Public Broadcasting Service's Web site offers a wide array of information on current issues.

Agre, Philip. *Computation and Human Experience.* 1997.

Bales, Kevin. *Disposable People: New Slavery in the Global Economy.* 1999.

*Emecheta, Buchi. *The Joys of Motherhood.* 1979.

Hoerder, Dirk. *Cultures in Contact: World Migrations in the 2nd Millennium.* 2002.

Iriye, Akira. *Cultural Internationalism and World Order.* 1997.

*Morrison, Toni. *Paradise.* 1998.

Public Broadcasting Service: **http://www.pbs.org**.

Smith, Andrea, ed. *Europe's Invisible Migrants.* 2002.

Turkle, Sherry. *Life on the Screen: Identity in the Age of the Internet.* 1995.

CHAPTER REVIEW

IMPORTANT EVENTS

1989	Chinese students revolt in Tiananmen Square and government suppresses them; fall of the Berlin Wall
1990s	Internet revolution
1990–1991	War in the Persian Gulf
1991	Civil war erupts in the former Yugoslavia; failed coup by Communist hard-liners in the Soviet Union
1992	Soviet Union is dissolved
1993	Toni Morrison becomes the first African American woman to win the Nobel Prize
1994	Nelson Mandela elected president of South Africa; Russian troops invade Chechnya; European Union officially formed
1995	International congress of women at Beijing
1997	Collapse of Thai currency launches economic problems for Pacific tigers
1999	Euro introduced in the European Union; world population reaches six billion
2000	Vladimir Putin becomes president of Russia
2001	Terrorist attack on the United States and declaration of a "war against terrorism"
2003	United State invades Iraq; the West divides on this policy; draft European Union constitution
2004	Ten countries join the European Union

KEY TERMS

ethnic cleansing (1189)
euro (1185)
European Union (EU) (1196)
global warming (1202)
Maastricht Treaty (1196)
nongovernmental organizations (NGOs) (1201)
Pacific tigers (1210)
postmodernism (1219)
World Bank (1201)

REVIEW QUESTIONS

1. What were the major issues facing the former Soviet world in the 1990s and early 2000s?
2. What trends suggest that the nation-state was a declining institution at the beginning of the twenty-first century?
3. What were the most important challenges facing the West in the new millennium?
4. What social and cultural questions has globalization raised?

MAKING CONNECTIONS

1. In what ways were global connections at the beginning of the twenty-first century different from the global connections at the beginning of the twentieth century?
2. How did the Western nation-state of early twenty-first century differ from the Western nation-state at the opening of the twentieth century?

FOR FURTHER EXPLORATION

To assess your mastery of the material in this chapter, see the Online Study Guide at **bedfordstmartins.com/hunt**.

To read additional primary-source material from this period, see Chapter 30 in *Sources of The Making of the West*, Second Edition.

Appendix

Useful Facts and Figures

PROMINENT ROMAN EMPERORS

Julio-Claudians

27 B.C.E.–14 C.E.	Augustus
14–37	Tiberius
37–41	Gaius (Caligula)
41–54	Claudius
54–68	Nero

Flavian Dynasty

69–79	Vespasian
79–81	Titus
81–96	Domitian

Golden Age Emperors

96–98	Nerva
98–117	Trajan
117–138	Hadrian
138–161	Antonius Pius
161–180	Marcus Aurelius

Severan Emperors

193–211	Septimius Severus
211–217	Antoninus (Caracalla)
217–218	Macrinus
222–235	Severus Alexander

Period of Instability

235–238	Maximinus Thrax
238–244	Gordian III
244–249	Philip the Arab
249–251	Decius
251–253	Trebonianus Gallus
253–260	Valerian
270–275	Aurelian
275–276	Tacitus
276–282	Probus
283–285	Carinus

Dominate

284–305	Diocletian
306	Constantius
306–337	Constantine I
337–340	Constantine II
337–350	Constans I

(Continued)

337–361	Constantius II
361–363	Julian
363–364	Jovian
364–375	Valentinian I
364–378	Valens
367–383	Gratian
375–392	Valentinian II
378–395	Theodosius I (the Great)

The Western Empire

395–423	Honorius
406–407	Marcus
407–411	Constantine III

409–411	Maximus
411–413	Jovinus
412–413	Sebastianus
423–425	Johannes
425–455	Valentinian III
455–456	Avitus
457–461	Majorian
461–465	Libius Severus
467–472	Anthemius
473–474	Glycerius
474–475	Julius Nepos
475–476	Romulus Augustulus

PROMINENT BYZANTINE EMPERORS

Dynasty of Theodosius

395–408	Arcadius
408–450	Theodosius II
450–457	Marcian

Dynasty of Leo

457–474	Leo I
474	Leo II
474–491	Zeno
475–476	Basiliscus
484–488	Leontius
491–518	Anastasius

Dynasty of Justinian

518–527	Justin
527–565	Justinian I
565–578	Justin II
578–582	Tiberius II
578–582	Tiberius II (I) Constantine
582–602	Maurice
602–610	Phocas

Dynasty of Heraclius

610–641	Heraclius
641	Heraclonas
641	Constantine III
641–668	Constans II
646–647	Gregory
649–653	Olympius
669	Mezezius
668–685	Constantine IV
685–695	Justinian II (banished)
695–698	Leontius

698–705	Tiberius III (II)
705–711	Justinian II (restored)
711–713	Bardanes
713–716	Anastasius II
716–717	Theodosius III

Isaurian Dynasty

717–741	Leo III
741–775	Constantine V Copronymus
775–780	Leo IV
780–797	Constantine VI
797–802	Irene
802–811	Nicephorus I
811	Strauracius
811–813	Michael I
813–820	Leo V

Phrygian Dynasty

820–829	Michael II
821–823	Thomas
829–842	Theophilus
842–867	Michael III

Macedonian Dynasty

867–886	Basil I
869–879	Constantine
887–912	Leo VI
912–913	Alexander
913–959	Constantine VII Porphrogenitos
920–944	Romanus I Lecapenus
921–931	Christopher
924–945	Stephen
959–963	Romanus II

963–969	Nicephorus II Phocas
976–1025	Basil II
1025–1028	Constantine VIII (IX) alone
1028–1034	Romanus III Argyrus
1034–1041	Michael IV the Paphlagonian
1041–1042	Michael V Calaphates
1042	Zoe and Theodora
1042–1055	Constantine IX Monomchus
1055–1066	Theodora alone
1056–1057	Michael VI Stratioticus

Prelude to the Comnenian Dynasty

1057–1059	Isaac I Comnenos
1059–1067	Constantine X (IX) Ducas
1068–1071	Romanus IV Diogenes
1071–1078	Michael VII Ducas
1078–1081	Nicephorus III Botaniates
1080–1081	Nicephorus Melissenus

Comnenian Dynasty

1081–1118	Alexius I
1118–1143	John II
1143–1180	Manuel I
1180–1183	Alexius II
1183–1185	Andronieus I
1183–1191	Isaac, Emperor of Cyprus

Dynasty of the Angeli

1185–1195	Isaac II
1195–1203	Alexius III
1203–1204	Isaac II (restored) with Alexius IV
1204	Alexius V Ducas Murtzuphlus

Lascarid Dynasty in Nicaea

1204–1222	Theodore I Lascaris
1222–1254	John III Ducas Vatatzes
1254–1258	Theodore II Lascaris
1258–1261	John IV Lascaris

Dynasty of the Paleologi

1259–1289	Michael VIII Paleologus
1282–1328	Andronicus II
1328–1341	Andronicus III
1341–1391	John V
1347–1354	John VI Cantancuzenus
1376–1379	Andronicus IV
1379–1391	John V (restored)
1390	John VII
1391–1425	Manuel II
1425–1448	John VIII
1449–1453	Constantine XI (XIII) Dragases

PROMINENT POPES

314–335	Sylvester	1492–1503	Alexander VI
440–461	Leo I	1503–1513	Julius II
590–604	Gregory I (the Great)	1513–1521	Leo X
687–701	Sergius I	1534–1549	Paul III
741–752	Zachary	1555–1559	Paul IV
858–867	Nicholas I	1585–1590	Sixtus V
1049–1054	Leo IX	1623–1644	Urban VIII
1059–1061	Nicholas II	1831–1846	Gregory XVI
1073–1085	Gregory VII	1846–1878	Pius IX
1088–1099	Urban II	1878–1903	Leo XIII
1099–1118	Paschal II	1903–1914	Pius X
1159–1181	Alexander III	1914–1922	Benedict XV
1198–1216	Innocent III	1922–1939	Pius XI
1227–1241	Gregory IX	1939–1958	Pius XII
1243–1254	Innocent IV	1958–1963	John XXIII
1294–1303	Boniface VIII	1963–1978	Paul VI
1316–1334	John XXII	1978	John Paul I
1447–1455	Nicholas V	1978–	John Paul II
1458–1464	Pius II		

THE CAROLINGIAN DYNASTY

687–714	Pepin of Heristal, Mayor of the Palace
715–741	Charles Martel, Mayor of the Palace
741–751	Pepin III, Mayor of the Palace
751–768	Pepin III, King
768–814	Charlemagne, King
800–814	Charlemagne, Emperor
814–840	Louis the Pious

West Francia

840–877	Charles the Bald, King
875–877	Charles the Bald, Emperor
877–879	Louis II, King

879–882	Louis III, King
879–884	Carloman, King

Middle Kingdoms

840–855	Lothair, Emperor
855–875	Louis (Italy), Emperor
855–863	Charles (Provence), King
855–869	Lothair II (Lorraine), King

East Francia

840–876	Ludwig, King
876–880	Carloman, King
876–882	Ludwig, King
876–887	Charles the Fat, Emperor

GERMAN KINGS CROWNED EMPEROR

Saxon Dynasty

962–973	Otto I
973–983	Otto II
983–1002	Otto III
1002–1024	Henry II

Franconian Dynasty

1024–1039	Conrad II
1039–1056	Henry III
1056–1106	Henry IV
1106–1125	Henry V
1125–1137	Lothair II (Saxony)

Hohenstaufen Dynasty

1138–1152	Conrad III
1152–1190	Frederick I (Barbarossa)
1190–1197	Henry VI
1198–1208	Philip of Swabia
1198–1215	Otto IV (Welf)
1220–1250	Frederick II
1250–1254	Conrad IV

Interregnum, 1254–1273: Emperors from Various Dynasties

1273–1291	Rudolf I (Habsburg)
1292–1298	Adolf (Nassau)

1298–1308	Albert I (Habsburg)
1308–1313	Henry VII (Luxemburg)
1314–1347	Ludwig IV (Wittelsbach)
1347–1378	Charles IV (Luxemburg)
1378–1400	Wenceslas (Luxemburg)
1400–1410	Rupert (Wittelsbach)
1410–1437	Sigismund (Luxemburg)

Habsburg Dynasty

1438–1439	Albert II
1440–1493	Frederick III
1493–1519	Maximilian I
1519–1556	Charles V
1556–1564	Ferdinand I
1564–1576	Maximilian II
1576–1612	Rudolf II
1612–1619	Matthias
1619–1637	Ferdinand II
1637–1657	Ferdinand III
1658–1705	Leopold I
1705–1711	Joseph I
1711–1740	Charles VI
1742–1745	Charles VII (not a Habsburg)
1745–1765	Francis I
1765–1790	Joseph II
1790–1792	Leopold II
1792–1806	Francis II

RULERS OF FRANCE

Capetian Dynasty

987–996	Hugh Capet
996–1031	Robert II
1031–1060	Henry I
1060–1108	Philip I
1108–1137	Louis VI
1137–1180	Louis VII
1180–1223	Philip II (Augustus)
1223–1226	Louis VIII
1226–1270	Louis IX (St. Louis)
1270–1285	Philip III
1285–1314	Philip IV
1314–1316	Louis X
1316–1322	Philip V
1322–1328	Charles IV

Valois Dynasty

1328–1350	Philip VI
1350–1364	John
1364–1380	Charles V
1380–1422	Charles VI
1422–1461	Charles VII
1461–1483	Louis XI
1483–1498	Charles VIII
1498–1515	Louis XII
1515–1547	Francis I
1547–1559	Henry II
1559–1560	Francis II
1560–1574	Charles IX
1574–1589	Henry III

Bourbon Dynasty

1589–1610	Henry IV
1610–1643	Louis XIII
1643–1715	Louis XIV
1715–1774	Louis XV
1774–1792	Louis XVI

After 1792

1792–1799	First Republic
1799–1804	Napoleon Bonaparte, First Consul
1804–1814	Napoleon I, Emperor
1814–1824	Louis XVIII (Bourbon Dynasty)
1824–1830	Charles X (Bourbon Dynasty)
1830–1848	Louis Philippe
1848–1852	Second Republic
1852–1870	Napoleon III, Emperor
1870–1940	Third Republic
1940–1944	Vichy government, Pétain regime
1944–1946	Provisional government
1946–1958	Fourth Republic
1958–	Fifth Republic

MONARCHS OF ENGLAND AND GREAT BRITAIN

Anglo-Saxon Monarchs

829–839	Egbert
839–858	Ethelwulf
858–860	Ethelbald
860–866	Ethelbert
866–871	Ethelred I
871–899	Alfred the Great
899–924	Edward the Elder
924–939	Ethelstan
939–946	Edmund I
946–955	Edred
955–959	Edwy
959–975	Edgar
975–978	Edward the Martyr
978–1016	Ethelred the Unready
1016–1035	Canute (Danish nationality)
1035–1040	Harold I
1040–1042	Hardicanute
1042–1066	Edward the Confessor
1066	Harold II

Norman Monarchs

1066–1087	William I (the Conqueror)
1087–1100	William II
1100–1135	Henry I

House of Blois

1135–1154	Stephen

House of Plantagenet

1154–1189	Henry II
1189–1199	Richard I

(Continued)

1199–1216	John
1216–1272	Henry III
1272–1307	Edward I
1307–1327	Edward II
1327–1377	Edward III
1377–1399	Richard II

House of Lancaster

1399–1413	Henry IV
1413–1422	Henry V
1422–1461	Henry VI

House of York

1461–1483	Edward IV
1483	Edward V
1483–1485	Richard III

House of Tudor

1485–1509	Henry VII
1509–1547	Henry VIII
1547–1553	Edward VI
1553–1558	Mary
1558–1603	Elizabeth I

House of Stuart

1603–1625	James I
1625–1649	Charles I

Commonwealth and Protectorate (1649–1660)

1653–1658	Oliver Cromwell
1658–1659	Richard Cromwell

House of Stuart (Restored)

1660–1685	Charles II
1685–1688	James II
1689–1694	William III and Mary II
1694–1702	William III (alone)
1702–1714	Anne

House of Hanover

1714–1727	George I
1727–1760	George II
1760–1820	George III
1820–1830	George IV
1830–1837	William IV
1837–1901	Victoria

House of Saxe-Coburg-Gotha

1901–1910	Edward VII

House of Windsor

1910–1936	George V
1936	Edward VIII
1936–1952	George VI
1952–	Elizabeth II

PRIME MINISTERS OF GREAT BRITAIN

Term	Prime Minister	Government
1721–1742	Sir Robert Walpole	Whig
1742–1743	Spencer Compton, Earl of Wilmington	Whig
1743–1754	Henry Pelham	Whig
1754–1756	Thomas Pelham-Holles, Duke of Newcastle	Whig
1756–1757	William Cavendish, Duke of Devonshire	Whig
1757–1761	William Pitt (the Elder), Earl of Chatham	Whig
1761–1762	Thomas Pelham-Holles, Duke of Newcastle	Whig
1762–1763	John Stuart, Earl of Bute	Tory
1763–1765	George Grenville	Whig
1765–1766	Charles Watson-Wentworth, Marquess of Rockingham	Whig
1766–1768	William Pitt, Earl of Chatham (the Elder)	Whig
1768–1770	Augustus Henry Fitzroy, Duke of Grafton	Whig
1770–1782	Frederick North (Lord North)	Tory
1782	Charles Watson-Wentworth, Marquess of Rockingham	Whig

Useful Facts and Figures

1782–1783	William Petty FitzMaurice, Earl of Shelburn	Whig
1783	William Henry Cavendish Bentinck, Duke of Portland	Whig
1783–1801	William Pitt (the Younger)	Tory
1801–1804	Henry Addington	Tory
1804–1806	William Pitt (the Younger)	Tory
1806–1807	William Wyndham Grenville (Baron Grenville)	Whig
1807–1809	William Henry Cavendish Bentinck, Duke of Portland	Tory
1809–1812	Spencer Perceval	Tory
1812–1827	Robert Banks Jenkinson, Earl of Liverpool	Tory
1827	George Canning	Tory
1827–1828	Frederick John Robinson (Viscount Goderich)	Tory
1828–1830	Arthur Wellesley, Duke of Wellington	Tory
1830–1834	Charles Grey (Earl Grey)	Whig
1834	William Lamb, Viscount Melbourne	Whig
1834–1835	Sir Robert Peel	Tory
1835–1841	William Lamb, Viscount Melbourne	Whig
1841–1846	Sir Robert Peel	Tory
1846–1852	John Russell (Lord)	Whig
1852	Edward Geoffrey–Smith Stanley Derby, Earl of Derby	Whig
1852–1855	George Hamilton Gordon Aberdeen, Earl of Aberdeen	Peelite
1855–1858	Henry John Temple Palmerston, Viscount Palmerston	Tory
1858–1859	Edward Geoffrey–Smith Stanley Derby, Earl of Derby	Whig
1859–1865	Henry John Temple Palmerston, Viscount Palmerston	Tory
1865–1866	John Russell (Earl)	Liberal
1866–1868	Edward Geoffrey–Smith Stanley Derby, Earl of Derby	Tory
1868	Benjamin Disraeli, Earl of Beaconfield	Conservative
1868–1874	William Ewart Gladstone	Liberal
1874–1880	Benjamin Disraeli, Earl of Beaconfield	Conservative
1880–1885	William Ewart Gladstone	Liberal
1885–1886	Robert Arthur Talbot, Marquess of Salisbury	Conservative
1886	William Ewart Gladstone	Liberal
1886–1892	Robert Arthur Talbot, Marquess of Salisbury	Conservative
1892–1894	William Ewart Gladstone	Liberal
1894–1895	Archibald Philip–Primrose Rosebery, Earl of Rosebery	Liberal
1895–1902	Robert Arthur Talbot, Marquess of Salisbury	Conservative
1902–1905	Arthur James Balfour, Earl of Balfour	Conservative
1905–1908	Sir Henry Campbell-Bannerman	Liberal
1908–1915	Herbert Henry Asquith	Liberal
1915–1916	Herbert Henry Asquith	Coalition
1916–1922	David Lloyd George, Earl Lloyd-George of Dwyfor	Coalition
1922–1923	Andrew Bonar Law	Conservative
1923–1924	Stanley Baldwin, Earl Baldwin of Bewdley	Conservative
1924	James Ramsay MacDonald	Labour
1924–1929	Stanley Baldwin, Earl Baldwin of Bewdley	Conservative
1929–1931	James Ramsay MacDonald	Labour
1931–1935	James Ramsay MacDonald	Coalition
1935–1937	Stanley Baldwin, Earl Baldwin of Bewdley	Coalition
1937–1940	Neville Chamberlain	Coalition
1940–1945	Winston Churchill	Coalition
1945	Winston Churchill	Conservative
1945–1951	Clement Attlee, Earl Attlee	Labour
1951–1955	Sir Winston Churchill	Conservative

(Continued)

PRIME MINISTERS OF GREAT BRITAIN (continued)

Term	Prime Minister	Government
1955–1957	Sir Anthony Eden, Earl of Avon	Conservative
1957–1963	Harold Macmillan, Earl of Stockton	Conservative
1963–1964	Sir Alec Frederick Douglas-Home, Lord Home of the Hirsel	Conservative
1964–1970	Harold Wilson, Lord Wilson of Rievaulx	Labour
1970–1974	Edward Heath	Conservative
1974–1976	Harold Wilson, Lord Wilson of Rievaulx	Labour
1976–1979	James Callaghan, Lord Callaghan of Cardiff	Labour
1979–1990	Margaret Thatcher (Baroness)	Conservative
1990–1997	John Major	Conservative
1997–	Tony Blair	Labour

RULERS OF PRUSSIA AND GERMANY

1701–1713	*Frederick I
1713–1740	*Frederick William I
1740–1786	*Frederick II (the Great)
1786–1797	*Frederick William II
1797–1840	*Frederick William III
1840–1861	*Frederick William IV
1861–1888	*William I (German emperor after 1871)
1888	Frederick III
1888–1918	*William II
1918–1933	Weimar Republic
1933–1945	Third Reich (Nazi dictatorship under Adolf Hitler)
1945–1952	Allied occupation
1949–1990	Division of Federal Republic of Germany in west and German Democratic Republic in east
1990–	Federal Republic of Germany (reunited)

*King of Prussia

RULERS OF AUSTRIA AND AUSTRIA-HUNGARY

1493–1519	*Maximilian I (Archduke)
1519–1556	*Charles V
1556–1564	*Ferdinand I
1564–1576	*Maximilian II
1576–1612	*Rudolf II
1612–1619	*Matthias
1619–1637	*Ferdinand II
1637–1657	*Ferdinand III
1658–1705	*Leopold I
1705–1711	*Joseph I
1711–1740	*Charles VI
1740–1780	Maria Theresa
1780–1790	*Joseph II
1790–1792	*Leopold II

1792–1835	*Francis II (emperor of Austria as Francis I after 1804)
1835–1848	Ferdinand I
1848–1916	Francis Joseph (after 1867 emperor of Austria and king of Hungary)
1916–1918	Charles I (emperor of Austria and king of Hungary)
1918–1938	Republic of Austria (dictatorship after 1934)
1945–1956	Republic restored, under Allied occupation
1956–	Free Republic

*Also bore title of Holy Roman Emperor

LEADERS OF POST-WORLD WAR II GERMANY

West Germany (Federal Republic of Germany), 1949–1990

Years	Chancellor	Party
1949–1963	Konrad Adenauer	Christian Democratic Union (CDU)
1963–1966	Ludwig Erhard	Christian Democratic Union (CDU)
1966–1969	Kurt Georg Kiesinger	Christian Democratic Union (CDU)
1969–1974	Willy Brandt	Social Democratic Party (SPD)
1974–1982	Helmut Schmidt	Social Democratic Party (SPD)
1982–1990	Helmut Kohl	Christian Democratic Union (CDU)

East Germany (German Democratic Republic), 1949–1990

Years	Communist Party Leader
1946–1971	Walter Ulbricht
1971–1989	Erich Honecker
1989–1990	Egon Krenz

Federal Republic of Germany (reunited), 1990–

1990–1998	Helmut Kohl	Christian Democratic Union (CDU)
1998–	Gerhard Schroeder	Social Democratic Party (SPD)

RULERS OF RUSSIA, THE USSR, AND THE RUSSIAN FEDERATION

c. 980–1015	Vladimir
1019–1054	Yaroslav the Wise
1176–1212	Vsevolod III
1462–1505	Ivan III
1505–1553	Vasily III
1553–1584	Ivan IV
1584–1598	Theodore I
1598–1605	Boris Godunov
1605	Theodore II
1606–1610	Vasily IV
1613–1645	Michael
1645–1676	Alexius
1676–1682	Theodore III
1682–1689	Ivan V and Peter I
1689–1725	Peter I (the Great)
1725–1727	Catherine I
1727–1730	Peter II
1730–1740	Anna
1740–1741	Ivan VI
1741–1762	Elizabeth
1762	Peter III
1762–1796	Catherine II (the Great)
1796–1801	Paul
1801–1825	Alexander I
1825–1855	Nicholas I
1855–1881	Alexander II
1881–1894	Alexander III
1894–1917	Nicholas II

Union of Soviet Socialist Republics (USSR)*

1917–1924	Vladimir Ilyich Lenin
1924–1953	Joseph Stalin
1953–1964	Nikita Khrushchev
1964–1982	Leonid Brezhnev
1982–1984	Yuri Andropov
1984–1985	Konstantin Chernenko
1985–1991	Mikhail Gorbachev

Russian Federation

1991–1999	Boris Yeltsin
1999–	Vladimir Putin

*USSR established in 1922

RULERS OF SPAIN

1479–1504	Ferdinand and Isabella
1504–1506	Ferdinand and Philip I
1506–1516	Ferdinand and Charles I
1516–1556	Charles I (Holy Roman Emperor Charles V)
1556–1598	Philip II
1598–1621	Philip III
1621–1665	Philip IV
1665–1700	Charles II
1700–1746	Philip V
1746–1759	Ferdinand VI
1759–1788	Charles III
1788–1808	Charles IV
1808	Ferdinand VII
1808–1813	Joseph Bonaparte
1814–1833	Ferdinand VII (restored)
1833–1868	Isabella II
1868–1870	Republic
1870–1873	Amadeo
1873–1874	Republic
1874–1885	Alfonso XII
1886–1931	Alfonso XIII
1931–1939	Republic
1939–1975	Fascist dictatorship under Francisco Franco
1975–	Juan Carlos I

RULERS OF ITALY

1861–1878	Victor Emmanuel II
1878–1900	Humbert I
1900–1946	Victor Emmanuel III
1922–1943	Fascist dictatorship under Benito Mussolini (maintained in northern Italy until 1945)
1946 (May 9–June 13)	Humbert II
1946–	Republic

SECRETARIES-GENERAL OF THE UNITED NATIONS

		Nationality
1946–1952	Trygve Lie	Norway
1953–1961	Dag Hammarskjöld	Sweden
1961–1971	U Thant	Myanmar
1972–1981	Kurt Waldheim	Austria
1982–1991	Javier Pérez de Cuéllar	Peru
1992–1996	Boutros Boutros-Ghali	Egypt
1997–	Kofi A. Annan	Ghana

UNITED STATES PRESIDENTIAL ADMINISTRATIONS

Term(s)	President	Political Party
1789–1797	George Washington	No party designation
1797–1801	John Adams	Federalist
1801–1809	Thomas Jefferson	Democratic-Republican
1809–1817	James Madison	Democratic-Republican
1817–1825	James Monroe	Democratic-Republican
1825–1829	John Quincy Adams	Democratic-Republican
1829–1837	Andrew Jackson	Democratic
1837–1841	Martin Van Buren	Democratic
1841	William H. Harrison	Whig
1841–1845	John Tyler	Whig
1845–1849	James K. Polk	Democratic
1849–1850	Zachary Taylor	Whig
1850–1853	Millard Filmore	Whig
1853–1857	Franklin Pierce	Democratic
1857–1861	James Buchanan	Democratic
1861–1865	Abraham Lincoln	Republican
1865–1869	Andrew Johnson	Republican
1869–1877	Ulysses S. Grant	Republican
1877–1881	Rutherford B. Hayes	Republican
1881	James A. Garfield	Republican
1881–1885	Chester A. Arthur	Republican
1885–1889	Grover Cleveland	Democratic
1889–1893	Benjamin Harrison	Republican
1893–1897	Grover Cleveland	Democratic
1897–1901	William McKinley	Republican
1901–1909	Theodore Roosevelt	Republican
1909–1913	William H. Taft	Republican
1913–1921	Woodrow Wilson	Democratic
1921–1923	Warren G. Harding	Republican
1923–1929	Calvin Coolidge	Republican
1929–1933	Herbert C. Hoover	Republican
1933–1945	Franklin D. Roosevelt	Democratic
1945–1953	Harry S. Truman	Democratic
1953–1961	Dwight D. Eisenhower	Republican
1961–1963	John F. Kennedy	Democratic
1963–1969	Lyndon B. Johnson	Democratic
1969–1974	Richard M. Nixon	Republican
1974–1977	Gerald R. Ford	Republican
1977–1981	Jimmy Carter	Democratic
1981–1989	Ronald W. Reagan	Republican
1989–1993	George H. W. Bush	Republican
1993–2001	William J. Clinton	Democratic
2001–	George W. Bush	Republican

MAJOR WARS OF THE MODERN ERA

1546–1555	German Wars of Religion
1526–1571	Ottoman wars
1562–1598	French Wars of Religion
1566–1609, 1621–1648	Revolt of the Netherlands
1618–1648	Thirty Years' War
1642–1648	English Civil War
1652–1678	Anglo-Dutch Wars
1667–1697	Wars of Louis XIV
1683–1697	Ottoman wars
1689–1697	War of the League of Augsburg
1702–1714	War of Spanish Succession
1702–1721	Great Northern War
1714–1718	Ottoman wars
1740–1748	War of Austrian Succession
1756–1763	Seven Years' War
1775–1781	American Revolution
1796–1815	Napoleonic wars
1846–1848	Mexican-American War
1853–1856	Crimean War
1861–1865	United States Civil War
1870–1871	Franco-Prussian War
1894–1895	Sino-Japanese War
1898	Spanish-American War
1904–1905	Russo-Japanese War
1914–1918	World War I
1939–1945	World War II
1946–1975	Vietnam wars
1950–1953	Korean War
1990–1991	Persian Gulf War
1991–1997	Civil War in the former Yugoslavia
2003	Iraq War

Glossary of Key Terms

This glossary of key terms contains definitions of words and ideas that are central to your understanding of the material covered in this textbook. Each term in the glossary is in boldface in the text when it is first defined, then listed again in the corresponding Chapter Review section to signal its importance. We have also included the page number on which the full discussion of the term appears so that you can easily locate the complete explanation to strengthen your historical vocabulary.

For words not defined here, two additional resources may be useful: the index, which will direct you to many more topics discussed in the text, and a good dictionary.

abolitionists (713): Advocates of the abolition of the slave trade and of slavery.

anarchism (907): The belief that people should not have government; it was popular among peasants and workers in the last half of the nineteenth century and the first decades of the twentieth.

appeasement (1075): The strategy of preventing a war by making concessions for legitimate grievances.

art nouveau (974): A successful style in the arts, household and fashion design, and graphics that featured flowing, sinuous lines that contrasted with the mechanical influence of the early twentieth century. It borrowed many of its motifs from Asian and African art and was internationally popular.

atheist (712): A person who does not believe in the existence of God.

Atlantic revolutions (749): A term historians use to refer to protest movements that appeared on both sides of the Atlantic in the late 1780s: the new United States prepared a new constitution after winning its independence from Great Britain, while organized revolts occurred in the Dutch Republic, the Austrian Netherlands, and France.

Blitzkrieg (1077): Literally, "lightning war"; a strategy for the conduct of war in which motorized firepower quickly and overwhelmingly attacks the enemy, leaving it in a state of shock and awe and unable to resist psychologically or militarily.

Boer War (985): The war between Britain and Boer (originally Dutch) inhabitants of South Africa for control of the region. Lasting between 1899 and 1902, the war convinced many British people that empire was wrong or at least too costly to maintain.

Bolshevik Revolution (1017): The overthrow of Russia's Provisional Government in the fall of 1917 by V. I. Lenin and his Bolshevik forces because of the government's continuing defeat in the war, its failure to bring political reform, and a further decline in the conditions of everyday life.

capital-intensive industry (920): A mid- to late-nineteenth-century development in industry that required great investments of money for machinery and infrastructure to make a profit; it contrasts with labor-intensive industry.

Chartism (855): The movement of supporters of the People's Charter (drawn up in Britain in 1838), which demanded universal manhood suffrage, vote by secret ballot, equal electoral districts, annual elections, and the elimination of property qualifications for and the payment of stipends to members of Parliament. Chartism attracted many working-class adherents.

cholera (829): An epidemic, usually fatal disease that appeared in the 1830s in Europe; it is caused by a waterborne bacterium that induces violent vomiting and diarrhea and leaves the skin blue, eyes sunken and dull, and hands and feet ice cold.

Christian Democrats (1110): Powerful center to center-right political parties that evolved in the late 1940s from former Catholic parties of the pre–World War II period.

Civil Code (792): The French legal code formulated by Napoleon in 1804 (hence also called the Napoleonic Code); it assured equal treatment under the law to all classes of men and guaranteed religious liberty but curtailed many of the rights of women.

civil disobedience (1054): Deliberately but peacefully breaking the law, a tactic used by Mohandas Gandhi in India and earlier by British suffragists to protest oppression and obtain political change.

cold war (1098): The rivalry between the United States and the Soviet Union following World War II that lead to massive growth in nuclear weapons on both sides.

communists (855): Those socialists who after 1840 (when the word was first used) advocated the abolition of private property in favor of communal, collective ownership.

conservatism (808): A political doctrine that emerged after 1815 and rejected much of the Enlightenment and the French Revolution, preferring monarchies over republics, tradition over revolution, and established religion over Enlightenment skepticism.

consuls (789): The title given to the three leaders of the new French government installed in 1799; in fact, Napoleon as First Consul held the reins of power.

Continental System (801): The system inaugurated by Napoleon's order in 1806 that France and its satellites boycott British goods; after some early successes in blocking British trade, the system was undermined by smuggling.

Corn Laws (853): Tariffs on grain in Great Britain that benefited landowners by preventing the import of cheap foreign grain; after agitation by the Anti–Corn Law League, the tariffs were repealed by the British government in 1846.

Cuban missile crisis (1133): The confrontation in 1962 between the United States and the USSR over Soviet installation of missiles off the American coast; both John F. Kennedy and Nikita Khrushchev backed down from using nuclear weapons to resolve the situation.

cult of the offensive (1006): A military strategy of constantly attacking the enemy, believed to be the key to winning World War I. Given the firepower of both sides, however, this strategy boosted casualties and failed to bring victory to either side.

daguerreotype (834): A form of photography named after its inventor, Jacques Daguerre.

de-Christianization (766): The campaign of extremist republicans against organized churches; militants forced priests to give up their vocations and marry, sold off the buildings of the Catholic church, and set up festivals of reason to compete with Catholicism.

Declaration of the Rights of Man and Citizen (757): The preamble to the French constitution drafted in August 1789; it established the sovereignty of the nation and the equality of rights of citizens and granted freedom of religion, freedom of the press, equality of taxation, and equality before the law.

decolonization (1118): The process—both violent and peaceful—by which colonies gained their independence from the imperial powers after World War II.

deist (712): A person who believes in God but gives him no active role in human affairs. Deists of the Enlightenment believed that a benevolent, all-knowing God had designed the universe and set it in motion but no longer intervened in the functioning of the universe. A deist might belong to no particular church (Catholic or Protestant).

DNA (1144): The genetic material that forms the basis of each cell; the discovery of its structure in 1952 revolutionized genetics, molecular biology, and other scientific and medical fields.

domesticity (847): The set of beliefs, prevailing in the early to mid-nineteenth century, purporting that women should live their lives within the domestic sphere and devote themselves to their families and the home.

Dual Alliance (953): A defensive alliance forged by German chancellor Otto von Bismarck between Germany and Austria-Hungary in 1879 as part of his system of alliances to prevent or limit war; joined by Italy in 1882 as a third partner and then called the Triple Alliance.

dual monarchy (887): A shared power arrangement between the Habsburg Empire and Hungary after the Prussian defeat of the Austrian Empire in 1867.

Duma (989): The Russian parliament set up in the aftermath of the outbreak of the Revolution of 1905. Few Russians could actually vote for representatives, but it held out promise to those of all classes.

economic miracle (1108): Europe's rapid recovery from the devastation in World War II and the striking prosperity of Germany in particular.

Enabling Act (1062): The legislation passed in 1933 suspending constitutional government for four years in order to meet the crisis in the German economy.

enlightened despots (729): A political term that refers to rulers who tried to promote reform without giving up their own supreme political power; the best examples were Catherine the Great of Russia, Frederick the Great of Prussia, and Joseph II of Austria. Also called enlightened absolutists.

Entente Cordiale (993): An alliance between Britain and France that began with an agreement in 1904 to honor colonial holdings.

Estates General (753): A body of deputies from the three estates, or orders, of France; the clergy (First Estate), the nobility (Second Estate), and everyone else (Third Estate); disputes about procedures of voting in this body in 1789 opened the way to the French Revolution.

ethnic cleansing (1189): The mass murder—genocide—of people of different ethnicities during the wars that developed when states declared themselves independent from Yugoslavia in the 1990s.

euro (1185): The common currency accepted by twelve of the fifteen members of the European Union. It went into effect gradually, becoming the denominator of business transfers in 1999 and entering public circulation in 2002.

European Economic Community (EEC or Common Market) (1112): A consortium of six European countries established to promote free trade and economic co-operation among its members. Since its founding in 1957, it has expanded its membership and also its sphere of activity.

European Union (EU) (1196): Formerly the European Economic Community (EEC, or Common Market), and then the European Community; formed in 1994 by the terms of the 1992 Maastricht Treaty. Its members have political ties through the European parliament as well as long-standing common economic, legal, and business mechanisms; as of 2004, it consists of twenty-five member countries.

existentialism (1126): A philosophy prominent after World War II that stressed the importance of action in the creation of an authentic self.

family allowance (1066): Government funds given to families with children in order to boost the birthrate in totalitarian and democratic countries alike.

Fascism (1041): A doctrine advocated by Benito Mussolini that glorified the state over the people and their individual or civil rights. Beginning in the 1920s, Fascism was politically grounded in an instinctual male violence and opposed to the so-called antinationalist socialist movement and parliamentary rule.

First Consul (781): The most important of the three consuls established by the French Constitution of 1800; the title, given to Napoleon Bonaparte, was taken from the ancient Roman republic.

five-year plans (1055): Centralized programs for long-range economic development first used by Joseph Stalin and copied by Adolf Hitler; these plans set production priorities and give production targets for individual industries and agriculture.

Fourteen Points (1022): A proposal by U.S. president Woodrow Wilson for peace during World War I. The Fourteen Points called for a peace based on settlement rather than on victory or a definitive conquest and thus helped bring about the surrender of the Central Powers.

Freemasons (723): Members of Masonic lodges, which were based on the rituals of stonemasons' guilds and provided a place where nobles and middle-class professionals (and even some artisans) shared interest in the Enlightenment and reform; lodges drew up constitutions and voted in elections. The movement began in Great Britain and spread eastward across Europe.

glasnost (1174): Literally, "openness" or "publicity"; a policy instituted in the 1980s by Soviet premier Mikhail Gorbachev calling for greater openness in speech and in thinking, which translated to the reduction of censorship in publishing, radio, television, and other media.

global warming (1202): An increase in the temperature of the earth's lower atmosphere resulting from a buildup of chemical emissions causing a greenhouse effect.

Great Fear (757): The term used by historians to describe the rural panic of 1789; fears of an aristocratic plot to pay beggars and vagrants to burn crops or barns sometimes turned into peasant attacks on aristocrats or on seigneurial records of peasants' dues.

Hasidim (721): A religious group within Judaism whose members pray in a highly emotional fashion and wear rustic clothing to emphasize their piety; founded by Ba'al Shem Tov in the 1740s and 1750s, and especially important in Poland-Lithuania. (The word is Hebrew for "most pious.")

Haussmannization (891): The process of urban renewal followed by many governments after the middle of the nineteenth century and named after its prime practitioner, Georges-Eugène Haussmann.

home rule (948): The right to an independent parliament demanded by the Irish and resisted by the British from the second half of the nineteenth century on.

ideology (812): A coherent set of beliefs (conservatism, liberalism, socialism, etc.) about the way the social and political order should be organized and changed; the word was coined during the French Revolution.

imperialism (848): European dominance of the non-West through economic exploitation and political rule (as distinct from the word *colonialism*, which usually implied establishment of settler colonies, often with slavery as the labor system); the word was coined in the mid-nineteenth century.

impressionism (944): A mid- to late-nineteenth-century artistic style that captured the sensation of light in images, derived from Japanese influences and from an opposition to the realism of photographs.

in vitro fertilization (1146): A process developed in the 1970s by which eggs are fertilized by sperm outside the human body and then implanted in a woman's uterus.

industrialization (728): The process of economic transformation that began in Great Britain in the 1770s and 1780s; its most striking features were the introduction of steam engines to power machinery and the concentration of those machines in factories that mass-produced cloth from cotton grown in the British colonies.

Jacobin Club (761): The first and most influential of the political clubs formed during the French Revolution; the Paris Jacobin Club inspired the formation of a national network of Jacobin clubs whose members dominated the revolutionary government during the period known as the Terror.

Kulturkampf (903): Literally, a "culture war," but in the 1870s the word indicated German chancellor Otto von Bismarck's attempt to fight the cultural power of the church through a series of injurious policies.

laissez-faire (716): An economic doctrine developed by Adam Smith based on his reading of the French physiocrats who advocated freeing the economy from government intervention and control. (The term is French for "to leave alone.")

League of Nations (1023): The international organization set up following World War I to maintain peace by arbitrating disputes and promoting collective security.

Lebensraum (1072): Literally, "living space"; the land that Adolf Hitler proposed to conquer so that true Aryans might have sufficient space to live their noble lives.

liberalism (812): An economic and political doctrine that emphasized free trade and the constitutional guarantees of individual rights such as freedom of speech and religion; liberals were favorable to the Enlightenment but critical of the violence of the French Revolution.

limited liability corporation (921): A legal entity developed in the mid- to late-nineteenth century in which the amount that owners of a factory or other enterprise owed creditors was restricted (limited) in case of financial failure.

lithograph (829): A mass-produced print using an inked stone (the Greek *lithos* means "stone"); lithographs played a key role in social commentary and political discussion in the 1830s–1850s.

Maastricht Treaty (1196): The agreement among the members of the European Community to have a closer alliance, including the use of common passports and eventually the development of a common currency; by the terms of this treaty, the European Community became the European Union (EU) in 1994.

mandate system (1026): The League of Nations covenant that granted the victors of World War I political control over Germany's former colonies.

march on Rome (1041): The threat by Benito Mussolini and his followers in 1922 to take over the Italian government in a military convergence on Rome; the march forced King Victor Emmanuel II to make Mussolini prime minister.

Marshall Plan (1103): A post–World War II program funded by the United States to get Europe back on its feet economically and thereby reduce the appeal of communism. It played an important role in the rebirth of European prosperity in the 1950s.

Marxism (907): A body of thought about the organization of production, social inequality, and the processes of revolutionary change as devised by the philosopher and economist Karl Marx.

Meiji Restoration (898): A change in the Japanese government in 1867 that reinstalled the emperor as legitimate ruler in place of the military leader, or shogun.

Methodism (721): A religious movement founded by John Wesley that broke away from the Anglican church in Great Britain and insisted on strict self-discipline and a "methodical" approach to religious study and observance. Wesley emphasized an intense personal experience of salvation and a life of thrift, abstinence, and hard work.

mir (880): A Russian farm community fortified by the emancipation of the serfs in 1861 that provided for holding the land in common and regulating the movements of any individual by the group. The mir hindered the free movement of labor and individual agricultural enterprise, including modernization.

Mitteleuropa (993): Literally, "central Europe," but used by influential military leaders in Germany before World War I to refer to land in both central and eastern Europe that they hoped to acquire as a substitute for vast colonial empires in Africa and Asia. This territory ultimately formed a war aim in World War I and for Hitler thereafter.

modernism (970): Changes in the arts at the end of the nineteenth century that featured a break with realism in art and literature and with lyricism in music.

multinational corporation (1146): A business that operates in many foreign countries by sending large segments of its manufacturing, finance, sales, and other business components abroad.

nationalism (814): A political doctrine that holds that all peoples derive their identities from their nations and should have states to express their common language and shared cultural traditions.

nation-state (881): A sovereign political entity of modern times based on representing a united people.

NATO (North American Treaty Organization) (1107): The security alliance formed in 1949 to provide a unified military force for the United States, Canada, and their allies in Western Europe and Scandinavia. The corresponding alliance of the Soviet Union and its allies was known as the Warsaw Pact.

Nazi-Soviet Pact (1077): The agreement reached in 1939 by Germany and the Soviet Union in which both agreed not to attack the other in case of war. The agreement secretly divided up territory that would later be conquered.

neoliberalism (1171): A theory promoted by Margaret Thatcher, Britain's prime minister from 1979 to 1990, and those who followed her calling for a return to liberal principles of the nineteenth century, including the reduction of welfare-state programs and the cutting of taxes for wealthy people in order to promote economic growth.

new unionism (946): A mid- to late-nineteenth-century development in working-class organizing that entailed nationwide unions with bureaucracies and a membership of all kinds of workers, including unskilled ones; they replaced local craft-based unions.

new woman (965): A woman of the turn of the twentieth century, often from the middle class, who dressed practically, moved about freely, lived apart from her family, and supported herself.

Nongovernmental organizations (NGOs) (1201): Charitable foundations and activist groups such as Doctors Without Borders that often work internationally on political, economic, and relief issues; also, philanthropic organizations such as the Rockefeller, Ford, and Open Society Foundations that shape economic and social policy and the course of political reform.

Nuremberg laws (1064): Legislation in 1935 that deprived Jewish Germans of their citizenship and imposed many other hardships on them.

OPEC (Organization of Petroleum Exporting Countries) (1167): A consortium that regulated the supply and export of oil and that acted with more unanimity after the United States supported Israel against the Arabs in the wars of the late 1960s and early 1970s.

opium (830): An addictive drug derived from the heads of poppy plants; it was imported to Europe from the Ottoman Empire and India, available in various forms, and often used by ordinary people until restricted in 1868.

Ostpolitik (1156): A policy initiated by Willy Brandt in the late 1960s in which West Germany sought better economic relations with the Communist countries of eastern Europe.

outwork (918): The process of having some aspects of industrial work done outside factories in individual homes.

Pacific tigers (1210): Countries of East Asia so named because of their massive economic growth, much of it from the 1980s on; foremost among these were Japan and China.

Pan-Slavism (888): A movement in the nineteenth century for the unity of all Slavs across national and regional boundaries.

Peace of Paris (1022): The series of peace treaties that provided the settlement of World War I. These treaties were resented, especially by Germany, Hungary, and states of the Middle East in which England and France took over the government.

perestroika (1174): Literally, "restructuring"; an economic policy instituted in the 1980s by Soviet premier Mikhail Gorbachev calling for the introduction of market mechanisms and the achievement of greater efficiency in manufacturing, agriculture, and services.

philosophes (708): Public intellectuals of the Enlightenment who wrote on subjects ranging from current affairs to art criticism with the goal of furthering reform in society. (The word in French means "philosophers.")

pop art (1152): A style in the visual arts that mimicked advertising and consumerism and that used ordinary objects as a part of paintings and other compositions.

Popular Front (1067): An alliance of political parties that joined together in the 1930s to resist fascism despite deep philosophical differences.

positivism (905): A theory, developed in the mid-nineteenth century, at the foundation of the social sciences that study of facts would generate accurate, or "positive," laws of society; these laws could, in turn, help in the formulation of policy and legislation.

postmodernism (1219): A term applied in the late twentieth century to both an intense stylistic mixture in the arts without a central unifying theme or privileged canon and a critique of Enlightenment and scientific beliefs in rationality and the possibility for precise knowledge.

proletariat (907): The working class or, in Marxist terms, those who do not control the means of production such as factories, tools, workshops, and machines.

Provisional Government (1016): The initial government to take control in Russia after the overthrow of the Romanov empire in 1917. The government was composed of aristocrats and members of the middle class, often deputies in the Duma, the assembly created after the Revolution of 1905.

psychoanalysis (967): Freud's theory of human mental processes and his method for treating their malfunctioning.

pump priming (1063): An economic policy used by governments to stimulate the economy through public works programs and other infusions to public funds.

purges (1058): The series of attacks instituted by Joseph Stalin on citizens of the USSR in the 1930s and later. The victims were accused of being "wreckers," or saboteurs of communism, while the public grew hysterical and pliable because of its fear.

realism (899): A style in the arts that arose in the mid-nineteenth century and was dedicated to depicting society realistically without romantic or idealistic overtones.

Realpolitik (873): Policies associated initially with nation building that are said to be based on hard-headed realities rather than the romantic notions of earlier nationalists. The term has come to mean any policy based on considerations of power alone.

Reform Act of 1884 (948): The British act that granted the right to vote to a mass male citizenry.

restoration (808): The Congress of Vienna's policy, after the fall of Napoleon, to "restore" as many regimes as possible to their former rulers.

romanticism (720, 815): An artistic movement of the early nineteenth century that glorified nature, emotion, genius, and imagination.

Russification (881): A program for the integration of Russia's many nationality groups involving the forced acquisition of Russian language and the practice of Russian orthodoxy as well as the settlement of ethnic Russians among other nationality groups.

salons (711): Informal gatherings, usually sponsored by middle-class or aristocratic women, that provided a forum for new ideas and an opportunity to establish new intellectual contacts among supporters of the Enlight-enment; works that could not be published officially were read aloud. (The word in French means "living rooms.")

samizdat (1156): A key form of dissident activity in the Soviet Union and its satellite countries of eastern Europe in the 1960s and 1970s; individuals reproduced uncensored publications by hand and passed them from reader to reader, thus building a foundation for the successful resistance of the 1980s.

sans-culottes (761): The name given to politically active men from the lower classes (French for "without breeches"); they worked with their hands and wore the long trousers of workingmen rather than the knee breeches of the upper classes.

Schlieffen Plan (1006): The strategy in World War I named for former chief of the German general staff Alfred von Schlieffen that called for attacks on two fronts—concentrating first on France to the west and then turning east to attack Russia.

Second International (946): A transnational organization of workers established in 1889, mostly committed to Marxian socialism.

social question (840): An expression common in the 1830s–1850s that reflected a widely shared concern about the effects of industrialization and urbanization on the fabric of social life.

socialism (813): A social and political doctrine that advocated the reorganization of society to overcome the new tensions created by industrialization; early socialists emphasized the need to restore social harmony through communities based on cooperation rather than competition.

Solidarity (1176): An outlawed Polish labor union of the 1980s that contested Communist Party programs and eventually succeeded in ousting the party from the Polish government.

soviets (1016): Councils of workers and soldiers first formed in Russia in the Revolution of 1905; they took shape to represent the people in the early days of the 1917 Russian Revolution. These groups saw themselves as a more legitimate political force than the Provisional Government.

stagflation (1168): The combination of a stagnant economy and soaring inflation; a period of stagflation occurred in the West in the 1970s as a result of an OPEC embargo on oil.

suffragists (977): Women around the turn of the twentieth century who worked actively for the right to vote.

temperance movement (845): A movement in the United States and Europe begun in the early nineteenth century to discourage consumption of alcohol.

Terror (763): The emergency government established under the direction of the Committee of Public Safety during the French Revolution; the government aimed to establish a republic of virtue, but to do so it arrested hundreds of thousands of political suspects and executed thousands of ordinary people.

terrorism (1168): Coordinated and targeted political violence by opposition groups.

thaw (1117): The climate of relative toleration for free expression in the Soviet bloc after the death of Joseph Stalin, in 1953. The thaw alternated with periods when the government returned to repression.

Thermidorian Reaction (770): The violent backlash against the rule of Robespierre that began with his arrest and execution; most of the instruments of the Terror were dismantled, and supporters of the Jacobins were harassed or even murdered.

Third Republic (949): The government that succeeded Napoleon III's Second Empire after its defeat in the Franco-Prussian War of 1870–1871 and lasted until France's defeat in World War II (1940).

third world (1098): A term devised after World War II to designate those countries outside either the capitalist world of the U.S. bloc or the socialist world of the Soviet bloc—most of them emerging from imperial domination.

total war (1003): A war built on full mobilization of soldiers, civilians, and the technological capacities of the nations involved. The term also refers to a highly destructive war and one that is both a physical war and a war for ideas and ideologies.

Truman Doctrine (1103): The United States' policy to limit communism after World War II by countering political crises with economic and military aid.

United Nations (UN) (1123): An organization for collective security and deliberation set up as World War II closed; it replaced the ineffective League of Nations and has proved active in resolving international conflicts both through negotiation and by the use of force.

Vatican II (1154): A Catholic Council held between 1962 and 1965 to modernize some aspects of church teachings (such as condemnation of Jews), to update the liturgy, and to promote cooperation among the faiths (i.e., ecumenism).

war guilt clause (1022): The part of the Treaty of Versailles that assigned blame for World War I to Germany.

Weimar Republic (1021): The parliamentary republic established in 1919 in Germany to replace the imperial form of government.

welfare state (1113): A system comprising state-sponsored programs for citizens, including veterans' pensions, social security, health care, family allowances, and disability insurance. Most highly developed after World War II, the welfare state intervened in society to bring economic democracy (to supplement political democracy) by setting a minimum standard of well-being.

working class (811): The term introduced in the early nineteenth century for those who worked in the new factories of industrial production.

World Bank (1201): An international institution of credit created in the 1940s. With the globalization of finances and of national economies from the 1980s on, it became increasingly powerful.

zemstvos (880): Regional councils of the Russian nobility established after the emancipation of the Serfs in 1861 to deal with education and local welfare issues.

Zionism (984): A movement that began in the late nineteenth century among European Jews to found a Jewish state.

Additional Credits

Index

A note about the index:

Names of individuals appear in bold face; biographical dates are included for major historical figures.

Letters in parentheses following pages refer to:
(i)   illustrations, including photographs and artifacts
(f)   figures, including charts, graphs, and tables
(m)   maps
(b)   boxed features (such as "Contrasting Views")

80 N

Greenland
(Den.)

Alaska

ICELAND

60 N

UNITE
KINGDO

CANADA

IRELAND

FRANCE

SPAI

40 N

PORTUGAL

UNITED STATES

ATLANTIC
OCEAN

Azores
(Port.)

MOROCC

Canary Is.
(Sp.)

BAHAMAS

Western Sahara
(Mor.)

20 N

DOMINICAN
REPUBLIC

Hawaii

HAITI

MEXICO

Puerto Rico (U.S.)

MAURITANIA

CUBA

ST. KITTS AND NEVIS

JAMAICA

ANTIGUA AND BARBUDA

CAPE
VERDE

SENEGAL

BELIZE

Guadeloupe (Fr.)

DOMINICA

MAL

HONDURAS

Martinique (Fr.)

ST. VINCENT AND THE GRENADINES

GAMBIA

GUATEMALA

ST. LUCIA

BARBADOS

GUINEA-BISSAU

EL SALVADOR

NICARAGUA

GRENADA

GUINEA

TRINIDAD AND TOBAGO

SIERRA LEONE

COSTA RICA

VENEZUELA

GUYANA

LIBERIA

PANAMA

SURINAME

CÔTE D'IVOIRE

PACIFIC OCEAN

COLOMBIA

French Guiana (Fr.)

BURKINA FASO

0

Equator

Galápagos Is.
(Ec.)

ECUADOR

GHANA

BRAZIL

PERU

SAMOA

BOLIVIA

20 S

TONGA

PARAGUAY

Easter I.
(Chile)

CHILE

ATLANTIC
OCEAN

URUGUAY

0   1,500   3,000 miles

ARGENTINA

0   1,500   3,000 kilometers

40 S

Falkland Is.
(U.K.)

60 S

80 S

160 W   140 W   120 W   100 W   80 W   60 W   40 W   20 W

ARCTIC OCEAN

NORWAY
SWEDEN
FINLAND
ESTONIA
LATVIA
LITHUANIA
DEN.
ETH.
GERMANY POLAND
BELARUS
LUX.
CZ. REP.
SLK.
UKRAINE
AUS.
HUNG.
MOLDOVA
SLN.
ROMANIA
WITZ.
CR.
S.M.
ITALY
B.H.
BULGARIA
MAC.
ALB.
GREECE
TUNISIA
MALTA

RUSSIAN FEDERATION

KAZAKHSTAN

MONGOLIA

N. KOREA
S. KOREA

JAPAN

PACIFIC OCEAN

GEORGIA
ARMENIA
UZBEKISTAN
KYRGYZSTAN
TURKMENISTAN
TAJIKISTAN
TURKEY
AZERBAIJAN
CYPRUS
SYRIA
LEBANON
ISRAEL
IRAQ
AFGHANISTAN
JORDAN
IRAN
KUWAIT
BAHRAIN
SAUDI ARABIA
QATAR
UNITED ARAB
EMIRATES
OMAN

CHINA

PAKISTAN

NEPAL
BHUTAN

TAIWAN

Mariana Is.
(U.S.)

MARSHALL
IS.

IA

LIBYA

EGYPT

BANGLADESH

INDIA

MYANMAR
(BURMA)
LAOS
VIETNAM

Guam
(U.S.)

NIGER

CHAD
SUDAN

YEMEN

THAILAND

CAMBODIA

PHILIPPINES

PALAU

FEDERATED STATES
OF MICRONESIA

NIGERIA
BENIN
TOGO
CENTRAL
AFRICAN REP.
CAMEROON
EQ.
UINEA
GABON
AO TOME
PRINCIPE
CONGO
ERITREA
DJIBOUTI
ETHIOPIA
SOMALIA

MALDIVES

SRI
LANKA

BRUNEI

MALAYSIA

NAURU

KIRIBATI

TUVALU

RWANDA
UGANDA
KENYA
DEM. REP. OF
THE CONGO
BURUNDI
TANZANIA
COMOROS
SEYCHELLES

SINGAPORE

INDONESIA

PAPUA
NEW
GUINEA

SOLOMON
IS.

ANGOLA
ZAMBIA
MALAWI
ZIMBABWE
NAMIBIA
BOTSWANA
MADAGASCAR

INDIAN OCEAN

MAURITIUS

EAST
TIMOR

VANUATU

FIJI

New Caledonia
(Fr.)

AUSTRALIA

SOUTH
AFRICA
MOZAMBIQUE
SWAZILAND
LESOTHO

NEW
ZEALAND

Tasmania
(Aust.)

N
W E
S

Abbreviations	
ALB.	ALBANIA
AUS.	AUSTRIA
BEL.	BELGIUM
B.H.	BOSNIA AND HERZEGOVINA
CR.	CROATIA
CZ. REP.	CZECH REPUBLIC
DEN.	DENMARK
HUNG.	HUNGARY
LUX.	LUXEMBOURG
MAC.	MACEDONIA
NETH.	NETHERLANDS
S.M.	SERBIA AND MONTENEGRO
SLK.	SLOVAKIA
SLN.	SLOVENIA
SWITZ.	SWITZERLAND

ANTARCTICA

20 E   40 E   60 E   80 E   100 E   120 E   140 E   160 E